The Essay

The Essay

Readings for
the Writing Process

Stephen H. Goldman

Bernard A. Hirsch

The University of Kansas

Houghton Mifflin Company   **Boston**

Dallas   Geneva, Illinois   Lawrenceville, New Jersey   Palo Alto

Acknowledgments

American Heritage Dictionary   Definition on page 154 © 1982 by Houghton Mifflin Company. Reprinted by permission from *The American Heritage Dictionary, Second College Edition*.

Roger Angell   Excerpt from *Five Seasons* by Roger Angell copyright © 1972, 1973, 1974, 1975, 1976 by Roger Angell. Reprinted by permission of Simon & Schuster, Inc.

James Baldwin   "Stranger in the Village" from *Notes of a Native Son* reprinted by permission of the author.

Arna Bontemps   "The Black Man Talks of Reaping" reprinted by permission of Harold Ober Associates, Inc.

Anthony Brandt   "The Gift of Gift-Giving" by Anthony Brandt reprinted by permission of the author.

Susan Brownmiller   Excerpt from *Against Our Will* copyright © 1975 by Susan Brownmiller. Reprinted by permission of Simon & Schuster, Inc.

Arthur C. Clarke   "Viking on the Plain of Gold," from *1984: Spring* by Arthur C. Clarke. Copyright © 1984 by Serendip BV. Reprinted by permission of Ballantine Books, a division of Random House, Inc.

Vine Deloria, Jr.   "The Artificial Universe" reprinted with permission of Macmillan Publishing Company from *We Talk, You Listen: New Tribes, New Turf* by Vine Deloria, Jr. Copyright © 1970 by Vine Deloria, Jr.

Annie Dillard   "Heaven and Earth in Jest" from *Pilgrim at Tinker Creek* by Annie Dillard copyright © 1974 by Annie Dillard. By permission of Harper & Row, Publishers, Inc.

Paul R. Ehrlich   "North America After the War" by Paul Ehrlich reprinted with permission from *Natural History*, Vol. 93, No. 3; copyright the American Museum of Natural History, 1984.

Acknowledgments continue on page 453.

Hope and Elaine,
without whom it would not
have been worth doing

Contents

Section Three / Structure 136

Drafting 139
Beginnings 141
Endings 144
Middles 147
Temporal Organization (Narrative) 147
Additive Organization (Lists, Comparison, Contrast, Classification, Division) 150
Conceptual Organization (Cause and Effect, Reason, Result, Purpose) 154
The Final Draft 156
Drafting and Structure 160

Section Four / Style 344

Preface

If we told you that writing is often a complicated activity that requires intense concentration, you would probably think we were merely stating the obvious. After all, you have had to write for most of your student years. Sometimes your experience may have been rewarding, and you wrote a paper you were satisfied with. At other times, you may have been frustrated, and you settled for handing in an awkward or an underdeveloped essay. Our aim in this textbook is to make the writing process rewarding and to increase your chances of writing essays that will please both you and your instructor.

Essentially, we want to give you some practical help in working through the writing process and in evaluating what you write. To do this, we have provided an analysis of the writing process and a selection of forty-three essays. Our analysis offers a number of techniques that other writers have used successfully—techniques for finding and developing ideas, organizing essays, and revising earlier drafts. The essays exemplify a rich variety of ideas, structures, and styles. They illustrate the possibilities you can explore as you develop your own writing skills. We have, in other words, tried to show you both the methods and goals of writing.

As a writer, you need to understand both. You need to develop a style with which you are comfortable but which is still within the conventions traditionally associated with the essay. Style will come most easily if you first understand the nature of the writing process. Once you have that understanding, however, you will also need some way of deciding whether the style you have chosen will work. Reading good essays by other writers will help you make such decisions. The more you learn about how others have approached the writing process, the better you will be able to appraise your own work.

The best way to understand the writing process is to practice. We have filled this textbook with exercises and writing assignments that we hope are interesting and challenging. We know that dull exercises will rarely produce decent results, and we hope that our assignments will engage both your intellect and your imagination. Good writing depends on your interest in what you are doing, on the value of your task, and on your willingness to see that task as worthwhile.

Because starting the writing process is so often complicated, we describe in Section One the many elements writers must consider as they begin their work. The *topic*, the *audience*, and the writer's own *personality* all shape the writing process. Each element influences the organization and language of the essay. Thus, the concepts and definitions we develop in this section will be used in every section that follows.

In Section Two our discussion of the writing process focuses on *meaning*. How do you find a topic? What do you do with a topic after you have found it? How do you know when you have enough information to start writing? You need to ask such basic questions before you start writing, and you need to answer them, at least tentatively, before you begin your first draft. These questions are not obstacles: they are opportunities to explore your topic and discover what you already know about it. The techniques we offer in this section are invitations to search for what is meaningful and worthwhile in the topic.

In Section Three we present methods for organizing your thoughts into a working draft of an essay. Finding an effective *organization* requires as much exploration as finding a worthwhile topic. No single method of organization works for all writers, even if they are dealing with the same topic. We discuss a variety of structures and techniques, and then provide opportunities for developing your own approaches to organizing your topic.

In our final section we discuss the language of the essay. The words, sentences, and mechanics of written language offer yet another opportunity for exploration and discovery. How you use language will influence how your readers understand and accept your message. Fascinating topics can be trivialized by tedious language, and commonplace topics can be made engaging through stimulating language. The techniques for *revision* we recommend in this section will help you review and rework what you have written so that it expresses your thoughts clearly and precisely. By the time you get to this final stage in the writing process, you will have done a great deal of work. By exploring various styles, you can ensure that what you want to say is not lost because of unclear or inconsistent use of language.

Although we have separated our discussions of meaning, structure, and language into three stages, we encourage you to re-examine each step throughout the entire writing process. For example, as you are exploring organization, you may want to reconsider your original topic. As you work through the writing process, however, you will find most of your attention shifting from meaning to structure to language.

Each of the sections contains essays that illustrate the techniques we discuss. We have selected them because we admire their authors' abilities to present their topics in fresh and often challenging ways. These essays express the diversity of human thought and experience. At their best, essays convey not only information, but personal beliefs. In this sense, the essays we have selected are essays at their best.

A project as ambitious as this textbook always owes whatever its success to many people. We would like to acknowledge the valuable insights and contributions of the following readers: Michael Allen, The College of Wooster, OH; John P. Bodnar, Prince George's Community College, MD; Helen Bridge, Chabot College, CA; Alma G. Bryant, University of South Florida; Lisa Ede, Oregon State University; C. R. Embry, Truckee Meadows Community College, NV; Francis A. Hubbard, Cleveland State University; Elaine L. Kleiner, Indiana State University; James A. Koger, Bemidji State University, MN; Andrew L. Mahon, Edinboro State College, PA; John McKernan, Marshall University, WV; Russell J. Meyer, University of Missouri–Columbia; George Otte, The University of Tulsa; Barbara Weaver, Ball State University, IN; Robert C. Wess, Southern Technical Institute, GA.

The staff of Houghton Mifflin Company helped us immeasurably as we first developed this text and then polished it for publication. Professor Peter Casagrande of the University of Kansas encouraged us in our work and helped us to find clerical support as we put together the final copy. Professors Michael Johnson of the University of Kansas and Randall Popken of Tarleton State University read an early version and gave us many timely suggestions. Ms. Pam LeRow of the University of Kansas Word Processing Center patiently produced four different drafts of the manuscript; and Ms. Jane Garrett of the University of Kansas English Department provided painstaking clerical assistance at crucial times.

Finally, we wish to thank our families. Melissa, Sarah, and Jessica Goldman spent two years quietly walking about the house as "that thing" was worked over again and again. Elaine Hirsch and Hope Goldman not only endured irregular hours and regular crises as we wrote, but also gave freely of their own time and energy to help us finish the manuscript. Their help and understanding will always be remembered.

S. H. G.
B. A. H.

The Essay

SECTION
ONE
Approaching Writing

"What I was going to say," said the Dodo in an offended tone, "was that the best thing to get us dry would be a Caucus-race."

"What is a Caucus-race?" said Alice, not that she much wanted to know, but the Dodo had paused as if it thought that *somebody* ought to speak, and no one else seemed inclined to say anything.

"Why," said the Dodo, "the best way to explain it is to do it."

Lewis Carroll, *Alice's Adventures in Wonderland*

We are going to take the Dodo's advice and explain the writing process by writing an essay. But we want to do more than simply take the Dodo's advice. We want to run the Caucus-race with you in this book, and we want to show you the finish line. In this way we hope to illustrate the strategies you can use when you need to fill a blank page with words that are supposed to make sense. In addition to running the race—or writing an essay—we want to show you a variety of essays to give you an idea of what you are reaching for when you write. Each section that follows contains instructions for a particular stage of the writing process and a selection of essays. By alternating discussions of the process with examples of completed works, we hope to show you how important a knowledge of both aspects is for your development as a writer. Developing your writing skills takes hard work, but that work can be made easier if you first learn how to slow down and make efficient use of each step in the process. And each step will make more sense to you if you understand what it contributes to the finished essay. The readings in each section will illustrate these contributions.

Before we turn to the work you must do, let's consider why many people find writing difficult and where these difficulties lie. If you understand why writing is troublesome, you will find the suggestions we make more helpful.

Writer, Audience, and Topic

Every piece of writing you do is shaped by the kind of person you are, the people you are writing to, and the topic you are writing about. To say that writers shape the things they write may seem obvious, but this simple statement implies a host of complications. Every time you write, you also tell your audience something about yourself. The words you choose imply many things about who you are and what you believe. How you appear to your readers is within your control, but only if you carefully consider how you express yourself. Do you wish to appear friendly or detached, thoughtful or spontaneous, cynical or optimistic, serious or humorous? The list could go on and on. Your decisions will influence what you write and how you express it.

The personality you choose should only be selected after considering your *purpose* for writing. Deciding on a purpose is often difficult for writers in college English courses. When you are assigned a topic for an essay, your only purpose may be to write that paper because you were told to. Such a purpose does not offer much help. When we talk about purpose, however, we mean something more than the immediate cause for writing an essay. To us, purpose is the goal you need to discover for yourself as you think over your assignment. Do you wish to emphasize some special feature of your topic? Do you want to persuade your readers that they need to act? Do you hope to explain why your beliefs are reasonable? Do you want to show the humorous side of the topic so others will be entertained? Again, the list could go on. Whatever your choice, your purpose will influence how you handle your topic and how you present yourself in your essay.

Audience is just as important to shaping your writing as your choice of personality and purpose. Whom you write to will, in fact, often determine what personality and purpose you select. Before you start writing, you should try to describe for yourself the people you are writing to. Are these people strangers who have no knowledge of you or your attitudes? How much can you expect them to know about the topic? Do they have a common background, or are they of different ages and educational levels? Will they sympathize with your position or will they be hostile? Writing is frequently a lonely act because your audience is not physically present. If you create some mental picture of your readers to guide you, you can make writing less lonely and less difficult than it might be.

Finally, the importance of your *topic* to shaping your writing may appear as obvious as the importance of the writer. But simply saying the topic is important is not enough: you need to consider how that topic will affect how you write. Is your topic so specialized that even well-educated readers will need many examples? Does your topic contain an extensive series of details that must be presented? Can your topic be handled from a single viewpoint, or must various viewpoints be covered? Are there implications to your topic that will require specific discussion? While you may know the topic for your essay, you still need to consider what you are going to say about it. Discovering a purpose and audience will help you make this decision, but the topic itself will be your ultimate source for making up your mind. Whatever you wish to say, it will be limited by the nature of your topic.

Whether you are writing a diary entry, a thank-you note to a distant relative, a letter to a friend, or an essay for an English class, you will always need to consider yourself (the writer), your readers, and your topic. In each case that entry, note, letter, or essay is different from all the others. As the role you play changes, your audience grows or narrows, and the topic becomes more or less complicated, your writing will change.

Most of us have learned to make these changes unconsciously. We adjust our words as our moods, audiences, and topics change, but we find it easier to make these adjustments when we speak than when we write. When we speak, our listeners are before us, and we are able to observe their reactions to our words. We can immediately address any questions or statements each person may make. Our audience is not some hypothetical construction, as in writing, but a real group of people whose very presence can guide us in choosing how we speak and what we speak about.

Dealing with Writing

Because an audience is not present when you write, it is much more difficult to anticipate how well your words will express your ideas. Writing usually requires you to cover your topic more clearly and in greater detail than speaking. The reason for this will become clear if you consider the differences between telling a friend about an accident in a conversation and writing about it in a letter. If you were to discuss the accident in a conversation, you could rely on your friend to ask for clarification when it was necessary. But if you were to describe it in a letter, you would need to anticipate the questions your friend might ask and include your answers as part of the description.

The consequences of being separated from your audience extend beyond the need for a fuller discussion of your topic. This separation also affects your sentence structure and organization. Written language is often more formal than spoken language because you have no way of knowing how your readers are reacting to your words. You don't know if your readers understand what you are saying. Although you may frequently feel frustrated by the conventions of grammar and punctuation that characterize much of written language, these conventions can actually help you to communicate with your audience. As a writer, you are expected to handle the complex task of balancing topic and audience, yet still give your readers some sense of your own personality. The larger and more unknown your audience, the greater is this task. For such forms of writing as the essay, it would be nearly impossible to handle this balancing without the guidance of the grammatical and mechanical conventions of written English. They allow writers and readers to speak the same "dialect" and therefore increase the chances of communication.

These conventions may often be frustrating because spelling does not always coincide with pronunciation, grammar is both complex and mysterious, and punctuation frequently appears inconsistent. But the frustration you feel is part of the process of learning to write well. You should not assume that learning these conventions represents the entire process of writing, but you do need to recognize the important function they serve. If you were to ignore the conventions, you would be giving yourself a serious handicap. A friend won't notice your violations of these conventions in a letter—and in fact might be disturbed if you were to follow them slavishly. But the executive of a company will notice them in your letter applying for a job. And the instructor of your history class will most certainly notice them in your term paper.

Do not try to use these conventions in the same way for every piece of writing. How you apply the conventions will vary as much as writer, audience, and topic vary. The following three examples illustrate the range of variations. In each case the audience, topic, and personality of the writer differ significantly, and these differences lead to different forms of written English.

The first passage is part of a personal letter to a sister whom the writer has not seen in almost a year.

Dear Hope—

First belated birthday greetings . . . did you know Mickey Rooney was also born on 9/23?

Enclosed are some pictures from this summer. The one of Nathaniel in front of his Busy Box was taken around Labor Day.

Nathaniel went in for his six-month check-up on 9/24, and we know he weighs 19 lbs 9 oz (or did on that date), measures 28¼" in length and according to the doctor, is "extraordinarily well proportioned."

His crawling attempts have been improved . . . up from lying on his tummy while flailing his arms & legs, to "bridges" a la what John did. Nathaniel will pull/drag and otherwise move along the ground when there is suitable incentive (a toy, newspaper, a deck of cards . . .), but he isn't crawling yet.

The letter starts, as so many letters do, with an apology for not writing sooner. The apology comes with a belated birthday greeting and an interesting bit of trivia. Such an opening promises that the rest of the letter will be "chatty." It will contain the latest news; and since the sisters see one another only once a year, there is plenty of news to share.

Certainly, the writer is cheerful, and she captures that tone in her writing. She will not be reporting any deaths in the family or financial disasters.

The punctuation, grammar, and vocabulary are part of the letter's tone. The writer is not overly concerned with the more formal conventions because this is not a formal letter. Her sentences are well formed, but the whimsical use of parentheses and ellipses gives her words a sense of spontaneity: "Nathaniel will pull/drag and otherwise move along the ground when there is suitable incentive (a toy, newspaper, or a deck of cards . . .), but he isn't crawling yet." And the vocabulary is consistent with the spontaneity. Mickey Rooney, Nathaniel, "his Busy Box," "flailing his arms & legs," "bridges a la what John did," and "pull/drag and otherwise move along the ground" are all reported in a cheerful manner.

Nevertheless, you have to be Hope to enjoy this letter fully. John, for example, is an older brother whose early attempts at crawling and walking have become the stuff of family legends. The writer is a fanatical solitaire player who likes to play while lying on the floor, so there is almost always an incentive for her son Nathaniel to move along the ground. Hope, of course, is aware of all of this, and her sister does not have to make this shared information explicit. She is not writing to anyone but Hope.

The second example does not assume as much shared information. Its coauthors, Rowland Evans and Robert Novak, are nationally syndicated columnists who must produce a daily piece for hundreds of newspapers throughout the United States.

His [Secretary of State George Schultz's] exit as the president's Mideast point man may be just what the doctor ordered for Ronald Reagan. It could convert the administration's Lebanon disaster to an election-year salvage job. The tool for that conversion may be at hand, thanks to the refusal of McFarlane, Reagan's national security adviser, and Baker, the White House chief of staff, to accept Schultz's edict that it is "their [Lebanon's] problem."

The president's strong statement that the U.S. would stick with Gamayel whatever he did with the May 17 accord now points toward U.S. acceptance of the eight-point plan sponsored by Saudi Arabia. It raises the probability once again that if Reagan cannot persuade Israel to withdraw its army, the two allies may be on a collision course.

The main purpose of a newspaper column is to present factual information or opinions in the clearest, most readable form. When we read a column, we expect to see short paragraphs, each centered around a single point. This journalistic style forces writers to break up their stories into small, essential bits of information and to arrange them in a sequence that gives the reader the essence of the news or the opinion. Such an arrangement affects the language the writers can use because it limits the length and complexity of their sentences.

But paragraphing is not the only factor that determines the shape of sentences in a column. The content is equally significant. Since most columns deal with current events, they frequently need to include background information so that the audience can follow the story or opinion. In the example, notice how the writers identify McFarlane and Baker: "The tool for that conversion may be at hand, thanks to the refusal of McFarlane, *Reagan's national security adviser,* and Baker, *the White House chief of staff,* to accept Schultz's edict that it is 'their problem.'" Sentences with short appositive phrases (phrases that rename or define a noun or pronoun) are common in news stories, because they provide background information quickly and efficiently.

Our second example also shows how audience helps shape the personality the writers choose and the language they use to project it. Because newspaper columnists write for a large and varied audience, their words must be readily understood by as many people as possible. These writers cannot afford to lecture in an overly learned language that might force many of their readers to rush for a dictionary. Not only will most readers refuse to read such a style, but they may also label the writers as "ivory-tower" snobs who probably have no practical idea of what is happening in the world. The language of our example is in no danger of such criticism. Its writers use words and phrases that will establish a familiar relationship between them and their audience. Phrases such as "just what the doctor ordered," "an election-year salvage job," and "on a collision course" may not impress you with their originality, but they clearly express the meanings the writers have in mind. More important, these phrases lead you to believe that the writers are direct, pragmatic men of the world, just the personality these columnists would want to project.

Our final example is taken from an essay written by F. H. Bronson for *Scientific American.* Mr. Bronson is writing for a general educated audience that is interested in the sciences.

The house mouse is an opportunistic commensal of human beings that has a spectacular history of global colonization. A commensal lives and feeds in close association with another species without either benefitting or harming it directly. *Mus domesticus* began its coexistence with humans perhaps 8,000 to 10,000 years ago on the steppes of Asia. Since then, in large part through transportation unwittingly provided by people, it has established itself on every major landmass and most minor ones. It infests homes, commercial establishments, granaries and other outbuildings from the Equator to the subpolar regions. It can live in man-made climates as different as central-heating ducts and frozen-food lockers.

Yet the house mouse is not a strict commensal. In many places it has reverted to a wild existence, where it lives in total independence of humans. In this feral pattern it can be found in a surprising diversity of habitats: coral atolls, grasslands, deserts, freshwater marshes, seashore dunes and alpine valleys.

Even a very quick reading of this passage indicates that we have a much more formal piece of writing than the personal letter or the newspaper column. Vocabulary, sentence structure, and paragraphing indicate this more formal style.

By defining the word *commensal* in the second sentence, Mr. Bronson anticipates that many of his readers will not know its meaning. Yet he uses this word and others like it because he knows his audience expects them. *Scientific American* is aimed at readers who are interested in this kind of material, even if they do not have an extensive technical vocabulary. If he had used simpler words that do not accurately reflect the complexity of his topic, the readers may have been insulted. Although the author cannot expect his readers to look up every unfamiliar word, he can assume they want to acquire a basic vocabulary of the subject. By introducing and then defining the important technical terms, the writer has responded to the demands of his readers and his topic.

The paragraphing and sentence structure also show how well Mr. Bronson understands the requirements of audience and topic. Because he is explaining a technical subject to a general audience, the sentences and paragraphs are longer and more complicated than those in our previous examples. The discussion must be more detailed so that specialized information can be shared. The writer must show how all these details are related to his message and purpose. For example, the third sentence continues the main topic, that the house mouse has successfully colonized most of the globe. The fourth sentence then adds details that illustrate the mouse's commensal nature: "Since then, *in large part through transportation unwittingly provided by people,* it has established itself on every major landmass and most minor ones." The more information you need to explain your topic, the more complicated your sentences will be. The longer and more complicated your sentences, the larger the paragraphs that contain them.

The short paragraphs you expect from a newspaper column are not suitable for this kind of essay. Readers expect the discussion to cover the topic fully, giving them as much background information as they need to understand the message. The writer is describing a complicated relationship between humans and the house mouse, and his description must present the numerous features of this relationship in as much detail as possible. Once again, we see how a writer has responded to the special requirements of his task.

The same thing should be said for anything you write. What you want to express, to whom you want to express it, and how you want to appear all have a part in shaping what you write.

The Writing Process

Given the complex demands writers must confront, it is easy to see why people find writing difficult. But these demands need not make your life miserable if you are willing to approach your writing in an orderly way.

No single method of writing works for all writers, or even a majority of them; every writer needs to find a method that will work best for him or her. However, all methods of writing must cover three broad areas: discovering a message and purpose *(meaning),* developing a method of presentation *(structure),* and finding suitable language *(style).* In our discussion of the writing process we consider each of these areas separately so that we can describe various techniques you may use as you work toward a finished essay. Keep in mind that these areas, although described separately, are closely interrelated. When working on purpose, for instance, most writers will also consider possible organizations and potential styles. When trying to organize their ideas, they will also rethink their original purpose. When writing out their thoughts, they will reexamine their intentions, consider new ideas, and abandon old ones. And when revising the essay to make sure that the words and the sentences are appropriate, most writers will again find new ideas and different organizations to consider.

Essays, in a sense, are like living things—they grow and evolve. All aspects of an essay—meaning, structure, and style—are subject to change at any time. You should therefore concern yourself with each aspect throughout the entire writing process. Even after you have finished, you may find yourself still wondering about choices you made.

The Essay

Throughout our discussion we have used the word *essay.* Since the sections that follow will deal almost exclusively with this kind of writing, we should describe what we mean by this word. You will probably have no trouble distinguishing an essay from a shopping list, an interoffice memo, a personal letter, or a short story. You would also probably agree that an essay is somehow different from a textbook or a nonfictional book. Although we may disagree about its specific characteristics, most of us can recognize an essay when we see one.

For example, most people would agree that the proper subject matter for an essay is fact rather than fiction. Even if the writer uses a story to illustrate an important point, the central purpose of the work remains the presentation of fact. Readers expect essays to be based on objective information that can be confirmed. If you found inaccuracies in an essay, you would probably not continue to read it, and you would certainly not take the writer's message seriously.

The range of possible topics for an essay is, of course, extremely broad. For example, you might choose to write about a new way of understanding a past event, argue for a solution to a common problem, describe a discovery, or explain an opinion. Your choice of topics is limited only by the requirement that there be a factual basis to what you write.

An essay must also appear to cover its topic fully. It is impossible to say how long an essay should be, but most people seem to think that essays vary in length from two hundred and fifty to twenty thousand words. The demands of purpose, personality, audience, and topic will determine the length of a specific essay. You need to give the appearance of fully developing your topic in an appropriate manner for your audience and purpose. We stress appearance here because no topic can ever be fully handled in even twenty thousand words, yet you need to convince your readers that your essay contains all the important points for understanding your message.

The key to appearance is organization. A strong organization will show your audience how all your points are connected. It will convince them that your discussion is complete, because there are no loose ends to distract them. Your readers are more likely to believe you are in control of both the facts and your conclusions. And because they believe this, they will be more willing to pay attention to what you write.

Finally, the audience for an essay is usually large and varied. The readers represent all regions, cultural backgrounds, and ages. As a result, the language we associate with essays is more formal than that of most other kinds of writing. It is, in fact, the closest thing we have to a national dialect. It is meant to cross the regional, social, and cultural boundaries that influence the way we speak. You may find differences in how writers use this "dialect," but they choose words and construct sentences in similar ways. They also tend to avoid words and constructions that are restricted to a specific area of the country or a single social group. When you write an essay, you will be trying to express your meaning to as many people as possible. The language you use will often determine how successful you are.

In this section we have tried to show you some of the more important forces that shape the writing you do. But simply knowing about them will not automatically help you to write well. That will come with the experience you gain from actually doing it. Each time you write and have people react to your work, you learn that much more. Reading examples of successful essays can also help. They illustrate how others have handled the writing process. Therefore we end this section with three essays that exemplify the writers' attention to personality, audience, and topic.

In the sections that follow we will discuss the writing process itself and suggest some ways of making it easier. We will also ask you to read a number of finished works that illustrate the rich variety of forms, topics, and language that is available just in this single type of writing: the essay.

The Two Cultures and Dr. Franklin's Fly

Joel J. Gold

S ome twenty-five years ago C. P. Snow pub- *1* lished a provocative little book decrying the separation of science and the humanities into "The Two Cultures." Committed as I already was to the study of English literature, I lamented the inability of scientists and humanists to discuss ideas together but went on happily burrowing into my own eighteenth-century niche. Little did I realize that a crumbling manuscript letter dated 1796 would lead me into that no-man's land between the two cultures.

Even now, as I sit here in my office, staring at three apparently very *2* dead flies floating—sunk actually—in a stoppered vial of Madeira wine, I marvel at the innocence with which it all began. I was writing a short article for one of the journals—they usually have "philology" or "philological" in the title—that publish humanists' work. To explain how I found myself between the two cultures, I had better lay out the main points of that essay. (And don't think I mind opening up my arcane researches to more than the half dozen or so scholarly souls who actually read the articles in such journals.)

Near the end of the eighteenth century a man who had been a dinner *3* guest at Benjamin Franklin's French residence related the following anecdote in a letter:

I remember one Day at Dinner, with Doctor Franklin at Passy, in the Year 1779, the Doctor produced a Fly, which had come out of a But of Madeira that Morning, and which by laying in the Sun was restored to Life.—The Doctor wish'd, that he cou'd, in like Manner, be bung'd up for fifty Years, and then restored to Life, to behold the flourishing State, in which America wou'd then be.

Naturally I wondered if others knew of this fey after-dinner story, and I began to poke around in a few books on Franklin. Without really expecting to find anything helpful, I glanced at the index to Carl Van Doren's massive biography and was startled by the entry: "Flies drowned in wine, BF on, 431." Back in 1773, some six years before the Passy dinner party, Franklin was writing from London about experiments designed to recall the dead to life. What was most intriguing, however, was a carefully detailed description of drowned flies. Three of them had fallen out of a Virginia-bottled Madeira into a glass. Ever the scientific inquirer, Franklin proposed an experiment to test whether or not the sun could indeed revive drowned flies. Within a few hours two of the three began to stir. Franklin's phrasing is rather stirring itself:

They commenced by some convulsive motions of the thighs, and at length they raised themselves upon their legs, wiped their eyes with their fore feet, beat and brushed their wings with their hind feet, and soon after began to fly, finding themselves in Old England, without knowing how they came thither. The third continued lifeless till sunset, when, losing all hopes of him, he was thrown away.

Franklin went on to wish such preservation were possible for humans, "for having a very ardent desire to see and observe the state of America a hundred years hence, I should prefer to any ordinary death, the being immersed in a cask of Madeira wine, with a few friends, till that time, to be then recalled to life by the solar warmth of my dear country!"

It seemed likely to me that puckish Dr. Franklin had carried out his   4
experiment in London in 1773 and then, for the amusement of his dinner guests at Passy six years later, *produced* a docile fly whose "revivification" allowed him to offer some "spontaneous" conjectures on coming back to see the flourishing state of America in fifty years. And so I wrote it up like that—a little Franklin anecdote for the delectation of my fellow philologists.

If I had been able to leave it at that, I would never have found myself   5
between the two cultures.

I mentioned the flies-in-Madeira to a fellow humanist at a wine and   6
cheese party. (It might not have been in very good taste, but you *can* see how the topic might come up.) "But is that possible?" he asked.

"Is what possible?"   7

"Can a fly drowned in wine be revived by drying it in the sun?"   8

Well, of course, I didn't know. Nor did he. Nor did anyone else at   9
our single culture cocktail party. My curiosity piqued, I decided to conduct a somewhat more extensive investigation on Monday.

The first phone calls were the worst. "Do you have a fly specialist,"   10
I asked the receptionist in the Entomology Department. She thought a moment.

"I don't think so. Not flies precisely. But we do have a bee man and   11
a cockroach man. Do you want either of them?"

I guess it was the unpleasant thought of cockroaches in Madeira that   12
led me to ask for the bee man. She rang his number.

Beginnings have always been difficult for me. "I know you're a spe-   13
cialist in bees," I started, "but do you know anything about flies?"

"Who *is* this anyway," he growled.   *14*

"Gold, English Department."   *15*

"Oh," he answered with what I, oversensitized I'm sure, took to be a *16* sneer. "Well, I suppose I know something about flies." (Probably compared to any dithering English professor.)

I didn't help the image at all when I launched into my question about *17* whether or not drowned flies could be recalled to life. He sputtered. "This *is* a joke, isn't it? Perkins, is that you?"

When I finally got the whole Benjamin Franklin-Madeira-America *18* story laid out, he said, "That Franklin always was a wag, wasn't he?" thus indicating that he was a whole lot closer to bridging the gap between the two cultures than I was ever likely to be. "Look," he said, "I don't think it can be done, but why don't you call my friend Baxter, who specializes in drosophilae." By this time I think he had accurately gauged the quality of his inquirer, and he added quickly—before the pause grew even the slightest bit awkward—"fruit flies." (This was before California made fruit flies front-page news.) "Drosophilae may be closer than bees."

I thanked him, reflecting that if fruit flies weren't closer than bees, *19* they were a darn sight nearer than cockroaches. I called the second man.

"Not fruit flies," he said witheringly, "Drosophilae."   *20*

"I beg your pardon."   *21*

"Drosophilae! D-r-o-"   *22*

I explained that I was in the English Department and that spelling was *23* not my problem. (You can see that my morning had made me a mite testy.) I explained the purpose of my phone call. He whooped. There is simply no other term for what he did into that telephone. He whooped.

Then, maybe because he had read C. P. Snow years ago and because *24* he wanted to reach out to his less fortunate brethren in the humanities, he offered what he assumed was a helping hand. "If they were larvae, they could have grown anaerobically."

It was my turn for the pregnant pause. "Right," I said slowly, "just *25* what do *you* mean when you use the word 'anaerobically?'" (a master stroke, implying, of course, that I was quite familiar with the word when used by *my* colleagues—say of Milton's Satan in the burning lake).

His measured response, which I suspected had been heard by gener- *26* ations of freshmen in Biology 101, told me that my master stroke hadn't fooled anyone. "A-nae-robi-cal-ly," he said (coming as close to spelling it as one could come without actually spelling it), "without air." He went on patiently: "If the flies were larvae, they might not have needed oxygen."

I read him the part where Franklin's anthropomorphic (*anaerobic*, *27* indeed!) flies moved their "thighs" convulsively, "wiped their eyes with their fore feet," and so forth. "No," he agreed, "they don't sound like larvae to me. They don't sound like flies either, but I guess you don't care about that."

I cared, but I was damned if I was going to waste any more time with 28 a fruit-fly freak. The cockroach man at least worked with larger creatures. Cockroaches, I thought, probably do have thighs and the rest of the apparatus. It was, however, all I could do to get quit of my now-cavorting scientist. "What are you working on?" he chortled. *"The Lord of the Flies?"* I knew I was driving another spike between the two cultures, but it *was* satisfying to hang up on Baxter the Fruit Fly.

I hesitated only a little before dialing the cockroach man. After all, I 29 thought, the Kafka specialists probably call him all the time. When I got through to his lab, however, I learned that he was in South America and would be gone for a year. If it was urgent, the secretary said (I considered briefly the kind of "urgent" calls a cockroach man would be getting), I might want to talk to his research assistant. The research assistant had a pleasant, sunny voice, and I found it easy to tell her the story of Dr. Franklin and the flies. I found her giggles much more encouraging than the disbelieving snorts of my first two scientists. I told her that I had talked to the bee expert and the drosophilist but that neither had seemed to understand. "No, I suppose not," she answered cryptically. When I asked her what she thought about the possibility that Franklin had actually revived his drowned flies, her response convinced me that I had finally found a kindred spirit: "We *could* try an experiment," she said. How marvelous that "we" sounded to me: I had been out there on the fringe alone for so long. And "experiment" sounded so, well, so scientific. I felt as if I had thrown my first bridge across the cultural gap.

"What kind of experiment?"   30

"Leave it to me," she said.   31

About a week later I opened my office door and immediately sensed 32 something new in the room, some intruder among the dusty books, unfiled notecards, and ungraded term papers. There was a stoppered vial of amber liquid sitting on my desk. A closer inspection revealed a tag around the sealed bottle top that read: "Contents: 3 adult *M. domestica* in 100 cc Paul Masson Madeira." Inside were three very dead—or very stoned, I amended with a bow to my new-found scientific spirit—flies.

There was an eight-and-a-half by eleven piece of paper under the vial. 33 It was a dittoed experiment sheet with space for details to be entered, and its very form, its specific categories, seemed to lend an aura of legitimacy and significance to my search for Truth:

Experimenter:

Date:

Pheromone Type: (whatever that meant)

Species:

Sample #:

Test: Qual.:

Dilutions:
  $C_0 =$
  Serial:

Test Results:

Sample History:

Comments:

Even as I scanned that impressive form and sloshed the Madeira around
a bit (setting up an interesting spiraling motion among the floating "*Musca
Domestica*"), I could not help thinking how unmethodical we humanists
were. There must be a way to study *Hamlet* or *Paradise Lost* or *The
Faerie Queene* more systematically.

Then I began to examine the entries made by my research assistant *34*
(how easily I appropriated her services: but the cockroach man *was* in
South America). The "Sample," I saw, consisted of "3 living adult *M.
Domestica*" (how she knew they were adult I did not know), which, I
learned under "Sample History," had been caught in Room 125 Snow
Hall. Apparently janitorial service was no better in Snow Hall than it
was in the Humanities Building. Somehow that thought pleased me.
The Paul Masson Madeira had been purchased at a local liquor store, I
saw, but its Previous History was "Unknown."

If *I* was beginning to show signs of a new scientific spirit, I suspected *35*
that my research assistant was crossing cultural boundaries too. One of
her entries went well beyond the requirements of the form. It was exactly
the kind of gratuitous tidbit I would tuck away in footnotes to philological
essays. According to the bottle label, she had written, "This wine has a
taste as rich as its place in early American history." How Benjamin
Franklin would have loved that! Had Paul Masson known Dr. Franklin
in France? No, no, there would be time enough for such questions when
this experiment was finished.

The Test Results were to be determined by me. And what were we *36*
testing? The "possible reviviscence of *M. domestica* bottled in Madeira;
said *M. Domestica* to be removed from wine two months hence." For
the next few weeks I examined the vial daily, observing the total inactivity
of the inhabitants and the unpleasant way the glass had of magnifying
their size. One of the departmental secretaries spotted the amber vial
one day and came in for a closer look. She went out quickly and has

refused to type anything for me since. Another secretary took to visiting my office and announcing for all to hear: "I've come to look at your fly." I seemed to be bridging two cultures, but they weren't science and humanism. I also noticed that the amount of time I was having to spend advising students was diminishing. They would be sitting in the chair opposite me, asking about what course in social science or mathematics they needed, when their eyes would be caught by a glint of light on the amber vial. They would look quickly back at me, but from then on it was only a matter of time before they would be looking at those dead flies steadily and then remembering a class they were late for or an appointment with a physician. I tried to explain the vial to one bright student, but she said it was all right—she understood. She worked during the summers at the state mental hospital.

As a matter of fact, none of this has worked out as I thought it would. *37* After the article appeared in *Modern Philology,* my own colleagues got a bit sniffy. They muttered about professional standards. Then, when they saw the flies in my office, they muttered about housekeeping standards. Nor could I bring myself to unseal the vial. I watched and I brooded. As fewer and fewer professors of literature would pass the time of day with me, I began phoning Professor Baxter—you remember the fruit-fly freak?—over in entomology. Baxter turned out to be rather a good sort and was quite interested when he heard I actually had an experiment brewing. After a few informative and pleasant phone conversations, we have taken to visiting each other. I go to his lab or he comes over here, and we discuss his flies or mine or Ben Franklin's—over a glass of aged Madeira, naturally.

Study Questions

1. Joel J. Gold opens his essay with a reference to C. P. Snow's *The Two Cultures,* a work that describes the inability of scientists and humanists to share with one another the basic concepts of their studies. In what ways does the essay illustrate this separation?
2. What personality does Gold project for himself in this essay? In what ways does it represent a commonly held notion of what English professors are like? How does that personality reflect Gold's opinion of the separation between scientists and humanists?
3. Gold presents a number of conversations between himself and members of the Entomology Department. How do these conversations help him to convey the personality he has chosen to present? What do these conversations show you about his impression of the personalities and attitudes of the scientists?

4. What other kinds of personalities might Gold have chosen for himself? If he had used one of these alternatives, how would that have changed his discussion of the separation between humanists and scientists? Discuss how appropriate such an alternative would have been for the message and purpose you see in this essay.

The Unglamorous But Worthwhile Duties of the Black Revolutionary Artist, or of the Black Writer Who Simply Works and Writes

Alice Walker

W hen I came to Sarah Lawrence in 1964, I was *1* fleeing from Spelman College in Atlanta, a school that I considered opposed to change, to freedom, and to understanding that by the time most girls enter college they are already women and should be treated as women. At Sarah Lawrence I found all that I was looking for at the time—freedom to come and go, to read leisurely, to go my own way, dress my own way, and conduct my personal life as I saw fit. It was here that I wrote my first published short story and my first book, here that I learned to feel what I thought had some meaning, here that I felt no teacher or administrator breathing down my neck.

I thought I had found happiness and peace in my own time.   *2*

And for that time, perhaps, I had. It was not until after I had graduated *3* and gone south to Mississippi that I began to realize that my lessons at Sarah Lawrence had left crucial areas empty, and had, in fact, contributed to a blind spot in my education that needed desperately to be cleared if I expected to be a whole woman, a full human being, a black woman full of self-awareness and pride. I realized, sometime after graduation, that when I had studied contemporary writers and the South at this college— taught by a warm, wonderful woman whom I much admired—the writings of Richard Wright had not been studied and that instead I had studied the South from Faulkner's point of view, from Feibleman's, from Flannery O'Connor's. It was only after trying to conduct the same kind of course myself—with black students—that I realized that such a course simply cannot *be* taught if *Black Boy* is not assigned and read, or if "The Ethics of Living Jim Crow" is absent from the reading list.

I realized further that when I had been yearning, while here, to do a *4* paper on pan-Africanism in my modern world history class, my Harvard-trained teacher had made no mention of W. E. B. Du Bois (who attended Harvard too, in the nineteenth century), no doubt because he had never heard of him.

I also realized that I had wasted five of my hard-to-come-by dollars 5 one semester when I bought a supposedly "comprehensive" anthology of English and American verse which had been edited by a Sarah Lawrence faculty member. A nice man, a handsome one even, who had not thought to include a single poem by a black poet. I believe this man, who *was* really very nice, did not know there *were* black poets, or, if he did, believed like Louis Simpson that "poetry that is identifiably Negro is not important." I've yet to figure out *exactly* what that means, but it sounds ugly and has effectively kept black poets out of "comprehensive" anthologies, where the reader would have the opportunity to decide whether their poems are "important" or not.

I began to feel that subtly and without intent or malice, I had been 6 miseducated. For where my duty as a black poet, writer, and teacher would take me, people would have little need of Keats and Byron or even Robert Frost, but much need of Hughes, Bontemps, Gwendolyn Brooks, and Margaret Walker.

So for the past four years I've been in still another college. This time 7 simply a college of books—musty old books that went out of print years ago—and of old people, the oldest old black men and women I could find, and a college of the young; students and dropouts who articulate in various bold and shy ways that they believe themselves to be without a valuable history, without a respectable music, without writing or poetry that speaks to them.

My enrollment in this newest college will never end, and for that I am 8 glad. And each day I look about to see what can and should be done to make it a bigger college, a more inclusive one, one more vital and long living. There are things our people should know, books they should read, poems they should know by heart. I think now of *Black Reconstruction* by Du Bois, of *Cane* by Jean Toomer, of *Mules and Men* by Zora Neale Hurston. Ten years ago, the one copy of *Black Reconstruction* that could be found in Atlanta was so badly battered and had been pasted back together so many times that a student could check it out of the library for only thirty minutes, and was then not allowed to take it outside the reading room. *Cane* by Jean Toomer and *Mules and Men* by Zora Neale Hurston I found tucked away behind locked doors in the library of Lincoln University. Knowing both books were out of print at the time, I Xeroxed them and stole somebody's rights, but it was the least I could do if I wanted to read them over and over again, which I did.

Today it gives me pleasure to see a Black Students' Association at 9 Sarah Lawrence. That must mean there are many black students to pay dues. When I was here there were six of us and none of us was entirely black. Much has clearly changed, here as in the rest of the country. But when I look about and see what work still remains I can only be mildly, though sincerely, impressed.

Much lip service has been given the role of the revolutionary black   *10* writer but now the words must be turned into work. For, as someone has said, "Work is love made visible." There are the old people, Toms, Janes, or just simply old people, who need us to put into words for them the courage and dignity of their lives. There are the students who need guidance and direction. Real guidance and real direction, and support that doesn't get out of town when the sun goes down.

I have not labeled myself yet. I would like to call myself revolutionary,   *11* for I am always changing, and growing, it is hoped for the good of more black people. I do call myself black when it seems necessary to call myself anything, especially since I believe one's work rather than one's appearance adequately labels one. I used to call myself a poet, but I've come to have doubts about that. The truest and most enduring impulse I have is simply to write. It seems necessary for me to forget all the titles, all the labels, and all the hours of talk and to concentrate on the mountain of work I find before me. My major advice to young black artists would be that they shut themselves up somewhere away from all debates about who they are and what color they are and just turn out paintings and poems and stories and novels. Of course the kind of artist we are required to be cannot do this. Our people are waiting. *But there must be an awareness of what is Bull and what is Truth,* what is practical and what is designed ultimately to paralyze our talents. For example, it is unfair to the people we expect to reach to give them a beautiful poem if they are unable to read it.

And so, what is the role of the black revolutionary artist? Sometimes   *12* it is the role of remedial reading teacher. I will never forget one of the girls in my black studies course last year at Jackson State. All year long she had been taught by one of the greatest black poets still living: Margaret Walker. I took over the class when Miss Walker was away for the quarter. We were reading "For My People" and this girl came to the section that reads:

Let a new earth rise. Let another world be born. Let a bloody peace be written in the sky. Let a second generation full of courage issue forth, let a people loving freedom come to growth, let a beauty full of healing and a strength of final clenching be the pulsing in our spirits and our blood. Let the martial songs be written, let the dirges disappear. Let a race of men now rise and take control!

"What do you think?" I asked the girl. (She had read the poem very   *13* well.) She shook her head. "What is the matter?" I asked. She said, "Oh, these older poets! They never write poems that tell us to fight!"

Then I realized that she had read the poem, even read it passionately, and had not understood a word of what it was about. "What is a 'martial song'"? I asked. "What is a disappearing dirge?" The girl was completely thrown by the words.

I recall a young man (bearded, good-looking), a Muslim, he said, who *14* absolutely refused to read Faulkner. "We in the revolution now," he said, "We don't have to read no more white folks." "Read thine enemy," I prodded, to no avail. And this same young man made no effort, either, to read Hughes or Ellison or McKay or Ernest Gaines, who is perhaps the most gifted young black writer working today. His problem was that the revolutionary rhetoric so popular today had convinced him of his own black perfection and of the imperfection of everybody and everything white, but it had not taught him how to read. The belief that he was already the complete man had stunted this young man's growth. And when he graduates from college, as he will, he will teach your children and mine, and still not know how to read, nor will he be inclined to learn.

The real revolution is always concerned with the least glamorous stuff. *15* With raising a reading level from second grade to third. With simplifying history and writing it down (or reciting it) for the old folks. With helping illiterates fill out food-stamp forms—for they must eat, revolution or not. The dull, frustrating work with our people is the work of the black revolutionary artist. It means, most of all, staying close enough to them to be there whenever they need you.

But the work of the black artist is also to create and to preserve what *16* was created before him. It is knowing the words of James Weldon Johnson's "Negro National Anthem" and even remembering the tune. It is being able to read "For My People" with tears in the eyes, comprehension in the soul. It is sending small tokens of affection to our old and ancient poets whom renown has ignored. One of the best acts of my entire life was to take a sack of oranges to Langston Hughes when he had the flu, about two weeks before he died.

We must cherish our old men. We must revere their wisdom, appre- *17* ciate their insight, love the humanity of their words. They may not all have been heroes of the kind we think of today, but generally it takes but a single reading of their work to know that they were all men of sensitivity and soul.

Only a year or so ago did I read this poem, by Arna Bontemps, "The *18* Black Man Talks of Reaping":

I have sown beside all waters in my day.
I planted deep within my heart the fear
That wind or fowl would take the grain away.
I planted safe against this stark, lean year.

I scattered seed enough to plant the land
In rows from Canada to Mexico.
But for my reaping only what the hand
Can hold at once is all that I can show.

Yet what I sowed and what the orchard yields
My brother's sons are gathering stalk and root,
Small wonder then my children glean in fields
They have not sown, and feed on bitter fruit.

It requires little imagination to see the author as a spiritual colossus, *19*
arms flung wide, as in a drawing by Charles White, to encompass all the
"Adams and the Eves and their countless generations," bearing the pain
of the reaping but brooding on the reapers with great love.

Where *was* this poem in all those poetry anthologies I read with eager *20*
heart and hushed breath? It was not there, along with all the others that
were not there. But it must, and will, be always in my heart. And if, in
some gray rushing day, all our black books are burned, it must be in my
head and I must be able to drag it out and recite it, though it be bitter to
the tongue and painful to the ears. For that is also the role of the black
revolutionary artist. He must be a walking filing cabinet of poems and
songs and stories, of people, of places, of deeds and misdeeds.

In my new college of the young I am often asked, "What is the place *21*
of hate in writing?" After all we have been through in this country it is
foolish and in any case useless to say hate has no place. Obviously, it
has. But we must exercise our noblest impluses with our hate, not to
let it destroy us or destroy our *truly precious heritage,* which is not, by
the way, a heritage of bigotry or intolerance. I've found, in my own
writing, that a little hatred, keenly directed, is a useful thing. Once
spread about, however, it becomes a web in which I would sit caught
and paralyzed like the fly who stepped into the parlor. The artist must
remember that some individual men, like Byron de la Beckwith or Sheriff
Jim Clark, should be hated, and that some corporations like Dow and
General Motors should be hated too. Also the Chase Manhattan Bank
and the Governor of Mississippi. However, there are men who should
be loved, or at least respected on their merits, and groups of men, like
the American Friends, who should not be hated. The strength of the
artist is his courage to look at every old thing with fresh eyes and his
ability to re-create, as true to life as possible, that great middle ground
of people between Medgar Evers's murderer, Byron de la Beckwith, and
the fine old gentleman John Brown.

I am impressed by people who claim they can see every person and *22*
event in strict terms of black and white, but generally their work is not,
in my long-contemplated and earnestly considered opinion, either black
or white, but a dull, uniform gray. It is boring because it is easy and

requires only that the reader be a lazy reader and a prejudiced one. Each story or poem has a formula, usually two-thirds "hate whitey's guts" and one-third "I am black, beautiful, strong, and almost always right." Art is not flattery, necessarily, and the work of any artist must be more difficult than that. A man's life can rarely be summed up in one word; even if that word is black or white. And it is the duty of the artist to present the man *as he is*. One should recall that Bigger Thomas was many great and curious things, but he was neither good nor beautiful. He was real, and that is sufficient.

Sometimes, in my anger and frustration at the world we live in, I ask *23* myself, What is real and what is not? And now it seems to me that what is real is what is happening. What is real is what did happen. What happened to me and happens to me is most real of all. I write then, out of that. I write about the old men that I knew (I love old men), and the great big beautiful women with arms like cushions (who would really rather look like Pat Nixon), and of the harried fathers and mothers and the timid, hopeful children. And today, in Mississippi, it seems I sometimes relive my Georgia childhood. I see the same faces, hear the same soft voices, take a nip, once in a while, of the same rich mellow corn, or wine. And when I write about the people there, in the strangest way it is as if I am not writing about them at all, but about myself. The artist then is the voice of the people, but she is also The People.

Study Questions

1. This essay was presented to the Black Students' Association of Sarah Lawrence College in 1970. Identify some of the words, phrases, and sentences that show Alice Walker's awareness of her intended audience. How do these words, phrases, and sentences create a bond between her and her listeners?
2. What problems might an all-white audience have with this work? What features of her essay would give such a group trouble? What features are understandable and appropriate to any group?
3. In paragraph 22 Walker states: "Art is not flattery, necessarily, and the work of any artist must be more difficult than that." In what ways does Walker not flatter her audience? How does she warn them about oversimplifications without alienating them?
4. This essay was first presented in 1970. If Walker were to rewrite this essay for presentation to the same Black Students' Association today, what changes do you feel she would have to make? To answer this question you may want to look at a few recent anthologies of American poetry to see which black writers are included. You may also want to consider the roles blacks have played in American politics since 1970.

Centering as Dialogue

Mary Caroline Richards

C entering: that act which precedes all others on *1* the potter's wheel. The bringing of the clay into a spinning, unwobbling pivot, which will then be free to take innumerable shapes as potter and clay press against each other. The firm, tender, sensitive pressure which yields as much as it asserts. It is like a handclasp between two living hands, receiving the greeting at the very moment that they give it. It is this speech between the hand and the clay that makes me think of dialogue. And it is a language far more interesting than the spoken vocabulary which tries to describe it, for it is spoken not by the tongue and lips but by the whole body, by the whole person, speaking and listening. And with listening too, it seems to me, it is not the ear that hears, it is not the physical organ that performs that act of inner receptivity. It is the total person who hears. Sometimes the skin seems to be the best listener, as it prickles and thrills, say to a sound or a silence; or the fantasy, the imagination: how it bursts into inner pictures as it listens and then responds by pressing its language, its forms, into the listening clay. To be open to what we hear, to be open in what we say. . . .

I am a question-asker and a truth-seeker. I do not have much in the *2* way of status in my life, nor security. I have been on quest, as it were, from the beginning. For a long time I thought there was something wrong with me: no ambition, no interest in tenure, always on the march, changing every seven years, from landscape to landscape. Certain elements were constant: the poetry, the desire for relationship, the sense of voyage. But lately I have developed also a sense of destination, or destiny. And a sense that if I am to be on quest, I must expect to live like a pilgrim; I must keep to the inner path. I must be able to be whoever I am.

For example, it seemed strange to me, as to others, that, having taken *3* my Ph.D. in English, I should then in the middle of my life, instead of taking up a college professorship, turn to the art of pottery. During one period, when people asked me what I did; I was uncertain what to answer; I guessed I could say I taught English, wrote poetry, and made pottery. What was my occupation? I finally gave up and said "Person."

Having been imbued with the ordinary superstitions of American *4* higher education, among which is the belief that something known as the life of the mind is more apt to take you where you want to go than any other kind of life, I busied myself with learning to practice logic, grammar, analysis, summary, generalization; I learned to make distinctions, to speculate, to purvey information. I was educated to be an intellectual of the verbal type. I might have been a philosophy major, a literature major, a language major. I was always a kind of oddball even in under-graduate circles, as I played kick-goal on the Reed College campus with President Dexter Keezer. And in graduate school, even more so. Examinations tended to make me merry, often seeming to me to be some kind of private game, some secret ritual compulsively played by the professors and the institution. I invariably became facetious in all the critical hours. All that solemnity for a few facts! I couldn't believe they were serious. But they were. I never quite understood it. But I loved the dream and the reality that lay behind those texts and in the souls of my teachers. I often felt like a kind of fraud, because I suspected that the knowledge I was acquiring and being rewarded for by academic diploma was wide wide of the truth I sensed to live somewhere, somewhere. I felt that I knew little of real importance; and when would the day come that others would realize it too, and I would be exposed? I have had dream after dream in which it turns out that I have not really completed my examinations for the doctorate and have them still to pass. And I sweat with anxiety. A sense of occupying a certain position without possessing the real thing: the deeper qualifications of wisdom and prophecy. But of course it was not the world who exposed me, it was my dreams. I do not know if I am a philosopher, but if philosophy is the love of wisdom, then I am a philosopher, because I love wisdom and that is why I love the crafts, because they are wise.

I became a teacher quite by chance. Liked it, found in education an 5
image through which I could examine the possibilities of growth, of nourishment, of the experiences that lead to knowledge of nature and of self. It was a good trade to be in if you were a question-asker.

But the trouble was that though the work absorbed my mind, it used 6
very little else. And I am by now convinced that wisdom is not the product of mental effort. Wisdom is a state of the total being, in which capacities for knowledge and for love, for survival and for death, for imagination, inspiration, intuition, for all the fabulous functioning of this human being who we are, come into a center with their forces, come into an experience of meaning that can voice itself as wise action. It is not enough to belong to a Society of Friends who believe in nonviolence if, when frustrated, your body spontaneously contracts and shoots out its fist to knock another man down. It is in our bodies that redemption takes place. It is the physicality of the crafts that pleases me: I learn through my hands and my eyes and my skin what I could never learn through my brain. I develop a sense of life, of the world of earth, air, fire, and water—and wood, to add the fifth element according to Oriental alchemy—which could be developed in no other way. And if it is life I am fostering, I must maintain a kind of dialogue with the clay, listening,

serving, interpreting as well as mastering. The union of our wills, like a marriage, it is a beautiful act, the act of centering and turning a pot on the potter's wheel; and the sexual images implicit in the forming of the cone and opening of the vessel are archetypal; likewise the give-and-take in the forming of a pot out of slabs, out of raw shards, out of coils; the union of natural intelligences: the intelligence of the clay, my intelligence, the intelligence of the tools, the intelligence of the fire.

You don't need me to tell you what education is. Everybody really 7 knows that education goes on all the time everywhere all through our lives, and that it is the process of waking up to life. Jean Henri Fabre said something just about like that, I think. He said that to be educated was not to be taught but to wake up. It takes a heap of resolve to keep from going to sleep in the middle of the show. It's not that we want to sleep our lives away. It's that it requires certain kinds of energy, certain capacities for taking the world into our consciousness, certain real powers of body and soul to be a match for reality. That's why knowledge and consciousness are two quite different things. Knowledge is like a product we consume and store. All we need are good closets. By consciousness I mean a state of being "awake" to the world throughout our organism. This kind of consciousness requires not closets but an organism attuned to the finest perceptions and responses. It allows experience to breathe through it as light enters and changes a room. When knowledge is transformed into consciousness and into will, ah then we are on the high road indeed. . . .

That which we consume, with a certain passivity, accepting it for the 8 most part from our teachers, who in turn have accepted it from theirs, is like the food we eat. And food, in order to become energy, or will, is transformed entirely by the processes of metabolism. We do not become the food we eat. Rather the food turns into us. Similarly with knowledge, at best. Hopefully, we do not turn into encyclopedias or propaganda machines or electric brains. Our knowledge, if we allow it to be transformed within us, turns into capacity for life-serving human deeds. If knowedge does not turn into life, it makes cripples and madmen and dunces. It poisons just as food would if it stayed in the stomach and was never digested, and the waste products never thrown off.

It is dangerous to seek to possess knowledge, as if it could be stored. 9 For one thing, it tends to make one impatient with ignorance, as people busy with money-seeking tend to be impatient with idlers. Though ignorance is the prime prerequisite for education, many teachers appear offended by it—or worse, contemptuous. Perhaps it is partly for this reason that many prefer to give advanced courses to select or "gifted" groups.

The possession of knowledge may create a materialism of its own. 10 Knowledge becomes property. Teachers compete with each other for status, wealth, influence. A professor of education was speaking to friends of education in the county where I live, and she was urging pay raises as bait for hiring good teachers, "for after all, the standard of success is the salary check." Naturally in this climate professional educators are apt to quarrel over tactics and to engage in pressure politics, motivated by a desire to protect their security and to establish their views as ruling policy. In other words, education may be sacrificed to knowledge-as-commodity. Just as life is sometimes sacrificed to art-as-arrangement. The quest is abandoned. Instead, property is bought at the site of the last dragon killed, and a ruling class is formed out of the heroes. The knights grow fat and lazy and conceited and petulant. They parade in their armor on special occasions to bedazzle the populace. But in their hearts are terror and duplicity. And when difficult times come, they fall upon each other with their rusty axes and try to divide the world into those who know and those who don't. There is nothing to equal in bitterness and gall, childishness and spite, the intramural warfare of the academic community. Where is honor? Where is devotion? Where is responsibility of soul?

Such an atmosphere brought me gradually to imagine possible short- *11* comings in the educational system I had docilely trusted. Initiative and imagination seemed sorely lacking. Teachers seemed to apply to their students the same pressures that had crippled them. Most of us have been brain-washed to think that knowledge and security make the world go round. And if the world seems to be going round very poorly, we do not think of questioning deeply its education. The need for creative imagination in the intellectually trained person is drastic. Also the need for spontaneous human feeling.

Fashionable thinking may dominate the scientist and artist and scholar *12* alike. For them, knowledge is the body of facts currently in fashion. Art is the image and compositional practice now in fashion. Since it is difficult to test the truth of most facts, faculty and students alike settle for "interesting," "original," and "self-consistent" theories. An ability to marshal and interpret "evidence" is highly esteemed, though evidence is often no more than opinions strongly held or secondary research. Very little stress is placed on developing powers of observation or on intuition. Thus, with primary experience held so at a distance, sensory life in particular, I find that my principal task in teaching adults is to win their trust. They tend to be overwhelmingly oriented to manipulation and to effect. It rarely occurs to them to work in a direct way with what they know and are. Their primary motivations are to please, to make a strong impression, to do either what is expected (if they are docile) or what is unexpected (if they are hostile). They assume that pretense and falsity are virtues. The whole thing sometimes seems like a massive confidence game.

Like other men, teachers tend to withhold themselves from naked *13* personal contact. They tend to pin their hopes on jargon and style. And this, I have observed, is what many students learn from them: afraid to reveal themselves, burdened with shame and dismay and hopelessness, or expertise and cunning.

A theory much in vogue is that Western man is sick with sexual 14 repression and pleasure anxiety. I believe that the squelching of the "person" and his spontaneous intuitive response to experience is as much at the root of our timidity, our falseness. Teachers and students who in the great school markets barter their learning for salaries and grades are hungry for respect, for personal relationship, for warmth. Unfortunately, they have the impression that these are extracurricular (like Newton's secondary qualities of color and so on)—and their capacity for balance between the life within and the world without shrinks or falters, or their desperation turns rank.

It is a sensitive matter, of course. I am not going to all these words 15 merely to insult the spirit of true research. But my life as a teacher and as a member of the human community advises me that education may estrange us from life-commitment as well as bind us firmly within it. There are all kinds of things to learn, and we had best learn them all. One of the reasons formal education is in danger today is that a sense of work is split off from human earnestness. How may this split be healed? Working with our materials as artist-craftsmen may help to engender a new health here.

An act of the self, that's what one must make. An act of the self, 16 from me to you. From center to center. We must mean what we say, from our innermost heart to the outermost galaxy. Otherwise we are lost and dizzy in a maze of reflections. We carry light within us. There is no need merely to reflect. Others carry light within them. These lights must wake to each other. My face is real. Yours is. Let us find our way to our initiative.

For must we not show ourselves to each other, and will we not know 17 then who are the teachers and who are the students? Do we not all learn from one another? My students at City College are worldly-wise and naive as lambs. I am sophisticated and uninformed. We make a good combination. They have never heard of e. e. cummings, who lived in their city, nor of the New York painters. They do not know that there are free art galleries where they may see the latest works of modern artists. They do not know very much about contemporary "culture." But they know well the life of the subway, the office, the factory, the union hall, the hassle for employment; they know what they did in the war or in their escape from Hungary or Germany, or in occupied France, or Israel. They know what it is like to be black in America. They are patient with my obtuseness, they check my too quick judgments, my sarcasm which is unperceptive. I help them to unmask, to be openly as tender and hopeful and generous as they inwardly are. I help them to open themselves to knowledge. They help me to open myself to life. We are equal in courage.

Must weakness be concealed in order that respect be won? Must love *18*
and fervor be concealed? Must we pretend to fearlessness? and certainty? Surely education should equip us to know what to fear and what
to be uncertain of. Surely it should equip us in personal honor.

Must. Should. Convenient words! Exhortations meant to loosen the *19*
grip of congealed behavior. . . . Perhaps these perceptions are not the
proper work of intellect, but of some other faculty deeply neglected in
our education. In any case, at a critical moment in life my hunger for
nakedness and realism and nobility turned to the clay of earth itself, and
to water and fire.

I took up pottery also, in a sense, by chance. Unforeseen opportunity *20*
joined with interest and readiness. Like teaching, not a consciously
sought but surely a destined union. For the materials and processes of
pottery spoke to me of cosmic presences and transformations quite as
surely as the pots themselves enchanted me. Experiences of the plastic
clay and the firing of the ware carried more than commonplace values.
Joy resonated deep within me, and it has stirred these thoughts only
slowly to the surface. I have come to feel that we live in a universe of
spirit, which materializes and dematerializes grandly; all things seem to
me to live, and all acts to contain meaning deeper than matter-of-fact;
and the things we do with deepest love and interest compel us by the
spiritual forces which dwell in them. This seems to me to be a dialogue
of the visible and the invisible to which our ears are attuned.

There was, first of all, something in the nature of the clay itself. You *21*
can do very many things with it, push this way and pull that, squeeze
and roll and attach and pinch and hollow and pile. But you can't do
everything with it. You can go only so far, and then the clay resists. To
know ourselves by our resistances—this is a thought first expressed to
me by the poet Charles Olson.

And so it is with persons. You can do very many things with us: push *22*
us together and pull us apart and squeeze us and roll us flat, empty us
out and fill us up. You can surround us with influences, but there comes
a point when you can do no more. The person resists, in one way or
another (if it is only by collapsing, like the clay). His own will becomes
active.

This is a wonderful moment, when one feels his will become active, *23*
come as a force into the total assemblage and dynamic intercourse and
interpenetration of will impulses. When one stands like a natural substance, plastic but with one's own character written into the formula, ah
then one feels oneself part of the world, taking one's shape with its
help—but a shape only one's own freedom can create.

And the centering of the clay, of which I have spoken. The opening *24*
of the form. And the firing of the pot. This experience has deep psychic
reverberations: how the pot, which was originally plastic, sets into dry
clay, brittle and fragile, and then by being heated to a certain temperature
hardens into stone. By natural law as it were, it takes its final form.

Ordeal by fire. Then, the form once taken, the pot may not last, the body may perish; but the inner form has been taken, and it cannot break in the same sense.

I, like everyone I know, am instinctively motivated toward symbols *25* of wholeness. What is a simpler, more natural one than the pot fired? Wholeness may be thought of as a kind of inner equilibrium, in which all our capacities have been brought into functioning as an organism. The potencies of the whole organism flow into the gestures of any part. And the sensation in any part reverberates throughout the soul. The unconscious and conscious levels of being can work together at the tasks of life, conveying messages to each other, assimilating one another. In wholeness I sense an integration of those characteristics which are uniquely *me* and those interests which I share with the rest of mankind. As for example any bowl is symbolic of an archetypal circular form, which I share with all, but which *I* make and which therefore contains those very qualities of myself which are active in the making. I believe that pots have the smell of the person who makes them: a smell of tenderness, of vanity or ambition, of ease and naturalness, of petulance, uncertainty, callousness, fussiness, playfulness, solemnity, exuberance, absent-mindedness. The pot gives off something. It gives off its innerness, that which it holds but which cannot be seen.

In pottery, by developing sensitivity in manipulating natural materials *26* by hand, I found a wisdom which had died out of the concepts I learned in the university: abstractions, mineralized and dead; while the minerals themselves were alive with energy and meaning. The life I found in the craft helped to bring to a new birth my ideals in education. Some secret center became vitalized in those hours of silent practice in the arts of transformation.

The experience of centering was one I particularly sought because I *27* thought of myself as dispersed, interested in too many things. I envied people who were "single-minded," who had one powerful talent and who knew when they got up in the morning what it was they had to do. Whereas I, wherever I turned, felt the enchantment: to the window for the sweetness of the air; to the door for the passing figures; to the teapot, the typewriter, the knitting needles, the pets, the pottery, the newspaper, the telephone. Wherever I looked, I could have lived.

It took me half my life to come to believe I was OK even if I did love *28* experience in a loose and undiscriminating way and did not know for sure the difference between good and bad. My struggles to accept my nature were the struggles of centering. I found myself at odds with the propaganda of our times. One is supposed to be either an artist or a homemaker, by one popular superstition. Either a teacher or a poet, by a theory which says that poetry must not sermonize. Either a craftsman or an intellectual, by a snobbism which claims either hand or head as the seat of true power. One is supposed to concentrate and not to spread oneself thin, as the jargon goes. And this is a jargon spoken by a cultural leadership from which it takes time to win one's freedom, if one is not lucky enough to have been born free. Finally, I hit upon an image: a seed-sower. Not to worry about which seeds sprout. But to give them as my gift in good faith.

But in spite of my self-acceptance, I still clung to a concept of purity *29* which was chaste and aloof from the fellowship of man, and had yet to center the image of a pure heart in whose bright warm streams the world is invited to bathe. A heart who can be touched and who stirs in response, bringing the whole body into an act of greeting.

Well then, I became a potter.   *30*

Study Questions

1. In "Centering as Dialogue," Mary Caroline Richards deals with the complex topic of education and individual development. How does her use of the term *centering* help her to explain what she believes a "whole" person should be? What parallels does she find between centering and teaching?
2. Richards deals with such abstractions as education, knowledge, wisdom, and intuition. Why are such terms needed? How does she help her readers understand what she means by them?
3. In paragraphs 7–13 Richards presents her view of academia. What is that view? What key words and phrases in these paragraphs express her attitude toward education as it now exists? Characterize the sentences in these paragraphs. Are they long or short, simple or complex? How does the topic help her shape these sentences?
4. As question 2 implies, Richards covers many subtopics in her essay. Do you feel that all of them are necessary for her discussion? Explain your answer.

SECTION
TWO

Meaning

T he Cat only grinned when it saw Alice. It looked good-natured, she thought: still it had *very* long claws and a great many teeth, so she thought it ought to be treated with respect.

"Cheshire-Puss," she began, rather timidly, as she did not at all know whether it would like the name; however, it only grinned a little wider. "Come, it's pleased so far," thought Alice, and she went on. "Would you tell me, please, which way I ought to go from here?"

"That depends a good deal on where you want to get to," said the Cat.

"I don't much care where ——" said Alice.

"Then it doesn't matter which way you go," said the Cat.

"—— so long as I get *somewhere*," Alice added as an explanation.

"Oh, you're sure to do that," said the Cat, "if you only walk long enough."

Lewis Carroll, *Alice's Adventures in Wonderland*

H ow often do all of us find ourselves so over-whelmed that, like poor Alice, we would rather be any place other than where we are now? If Alice is confused by fantastic Wonderland, we are frequently just as confused by our own world. And what about those writers who face a blank sheet of paper that grins back at them like a Cheshire Cat? Wouldn't they rather be washing the car or alphabetizing record collections? Sane human beings will avoid pain whenever possible, and confusion is painful whether it comes from visiting an absurd world or from being forced to write.

Alice and writers have much in common. Alice finds herself in a world of nonsense populated with characters who seem ridiculous. Yet these characters appear to be perfectly logical to one another. As far as they are concerned, it is Alice who has the problems. Writers must deal with worlds of information that may seem equally nonsensical. Although each piece of information may be accurate, it is left to the writer to somehow gather all the bits and pieces together and make sense of it all. Like Alice, we may know a great deal about the world we're in, but we would find it impossible to explain it fully. How would we begin? What would we emphasize? What must be included? What could be left out?

Alice has one distinct advantage over writers. She can awake from her dream and Wonderland disappears. But an assigned theme does not evaporate. It will be there even after a good night's sleep. Unlike Alice, writers must finally confront their confusion and discover ways to transform it into orderly prose that conveys meaning.

The essays at the end of this section are intended to aid you in your search for ways of overcoming confusion. They illustrate various methods other writers have used to make sense out of vast amounts of information. These writers have discovered within all that information a statement worth making and a reason for making it: that is, they have found a *meaning*. Sometimes the meaning a writer deals with will contain complex philosophies that will challenge even the most learned readers. At other times it deals with some trivial topic that turns out to be both delightful and exciting. All of the essays, however, have one thing in common: their writers have cut through the chaos of facts and found something to say about the topic.

In order to make effective use of the essays, we will ask you to read them as if you had to write on the same topic:

What do you learn in each essay that would help you deal with the topic in your own paper?

What did you already know?

Do you agree or disagree with the writer?

What did the writer include that you would not?

What examples can you think of that would support the writer's opinions?

What examples would oppose those opinions?

What information would you need before you would tackle the same topic?

What other information would make the meaning of the essay clearer to you?

By asking these questions and seeking honest answers, you will learn how to adapt these same questions to your own writing and in this way begin to gather together the bits and pieces and create your own meaning.

Before we ask you to read the essays, however, we want to describe several methods that can help you discover possible meanings for your essays. Each method will help you look at your topic and explore your reactions to it before you commit yourself to any particular message. In fact, you may find that by using one or more of these techniques you will discover you actually do have something to say on topics that first appeared completely unmanageable. Many of the questions following the essays in this section will give you practice in using these discovery techniques.

Prewriting

As was mentioned in Section 1, one broad area of the writing process involves the search for the various possible meanings a topic might suggest. This stage is usually called *prewriting*. There are many different ways of doing this, but they generally fall into two categories: unstructured and structured prewriting.

Although you may never have been aware of it, it is very likely that you already know one very common method of unstructured prewriting.

Many writers search for meaning by first writing a draft of the essay and then continually redrafting until they are satisfied. These writers feel most comfortable when they see how each part fits into a whole. They do prewriting and organizing simultaneously.

Such a method has rather serious drawbacks. It will only work if the writer is willing to alter constantly the completed drafts and occasionally scrap unsuccessful ones—but radically changing a draft can be very difficult. Once you have spent your time and energy in writing a paper, you may find that you are too exhausted to face such a task. You have made a large commitment to that draft, and it may be extremely difficult for you to consider effective alternate meanings or structures. You are locked into seeing the topic as it was developed in that draft, and any further reshaping of the paper is usually only a "refinement" of your first version.

In order to avoid such a premature commitment, a number of writers use a scaled-down version of this technique: *free writing*. When faced with a topic that brings with it no immediate inspiration, they will start writing down any random thoughts they have. This method frees them from worrying about organization and allows them to concentrate on what they might have to say. Because free writing is simply recording thoughts as they occur, the result looks nothing like a finished essay.

One particular variation of free writing is effective in easing writers into the entire writing process. This method requires them to write continuously on a topic for a set time, usually five to ten minutes. During that time the writers must never stop writing. If they can't think of anything to say, they write "can't think" or some other such phrase. For example, the following might have been produced by a writer who had been assigned the topic of describing someone he or she respects.

How about some political figure or a scientist or an artist. I really don't know many people who fit any of those descriptions, but their must be someone. Can't think, can't think. Why can't I think? What's so hard about this? I wonder if there is anyone I really respect. I wonder what it means to respect someone in the first place. Can't think, can't think. I think i would have to believe that person is honest, that he doesn't lie to make things easy for himself. That lets out the politicans. What about scientists? Can't think, can't think, can't think, can't think. Don't know much about science and nothing about scientists. How about artists? I like a lot of Picasso's work and was really impressed with that painting of his in the United Nations. It told the truth and the guide pointed out that Picasso was forced into exile from Spain because of his views. Can't think, can't think, can't think, can't think, can't think, can't think.

While our hypothetical writer might never use Picasso, the exercise has accomplished a number of valuable things: certain figures have been eliminated; a requirement for respecting a person has been identified;

and the issue of how to define respect has been raised. Each of these points gives the writer clues to what might be considered next. While it is only a bare beginning, the exercise has started the writing process. The writer's feet are wet.

Brainstorming

You may find that free writing produces so many different random thoughts or too many "can't thinks" to be very helpful. *Brainstorming,* another type of unstructured prewriting, might therefore be more helpful, because it requires greater concentration on the topic. Since it is also meant to ease you into the writing process, brainstorming is best done with pencil and paper.

As an example, suppose we were to write on the topic of where we like to go when we want to relax, and suppose we have chosen zoos. Knowing what the topic is will not immediately suggest either an exciting theme or a specific meaning. With brainstorming you can begin the process of discovering both. Initially, all that is required is to write down the words and phrases that occur to you as you consider the subject. You don't need complete sentences at this point or even reasons for including particular items on the list. You are merely collecting your thoughts. Such a list might look like the following:

ZOOS

lions and tigers	smelly cages
apes	exotic animals
elephants	petting parks/children's zoos
bears	families
African plains	babies in strollers
rain forests	food to feed the animals
special exhibits	food to feed the visitors
Bronx Zoo	commercialization
San Diego Zoo	special/tourist rides
small zoos	souvenirs
private zoos	cameras
Safari Park	"feeding" the animals
couples on dates	sick animals
hordes of children running around	plastic cups

This list is not particularly unusual or exciting, and at first you may think that we have not really accomplished very much. The list, however, is only the first step. It supplies us with some concrete notions to work with.

The next step is to concentrate on the items in the list to see what possibilities they suggest. Our list suggests that we have both positive and negative feelings toward zoos. On the positive side are the animals, the people, and several methods of displaying the animals so that the visitors can see them in special habitats. On the negative side are the costs, the commercialization of many zoos, and the inevitable sick animals. Keeping these two aspects in mind, we need to rewrite our original list. The terms that appear to address similar subjects should be grouped together. We may also add new terms and drop the ones we no longer like. Our revised list might look like this:

ZOOS

A. lions and tigers

apes

elephants

bears

exotic animals

animals in danger of extinction

B. special exhibits

African plains

rain forests

petting parks

children's zoos

Animals of the Night

C. Bronx Zoo

San Diego Zoo

small zoos

private zoos

Safari Park

D. commercialization of zoos

souvenirs

plastic cups

special/tourist rides

T-shirts and caps

E. couples on dates

hordes of children running around

families

babies in strollers

people passing time

older couples

F. smelly cages

"feeding" the animals

sick animals

rise in costs for food

inadequate enclosures

animals dying from improper care

The groups we have formed in the revised list will suggest specific thoughts. Now we need to shape these thoughts more precisely by giving each group a short descriptive title, usually a simple sentence. Once again, we may want to add or delete items.

ZOOS

A. Nowhere but in a zoo will you see so many different kinds of animals
   the usual animals—lions, tigers, elephants, and bears.
   exotic animals
   animals in danger of extinction
   baby animals
B. Many zoos have built special exhibits for their animals that draw huge crowds.
   African plains/rain forests
   children's zoos
   new ape houses
   Animals of the Night
C. There are many different kinds of zoos.
   large, metropolitan zoos—Bronx and San Diego zoos
   small zoo
   private zoos
   Safari Park
   petting zoos
D. In order to draw larger crowds zoos have become commercialized.
   souvenirs
   T-shirts and caps
   plastic cups
   special/tourist rides
E. Zoos are for people, too.
   couples on dates
   hordes of children running around
   families
   babies in strollers
   people passing time
   older couples
F. Zoos are threatened by many serious problems.
   "feeding" the animals
   sick animals—expensive care
   rise in cost of food
   inadequate enclosures
   animals dying from improper care

The short sentences we have written for the titles are our potential subtopics. We now have to decide whether these subtopics will suit our needs. Do we have enough ideas to develop a paper? Are there perhaps too many? What is our attitude toward zoos? Although we haven't written a paragraph yet, now is the time to ask these questions. The answers will give us a better idea of what to focus on, so that we will be working toward a specific goal rather than waiting for inspiration.

In our example it is most likely that some groups will have to be cut out; it would be impossible to cover so many subtopics in a standard freshman essay. If we later find that more material is needed, one or more of the groups that we've dropped can always be added again.

Three of the groups in the list deal with positive aspects of the zoos; two, with negative ones. One, group C, seems neutral; no attitude is expressed. Let's say that we first choose to drop group C because it does not seem very promising. This still leaves five subtopics, and that is still too many. We need to choose between the two aspects of zoos these groups represent. While both are valid, dealing with both would demand far more space than is available. We must therefore decide whether to focus on the positive or negative aspect; let's say we choose the positive.

We have reached the point at which we can control our essay, because we will not have to discover meaning while writing the first draft. We can now evaluate our thoughts and random ideas before we commit ourselves to a method of organization. None of the lists required much time or energy to produce, and they are much easier to change than completed drafts. But we still know precisely what ideas we are toying with.

Two steps remain before we are finished with brainstorming. First, we need to look over the remaining groups and add a title that will represent our general attitude toward all of them. This need not be the final title of our essay, but it will give us a concrete statement to work with.

Finally, we need to arrange the groups in the order we want them to appear in the essay. That order will probably change once we begin writing, but at least we will start with a definite idea of what begins the essay, what ends it, and what will come in the middle. Reordering the groups before we begin the first draft allows us even more control over our subtopics and the meaning we are working toward. Our final list might go something like this:

THERE IS NOTHING LIKE A GOOD ZOO

1. Nowhere but in a zoo will you see so many different
   kinds of animals.
   the usual—lions, tigers, elephants, and bears
   exotic animals

animals in danger of extinction
baby animals
2. Many zoos have built exciting exhibits for their animals.
African plains
rain forests
children's zoos
new ape houses
animals of the night
3. Zoos are for people, too.
couples on dates
hordes of children running around
families
babies in strollers

Group 1 is a logical place for the essay to begin. After all, animals are usually the first things that come to mind when zoos are mentioned. It is again quite logical to follow mention of the animals with a discussion of how they are kept. Group 2 will allow us to expand on the idea of a good zoo. Finally, group 3, with its focus on the people who visit zoos, will enable us to end on a high note. The pleasure zoos offer can be emphasized by showing how pleased these people are by their visits.

Now we are ready to start our first draft, and we already have a firm idea of what we want our message to be. We still have the writing before us, and we should expect to make further changes, but brainstorming has given us a specific direction to explore.

Item Analysis

Brainstorming will not work all the time for all writers. The technique assumes that you do have something to say about the topic and that by focusing on key words and phrases you will eventually develop a workable meaning and find an appropriate organization.

On the other hand, if you must deal with an extremely broad topic or if the topic demands particularly careful analysis, a structured form of prewriting may be preferable. *Item analysis* is a structured prewriting technique that is useful for complex topics. This method will lead you to examine the subject closely.

Item analysis is especially helpful when you need to decide if you have sufficient information about your topic, and it will identify those areas that require further research. In effect, item analysis probes your background knowledge and reveals its strengths and weaknesses.

Like brainstorming, item analysis should be done with paper and pencil. You will write down a standard set of questions that you then apply to your topic.

These questions look innocent enough to start with: Who? What? Where? When? Why? How? Teachers have been giving this same set of questions to writing students throughout grade school, high school, and beyond. If used correctly, they test your understanding of the topic:

Who? Is there a person involved who is essential to the topic? Why is this person essential? What would this topic be like without this person? How would the majority of people react to this person? How would I react to this person? Who else might be involved with the topic? How might they be affected by the topic?

What? What specific details are essential to this topic? How would the topic change if one or more of these details were left out? Are these changes significant? What changes in the topic would occur if one or more of these details were altered? Are these changes important? What can most people be expected to know about this topic? How much can I depend upon my own understanding of these details?

Where? Is this topic dependent on a particular place? Would a change in place alter the details of the topic? Would other people know much about this place?

When? Is this topic dependent on a particular time or age? Would a change in the time or age change the details of the topic? What would other people be expected to know about that time or age? How well known is that information?

Why? Are there obvious factors that have influenced this topic? Are these important in understanding the topic? Where would I go to learn more about them? What would the topic be like without them? Why should people be concerned with the topic? Will identifying these reasons be sufficient incentive for writing an essay on the topic?

How? How has this topic affected poeple? How is it important for my own life? How are people and/or events in the topic worth reading about? How is anything changed by understanding the topic? How are the events in the topic related to one another?

These six questions are focusing devices meant to center your attention on the topic and on various possible approaches. The questions listed under each category are only a small sample of the many that could be asked.

Not all of these questions will be equally useful for each topic, but you should force yourself to apply them all. If you have trouble getting started, you might try free writing on each question for five to ten minutes. Prewriting is a stage for discovering what you have to say and what you need to say about a topic. What you discover depends on how sincerely you approach the work involved.

Because item analysis will vary greatly from topic to topic, we cannot give a "typical" example. The following illustration, however, shows the process in operation.

Suppose you are trying to write an essay that is to describe what life will be like after a major nuclear war. Such a complex topic will require rather careful consideration. The two major difficulties here are the huge range of subtopics and the many opportunities for unthinking, emotional responses. So, "life after nuclear war" is a fine candidate for item analysis. Using the six questions will keep your mind focused on the subject matter while you explore the possibilities. And as you attempt to answer the questions you will better understand which of your ideas are based on fact and which are based on emotions.

Let's look at one possible result of item analysis:

LIFE AFTER A MAJOR NUCLEAR WAR

Who?   Human survivors—if a major nuclear war, the vast majority of people would be casualties, especially in Europe, Asia, and North America—the nuclear powers would be hardest hit—aftereffects would kill many more—so people may not play much of a role in the future

Other survivors—certain kinds of insects are believed to be resistant to radiation—others simply exist in too large numbers to be wiped out—try to find out whether there are some kinds of plants and animals that are also immune to radiation—or, at least, resistant

Should I show my feelings toward the destruction? Is it a tragedy—so many people killed—or do we deserve it—after all we dropped the bombs. Perhaps the description of the destruction will be enough emotion

What?   The actual explosions from the bombs will account for only a small number of deaths. Radiation poisoning, climatic changes, destruction of food sources, diminished living space will be the most important features. Must check on half-lives and find out how long before radiation is at a "safe" level for "normal" life—normal life will not be the same—if people exist, there will be relatively few—these people, and the plants, insects, and animals, will probably be mutations—Must check to see if anyone has tried to predict what kinds of mutations

Where? The whole world, of course—but this will complicate things for me—the changes will probably not be the same everywhere—there will be "hot spots"—will there be "cool spots"?—check: will radiation be distributed evenly all over the world?—no matter what, no place would be very nice to live in—with all the possible variations—better choose one area—can't be too small because I don't want it to appear too local—maybe North America

When? It couldn't be for now—the readers will know no such thing has happened—makes no sense for it to be in the past for the same reason—must be the future, but no exact date—the way things are going it could be in the next few years—I won't specify when in the future—let the reader decide

Why? Should I discuss the reasons for it?—maybe, simply state it happened—too much detail could raise political issues that would be distracting—everyone, anywhere can come up with his or her own reasons for the war

How? The world would change because (1) radiation will reshape some forms of life and kill most others—(2) the dust kicked up from the explosions should affect the climate in the same way as the dirt thrown up by volcanoes, only worse—there will be a "nuclear winter"—check how long—that takes care of the crops, even if radiation in the soil could be handled—(3) check what massive radiation will do to the ozone layer—if it's messed up, a lot of heat could follow the cold—(4) deaths of a whole lot of species and mutations of others will destroy the old food chain—(5) can people really survive all this?

Item analysis requires you to begin with detailed writing, but the amount is still far less than a first draft. Item analysis allows you to think out loud while you are writing in a form that is easily changed. With practice, you will learn to consider how your various points might fit together as you write them down. In the example, we narrow the discussion to North America during the answer to where. And during the consideration of why, we decide to keep the description of the war to a minimum.

Again, item analysis will help you see what further information you need before you begin to write. Our illustration is filled with reminders to check out certain possibilities, to see what others might have to say about particular points. If you follow up on these reminders, the search for information can be carried out efficiently. Instead of simply reading anything that looks good, you know what holes need to be filled and can better spend the time seeking out works that will answer specific "checks."

Finally, item analysis also shows you where to concentrate your thoughts after you have found the information you need. In the example, the answers to where, when, and why show little material; they only serve to narrow our focus on time and place. The answers to who, what, and how, on the other hand, focus on the issues of what life will remain after the war and how it will have been affected.

A number of key terms that arise in the answers to the questions who, what, and how can be used for brainstorming. "Those that live," "those that die," "climatic changes," "nuclear winter," "mutations," and "destruction of food sources" can form the nucleus of a good brainstorming list, which should be the next step. (Item analysis allows you to list what you know about the topic and to identify what needs to be learned. After the new information is found, brainstorming will help you explore the meanings implied by that knowledge.) Brainstorming remains important because it leads you to a more specific view of possible ideas.

After brainstorming comes the attempt at a first draft. And, as in the earlier case, it should come as no surprise that writing a first draft will bring about changes in the meaning. Meanings that come from structured prewriting methods like item analysis are very susceptible to such changes. New connections will occur to you as you write, and you will find yourself reanswering many of the six questions. You may even find it necessary to seek out new information and redo part of your brainstorming. The search for meaning does not stop when you have finished the prewriting stage.

Meaning and Prewriting

Free writing, brainstorming, and item analysis are only three out of many possible methods of prewriting. The method you use is less important than the fact that you find some way of focusing your attention on meaning. Whatever specific method you use, the principle remains the same: prewriting will free you from worry about the way to present your message and allow you to concentrate on the message itself.

The essays that follow deal with a broad range of ideas. Remember to read them as if some day you might also have to write on their respective topics. Combined with the study questions and exercises that follow each essay, this active reading will open up to you the many possibilities you have when you start at the beginning of the process rather than in the middle—that is, when you take the time to prewrite.

The Gift of Gift-Giving

Anthony Brandt

I dated a woman for a while—a literary type, *1* well-read, lots of books in her place—whom I admired a bit too extravagantly, and one Christmas I decided to give her something unusually nice and, I'm afraid, unusually expensive. I bought her a set of Swift's *Works*—not just any set but a scarce early-eighteenth-century edition; then I wrapped each leather-bound volume separately and made a card for each volume, each card containing a carefully chosen quotation from Swift himself. I thought it was terribly romantic; I had visions of her opening the set, volume by volume, while we sat by the fire Christmas Eve sipping cognac and listening to the Brandenburg Concertos.

How stupid I am sometimes! She, practical woman that I should have *2* known she was, had bought me two pairs of socks and a shirt, plus a small volume of poems by A. R. Ammons. She cried when she opened the Swift. I thought they were tears of joy, but they weren't. "I can't accept this," she said. "It's totally out of proportion." She insisted that I take the books back or sell them or keep them for myself. When I protested she just got more upset, and finally she asked me to leave and to take the books with me. Hurt and perplexed, I did. We stopped seeing each other soon after that. It took me weeks to figure out what I had done wrong. "There's a goat in all of us," R. P. Blackmur wrote somewhere, "a stupid, stubborn goat."

To my credit, I'm normally more perspicacious about the gifts I give, *3* and less of a show-off. But I have it in me, obviously, to be, as my ex-girlfriend said, totally out of proportion: to give people things I can't afford, or things that betoken an intimacy that doesn't exist, or things that bear no relation to the interests or desires of the person I'm giving them to. I've kicked myself too often not to know it's there, this insensitivity to the niceties of gift-giving.

The niceties, of course, not the raw act of giving (and certainly not *4* the thought) are what count. In most cultures, most of them more sensible than our own, the giving of gifts is highly ritualistic—that is, it is governed by rules and regulations; it is under strict social control. It is also, more or less explicitly, an exchange. None of this giving with no thought of receiving; on the contrary, you give somebody something and you expect something back in return—maybe not right away but soon enough. And it is expected to be of more or less equivalent value; you can be fairly certain that nobody is going to one-up you with something really extravagant like a scarce set of Swift, or else turn greedy on you and give you a penny whistle in return for a canoe. And once that's under control, the giving and receiving of gifts is free to become cere-monious, an occasion for feasting and celebration. You can finish your cognacs, in other words, and get down to the real business of the evening.

Gift-giving involves the expectation of reciprocity therefore, but we 5 wise men of the Western world avoid this fact: we paper it over with rhetoric about selflessness, about how much better it is to give than to receive. "An honorable benefactor never thinks on the good turn he does," wrote Seneca nearly two thousand years ago. Indeed. The hon-orable, the noble thing to do, we like to tell ourselves, is to give it and forget it, to expect nothing at all in return, not even gratitude. To give freely, spontaneously, like nature in her abundance. ("How many are unworthy the light, and yet the day rises to them," Seneca also wrote.) Like some happy hooker who neglects to charge her customers. Like God's own fool.

I've given some thought to my own proclivities in this matter and have 6 concluded that even at my most ridiculously generous, my most spon-taneously giving, I expect something in return as much as the next man does. I'm trying literally to buy something: affection, maybe love. Someone's admiration. Or to establish my chosen identity as a romantic, capable of making the grand gesture. Or to inspire guilt: See, I've thought hard and gone to a lot of trouble to get you what you might want, to penetrate to your heart and give it its desire. Have you done the same for me? My girlfriend saw through all this right away. As I said, it took me weeks.

The niceties. What are the niceties? I used to think there were no 7 niceties, that the thought really was all that counted. I might have gotten this from my mother, who every Christmas spent exactly the same amount of money on my brother and me—no favorite sons in this house-hold—and made sure we knew it. My mother seldom wrapped gifts, or if she did, she used the cheapest possible tissue paper and no ribbons. We had no-frills birthdays, a no-frills Christmas. I forgot her birthday once, even after she had dropped numerous hints that it was imminent, and she made me feel quite ashamed about it. The overall lesson was that you remembered—you might give foolish things, but you remem-bered—and you gave generously; there was always an abundance of presents. But you didn't have to wrap them, and cards were unneces-sary. She had a puritan mentality. Decoration was frivolous.

I haven't gone quite to the other extreme, but—eighteenth-century 8 literature aside—it now seems to me that decoration is most of it. When I first started living with my wife and we began giving each other things, as lovers are wont to do, it gradually came out that most of her previous boyfriends were, shall we say, unimaginative when it came to gifts. One of them gave her a salad spinner for Christmas, a baked ham for her birthday. Why not a broom? Why not a month's supply of Wonder Bread? With one exception, nobody had given her flowers since she was in high school, and that was more than a few years ago. I didn't need to be told twice. She got flowers on Easter Sunday, which was the first major occasion we shared together, and they were delivered, which is definitely the best way to get flowers. She got flowers this last birthday. She gets flowers sometimes for no reason at all. She cries every time, but these tears are tears of joy.

I'm not bragging: any idiot could see how to win this woman's heart. 9 She told me how; she was explicit about it. My point is not what a swell fellow I am, it's the flowers. They're nothing but decoration. They're entirely useless; in my allergy-prone family, they can even cause discomfort. But they're an ideal gift. Purely symbolic. Pure cliché. We want those clichés. We want what everybody wants: the timeless, unchangeable gestures; the rituals; the beautiful wrapping paper; the ribbons— ironed, no less, and chosen to go with the color of the paper. I'm slowly learning these arts. A last-minute shopper by habit, I'm learning to plan ahead, to ask well in advance precisely what she wants, and to get it for her; I'm abandoning, slowly, my wish to surprise her, to find some fabulous object she hadn't thought of but would instantly see is just right for her. It's an ego trip: I'm so clever, so thoughtful, so imaginative that I know her mind better than she knows it herself. I'm giving it up. And I'm even learning to give her things she wants that I don't like, things that seem to me tacky or unneeded or that won't last the way I like things to last. And for the really important things, the jewelry she will keep and wear all her life, we now go shopping together. The jewelry, please take note, is decoration. I'm beginning to take her to rare-book shops so she can buy me what I want for Christmas. More decoration. You don't read rare books; you shelve them. She thinks they're silly, but she goes along with me. And why not? We pamper each other. We don't have the nerve to pamper ourselves.

There's precious little genuine altruism in the world. There are profes- 10 sional altruists, it's true—nurses, social workers, all these so-called "helping professions"—but they get paid to dispense their services; as for governmental largess, ask any welfare recipient whether it's given freely or grudgingly. Even institutionalized giving is a kind of exchange: some kind of payoff is expected. During my years with Sherman Fairchild I spent some time working for his philanthropic foundation; my job was to find worthy projects to which Fairchild might donate a few of his millions. The experience taught me a great deal about the power of money, the power of the gift. Everywhere I went, and that was all over the country, potential donees treated me with a respect far out of proportion to my callow abilities. Talk about ego trips: deans of medical schools asked for my opinions and advice; presidents of universities invited me to tea; the then director of the National Institutes of Health gave me an hour of his time. At one university a department chairman even asked me to write a critique of his department, which he then distributed to his faculty. I tried to tell all these people that I could only make recommendations, that I had no power to decide on contributions. But it made no difference; I was in demand.

None of the above, however, caught my interest; that belonged to *11* Cesar Chavez, whom I met on the ninth day of his famous fast as he lay in his austere room in the farm-workers' center in Delano, California, watching the sunlight fade. I had never encountered so much charisma before, and I was overwhelmed. But Fairchild would have none of it. A small grant for their health center? No way. Too controversial. I spent months trying to help raise money for Chavez at other foundations. Not a dime. Foundation money goes to university or hospital buildings, which then get named after the donors; to fellowships or professorial chairs, similarly named; to museums, which thoughtfully chisel the names of major donors on the walls. Money buys prestige. Foundation exec- utives talk about their gifts as "investments" and look for a return of sorts, for the kind of success in a project or program they can then point to and call "mine." Some of them wind up thinking very well of them- selves indeed.

Yet Joe Delaney, the football player, gave his life trying to save two *12* drowning boys. My parents gave up a great deal in the way of material comfort so that my brother and I could go to Cornell and Princeton. Some people regularly give blood; it's anonymous, a gift for which they receive no credit, and it temporarily weakens them. As soon as one becomes cynical about the possibility of altrusim, counterinstances come to mind. We live in tension between the possibility of altruism and the reality of egoism. And whichever way we lean, we ultimately want to think well of ourselves.

I don't suppose I'm really a cynic; my wife tells me I'm more of an *13* ironist. Maybe so. Look into human motivation long enough, I am convinced, and you come away unwilling to take anything at face value. But that doesn't necessarily destroy your faith in human nature. I think most of us want to get beyond our selfishness. We want to give; beneath the neuroses, the compulsions, the fears, anxieties, desires, the self-pity, we harbor generous impulses, spontaneous warmth. There is much good nature in the human animal. "As a general rule, people, even the wicked," wrote Dostoevsky, "are much more naive and simplehearted than we suppose. And we ourselves are, too." And Whitman wrote, without any irony at all, "When I give I give myself."

Whitman found a way to resolve the tension; he also wrote, "The gift *14* is to the giver, and comes back most to him—it cannot fail. . . ." Whit- man gave himself to the world and made the bold, massively egoistic assumption that the gift measured up. This is spiritual theory: you pass on the gifts God has given you, and the more you give, the more you

will receive. The bargain is elevated to a higher plane; by keeping nothing
for yourself, everything comes to you. You become a conduit for largess;
altrusim and egoism become one.

   But who's up to such spiritual heroics? Not many of us. We who are   *15*
not poets live in the tension for the most part; we do our best to give
our children an education, to share the wealth at Christmas or on other
sacrificial occasions, and to be gracious about it—to find a style that
pleases, to observe the niceties—while one eye looks to what we may
be getting back. As long as we don't deceive ourselves and imagine we
don't *want* anything back—when we all do—there's no danger of feeling
the kind of unacknowledged disappointment over unacknowledged expectations that does turn people cynical.

Study Questions

1. What sentence in "The Gift of Gift-Giving" first clearly states Brandt's
   thesis? Is it placed before or after his anecdote about his extravagant
   Christmas gift? How does that anecdote help the readers to understand Brandt's thesis?
2. "The Gift of Gift-Giving" deals with a topic that Brandt takes seriously. What words and phrases does he use to impress his attitude
   upon his readers?
3. "The Gift of Gift-Giving" was published in *Esquire*. Examine an issue
   of this magazine and pay close attention to its advertising. How would
   you characterize the audience *Esquire* aims for? Given such a characterization, why would the editors think the audience would read
   this essay?
4. How do you feel Brandt's readers will react to the following sentence
   in his last paragraph?

   We who are not poets live in tension for the most part; we do our
   best to give our children an education, to share the wealth at Christmas
   or other sacrificial occasions, and to be gracious about it—to find a
   style that pleases, to observe the niceties—while one eye looks to
   what we may be getting back.

   Why do you think he waited until the end to state his opinion so
   clearly?

Suggestions for Prewriting

1. By the end of "The Gift of Gift-Giving," you should have a clear idea
   of Brandt's opinion of why people give gifts; but Brandt barely discusses why people accept gifts. In a ten-minute free-writing exercise,

write about your own feelings about receiving presents. Any gift, occasion, or specific incident can be used for this free writing. Remember, free writing is meant to help you collect your thoughts and start you writing. Usually you will be the only one to see the results.

2. "The Gift of Gift-Giving" can be called an *evaluative* essay, because it tries to judge the reasons that people give presents. When you attempt an essay of this type, you may find a directed kind of item analysis useful in the prewriting stage. Instead of asking the general questions who, what, where, when, why and how, use a more specific set of questions that directs your attention to evaluating the topic:

Why do I do _____ ?
How do I react to _____ ?
What do I think of people who do or believe in _____ ?
What difference in my life or in other people's lives will _____ make?
How would I argue for or against _____ ?

Depending on how you fill in the blanks, each of these questions can give you specific leads to follow as you try to develop a topic. You might also find new questions to ask as you answer one or more of them.

Choose one or more of the above questions and do the prewriting for an essay on one of the following ideas:

accepting gifts	a specific television series
horror films	required foreign language courses
opinion polls	family vacations
alcoholic drinks	special holidays

To help guide your prewriting, suppose that the essay you are to produce will be submitted to a popular magazine like *Esquire.*

On the Ball

Roger Angell

I t weighs just over five ounces and measures *1* between 2.86 and 2.94 inches in diameter. It is made of a composition-cork nucleus encased in two thin layers of rubber, one black and one red, surrounded by 121 yards of tightly wrapped blue-gray wool yarn, 45 yards of white wool yarn, 53 more yards of blue-gray wool yarn, 150 yards of fine cotton yarn, a coat of rubber cement, and a cowhide (formerly horsehide) exterior, which is held together with 216 slightly raised red cotton stitches. Printed certifications, endorsements, and outdoor advertising spherically attest to its authenticity. Like most institutions, it is considered inferior in its present form to its ancient archetypes, and in this case the complaint is probably justified; on occasion in recent years it has actually been known to come apart under the demands of its brief but rigorous active career. Baseballs are assembled and handstitched in Taiwan (before this year the work was done in Haiti, and before 1973 in Chicopee, Massachusetts), and contemporary pitchers claim that there is a tangible variation in the size and feel of the balls that now come into play in a single game; a true peewee is treasured by hurlers, and its departure from the premises, by fair means or foul, is secretly mourned. But never mind: any baseball is beautiful. No other small package comes as close to the ideal in design and utility. It is a perfect object for a man's hand. Pick it up and it instantly suggests its purpose; it is meant to be thrown a considerable distance—thrown hard and with precision. Its feel and heft are the beginning of the sport's critical dimensions; if it were a fraction of an inch larger or smaller, a few centigrams heavier or lighter, the game of baseball would be utterly different. Hold a baseball in your hand. As it happens, this one is not brand-new. Here, just to one side of the curved surgical welt of stitches, there is a pale-green grass smudge, darkening on one edge almost to black—the mark of an old infield play, a tough grounder now lost in memory. Feel the ball, turn it over in your hand; hold it across the seam or the other way, with the seam just to the side of your middle finger. Speculation stirs. You want to get outdoors and throw this spare and sensual object to somebody or, at the very least, watch somebody else throw it. The game has begun.

Thinking about the ball and its attributes seems to refresh our appre- *2* ciation of this game. A couple of years ago, I began to wonder why it was that pitchers, taken as a group, seemed to be so much livelier and more garrulous than hitters. I considered the possibility of some obscure physiological linkage (the discobologlottal syndrome) and the more obvious occupational discrepancies (pitchers have a lot more spare time than other players), but then it came to me that a pitcher is the only man in baseball who can properly look on the ball as being his instrument, his accomplice. He is the only player who is granted the privilege of making offensive plans, and once the game begins he is (in concert with his catcher) the only man on the field who knows what is meant to happen next. Everything in baseball begins with the pitch, and every other part of the game—hitting, fielding, and throwing—is reflexive and defensive. (The hitters on a ball team are referred to as the "offense," but almost three quarters of the time this is an absolute misnomer.) The batter tapping the dirt off his spikes and now stepping into the box looks sour and glum, and who can blame him, for the ball has somehow been granted in perpetuity to the wrong people. It is already an object of suspicion and hatred, and the refex that allows him occasionally to deflect that tiny onrushing dot with his bat, and sometimes even to relaunch it violently in the opposite direction, is such a miraculous response of eye and body as to remain virtually inexplicable, even to him. There are a few dugout flannelmouths (Ted Williams, Harry Walker, Pete Rose) who can talk convincingly about the art of hitting, but, like most arts, it does not in the end seem communicable. Pitching is different. It is a craft ("the crafty portsider . . .") and is thus within reach.

The smiling pitcher begins not only with the advantage of holding his *3* fate in his own hands, or hand, but with the knowledge that every advantage of physics and psychology seems to be on his side. A great number of surprising and unpleasant things can be done to the ball as it is delivered from the grasp of a two-hundred-pound optimist, and the first of these is simply to transform it into a projectile. Most pitchers seem hesitant to say so, but if you press them a little they will admit that the prime ingredient in their intense personal struggle with the batter is probably fear. A few pitchers in the majors have thrived without a real fastball— junk men like Eddie Lopat and Mike Cuellar, superior control artists like Bobby Shantz and Randy Jones, knuckleballers like Hoyt Wilhelm and Charlie Hough—but almost everyone else has had to hump up and throw at least an occasional no-nonsense hard one, which crosses the plate at eighty-five miles per hour, or better, and thus causes the hitter to—well, to *think* a little. The fastball sets up all the other pitches in the hurler's repertoire—the curve, the slider, the sinker, and so on— but its other purpose is to intimidate. Great fastballers like Bob Gibson, Jim Bunning, Sandy Koufax, and Nolan Ryan have always run up high strikeout figures because their money pitch was almost untouchable, but their deeper measures of success—twenty-victory seasons and low earned-run averages—were due to the fact that none of the hitters they faced, not even the best of them, was immune to the thought of what a 90-mph missile could do to a man if it struck him. They had been ever so slightly distracted, and distraction is bad for hitting. The intention of the pitcher has almost nothing to do with this; very few pitches are delivered with intent to maim. The bad dream, however, will not go away. Walter Johnson, the greatest fireballer of them all, had almost absolute control, but he is said to have worried constantly about what might happen if one of his pitches got away from him. Good hitters know all this and resolutely don't think about it (a good hitter is a man who can keep his back foot firmly planted in the box even while the rest of him is pulling back or bailing out on an inside fastball), but even these icy customers are less settled in their minds than they would like to be, just because the man out there on the mound is hiding that cannon behind his hip. Hitters, of course, do not call this fear. The word is "respect."

It should not be inferred, of course, that major-league pitchers are 4 wholly averse to hitting batters, or *almost* hitting batters. A fastball up around the Adam's apple not only is a first-class distracter, as noted, but also discourages a hitter from habitually leaning forward in order to put more of his bat on a dipping curve or a slider over the outer rim of the plate. The truth of the matter is that pitchers and batters are engaged in a permanent private duel over their property rights to the plate, and a tough, proud hurler who senses that the man now in the batter's box has recently had the better of things will often respond in the most direct manner possible, with a hummer to the ribs. Allie Reynolds, Sal Maglie, Don Drysdale, Early Wynn, and Bob Gibson were cold-eyed lawmen of this stripe, and the practice has by no means vanished, in spite of strictures and deplorings from the high chambers of baseball. Early this year, Lynn McGlothen, of the Cards, routinely plunked the Mets' Del Unser, who had lately been feasting on his pitches, and then violated the ancient protocol in these matters by admitting intent. Dock Ellis, now a Yankee but then a Pirate, decided early in the 1974 season that the Cincinnati Reds had somehow established dominance over his club, and he determined to set things right in his own way. (This incident is described at length in a lively new baseball book, *Dock Ellis in the Country of Baseball,* by Donald Hall.) The first Cincinnati batter of the game was Pete Rose, and the first pitch from Ellis was at his head—"not actually to *hit* him," Ellis said later, but as a "*message* to let him know that he was going to be hit." He then hit Rose in the side. The next pitch hit the next Red batter, Joe Morgan, in the kidney. The third batter was Dan Driessen, who took Ellis's second pitch in the back. With the bases loaded, Dock now threw four pitches at Tony Perez (one behind his back), but missed with all of them, walking in a run. He then missed Johnny Bench (and the plate) twice, whereupon Pirate manager Danny Murtaugh came out to the mound, stared at Ellis with silent surmise, and beckoned for a new pitcher.

Hitters can accept this sort of fugue, even if they don't exactly enjoy 5 it, but what they do admittedly detest is a young and scatter-armed smoke-thrower, the true wild man. One famous aborigine was Steve Dalkowski, an Oriole farmhand of the late nineteen fifties and early sixties who set records for strikeouts and jumpy batters wherever he played. In one typical stay with a Class D league, he threw 121 strikeouts and gave up 129 walks and 39 wild pitches, all in the span of 62 innings. Dalkowski never made it to the majors, but, being a legend, he is secure for the ages. "Once I saw him work a game in the Appalachian League," a gravel-voiced retired coach said to me not long ago, "and nothing was hit *forward* for seven innings—not even a foul ball." An attempt was once made to clock Dalkowski on a recording device, but his eventual mark of 93.5 mph was discounted, since he threw for forty minutes before steering a pitch into the machine's recording zone.

Better-known names in these annals of anxiety are Rex Barney, a 6 briefly flaring Brooklyn nova of the nineteen forties, who once threw a no-hit game but eventually walked and wild-pitched his way out of base-ball; Ryne Duren, the extremely fast and extremely nearsighted reliever for the Yankees and other American League clubs in the fifties and sixties, whose traditional initial warm-up pitch on his being summoned to the mound was a twelve-foot-high fastball to the foul screen; and a pair of rookies named Sandy Koufax and Bob Feller. Koufax, to be sure, eventually became a superb control artist, but it took him seven years before he got his great stuff entirely together, and there were times when it seemed certain that he would be known only as another Rex Barney. Sandy recalls that when he first brought his boyish assortment of fiery sailers and bouncing rockets to spring-training camp he had difficulty getting in any mound work, because whenever he picked up his glove all the available catchers would suddenly remember pressing ap-pointments in some distant part of the compound. Feller had almost a career-long struggle with *his* control, and four times managed to lead his league simultaneously in walks and in strikeouts. His first appearance against another major-league club came in an exhibition game against the Cardinals in the summer of 1936, when he was seventeen years old; he entered the game in the fourth inning, and eventually struck out eight batters in three innings, but when his searing fastball missed the plate it had the batters jumping around in the box like roasting popcorn. Frank Frisch, the St. Louis player-manager, carefully observed Feller's first three or four deliveries and then walked down to the end of the dugout, picked up a pencil, and removed himself from the Cardinal lineup.

The chronically depressed outlook of major-league batters was pushed 7 to the edge of paranoia in the nineteen fifties by the sudden and utterly unexpected arrival of the slider, or the Pitcher's Friend. The slider is an easy pitch to throw and a hard one to hit. It is delivered with the same motion as the fastball, but with the pitcher's wrist rotated approximately ninety degrees (to the right for a right-hander, to the left for a southpaw), which has the effect of placing the delivering forefinger and middle finger slightly off center on the ball. The positions of hand, wrist, and arm are almost identical with those that produce a good spiral forward pass with a football. The result is an apparent three-quarter-speed fastball that suddenly changes its mind and direction. It doesn't break much—in its early days it was slightingly known as the "nickel curve"—but a couple of inches of lateral movement at the plateward end of the ball's brief sixty-foot-six-inch journey can make for an epidemic of pop-ups, foul balls, and harmless grounders. "Epidemic" is not an exaggeration. The slider was the prime agent responsible for the sickening and decline of major-league batting averages in the two decades after the Second World War, which culminated in a combined average of .237 for the two leagues in 1968. A subsequent crash program of immunization and prevention by the authorities produced from the laboratory a smaller strike zone and a lowering of the pitcher's mound by five inches, but the hitters, while saved from extermination, have never regained their state of rosy-cheeked, pre-slider good health.

For me, the true mystery of the slider is not its flight path but the 8 circumstances of its discovery. Professional baseball got under way in the eighteen-seventies, and during all the ensuing summers uncounted thousands of young would-be Mathewsons and Seavers spent their after-noons flinging the ball in every conceivable fashion as they searched for magic fadeaways and flutter balls that would take them to Cooperstown. Why did eighty years pass before anybody noticed that a slight cocking of the wrist would be sufficient to usher in the pitchers' Golden Age? Where were Tom Swift and Frank Merriwell? What happened to Amer-ican Know-How? This is almost a national disgrace. The mystery is deepened by the fact that—to my knowledge, at least—no particular pitcher or pitching coach is given credit for the discovery and propagation of the slider. Bob Lemon, who may be the first man to have pitched his way into the Hall of Fame with a slider, says he learned the pitch from Mel Harder, who was an elder mound statesman with the Indians when Lemon came up to that club, in 1946. I have also heard some old-timers say that George Blaeholder was throwing a pretty fair slider for the St. Louis Browns way back in the nineteen-twenties. But none of these worthies ever claimed to be the Johnny Appleseed of the pitch. The thing seemed to generate itself—a weed in the bullpen which overran the field.

The slider has made baseball more difficult for the fan as well as for 9 the batter. Since its action is late and minimal, and since its delivery does not require the easily recognizable armsnap by the pitcher that heralds the true curve, the slider can be spotted only by an attentive spectator seated very close to home plate. A curve thrown by famous old pretzel-benders like Tommy Bridges and Sal Maglie really used to *curve;* you could see the thing break even if you were way out in the top deck of Section 31. Most fans, however, do not admit the loss. The contemporary bleacher critic, having watched a doll-size distant slugger swing mightily and tap the ball down to second on four bounces, smiles and enters the out in his scorecard. "Slider," he announces, and everybody nods wisely in agreement.

The mystery of the knuckleball is ancient and honored. Its practition- *10* ers cheerfully admit that they do not understand why the pitch behaves the way it does; nor do they know, or care much, which particular lepidopteran path it will follow on its way past the batter's infuriated swipe. They merely prop the ball on their fingertips (not, in actual fact, on the knuckles) and launch it more or less in the fashion of a paper airplane, and then, most of the time, finish the delivery with a faceward motion of the glove, thus hiding a grin. Now science has confirmed the phenomenon. Writing in *The American Journal of Physics,* Eric Sawyer and Robert G. Watts, of Tulane University, recently reported that wind-tunnel tests showed that a slowly spinning baseball is subject to forces capable of making it swerve a foot or more between the pitcher's mound and the plate. The secret, they say, appears to be the raised seams of the ball, which cause a "roughness pattern" and an uneven flow of air, resulting in a "nonsymmetric lateral force distribution and . . . a net force in one direction or another."

Like many other backyard baseball stars, I have taught myself to *11* throw a knuckleball that moves with so little rotation that one can almost pick out the signature of Charles S. Feeney in midair; the pitch, however, has shown disappointingly few symptoms of last-minute fluttering and has so far proved to be wonderfully catchable or hittable, mostly by my wife. Now, at last, I understand the problem. In their researches, Sawyer and Watts learned that an entirely spinless knuckler is *not* subject to varying forces, and thus does not dive or veer. The ideal knuckler, they say, completes about a quarter of a revolution on its way to the plate. The speed of the pitch, moreover, is not critical, because "the magnitude of the lateral force increases approximately as the square of the velocity," which means that the total lateral movement is "independent of the speed of the pitch."

All this has been perfectly understood (if less politely defined) by any *12* catcher who has been the battery mate of a star knuckleballer, and has thus spent six or seven innings groveling in the dirt in imitation of a bulldog cornering a nest of field mice. Modern catchers have the assistance of outsized gloves (which lately have begun to approach the diameter of tea trays), and so enjoy a considerable advantage over some of their ancient predecessors in capturing the knuckler. In the middle nineteen-forties, the receivers for the Washington Senators had to deal with a pitching staff that included *four* knuckleball specialists—Dutch

Leonard, Johnny Niggeling, Mickey Haefner, and Roger Wolff. Among
the ill-equipped Washington catchers who tried to fend off almost daily
midafternoon clouds of deranged butterflies were Rick Ferrell and Jake
Early; Early eventually was called up to serve in the armed forces—
perhaps the most willing inductee of his day.

The spitball was once again officially outlawed from baseball in 1974,   *13*
and maybe this time the prohibition will work. This was the third, and
by far the most severe, edict directed at the unsanitary and extemely
effective delivery, for it permits an umpire to call an instantaneous ball
on any pitch that even looks like a spitter as it crosses the plate. No
evidence is required; no appeal by the pitcher to higher powers is permissible. A subsequent spitball or imitation thereof results in the expulsion of the pitcher from the premises, *instanter,* and an ensuing fine.
Harsh measures indeed, but surely sufficient, we may suppose, to keep
this repellent and unfair practice out of baseball's shining mansion forever. Surely, and yet . . . Professional pitchers have an abiding fondness
for any down-breaking delivery, legal or illegal, that will get the job done,
and nothing, they tell me, does the job more effectively or more enter-
tainingly than a dollop of saliva or slippery-elm juice, or a little bitty dab
of lubricating jelly, applied to the pitching fingers. The ball, which is
sent off half wet and half dry, like a dilatory schoolboy, hurries innocently
toward the gate and its grim-faced guardians, and at the last second darts
under the turnstile. Pitchers, moreover, have before them the inspiring
recent example of Gaylord Perry, whose rumored but unverified Fagin-
esque machinations with K-Y Jelly won him a Cy Young Award in 1972
and led inevitably to the demand for harsher methods of law enforcement.
Rumor has similarly indicted other highly successful performers, like
Don Drysdale, Whitey Ford, and Bill Singer. Preacher Roe, upon retiring
from the Dodgers, in 1954, after an extended useful tenure on the mound
at Ebbets Field, published a splendidly unrepentant confession, in which
he gave away a number of trade secrets. His favorite undryer, as I recall,
was a full pack of Juicy Fruit gum, and he loaded up by straightening
the bill of his cap between pitches and passing his fingers momentarily
in front of his face—now also illegal, alas.
  It may be perceived that my sympathies, which lately seemed to lie   *14*
so rightly on the side of the poor overmatched hitters, have unaccount-
ably swung the other way. I admit this indefensible lapse simply because
I find the spitter so enjoyable for its deviousness and skulking disrespect.
I don't suppose we should again make it a fully legal pitch (it was first
placed outside the pale in 1920), but I would enjoy a return to the era
when the spitter was treated simply as a misdemeanor and we could all
laugh ourselves silly at the sight of a large, outraged umpire suddenly
calling in a suspected wetback for inspection (and the pitcher, of course,

rolling the ball to him across the grass) and then glaring impotently out at the innocent ("Who—*me?*") perpetrator on the mound. Baseball is a hard, rules-dominated game, and it should have more room in it for a little cheerful cheating.

All these speculations, and we have not yet taken the ball out of the 15 hands of its first friend, the pitcher. And yet there is always something more. We might suddenly realize, for instance, that baseball is the only team sport in which the scoring is not done with the ball. In hockey, football, soccer, basketball, lacrosse, and the rest of them, the ball or its equivalent actually scores or is responsible for the points that determine the winner. In baseball, the score is made by the base runner—by the man down there, just crossing the plate—while the ball, in most cases, is a long way off, doing something quite different. It's a strange business, this unique double life going on in front of us, and it tells us a lot about this unique game. A few years ago, there was a suddenly popular thesis put forward in some sports columns and light-heavy-weight editorial pages which proposed that the immense recent popularity of professional football could be explained by the fact that the computerlike complexity of its plays, the clotted and anonymous masses of its players, and the intense violence of its action constituted a perfect Sunday parable of contemporary urban society. It is a pretty argument, and perhaps even true, especially since it is hard not to notice that so many professional football games, in spite of their noise and chaos, are deadeningly repetitious, predictable, and banal. I prefer the emotions and suggestions to be found in the other sport. I don't think anyone can watch many baseball games without becoming aware of the fact that the ball, for all its immense energy and unpredictability, very rarely escapes the control of the players. It is released again and again—pitched and caught, struck along the ground or sent high in the air—but almost always, almost instantly, it is recaptured and returned to control and safety and harmlessness. Nothing is altered, nothing has been allowed to happen. This orderliness and constraint are among the prime attractions of the sport; a handful of men, we discover, can police a great green country, forestalling unimaginable disasters. A slovenly, error-filled game can sometimes be exciting, but it never seems serious, and is thus never truly satisfying, for the metaphor of safety—of danger subdued by skill and courage—has been lost. Too much civilization, however, is deadly—in this game, a deadly bore. A deeper need is stifled. The ball looks impetuous and dangerous, but we perceive that in fact it lives in a slow, guarded world of order, vigilance, and rules. Nothing can ever happen here. And then once again the ball is pitched—sent on its quick, planned errand. The bat flashes, there is a new, louder sound, and suddenly we see the ball streaking wild through the air and then bounding along distant and untouched in the sweet green grass. We leap up, thousands of us, and shout for its joyful flight—free, set free, free at last.

Study Questions

1. In "On the Ball" Roger Angell says in the first paragraph, "any baseball is beautiful. No other small package comes as close to the ideal in design and utility." In Section 1 we stated that any piece of writing must be shaped by its topic and audience. In other words, it must have a design and utility. What do you think Angell's purpose was in writing this essay? Where do you see that purpose most clearly stated?

2. Angell tells a number of stories about both well-known and obscure baseball players. How do these stories help Angell achieve the purpose you identified in your answer to question 1?

3. Do people have to know baseball well in order to understand this essay? Would the essay make sense to someone from France? to someone in the United States who knew very little about baseball? What passages might confuse each of these readers? What parts of Angell's meaning might they still understand despite their confusion?

4. Where do you think this essay was first published? Explain your answer by characterizing the audience the words and phrases best seem to suit.

Suggestions for Prewriting

Roger Angell begins his essay with a detailed description of a baseball. You may also find that description is a good way to begin thinking about a topic for a paper. As in the case of evaluative essays, there are a number of questions you can ask yourself as you start the prewriting stage:

What features do I remember most when I think of _____ ?
What features do I see first when I look at _____ ?
What features make _____ unique?
What does _____ remind me of ?
What features of _____ do I like the most (or the least)?

As is clear from "On the Ball," description in an essay is rarely an end in itself. However, when you are dealing with even abstract topics in prewriting, it may be useful to "see" the subject first. This will frequently trigger thoughts beyond the description and lead to interesting possibilities. You will usually need to follow the answers to the above questions with further prewriting. Nevertheless, by beginning with them your later work will be made easier.

Choose some piece of sporting equipment that you think is "perfect" for its purpose. Practice prewriting by answering as many of the model questions as possible and follow up your answers by applying free writing, brainstorming, or item analysis to them.

The Old Stone House

Edmund Wilson

A s I go north for the first time in years, in the *1* slow, the constantly stopping, milk train— which carries passengers only in the back part of the hind car and has an old stove to heat it in winter—I look out through the dirt-yellowed double pane and remember how once, as a child, I used to feel thwarted in summer till I had got the windows open and there was nothing between me and the widening pastures, the great boulders, the black and white cattle, the rivers, stony and thin, the lone elms like feather-dusters, the high air which sharpens all outlines, makes all colors so breathtakingly vivid, in the clear light of late afternoon.

The little stations again: Barnevald, Stittville, Steuben—a tribute to *2* the Prussian general who helped drill our troops for the Revolution. The woman behind me in the train talks to the conductor with a German accent. They came over here for land and freedom.

Boonville: that pale boxlike building, smooth gray, with three floors *3* of slots that look in on darkness and a roof like a flat overlapping lid— cold dark clear air, fresh water. Like nothing else but upstate New York. Rivers that run quick among stones, or, deeper, stained dark with dead leaves. I used to love to follow them—should still. A fresh breath of water off the Black River, where the blue closed gentians grow. Those forests, those boulder-strewn pastures, those fabulous distant falls!

There was never any train to Talcottville. Our house was the center *4* of the town. It is strange to get back to this now: it seems not quite like anything else that I have ever known. But is this merely the apparent uniqueness of places associated with childhood?

The settlers of this part of New York were a first westward migration *5* from New England. At the end of the eighteenth century, they drove ox-teams from Connecticut and Massachusetts over into the wild northern country below Lake Ontario and the St. Lawrence River, and they established here an extension of New England.

Yet an extension that was already something new. I happened last *6* week to be in Ipswich, Mass., the town from which one branch of my family came; and, for all the New England pride of white houses and green blinds, I was oppressed by the ancient crampedness. Even the House of the Seven Gables, which stimulated the imagination of Hawthorne, though it is grim perhaps, is not romantic. It, too, has the tightness and the self-sufficiency of that little provincial merchant society, which at its best produced an intense little culture, quite English in its concreteness and practicality—as the block letters of the signs along the docks make Boston look like Liverpool. But life must have hit its head on those close and low-ceilinged coops. That narrowness, that meagerness, that stinginess, still grips New England today: the drab summer cottages along the shore seem almost as slit-windowed and pinched as the gray twin-houses of a mill town like Lawrence or Fall River. I can feel the relief myself of coming away from Boston to these first uplands of the Adirondacks, where, discarding the New England religion but still speaking the language of New England, the settlers found limitless space. They were a part of the new America, now forever for a century on the move; and they were to move on themselves before they would be able to build here anything comparable to the New England civilization. The country, magnificent and vast, has never really been humanized as New England has: the landscape still overwhelms the people. But this house, one of the few of its kind among later wooden houses and towns, was an attempt to found a civilization. It blends in a peculiar fashion the amenities of the eastern seaboard with the rudeness and toughness of the new frontier.

It was built at the end of the eighteenth century: the first event recorded in connection with it is a memorial service for General Washington. It took four or five years in the building. The stone had to be quarried and brought out of the river. The walls are a foot and a half thick, and the plaster was applied to the stone without any intervening lattice. The beams were secured by enormous nails, made by hand and some of them eighteen inches long. Solid and simple as a fortress, the place has also the charm of something which has been made to order. There is a front porch with white wooden columns which support a white wooden balcony that runs along the second floor. The roof comes down close over the balcony, and the balcony and the porch are draped with vines. Large ferns grow along the porch, and there are stone hitching-posts and curious stone ornaments, cut out of the quarry like the house: on one side, a round-bottomed bowl in which red geraniums bloom, and on the other, an unnamable object, crudely sculptured and vaguely pagoda-like. The front door is especially handsome: the door itself is dark green and equipped with a brass knocker, and the woodwork which frames it is white; it is crowned with a wide fanlight and flanked by two narrow panes of glass, in which a white filigree of ironwork makes a webbing like ice over winter ponds. On one of the broad sides of the buiding, where the mortar has come off the stone, there is a dappling of dark gray under pale gray like the dappling of light in shallow water, and the feathers of the elms make dapplings of sun among their shadows of large lace on the grass.

The lawn is ungraded and uneven like the pastures, and it merges *8* eventually with the fields. Behind, there are great clotted masses of myrtle-beds, lilac-bushes, clumps of pink phlox and other things I cannot identify; pink and white hollyhocks, some of them leaning, fine blue and purple dye of larkspur; a considerable vegetable garden, with long rows of ripe gooseberries and currants, a patch of yellow pumpkin flowers, and bushes of raspberries, both white and red—among which are sprinkled like confetti the little flimsy California poppies, pink, orange, white and red. In an old dark red barn behind, where the hayloft is almost collapsing, I find spinning-wheels, a carder, candle-molds, a patent boot-jack, obsolete implements of carpentry, little clusters of baskets for berry-picking and a gigantic pair of scales such as is nowadays only seen in the hands of allegorical figures.

The house was built by the Talcotts, after whom the town was named. 9
They owned the large farm in front of the house, which stretches down to the river and beyond. They also had a profitable grist mill, but—I learn from the county history—were thought to have "adopted a policy adverse to the building up of a village at the point where natural advantages greatly favored," since they "refused to sell village lots to mechanics, and retained the water power on Sugar River, although parties offered to invest liberally in manufactures." In time, there were only two Talcotts left, an old maid and her widowed sister. My great-grandfather, Thomas Baker, who lived across the street and had been left by the death of his wife with a son and eight daughters, paid court to Miss Talcott and married her. She was kind to the children, and they remembered her with affection. My great-grandfather acquired in this way the house, the farm and the quarry.

All but two of my great-grandfather's daughters, of whom my grand- 10
mother was one—"six of them beauties," I understand—got married and went away. Only one of them was left in the house at the time when I first remember Talcottville: my great-aunt Rosalind, a more or less professional invalid and a figure of romantic melancholy, whose fiancé had been lost at sea. When I knew her, she was very old. It was impressive and rather frightening to call on her—you did it only by special arrangement, since she had to prepare herself to be seen. She would be beautifully dressed in a lace cap, a lavender dress and a white crocheted shawl, but she had become so bloodless and shrunken as dreadfully to resemble a mummy and reminded one uncomfortably of Miss Haversham in Dickens's *Great Expectations*. She had a certain high and formal coquetry and was the only person I ever knew who really talked like the characters in old novels. When she had been able to get about, she had habitually treated the townspeople with a condescension almost baronial. According to the family legend, the great-grandmother of great-grandmother Baker had been a daughter of one of the Earls of Essex, who had eloped with a gardener to America.

Another of my Baker great-aunts, who was one of my favorite rela- *11*
tives, had married and lived in the town and had suffered tragic disap-
pointments. Only her strong intellectual interests and a mind capable of
philosophic pessimism had maintained her through the wreck of her
domestic life. She used to tell me how, a young married woman, she
had taught herself French by the dictionary and grammar, sitting up at
night alone by the stove through one of their cold and dark winters. She
had read a great deal of French, subscribed to French magazines, without
ever having learned to pronounce it. She had rejected revealed religion
and did not believe in immortality; and when she felt that she had been
relieved of the last of her family obligations—though her hair was now
turning gray—she came on to New York City and lived there alone for
years, occupying herself with the theater, reading, visits to her nephews
and nieces—with whom she was extremely popular—and all the spectacle
and news of the larger world which she had always loved so much but
from which she had spent most of her life removed.

When she died, only the youngest of the family was left, the sole *12*
brother, my great-uncle Tom. His mother must have been worn out with
childbearing—she died after the birth of this ninth child—and he had not
turned out so well as the others. He had been born with no roof to his
mouth and was obliged to wear a false gold palate, and it was difficult to
understand him. He was not really simple-minded—he had held a small
political job under Cleveland, and he usually beat me at checkers—but
he was childlike and ill-equpped to deal with life in any very effective
way. He sold the farm to a German and the quarry to the town. Then
he died, and the house was empty, except when my mother and father
would come here to open it up for two or three months in the summer.

I have not been back here in years, and I have never before examined *13*
the place carefully. It has become for me something like a remembered
dream—unearthly with the powerful impressions of childhood. Even
now that I am here again, I find I have to shake off the dream. I keep
walking from room to room, inside and outside, upstairs and down, with
uneasy sensations of complacency that are always falling through to
depression.

These rooms are very well proportioned; the white mantel-pieces are *14*
elegant and chaste, and the carving on each one is different. The larger
of the two living rooms now seems a little bare because the various
members of the family have claimed and taken away so many things; and
there are some disagreeable curtains and carpets, for which the wife of
my great-uncle Tom is to blame. But here are all the things, I take note,
that are nowadays sold in antique stores: red Bohemian-glass decanters;
a rusty silver snuff-box; a mirror with the American eagle painted at the
top of the glass. Little mahogany tables with slim legs; a set of curly-
maple furniture, deep seasoned yellow like satin; a yellow comb-backed

rocker with a design of green conch-shells that look like snails. A small bust of Dante with the nose chipped, left behind as defective by one of my cousins when its companion piece, Beethoven, was taken away; a little mahogany melodeon on which my Aunt "Lin" once played. Large engravings of the family of Washington and of the "Reformers Presenting Their Famous Protest before the Diet of Spires"; a later engraving of Dickens. Old tongs and poker, impossibly heavy. A brown mahogany desk inlaid with yellow birdwood, which contains a pair of steel-rimmed spectacles and a thing for shaking sand on wet ink. Daguerreotypes in fancy cases: they seem to last much better than photographs—my grandmother looks fresh and cunning—I remember that I used to hear that the first time my grandfather saw her, she was riding on a load of hay—he came back up here to marry her as soon as he had got out of medical school. An old wooden flute—originally brought over from New England, I remember my great-uncle's telling me, at the time when they traveled by ox-team—he used to get a lonely piping out of it—I try it but cannot make a sound. Two big oval paintings, in tarnished gilt frames, of landscapes romantic and mountainous: they came from the Utica house of my great-grandfather Baker's brother—he married a rich wife and invented excelsior—made out of the northern lumber—and was presented with a solid-silver table service by the grateful city of Utica.

Wallpaper molded by the damp from the stone; uninviting old black *15* haircloth furniture. A bowl of those enormous up-country sweet peas, incredibly fragrant and bright—they used to awe and trouble me—why?

In the dining room, a mahogany china closet, which originally—in the *16* days when letters were few and great-grandfather Baker was postmaster—was the whole of the village post office. My grandmother's pewter tea-service, with its design of oak-leaves and acorns, which I remember from her house in New Jersey. Black iron cranes, pipkins and kettles for cooking in the fireplace; a kind of flat iron pitchfork for lifting the bread in and out, when they baked at the back of the hearth. On the sideboard, a glass decanter with a gilt black-letter label: "J. Rum." If there were only some rum in the decanter!—if the life of the house were not now all past!—the kitchens that trail out behind are almost too old-smelling, too long deserted, to make them agreeable to visit—in spite of the delightful brown crocks with long-tailed blue birds painted on them, a different kind of bird on each crock.

In the ample hall with its staircase, two large colored pictures of trout, *17* one rising to bait, one leaping. Upstairs, a wooden pestle and mortar; a perforated tin box for hot coals to keep the feet warm in church or on sleigh-rides; a stuffed heron; a horrible bust of my cousin Dorothy Read in her girlhood, which her mother had done of her in Germany. The hair-ribbon and the ruffles are faithfully reproduced in marble, and the eyes have engraved pupils. It stands on a high pedestal, and it used to be possible, by pressing a button, to make it turn around. My Cousin

Grace, Dorothy's mother, used to show if off and invite comparison with the original, especially calling attention to the nose; but what her mother had never known was that Dorothy had injured her nose in some rather disgraceful row with her sister. One day when the family were making an excursion, Dorothy pleaded indisposition and bribed a man with a truck to take the bust away and drop it into a pond. But Uncle Tom got this out of the man, dredged the statue up and replaced it on its pedestal. An ugly chair with a round rag back; an ugly bed with the head of Columbus sticking out above the pillows like a figurehead. Charming old bedquilts, with patterns of rhomboids in softened browns, greens and pinks, or of blue polka-dotted hearts that ray out on stiff phallic stalks. A footstool covered in white, which, however, when you step on a tab at the side, opens up into a cuspidor—some relic, no doubt, of the times when the house was used for local meetings. (There used to be a musical chair, also brought back from Germany, but it seems to have disappeared.) A jar of hardly odorous dried rose-leaves, and a jar of little pebbles and shells that keep their bright colors in alcohol.

The original old panes up here have wavy lines in the glass. There   18 are cobweb-filthy books, which I try to examine: many religious works, the annals of the state legislature, a book called *The Young Wife, or Duties of Women in the Marriage Relation,* published in Boston in 1838 and containing a warning against tea and coffee, which "loosen the tongue, fire the eye, produce mirth and wit, excite the animal passions, and lead to remarks about ourselves and others, that we should not have made in other circumstances, and which it were better for us and the world, never to have made." But there is also, I noticed downstairs, Grant Allen's *The Woman Who Did* from 1893.

I come upon the *History of Lewis County* and read it with a certain   19 pride. I am glad to say to myself that it is a creditable piece of work— admirably full in its information on geology, flora and fauna, on history and local politics; diversified with anecdotes and biographies never over-flattering and often pungent; and written in a sound English style. Could anyone in the county today, I wonder, command such a sound English style? I note with gratification that the bone of a prehistoric cuttlefish, discovered in one of the limestone caves, is the largest of its kind on record, and that a flock of wild swans was seen here in 1821. In the eighties, there were still wolves and panthers. There are still bears and deer today.

I also look into the proceedings of the New York State Assembly. My   20 great-grandfather Thomas Baker was primarily a politician and at that time a member of the Assembly. I have heard that he was a Jacksonian Democrat, and that he made a furious scene when my grandmother came back from New Jersey and announced that she had become a Republican: it "spoiled her whole visit." There is a photograph of great-grandfather

Baker in an oval gilt frame, with his hair sticking out in three spikes and a wide and declamatory mouth. I look through the Assembly record to see what sort of role he played. It is the forties; the Democrats are still angry over the Bank of United States. But when I look up Thomas Baker in the index, it turns out that he figures solely as either not being present or as requesting leave of absence. They tell me he used to go West to buy cattle.

That sealed-up space on the second floor which my father had knocked 21 out—who did they tell me was hidden in it? I have just learned from one of the new road-signs which explain historical associations that there are caves somewhere here in which slaves were hidden. Could this have been a part of the underground route for smuggling Negroes over the border into Canada? Is the attic, the "kitchen chamber," which is always so suffocating in summer, still full of those carpetbags and crinolines and bonnets and beaver-hats that we used to get out of the old cowhide trunks and use to dress up for charades?

It was the custom for the married Baker daughters to bring their 22 children back in the summer; and their children in time brought their children. In those days, how I loved coming up here! It was a reunion with cousins from Boston and New York, Ohio and Wisconsin, as well as with the Talcottville and Utica ones: we fished and swam in the rivers, had all sorts of excursions and games. Later on, I got to dislike it: the older generation died, the younger did not much come. I wanted to be elsewhere, too. The very fullness with life of the past, the memory of those many families of cousins and uncles and aunts, made the emptiness of the present more oppressive. Isn't it still?—didn't my gloom come from that, the night of my first arrival? Wasn't it the dread of that that kept me away? I am aware, as I walk through the rooms, of the amplitude and completeness of the place—the home of a big old-fashioned family that had to be a city in itself. And not merely did it house a clan: the whole life of the community passed through it. And now for five sixths of the year it is nothing but an unheated shell, a storehouse of unused antiques, with no intimate relation to the county.

The community itself today is somewhat smaller than the community 23 of those days, and its condition has very much changed. It must seem to the summer traveler merely one of the clusters of houses that he shoots through along the state highway: and there may presently be little left save our house confronting, across the road, the hot-dog stand and the gasoline station.

For years I have had a recurrent dream. I take a road that runs toward 24 the west. It is summer; I pass by a strange summer forest, in which there are mysterious beings, though I know that, on the whole, they are shy and benign. If I am fortunate and find the way, I arrive at a wonderful

river, which runs among boulders, with rapids, between alders and high
spread trees, through a countryside fresh, green and wide. We go in
swimming; it is miles away from anywhere. We plunge in the smooth
flowing pools. We make our way to the middle of the stream and climb
up on the pale round gray stones and sit naked in the sun and the air,
while the river glides away below us. And I know that it is the place for
which I have always longed, the place of wildness and freedom, to find
which is the height of what one may hope for—the place of unalloyed
delight.

As I walk about Talcottville now, I discover that the being-haunted   25
forest is a big grove which even in daytime used to be lonely and dark
and where great white Canadian violets used to grow out of the deep
black leaf-mold. Today it is no longer dark, because half the trees have
been cut down. The river of my dream, I see, is simply an idealized
version of the farther and less frequented and more adventurous bank of
Sugar River, which had to be reached by wading. Both river and forest
are west of the road that runs through the village, which accounts for
my always taking that direction in my dream. I remember how Sugar
River—out of the stone of which our house is built—used, in my boy-
hood, so to fascinate me that I had an enlargement made of one of the
photographs I had taken of it—a view of "the Big Falls"—and kept it in
my room all winter. Today the nearer bank has been largely blasted
away to get stone for the new state highway, and what we used to call
"the Little Falls" is gone.

I visit the house of my favorite great-aunt, and my gloom returns and   26
overwhelms me. The huge root of an elm has split the thick slabs of the
pavement so that you have to walk over a hump; and one of the big
square stone fence-posts is toppling. Her flowers, with no one to tend
them, go on raggedly blooming in their seasons. There has been nobody
in her house since she died. It is all too appropriate to her pessimism—
that dead end she always foresaw. As I walk around the house, I remember how, once on the back porch there, she sang me old English
ballads, including that gruesome one, "Oh, where have you been, Randall, my son?"—about the man who had gone to Pretty Peggy's house
and been given snakes to eat:

"What had you for supper, Randall, my son?"
"Fresh fish fried in butter. Oh, make my bed soon!
For I'm sick at my heart and I fain would lie down!"

She was old then—round-shouldered and dumpy—after the years   27
when she had looked so handsome, straight-backed and with the fashionable aigrette in her hair. And the song she sang seemed to have been
drawn out of such barbarous reaches of the past, out of something so

surprisingly different from the college-women's hotels in New York in
which I had always known her as living: that England to which, far
though she had come from it, she was yet so much nearer than I—that
queer troubling world of legend which I knew from Percy's *Reliques* but
with which she had maintained a real contact through centuries of wom-
en's voices—for she sang it without a smile, completely possessed by its
spirit—that it made my flesh creep, disconcerted me.

My great-aunt is dead, and all her generation are dead—and the new   28
generations of the family have long ago left Talcottville behind and have
turned into something quite different. They were already headed for the
cities by the middle of the last century, as can be seen by the rapid
dispersal of great-grandfather Baker's daughters. Yet there were still, in
my childhood, a few who stayed on in this country as farmers. They
were very impressive people, the survivors of a sovereign race who had
owned their own pastures and fields and governed their own community.
Today the descendants of these are performing mainly minor functions
in a machine which they do not control. They have most of them become
thoroughly urbanized, and they are farther from great-grandfather Baker
than my grandmother, his daughter, was when she came back from New
Jersey a Republican. One of her children, a retired importer in New
York, was complaining to me the other day that the outrageous demands
of the farmers were making business recovery impossible, and protesting
that if the advocates of the income tax had their way, the best people
would no longer be able to live up to their social positions. A cousin,
who bears the name of one of his Ipswich ancestors, a mining engineer
on the Coast and a classmate and admirer of Hoover, invested and has
lost heavily in Mexican real estate and the industrial speculations of the
boom. Another, with another of the old local names, is now at the head
of an organization whose frankly avowed purpose is to rescue the New
York manufacturers from taxation and social legislation. He has seen
his native city of Utica decline as a textile center through the removal
of its mills to the South, where taxes are lighter and labor is cheaper;
and he is honestly convinced that his efforts are directed toward civic
betterment.

Thus the family has come imperceptibly to identify its interests with   29
those of what my great-grandfather Baker would have called the "money
power." They work for it and acquiesce in it—they are no longer the
sovereign race of the first settlers of Lewis County, and in the cities they
have achieved no sovereignty. They are much too scrupulous and decent, and their tastes are too comparatively simple for them ever to have
rolled up great fortunes during the years of expansion and plunder. They
have still the frank accent and the friendly eye of the older American

world, and they seem rather taken aback by the turn that things have been taking.

And what about me? As I come back in the train, I find that—other *30* causes contributing—my depression of Talcottville deepens. I did not find the river and the forest of my dream—I did not find the magic of the past. I have been too close to the past: there in that house, in that remote little town which has never known industrial progress since the Talcotts first obstructed the development of the water power of Sugar River, you can see exactly how rural Americans were living a century and a half ago. And who would go back to it? Not I. Let people who have never known country life complain that the farmer has been spoiled by his radio and his Ford. Along with the memory of exaltation at the immensity and freedom of that countryside, I have memories of horror at its loneliness: houses burning down at night, sometimes with people in them, where there was no fire department to save them, and husbands or wives left alone by death—the dark nights and the prisoning winters. I do not grudge the sacrifice of the Sugar River falls for the building of the new state highway, and I do not resent the hot-dog stand. I am at first a little shocked at the sight of a transformer on the road between Talcottville and Boonville, but when I get to the Talcottville house, I am obliged to be thankful for it—no more oil-lamps in the evenings! And I would not go back to that old life if I could: that civilization of northern New York—why should I idealize it?—was too lonely, too poor, too provincial.

I look out across the Hudson and see Newburgh: with the neat- *31* windowed cubes of its dwellings and docks, distinct as if cut by a burin, built so densely up the slope of the bank and pierced by an occasional steeple, undwarfed by tall modern buildings and with only the little old-fashioned ferry to connect it with the opposite bank, it might still be an eighteenth-century city. My father's mother came from there. She was the granddaughter of a carpet-importer from Rotterdam. From him came the thick Spanish coins which the children of my father's family were supposed to cut their teeth on. The business, which had been a considerable one, declined as the sea trade of the Hudson became concentrated in New York. My father and mother went once—a good many years ago—to visit the old store by the docks, and were amazed to find a solitary old clerk still scratching up orders and sales on a slate that hung behind the counter.

And the slate and the Spanish coins, though they symbolize a kind of *32* life somewhat different from that evoked by Talcottville, associate themselves in my mind with such things as the old post office turned china closet. And as I happen to be reading Herndon's *Life of Lincoln*, that, too, goes to flood out the vision with its extension still further west, still further from the civilized seaboard, of the life of the early frontier. Through Herndon's extraordinary memoir, one of the few really great American books of its kind, which America has never accepted, preferring to it the sentimentalities of Sandburg and the ladies who write Christmas stories—the past confronts me even more plainly than through the bootjacks and daguerreotypes of Talcottville, and makes me even more uneasy. Here you are back again amid the crudeness and the poverty of the American frontier, and here is a man of genius coming out of it and perfecting himself. The story is not merely moving, it becomes almost agonizing. The ungainly boorish boy from the settler's clearing, with nobody and nothing behind him, hoping that his grandfather had been a planter as my great-aunt Rosalind hoped that she was a descendant of the Earls of Essex, the morbid young man looking passionately toward the refinement and the training of the East but unable to bring himself to marry the women who represented it for him—rejoining across days in country stores, nights in godforsaken hotels, rejoining by heroic self-discipline the creative intelligence of the race, to find himself the conscious focus of its terrible unconscious parturition—his miseries burden his grandeur. At least they do for me at this moment.

Old Abe Lincoln came out of the wilderness,
Out of the wilderness, out of the wilderness—

The echo of the song in my mind inspires me with a kind of awe—I can hardly bear the thought of Lincoln.

Great-grandfather Baker's politics and the Talcottville general store, *33* in which people sat around and talked before the new chain store took its place—Lincoln's school was not so very much different. And I would not go back to that.

Yet as I walk up the steps of my house in New York, I am forced to *34* recognize, with a sinking, that I have never been able to leave it. This old wooden booth I have taken between First and Second Avenues—what is it but the same old provincial America? And as I open the door with its loose knob and breathe in the musty smell of the stair-carpet, it seems to me that I have not merely stuck in the world where my fathers lived but have actually, in some ways, lost ground in it. This gray paintless clapboarded front, these lumpy and rubbed yellow walls—they were probably once respectable, but they must always have been commonplace. They have never had even the dignity of the house in Lewis County. But I have rented them because, in my youth, I had been used to living in houses and have grown to loathe city apartments.

So here, it seems, is where I must live: in an old cramped and sour *35* frame-house—having failed even worse than my relatives at getting out of the American big-business era the luxuries and the prestige that I unquestionably should very much have enjoyed. Here is where I end by living—among the worst instead of the best of this city that took the trade away from Newburgh—the sordid and unhealthy children of my sordid and unhealthy neighbors, who howl outside my windows night and day. It is this, in the last analysis—there is no doubt about it now!— which has been rankling and causing my gloom: to have left that early world behind yet never to have really succeeded in what was till yesterday the new.

Study Questions

1. "The Old Stone House" appears to be an essay of *personal description*; that is, Edmund Wilson describes the house in terms of the personal feelings and memories it invokes. Why would readers be interested in this kind of essay? What might they learn about themselves from reading it?
2. In describing the house, Wilson frequently interrupts his description to give anecdotes. How are these anecdotes connected with his description? What added information do they give the readers?
3. How formal is the language in "The Old Stone House"? Why do you think Wilson chose this level of formality? How does it balance the "personal" nature of the description of the house?
4. Compare and contrast the use of anecdotes in "The Old Stone House" and "On the Ball." In both essays the authors use anecdotes to illustrate their feelings toward their topics. In what way are the anecdotes similar? In what way are they different? How does the difference in subject matter affect the kinds of anecdotes used in each?

Suggestion for Prewriting

Trying to describe a place you are familiar with may not be as easy as it at first appears. What to describe and how to describe it are two questions that may cause considerable uncertainty. *Mapping* is a prewriting technique that can help you handle that uncertainty by focusing your attention on the place you wish to describe before you start writing. It gives you time to "see" the place without worrying about what you will write or how you will express your thoughts.

You begin mapping by drawing a diagram of the place you want to describe. Start by simply drawing its outline, and then either physically or mentally walking around that place. As you tour it, write down on the diagram those objects and features that you notice and add a few phrases that summarize the most salient characteristics and your personal reaction to them (see fig. 3.1, p. 148, for an illustration of such a map).

Your annotated diagram will give you concrete material on which to base your description.

To practice this form of prewriting, choose a single room (of some familiar house, store, or building) and make an annotated map of it. Since your goal is to prepare yourself for writing an essay on how that room evokes for you a specific emotion (fear, pleasure, depression, delight), be sure that the remarks you record deal with those features and objects you associate with the feeling you have chosen. If at all possible, annotate your diagram while you are actually in the room.

Teaching Language in Open Admissions

Adrienne Rich

M y first romantic notion of teaching came, I *1* think, from reading Emlyn Williams's play *The Corn Is Green,* sometime in my teens. As I reconstruct it now, a schoolteacher in a Welsh mining village is reading her pupils' essays one night and comes upon a paper which, for all its misspellings and dialect constructions, seems to be the work of a nascent poet. Turning up in the midst of the undistinguished efforts of her other pupils, this essay startles the teacher. She calls in the boy who wrote it, goes over it with him, talks with him about his life, his hopes, and offers to tutor him privately, without fees. Together, as the play goes on, they work their way through rhetoric, mathematics, Shakespeare, Latin, Greek. The boy gets turned on by the classics, is clearly intended to be, if not a poet, at least a scholar. Birth and family background had destined him for a life in the coal mines; but now another path opens up. Toward the end of the play we see him being coached for the entrance examinations for Oxford. I believe crisis strikes when it looks as if he has gotten one of the village girls pregnant and may have to marry her, thus cutting short a career of dazzling promise before it has begun. I don't recall the outcome, but I suspect that the unwed mother is hushed up and packed away (I would be more interested to see the play rewritten today as *her* story) and the boy goes off to Oxford, with every hope of making it to donhood within the decade.

Perhaps this represents a secret fantasy of many teachers: the ill- *2* scrawled essay, turned up among so many others, which has the mark of genius. And looking at the first batch of freshman papers every semester can be like a trip to the mailbox—there is always the possibility of something turning up that will illuminate the weeks ahead. But behind the larger fantasy lie assumptions which I have only gradually come to recognize; and the recognition has to do with a profound change in my conceptions of teaching and learning.

Before I started teaching at City College I had known only elitist *3* institutions: Harvard and Radcliffe as an undergraduate, Swarthmore as a visiting poet, Columbia as teacher in a graduate poetry workshop that included some of the best young poets in the city. I applied for the job at City in 1968 because Robert Cumming had described the SEEK program to me after Martin Luther King was shot, and my motivation was complex. It had to do with white liberal guilt, of course; and a political decision to use my energies in work with "disadvantaged" (black and Puerto Rican) students. But it also had to do with a need to involve myself with the real life of the city, which had arrested me from the first weeks I began living here.

In 1966 Mayor John Lindsay had been able, however obtusely, to coin 4 the phrase "Fun City" without actually intending it as a sick joke. By 1968, the uncollected garbage lay bulging in plastic sacks on the north side of Washington Square, as it had lain longer north of 110th Street; the city had learned to endure subway strikes, sanitation strikes, cab strikes, power and water shortages; the policeman on the corner had become a threatening figure to many whites as he had long been to blacks; the public school teachers and the parents of their pupils had been in pitched battle. On the Upper West Side poor people were being evicted from tenements which were then tinned-up and left empty, awaiting unscheduled demolition to make room for middle-income housing, for which funds were as yet unavailable; and a squatter movement of considerable political consciousness was emerging in defiance of this uprooting.

There seemed to be three ways in which the white middle class could 5 live in New York: the paranoiac, the solipsistic, and a third, which I am more hesitant to define. By the mid-sixties paranoia was visible and audible: streets of brownstones whose occupants had hired an armed guard for the block and posted notices accordingly; conversations on park benches in which public safety had replaced private health as a topic of concern; conversion of all personal anxieties into fear of the mugger (and the mugger was real, no doubt about it). Paranoia could become a life-style, a science, an art, with the active collaboration of reality. Solipsism I encountered first and most concretely in a conversation with an older European intellectual who told me he liked living in New York (on the East Side) because Madison Avenue reminded him of Paris. It was, and still is, possible to live, if you can afford it, on one of those small islands where the streets are kept clean and the pushers and nodders invisible, to travel by cab, deplore the state of the rest of the city, but remain essentially aloof from its causes and effects. It seems about as boring as most forms of solipsism, since to maintain itself it must remain thick-skinned and ignorant.

But there was, and is, another relationship with the city which I can 6 only begin by calling love. The city as object of love, a love not unmixed with horror and anger, the city as Baudelaire and Rilke had previsioned it, or William Blake for that matter, death in life, but a death emblematic of the death that is epidemic in modern society, and a life more edged, more costly, more charged with knowledge, than life elsewhere. Love as one knows it sometimes with a person with whom one is locked in struggle, energy draining but also energy replenishing, as when one is fighting for life, in oneself or someone else. Here was this damaged, self-destructive organism, preying and preyed upon. The streets were rich with human possibility and vicious with human denial (it is breath-taking to walk through a street in East Harlem, passing among the lithe, alert, childish bodies and attuned, observant, childish faces, playing in the spray of a hydrant, and to know that addiction awaits every brain and body in that block as a potential killer). In all its historic, over-crowded, and sweated poverty, the Lower East Side at the turn of the century had never known this: the odds for the poor, today, are weighted by heroin, a fact which the middle classes ignored until it breathed on their own children's lives as well.

In order to live in the city, I needed to ally myself, in some concrete, 7 practical, if limited way, with the possibilities. So I went up to Convent Avenue and 133rd Street and was interviewed for a teaching job, hired as a poet-teacher. At that time a number of writers, including Toni Cade Bambara, the late Paul Blackburn, Robert Cumming, David Henderson, June Jordan, were being hired to teach writing in the SEEK program to black and Puerto Rican freshmen entering from substandard ghetto high schools, where the prevailing assumption had been that they were of inferior intelligence. (More of these schools later.) Many dropped out (a lower percentage than the national college dropout rate, however); many stuck it out through several semesters of remedial English, math, reading, to enter the mainstream of the college. (As of 1972, 208 SEEK students—or 35 to 40 percent—have since graduated from City College; 24 are now in graduate school. *None* of these students would have come near higher education under the regular admissions programs of the City University; high-school guidance counselors have traditionally written off such students as incapable of academic work. Most could not survive economically in college without the stipends which the SEEK program provides.)

My job, that first year, was to "turn the students on" to writing by 8 whatever means I wanted—poetry, free association, music, politics, drama, fiction—to acclimate them to the act of writing, while a grammar teacher, with whom I worked closely outside of class, taught sentence structure, the necessary mechanics. A year later this course was given up as too expensive, since it involved two teachers. My choice was to enlarge my scope to include grammar and mechanics or to find a niche elsewhere and teach verse writing. I stayed on to teach, and learn, grammar—among other things.

The early experience in SEEK was, as I look back on it, both un- 9 nerving and seductive. Even those who were (unlike me) experienced teachers of remedial English were working on new frontiers, trying new methods. Some of the most rudimentary questions we confronted were:

How do you make standard English verb endings available to a dialect-speaker? How do you teach English prepositional forms to a Spanish-language student? What are the arguments for and against "Black English"? The English of academic papers and theses? Is standard English simply a weapon of colonization? Many of our students wrote in the vernacular with force and wit; others were unable to say what they wanted on paper in or out of the vernacular. We were dealing not simply with dialect and syntax but with the imagery of lives, the anger and flare of urban youth—how could this be *used,* strengthened, without the lies of artificial polish? How does one teach order, coherence, the structure of ideas while respecting the student's experience of his or her thinking and perceiving? Some students who could barely sweat out a paragraph delivered (and sometimes conned us with) dazzling raps in the classroom: How could we help this oral gift transfer itself onto paper? The classes were small—fifteen at most; the staff, at that time, likewise; we spent hours in conference with individual students, hours meeting together and with counselors, trying to teach ourselves how to teach and asking ourselves what we ought to be teaching.

So these were classes, not simply in writing, not simply in literature, 10 certainly not just in the correction of sentence fragments or the redemptive power of the semicolon; though we did, and do, work on all these. One teacher gave a minicourse in genres; one in drama as literature; teachers have used their favorite books from *Alice in Wonderland* to Martin Buber's *The Knowledge of Man;* I myself have wandered all over the map of my own reading: D. H. Lawrence, W. E. B. DuBois, LeRoi Jones, Plato, Orwell, Ibsen, poets from W. C. Williams to Audre Lorde. Sometimes books are used as a way of learning to look at literature, sometimes as a provocation for the students' own writing, sometimes both. At City College all Basic Writing teachers have been free to choose the books they would assign (always keeping within the limits of the SEEK book allowance and considering the fact that non-SEEK students have no book allowance at all, though their financial need may be as acute). There has never been a set curriculum or a required reading list; we have poached off each others' booklists, methods, essay topics, grammar-teaching exercises, and anything else that we hoped would "work" for us.

Most of us felt that students learn to write by discovering the validity 11 and variety of their own experience; and in the late 1960s, as the black classics began to flood the bookstores, we drew on the black novelists, poets, and polemicists as the natural path to this discovery for SEEK students. Black teachers were, of course, a path; and there were some who combined the work of consciousness-raising with the study of Sophocles, Kafka, and other pillars of the discipline oddly enough known as "English." For many white teachers, the black writers were a relatively new discovery: the clear, translucent prose of Douglass, the sonorities of *The Souls of Black Folk,* the melancholy sensuousness of Toomer's poem-novel *Cane.* In this discovery of a previously submerged culture we were learning from and with our students as rarely happens in the university, though it is happening anew in the area of women's studies. We were not merely exploring a literature and a history which had gone virtually unmentioned in our white educations (particularly true for those over thirty); we were not merely having to confront in talk with our students and in their writings, as well as the books we read, the bitter reality of Western racism: we also found ourselves reading almost any piece of Western literature through our students' eyes, imagining how this voice, these assumptions, would sound to us if we were they. "We learned from the students"—banal cliché, one that sounds pious and patronizing by now; yet the fact remains that our white liberal assumptions *were* shaken, our vision of both the city and the university changed, our relationship to language itself made both deeper and more painful.

Of course the students responded to black literature; I heard searching *12* and acute discussions of Jones's poem "The Liar" or Wright's "The Man Who Lived Underground" from young men and women who were in college on sufferance in the eyes of the educational establishment; I've heard similar discussions of *Sons and Lovers* or the *Republic.* Writing this, I am conscious of how obvious it all seems and how unnecessary it now might appear to demonstrate by little anecdotes that ghetto students can handle sophisticated literature and ideas. But in 1968, 1969, we were still trying to prove this—we and our students felt that the burden of proof was on us. When the Black and Puerto Rican Student Community seized the South Campus of C.C.N.Y. in April 1969, and a team of students sat down with the president of the college and a team of faculty members to negotiate, one heard much about the faculty group's surprised respect for the students' articulateness, reasoning power, and skill in handling statistics—for the students were negotiating in exchange for withdrawal from South Campus an admissions policy which would go far beyond SEEK in its inclusiveness.

Those of us who had been involved earlier with ghetto students felt *13* that we had known their strength all along: an impatient cutting through of the phony, a capacity for tenacious struggle with language and syntax and difficult ideas, a growing capacity for political analysis which helped counter the low expectations their teachers had always had of them and which many had had of themselves; and more, their knowledge of the naked facts of society, which academia has always, even in its public urban form, managed to veil in ivy or fantasy. Some were indeed chronologically older than the average college student; many, though eighteen or twenty years old, had had responsibility for themselves and their families for years. They came to college with a greater insight into the actual workings of the city and of American racial oppression than most of their teachers or their elite contemporaries. They had held dirty jobs, borne children, negotiated for Spanish-speaking parents with an English-speaking world of clinics, agencies, lawyers, and landlords, had their sixth senses nurtured in the streets, or had made the transition from southern sharehold or Puerto Rican countryside to Bedford-Stuyvesant or the *barrio* and knew the ways of two worlds. And they were becoming, each new wave of them, more lucidly conscious of the politics of their situation, the context within which their lives were being led.

It is tempting to romanticize, at the distance of midsummer 1972, what the experience of SEEK—and by extension, of all remedial freshman programs under Open Admissions—was (and is) for the students themselves. The Coleman Report and the Moynihan Report have left echoes and vibrations of stereotypical thinking which perhaps only a first-hand knowledge of the New York City schools can really silence. Teaching at City I came to know the intellectual poverty and human waste of the public school system through the marks it had left on students—and not on black and Puerto Rican students only, as the advent of Open Admissions was to show. For a plain look at the politics and practices of this system, I recommend Ellen Lurie's *How to Change the Schools,* a handbook for parent activists which enumerates the conditions she and other parents, black, Puerto Rican, and white, came to know intimately in their struggles to secure their children's right to learn and to be treated with dignity. The book is a photograph of the decay, racism, and abusiveness they confronted, written not as muckraking journalism but as a practical tool for others like themselves. I have read little else, including the most lyrically indignant prose of radical educators, that gives so precise and devastating a picture of the life that New York's children are expected to lead in the name of schooling. She writes of "bewildered angry teenagers, who have discovered that they are in classes for mentally retarded students, simply because they cannot speak English," of teachers and principals who "behaved as though every white middle-class child was gifted and was college material, and every black and Puerto Rican (and sometimes Irish and Italian) working-class child was slow, disadvantaged, and unable to learn anything but the most rudimentary facts." She notes that "81 elementary schools in the state (out of a total 3,634) had more than 70 percent of their students below minimum competence, and 65 *of these were New York City public schools!*" Her findings and statistics make it clear that tracking begins at kindergarten (chiefly on the basis of skin color and language) and that nonwhite and working-class children are assumed to have a maximum potential which fits them only for the so-called general diploma, hence are not taught, as are their middle-class contemporaries, the math or languages or writing skills needed to pass college entrance examinations or even to do academic-diploma high-school work. I have singled out these particular points for citation because they have to do directly with our students' self-expectations and the enforced limitation of their horizons years before they come to college. But much else has colored their educational past: the drug pushers at the school gates, the obsolete texts, the punitive conception of the teacher's role, the ugliness, filth, and decay of the buildings, the demoralization even of good teachers working under such conditions. (Add to this the use of tranquilizing drugs on children who are considered hyperactive or who present "behavior problems" at an early age.)

To come out of scenes like these schools and be offered "a chance" 15 to compete as an equal in the world of academic credentials, the white-collar world, the world beyond the minimum wage or welfare, is less romantic for the student than for those who view the process from a distance. The student who leaves the campus at three or four o'clock after a day of classes, goes to work as a waitress, or clerk, or hash-slinger, or guard, comes home at ten or eleven o'clock to a crowded apartment with TV audible in every corner—what does it feel like to this student to be reading, say, Byron's "Don Juan" or Jane Austen for a class the next day? Our students may spend two or three hours in the subway going to and from college and jobs, longer if the subway system is more deplorable than usual. To read in the New York subway at rush hour is impossible; it is virtually impossible to think.

How does one compare this experience of college with that of the 16 Columbia students down at 116th Street in their quadrangle of gray stone dormitories, marble steps, flowered borders, wide spaces of time and architecture in which to talk and think? Or that of Berkeley students with their eucalyptus grove and tree-lined streets of bookstores and cafés? The Princeton or Vassar students devoting four years to the life of the mind in Gothic serenity? Do "motivation" and "intellectual competency" mean the same for those students as for City College undergraduates on that overcrowded campus where in winter there is often no place to sit between classes, with two inadequate bookstores largely filled with required texts, two cafeterias and a snack bar that are overpriced, dreary, and unconducive to lingering, with the incessant pressure of time and money driving at them to rush, to get through, to amass the needed credits somehow, to drop out, to stay on with gritted teeth? Out of a graduating class at Swarthmore or Oberlin and one at C.C.N.Y., which students have demonstrated their ability and commitment, and how do we assume we can measure such things?

Sometimes as I walk up 133rd Street, past the glass-strewn doorways 17 of P.S. 161, the graffiti-sprayed walls of tenements, the uncollected garbage, through the iron gates of South Campus and up the driveway to the prefab hut which houses the English department, I think wryly of John Donne's pronouncement that "the University is a Paradise; rivers of Knowledge are there; Arts and Sciences flow from thence." I think that few of our students have this Athenian notion of what college is going to be for them; their first introduction to it is a many hours' wait in line at registration, which only reveals that the courses they have been advised or wanted to take are filled, or conflict in hours with a needed job; then more hours at the cramped, heavily guarded bookstore; then perhaps, a semester in courses which they never chose, or in which the pace and allusions of a lecturer are daunting or which may meet at opposite ends of an elongated campus stretching for six city blocks and spilling over into a former warehouse on Broadway. Many have written of their first days at C.C.N.Y.: "I only knew it was different from high school." What was different, perhaps, was the green grass of early September with groups of young people in dashikis and gelés, jeans and tie-dye, moving about with the unquenchable animation of the first days of the fall semester; the encounter with some teachers who seem to respect them as individuals; something at any rate less bleak, less violent, less mean-spirited, than the halls of Benjamin Franklin or Evander Childs or some other school with the line painted down the center of the corridor and a penalty for taking the short-cut across that line. In all that my students have written about their high schools, I have found bitterness, resentment, satire, black humor; never any word of nostalgia for the school, though sometimes a word of affection for a teacher "who really tried."

The point is that, as Mina Shaughnessy, the director of the Basic 18 Writing Program at City, has written, "the first stage of Open Admissions involves *openly admitting* that education has failed for too many students." Professor Shaughnessy writes in her most recent report of the increase in remedial courses of white, ethnic students (about two-thirds of the Open Admissions freshmen who have below-80 high school averages) and of the discernible fact, a revelation to many, that these white students "have experienced the failure of the public schools in different ways from the black and Puerto Rican students." Another City College colleague, Leonard Kriegel, writes of this newest population: "Like most blue-collar children, they had lived within the confines of an educational system without ever having questioned that system. They were used to being stamped and categorized. Rating systems, grades, obligations to improve, these had beset them all their lives. . . . They had few expectations from the world-at-large. When they were depressed, they had no real idea of what was getting them down, and they would have dismissed as absurd the idea that they could make demands. They accepted the myths of America as those myths had been presented to them."

Meeting some of the so-called ethnic students in class for the first time 19 in September 1970, I began to realize that: there *are* still poor Jews in New York City; they teach English better to native speakers of Greek on the island of Cyprus than they do to native speakers of Spanish on the island of Manhattan; the Chinese student with acute English-language difficulties is stereotyped as "nonexpressive" and channeled into the

physical sciences before anyone has a chance to find out whether he or
she is a potential historian, political theorist, or psychologist; and (an
intuition, more difficult to prove) white, ethnic working-class young
women seem to have problems of self-reliance and of taking their lives
seriously that young black women students as a group do not seem to
share.

There is also a danger that, paradoxically or not, the white middle- 20
class teacher may find it easier to identify with the strongly motivated,
obviously oppressed, politically conscious black student than with the
students of whom Kriegel has written. Perhaps a different set of prejudices exists: if you're white, why aren't you more hip, more achieving,
why are you bored and alienated, why don't you *care* more? Again, one
has to keep clearly in mind the real lessons of the schools—both public
and parochial—which reward conformity, passivity, and correct answers
and penalize, as Ellen Lurie says, the troublesome question "as trouble-
making," the lively, independent, active child as "disruptive," curiosity
as misbehavior. (Because of the reinforcement in passivity received all
around them in society and at home, white women students seem particularly vulnerable to these judgments.) In many ways the damage is more
insidious because the white students have as yet no real political analysis
going for them; only the knowledge that they have not been as successful
in school as white students are supposed to be.

Confronted with these individuals, this city, these life situations, these 21
strengths, these damages, there are some harsh questions that have to
be raised about the uses of literature. I think of myself as a teacher of
language: that is, as someone for whom language has implied freedom,
who is trying to aid others to free themselves through the written word,
and above all through learning to write it for themselves. I cannot know
for them what it is they need to free, or what words they need to write;
I can only try with them to get an approximation of the story they want
to tell. I have always assumed, and I do still assume, that people come
into the freedom of language through reading, before writing; that the
differences of tone, rhythm, vocabulary, intention, encountered over
years of reading are, whatever else they may be, suggestive of many
different possible modes of being. But my daily life as a teacher confronts
me with young men and women who have had language and literature
used against them, to keep them in their place, to mystify, to bully, to
make them feel powerless. Courses in great books or speed-reading are
not an answer when it is the meaning of literature itself that is in question.
Sartre says: "the literary object has no other substance than the reader's
subjectivity; Raskolnikov's waiting is *my* waiting which I lend him. . . .
His hatred of the police magistrate who questions him is my hatred,
which has been solicited and wheedled out of me by signs. . . . Thus,
the writer appeals to the reader's freedom to collaborate in the production

of his work." But what if it is these very signs, or ones like them, that have been used to limit the reader's freedom or to convince the reader of his or her unworthiness to "collaborate in the production of the work"?

I have no illuminating answers to such questions. I am sure we must *22* revise, and are revising, our notion of the "classic," which has come to be used as a term of unquestioning idolatry instead of in the meaning which Sartre gives it: a book written by someone who "did not have to decide with each work what the meaning and value of literature were, since its meaning and value were fixed by tradition." And I know that the action from the other side, of becoming that person who puts signs on paper and invokes the collaboraton of a reader, encounters a corresponding check: in order to write I have to believe that there is someone willing to collaborate subjectively, as opposed to a grading machine out to get me for mistakes in spelling and grammar. (Perhaps for this reason, many students first show the writing they are actually capable of in an uncorrected journal rather than in a "theme" written "for class.") The whole question of *trust* as a basis for the act of reading or writing has only opened up since we began trying to educate those who have every reason to mistrust literary culture. For young adults trying to write seriously for the first time in their lives, the question "Whom can I trust?" must be an underlying boundary to be crossed before real writing can occur. We who are part of literary culture come up against such a question only when we find ourselves writing on some frontier of self-determination, as when writers from an oppressed group *within* literary culture, such as black intellectuals, or, most recently, women, begin to describe and analyze themselves as they cease to identify with the dominant culture. Those who fall into this category ought to be able to draw on it in entering into the experience of the young adult for whom writing itself—as reading—has been part of the not-me rather than one of the natural activities of the self.

At this point the question of method legitimately arises: How to do it? *23* How to develop a working situation in the classroom where trust becomes a reality, where the students are writing with belief in their own validity, and reading with belief that what they read has validity for them? The question is legitimate—How to do it?—but I am not sure that a description of strategies and exercises, readings, and writing topics can be, however successful they have proven for one teacher. When I read such material, I may find it stimulating and heartening as it indicates the varieties of concern and struggle going on in other classrooms, but I end by feeling it is useless to me. X is not myself and X's students are not my students, nor are my students of this fall the same as my students of last spring. A couple of years ago I decided to teach *Sons and Lovers,* because of my sense that the novel touched on facts of existence crucial to people in their late teens, and my belief that it dealt with certain aspects of family life, sexuality, work, anger, and jealousy which carried over to many cultures. Before the students began to read, I started talking about the time and place of the novel, the life of the mines, the process of industrialization and pollution visible in the slag heaps; and I gave the students (this was an almost all-black class) a few examples of the dialect they would encounter in the early chapters. Several students challenged the novel sight unseen: it had nothing to do with them, it was about English people in another era, why should they expect to find it meaningful to them, and so forth. I told them I had asked them to read it because I believed it was meaningful for them; if it was not, we could talk and write about why not and how not. The following week I reached the classroom door to find several students already there, energetically arguing about the Morels, who was to blame in the marriage, Mrs. Morel's snobbery, Morel's drinking and violence—taking sides, justifying, attacking. The class never began; it simply continued as other students arrived. Many had not yet read the novel, or had barely looked at it; these became curious and interested in the conversation and did go back and read it because they felt it must have something to have generated so much heat. That time, I felt some essential connections had been made, which carried us through several weeks of talking and writing about and out of *Sons and Lovers,* trying to define our relationships to its people and theirs to each other. A year or so later I enthusiastically started working with *Sons and Lovers* again, with a class of largely ethnic students—Jewish, Greek, Chinese, Italian, German, with a few Puerto Ricans and blacks. No one initially challenged the novel, but no one was particularly interested—or, perhaps, as I told myself, it impinged too dangerously on materials that this group was not about to deal with, such as violence in the family, nascent sexual feelings, conflicting feelings about a parent. Was this really true? I don't know; it is easy to play sociologist and make generalizations. Perhaps, simply, a different chemistry was at work, in me and in the students. The point is that for the first class, or for many of them, I think a trust came to be established in the novel genre as a possible means of finding out more about themselves; for the second class, the novel was an assignment, to be done under duress, read superficially, its connections with themselves avoided wherever possible.

Finally, as to trust: I think that, simple as it may seem, it is worth 24 saying: a fundamental belief in the students is more important than anything else. We all know of those studies in education where the teacher's previously induced expectations dramatically affect the learning that goes on during the semester. This fundamental belief is not a sentimental matter: it is a very demanding matter of realistically conceiving the student where he or she is, and at the same time never losing sight of where he or she *can* be. Conditions at a huge, urban, overcrowded, noisy, and pollution-soaked institution can become almost physically overwhelming at times, for the students and for the staff: sometimes apathy, accidia, anomie seem to stare from the faces in an overheated basement classroom, like the faces in a subway car, and I sympathize with the rush to get out the moment the bell rings. This, too, is our context—not merely the students' past and my past, but this present moment we share. I (and I don't think I am alone in this) become angry with myself for my ineffectualness, angry at the students for their apparent resistance or their acceptance of mediocrity, angriest at the political conditions which dictate that we have to try to repair and extend the fabric of language under conditions which tend to coarsen our apprehensions of everything. Often, however, this anger, if not driven in on ourselves, or converted to despair, can become an illuminating force: the terms of the struggle for equal opportunity are chalked on the blackboard: this is what the students have been up against all their lives.

I wrote at the beginning of this article that my early assumptions about　25 teaching had changed. I think that what has held me at City is not the one or two students in a class whose eyes meet mine with a look of knowing they were born for this struggle with words and meanings; not the poet who has turned up more than once; though such encounters are a privilege in the classroom as anywhere. What has held me, and what I think holds many who teach basic writing, are the hidden veins of possibility running through students who don't know (and strongly doubt) that this is what they were born for, but who may find it out to their own amazement, students who, grim with self-depreciation and prophecies of their own failure or tight with a fear they cannot express, can be lured into sticking it out to some moment of breakthrough, when they discover that they have ideas that are valuable, even original, and can express those ideas on paper. What fascinates and gives hope in a time of slashed budgets, enlarging class size, and national depression is the possibility that many of these young men and women may be gaining the kind of critical perspective on their lives and the skill to bear witness that they have never before had in our country's history.

At the bedrock level of my thinking about this is the sense that lan-　26 guage is power, and that, as Simone Weil says, those who suffer from injustice most are the least able to articulate their suffering; and that the silent majority, if released into language, would not be content with a perpetuation of the conditions which have betrayed them. But this notion hangs on a special conception of what it means to be released into language: not simply learning the jargon of an elite, fitting unexceptionably into the status quo, but learning that language can be used as a means of changing reality. What interests me in teaching is less the emergence of the occasional genius than the overall finding of language by those who did not have it and by those who have been used and abused to the extent that they lacked it.

The question can be validly raised: Is the existing public (or private) 27
educational system, school, or university the place where such a relationship to language can be developed? Aren't those structures already
too determined, haven't they too great a stake in keeping things as they
are? My response would be, yes, but this is where the *students* are. On
the one hand, we need alternate education; on the other, we need to
reach those students for whom unorthodox education simply means too
much risk. In a disintegrating society, the orthodox educational system
reflects disintegration. However, I believe it is more than simply reform-
ist to try to use that system—while it still exists in all its flagrant defici-
ences—to use it to provide essential tools and weapons for those who
may live on into a new integration. Language is such a weapon, and
what goes with language: reflection, criticism, renaming, creation. The
fact that our language itself is tainted by the quality of our society means
that in teaching we need to be acutely conscious of the kind of tool we
want our students to have available, to understand how it has been used
against them, and to do all we can to insure that language will not
someday be used by them to keep others silent and powerless.

Study Questions

1. In the first paragraph of "Teaching Language in Open Admissions,"
   Adrienne Rich presents a romantic view of teaching. What purpose
   does this view serve as she prepares her readers for her message?
   Reread the final sentence of this paragraph before you attempt an
   answer.
2. In her discussion of the open admissions program, Rich points out
   that few of the teachers were really prepared to teach in the program. How do you think these instructors would react to this statement? How do you think the students would react? What does Rich
   add to her discussion that shows that she anticipates such reactions?
3. Why does Rich frequently give anecdotes about her own classes?
   How do these anecdotes help the readers better understand her points?
4. Rich often describes the kind of life most of the students in the
   program lead. What purpose does this description serve? Why is this
   description needed for a proper understanding of her message?

Suggestion for Prewriting

In "Teaching Language in Open Admissions," Adrienne Rich uses many
anecdotes, or short narratives, to illustrate the points she considers important. Anecdotes can also be useful in prewriting. Because they give

you concrete illustrations of your topic, these narratives help you to concentrate on the possible statements you can make.

Choose some family event that you believe exemplifies your family's character and write out a brief description of what happened. Describe that incident as if you are writing to a stranger who knows nothing about you. Once you have written the brief description, use any of the pre-writing methods you wish and consider how you might use the incident in an essay on the special qualities you see in your family.

The Nature of
Symbolic Language

Erich Fromm

L et us assume you want to tell someone the *1*
difference between the taste of white wine and
red wine. This may seem quite simple to you.
You know the difference very well; why should it not be easy to explain
it to someone else? Yet you find the greatest difficulty putting this taste
difference into words. And probably you will end up by saying, "Now
look here, I can't explain it to you. Just drink red wine and then white
wine, and you will know what the difference is." You have no difficulty
in finding words to explain the most complicated machine, and yet words
seem to be futile to describe a simple taste experience.

Are we not confronted with the same difficulty when we try to explain *2*
a feeling experience? Let us take a mood in which you feel lost, deserted,
where the world looks gray, a little frightening though not really dangerous. You want to describe this mood to a friend, but again you find
yourself groping for words and eventually feel that nothing you have said
is an adequate explanation of the many nuances of the mood. The
following night you have a dream. You see yourself in the outskirts of
a city just before dawn, the streets are empty except for a milk wagon,
the houses look poor, the surroundings are unfamiliar, you have no means
of accustomed transportation to places familiar to you and where you
feel you belong. When you wake up and remember the dream, it occurs
to you that the feeling you had in that dream was exactly the feeling of
lostness and grayness you tried to describe to your friend the day before.
It is just one picture, whose visualization took less than a second. And
yet this picture is a more vivid and precise description than you could
have given by talking *about* it at length. The picture you see in the
dream is a *symbol* of something you felt.

What is a symbol? A symbol is often defined as "something that *3*
stands for something else." This definition seems rather disappointing.
It becomes more interesting, however, if we concern ourselves with those
symbols which are sensory expressions of seeing, hearing, smelling,
touching, standing for a "something else" which is an inner experience,
a feeling or thought. A symbol of this kind is something outside ourselves; that which it symbolizes is something inside ourselves. Symbolic
language is language in which we express inner experience as if it were

a sensory experience, as if it were something we were doing or something that was done to us in the world of things. Symbolic language is language in which the world outside is a symbol of the world inside, a symbol for our souls and our minds.

If we define a symbol as "something which stands for something else," *4* the crucial question is: *What is the specific connection between the symbol and that which it symbolizes?*

In answer to this question we can differentiate between three kinds of *5* symbols: the *conventional,* the *accidental* and the *universal* symbol. As will become apparent presently, only the latter two kinds of symbols express inner experiences as if they were sensory experiences, and only they have the elements of symbolic language.

The *conventional* symbol is the best known of the three, since we *6* employ it in everyday language. If we see the word "table" or hear the sound "table," the letters T-A-B-L-E stand for something else. They stand for the thing table that we see, touch and use. What is the connection between the *word* "table" and the *thing* "table"? Is there any inherent relationship between them? Obviously not. The thing table has nothing to do with the sound table, and the only reason the word symbolizes the thing is the convention of calling this particular thing by a particular name. We learn this connection as children by the repeated experience of hearing the word in reference to the thing until a lasting association is formed so that we don't have to think to find the right word.

There are some words, however, where the association is not only *7* conventional. When we say "phooey," for instance, we make with our lips a movement of dispelling the air quickly. It is an expression of disgust in which our mouths participate. By this quick expulsion of air we imitate and thus express our intention to expel something, to get it out of our system. In this case, as in some others, the symbol has an inherent connection with the feeling it symbolizes. But even if we assume that originally many or even all words had their origins in some such inherent connection between symbol and the symbolized, most words no longer have this meaning for us when we learn a language.

Words are not the only illustration for conventional symbols, although *8* they are the most frequent and best-known ones. Pictures also can be conventional symbols. A flag, for instance, may stand for a specific country, and yet there is no connection between the specific colors and the country for which they stand. They have been accepted as denoting that particular country, and we translate the visual impression of the flag into the concept of that country, again on conventional grounds. Some pictorial symbols are not entirely conventional; for example, the cross. The cross can be merely a conventional symbol of the Christian church and in that respect no different from a flag. But the specific content of the cross referring to Jesus' death or, beyond that, to the interpenetration of the material and spiritual planes, puts the connection between the symbol and what it symbolizes beyond the level of mere conventional symbols.

The very opposite to the conventional symbol is the *accidental* sym-   9
bol, although they have one thing in common: there is no intrinsic relationship between the symbol and that which it symbolizes. Let us assume that someone has had a saddening experience in a certain city; when he hears the name of that city, he will easily connect the name with a mood of sadness, just as he would connect it with a mood of joy had his experience been a happy one. Quite obviously there is nothing in the nature of the city that is either sad or joyful. It is the individual experience connected with the city that makes it a symbol of a mood.

The same reaction could occur in connection with a house, a street,   10
a certain dress, certain scenery, or anything once connected with a specific mood. We might find ourselves dreaming that we are in a certain city. In fact, there may be no particular mood connected with it in the dream; all we see is a street or even simply the name of the city. We ask ourselves why we happened to think of that city in our sleep and may discover that we had fallen asleep in a mood similar to the one symbolized by the city. The picture in the dream represents this mood, the city "stands for" the mood once experienced in it. Here the connection between the symbol and the experience symbolized is entirely accidental.

In contrast to the conventional symbol, the accidental symbol cannot   11
be shared by anyone else except as we relate the events connected with the symbol. For this reason accidental symbols are rarely used in myths, fairy tales, or works of art written in symbolic language because they are not communicable unless the writer adds a lengthy comment to each symbol he uses. In dreams, however, accidental symbols are frequent.

The *universal* symbol is one in which there is an intrinsic relationship   12
between the symbol and that which it represents. We have already given one example, that of the outskirts of the city. The sensory experience of a deserted, strange, poor environment has indeed a significant relationship to a mood of lostness and anxiety. True enough, if we have never been in the outskirts of a city we could not use that symbol, just as the word "table" would be meaningless had we never seen a table. This symbol is meaningful only to city dwellers and would be meaningless to people living in cultures that have no big cities. Many other universal symbols, however, are rooted in the experience of every human being. Take, for instance, the symbol of fire. We are fascinated by certain qualities of fire in a fireplace. First of all, by its aliveness. It changes continuously, it moves all the time, and yet there is constancy in it. It remains the same without being the same. It gives the impression of power, of energy, of grace and lightness. It is as if it were dancing and had an inexhaustible source of energy. When we use fire as a symbol,

we describe the inner experience characterized by the same elements which we notice in the sensory experience of fire; the mood of energy, lightness, movement, grace, gaiety—sometimes one, sometimes another of these elements being predominant in the feeling.

Similar in some ways and different in others is the symbol of water— *13* of the ocean or of the stream. Here, too, we find the blending of change and permanence, of constant movement and yet of permanence. We also feel the quality of aliveness, continuity and energy. But there is a difference; where fire is adventurous, quick, exciting, water is quiet, slow and steady. Fire has an element of surprise; water an element of predictability. Water symbolizes the mood of aliveness, too, but one which is "heavier," "slower," and more comforting than exciting.

That a phenomenon of the physical world can be the adequate ex- *14* pression of an inner experience, that the world of things can be a symbol of the world of the mind, is not surprising. We all know that our bodies express our minds. Blood rushes to our heads when we are furious, it rushes away from them when we are afraid; our hearts beat more quickly when we are angry, and the whole body has a different tonus if we are happy from the one it has when we are sad. We express our moods by our facial expressions and our attitudes and feelings by movements and gestures so precise that others recognize them more accurately from our gestures than from our words. Indeed, the body is a symbol—and not an allegory—of the mind. Deeply and genuinely felt emotion, and even any genuinely felt thought, is expressed in our whole organism. In the case of the universal symbol, we find the same connection between mental and physical experience. Certain physical phenomena suggest by their very nature certain emotional and mental experiences, and we express emotional experiences in the language of physical experiences, that is to say, symbolically.

The universal symbol is the only one in which the relationship between *15* the symbol and that which is symbolized is not coincidental but intrinsic. It is rooted in the experience of the affinity between an emotion or thought, on the one hand, and a sensory experience, on the other. It can be called universal because it is shared by all men, in contrast not only to the accidental symbol, which is by its very nature entirely personal, but also to the conventional symbol, which is restricted to a group of people sharing the same convention. The universal symbol is rooted in the properties of our body, our senses, and our mind, which are common to all men and, therefore, not restricted to individuals or to specific groups. Indeed, the language of the universal symbol is the one common tongue developed by the human race, a language which it forgot before it succeeded in developing a universal conventional language.

There is no need to speak of a racial inheritance in order to explain *16* the universal character of symbols. Every human being who shares the essential features of bodily and mental equipment with the rest of mankind is capable of speaking and understanding the symbolic language that is based upon these common properties. Just as we do not need to learn to cry when we are sad or to get red in the face when we are angry, and just as these reactions are not restricted to any particular race or group of people, symbolic language does not have to be learned and is not restricted to any segment of the human race. Evidence for this is to be found in the fact that symbolic language as it is employed in myths and dreams is found in all cultures—in so-called primitive as well as such highly developed cultures as Egypt and Greece. Furthermore, the symbols used in these various cultures are strikingly similar since they all go back to the basic sensory as well as emotional experiences shared by men of all cultures. Added evidence is to be found in recent experiments in which people who had no knowledge of the theory of dream interpretation were able, under hypnosis, to interpret the symbolism of their dreams without any difficulty. After emerging from the hypnotic state and being asked to interpret the same dreams, they were puzzled and said, "Well, there is no meaning to them—it is just nonsense."

The foregoing statement needs qualification, however. Some symbols *17* differ in meaning according to the difference in their realistic significance in various cultures. For instance, the function and consequently the meaning of the sun is different in northern countries and in tropical countries. In northern countries, where water is plentiful, all growth depends on sufficient sunshine. The sun is the warm, life-giving, protecting, loving power. In the Near East, where the heat of the sun is much more powerful, the sun is a dangerous and even threatening power from which man must protect himself, while water is felt to be the source of all life and the main condition for growth. We may speak of dialects of universal symbolic language, which are determined by those differences in natural conditions which cause certain symbols to have a different meaning in different regions of the earth.

Quite different from these "symbolic dialects" is the fact that many *18* symbols have more than one meaning in accordance with different kinds of experiences which can be connected with one and the same natural phenomenon. Let us take up the symbol of fire again. If we watch fire in the fireplace, which is a source of pleasure and comfort, it is expressive of a mood of aliveness, warmth, and pleasure. But if we see a building or forest on fire, it conveys to us an experience of threat or terror, of the powerlessness of man against the elements of nature. Fire, then, can be the symbolic representation of inner aliveness and happiness as well as of fear, powerlessness, or of one's own destructive tendencies. The same holds true of the symbol water. Water can be a most destructive force when it is whipped up by a storm or when a swollen river floods its banks. Therefore, it can be the symbolic expression of horror and chaos as well as of comfort and peace.

Another illustration of the same principle is a symbol of a valley. The *19* valley enclosed between mountains can arouse in us the feeling of security and comfort, of protection against all dangers from the outside. But the protecting mountains can also mean isolating walls which do not permit us to get out of the valley and thus the valley can become a symbol of imprisonment. The particular meaning of the symbol in any given place can only be determined from the whole context in which the symbol appears, and in terms of the predominant experiences of the person using the symbol.

A good illustration of the function of the universal symbol is a story, *20* written in symbolic language, which is known to almost everyone in Western culture: the Book of Jonah. Jonah has heard God's voice telling him to go to Nineveh and preach to its inhabitants to give up their evil ways lest they be destroyed. Jonah cannot help hearing God's voice and that is why he is a prophet. But he is an unwilling prophet, who, though knowing what he should do, tries to run away from the command of God (or, as we may say, the voice of his conscience). He is a man who does not care for other human beings. He is a man with a strong sense of law and order, but without love.

How does the story express the inner processes in Jonah?   *21*

We are told that Jonah went down to Joppa and found a ship which *22* should bring him to Tarshish. In mid-ocean a storm rises and, while everyone else is excited and afraid, Jonah goes into the ship's belly and falls into a deep sleep. The sailors, believing that God must have sent the storm because someone on the ship is to be punished, wake Jonah, who had told them he was trying to flee from God's command. He tells them to take him and cast him forth into the sea and that the sea would them become calm. The sailors (betraying a remarkable sense of humanity by first trying everything else before following his advice) eventually take Jonah and cast him into the sea, which immediately stops raging. Jonah is swallowed by a big fish and stays in the fish's belly three days and three nights. He prays to God to free him from this prison. God makes the fish vomit out Jonah unto the dry land and Jonah goes to Nineveh, fulfills God's command, and thus saves the inhabitants of the city.

The story is told as if these events had actually happened. However, *23* it is written in symbolic language and all the realistic events described are symbols for the inner experiences of the hero. We find a sequence of symbols which follow one another; going into the ship, going into the ship's belly, falling asleep, being in the ocean, and being in the fish's belly. All these symbols stand for the same inner experience: for a condition of being protected and isolated, of safe withdrawal from communication with other human beings. They represent what could be represented in another symbol, the fetus in the mother's womb. Different as the ship's belly, deep sleep, the ocean, and a fish's belly are realistically, they are expressive of the same inner experience, of the blending between protection and isolation.

In the manifest story events happen in space and time: *first,* going into   24 the ship's belly; *then,* falling asleep; *then,* being thrown into the ocean; *then,* being swallowed by the fish. One thing happens after the other and, although some events are obviously unrealistic, the story has its own logical consistency in terms of time and space. But if we understand that the writer did not intend to tell us the story of external events, but of the inner experience of a man torn between his conscience and his wish to escape from his inner voice, it becomes clear that his various actions following one after the other express the same mood in him; and that *sequence in time* is expressive of a *growing intensity* of the same feeling. In his attempt to escape from his obligation to his fellow men Jonah isolates himself more and more until, in the belly of the fish, the protective element has so given way to the imprisoning element that he can stand it no longer and is forced to pray to God to be released from where he had put himself. (This is a mechanism which we find so characteristic of neurosis. An attitude is assumed as a defense against a danger, but then it grows far beyond its original defense function and becomes a neurotic symptom from which the person tries to be relieved.) Thus Jonah's escape into protective isolation ends in the terror of being imprisoned, and he takes up his life at the point where he had tried to escape.

There is another difference between the logic of the manifest and of   25 the latent story. In the manifest story the logical connection is one of causality of external events. Jonah wants to go overseas *because* he wants to flee from God, he falls asleep *because* he is tired, he is thrown overboard *because* he is supposed to be the reason for the storm, and he is swallowed by the fish *because* there are man eating fish in the ocean. One event occurs because of a previous event. (The last part of the story is unrealistic but not illogical.) But in the latent story the logic is different. The various events are related to each other by their association with the same inner experience. What appears to be a causal sequence of external events stand for a connection of experiences linked with each other by their association in terms of inner events. This is as logical as the manifest story—but it is a logic of a different kind.

Study Questions

1. In "The Nature of Symbolic Language," Erich Fromm handles a far more abstract topic than does Angell ("On the Ball"). What does Fromm do to try to make his readers comfortable with his topic?

2. How much knowledge does Fromm assume his readers have about the nature of symbols? Identify specific passages that suggest what he is or is not taking for granted.
3. What reason for reading an essay that deals with the nature of symbolic language does Fromm give or suggest to his audience? Where does that statement or suggestion come? Why do you think Fromm has placed it there?
4. Contrast the language (words and sentence structure) of "The Nature of Symbolic Language" with that of "The Gift of Gift-Giving." How can the differences in language be explained by the differences in topics?

Suggestion for Prewriting

Erich Fromm defines a universal symbol as an "intrinsic relationship between the symbol and that which it represents" and states that "many symbols have more than one meaning in accordance with different kinds of experiences." His example of fire as a universal symbol makes an effective illustration of a prewriting technique known as *clustering*.

Developed by Gabriel Rico, clustering is a variation of brainstorming. You begin by writing down a key word or phrase in the center of a sheet of paper and circling it. Next, you write down around that circle ideas that are suggested by the key word or phrase, circle them, and link each to the first (see fig. 2.1). For each new idea, you then write down other words or phrases; and the process continues until you find no more associations. By using lines to link each new idea with the word or phrase that inspired it, clustering more clearly shows the relationships among all the ideas than simple brainstorming can.

To practice clustering, choose a universal symbol such as the sun, the moon, water, soil, or one of the seasons and explore the various meanings you associate with your choice.

Fig. 2.1: Clustering

Of Truth

Francis Bacon

W hat is truth?" said jesting Pilate; and would *1* not stay for an answer. Certainly there be that delight in giddiness, and count it a bondage to fix a belief; affecting free-will in thinking, as well as in acting. And though the sects of philosophers of that kind be gone, yet there remain certain discoursing wits, which are of the same veins, though there be not so much blood in them as was in those of the ancients. But it is not only the difficulty and labor which men take in finding out of truth; nor again, that when it is found, it imposeth upon men's thoughts, that doth bring lies in favor; but a natural though corrupt love of the lie itself. One of the later school of the Grecians examineth the matter, and is at a stand to think what should be in it, that men should love lies; where neither they make for pleasure, as with poets; nor for advantage, as with the merchant, but for the lie's sake. But I cannot tell: this same truth is a naked and open daylight, that doth not show the masks and mummeries and triumphs of the world half so stately and daintily as candle lights. Truth may perhaps come to the price of a pearl, that showeth best by day, but it will not rise to the price of a diamond or carbuncle, that showeth best in varied lights. A mixture of a lie doth ever add pleasure. Doth any man doubt that if there were taken out of men's minds vain opinions, flattering hopes, false valuations, imaginations as one would, and the like, but it would leave the minds of a number of men poor shrunken things, full of melancholy and indisposition, and unpleasing to themselves? One of the fathers, in great severity, called poesy *vinum daemonum,* because it filleth the imagination, and yet it is but with the shadow of a lie. But it is not the lie that passeth through the mind, but the lie that sinketh in, and settleth in it, that doth the hurt, such as we spake of before. But howsoever these things are thus in men's depraved judgments and affections, yet truth, which only doth judge itself, teacheth that the inquiry of truth, which is the love-making, or wooing of it, the knowledge of truth, which is the presence of it, and the belief of truth, which is the enjoying of it, is the sovereign good of human nature. The first creature of God, in the works of the days, was the light of the sense; the last was the light of reason; and His sabbath work ever since is the illumination of His Spirit. First, He breathed light upon the face of the matter, or chaos; then He breathed light into the face of man; and still He breatheth and inspireth light into the face of His chosen. The poet that beautified the sect that was otherwise inferior to the rest saith yet excellently well: "It is a pleasure to stand upon the shore, and to see ships tossed upon the sea: a pleasure to stand in the window of a castle, and to see a battle, and the adventures thereof below: but no pleasure is comparable to the standing upon the vantage ground of truth" (a hill not to be commanded, and where the air is always clear and serene), "and to see the errors, and wanderings, and mists, and tempests, in the vale below": so always that this prospect be with pity, and not with swelling or pride. Certainly, it is heaven upon earth to have a man's mind move in charity, rest in providence, and turn upon the poles of truth.

To pass from theological and philosophical truth to the truth of civil 2 business; it will be acknowledged even by those that practice it not, that clear and round dealing is the honor of man's nature, and that mixture of falsehood is like alloy in coin of gold and silver, which may make the metal work the better, but it embaseth it. For these winding and crooked courses are the goings of the serpent; which goeth basely upon the belly, and not upon the feet. There is no vice that doth so cover a man with shame as to be found false and perfidious; and therefore Montaigne saith prettily, when he inquired the reason why the word of the lie should be such a disgrace, and such an odious charge, saith he, "If it be well weighed, to say that a man lieth is as much as to say that he is brave towards God and a coward towards men."* For a lie faces God, and shrinks from man. Surely the wickedness of falsehood and breach of faith cannot possibly be so highly expressed, as in that it shall be the last peal to call the judgments of God upon the generations of men, it being foretold that when Christ cometh, he shall not "find faith upon the earth."†

Study Questions

1. Bacon has chosen "Of Truth" as the title of this essay, yet he discusses lies as much as he does truth. Has something gone wrong with his presentation? What reasons might he have for giving equal time to lies? How does that part of his discussion clarify what he has to write about truth?
2. According to Bacon, "it is heaven upon earth to have a man's mind move in charity, rest in providence, and turn upon the poles of truth." Go to the *Oxford English Dictionary* and check what meanings Bacon had in mind for the words *providence* and *rest*. How have the meanings of these words changed since Bacon's time? If readers are not

* *Essays* II.18.
† Luke xviii.8.

aware of the older meanings, how much of Bacon's message, if any, will they miss?

3. In Section 1 we called sentence structure a "convention of the written language." Choose a passage from "Of Truth" and contrast the sentences in it with those of any of the more recent essays in this section. What differences do you notice? Do these differences cause difficulties for you in understanding Bacon's essay? Why or why not?

4. Writers of essays often use quotations to support or illustrate a point they want to emphasize. In "Of Truth" Bacon quotes from the Bible and from the works of Lucretius, Montaigne, and Saint Augustine. Would readers who were not aware of these sources be put off by such references? Why do you think Bacon makes use of so many quotations? What does he assume about his audience and what they would consider valid support of his statements?

Suggestion for Prewriting

Quotations can be of help to you when you are doing prewriting. If you are having trouble focusing on a topic or discovering your attitude toward it, search for a quotation dealing with your topic that seems to express your own thoughts or opinions. With that quotation as the point of departure, try either free writing or brainstorming on your reactions to it.

Abstract concepts are frequently difficult to define because we use them constantly without thinking much about them. For example, we may often use words like *truth, honesty, democracy,* and *freedom,* but most of us would be hard pressed to explain what we mean by them. Choose an abstract word like one of the four just mentioned and find a quotation in which the word is used. Then do the prewriting for an essay that gives your personal definition of your choice.

The Image World

Susan Sontag

R eality has always been interpreted through the *1* reports given by images; and philosophers since Plato have tried to loosen our dependence on images by evoking the standard of an image-free way of apprehending the real. But when, in the mid-nineteenth century, the standard finally seemed attainable, the retreat of old religious and political illusions before the advance of humanistic and scientific thinking did not—as anticipated—create mass defections to the real. On the contrary, the new age of unbelief strengthened the allegiance to images. The credence that could no longer be given to realities understood *in the form of* images was now being given to realities understood *to be* images, illusions. In the preface to the second edition (1843) of *The Essence of Christianity,* Feuerbach observes about "our era" that it "prefers the image to the thing, the copy to the original, the representation to the reality, appearance to being"—while being aware of doing just that. And his premonitory complaint has been transformed in the twentieth century into a widely agreed-on diagnosis: that a society becomes "modern" when one of its chief activities is producing and consuming images, when images that have extraordinary powers to determine our demands upon reality and are themselves coveted substitutes for firsthand experience become indispensable to the health of the economy, the stability of the polity, and the pursuit of private happiness.

Feuerbach's words—he is writing a few years after the invention of *2* the camera—seem, more specifically, a presentiment of the impact of photography. For the images that have virtually unlimited authority in a modern society are mainly photographic images; and the scope of that authority stems from the properties peculiar to images taken by cameras.

Such images are indeed able to usurp reality because first of all a *3* photograph is not only an image (as a painting is an image), an interpretation of the real; it is also a trace, something directly stenciled off the real, like a footprint or a death mask. While a painting, even one that meets photographic standards of resemblance, is never more than the stating of an interpretation, a photograph is never less than the registering of an emanation (light waves reflected by objects)—a material vestige of its subject in a way that no painting can be. Between two fantasy alternatives, that Holbein the Younger had lived long enough to have painted Shakespeare or that a prototype of the camera had been invented early enough to have photographed him, most Bardolators would choose the photograph. This is not just because it would presumably show what Shakespeare really looked like, for even if the hypothetical photograph were faded, barely legible, a brownish shadow, we would probably still prefer it to another glorious Holbein. Having a photograph of Shakespeare would be like having a nail from the True Cross.

Most contemporary expressions of concern that an image-world is *4* replacing the real one continue to echo, as Feuerbach did, the Platonic depreciation of the image: true insofar as it resembles something real, sham because it is no more than a resemblance. But this venerable naïve realism is somewhat beside the point in the era of photographic images, for its blunt contrast between the image ("copy") and the thing depicted (the "original")—which Plato repeatedly illustrates with the example of a painting—does not fit a photograph in so simple a way. Neither does the contrast help in understanding image-making at its origins, when it was a practical, magical activity, a means of appropriating or gaining power over something. The further back we go in history, as E. H. Gombrich has observed, the less sharp is the distinction between images and real things; in primitive societies, the thing and its image were simply two different, that is, physically distinct, manifestations of the same energy or spirit. Hence, the supposed efficacy of images in propitiating and gaining control over powerful presences. Those powers, those presences were present in *them*.

For defenders of the real from Plato to Feuerbach to equate image *5* with mere appearance—that is, to presume that the image is absolutely distinct from the object depicted—is part of that process of desacralization which separates us irrevocably from the world of sacred times and places in which an image was taken to participate in the reality of the object depicted. What defines the originality of photography is that, at the very moment in the long, increasingly secular history of painting when secularism is entirely triumphant, it revives—in wholly secular terms—something like the primitive status of images. Our irrepressible feeling that the photographic process is something magical has a genuine basis. No one takes an easel painting to be in any sense co-substantial with its subject; it only represents or refers. But a photograph is not only like its subject, a homage to the subject. It is part of, an extension of that subject; and a potent means of acquiring it, of gaining control over it.

Photography is acquisition in several forms. In its simplest form, we *6* have in a photograph surrogate possession of a cherished person or thing, a possession which gives photographs some of the character of unique objects. Through photographs, we also have a consumer's relation to events, both to events which are part of our experience and to those which are not—a distinction between types of experience that such habit-forming consumership blurs. A third form of acquisition is that, through image-making and image-duplicating machines, we can acquire something as information (rather than experience). Indeed, the importance of photographic images as the medium through which more and more events enter our experience is, finally, only a byproduct of their effectiveness in furnishing knowledge dissociated from and independent of experience.

This is the most inclusive form of photographic acquisition. Through 7 being photographed, something becomes part of a system of information, fitted into schemes of classification and storage which range from the crudely chronological order of snapshot sequences pasted in family albums to the dogged accumulations and meticulous filing needed for photography's uses in weather forecasting, astronomy, microbiology, geology, police work, medical training and diagnosis, military reconnaissance, and art history. Photographs do more than redefine the stuff of ordinary experience (people, things, events, whatever we see—albeit differently, often inattentively—with natural vision) and add vast amounts of material that we never see at all. Reality as such is redefined—as an item for exhibition, as a record for scrutiny, as a target for surveillance. The photographic exploration and duplication of the world fragments continuities and feeds the pieces into an interminable dossier, thereby providing possibilities of control that could not even be dreamed of under the earlier system of recording information: writing.

That photographic recording is always, potentially, a means of control 8 was already recognized when such powers were in their infancy. In 1850, Delacroix noted in his *Journal* the success of some "experiments in photography" being made at Cambridge, where astronomers were photographing the sun and the moon and had managed to obtain a pinhead-size impression of the star Vega. He added the following "curious" observation:

Since the light of the star which was daguerreotyped took twenty years to traverse the space separating it from the earth, the ray which was fixed on the plate had consequently left the celestial spherc a long time before Daguerre had discovered the process by means of which we have just gained control of this light.

Leaving behind such puny notions of control as Delacroix's, photog- 9 raphy's progress has made ever more literal the senses in which a photograph gives control over the thing photographed. The technology that has already minimized the extent to which the distance separating photographer from subject affects the precision and magnitude of the image; provided ways to photograph things which are unimaginably small as well as those, like stars, which are unimaginably far; rendered picture-taking independent of light itself (infrared photography) and freed the picture-object from its confinement to two dimensions (holography); shrunk the interval between sighting the picture and holding it in one's hands (from the first Kodak, when it took weeks for a developed roll of film to be returned to the amateur photographer, to the Polaroid, which ejects the image in a few seconds); not only got images to move (cinema) but achieved their simultaneous recording and transmission (video)—this technology has made photography an incomparable tool for deciphering behavior, predicting it, and interfering with it.

Photography has powers that no other image-system has ever enjoyed *10* because, unlike the earlier ones, it is *not* dependent on an image maker. However carefully the photographer intervenes in setting up and guiding the image-making process, the process itself remains an optical-chemical (or electronic) one, the workings of which are automatic, the machinery for which will inevitably be modified to provide still more detailed and, therefore, more useful maps of the real. The mechanical genesis of these images, and the literalness of the powers they confer, amounts to a new relationship between image and reality. And if photography could also be said to restore the most primitive relationship—the partial identity of image and object—the potency of the image is now experienced in a very different way. The primitive notion of the efficacy of images presumes that images possess the qualities of real things, but our inclination is to attribute to real things the qualities of an image.

As everyone knows, primitive people fear that the camera will rob *11* them of some part of their being. In the memoir he published in 1900, at the end of a very long life, Nadar reports that Balzac had a similar "vague dread" of being photographed. His explanation, according to Nadar, was that

every body in its natural state was made up of a series of ghostly images superimposed in layers to infinity, wrapped in infinitesimal films. . . . Man never having been able to create, that is to make something material from an apparition, from something impalpable, or to make from nothing, an object—each Daguerreian operation was therefore going to lay hold of, detach, and use up one of the layers of the body on which it focused.

It seems fitting for Balzac to have had this particular brand of trepidation—"Was Balzac's fear of the Daguerreotype real or feigned?" Nadar asks. "It was real . . ."—since the procedure of photography is a materializing, so to speak, of what is most original in his procedure as a novelist. The Balzacian operation was to magnify tiny details, as in a photographic enlargement, to juxtapose incongruous traits or items, as in a photographic layout: made expressive in this way, any one thing can be connected with everything else. For Balzac, the spirit of an entire milieu could be disclosed by a single material detail, however paltry or arbitrary-seeming. The whole of a life may be summed up in a momentary appearance. And a change in appearances is a change in the person, for he refused to posit any "real" person ensconced behind these appearances. Balzac's fanciful theory, expressed to Nadar, that a body is composed of an infinite series of "ghostly images," eerily parallels the supposedly realistic theory expressed in his novels, that a person is an aggregate of appearances, appearances which can be made to yield, by proper focusing, infinite layers of significance. To view reality as an endless set of situations which mirror each other, to extract analogies from the most dissimilar things, is to anticipate the characteristic form of perception stimulated by photographic images. Reality itself has started to be understood as a kind of writing, which has to be decoded— even as photographed images were themselves first compared to writing. (Niepce's name for the process whereby the image appears on the plate was heliography, sun-writing; Fox Talbot called the camera "the pencil of nature.")

The problem with Feuerbach's contrast of "original" with "copy" is its static definitions of reality and image. It assumes that what is real persists, unchanged and intact, while only images have changed: shored up by the most tenuous claims to credibility, they have somehow become more seductive. But the notions of image and reality are complementary. When the notion of reality changes, so does that of the image, and vice versa. "Our era" does not prefer images to real things out of perversity but partly in response to the ways in which the notion of what is real has been progressively complicated and weakened, one of the early ways being the criticism of reality as façade which arose among the enlightened middle classes in the last century. (This was of course the very opposite of the effect intended.) To reduce large parts of what has hitherto been regarded as real to mere fantasy, as Feuerbach did when he called religion "the dream of the human mind" and dismissed theological ideas as psychological projections; or to inflate the random and trivial details of everyday life into ciphers of hidden historical and psychological forces, as Balzac did in his encyclopedia of social reality in novel form—these are themselves ways of experiencing reality as a set of appearances, an image.   12

Few people in this society share the primitive dread of cameras that comes from thinking of the photograph as a material part of themselves. But some trace of the magic remains: for example, in our reluctance to tear up or throw away the photograph of a loved one, especially of someone dead or far away. To do so is a ruthless gesture of rejection. In *Jude the Obscure* it is Jude's discovery that Arabella has sold the maple frame with the photograph of himself in it which he gave her on their wedding day that signifies to Jude "the utter death of every sentiment in his wife" and is "the conclusive little stroke to demolish all sentiment in him." But the true modern primitivism is not to regard the image as a real thing; photographic images are hardly that real. Instead, reality has come to seem more and more like what we are shown by cameras. It is common now for people to insist about their experience of a violent event in which they were caught up—a plane crash, a shoot-   13 out, a terrorist bombing—that "it seemed like a movie." This is said, other descriptions seeming insufficient, in order to explain how real it was. While many people in non-industrialized countries still feel apprehensive when being photographed, divining it to be some kind of trespass, an act of disrespect, a sublimated looting of the personality or the culture, people in industrialized countries seek to have their photographs taken—feel that they are images, and are made real by photographs.

Study Questions

1. In this essay Susan Sontag claims: "But a photograph is not only like its subject, a homage to the subject. It is part of, an extension of that subject; and a potent means of acquiring it, of gaining control over it." How does this claim help explain why Sontag called her essay "The Image World"?
2. Sontag quotes from a number of writers (e.g., Feuerbach, Delacroix, Nadar) who are not well-known to many readers. Why do you think she used these quotations? Will readers be confused because they do not know the people she quotes from? Why or why not?
3. How much experience do you believe Sontag has had with photography. Point out specific passages in the essay that support your answer.
4. What do you think Sontag's attitude is toward photography? Where in the essay is this attitude made clear? Why did she place this passage where she did?

Suggestions for Prewriting

Susan Sontag develops her essay by comparing and contrasting painting and photography. This is an organizational technique that is discussed in Section 3. Comparison and contrast can also be used in prewriting. By finding similarities and differences between your topic and a related object or idea, you will often identify important points you need to make in your discussion, whether or not you use comparison and contrast in the essay itself. There are a number of questions you can ask yourself to start off this search:

What other objects or ideas are my readers likely to think of when I mention this topic?

What features of these other objects or ideas are similar to my topic?

In what ways are these similarities significant?

In what ways are these similarities superficial?

What features of these other objects or ideas are different from my topic?

In what ways are these differences significant?

In what ways are these differences superficial?

How can I use these similarities and differences to emphasize the importance of my topic?

   Choose one of the topics listed below and practice prewriting based on comparison and contrast:

writing an essay   choosing a college
reading a story   preparing a meal
taking a test   baby-sitting

Remember, your goal is to find an object or idea that seems related to one of these topics and to use comparison and contrast to help you learn more about your choice.

The Boston Photographs

Nora Ephron

"I made all kinds of pictures because I thought 1
it would be a good rescue shot over the ladder
. . . never dreamed it would be anything
else. . . . I kept having to move around because of the light set. The
sky was bright and they were in deep shadow. I was making pictures
with a motor drive and he, the fire fighter, was reaching up and, I don't
know, everything started falling. I followed the girl down taking pictures
. . . I made three or four frames. I realized what was going on and I
completely turned around, because I didn't want to see her hit."

You probably saw the photographs. In most newspapers, there were 2
three of them. The first showed some people on a fire escape—a fireman,
a woman and a child. The fireman had a nice strong jaw and looked very
brave. The woman was holding the child. Smoke was pouring from the
building behind them. A rescue ladder was approaching, just a few feet
away, and the fireman had one arm around the woman and one arm
reaching out toward the ladder. The second picture showed the fire
escape slipping off the building. The child had fallen on the escape and
seemed about to slide off the edge. The woman was grasping desperately
at the legs of the fireman, who had managed to grab the ladder. The
third picture showed the woman and child in midair, falling to the ground.
Their arms and legs were outstretched, horribly distended. A potted
plant was falling too. The caption said that the woman, Diana Bryant,
nineteen, died in the fall. The child landed on the woman's body and
lived.

The pictures were taken by Stanley Forman, thirty, of the *Boston* 3
Herald American. He used a motor-driven Nikon F set at 1/250, f 5.6–
8. Because of the motor, the camera can click off three frames a second.
More than four hundred newspapers in the United States alone carried
the photographs; the tear sheets from overseas are still coming in. The
New York Times ran them on the first page of its second section; a paper
in south Georgia gave them nineteen columns; the *Chicago Tribune,* the
Washington Post and the *Washington Star* filled almost half their front
pages, the *Star* under a somewhat redundant headline that read:
SENSATIONAL PHOTOS OF RESCUE ATTEMPT THAT FAILED.

The photographs are indeed sensational. They are pictures of death 4
in action, of that split second when luck runs out, and it is impossible to
look at them without feeling their extraordinary impact and remembering,
in an almost subconscious way, the morbid fantasy of falling, falling off

a building, falling to one's death. Beyond that, the pictures are classics, old-fashioned but perfect examples of photojournalism at its most spectacular. They're throwbacks, really, fire pictures, 1930s tabloid shots; at the same time they're technically superb and thoroughly modern—the sequence could not have been taken at all until the development of the motor-driven camera some sixteen years ago.

Most newspaper editors anticipate some reader reaction to photo- 5 graphs like Forman's; even so, the response around the country was enormous, and almost all of it was negative. I have read hundreds of the letters that were printed in letters-to-the-editor sections, and they repeat the same points. "Invading the privacy of death." "Cheap sensationalism." "I thought I was reading the *National Enquirer.*" "Assigning the agony of a human being in terror of imminent death to the status of a side-show act." "A tawdry way to sell newspapers." The *Seattle Times* received sixty letters and calls; its managing editor even got a couple of them at home. A reader wrote the *Philadelphia Inquirer:* "*Jaws* and *Towering Inferno* are playing downtown; don't take business away from people who pay good money to advertise in your own paper." Another reader wrote the *Chicago Sun-Times:* "I shall try to hide my disappointment that Miss Byrant wasn't wearing a skirt when she fell to her death. You could have had some award-winning photographs of her underpants as her skirt billowed over her head, you voyeurs." Several newspaper editors wrote columns defending the pictures: Thomas Keevil of the *Costa Mesa* (California) *Daily Pilot* printed a ballot for readers to vote on whether they would have printed the pictures; Marshall L. Stone of Maine's *Bangor Daily News,* which refused to print the famous assassination picture of the Vietcong prisoner in Saigon, claimed that the Boston pictures showed the dangers of fire escapes and raised questions about slumlords. (The burning building was a five-story brick apartment house on Marlborough Street in the Back Bay section of Boston.)

For the last five years, the *Washington Post* has employed various 6 journalists as ombudsmen, whose job is to monitor the paper on behalf of the public. The *Post*'s current ombudsman is Charles Seib, former managing editor of the *Washington Star;* the day the Boston photographs appeared, the paper received over seventy calls in protest. As Seib later wrote in a column about the pictures, it was "the largest reaction to a published item that I have experienced in eight months as the *Post*'s ombudsman. . . .

"In the *Post*'s newsroom, on the other hand, I found no doubts, no 7 second thoughts . . . the question was not whether they should be printed but how they should be displayed. When I talked to editors . . . they used words like 'interesting' and 'riveting' and 'gripping' to describe them. The pictures told something about life in the ghetto, they said (although the neighborhood where the tragedy occurred is not a ghetto, I am told). They dramatized the need to check on the safety of fire escapes. They dramatically conveyed something that had happened, and that is the business we're in. They were news. . . .

"Was publication of that [third] picture a bow to the same taste for *8* the morbidly sensational that makes gold mines of disaster movies? Most papers will not print the picture of a dead body except in the most unusual circumstances. Does the fact that the final picture was taken a millisecond before the young woman died make a difference? Most papers will not print a picture of a bare female breast. Is that a more inappropriate subject for display than the picture of a human being's last agonized instant of life?" Seib offered no answers to the questions he raised, but he went on to say that although as an editor he would probably have run the pictures, as a reader he was revolted by them.

In conclusion, Seib wrote: "Any editor who decided to print those *9* pictures without giving at least a moment's thought to what purpose they served and what their effect was likely to be on the reader should ask another question: Have I become so preoccupied with manufacturing a product according to professional traditions and standards that I have forgotten about the consumer, the reader?"

It should be clear that the phone calls and letters and Seib's own *10* reaction were occasioned by one factor alone: the death of the woman. Obviously, had she survived the fall, no one would have protested; the pictures would have had a completely different impact. Equally obviously, had the child died as well—or instead—Seib would undoubtedly have received ten times the phone calls he did. In each case, the pictures would have been exactly the same—only the captions, and thus the responses, would have been different.

But the questions Seib raises are worth discussing—though not exactly *11* for the reasons he mentions. For it may be that the real lesson of the Boston photographs is not the danger that editors will be forgetful of reader reaction, but that they will continue to censor pictures of death precisely because of that reaction. The protests Seib fielded were really a variation on an old theme—and we saw plenty of it during the Nixon-Agnew years—the "Why doesn't the press print the good news?" argument. In this case, of course, the objections were all dressed up and cleverly disguised as righteous indignation about the privacy of death. This is a form of puritanism that is often justifiable; just as often it is merely puritanical.

Seib takes it for granted that the widespread though fairly recent *12* newspaper policy against printing pictures of dead bodies is a sound one; I don't know that it makes any sense at all. I recognize that printing pictures of corpses raises all sorts of problems about taste and titillation and sensationalism; the fact is, however, that people die. Death happens to be one of life's main events. And it is irresponsible—and more than that, inaccurate—for newspapers to fail to show it, or to show it only when an astonishing set of photos comes in over the Associated Press wire. Most papers covering fatal automobile accidents will print pictures of mangled cars. But the significance of fatal automobile accidents is not that a great deal of steel is twisted but that people die. Why not show it? That's what accidents are about. Throughout the Vietnam war, editors were reluctant to print atrocity pictures. Why *not* print them? That's what that war was about. Murder victims are almost never photographed; they are granted their privacy. But their relatives are relentlessly pictured on their way in and out of hospitals and morgues and funerals.

I'm not advocating that newspapers print these things in order to teach *13* their readers a lesson. The *Post* editors justified their printing of the Boston pictures with several arguments in that direction; every one of them is irrelevant. The pictures don't show anything about slum life; the incident could have happened anywhere, and it did. It is extremely unlikely that anyone who saw them rushed out and had his fire escape strengthened. And the pictures were not news—at least they were not national news. It is not news in Washington, or New York, or Los Angeles that a woman was killed in a Boston fire. The only newsworthy thing about the pictures is that they were taken. They deserve to be printed because they are great pictures, breathtaking pictures of something that happened. That they disturb readers is exactly as it should be: that's why photojournalism is often more powerful than written journalism.

Study Questions

1. The photographs Nora Ephron describes in "The Boston Photographs" were taken in 1978. It is unlikely that most readers of today will have seen them or remembered them. How important is seeing the photographs for the message of this essay? Will readers still be interested in what Ephron has to say about them? Why or why not?
2. Ephron claims that "had the child died as well—or instead—Seib would undoubtedly have received ten times the phone calls he did." Do you agree or disagree with this claim? What does your answer tell you about how photographers—and writers—decide on the material they put before an audience?
3. In her final paragraph, Ephron states: "They deserve to be printed because they are great pictures, breathtaking pictures of something that happened. That they disturb readers is exactly as it should be: that's why photojournalism is often more powerful than written journalism." What differences between writing and photography do you think she has in mind? How do these differences allow photojournalism to be "more powerful"? In what ways does the relationship between photographer and audience differ from the one between

writer and audience? How do these differences allow photojournalism
to be "more powerful"?

4. How long after seeing the Boston photographs do you think it was
   before Ephron started writing her essay? Do you think it would have
   been possible for her to write this essay immediately after seeing
   them? Why or why not? What do your answers tell you about the
   need for prewriting?

Suggestion for Prewriting

Almost everyone has a special photograph that is important to him or
her because of the memories it evokes; and even those who cannot think
of one particular picture still will be able to find at least one to which
they react strongly. Choose a photograph which is important to you or
which evokes strong feelings; practice prewriting by trying to explain to
total strangers why you have those feelings. For this exercise, you may
find both item analysis and brainstorming helpful.

Man at the Mercy of His Language

Peter Farb

L inguistically speaking, man is not born free. *1* He inherits a language full of quaint sayings, archaisms, and a ponderous grammar; even more important, he inherits certain fixed ways of expression that may shackle his thoughts. Language becomes man's shaper of ideas rather than simply his tool for reporting ideas. An American's conventional words for directions often limit his ability to read maps: It is an apt youngster indeed who can immediately grasp that the *Upper* Nile is in the *south* of Egypt and the *Lower* Nile is in the *north* of Egypt. Another example: English has only two demonstrative pronouns ("this" and "that," together with their plurals) to refer either to something near or to something far away. The Tlingit Indians of the Northwest Coast can be much more specific. If they want to refer to an object very near and always present, they say *he; ya* means an object also near and present, but a little farther away; *yu* refers to something still farther away, while *we* is used only for an object so far away that it is out of sight. So the question arises whether even the most outspoken member of American society can "speak his mind." Actually, he has very little control over the possible channels into which his thoughts can flow. His grammatical mind was made up for him by his culture before he was born.

The way in which culture affects language becomes clear by comparing *2* how the English and Hopi languages refer to H_2O in its liquid state. English, like most other European languages, has only one word—"water"—and it pays no attention to what the substance is used for or its quantity. The Hopi of Arizona, on the other hand, use *pahe* to mean the large amounts of water present in natural lakes or rivers, and *keyi* for the small amounts in domestic jugs and canteens. English, though, makes other distinctions that Hopi does not. The speaker of English is careful to distinguish between a lake and a stream, between a waterfall and a geyser; but *pahe* makes no distinction among lakes, ponds, rivers, streams, waterfalls, and springs.

A Hopi speaker, of course, knows that there is a difference between *3* a geyser, which spurts upward, and a waterfall, which plunges downward, even though his vocabulary makes no such distinction. Similarly, a speaker of English knows that a canteen of water differs from a river of water. But the real point of this comparison is that neither the Hopi nor the American uses anywhere near the possible number of words that could be applied to water in all of its states, quantities, forms, and functions. The number of such words is in the hundreds and they would hopelessly encumber the language. So, to prevent the language from becoming unwieldy, different kinds of water are grouped into a small number of categories. Each culture defines the categories in terms of the similarities it detects; it channels a multitude of ideas into the few categories that it considers important. The culture of every speaker of English tells him that it is important to distinguish between oceans, lakes, rivers, fountains, and waterfalls—but relatively unimportant to make the distinction between the water in a canteen in his canoe and the water underneath the same canoe. Each culture has categorized experience through language in a quite unconscious way—at the same time offering anthropologists commentaries on the differences and similarities that exist in societies.

The possibility of such a relationship between language and culture 4 has been formulated into a hypothesis by two American linguists, Sapir and Whorf. According to Sapir, man does not live in the midst of the whole world, but only in a part of it, the part that his language lets him know. He is, says Sapir, "very much at the mercy of the particular language which has become the medium of expression" for his group. The real world is therefore "to a large extent unconsciously built up on the language habits of the group . . . The worlds in which different societies live are distinct worlds, not merely the same world with different labels attached." To Sapir and Whorf, language provides a different network of tracks for each society, which, as a result, concentrates on only certain aspects of reality.

According to the hypothesis, the differences between languages are 5 much more than mere obstacles to communication; they represent basic differences in the "world view" of the various peoples and in what they understand about their environment. The Eskimo can draw upon an inventory of about twenty very precise words for the subtle differences in a snowfall. The best a speaker of English can manage are distinctions between sticky snow, sleet, hail, and ice. Similarly, to most speakers of English, a seal is simply a seal, and they have only that one word to describe it; if they want to say anything else about the seal, such as its sex or its color, then they have to put an adjective before the word "seal." But the Eskimo has a number of words with which to express various kinds of sealdom: "a young swimming seal," "a male harbor seal," "an old harbor seal," and so forth. A somewhat similar situation exists in English with the word "horse." This animal may be referred to as "chestnut," "bay mare," "stallion," and other names that one would not expect to find in the vocabulary of the horseless Eskimo.

The Eskimo, of course, is preoccupied with seals, a primary food 6 source for him, whereas some speakers of English seem to be taken up with the exact particulars of the domesticated horse. The real question is: Do these different vocabularies restrict the Eskimo and the speaker of English, and do they force the speakers of different languages to conceptualize and classify information in different ways? Can an Eskimo look at a horse and in his own mind classify it as "a bay mare"? Or, because he lacks the words, is he forever blind to the fact that this kind of animal exists? The answer is that with a little practice an Eskimo can learn to tell apart the different kinds of horses, just as an American can learn about the various seals, even though the respective languages lack the necessary vocabularies. So vocabulary alone does not reveal the cultural thinking of a people.

But does the *totality* of the language tell anything about the people 7 who speak it? To answer that, look at the English verb "grab." An English speaker says, "I grab it," "I grabbed it," "I will grab it," and so on. Only the context of the situation tells the listener what it is that is being grabbed and how it is being done. "I grab it" is a vague sentence— except in one way. English is remarkably concerned about the tense of the verb. It insists on knowing whether I grab it now, or grabbed it some time in the past, or will grab it at a future time. The English language is preoccupied with time, and so is the culture of its speakers, who take considerable interest in calendars, record-keeping, diaries, history, almanacs, stock-market forecasts, astrological predictions, and always, every minute of the waking day, the precise time.

No such statement as "I grab it" would be possible in Navaho. To 8 the Navaho, tense is of little importance, but the language is considerably more discriminating in other ways. The Navaho language would describe much more about the pronoun "I" of this sentence; it would tell whether the "I" initiated the action by reaching out to grab the thing, or whether the "I" merely grabbed at a horse that raced by. Nor would the Navaho be content merely with "grab"; the verb would have to tell him whether the thing being grabbed is big or little, animate or inanimate. Finally, a Navaho could not say simply "it"; the thing being grabbed would have to be described much more precisely and put in a category. (If you get the feeling that Navaho is an exceedingly difficult language, you are correct. During World War II in the Pacific, Navaho Indians were used as senders and receivers of secret radio messages because a language, unlike a code, cannot be broken; it must be learned.)

Judging by this example and by other linguistic studies of Navaho, a 9 picture of its speakers emerges: They are very exacting in their perception of the elements that make up their universe. But is this a true picture of the Navaho? Does he perceive his world any differently from a White American? Anthropological and psychological studies of the Navaho show that he does. He visualizes himself as living in an eternal and unchanging universe made up of physical, social, and supernatural forces, among which he tries to maintain a balance. Any accidental failure to observe rules or rituals can disturb this balance and result in some

misfortune. Navaho curing ceremonies, which include the well-known
sandpainting, are designed to put the individual back into harmony with
the universe. To the Navaho, the good life consists of maintaining intact
all the complex relationships of the universe. It is obvious that to do so
demands a language that makes the most exacting discriminations.

Several words of caution, though, about possible misinterpretations 10
of the Sapir–Whorf Hypothesis. It does not say that the Navaho holds
such a world view because of the structure of his language. It merely
states that there is an interaction between his language and his culture.
Nor does the hypothesis maintain that two cultures with different languages and different world views cannot be in communication with each
other (the Navaho and the White American are very much in communication today in Arizona and New Mexico). Instead, the hypothesis
suggests that language is more than a way of communicating. It is a
living system that is a part of the cultural equipment of a group, and it
reveals a culture at least as much as do spear points, kinship groups, or
political institutions. Look at just one of the clues to culture that the
Sapir–Whorf Hypothesis has already provided: Shortly after the hypothesis was proposed, it was attacked on the basis that the Navaho speak
an Athabaskan language and the Hopi a Uto-Aztecan one, yet they live
side by side in the Southwest and share a culture. So, after all, asked
the critics, what difference can language make in culture? Instead of
demolishing the hypothesis, this comparison actually served to reveal its
value. It forced anthropologists to take another look at the Navaho and
the Hopi. As the hypothesis had predicted, their world views are quite
far apart—and so are their cultures.

The Sapir–Whorf Hypothesis has alerted anthropologists to the fact 11
that language is keyed to the total culture, and that it reveals a people's
view of its total environment. Language directs the perceptions of its
speakers to certain things; it gives them ways to analyze and to categorize
experience. Such perceptions are unconscious and outside the control
of the speaker. The ultimate value of the Sapir–Whorf Hypothesis is that
if offers hints to cultural differences and similarities among peoples. . . .

Study Questions

1. Peter Farb's "Man at the Mercy of His Language," like Fromm's "The
   Nature of Symbolic Language," deals with the relationship between
   language and culture. Yet Farb seems to deal with this topic in a
   more concrete way. What differences in the way each writer narrows
   his topic might account for this appearance?
2. In this essay what information on language is new to you? Does Farb
   assume that you have this information before you start reading the
   essay? Defend your answer by referring to specific passages.

3. Many linguists consider the Sapir–Whorf hypothesis to be a rather dangerous concept. They point out that some people, Adolf Hitler among them, have tried to use it to prove that one language culture is inherently superior to others. How has Farb tried to anticipate this danger and warn his readers against it?
4. Farb writes: "Linguistically speaking, man is not born free. He inherits a language full of quaint sayings, archaisms, and a ponderous grammar; even more important, he inherits fixed ways of expression that may shackle his thoughts." In what ways does this view on the limitations imposed by language compare with your own view of having to write for an English class?

Suggestion for Prewriting

Peter Farb uses numerous examples from the English, Hopi, Eskimo, and Navaho languages to illustrate his points about the Sapir–Whorf hypothesis. But the value of using examples should not be limited to the role they play in finished essays. Like quotations, examples can often help you in prewriting, especially when combined with a directed form like item analysis. The more complex your topic, the more useful examples will be, because they can serve as specific focuses for your questions. For example, it is far easier to apply the who, what, why, where, how, and when questions to an example that illustrates the various Hopi terms for water than to the simple generalization that different languages have different ways of talking about the world.

Suppose that you were going to write a paper on how parents and children often misunderstand each other because they do not speak the same language. List some of the words students use when they talk to one another about music, dating, classes, or another area of your own choosing, which would probably not be understood by their parents. Briefly describe why you believe these words would cause problems for the parents. Then use that description as the basis for an exercise in item analysis.

Dick Cook

John McPhee

R ichard Okey Cook came into the country* in *1*
1964, and put up a log lean-to not far from the
site where he would build his present cabin.
Trained in aspects of geophysics, he did some free-lance prospecting that
first summer near the head of the Seventymile River, which goes into the
Yukon a few bends below Eagle. His larger purpose, though, was to
stay in the country and to change himself thoroughly "from a professional
into a bum"—to learn to trap, to handle dogs and sleds, to net fish in
quantities sufficient to feed the dogs. "And that isn't easy," he is quick
to say, claiming that to lower his income and raise his independence he
has worked twice as hard as most people. Born and brought up in Ohio,
he was a real-estate appraiser there before he left for Alaska. He had
also been to the Colorado School of Mines and had run potentiometer
surveys for Kennecott Copper in Arizona. Like many Alaskans, he came
north to repudiate one kind of life and to try another. "I wanted to get
away from paying taxes to support something I didn't believe in, to
get away from big business, to get away from a place where you can't
be sure of anything you hear or anything you read. Doctors rip you off
down there. There's not an honest lawyer in the Lower Forty-eight.
The only honest people left are in jail." Toward those who had held
power over him in various situations his reactions had sometimes been
emphatic. He took a poke at his high-school principal, in Lyndhurst,
Ohio, and was expelled from school. In the Marine Corps, he became a
corporal twice and a private first class three times. His demotions resulted from fistfights—on several occasions with sergeants, once with a
lieutenant. Now he has tens of thousands of acres around him and no
authorities ordinarily proximitous enough to threaten him—except nature, which he regards as God. While he was assembling his wilderness
dexterity, he spent much of the year in Eagle, and he became, for a
while, its mayor. A single face, a single vote, counts for a lot in Alaska,
and especially in the bush.

The traplines Cook has established for himself are along several *2*
streams, across the divides between their headwaters and on both banks
of the Yukon—upward of a hundred miles in all, in several loops. He

---

* McPhee writes: "People in the region of the upper Yukon refer to their part
of Alaska as 'the country.' A stranger appearing among them is said to have
'come into the country.'"

runs them mainly in November and December. He does not use a snow machine, as many trappers in Alaska do. He says, "The two worst things that ever happened to this country are the airplane and the snow machine." His traplines traverse steep terrain, rocky gullies—places where he could not use a machine anyway. To get through, he requires sleds and dogs. Generally, he has to camp out at least one night to complete a circuit. If the temperature is colder than thirty below, he stays in his cabin and waits for the snap to pass. As soon as the air warms up, he hits the trail. He has built lean-tos in a few places, but often enough he sleeps where he gets tired—under an orange canvas tarp. It is ten feet by ten, and weighs two and a half pounds, and is all the shelter he needs at, say, twenty below zero. Picking out a tree, he ties one corner of the tarp to the trunk, as high as he can reach. He stakes down the far corner, then stakes down the two sides. Sometimes, he will loft the center by tying a cord to a branch above. He builds a lasting fire between the tree and himself, gets into his sleeping bag, and drifts away. Most nights are calm. Snow is light in the upper Yukon. The tarp's configuration is not so much for protection as to reflect the heat of the fire. He could make a closed tent with the tarp, if necessary. His ground cloth, or bed pad, laid out on the snow beneath him, is the hide of a caribou.

He carries dried chum salmon for his dogs, and his own food is dried 3 moose or bear meat and pinole—ground parched corn, to which he adds brown sugar. In the Algonquin language, pinole was "rockahominy." "It kept Daniel Boone and Davy Crockett going. It keeps me going, too." He carries no flour. "Flour will go rancid on you unless you buy white flour, but you can't live and work on that. I had a friend who died of a heart attack from eating that crap. It's not news that the American people are killing themselves with white flour, white sugar, and soda pop. If you get out and trap thirty miles a day behind dogs, you can damned well tell what lets you work and what doesn't." From a supplier in Seattle he orders hundred-pound sacks of corn, pinto beans, unground wheat. He buys cases of vinegar, tomato paste, and tea. Forty pounds of butter in one-pound cans. A hundred pounds of dried milk, sixty-five of dried fruit. Twenty-five pounds of cashews. Twenty-five pounds of oats. A forty-pound can of peanut butter. He carries it all down the Yukon from Eagle by sled or canoe. He uses a couple of moose a year, and a few bear, which are easier to handle in summer. "A moose has too much meat. The waste up here you wouldn't believe. Hunters that come through here leave a third of the moose. Indians don't waste, but with rifles they are overexcitable. They shoot into herds of caribou and wound some. I utilize everything, though. Stomach. Intestines. Head. I feed the carcasses of wolverine, marten, and fox to the dogs. Lynx is another matter. It's exceptionally good, something like chicken or pork."

With no trouble at all, Dick Cook remembers where every trap is on 4 his lines. He uses several hundred traps. His annual food cost is somewhere under a thousand dollars. He uses less than a hundred gallons of fuel—for his chain saws, his small outboards, his gasoline lamps. The furs bring him a little more than his basic needs—about fifteen hundred dollars a year. He plants a big garden. He says, "One of the points I live by is not to make any more money than is absolutely necessary." His prospecting activity has in recent years fallen toward nil. He says he now looks for rocks not for the money but "just for the joy of it—a lot of things fall apart if you are not after money, and prospecting is one of them."

In winter on the trail, he wears a hooded cotton sweatshirt, no hat. 5 He does use an earband. He has a low opinion of wool. "First off, it's too expensive. Second off, you don't have the moisture problem up here you have in the States." He wears Sears' thermal long johns under cotton overalls, and his feet are kept warm by Indian-made mukluks with Bean's felt insoles and a pair of wool socks. He rarely puts on his parka. "You have to worry up here more about overdressing than about under- dressing. The problem is getting overheated." Gradually, his clothes have become rags, with so many shreds, holes, and rips that they seem to cling to him only through loyalty. Everything is patched, and loose bits flap as he walks. His red chamois-cloth shirt has holes in the front, the back, and the sides. His green overalls are torn open at both knees. Half a leg is gone from his corduroy pants. His khaki down jacket is quilted with patches and has a long rip under one arm. His hooded sweatshirt hangs from him in tatters, spreads over him like the thrums of a mop. "I'll tell you one thing about this country," he says. "This country is hard on clothes."

Cook is somewhat below the threshold of slender. He is fatless. His 6 figure is a little stooped, unprepossessing, but his legs and arms are strong beyond the mere requirements of the athlete. He looks like a scarecrow made of cables. All his features are feral—his chin, his nose, his dark eyes. His hair, which is nearly black, has gone far from his forehead. His scalp is bare all the way back to, more or less, his north pole. The growth beyond—dense, streaked with gray—cantilevers to the sides in unbarbered profusion, so that his own hair appears to be a parka ruff. His voice is soft, gentle—his words polite. When he is being pedagogical, the voice goes up several registers, and becomes hortative, and sharp. He is not infrequently pedagogical.

A decade and more can bring deep seniority in Alaska. People arrive 7 steadily. And people go. They go from Anchorage and Fairbanks—let alone the more exacting wild. Some, of course, are interested only in a year or two's work, then to return with saved high wages to the Lower Forty-eight. Others, though, mean to adapt to Alaska, hoping to find a sense of frontier, a fresh and different kind of life. They come continually to Eagle, and to Circle, the next settlement below Eagle down the Yukon. The two communities are about a hundred and sixty river miles apart, and in all the land between them live perhaps thirty people. The state of New Jersey, where I happen to live, could fit between Eagle and Circle. New Jersey has seven and a half million people. Small wonder that the Alaskan wild has at least a conceptual appeal to certain people from a place like New Jersey. Beyond Circle are the vast savannas of the Yukon Flats—another world. Upstream from Circle are the bluffs, the mountains, the steep-falling streams—the country. Eagle and Circle are connected only by river, but each of them is reachable, about half the year, over narrow gravel roads (built for gold mines) that twist through the forest and are chipped out of cliffsides in high mountain passes. If you get into your car in Hackensack, Circle is about as far north as you can go on North America's network of roads. Eagle, with its montane setting, seems to attract more people who intend to stay. In they come— young people in ones and twos—from all over the Lower Forty-eight. With general trapping catalogues under their arms, they walk around wondering what to do next. The climate and the raw Alaskan wild will quickly sort them out. Some will not flinch. Others will go back. Others will stay on but will never get past the clustered cabins and gravel streets of Eagle. These young people, for the most part, are half Cook's age. He is in his middle forties. He is their exemplar—the one who has done it and stuck. So the newcomers turn to him, when he is in town, as sage and mentor. He tells them that it's a big but hungry country out there, good enough for trapping, maybe, but not for too much trapping, and they are to stay the hell off his traplines. He does not otherwise discourage people. He wants to help them. If, in effect, they are wearing a skin and carrying a stone-headed club, he suggests that technology, while it can be kept at a distance, is inescapable. "The question," he will say, "is how far do you want to go? I buy wheat. I use axes, knives, I have windows. There's a few things we've been trained to need and can't give up. You can't forget the culture you were raised in. You have to satisfy needs created in you. Almost everyone needs music, for instance. Cabins may be out of food, but they've all got books in them. Indian trappers used deadfalls once—propped-up logs. I wouldn't want to live without my rifle and steel traps. I don't want to have to live on a bow and arrow and a deadfall. Somewhere, you have to make some sort of compromise. There is a line that has to be drawn. Most people feel around for it. Those that try to be too Spartan generally back off. Those who want to be too luxurious end up in Eagle—or in Fairbanks, or New York. So far as I know, people who have tried to get away from technology completely have always failed. Meanwhile, what this place has to offer is wilderness that is nowhere else."

A favorite aphorism of Cook's is that a farmer can learn to live in a *8* city in six months but a city person in a lifetime cannot learn to live on a farm. He says of newcomers, "A lot of them say they're going to 'live off the land.' They go hungry. They have ideas about everything—on arrival. And they've got no problems. But they're diving off too high a bridge. Soon they run into problems, so they come visiting. They have too much gear and their sleeping bags are too heavy to carry around. They are wondering where to get meat, where and how to catch fish, how to protect their gear from bears. You can't tell them directly. If you tell them to do something, they do the opposite. But there are ways to let them know."

Cook seems to deserve his reputation. In all the terrain that is more 9 or less focussed on the post office at Eagle, he is the most experienced, the best person to be sought out by anyone determined to live much beyond the outermost tip of the set society. He knows the woods, the animals, sleds, traps, furs, dogs, frozen rivers, and swift water. He is the sachem figure. And he had long since achieved this status when a day arrived in which a tooth began to give him great pain. He lay down in his cabin and waited for the nuisance to pass. But the pain increased and was apparently not going to go away. It became so intense he could barely stand it. He was a couple of hundred miles from the most accessible dentist. So he took a pair of channel-lock pliers and wrapped them with tape, put the pliers into his mouth, and clamped them over the hostile tooth. He levered it, worked it awhile, and passed out. When he came to, he picked up the pliers and went back to work on the tooth. It wouldn't give. He passed out again. Each time he attacked the tooth with the pliers, he passed out. Finally, his hand would not move. He could not make his arm lift the pliers toward his mouth. So he set them down, left the cabin, and—by dogsled and mail plane—headed for the dentist, in Fairbanks.

Study Questions

1. In the first paragraph of "Dick Cook," Cook says: "I wanted to get away from paying taxes to support something I didn't believe in, to get away from big business, to get away from a place where you can't be sure of anything you hear or anything you read. Doctors rip you off down there. There's not an honest lawyer in the Lower Forty-eight. The only honest people left are in jail." Will most readers agree with this characterization of the "Lower Forty-eight"? What does this quotation tell them about Dick Cook's character?
2. What does John McPhee think of Dick Cook? Point to specific passages that suggest this attitude.
3. Reread paragraphs 4–6 and pay close attention to the structure of the sentences. How complex are they? How difficult are they to read? Explain how the structure of these sentences supports the attitude toward Dick Cook that you identified in question 2.

4. After reading "Dick Cook," are you interested in "going into the country"? What in the essay either encouraged or discouraged you? Do you think McPhee wanted you to react this way?

Suggestion for Prewriting

We have already discussed using examples as a basis for prewriting. Even negative examples can be effective aids to prewriting. In "Dick Cook" we have the case of a man who is obviously capable of surviving and succeeding in the Alaskan wild, but what if we wanted to describe a person who could not?

Reread the essay and note the characteristics that you believe allowed Dick Cook to come into the country and stay there. With these traits in mind, prepare to write an essay describing Dick Cook's opposite. For this exercise you may want to use the descriptive questions suggested on p. 61, clustering, or item analysis.

North America After the War

Paul R. Ehrlich

I t was almost the end of the century when *1* humanity's luck ran out. Most of the nuclear war scenarios had been optimistic. Three-quarters of the American and Soviet arsenals, more than 30,000 nuclear devices, exploded with power in excess of 9,000 megatons (9 billion tons) of TNT. The large cities of North America, Europe, Russia, China, and Japan, as well as huge areas of dense forest, fueled fire storms. Soot from these fire storms joined dust lofted into the stratosphere by thousands of ground bursts. Smoke from myriad smaller fires choked the lower atmosphere and darkness enshrouded the Northern Hemisphere from a few days after the early July war until October, when substantial sunlight again began to reach the earth's surface.

Soot and smoke absorbed large amounts of solar energy; dust reflected *2* more back into space. This plunged temperatures in all inland areas to below zero for virtually the entire dark summer. Except for small refugia on the coastlines, temperatures across the North American continent fell below 10°F for several months, going well below zero in many places for extended periods. No place in the Northern Hemisphere escaped severe frosts. Although far fewer weapons were detonated in the Southern Hemisphere, plumes of soot moved rapidly across the equator from the North, creating quick freezes in many places. Dusky skies, lower than normal temperatures, and radioactive fallout eventually covered the entire planet. The "nuclear winter" predicted by the world's top atmospheric scientists in late 1983 had come to pass.

By January, much of the debris had cleared from the skies, but lin- *3* gering smoke, stratospheric dust, and material from still-burning fires prolonged an unusually cold winter. Spring and summer were also colder than usual. Nitrogen oxides, produced when thermonuclear fireballs burned atmospheric nitrogen, had severely damaged the stratospheric ozone layer, which normally filters out ultraviolet rays harmful to plants and animals. This made the return of sunlight a mixed blessing.

Blast, fire, prompt radiation and delayed fallout, subzero tempera- *4* tures, toxic smog, and lack of food eliminated the vestiges of human life. Even in the warmer places—the coastlines where the cold had been ameliorated by the thermal inertia of the oceans—people could not survive. The few officials and military personnel in the United States and Canada whose deep shelters had not been "dug out" by Soviet missiles, and who had passed the nuclear winter underground, starved soon after emerging in the frigid spring. Tropical peoples, even in coastal areas of Mexico, succumbed to exposure, radiation sickness, hunger, civil disorder, and epidemic disease. Starvation finished the Eskimo. Human beings were gone from North America—indeed, from the entire Northern Hemisphere.

But not all life was extinct. Scattered pockets of severely frost-dam- 5 aged chaparral along the coast had escaped the great fires that had swept most of California bare. Even after the erosion of bare slopes in the postwar rain, many seeds survived. The Olympic Peninsula and parts of coastal British Columbia and Alaska had suffered less than inland areas because, as in California, the adjacent sea had moderated the long cold period. Even in coastal areas many plants died from a combination of low light, toxic air pollution, high radiation (the last especially affected the sensitive conifers), and from the continual violent storms generated by the sharp sea-land temperature gradient.

Inland in the subarctic and arctic North, virtually all of the growing 6 plants had died. Cold-resistant boreal trees, deprived of the normal environmental cues that induce cold hardiness, were not prepared for the nuclear aftermath. Paper birches and aspens, which can tolerate temperatures of −100°F when acclimatized, died when midsummer temperatures dropped in a few days to −20°F. In the Rocky Mountains and sections of the East, substantial areas of forest had not burned, but most of the standing trees had succumbed to the extreme, unseasonable cold. Persistence of plant populations in most parts of what had been the United States and Canada depended on the survival of seeds and roots (or other subterranean organs) in the frozen ground.

Due to vagaries in wind patterns, vegetation survived in a few enclaves 7 along the west coast of Florida, parts of Yucatan and Chiapas in Mexico, and the Osa Peninsula of Costa Rica. But in most of Florida, Mexico, and Central America, the devastation of growing plants was virtually complete. Subtropical and tropical floras, unfortunately, had had much less evolutionary experience with extreme cold: only a very few relatively hardy seeds and subterranean parts survived outside of the enclaves.

Most of the higher vertebrates went the way of *Homo sapiens*. The 8 cold alone killed many animals before radiation, thirst (lakes, rivers, and streams were covered with several feet of ice), and starvation could affect them. In the smoggy darkness, many had a reduced ability to find food, preventing them from adequately stoking their metabolic fires. Nearly every species of migratory land bird went extinct. But in places in the Northwest, a few warmblooded creatures—crows, ravens, starlings, ptarmigan, gulls, black bears, coyotes, rabbits, and rodents—managed to survive. So did some of the hardier denizens of the coastal chaparral pockets in California—but the extremely high radiation levels gradually pushed many populations to extinction.

In the continental interior, a handful of vertebrates survived the cold, 9 mostly reptiles, amphibians, and fishes whose physiological plasticity allowed their body temperatures to drop to near freezing. Warmblooded animals that hibernate had no opportunity to build reserves for a normal winter, let alone a nuclear winter. The lower metabolic rates of the lower vertebrates permitted scattered individuals to survive in deep crevices, burrows, or beneath the ice of large lakes. Most of those few survivors starved the following spring.

The majority of insects were even less fortunate. In seasonal envi-   *10* ronments, insects normally pass the winter (or other stressful seasons) in a specific developmental stage—and virtually all were caught in the wrong stage. Only in arctic and alpine areas, where insects are adapted to summer frosts, did some insect fauna survive the freezing.

During the first postwar summer, seeds began to sprout in areas where   *11* fire storms had not sterilized the soil. Surviving perennials in coastal pockets also began to produce new growth. But continuing cold weather and strong ultraviolet radiation damaged the tender young plant tissues. Many desert spring annuals that depended on now-extinct insects for pollination failed to reproduce. In refugia where insect pollinators did survive, they often were disoriented by the ultraviolet light, which though invisible to mammals was visible to them. This not only reduced their capacity to pollinate but also to reproduce themselves.

In arctic and alpine areas, many surviving insect populations dwindled   *12* further or went extinct from lack of food. The growing season was extremely short and frosts frequently damaged plants struggling to recover. The abundant female mosquitoes had few vertebrates to feed on, and the males found little nectar in the few surviving flowers. Only a small fraction of the boreal insect fauna that had survived the first winter went into diapause for the next.

Not only was spring silent over most of the continent that first year   *13* following the war, but summer was silent as well. In much of what had been the United States, no birds sang, no dogs barked, no frogs croaked, no fishes leaped. As they emerged into the desolation, most of the scattered lizards, snakes, turtles, and toads starved. Most areas were utterly devoid of organic motion beyond the wind-induced flutter of the leaves of scattered plants. There were exceptions, though. In mines, caves, and deep underground shelters, flies, roaches, rats, and mice had survived and in some had even thrived on the cadavers of people who had sought shelter there. When some of these survivors emerged at night, they found a similar resource in the abundant thawing cadavers of people and domestic animals. These scavengers built large local populations. But they soon crashed when they exhausted their grim resources.

All in all, life was in worse shape at the end of the first postwar   *14* summer than it had been in the spring. Only where substantial plant communities remained—on the northwest coast, in the coastal California chaparral, and in the tropical and subtropical pockets—did relatively diverse vertebrate and invertebrate populations survive. And even there losses were substantial. The last North American mountian lions, lynxes, large hawks, golden eagles, and other large predators went extinct; the refugia were not big enough to save the decimated populations of most animals that require large home ranges. Vultures did survive on the abundant carrion as did the once endangered bald eagle, outlasting—and even dining on—the species that had endangered them. Kestrels also made it, dining on grasshoppers. Most herbivorous insects that specialized on the less hardy plants were incapable of switching to plants with different suites of chemical feeding stimulants and toxic defenses. So they followed their plants into oblivion.

For several years after the war, dust from the partly denuded conti- 15 nents and smoke from lightning-ignited fires in forest remnants, smoldering peat bogs, coal stocks and seams, and burning oil and gas wells produced cool summers and unusually harsh winters. But gradually the climate returned more or less to normal, except that, in the near absence of vegetation, much of the central continent was more arid than before the war.

Over the next decades, plants began to reconquer the desolate conti- 16 nent. In the normally cooler latitudes many seeds in the soil were largely undamaged by cold and radiation. During each growing season for the first few postwar years, some prewar seeds germinated. And each year some of the seedlings survived.

Species adapted to disturbed areas did best. Kudzu vine, crab grass, 17 stork's bill, dandelions, and similar weeds quickly covered large areas, often choking out species that people had once considered "more desirable." In California, an impoverished chaparral community slowly reclaimed the denuded hillsides, aided to some extent by its natural adaptation to fire. A rare survivor in that community was the gypsy moth. In the subarctic and the arctic, grasses, sedges, and dwarf willows regenerated relatively rapidly in spite of the short growing season. Some of the growing herbaceous and shrubby plants, accustomed to summer frosts, had only been set back, not killed, by the nuclear winter and subsequent frosty summers.

Forests returned slowly, since many trees require more than a decade 18 to complete a generation. In the West, aspens from the coastal refugia and from surviving roots spread in a few hundred years to cover large portions of their previous range. Simultaneously, scrubby Gambel's oak reappeared and formed dense local stands. No significant herbivores took advantage of the oak's periodic years of heavy acorn production; concomitantly, relatively few animals were available to disperse the acorns until feral rat populations began to transport and store them. Then the oaks spread rapidly.

In the East, the turkey oak, a denizen of poor soils, underwent a 19 similar explosion. Several species of wind-pollinated pines also made a comeback. Widespread, previously common species—white and south-

ern pines in the East, and piñon, lodgepole, and ponderosa in the West—
were the most successful.

Vegetation recovered most slowly in the subtropical and tropical areas. 20
There, wherever intense cold had prevailed, virtually all the plants—like
the animals—had been destroyed. Most species could not tolerate chill-
ing even to a few degrees *above* freezing, and their seeds were not cold
hardy. Those plants that survived in refugia began gradually to spread
into the debris-littered wastelands, but progress was slow—especially for
the many plants that depended on now-extinct animals to disperse their
seeds. This was much more important in tropical than in temperate
ecosystems.

The first animals to repopulate substantial areas of North America 21
were also "weeds." Roaches, rats, and houseflies suffered setbacks in
the early years, but they persisted and increased, free of significant
natural enemies and able to feed on a variety of plant materials and
organic debris. Crickets and grasshoppers, both relatively generalized
feeders, spread back fast from coastal refugia. Fire ants, having taken
in stride massive attacks with pesticides before the war, survived the
ultimate human assault in pockets along the Gulf Coast and spread once
more over what had been the southeastern United States. As the flora
recovered, snowshoe hares reinvaded much of their old territory, fanning
out from surviving northwestern populations and reaching the east coast
in a few hundred years. They renewed their famous cycling behavior—
population outbreaks followed by crashes. That they did so in the total
absence of their lynx predators (long thought to have been a cause of the
cycles) would have fascinated population biologists—if there had been
any around.

The first predators to reoccupy the desolate areas were spiders, bal- 22
looning in from refugia and emerging from underground burrows. Coyotes also thrived, learning to hunt the rats and following the spreading
front of snowshoe hares. Wolves faded away; there were too few survivors. Because of the vagaries of fallout patterns, wolves had suffered
more than most species from radiation effects, and they did not successfully adapt to a diet of rats and hares.

A casual observer might have missed the most significant change in 23
predator trophic levels: the near absence of predacious and parasitic
insects. The impact of toxins from the war, together with the cold, was
similar to spraying the entire continent with insecticides. In many cases,
the smaller populations at the predator trophic levels died off even though
their plant-eating insect hosts had survived. One result was huge outbreaks of locusts, gypsy moths, cutworms, and Japanese beetles, which
decimated the foliage over large areas. Another was that some previously
rare herbivorous insects, freed from natural controls, developed huge,
destructive populations, just as new pests had often been created by the
misuse of pesticides before the war.

Although most insectivorous birds were extinct, cattle egrets, dining 24
on the larger insects, gradually spread throughout North America. They
were joined by ravens, crows, starlings, and gulls, all of which shifted
their diets to a heavy emphasis on insects. Robins also reinvaded from
refugia, but in the absence of lawns and with a severe shortage of earth-
worms, their populations grew with glacial slowness.

Some three thousand years after the war, the first human beings set 25
foot on what had once been the United States. A handful of people had
persisted through the postwar chaos in the Southern Hemisphere; the
scattered groups of survivors had not all dwindled to extinction as many
biologists had feared they might. But all had reverted to subsistence
farming, mostly with stone and wooden implements. Most libraries had
been destroyed by the war or in the subsequent social breakdown; the
few that remained decayed in the deserted cities. People had had no
time to preserve cultural artifacts that were peripheral to the daily struggle for existence.

Almost three thousand years elapsed before human populations grew 26
large enough to form small, rudimentary cities and to begin exploratory
moves into the mysterious and devastated North. Both the knowledge
and the implements of industrial civilization were long gone. The new
pioneers came in simple sailboats, moving along the Gulf Coast into ex-
Texas. Over the next several millennia, they repopulated the transformed continent, farming the primitive maize and potato strains they
had brought with them; hunting rats, hares, muskrats, beavers, and coyotes; and gathering locusts. Deer had not survived in North America,
and the few that did in South America had been hunted to extinction.

To its prewar residents, North America of the year 5000 would have 27
seemed a strange and unstable land indeed. Populations of the common-
est organisms were still fluctuating violently. When grasshoppers had a
good sequence of years, hordes of ravens, crows, starlings, gulls, and
egrets made the vast plains a study in black and white. Then, as the
foliage was exhausted, the grasshoppers died out, the birds succumbed
or moved on, and dust storms swept the land—often leading to many
decades of desolation before plants restored the ground cover.

Biologists transported in time would have been depressed at the low 28
diversity in forests, grasslands, and deserts, but they would have been
astounded at some of the organisms in abundance. Eastern diamondback
rattlesnakes were everywhere, having spread from their Florida refugia
and adapted to colder climates while feasting on rats. Monarch butterflies
and tiger swallowtails were nowhere to be seen. The most common
butterfly on the eastern coast was *Cissia joyceae,* an attractive little wood
nymph once known from only a single specimen from Costa Rica. With
unusual rapidity, it had evolved the ability to pass winters as a caterpillar
in diapause and now had several generations a year, thriving on a diet of
grasses.

In the West, a tiny beige hairstreak butterfly, *Strymon avalona,* sur- *29* vived the war on Santa Catalina Island, to which it had previously been restricted. The hairstreak crossed to the mainland after the war and became widespsread and common. It too evolved a broadened diet, thriving on locoweeds, vetches, and other weedy plants, as well as on lupines, which had become extremely common as disturbances remained widespread.

Giant land snails and walking catfishes had become prominent features *30* of the warmer parts of the continent. These were not strange mutants but simply exotic organisms that had gained a foothold before the war. Such tough, competitive organisms had become dominant in the absence of many previous predators and competitors. Indeed, contrary to popular mythology, increased mutation rates due to high levels of ionizing radiation had not significantly speeded evolution. Prewar mutation rates and genetic recombination had provided all the genetic variability needed for evolution to proceed rapidly under strong selection pressures. The genetic damage done by radiation-induced mutations only weakened populations; the mutations did not produce any "hopeful monsters" that rapidly replaced previous types.

Only minor evolutionary changes occurred during the time between *31* the war and the human reinvasion. Resistance to pesticides, for example, which had been common in the old days, disappeared. Some specialists broadened their niches. Camouflage and other protective mechanisms of many smaller insects declined because the previous great diversity of insectivorous birds—including most of the species that searched carefully for their prey—had been largely lost. Three millennia had not been enough time for North American ecosystems to make substantial evolutionary progress toward rediversifying the biota. That would require a thousandfold greater time.

Homo sapiens was barred from one cultural evolutionary course it *32* had once taken. The human groups that went through the first industrial revolution had thoroughly depleted the nonrenewable resources of the planet before they blew it up. No nearly pure copper lay around on the surface as it had in the Old Stone Age; it had to be extracted by the smelting of low-grade ores. Oil could no longer be had by drilling down a few feet; it could be obtained only by drilling several thousand feet. High technology was requred to obtain the resources needed by technological civilization. And high technology did not exist in the postwar Stone Age.

The war and its aftermath had destroyed most of the stocks of re- *33* sources and much of the knowledge of how to use them. During the millennia that followed, while *Homo sapiens* barely hung on, remaining stockpiles of materials rusted away, decayed, and dispersed—and scientific knowledge was forgotten. Whether this was a blessing or curse might have been debated if there were time travelers, but the result was final. The technology that had produced automobiles, airplanes, television, computers, ICBMs, and thermonuclear devices would never be regained.

Study Questions

1. Although "North America After the War" appears to be objective, Ehrlich has a personal message to express. What is his message? Where has he stated it? Why has Ehrlich placed it in that position?
2. Compare this essay with McPhee's "Dick Cook." Erhlich deals exclusively with an area, North America, while McPhee focuses on a human, Dick Cook. How does each writer's choice of subject matter cause differences in language and tone?
3. In Section 2 we said that item analysis could show you where you need to have further information before you start drafting. What information in the Ehrlich essay is new to you? If you had to write on the same topic and did not know about this essay, where could you go to learn the information? Try to find the titles of books and articles that deal with this topic.
4. In Section 2, we said that the search for meaning did not end once drafting began. Compare "North America After the War" with the example of item analysis on pp. 44–45. Pretend that Ehrlich did this analysis in preparation for writing his essay. Although they deal with many of the same questions, the item analysis and the essay show key differences. Identify them and speculate on how they might have arisen as the writer went from prewriting to drafting his essay.

Suggestion for Prewriting

In "North America After the War," Paul Ehrlich ends with a question that seems to call for further development: Would the loss of technology be a curse or a blessing for future generations? Prepare to write an essay in which you answer this question. Use any form of prewriting you wish, but pay particular attention to areas in which you would need further information. As part of this exercise, follow up on one of these areas by finding the additional information you need.

Essay Assignments

At the end of each section that deals with a stage in the writing process, we will include assignments that ask for completed essays. Although we will not have described the entire writing process until the final section, we feel that you will benefit from regularly trying to handle these assignments in two ways. First, there is no better way of learning to do something than by trying to do it. If you restrict your work to only the isolated stages, you run the risk of not seeing how each stage is closely related to the others. Second, if you try to write full essays at once, you will have a better appreciation for how the techniques we describe later can help you with the problems you encounter.

1. On p. 89 we asked you to describe an event in your family that illustrated its character and to do some prewriting based on that anecdote. Using that work as a basis, write an essay of four hundred to five hundred words in which you relate the incident and clearly explain how it illustrates your family's character. Keep in mind that you are not writing a "true confessions" story but are trying to show strangers something about your family and your feelings toward it. Remember that your goal is not simply to describe what happened. You are using the description to make a point about your family.

2. The editors of *Time* magazine are under the mistaken impression that you have just returned from the Island of Mingori, where you saw the bandersnatch, a creature that had never been seen before. They have offered you five hundred dollars for a short essay (400–500 words) describing this creature. Since no one can challenge your description, you have decided to take a shot at the essay. Write in such a way that the editors will believe you. Keep in mind that your essay must describe the bandersnatch and not simply your trip to Mingori.

3. "'What is truth?' asked jesting Pilate and did not stay for an answer." The term *truth* means many things to many people, and the debate over its importance may never end. Many people, however, have never made the attempt to consider what they mean by the word. *Truth* is a frequently used word that is often employed without much thought. And the same can be said of such terms as *honesty, generosity*, and *sympathy*.

   In this assignment we want you to try to describe what one of the four words mentioned above, or another to your own liking, means to you. To help you concentrate on possible meanings, find a quotation in which your word is used in a way that you find effective. Then use one or more prewriting exercises to investigate why you are attracted to the quotation. Your goal will be to write a six-hundred to eight-hundred word essay that explains to a wide audience what you think your word means and why. Since you will be dealing with an audience of strangers, it is important that you make your meaning as clear and as concrete as possible and that you illustrate your points so that your readers will be able to see exactly what you have in mind.

Remember that the only reason your audience will have to read your essay is an interest in what you have to say about the meaning of the word. You should not try to convince your readers to believe as you believe; your aim is to describe your opinions in such a way that they will understand your point of view.

4. Thomas Jefferson University (TJU) is a moderately sized (15,000) institution of higher education, long known for its demanding degree programs and its excellent graduates. The university offers bachelor degrees in almost every field of study, and each degree has a strict set of requirements. TJU is now in the middle of a sharp decline in enrollments, and if the decline continues, the university may not be able to stay open. Enrollments have dropped 20 percent in five years, and there is no indication that the trend will stop.

Because of their concern over this situation, a number of faculty members have proposed a revision in degree requirements as a solution. These people point out that the university has a superior reputation in such areas as computer science, chemistry, and the biological sciences. They feel that the present requirement that all first- and second-year students concentrate on general courses be revised to permit them to begin their majors immediately. They point out that students now must take 76 of the 130 credit hours needed for graduation in required courses. They believe such requirements discourage bright students from enrolling at TJU because other universities allow earlier and greater specialization.

Those faculty members favoring a revision in the requirements have made the following suggestions:

1. Allow students to take upper-level courses in their chosen field immediately
2. Reduce the composition and literature requirement from four courses (12 hours) to two (6 hours)
3. Reduce the Western civilization requirement from four courses (12 hours) to two (6 hours)
4. Eliminate both the history of art (6 hours) and history of music (3 hours) requirements
5. Excuse all students with science majors from the foreign language requirement (16 hours)
6. Reduce the distribution requirement of three courses in each area (mathematics and natural science, social science, and humanities) to two courses in each, including the required course in calculus (18 hours instead of the required 27 hours)

They argue that these changes will make the programs at TJU far more attractive to potential students without harming the quality of the education available.

Another group of faculty members opposes all of these changes. They feel that TJU offers a very special kind of education that would be lost if students were allowed to specialize. They point out that the breadth of the education students receive is every bit as important as its depth and that few students will ever have the chance to study so many different areas again. Once people graduate, they argue, they spend their lives concentrating on their professions, and the opportunity for exploring unrelated fields is lost. For these faculty members, the proposed changes represent a turn toward job training rather than education. While they recognize that the enrollment decline is serious, they want to find other solutions to it (although they have proposed none themselves).

The dispute between these two groups is now receiving national attention, but so far the only opinions covered are those of the faculty. As a student at TJU, you wish to give a student's opinion of the proposed changes in a short essay (800–1,000 words) for a national newspaper that covers higher education. You plan to discuss what your own goals are and how the proposed changes will affect them. Write that essay for a national audience that is only vaguely aware of what is happening at TJU. Concentrate on what you feel a college program should do for you and how the proposed revisions in degree requirements would either help or hurt you as you try to attain your goals.

SECTION THREE
Structure

The White Rabbit put on his spectacles. "Where shall I begin, please your Majesty?" he asked.

"Begin at the beginning," the King said, very gravely, "and go on till you come to the end: then stop."

There was dead silence in the court, whilst the White Rabbit read out these verses:—

"They told me you had been to her,
  And mentioned me to him:
She gave me a good character,
  But said I could not swim.
He sent them word I had not gone
  (We know it to be true):
If she should push the matter on,
  What would become of you?
I gave her one, they gave him two,
  You gave us three or more;
They all returned from him to you,
  Though they were mine before.
If I or she could chance to be
  Involved in this affair,
He trusts to you to set them free,
  Exactly as we were.
My notion was that you had been
  (Before she had this fit)
An obstacle that came between
  Him, and ourselves, and it.
Don't let him know she liked them best,
  For this must ever be
A secret, kept from all the rest,
  Between yourself and me."

"That's the most important piece of evidence we've heard yet," said the King, rubbing his hands; "so now let the jury—"

"If anyone can explain it," said Alice (she had grown so large in the last few minutes that she wasn't a bit afraid of interrupting him,) "I'll give him a sixpence. *I* don't believe there is an atom of meaning in it."

Lewis Carroll, *Alice's Adventures in Wonderland*

A lice speaks for us all when she challenges anyone to make sense of the poem. If there is
any meaning in it, it is known only to the
poet—and perhaps the mad inhabitants of Wonderland. But the poem
looks as if it should mean something. The sentences are grammatical,
and the words are familiar. Nothing in the lines themselves signals that
this is utter nonsense. Why then do Alice and we agree that there is not
"an atom of meaning in it"?

We agree because, ironically, we cannot read the poem as the King
told the White Rabbit to read it: "Begin at the beginning, and go on till
you come to the end: then stop." For us, there is no beginning, middle,
or end. The poem appears to be someone's brainstorming list or perhaps
the random thoughts inspired by item analysis. What these thoughts
represent and how they are related to one another is still in the mind of
the poet, and he or she does not seem ready to share them with an
audience.

Audience is the key term in the second stage of the writing process.
It is here that you will be trying to present to potential readers the
meaning you discovered in prewriting, and that presentation will need to
be organized. In prewriting you were able to concentrate on your ideas;
in drafting you must start to worry about how others will understand
them.

The essay selections in this section illustrate a wide variety of methods
for organizing your thoughts. As you read them, look for the signals the
writers use to show their readers how their essays are structured and
how each part is related to the whole.

What does the opening of the essay tell me to expect?

Does the writer give me a reason for reading the essay?

Does the writer give a reason for writing it?

What logic is there to the order in which the points are presented?

What changes would I make in that order if I were writing the essay?

What key terms does the writer use to show me how the essay is organized?

If I were to write on this same topic, would I use the same method of organization?

Is there a single method of organization, or does the writer use a number of different methods?

If the writer uses various methods, how are the variations connected with the different subtopics in the essay?

These questions will help you to focus on how the writers found their own answers to the problem of making their meanings public. Combined with the exercises following each essay, your answers will show you the wide range of possible organizations you might use and give you some broad guidelines for your own writing.

In order to help you best use the questions and the exercises, we first want to discuss in greater detail the second stage of the writing process, *drafting*. It is at this stage that you begin to experiment with possible organizations. Just as prewriting helps you to discover a message, drafting will help you discover a form.

Drafting

When it comes to writing the first draft of a paper, few alternatives exist to plunging right in. Whether you use a formal outline first or simply write off of the final brainstorming list is a matter of personal choice. But you have no choice when it comes to writing a first draft.

To demonstrate what we mean by a first draft, we will return to our final brainstorming list on the topic of zoos. Having produced a final list with the descriptive title "There is nothing like a good zoo," it is now time to write a first version of that paper:

THERE IS NOTHING LIKE A GOOD ZOO

I have always enjoyed my visits to the zoo, no matter what zoo I visit. All zoos offer me many enjoyable sights, but the three things I enjoy most are the animals, the special exhibits, and my fellow visitors. Zoos give me a place to go when I am tired of dealing with this over complicated world. A place that cannot be found anywhere else.

The first, and most basic, ingredient of a zoo is, of course, the animals. These animals don't have to be very exotic either. Lions, tigers, elephants, bears, and monkeys can be found in almost any zoo, and I always enjoy them even if I have seen them hundreds of times before. They go about living their lives before the eyes of hundreds of people every day and they don't seem to care. They show me that no matter what problems I face life goes on. They are able to manage under terrible conditions and they adapt. They show me that people should be able to adapt if animals can. I feel peaceful seeing how they can remain calm in the situation they are in.

Another important feature to me that zoos have are the special exhibits. African plains, tropical rainforests, and special "night" houses are just three kinds. All of these exhibits take me out of my limited world and show me there is a lot more to this planet than where I live. I go on adventures to places I never was and forget the problems I have. Going through these exhibits gives me time off and you get to rest for a little while. You need rest occassionally or everything gets too depressing.

Finally, I enjoy the people who visit the zoo too. I see young and old people in love, married families with hordes of children running around, and people like myself who are alone and just killing time. They all enjoy the zoo. Snapping pictures right and left with every kind of camera. Laughing at the actions of many of the animals. Being amazed at the unusual animals. They too are wrapped up in the zoo, and it is fun to share the enjoyment with them. Even though we don't know each other, we all seem to be friends in the zoo.

Zoos allow you to escape from the real world for a little while and forget your own problems. They are able to do this because of the animals, special exhibits, and people that are there. We should all take time off and go to a zoo.

Notice that we have produced a draft that has some similarities to the example of controlled free writing in Section 1. Although our draft is longer and contains no "can't thinks," it is clear that we are still thinking over the topic. Many of the ideas in the draft can be found in the brainstorming list, but one major point is new. We have included a reason for enjoying zoos: they are an escape from the "real world." It is not surprising that new information like this should surface during a first draft. As writers concentrate on writing, new ideas will appear, particularly ideas that help them focus on a message.

Our first draft illustrates two important features of the beginning of drafting. First, as we begin to set down our ideas, the organization is very tentative, following almost exactly the final brainstorming list. Our draft is easier to understand than the poem read by the White Rabbit, but it will need further work before we can communicate effectively. For example, we will need to rework the ideas in the second paragraph so our audience will be better able to understand how watching caged animals produces a sense of calm. Many readers would see such a scene as an instance of cruel treatment to creatures that should be allowed to roam free. To get our point across, we will have to anticipate such reactions.

Second, our first draft lacks a *context*. We have not given our audience a reason to read the essay. The draft has a beginning, middle, and end, but these parts do not engage the reader. Like most first drafts, ours seems to have been stuffed into a formula. In this case the formula is the five-paragraph essay: we introduce our topic, discuss it in three paragraphs, and conclude by repeating what we wrote. When you begin to draft an essay, such formulas are very useful: they give you prepackaged organizations that free you to concentrate on what you wish to say. Eventually, however, these formulas need to be discarded. The time will come when you have to consider how to reorganize the essay so that your readers will not feel that they are dealing with just another classroom exercise, even if the essay you are writing is a classroom exercise. In other words, you will have to create a context for your essay that is more than "here are some of my thoughts on this topic" or "here is the paper you assigned me."

Beginnings

How you open and close your essay will go far in determining its effect on your readers. Openings and closings have particular roles to play, and these roles help the readers follow both your individual points and your meaning.

A good beginning puts the readers in the right frame of mind for the rest of the essay. It establishes a context for the ideas you wish to present. With a proper context your audience will be more likely to understand your intended message.

The opening paragraph in our sample does hint at a context. But is it an effective one? Will it encourage readers to go further? Will it interest them in the essay? Probably not. The opening paragraph is typical of many essays in which the writer begins by merely announcing the topic without trying to involve the readers. For a first draft, where we are still collecting our thoughts, the opening paragraph is fine, but in a finished paper its effect could be deadly.

As the drafting stage continues, therefore, we will need to concentrate on the opening and rework it with the possible reactions of the readers in mind. Having collected our thoughts, we now need to present those thoughts to others.

The beginnings of essays can take many different forms, but all of them perform the same task of establishing a context for your message. If you have taken the time to do some prewriting and have bothered to write a first draft, you have one advantage over those who have not: you will have a much better idea of what it is you are trying to introduce.

There are three general kinds of introductions you will find useful for most of the essays you will be called upon to write. The first is a direct statement of the message. You don't want to state it so directly, however, that you end up with something like the first paragraph in our example. You also need to include enough information to interest your readers and give them some idea of your attitude toward the topic.

Imagine that we are now continuing the drafting stage and want to redraft the opening. We should focus on the sentence "Zoos give me a place to go when I am tired of dealing with this over complicated world," because it seems to be the clearest statement of the message. And we need to add information that will engage the readers' interest.

The redraft might look something like this:

I have just had six days of screaming headlines that have announced murders, increased international tension, and unimagible suffering. I have also had six days of huge electric bills, rising food costs, and boring work. Six days are enough. It is time to go to the zoo. Zoos give me a place to go when I am tired of dealing with this over-complicated world. It is not that I will be able to permanently escape the world's and my problems, but it will give me a rest. And an occasional rest does help.

Although you would probably have little trouble finding ways to improve the sentences in this redraft, to suggest different words, or to correct some of its mechanics, remember that we are still drafting the essay. If we see a fault, it is fine to correct it; but if misspellings like *occassional* go unnoticed, there will be time to find them later. All will go well as long as we remember that this is a draft and not a finished work.

Certainly you can easily understand our message after reading this paragraph. You may even be able to predict most of the points we will make in the body of the essay to support it. But the message was equally clear in the original example. What is noticeably different is that we have created a more interesting context for our readers. They will be able to sympathize with our desire for a rest because the problems mentioned here are problems faced by everyone. Most people would like a rest from them. Perhaps a visit to a zoo could help us all.

The new material was not, of course, on our final brainstorming list. The need to consider the readers has forced us to find additional material. The original brainstorming list might have made the message clear to us, but more detail was needed for it to interest others. By focusing on "this over-complicated world," we can establish a common ground for all readers to share. They can now understand why we want to escape, and this prepares them for the kinds of subtopics and examples that will follow.

Not all introductions directly state the message of the essay. In a second type of introduction, the writer delays the statement of the message and leads up to it slowly. Such organizations allow readers to reason along with you as you first support or illustrate your message. These introductions need to interest the readers to such an extent that they are willing to suspend their usual insistence on knowing your intentions. The writers focus on a careful presentation of context, on why the topic is interesting or important.

Suppose we decide that we would like to try out such an opening. Although our first redraft seems promising, we want to look at a number of possibilities. After all the drafting process is as much an exploration of potential forms as prewriting is of potential meanings. The new introduction might take this form:

It is December, and a small, but ever-increasing number of people are about to do something irrational. Faced with large utility, food, and creit card bills, they are going to increase their debts even more. They are not going to spend that money on gifts although December is the season of gift giving. They are going to use their MasterCard or VisaCard to join their local zoological societies. Why would anyone want to give money to a zoo, especially in December? What is there about a zoo that would encourage people from all kinds of backgrounds to further overextend their credit?

Notice how we have tried in this new opening to personalize the introduction. Openings that do not state the thesis directly need to give the readers some good reason for reading on. In this case, we raise a question; Why do people contribute to zoos? And we raise it in what we hope is an interesting manner. By suggesting that such contributions appear to be irrational, we are creating a specific context for our meaning. This opening adds a new perspective to the discussion, and this perspective will shape the readers' responses to what we will say in the body of the essay.

Once again, new material has been added. In order to suggest the "irrational" appearance of giving money to zoos, we have focused on credit cards and increases in the cost of living. Moreover, we have all of this take place in December, because most people do not think of going to zoos in the winter; yet it is a popular time for many organizations to ask for contributions.

In the third type of opening, a special form of the indirect method, the writer begins with a brief anecdote that dramatizes the point that he or she wishes to make. Such an opening can help the reader to imagine more vividly the context of the essay. For example, we might try out the following anecdote for our essay on zoos:

Not too long ago a group of seven and eight year olds were on a guided tour of the Woodland Park Zoo in Seattle. Their guide, the director of the zoo, had clearly captured the children's attention as he showed them one wonder after another. Now it was time for the climax, for the star attraction the zoo had to offer. Throughout their tour the guide had tried to heighten their interest by promising them a visit to Woodland Park's unique exhibit, the Marsh and Swamp. No matter what exciting exhibits they saw, he constantly reminded them that they had not yet seen the Marsh and Swamp.

As the children approached this long promised cap to their day, their excitment was obvious. They yelled, screamed, laughed, jumped, and ran to be the first into the enclosure. Just as the last child entered the exhibit, however, their noise stopped. They were disappointed with the sights that greeted them. The guide tried to find out why his favorite part of the entire zoo failed to impress the students, and finally one of the seven year olds saddly replied to his questions, "You promised to show us the Martian swamp."

Perhaps you might think that only a child would believe that a zoo could have a Martian swamp, yet many adults find marvels to equal this in a visit to a zoo. The exhibit in the Woodland Park Zoo for example may not represent a swamp in Mars but it does offer its visitors an exact reproduction of the wooded swamp and freshwater marsh in New England, thousands of miles away.

Anecdotes are not always easy to find. In this case we had to read through several magazines devoted to zoos before we found the one we used here. A good anecdote, however, can be well worth the effort. Its details will hold the attention of your readers during that crucial moment when they are still deciding whether or not to read your essay.

The essay selections in this section will have many different types of openings. Our "zoo" examples represent only three general types, and even within these there is a great deal of variation. Nevertheless, all introductions have a common characteristic: they establish the special context the writer needs for his or her meaning. A successful introduction will prepare the reader for the specific ideas the writer wants to present.

Endings

As with openings, you will write better endings if you have taken the time to do some prewriting. Since you have some idea of what you want to say and what you think is important, you might try to write the ending of your essay before you have written the middle. By trying to write your conclusion right after you have explored various openings but before you have drafted the body of your essay, you will avoid a serious problem that almost everyone encounters—running out of things to say. In haste to reach the end, some writers are content just to stop. To tired writers, endings frequently appear to be needless elaborations, or even repetitions, of what has already been written. In fact, our first draft of "There Is Nothing like a Zoo" had just such an ending. If you write your ending soon after you have finished the opening, you may have a better chance of developing an effective conclusion.

Because the ending to your essay is the last thing your readers see, it will usually be the first thing they will recall. How you leave them often determines what they will remember best. Thus, you must make certain that your conclusion both signals the end of your discussion and highlights your message.

Telling your readers that you have finished is never easy. You are, in effect, saying that you have dealt with the topic as fully as you want to and that you believe your discussion is complete. Such a statement cannot be given lightly, and you might sound a rather sour concluding note if all you do is weakly repeat earlier remarks because you cannot think of anything else to say. Such endings will rarely impress your readers with the significance of your meaning. By mere repetition you will not take advantage of the special position conclusions hold.

Let us return to our first draft to see what can be done with the final paragraph so that it might better express both completion and importance of meaning.

Happily, a number of the techniques we discussed for beginning essays also work for ending them. Because in both parts we need to emphasize the context of the message, this should not be surprising. However, you do need to remember that whereas introductions open up that context to your readers, endings close it. Thus, the words and phrases you use in each will differ.

Suppose, for example, we want to restate our thesis in the conclusion. Such a restatement can be effective if we are dealing with a particularly complex idea, but we should not let it appear too repetitious. We might introduce new information in our conclusion that would extend the significance of our major point. For "There Is Nothing like a Good Zoo," this method could produce the following ending:

According to the *Encyclopaedia Britannica* zoos are places that have as their chief purpose "to gratify the pleasure most persons feel in viewing at close range the curious and beautiful living products of nature, but they serve also as a means of instruction in natural history, providing material for museums and for investigations in comparative anatomy and pathology." While I do not wish to argue with the writer of this description, I feel that he has missed an even more important purpose that zoos serve. They allow us to broaden our view of the world by showing there is much more to our planet than screaming headlines and this week's bills. Zoos are an escape into a larger world than the one our constant worries shows us. They remind us that there are still things left to enjoy if only we give them a chance.

Here, we begin our redraft by using a quotation that presents a slightly different picture of zoos. This enables us to restate our own point and emphasize it. Encyclopedias are well worth mining for short quotations. You will usually find some statement that you can make use of or some further bit of information that you can add to your draft.

Notice that we try to avoid being repetitious by expanding the point we made earlier in our drafts of the introduction. We have moved from our opening suggestion that zoos are an escape from daily problems to the statement that zoos are "an escape into a larger world than our worries show us." Instead of picturing zoos as fantasy worlds, we open up our message to a broader meaning: "They remind us that there are still things left for us to enjoy if only we give them a chance." In this way the essay ends on a strong positive note that will please the readers. And if you manage to please your readers, they will remember your essay longer and more fondly than if you only repeat earlier sentences.

Anecdotes can also make effective conclusions if you choose one that leaves the readers with a vivid image of the point you are stressing. Although we could be satisfied with the first redraft of our conclusion, we should try out other possibilities. An ending with an anecdote might look like this:

Seven years ago the newspapers were filled with reports about a University of Michigan freshman who had dropped out of sight. He was a remarkably intelligent young man who had entered the university at the age of fifteen. Naturally everyone from the university officials to his friends to his parents were worried, and his picture was carried in almost every newspaper in a five state area. But for two days no new information was heard.

Finally, a close friend came forward and told one of the strangest stories imaginable. The missing freshman was a fanatic player of Dungeons and Dragons. He had decided to invent the ultimate playing field for this game, and he had gone into the old heating tunnels that criss-crossed the campus underground. Twenty people immediately took to the tunnel in search of the lost student. A day later they found him still wandering the tunnels completely involved in his private game, happily ignoring all the pressures of student life that had driven him to his game in the first place and ignorant of how much time had passed.

Wasn't this young man doing what many people do when they look for new sight and experiences to escape from their own pressure? Perhaps everyone needs to recognize this need for a rest before things become too much and the mind snaps. Perhaps it would have helped that student if he had visited a zoo occasionally.

We chose for this ending an anecdote that dramatically described one way of escaping from problems, other than visiting a zoo. We wanted to contrast the serious consequences for this young man of fantasizing with the lighter relaxation a zoo offers. This contrast, in turn, stresses that our meaning has a serious side to it. The final note is certainly not the positive one of our first example, but it does emphasize the importance of the message. The story of the freshman should keep this point in our readers' minds for some time to come.

You will see in the following selections many distinct ways of ending an essay. Each is successful because its writer took care with it. He or she found an ending that effectively completed the essay and left the reader with a vivid sense of its importance.

Middles

No opening or ending will be effective if there is no middle. Introductions and conclusions are frames for your essay, and they must enclose something. In our earlier discussion of the sample first draft, we pointed out that we would have to work on presenting the information in the body of the essay and that we needed to improve upon our tentative organization. Three general types of organization are available to writers as they redraft their works into more effective versions. Although an essay will rarely follow only one of these types, we will present each of them separately and illustrate each with possible redrafts of "There Is Nothing like a Good Zoo."

Temporal organization

Writers use temporal organization to arrange their ideas in a time sequence. In its simplest form, temporal organization is narrative (as in the anecdotes in the third example of openings and the second example of endings). But you may find it useful to use this type of organization even when there is no obvious time sequence to follow. In such cases you will have to invent your own sequence and mark it clearly for the reader.

The topic of zoos, for example, does not immediately suggest any specific time sequence, nor does the brainstorming list in Section 2 suggest how one might be applied to it. Yet by organizing our presentation as a walk through the zoo, we would be able to discuss the animals, exhibits, and visitors in an orderly way. First, of course, we should do some more research and either find a map of a zoo or create our own. Having a concrete diagram in front of us will be far more helpful than our simply winging it. Next, we should write a few notes on the map suggesting the areas that we want to use and outlining the best route to follow. Third, we should, if at all possible, visit that zoo and follow our chosen route in order to elaborate on our notes. Figure 3.1 illustrates the map we produced after following each of these steps:

Having planned our organization, we can now turn to redrafting the middle of our essay so that our discussion follows the order suggested by the annotated map:

I am not sure why it is true, but the simple act of entering a zoo makes me feel that I have left my world of troubles behind. As soon as I am through the main gate I feel that I am about to enter an exotic world that I only vaguely remember from past visits. Even the areas of the zoo right after the main gate seems new to me although at the zoo I am now visiting, the Kansas City Zoo, it is crowd with people and there is nothing to see but concrete walks and minature railroad tracks. Somehow these usual sights seem different and new. The old and young couples, the children, the lovers, and the loners seem caught up in the excitement. Each concrete walk and even the railroad tracks seem to me to lead to new sights and sounds that leave the city behind.

I get caught up in this excitement because it is catching. The people around me do not appear to be worrying about how to pay their bills, or the crime rate, or possible nuclear war. I start to forget these problems also. I choose the path to my left and start out on my adventure.

As I walk down that path I ignore the sights on my right. There are only a few animals there and they are too far back in their enclosures to see. On my left, however, is another story. For as far down the walk as I can go there is an open plain with herds of animals clearly in sight. First come the buffalo. Although I have seen them many times before, I am still amazed at their size. These beasts simply stand in a herd and ignore the activity around them as they quietly graze on the grasses. No matter what happens near them, they remain intent on their single task of eating.

Next, some fifty yards from the buffalo, is a herd of deer. They are more spread out than the buffalo and seem far more delicate. But they also seem intent on the single thing each member is doing. Some are quietly eating, just like the buffalo. Some are taking care of their young. But all of them seem calm despite the noise around them as a crowd of children rush to the fence to see the young deer. The deer are so quiet and calm that the children soon quiet down themselves and concentrate on the way in which the parent deer are taking care of their young.

I now feel as quite and calm myself and am really enjoying the sights. Slowly I continue my walk and watch the camels, lions, tigers, and even a troop of baboons going about their tasks. They are all concentrating on what they are doing and refuse to be distracted. Finally the path turns to the right. I see in the distance my favorite exhibition and I start walking past it. Passing the ape house, the antelope, and turtles, I arrive at the Tropical Habitat Building. Inside this building is a reproduction of a tropical

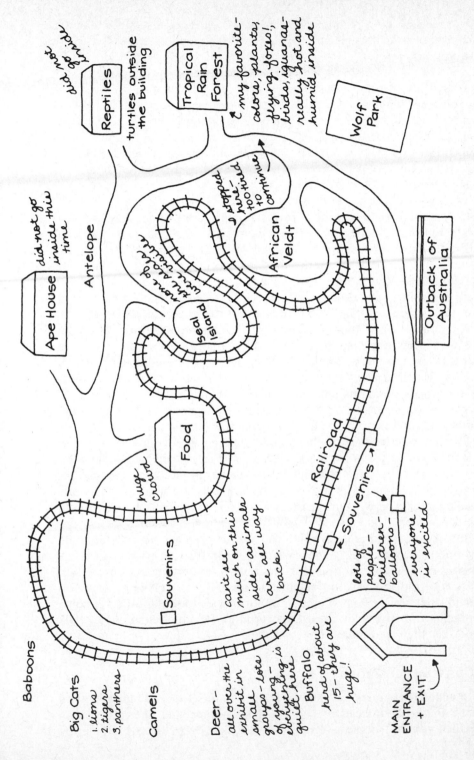

Baboons

Big Cats
1. lions
2. tigers
3. panthers

Camels

Deer —
all over the exhibit in small groups – lots of young – everything is quiet here

Buffalo
herd of about 15 – they are huge!

lots of people – children – balloons –

everyone is excited

MAIN
ENTRANCE
+ EXIT

Souvenirs

can't see much on this side – animals are all way in back.

huge crowd

Food

Seal Island
went to show at noon

Ape House
did not go inside this time

Antelope

Reptiles
did not go inside
turtles outside the building

Tropical Rain Forest
→ my favorite – colors, plants, flying foxes!, birds, iguanas – really hot and humid inside

I stopped here – too tired to continue

African Veldt

Wolf Park

Railroad

Souvenirs

Outback of Australia

Fig. 3.1: Map of the Zoo

rain forest complete with brightly colored birds, dark green iguanas, and even flying foxes. Everywhere they are free to roam about the exhibit.

It does not take much for me to imagine myself in a real rain forest. The fantastic plants and animals on every side quickly grab my attention and I soon forget that not half a mile away are twenty story buildings. Even the heat and the humidity of the building contribute to this illusion. In my own house I would find this climate uncomfortable, here it feels natural and I actually like it. I find a tree stump, supplied by the zoo for visitors who want to rest, and I sit down to enjoy the sights. Somewhere in the world there is an actual rainforest, and for the time I rest on that stump I can believe that I am there.

If you compare this draft with the original draft of the body of our essay, you should notice that the new version is both smoother and more detailed. The temporal order allows us to be far less stiff. We are able to discuss each point in the original without appearing to lecture our readers. Instead, we take them on a tour of the zoo with us, and we share with them our thoughts as we view the exhibits. This sense of "sharing" produces a far less formal tone than the earlier draft. "The first, and most basic, ingredient of a zoo . . ." is replaced with "As soon as I am through the main gate. . . ." The organization of the new draft is at least as rigorous as that of the first. Time phrases such as "as soon as," "as I walk down," "next," "now," and "finally" show our readers the sequence of exhibits and unite the thoughts each new view inspires. Moreover, such verbs as "enter," "continue," and "sit" echo this organization and help the readers fit each action into the sequence.

The increased detail of the second version is a result of our new organization. In the first version we simply listed the elements that were most important to us. Although they can be an effective way of presenting information, lists are very restrictive. After listing the points what more can be written? Lists seem to be complete once each item has been written down, and extended discussion frequently seems unnecessary. Presenting each exhibit as we see it seems to call for some description of each sight. Thus, when we redrafted our paper, our problem was not searching for more to say but rather limiting our description so that we did not say too much. Because we were able to focus on individual exhibits, we had greater opportunities for detail—good choice of organization gives you these opportunities. If a particular choice fails to do this, then try another one.

Additive organization

With additive organization the writer does not use time to bind the parts of the topic but instead presents a list of items that seem to belong together. In the simplest form, as in our first draft, the writer merely lists the ideas without much discussion of their common or distinct features. More often, however, the writer who uses this technique will make use of comparison and contrast, a method of organization in which similarities and differences among the items are emphasized. Let us return to the new draft of the body of our essay and use this method in describing the herd of deer in paragraph 4. Since we have already pointed out that different groups of deer are doing different things, comparison and contrast could improve this passage.

Next, some fifty yards from the buffalo, is a herd of deer. They are in three groups, and each group is engaged in a spearate activity. The one nearest to me consists of only mothers and their young. The mothers are quietly feeding their fawns and appear completely unaware of anything but them. They have eyes only for their young who are equally unconcerned with anything but getting as much of their mothers' milk as they can. Only a short distance from them, a second group is behaving quite differently. This group consists of three large males who seem to be guarding the first group. They are very aware of the world around them as they check out one area after another to see if anything holds danger for the mothers and their young. Standing every ready to give warning or do battle, they gaze intently, never distracted from their task. Further back from these two groups is most of the herd. Like the buffalo they are quietly eating and sunning themselves. Free from caring for fawns or guarding them, they ignore everything else but the grasses and the sun.

Yet despite the different behavior of each group, the over-all effect is a picture of calm. Each member does what needs to be done and is only concerned with what it is doing at that moment. When a crowd of children rush to the fence to see the young deer, there is no change in the animals behavior. Soon the children themselves either quiet down or rush off to some other enclosure.

Here we have experimented with comparison and contrast to emphasize two points. First, we described the differences among the three groups of deer so that the readers might see that the animals do not behave the same. We did this to avoid boring repetition of the same description, animal after animal. The differences were underscored by such words as "differently," "unaware" as opposed to "very aware," and "gazing intently" versus "ignore everything."

Nevertheless, we did not want to emphasize the differences so much that the readers would lose sight of the essential similarities. Therefore we end the passage with a comparison: they all present a "picture of calm." In this way, we are able to use comparison and contrast to fill out our description with individual details without weakening the general point. In other words, we try to make an organizational technique work for us rather than force our meaning to fit a technique. Throughout the drafting process, this should be your goal in experimenting with various organizations. You should be trying out different methods to find out which work best for what you are trying to express.

Sometimes the list of items you are working with will be far more extensive than three groups of deer; and long lists are too awkward to control by comparison and contrast. Frequently in these situations, classification is the additive organization that works best. When using this method, the writer usually starts by establishing a general category and then divides that category into smaller ones. If necessary, these subcategories can be divided even further. At its best, you can use classification to present large blocks of information in readable units. Rarely should you use classification as an end in itself. If your goal, for instance, is only to describe how an office staff is organized, a chart will show that chain of command far more simply and clearly than a group of sentences arranged in a paragraph.

Suppose that we decide that the temporal organization used earlier does not allow us to dwell long enough on individual exhibits and that instead of giving a tour of the zoo we prefer to use only two or three of the attractions. If one of these is an exhibit filled with various kinds of gorillas, we might try out the following draft as part of our body:

Yet another diversion zoos can offer is their own version of trivial pursuit. For example the San Diego Zoo is one of the few that has one exhibit entirely devoted to gorillas. The exhibit is contained in a huge area that has been especially designed for the animals special needs. It reproduces the tree tops of the gorillas natural habitat complete with vines and plenty of room to swing on them. Visitors can spend hours watching the gorillas do exactly what they please completely ignorant of the people watching them.

While it is fun to spend time simply watching the gorillas, this fun is increased by the large sign in front of the exhibit which informs the viewers that there are actually three kinds of gorillas. First of all gorillas are divided into two major kinds, lowland and mountain gorillas. Mountain gorillas, the sign states, are the largest of all, often weighing more than five hundred pounds. They are very black and have very long hair. As their name implies, they live in the mountains and need the black coloring to absorb as much heat as possible and the long hair to keep that heat as long as possible. The sign goes on to tell that there are only about five hundred gorillas in the wild and there are none in zoos. As a result the visitors must be content with a photograph of a mountain gorilla attached to the sign.

Lowland gorillas make up the other kind, and there are two types. First the sign describes the Western Lowland Gorilla with the scientific name of *gorilla gorilla gorilla*. This species has very short hair and ranges in color from black to grayish-brown. They average about one hundred pounds less than the mountain gorillas but they are far more abundant, relatively speaking. The sign states that there are about 35,000 western lowland gorillas in the wild and that they are the most common gorillas people see in zoos.

The second type of lowland gorilla, the Eastern Lowland Gorilla, looks like the western type, but actually its features lie somewhere between the mountain and western gorillas. Its scientific name is *gorilla gorilla graueri*. Its hair is longer than the western but shorter than the mountain. It is darker than the western lowland gorilla, but not as black as the mountain. It weighs more than the western, but not as much as the mountain. Finally, the sign points out, there are more eastern lowland gorillas, about 5,000, living in the wild than mountain gorillas, but there are far fewer of them than western lowland gorillas. The San Diego zoo is one of only a handful of zoos in the world to have eastern lowland gorillas.

Equiped with this information, the visitor can now turn to the actual animals and play the game of "Which Is Which?" Scanning the gorillas in tree tops, swinging on vines, feeding off in corners, and gathered in groups, the game begins. Which are the darker ones? Which have the longer hair? Is the one resting on that branch heavier than the ones at the base of this tree? Are all three of those gorillas sitting together eastern lowland gorillas? Or is the middle one actually a western lowland gorilla? How black does a gorilla have to be before it is an eastern lowland gorilla? It is not difficult to see how people can get caught up in this game and actively seek out the various types. They can lose themselves in their quest for that rare eastern lowland gorilla and for that time, at least, forget about the problems that drove them to the zoo in the first place. Once they have mastered the differences between the two kinds of gorillas, moreover, they can advance to the next level and try to distinguish among the two kinds of lions or the seven types of tigers or even the five (perhaps more) kinds of zebras. Such skills may never help pay the bills, but for many it is nice to have them.

In this draft we try to give a concrete illustration of one kind of entertainment zoos offer. To make that example clear, we first need to explain to our readers what to look for, so we use classification to cover the basic facts. In effect, we are setting up the points in the last paragraph by first giving our readers important background information. The questions in paragraph 5 will then make more sense to them, and they will be able to see more clearly why some people might enjoy playing the game.

This redraft illustrates once again that prewriting never really ends. As you experiment with different organizations, you will frequently find you need more information. Each method requires specific kinds of information that you might never have considered until you began the drafting.

Finally, you may occasionally find that you need to clarify a point in your draft by defining a word or concept. Definition is an additive organization that is normally used for rather brief passages to make sure that the readers understand exactly what you mean. The first example of endings (p. 145) illustrates this: we not only quote from the *Encyclopaedia Britannica* but add our own definitions as well.

Within the body of the essay, we can make similar use of definition to clarify some particular reaction to an exhibit. Compare our description of rain forests in the redraft using temporal organization (p. 150) with the following:

No dictionary will ever be able to define a rain forest, especially a rain forest that has been carefully built by a good zoo. The *American Heritage Dictionary*, for example, defines a rain forest as "a dense evergreen forest occupying a tropical region with an annual rainfall of at least 100 inches." The South American Rainforest of the Bronx Zoo would seem to fit that definition, although the rainfall is like the exhibit itself artificial and New York City is certainly not in a tropical region. But once inside the exhibit its visitors quickly realize that there is much more to a rain forest than location, trees, and rain.

A rain forest is part of a world most will never see. It is so removed from where and how the majority of people live that it might as well be labelled a Venusian forest. Here the zoo visitor is immediately lost in a riot of greens, browns, yellows and reds. Flying birds fill the air, crawling reptiles inhabit the ground, and snakes hang from the branches. Everywhere there is something extraordinary to see if only care is taken to look. What is a rain forest exhibition in a zoo? It is a place to remind people that there are still strange things to see and enjoy in this world.

As you can see, definition is most effective when it is not used as an end in itself. Here we use a rather common dictionary definition so that we can discuss how inadequate it is and propose our own subjective one. By adding our own definition, we are able to once again emphasize our theme about the value of zoos.

Conceptual organization

The final general category of organization we will deal with here is conceptual organization. When using a conceptual organization the writer emphasizes such logical relationships as cause and effect, result, reason, and purpose. It is a more abstract method in that it deals with mental associations. Unlike temporal and additive organizations, based on time sequence or membership in a group, conceptual organization demands that the writers find deeper connections among the details, connections that require more than merely identifying a sequence or finding similarities and differences. Conceptual organization can also be used to highlight relationships in which the elements actually contradict one another or lack any logical connection.

You will find conceptual organization helpful for passages in which you need to discuss abstract ideas or defend your point of view. Such passages usually require this technique because they contain concepts rather than concrete objects. Suppose that after reading our various drafts of "There Is No Place like a Good Zoo," we are concerned that we have spent too much of our time on describing the exhibits and not enough on our theme that visiting zoos is a healthy way of coping with daily problems because it allows us to rest for a while. We need to present our theme directly so that our readers will not forget why we are writing the essay. Conceptual organization is effective for such a presentation:

No matter what the exhibit, the diversions they offer us are not only pleasant but healthful as well. Living each day forces us to deal with problems that can get the best of anyone. Worrying about bills, the next exam, how the boss feels, the repairs the car needs, the danger of walking the streets, or the quality of the air we breathe gives us all a warped view of our lives and the world we live in. We become so naturally preoccupied with our problems that we can only see our world as nothing more than one big problem with no solution. Because we see the world that way, we give in and start to withdraw. We see nothing worth all the aggravation.

How do rain forests and gorillas help? Few people seem to realize their value. They see zoos as basically for children, not adults, or they think they are luxuries that drain off tax money for more important projects. Zoos, however, are not luxuries, and the tax money spent on them is well spent. They give us the chance to wonder about our world and to learn more about it, and these chances are rare. Rain forests show us that there is much more to our world than the street that we live on or the headlines in the local newspaper. They give us not an escape but a more complete view of our world. They give us a chance to be curious about the colors, plants, and animals. The various types of gorillas give us a chance to learn to prove to ourselves that we can still learn new things just for the sake of learning. We can't pay our bills by identifying a western lowland gorilla or a subtype of zebra or tiger, but at least for that moment we have shown ourselves that we can still learn. We have also proven to ourselves that we can still notice details around us. Zoos can be for adults if they only give them a chance.

This paragraph is our most extensive discussion of the theme so far. Our attempt at conceptual organization is filled with awkward words and phrases and faulty mechanics, but it has forced us to examine our meaning and defend it by explaining how visits to zoos cause us to relax. We can worry later about cleaning up its faulty spelling, poor punctuation, and incorrect grammar.

This redraft illustrates one final point about trying out different methods of organization when drafting. Notice that in the second paragraph we echo two other drafts we produced earlier, concerning rain forests and gorillas. As you continue drafting, it is wise to consider how your various attempts might fit together. You will then have a clearer idea of the final form your essay will take.

The Final Draft

Deciding when you have done enough is never easy. You can always think of one more thing that might make an important difference. But an end must come to drafting. Perhaps you will know when to stop because you are completely satisfied with what you have produced in your different experiments. Perhaps you will have exhausted all the possibilities you can think of in the time you have. Whatever the reason, you will reach a point when you need to pull your various attempts together, pick the ones that look most promising, and write what might be the final draft. We say that it *might* be the final draft because, in fact, you may go through several versions before you have one that you like. We call it a final *draft* because even when you have produced a version you like, it is not yet a finished essay. Revision still lies ahead. Nevertheless, in order to refine a paper it is necessary to have it before you in as complete a form as possible.

Because in the following section we will discuss the techniques of revision, we will present here our choice for a final draft. Compare it with the earlier attempts in this section. You will notice we have used parts of most of them here, but we have introduced new material as well. The process of writing is never static and new ideas will always occur. Examine the organization of the entire draft. You will find that there is no single method used throughout. In most essays, the author will make use of many different techniques as he or she goes from point to point, and we have tried to make our draft reflect this mixture.

THERE IS NOTHING LIKE A GOOD ZOO

It is December, and a small, but ever-increasing number of people are about to do something irrational. Faced with high utility bills, soaring food costs, and huge credit-card balances, they are going to increase their debts even more. They are not, however, going to spend that money on gifts although December is the season of gift giving. They are going to use those credit cards to join their local zoological societies. Why would anyone want to give money to a zoo, especially in December? What is there about a zoo that would encourage people to further over extend their credit.

Some would argue that these people are going through a second childhood, after all zoos, according to them, are for children. They might even defend their argument by saying that these people are trying to escape the real world by visiting the zoos and acting like children for a while.

Zoos do have many diversions for people who wish to escape. I know that as soon as I enter the main gate of a zoo I feel I have left the city behind. The crowds gathered around the gate and the souvenir shops seem somehow to be different to me than similar crowds on the city streets. The concrete walks and the asphalt roads of a zoo seem more wonderous than the walks and roads of a city. The people on them are not the same threatening crowds blocking my way. In the zoo these people become to me families, loving couples, happy children, and tired loners who are all caught up in the same excitement. I like these people more in the zoo than I do in the city.

The first special exhibit I always try to visit is a favorite diversion of mine. If the zoo has a rain forest that is where I head first. No dictionary definition of a rain forest will ever prepare a person for a well-planned exhibit. The *American Heritage Dictionary*, for example, defines a rain forest as "a dense evergreen forest occupying a tropical region with an annual rainfall of at least 100 inches." The Rain Forest of the Topeka Zoo would seem to be modelled on that definition, although the rainfall is artificial and the Kansas climate cannot really be called tropical. But once inside the exhibit visitors quickly realize that there is much more to rain forests than location, trees, and rain.

It is a world that most of us will never get to see except at a zoo. It is so removed from where and how the majority of people live that it might as well be called a Venusian forest. The visitor is immediately lost in a riot of greens, browns, yellows, and reds as soon as he or she enters the exhibit. Colorful flying birds fill the air, crawling reptiles litter the ground, and snakes hang from the branches. Everywhere there is something extraordinary. If you look carefully you will even see flying foxes hanging from the supports of the roof. What is a rain forest exhibition? It is really a place to forget your problems and enjoy unique sights.

Yet another diversion zoos can offer visitors is the version of trivial pursuit. For example the San Diego Zoo has an elaborate gorilla exhibit that tries to reproduce the right habitat for the animals. While it is fun to spend the time simply watching the gorillas, this fun can be considerably increased by reading the large sign in front of the exhibit that explains to the viewers that there are actually three kinds of gorillas. Gorillas are divided, first of all into two major classes, mountain and lowland gorillas. Mountain gorillas are the largest of all often weighing more than five hundred pounds. They are very black and have very long hair. As their name implies, they live in the mountains and need the black coloring to absorb as much heat as possible and the long hair to keep that heat as long as possible. There are only about five hundred mountain gorillas now in the wild, and there are none in any zoo. As a result the visitors must be content with a photograph attached to the sign.

Lowland gorillas come in two types. The western lowland gorilla averages about a hundred pounds less than mountain gorillas. This type ranges in color from black to grayish brown and has very short hair. They are far more abundant, relatively speaking, than mountain gorillas with about 35,000 now living in the wild. Western lowland gorillas are the most common gorillas people see in zoos.

Eastern lowland gorillas have characteristics that place them somewhere between western lowland gorillas and mountain gorillas. They weigh more than the western but less than the mountain gorillas. It is darker than the western but not as black as the mountain and the hair length is also in between that of the other two types. About 5,000 eastern gorillas now live in the wild, and very few zoos have them.

Equipped with this information, the visitor can now turn to the game of "Which Is Which?" Looking over the gorillas carefully, the game begins. Which are the darker ones? Which have longer hair? Is the one resting on that branch heavier than the ones at the base of this tree? Are all three gorillas feeding in that corner western lowland gorillas? Or is the middle one actually an eastern one? How black does a gorilla have to be before it qualifies as an eastern one? People can quickly get caught up in this game as they seek out that rare eastern lowland gorilla, and for that time forget the city outside the zoo. Identifying a particular kind of gorilla will not pay the bills, but it is nice to do anyhow.

But these diversions are more than fun for the people doing them, they are healthful as well. Living each day forces us to deal with problems that can seriously depress us. Worrying about money, the next exam, what the boss is thinking, the repairs the car needs, the crime rate, or the quality of our air and water can give us a warped view of our lives and the world we live in. We become so preoccupied with our worries that we begin to think that they are all there is to life, and that is when we begin to withdraw. Nothing seems worthwhile.

How do rain forests and gorilla help? Many people do not seem to realize their value. These are the ones who think zoos are only for children. Many of them would go so far as to say that zoos are a drain on tax money that should go to more important projects. Zoos, however, are not luxuries. The taxes spent on them are well spent.

They give us a chance to wonder about our world and to learn more about it than the limited spot we choose for our homes and jobs. Rain forests show us that there is much more to our world than the streets that we live on or the headlines in the local newspaper. They don't give us an escape but a more complete view of our world. They give us a chance to be curious about sights we have never seen before and a sense of amazement that such things really exist on this planet.

And trying to identify the different kinds of gorillas gives us a chance to prove to ourselves that we are capable of learning for the pleasure of learning. There may be no practical benefit from being able to tell the difference between eastern and western lowland gorilla, but who cares. We should be allowed to enjoy some things for their own sake and to notice details simply because they are there.

Several years ago the newspapers were filled with stories about a University of Michigan freshman who had suddenly dropped out of sight. He was a remarkably intelligent young man who had entered the university at the age of fifteen. The papers throughout the midwest carried the story and his picture, but for three days there was no new information.

Finally, a friend came forward and told one of the strangest stories imaginable. The missing student was a fanatic player of Dungeons and Dragons. He had decided to invent the ultimate playing field for this game, and he had gone into the old heating tunnels that criss-crossed the campus. People immediately took up the search and they found him a day later still wandering the tunnels completely involved in his private game.

Wasn't this freshman doing what many people do when they seek out new sights and experiences in order to escape from the pressures of their lives? Perhaps everyone needs to recognize this need for a rest before things become too much and the mind snaps. Perhaps it would have helped that student if he had visited a zoo occassionally. Perhaps he should have joined a zoological society.

The most noticeable feature of this final draft is its length. Like most final drafts, it is too long, and we will have to do some cutting when we revise.

Once you have gotten over the length, we hope you also notice what we selected to include and what we left out. Selection is the key to writing final drafts. For example, we chose our second opening because we liked the question it raised. We felt that the question directly confronted an attitude that many readers would hold about zoos. By raising it early, we acknowledged that impression and implied that we would deal with it in the body of the essay. Such a tactic gave us a chance of holding on to those readers.

We selected the second ending for our final draft because its dramatic anecdote highlighted the serious side of our meaning: zoos are not an escape from reality; they supply a corrective to our narrow view of the world. The contrast between the rich variety of sights in a zoo and the freshman walking through the confining underground tunnels was too good to pass up.

Our decision to delete most of the walk through the zoo and all mention of buffalo, deer, camels, lions, and tigers may be surprising. We felt that this part of our drafting did not advance our meaning very well. Because we had spent so much time describing the animals, we said little about how we found watching them relaxing. All we managed to say was that, because the animals appeared calm, we felt calm. And we said that over and over again.

We kept the descriptions of the rain forest and the gorilla exhibit because they dealt more concretely with our reactions. In each case we were able to explain why we found the exhibit both relaxing and thought provoking. Although the discussion of the gorillas in particular will need further refinement, both passages support our meaning more clearly than the narrative does.

Moreover, by keeping the passages on the rain forest and the gorillas, we are able to keep the conceptual redraft as well. It makes the most direct statement of our message and explains how these two exhibits support it. Thus, all three choices are closely related to one another.

Writing a final draft, of course, involves more than choosing among paragraphs and whole passages. Paragraph 2, for instance, is new. We wrote it because we felt we needed something between the question raised in the first paragraph and the entrance into the zoo in the third. By detailing the negative attitudes that some people hold before we offered our positive one, we hoped to forestall later objections. In effect, we said, "We know that some of you might believe this, but give us a chance to tell you what we think."

Working on the final draft for an essay is the critical point in the writing process. It is then that you make commitments to your message and its form. These commitments should not be made lightly. You should try to have reasons for keeping every part you include and for omitting those you leave out. You can always change your mind and rewrite part or all of the draft, but revision will go more smoothly if you can first explain to yourself why you like your final draft.

Drafting and Structure

In this section we have illustrated some of the most common methods of organization and how they can help you as you shape your meaning in the drafting stage. Many other organizational techniques exist; as you practice drafting, you will naturally develop your own versions of each of them. Drafting is, after all, as much a process of discovery as is prewriting.

We have included in this section a group of essays that illustrate just how diverse organizational techniques can be. As you read, consider these techniques carefully. The study questions and exercises will aid you in experimenting with as many methods as possible. Few topics demand only one kind of organization. As a result, the choices you make will often be personal ones, based on what you think works best. If you explore a number of possibilities rather than grab the first organizational technique you can think of, your choices have a better chance of being good ones.

Mary and Joe, Chicago-Style

Mike Royko

M ary and Joe were flat broke when they got off *1* the bus in Chicago. They didn't know anybody and she was expecting a baby.

They went to a cheap hotel. But the clerk jerked his thumb at the *2* door when they couldn't show a day's rent in advance.

They walked the streets until they saw a police station. The desk *3* sergeant said they couldn't sleep in a cell, but he told them how to get to the Cook County Department of Public Aid.

A man there said they couldn't get regular assistance because they *4* hadn't been Illinois residents long enough. But he gave them the address of the emergency welfare office on the West Side.

It was a two-mile walk up Madison Street to 19 S. Damen. Someone *5* gave them a card with a number on it and they sat down on a bench, stared at the peeling green paint and waited for their number to be called.

Two hours later, a caseworker motioned them forward, took out blank *6* forms and asked questions: Any relatives? Any means of getting money? Any assets?

Joe said he owned a donkey. The caseworker told him not to get *7* smart or he'd be thrown out. Joe said he was sorry.

The caseworker finished the forms and said they were entitled to *8* emergency CTA fare to County Hospital because of Mary's condition. And he told Joe to go to an Urban Progress Center for occupational guidance.

Joe thanked him and they took a bus to the hospital. A guard told *9* them to wait on a bench. They waited two hours, then Mary got pains and they took her away. Someone told Joe to come back tomorrow.

He went outside and asked a stranger on the street for directions to *10* an Urban Progress Center. The stranger hit Joe on the head and took his overcoat. Joe was still lying there when a paddy wagon came along so they pinched him for being drunk on the street.

Mary had a baby boy during the night. She didn't know it, but three *11* foreign-looking men in strange, colorful robes came to the hospital asking about her and the baby. A guard took them for hippies and called the police. They found odd spices on the men so the narcotics detail took them downtown for further questioning.

The next day Mary awoke in a crowded ward. She asked for Joe. *12* Instead, a representative of the Planned Parenthood Committee came by to give her a lecture on birth control.

Next, a social worker came for her case history. She asked Mary who *13* the father was. Mary answered and the social worker ran for the nurse. The nurse questioned her and Mary answered. The nurse stared at her and ran for the doctor. The doctor wrote "Post partum delusion" on her chart.

An ambulance took Mary to the Cook County Mental Health Clinic *14* the next morning. A psychiatrist asked her questions and pursed his lips at the answers.

A hearing was held and a magistrate commited her to the Chicago *15* State Hospital, Irving Park and Narragansett.

Joe got out of the House of Correction a couple of days later and went *16* to the County Hospital for Mary. They told him she was at Chicago State and the baby had been placed in a foster home by the State Department of Children and Family Services.

When Joe got to Chicago State, a doctor told him what Mary had said *17* about the baby's birth. Joe said Mary was telling the truth. They put Joe in a ward at the other end of the hospital.

Meanwhile, the three strangely dressed foreign-looking men were re- *18* leased after the narcotics detail could find no laws prohibiting the possession of myrrh and frankincense. They returned to the hospital and were taken for civil rights demonstrators. They were held in the County Jail on $100,000 bond.

By luck, Joe and Mary met on the hospital grounds. They decided to *19* tell the doctors what they wanted to hear. The next day they were declared sane and were released.

When they applied for custody of Mary's baby, however, they were *20* told it was necessary for them to first establish a proper residence, earn a proper income and create a suitable environment.

They applied at the Urban Progress Center for training under the *21* Manpower Development Program. Joe said he was good at working with wood. He was assigned to a computer data-processing class. Mary said she'd gladly do domestic work. She was assigned to a course in key-punch operating. Both got $20-a-week stipends.

Several months later they finished the training. Joe got a job in a gas *22* station and Mary went to work as a waitress.

They saved their money and hired a lawyer. Another custody hearing *23* was held and several days later the baby was ordered returned to them.

Reunited finally, they got back to their two-room flat and met the *24* landlord on the steps. He told them Urban Renewal had ordered the building torn down. The City Relocation Bureau would get them another place.

They packed, dressed the baby and hurried to the Greyhound bus *25* station.

Joe asked the ticket man when the next bus was leaving. *26*

"Where to?" the ticket man asked. *27*

"Anywhere," Joe said, "as long as it is right now."   *28*

He gave Joe three tickets and in five minutes they were on a bus *29* heading for southern Illinois—the area known as "Little Egypt."

Just as the bus pulled out, the three strangely dressed men ran into *30* the station. But they were too late. It was gone.

So they started hiking down U.S. 66. But at last report they were *31* pinched on suspicion of being foreigners in illegal possession of gold.

Study Questions

1. At first reading, "Mary and Joe, Chicago-Style" might seem to be more like a short story than an essay. Why might Royko have chosen to discuss the treatment of the poor in this manner? What kind of a response is he trying to elicit from his audience?
2. Royko clearly wants his readers to see the parallels between Mary and Joe and the biblical Mary and Joseph. How much of the bible story does his audience need to know in order to appreciate his meaning? How much of his meaning would be missed if readers failed to make the connection?
3. Since he makes use of the Bible, is it Royko's point that people have not changed since the birth of Christ? What differences between the biblical story and his own does he try to emphasize? How important are these differences for a proper understanding of his message?
4. In "Mary and Joe, Chicago-Style," Royko's chief method of organization is temporal. Identify the words and phrases used to signal that organization to his readers.

Suggestion for Drafting

By presenting his essay as a narrative, Royko takes the risk that readers will miss his point. He implies his theme rather then explicitly states it, and he depends on his readers to interpret him correctly. When it works, this indirect method can make writing fun and reading enjoyable, but its success depends on both the writer's ability to give clear clues to his meaning and the reader's skill in using them.

Suppose you want to write an essay that covers the same topic as "Mary and Joe, Chicago-Style," but you prefer to take the safer route of directly stating your message. Choose a single passage in Royko's essay that suggests some bureaucratic attitude toward the poor. First state what that attitude is, and then give a "modern" example. Compare your draft with the original passage. What changes in language and "personality" does your redrafting produce?

Days of Valor

Fighting the Wild

Joanna L. Stratton

"Imagine, if you can, these pioneer women so suddenly transplanted from homes of comforts in eastern states to these bare, treeless, wind-swept, sun-scorched prairies with no comforts, not even a familiar face."

Lizzie Anthony Opdyke

F or settlers like the Opdykes, Kansas was a 1 harsh and formidable environment. Settling miles apart from one another, the emigrants faced the starkness of the wilderness alone. Deprivation, isolation and desolation were facets of everyday life for men and women alike.

To the pioneer woman, the day-to-day uncertainties of wilderness life 2 proved especially harrowing. During the working hours of the day, her husband was frequently too far out of range to respond to any call for assistance. Furthermore, circumstances often required him to leave his family for days or weeks at a time. Setting off on trading or hunting expeditions, the frontiersman left his family unguarded with only the hope of his safe return.

Such long absences were wearing for the waiting mother. Burdened 3 with both the maintenance and the protection of the family homestead, she could rely on no one but herself. In these lonely circumstances, she fought the wilderness with her own imagination, skill, common sense and determination.

Allena A. Clark had her own ways of coping with a lonely day or a 4 sudden emergency. Her daughter Esther remembered:

". . . the unbroken prairies stretched for miles outside, and the wistful- 5 faced sheep were always near at hand. Often mother used to go out and lie down among them, for company, when she was alone for the day.

"When the spring freshets came, the sheep were on the wrong side of 6 the river, and it was my mother who manned one of the three wagons that went back and forth across the rising waters until the last sheep was safely on the home side. She has told me of the terror that possessed her during those hours, with the water coming up steadily to the wagon bed. To this day, there is a superstitious dread of water in the heart of every one of our family.

"Mother has always been the gamest one of us. I can remember her *7* hanging on to the reins of a runaway mule team, her black hair tumbling out of its pins and over her shoulders, her face set and white, while one small girl clung with chattering teeth to the sides of the rocking wagon and a baby sister bounced about on the floor in paralyzed wonder. I remember, too, the things the men said about 'Leny's nerve.' But I think, as much courage as it took to hang on to the reins that day, it took more to live twenty-four hours at a time, month in and out, on the lonely and lovely prairie, without giving up to the loneliness."

That loneliness, usually borne with dignity and silence, could at times *8* express itself in unexpected ways. Mary Furguson Darrah recalled a time when "Mr. Hilton, a pioneer, told his wife that he was going to Little River for wood. She asked to go with him . . . She hadn't seen a tree for two years, and when they arrived at Little River she put her arms around a tree and hugged it until she was hysterical."

Nightfall, blanketing the prairie in a dense, boundless blackness, *9* brought an even keener sense of solitude to the pioneer home. The profound silence was broken only by the occasional chirr of a cricket or the gentle swish of the tall prairie grass—or by the call of the wild. For it was during the black nights that the howl of the coyote and the wolf spread terror through every frontier homestead. Often roaming the plains in packs, these rapacious animals would attack without provocation or mercy.

"In the summer of 1872 and '73," recalled S. N. Hoisington, "the gray *10* wolves and coyotes were very numerous. It was not safe to go out across the prairies without a weapon of some kind. My mother was a nurse and doctor combined. In early girlhood she used to help her brother mix his medicines, and after she came to Kansas people came for miles for her to doctor their families.

"A man by the name of Johnson had filed on a claim just west of us, *11* and had built a sod house. He and his wife lived there two years, when he went to Salina to secure work. He was gone two or three months, and wrote home once or twice, but his wife grew very homesick for her folks in the east, and would come over to our house to visit mother.

"Mother tried to cheer her up, but she continued to worry until she *12* got bed fast with the fever. At night she was frightened because the wolves would scratch on the door, on the sod and on the windows, so my mother and I started to sit up nights with her. I would bring my revolver and ammunition and axe, and some good-sized clubs.

"The odor from the sick woman seemed to attract the wolves, and *13* they grew bolder and bolder. I would step out, fire off the revolver and they would settle back for a while when they would start a new attack. I shot one through the window and I found him lying dead in the morning.

"Finally the woman died and mother laid her out. Father took some *14* wide boards that we had in our loft and made a coffin for her. Mother made a pillow and trimmed it with black cloth, and we also painted the coffin black.

"After that the wolves were more determined than ever to get in. One *15* got his head in between the door casing and as he was trying to wriggle through, mother struck him in the head with an axe and killed him. I shot one coming through the window. After that they quieted down for about half an hour, when they came back again. I stepped out and fired at two of them but I only wounded one. Their howling was awful. We fought these wolves five nights in succession, during which time we killed and wounded four gray wolves and two coyotes.

"When Mr. Johnson arrived home and found his wife dead and his *16* house badly torn down by wolves he fainted away. . . . After the funeral he sold out and moved away."

To apprehensive settlers, the coyote was not the only terror of the *17* night. Prairie fires, sweeping furiously across the plains, were a constant worry to families isolated on separate homesteads. From late summer through the autumn months, the endless miles of tall prairie grass became a vast tinderbox, dry and brown from the scorching summer weather. It took only a quick spark from an untended campfire or a passing train engine, or a stroke of lightning, to set the countryside ablaze. Within minutes, great clouds of heavy black smoke would fill the autumn air, and the skies would redden from the brilliant inferno below.

"In those days of endless sweep of prairies," wrote Agnes Barry, *18* "when the tall grass became dry from premature drying from drought or early frost, it was a signal for close vigilance in watching the horizon all around for prairie fires. A light against the sky told of a prairie fire in that direction and great anxiety was felt if the wind happened to be in your direction. At times the fires would be such that the flames could be seen creeping up the hillsides, and would spread over great stretches of ground. The Saline River which almost surrounded our place was considered a security, but sometimes the gales of wind blowing masses of loose grass or weeds would cause the fire to 'jump' the river. Excitement was keen whenever the fires were seen, and the men always took wet sacks and hastened to fight the flames, sometimes working for hours before it was under control."

For protection against the fires, most homesteaders plowed wide strips *19* of ground around their property. Although these furrows were designed to halt the spread of any fire, they were not always foolproof. Sweeping flames carried by a stiff wind could easily jump a fire guard and threaten homes and fields alike. In this regard, the frontier family was always on guard and stood ready to battle any sudden fire. At the first sign of smoke or flames, they raced forward with buckets of water, pails of dirt, and wet blankets or grain sacks to help douse the flames.

Lillian Smith well remembered the many nights spent fighting fires 20 which threatened her family's farm. "Many a time my mother stayed up all night watching the red glare of the prairie fires in more than one direction, in fear and trembling that they might come swooping down upon us asleep in our little log cabin. However, she was always prepared. As soon as she would see the fire getting close, away we would go with our buckets of water and rags tied to hoes, rakes and sticks, wet them and set a back fire to meet the monster coming, so when it reached our line we would stand still and wait until we knew it had passed us by for that time.

"There were no barns then, so frames for sheds and stables were 21 constructed of small trees cut from the timber, and haystacks were built beside them for walls, the tops covered with hay, in that way making good shelters for cows and horses. With such things that close to the house, one can realize in what a position we would be in case one of those prairie fires had reached them."

Harriet Walter also had vivid memories of the fires which threatened 22 her family's farm in Lincoln. "One spring a heavy smoke was seen in the southeast over towards Minersville, and Mr. McIntyre, as was the custom of every man when the fire was not near his home, grabbed a sack and went to meet it. His neighbor, George, living a mile south, had a very cross cow and everyone in the community was afraid of her, as she did not hesitate at all to use her horns on anyone except her owner. So, when Mr. McIntyre came bounding down the hill from the north, he was frightened nearly to death to find that he had almost leaped on this cow. It was hard to tell which was the more frightened, the cow or himself, but he certainly felt a great relief to see the cow turn tail and flee.

"As he advanced to meet the fire he found a great many of the neigh- 23 bors already fighting, with blackened faces and smarting eyes. Before it was put out an old Irish woman, by the name of Porter, was burned trying to save her possessions, and our home was saved with the fire a little more than a mile away. Another time one came from the northeast crossing our farm diagonally, burning quite a bit of hay and the hedge trees which had been set with a great deal of care and labor around each forty of land.

"One day in May I was gathering wild flowers on a hill opposite our 24 house when I discovered fire creeping along the roadside and almost to a meadow which was in front of our house. The grass there was very tall and rank, and I knew, child that I was, that if the fire ever got in there our home was doomed. What would you have done? Well, I took off my petticoat and beat till I was exhausted but every spark was out.

"The worst scare that I ever had by fire, though, was when a little girl *25*
of eight. We had been out with father burning off the pasture as was the
custom of every spring, because the grass grew so rank and the new
growth would come on quicker if the old was burned off. So on Saturday
evening, as there was no wind, we all assisted in the 'burning off.' Sunday
afternoon the wind veered to the north and a cowchip which had smoul-
dered unnoticed was blown into some trash along the hedge row and the
mischief was done.

"My father's feed lots were perhaps an eighth of a mile south of this *26*
hedge row. I've forgotten what the fence was made of, but I think of
six-inch plank. One thing I remember vividly and that was the wind
break which was one hundred feet long, and the sheds were of prairie
hay. I realized only too well what that meant. My childish mind was
filled with horror as I ran to my father to tell him the awful news. He
sent me to a neighbor a quarter of a mile away for help and I ran, gasping
for breath when I arrived. The men succeeded in saving all the stock
except one small calf which ran back into the flames. My, what a
brawling and turmoil there was though, because all animals seem to be
crazed by fire."

In 1877, Anna and Jacob Ruppenthal brought their five children to a *27*
homestead ten miles north of Wilson, Kansas. Like other families, the
Ruppenthals experienced the trials and tribulations of farming on the
wide-open prairie. As J. C. Ruppenthal later explained, prairie fires were
a constant source of worry:

"In the days of endless sweep of prairie, of grass without limit for *28*
many, many miles, the ripening of the grass in early fall or its premature
drying from drought was signal for renewal of nightly vigilance in watching the horizon all around. Every light against the sky told of a prairie
fire in that direction. The direction of the wind, either from or opposite
the direction of such fire, or sidewise, the unsteadiness of wind with
possibility of veering so as to bring fire toward the home—all these were
noted. The last act at night, after seeing that the children were all asleep,
and all quiet among the livestock in sheds, pens and corrals, was to
sweep the entire horizon for signs of flame.

"Many times, on awakening in the dead of night, the room was light *29*
with reflection from the sky, shining thru uncurtained windows from some
fire ten or twenty or fifty miles away. Often in the small hours mother
watched from window to window to see if the light died away, indicating
that the fire had gone out, or had grown brighter threatening a wider
scope of blackened prairie behind it.

"At times the flames themselves were visible at night up to twenty or *30*
twenty-five miles away, as they crept up hills in the buffalo grass, or
flared longer in redtop bunch grass, and when the fire rolled down into
a hollow in big blue stem grass, though the flames might not be seen, the
general red glare in the sky told somewhat of the heat and light from the

tall grass below. Despite the fear inspired by a prairie fire, there was a fascination to watch a fire by night, advancing, brightening, showing masses of solid flame or myriads of tiny jets that flickered and went out, to flash again farther along. At times the silhouettes of men fighting could be seen against the background of distant flames.

"Some freighters, in revenge for the shutting off of the road by the *31* Twin Groves by Philip Gabel, set fire to the dry grass between Dry Hollow and our log house. We new settlers were without the slightest notion what to do. Father hastily turned the livestock loose. The wagon was drawn onto a patch of plowed ground near the house. Household goods were hastily carried out to the same place of refuge.

"Then father took a shovel and started toward the fire raging in flames *32* in tall blue stem grass in the creek bottom 80 rods away. A man dashed up on horseback and called to him to drop his shovel and get some wet grain sacks. At once the five children huddled on the plowed patch were admonished to stay there. Mother and father each seized the 'American extra heavy A seamless' white grain sacks, dipped them into water to wet them well, and then hastened toward the fire.

"A number of neighbors came too, and perhaps a dozen or so in all *33* fought the flames for hours and finally subdued them, though considerable good timber was burned over and fine young trees killed. In this fight with fire, fear lent power to mother and she fought without stopping, heeding nothing of the admonitions of the men fighters who assured her she need not work so hard. She wet sacks and carried sacks and smote the flames of burning grass, even as any of the men, and ventured to the thickest and hottest of the line where the fire ate steadily into the dry grass.

"Several years later a similar prairie fire swept down on the east side *34* of the homestead. Again mother pressed to the front and labored there until all danger was past. For the several women who gathered but took no part she had a feeling very akin to contempt, tho not disclosed to them. For her, there was danger and she saw nothing but to exert every ounce of strength to beat out the fire."

Women gradually learned to cope with prairie loneliness and to cherish *35* whatever neighboring was possible. "There was just a cotton-wood cabin on the farm," recalled Anne Bingham, "with one room and a loft reached by a ladder. There was not a tree nearer than the little creek, and our nearest neighbor lived in a 'ravine' out of sight about a half a mile away. We were as much isolated as if we were miles from a neighbor, and not a dwelling in sight. I never saw a light from a home at night all the time we lived on the farm.

"Our home in the ravine was miles from the highway, but I had the *36* satisfaction of knowing that when anyone came to see us, they did not come from convenience on the way, but really did want to see us. Then we were not troubled with tramps. But I did wish many times that we lived on the road to relieve the loneliness and besides in case of accident or sudden illness or snake bite."

The isolation of frontier living seemed particularly alarming during *37* times of unforeseen crisis. Sudden accidents, illness, or death often became terrifying ordeals when the nearest neighbor or town lay many miles away. Pregnancy and childbirth involved particular apprehension for the pioneer woman and her family. During pregnancy, adequate medical suervision was totally lacking. Likewise, the expectant mother often had very little female company to console and guide her through any difficult times. Worse yet, an unbalanced diet, a heavy work load and poor housing conditions placed serious physical handicaps on the pregnant woman and her unborn child as well.

Childbirth itself was often the most difficult time of all. For the most *38* part, women struggled through labor and delivery with little assistance. While a practicing physician was occasionally available to them, blizzards, floods or other mishaps often delayed him unitl it was too late. In many communities, the tireless hands of an experienced midwife brought some relief to the new mother. Yet all too often the woman isolated on her homestead found no medical help forthcoming. Instead, she relied only on the assistance of an anxious husband, a concerned neighbor or an older son or daughter.

One woman, Mrs. A. S. Lecleve, did not have even this much help. *39* As her daughter, Annette Lecleve Botkin, shyly explained, "My parents settled in Rice County, Kansas, in 1873. Their house was three miles from the nearest neighbor. Ellsworth or Sterling was their nearest trading point, both over sixteen miles away.

"It was the last of July, and my father was thinking of the long winter *40* ahead, and perhaps the blizzards to come. And at that time there was not a tree in sight. The little four-room frame house (at that time the only frame house in the county) had to be kept warm, for there were a couple of little children already in the home and the stork was expected to make his appearance again in a short time. So my father arose early and started on his all-day trip to Mule Creek to get a load of wood. Mule Creek was about seventeen miles away.

"He had no sooner gotten out of sight, than my mother knew that the *41* stork, being an undependable sort of bird, had decided that it was time to leave his precious bundle. Now that was a terrifying situation. Alone with two babies, one four and the other eighteen months, not a neighbor that could be called, no doctor to be gotten.

"So my brave mother got the baby clothes together on a chair by the *42* bed, water and scissors and what else was needed to take care of the baby; drew a bucket of fresh water from a sixty-foot well; made some bread-and-butter sandwiches; set out some milk for the babies. And when Rover had orders to take care of the babies he never let them out of his sight, for at that time any bunch of weeds might harbor a rattle-snake.

"So, at about noon the stork left a fine baby boy. My father arrived 43 home about dusk with a big load of wood and congratulating himself that he would at least have some wood to burn on very cold days. My mother, having fainted a number of times in her attempt to dress the baby, had succeeded at last; and when my father came in he found a very uncomfortable but brave and thankful mother, thankful that he had returned home with the precious wood, and that she and the baby were alright."

In these difficult times, the pioneer mother experienced many such 44 long and lonely hours awaiting the return of her husband from his daily expeditions. During her first years of pioneering, Anne Bingham composed, in the romantic diction of the time, an account of the quiet expectancy and dread she felt as a young wife. Fifty years later she sent the account to Lilla Day Monroe, noting that she spent "days and days of it when my husband was obliged to go to town":

"The day is gone. The sunbeams slant across the room and shadows 45 lengthening out of doors are further thrown upon the grassy hillsides, almost enfolding them in fond embrace.

"A woman sits alone. Her work is done and she looks anxiously at 46 the time to see if the hour has not arrived when her loved one will be at home, for she has been alone all day with just a little child to bear her company.

"The hours fly fast when work employs, but tired hands and anxious 47 heart must give up now, and watch the distance down the road as far as eye can reach. The dear one is so prompt to come, that she can measure out the time almost that he will be away.

"He is not yet in sight. She rests her straining eyes, shading them 48 with her hands from the rays of the setting sun.

"The minutes go so slow and he should be here now. Oh, what if 49 something may have happened and she would never look into those dear eyes again. She cannot bear the thought and her own eyes grow dim with gathering tears.

"The little child draws near and seeing the anxious look tries to com- 50 fort, saying, 'Don't worry, Mama, Papa'll come soon.' The dog shares in the longing for his master, and trots along the path, stopping to listen for the tread of the horses' feet. He crouches low, and finally springing up, pricks up his ears and barking joyously, bounds away to meet the moving object just coming into view, across the span between the clumps of trees.

"As the fond absent one draws nearer, the woman's anxious look is 51 lessening and tears are almost falling in blessed thankfulness.

"The sun has gone below the western horizon and dewy fragrance falls 52 upon the valley. She whose lonely hours were filled with loving thoughts and anxious heart wears now a happy look and says when he is near enough to hear, 'I am so glad that you are safe at home.' The loving child raises her tiny face to get the welcome kiss and greets her papa with 'I knew that you would come, dear papa, I knew that you could come.'

"The scene is changed and now the woman looks no longer, for her *53* dear family is all away, to come no more. She now looks forward to the time when she will go to them. All her hours are lonely now and memory only brings her sad and mournful thoughts of bygone days."

Study Questions

1. What are Joanna Stratton's feelings toward the women she describes in "Days of Valor: Fighting the Wild"? How does she make these feelings clear to her readers?
2. A quick glance at the punctuation of the essay shows that well over two-thirds of the text is actually from other writers and speakers. What effect does such a heavy dependence on quotations have on the readers' attitude toward Stratton's topic? How is her message clarified by these quotations?
3. Temporal organization is used in each of the quotations, but Stratton employs a different type of organization to integrate them into the essay. What is that method? What words and phrases signal this organization to the readers?
4. Is there a formal conclusion to this essay? If there is, how does Stratton signal its beginning? If there is not, how does the lack of one affect the readers?

Suggestion for Drafting

The key to Joanna Stratton's "Days of Valor: Fighting the Wild" lies in two sentences in her introductory paragraphs:

Deprivation, isolation and desolation were facets of everyday life for men and women alike.
To the pioneer woman, the day-to-day uncertainties of wilderness life proved especially harrowing.

Through these two sentences Stratton suggests the scope of her meaning and the special emphasis it will have. The many quotations that follow illustrate the "day-to-day uncertainties of wilderness life" for the pioneer women.

What if Stratton had confined her discussion to just one of these uncertainties: the threat of fire? Such a narrowing of the body of the essay would require changes in her opening and closing paragraphs. After rereading the passage on fires (paragraphs 17–34), write a new introduction and conclusion that would be appropriate if only that section were the body of the essay.

The Education of a Feminist: Part One

Susan Jacoby

The problem lay buried, unspoken, for many years in the minds of American women. It was a strange stirring, a sense of dissatisfaction, a yearning that women suffered in the middle of the twentieth century in the United States. Each suburban wife struggled with it alone. As she made beds, shopped for groceries, matched slip-cover material, ate peanut butter sandwiches with her children, chauffeured Cub Scouts and Brownies, lay beside her husband at night—she was afraid to ask even of herself the silent question—"Is this all?"

T he opening lines of *The Feminine Mystique* 1 did not, I confess, grip the imagination of a nineteen-year-old "comp lit" student with the familiar lyricism of "it was the best of times, it was the worst of times"; the appealing, if cockeyed, certainty that "happy families are all alike," or the blunt force of "I am an American, Chicago-born." Nor did they fit into an intellectual framework that was being formed not only by an eccentric, self-selected course of fiction (Michigan State University, in 1964, gave its honor students complete freedom to avoid a well-rounded education if they would only read *something* and pay no attention to the rumbles of discontent being heard from a far-off place called Berkeley) but by the more predictable collegiate influences of Freud, Marx, Hegel, Kant, *et al.*

Nevertheless, it was Betty Friedan's book (not, of course, recom- 2 mended or required for any college course) which initiated a slow intellectual process that was to change my mind and my life. It has been just fifteen years since I picked up a copy of the first paperback edition of *The Feminine Mystique*; in this short epoch, as epochs go, modern feminism has become a movement with so many powerful political and emotional implications that many Americans have forgotten, if they ever knew, about the intellectual void that had to be filled before a "women's movement" could exist.

The tumultuous activism of the movement is not the only factor that 3 has obscured the intellectual foundations of contemporary feminism. It has become unfashionable to speak of intellectualism with respect in almost any context. The very word "intellectual," battered from the left and from the right (remember *The Greening of America* on one hand and the collected speeches of Spiro Agnew on the other), has acquired fusty, pejorative connotations. The Oxford English Dictionary's definition of an intellectual as an "enlightened person" is no longer in favor, even among people who would at one time have been proud to consider themselves intellectuals. At best, the once-honorable word conjures up visions of an owlish, irrelevant, hopelessly *middle-class* professor entombed by a wall of books. Many feminists, stung by charges that the movement is meaningful only to middle-class women, are particularly uneasy about the intellectual (and social) origins of the current wave of feminism. But the fact is plain: The unfinished feminist revolution began—though it has not ended—with a book written by a privileged middle-class woman who had enjoyed the benefits of an elite education (in contrast to other modern revolutions, which began with books written by privileged middle-class men).

The dog-eared pages of my old copy of *The Feminine Mystique* are 4 smeared with dried ketchup stains and undergraduate exclamation points in the margins—testimony to the fact that the book was well read. I look at those pages, and I have no trouble remembering my excitement at the title of the first chapter: "The Problem That Has No Name." Not that a light bulb flashed on over my head in comic-strip fashion; it took some years for me to realize that feminism might be as valuable an intellectual tool as any other set of ideas. But I recognized the problem that had no name—right from the start. I had grown up with it, but what is one to do or think about a "problem" that lacks a definition?

It is difficult to describe, without seeming to exaggerate, the condition 5 of anger and bewilderment that was the lot of a bright, ambitious girl growing up in an ordinary American town, receiving an ordinary American education, in the 1950s. I stress the word "ordinary." It is no accident that most leaders and theoreticians of the feminist movement either grew up in the large cities that are the centers of culture in the United States or were educated at the old Eastern women's colleges which, whatever their deficiencies, had the singular virtue of exposing young women to a concentration of brilliant female minds not to be found in other American institutions.*

* The chief drawback of these institutions, before most of them shifted to co-education in the late 1960's, was hopelessly entangled with their major asset. Surrounded by extremely bright young women as classmates, encouraged to express themselves by the presence of so many accomplished older women, the graduates of these prestigious colleges went out into the world with almost no experience of speaking up in front of or competing with men. Given the outstanding intellectual qualifications and privileged economic backgrounds of so many of the students, the surprising fact is not that the Seven Sisters produced so many women leaders but that they produced so few.

Again, I stress the ordinariness of the environment in which I lived 6
until, at age twenty, I went forth to pursue the fantasies of newspaper
reporting inspired by the first movie version of *The Front Page*. Lansing,
Michigan, is neither the center of the universe nor a backward hamlet.
When I was a girl, Lansing was a city of more than 100,000 people—
then, as now, the capital of the state, headquarters of the Oldsmobile
division of General Motors, and home of Michigan State University. My
family lived in Okemos, a suburb of professors, businessmen, and civil
servants who had scraped up enough money to move out of the aging
central city. Named after the last Indian chief who inhabited the area,
Okemos was separated into what the realtors called "subdivisions": Indian Hills, Chippewa Hills, Tacoma Hills, Ottawa Hills, Forest Hills
and—an afterthought—Hiawatha Park. We lived in Forest Hills, which
was neither the richest nor the poorest of the subdivisions. A few of the
rich kids, who lived in Tacoma Hills and Indian Hills, had swimming
pools. The poorer kids, in Ottawa Hills and Chippewa Hills, had to share
bedrooms with brothers and sisters. We Forest Hills kids had our own
bedrooms but no pools in the back yard.

In this middle-class milieu, the only working women I knew were 7
grade school or high school teachers. Until I graduated from college, I
had *never* known a woman who did anything else—no women doctors,
lawyers, journalists, or veterinarians—no secretaries or waitresses or
cooks, either. Of course, I was aware that a great many women did
secretarial work, but I assumed that they were young and waiting to
catch a husband or unlucky enough to be divorced. Only one of my
friends had a working mother, and she was a first-grade teacher. Another
friend had a mother who, it was said, had been a researcher for *Time*
magazine before she came home to Michigan to marry a doctor. My own
mother did not have a job, and she made it clear that the "wildness" of
a few kids in the neighborhood—those who turned their record players
up too loud and rode their bikes across the neighbors' lawns—was at-
tributable to the fact that they had mothers who "worked." I had no way
of checking out this information, because I didn't know the wild kids or
their mothers. To this day, I don't know whether they were real people
or whether, in my mother's mythology, they occupied the position of
Sophie Portnoy's errant neighbor, the one who was responsible for her
son's colitis because she gadded about in the local stores and failed to
prevent her little boy from eating hot dogs and doughnuts in greasy
spoons.

So the only women I knew when I was growing up were housewives. 8
And there I was, wanting to be "a writer" from the age of eleven (when
I gave up the impractical dream of becoming a baseball player). I didn't
want to be a housewife; I had taken note of The Problem That Had No
Name before Betty Friedan named it, but I had no frame of reference to
make sense out of what I saw. I didn't know any women who worked,
but I knew women who drank. And women who took barbiturates. And

women who slept the day away, still in their nightgowns when their children returned home after school. One Friday afternoon, I went home with a girlfriend to spend the night and we found her mother staring glassy-eyed into an empty bottle of Scotch. "Mom, you promised not to do that any more," my friend said. "It's because you don't have a date for the dance tonight," Mom replied. Then, turning to me, "And you, Susan, you don't have a date either. Your mother must feel terrible too."

It has been suggested, by women as well as men, that the hindsight 9 of feminist conviction has cast the lives of the women of my childhood in a worse light than they could have appeared to me at the time. Not so. Only since the feminist movement have I been able to bring any understanding to bear on the question of why those suburban women locked themselves into, or permitted themselves to be locked into, what seemed to me such a stultifying existence. My mother, who found herself a job after my younger brother entered college, has told me she now feels that she and our entire family would have been better off if she had gone to work much earlier. "In those days," she said, "it wasn't even a question you could ask yourself—whether you'd be better off, even whether you might be a better mother, if you had real interests outside of your home."

That my mother's repressed questions might be related to my own 10 limitless ambitions was not something that could have occurred to me when I was a teen-ager. I only knew, by age fifteen, that I had a boundless contempt for women who wrote "Occupation: Housewife" on the census form. The conclusion I drew, from the narrow vision of my girlfriends as well as from their mothers' lives, was that women were, as a group, quite stupid. *I,* of course, was an exception. In high school and college, I was often told that I thought and/or wrote like a man, and I was always pleased to hear it. If this sounds like an emotional rather than an intellectual conundrum, I can only say I did not see it that way at the time. The one question that bothered me was why other women were so dumb.

I was a pushy, nervy, hard-working kid, and everything conspired to 11 reinforce my thinking. When a high school counselor suggested that I major in education because I would make an excellent English teacher and teaching was always a good fall-back position for a woman, I snorted and paid no attention: The counselor was a woman, and I took her advice as one more proof of female stupidity. In my senior year, I became the first girl to win a college scholarship from the local chapter of Sigma Delta Chi (then an all-male journalism fraternity, now just another coed organization). The award was presented by Helen Thomas, then a junior White House correspondent for United Press International. Thomas was, as it happened, the first female reporter I had ever met, but she was also an example of what I did not want to become. Now a respected senior political correspondent, Thomas was, in 1963, assigned chiefly to stories about Jackie, John-John, and Caroline Kennedy, and Caroline's pony, Macaroni. No doubt she could have told me some interesting stories about what it was really like, being a woman in a man's world. But she didn't tell any tales and I certainly didn't ask for any. The race, as far as I was concerned, was still to the swift.

So I moved fifteen minutes away from home to Michigan State University, an institution of twenty-six thousand students, give or take a few hundred. All of my professors were men. At a university of that size, there must have been a few women faculty members, but I didn't run into any of them—either as a student or a reporter for the campus newspaper.   *12*

One of my professors, a journalism instructor who was in fact the only good teacher of English composition at the university, did me the invaluable favor of suggesting that I might just find the going a little harder in my chosen profession because I was a woman. Naïve as it may have been for someone who thought she was so smart, I had simply never considered the possibility that I might be defeated in anything that mattered to me. I already had a plan: I would get a job as a reporter for a big-city newspaper and support myself until, like Twain and Hemingway, I was ready to forsake the transitory excitement of news in order to produce masterpieces of fiction. My professor pointed out that newspapers were not as eager to hire young women as young men, because they were afraid the women would quit work as soon as they got married and had children. Therefore, he admonished, I must have a thick collection of professional clippings when it came time to apply for a job. He too had a plan: His best student was graduating and leaving a job as a campus "stringer" for *The Detroit Free Press*. I would be good at the job and the professor would recommend me. A university the size of Michigan State is an important source of news; at eighteen, my byline began appearing regularly over prominently displayed stories in the second largest newspaper in the state.   *13*

Why, in the course of these triumphs, was I bothered enough about the "woman question" to pick up a copy of *The Feminine Mystique?* My interest was due in part to the education I was getting and in part to the eduation I was not getting. I had heard enough about Freud in Psych. 101 to make me want to read more of him. It didn't make any sense to me, a theory of feminine nature based entirely on the behavior of patients in nineteenth-century Vienna. If Freud was to be believed, most of what I wanted in life was perfectly normal for a man and perfectly crazy for a woman.   *14*

But it was literature, not psychiatry (a discipline bearing much too marked a resemblance to religion to have a significant impact on a nineteen-year-old agnostic) which posed a genuinely serious and troubling intellectual problem. It had begun to dawn on me that the statement "you write like a man" was not an unmixed compliment. How could I   *15* "write like a man" when I was a woman, albeit an odd sort of woman by most people's definitions (my own included)? By 1964, the mid-point of my college years, I had read only two books by women regarded as important writers—the painfully dull *Silas Marner* and *Jane Eyre*. A partial list of the writers I had not read (most of whose names I did not even know at the time) should suffice: Jane Austen, Simone de Beauvoir, the Brontë sisters (*Jane Eyre* excepted), Willa Cather, Colette, Carson McCullers, Doris Lessing, Flannery O'Connor, George Sand, Eudora Welty, Edith Wharton.

A lousy education? Perhaps. Certainly, I never could have gotten a *16* diploma from Radcliffe or Sarah Lawrence without having read Jane Austen. Nevertheless, my literary education acquired on my own as well as through the admittedly minimal demands of Michigan State, was considerably more advanced than that of most American college students. Ignorant as I was of writing by women, I was well versed in the works of male major writers. Dostoevsky, Tolstoy, Checkhov, Turgenev, Flaubert, Proust, Dickens, Hardy, Faulkner, James: I had read them all. And, because I could never control the habit of reading for pleasure even while I was limping toward a college degree, I was even familiar with books by living writers. Saul Bellow and Philip Roth (neither of whom appeared in my *goyische* lit courses) were my favorites. I remember reading Roth's brilliant short story "Defender of the Faith" and wishing (a) that I had written it myself or (b) that some woman would publish a short story of that high caliber in a women's magazine. But that was silly. Literary quality and "women's magazine" offered a contradiction in terms.

I recently read a passage from a 1960 *Ladies' Home Journal* (cited in *17* *The Feminine Mystique*) to a twenty-one-year-old woman I know. She laughed and laughed and refused to believe that such an article had ever been published. The passage described the happy life of a Texas house-wife named Janice in a regular feature called "How America Lives."

Sometimes, she washes and dries her hair before sitting down at a *18* bridge table at 1:30. Mornings she is having bridge at her house are the busiest, for then she must get out the tables, cards, tallies, prepare fresh coffee and organize lunch . . . During the winter months, she may play as often as four days a week from 9:30 to 3 p.m. . . . Janice is careful to be home before her sons return from school at 4 p.m.

She is not frustrated, this new young housewife. An honor student *19* at high school, married at eighteen, remarried and pregnant at twenty, she has the house she spent seven years dreaming and planning in detail. She is proud of her efficiency as a housewife, getting it all done by 8:30 . . .

"I love my home," she says . . . The pale gray paint in her L-shaped *20* living and dining room is five years old, but still in perfect condition

. . .The pale peach and yellow and aqua damask upholstery looks spotless after eight years' wear. "Sometimes I feel I'm too passive, too content," remarks Janice, fondly regarding the wristband of large family diamonds she wears even when the watch itself is being repaired . . . Her favorite possession is her four-poster spool bed with a pink taffeta canopy. "I feel just like Queen Elizabeth sleeping in that bed," she says happily. (Her husband sleeps in another room, since he snores.)

"I'm so grateful for my blessings," she says. "Wonderful husband, 21 handsome sons with dispositions to match, big comfortable house . . . I'm thankful for my good health and faith in God and such material possessions as two cars, two TV's and two fireplaces."

The inability of a twenty-one-year-old to see such a passage as any- 22 thing other than a parody is a tribute to the profound changes in thought and behavior that have taken place during the past fifteen years. It is difficult to explain to anyone under the age of twenty-five what feminism meant to women of my generation, reared at the height of the "back to the home" movement after the Second World War.

During the first year of my feminist education, which began on the 23 spring day in 1964 when I bought a copy of *The Feminine Mystique,* I learned a variety of amazing things:

1. There was indeed a "back to the home" movement after the war—a 24 movement which wiped out many of the educational and professional gains women had made in the 1920's, 30's, and early 40's. Women's magazines in the 30's and early 40's had published serious fiction and non-fiction, by male and female authors, instead of the drivel exemplified by "How America Lives."
2. There was an alternative—in fact, there were many alternatives—to 25 the Freudian view of feminine nature and feminine sexuality.
3. Contrary to what I had heard in school, the nineteenth-century femi- 26 nists were not a bunch of loony, frustrated hags. Their thoughts were worth reading. (At the time, Susan B. Anthony was the only "suffragette" whose name I knew. In the history textbook my school had used, the women's suffrage movement occupied half a paragraph.)
4. The educational system was geared to discourage girls from pursuing 27 serious "masculine" goals. Stupidity was not an adequate explanation of why so many counselors encouraged girls to teach elementary school and why so many girls faithfully followed their advice.
5. There was a body of great literature by women. I knew nothing about 28 it.

Again, there are those who would contend that my ignorance was the 29 result of a particularly horrible education. Again, I say I had an education that was, in some respects, better than average. Insofar as the history of women was concerned, it was certainly no worse than the American norm.

Imagine the heady discoveries of 1964! Emily Dickinson was not, it *30* seemed, a saccharine nature poet. But wasn't she a hermit, a complete weirdo, like all great women who "wrote"? Perhaps she was, but there were others who weren't—women who, in much harder times, insisted on their right to both love and work. George Sand. Colette. Margaret Fuller. Anna Akhmatova (a spur to learn Russian). During that year, I encountered the idea that it was not necessary to deny I was a woman like other women in order to become a person of worldly achievement. I greeted this idea with a good deal of suspicion and was unable to absorb it emotionally for many years. One does not lightly cast off habits of the mind that have been extremely useful in the past; the idea that I had nothing in common with other dumb women had played no small role in helping me avoid snares ranging from the bad advice of school counselors to the accidental teen-age pregnancies that aborted the development of so many of the girls I knew.

But I was one of the lucky ones. My feminist education began just *31* before life handed me an unforgettable (unforgettable only because it was the first) setback based solely on the fact that I was, in the end, only a woman. I had intended, logically enough, to go to work for *The Detroit Free Press* after I graduated in the summer of 1965. In January, I showed up for a job interview that I thought was only a formality. I had, after all, been writing for the paper for two years. The editor greeted me cheerfully, told me how happy he would be to have me working full time for the paper, and started describing the duties of a society reporter. "*Society* reporter." I gulped. He explained that I would start by writing up weddings but, with my demonstrated talent, I would soon progress to writing feature articles about women's charities and child care. I had assumed, I said, that I would be hired for general assignment since that was what I had been doing in Lansing. No, he answered, the paper never hired women for anything but society news. Women couldn't be hired for general assignment, because it was too dangerous to send women out on night stories.

Believe it or not, this was the first indication I had ever received that *32* anything more than talent and hard work was required for success. Thanks to the beginnings of feminism in my own mind, I was able to understand that the editor was part of the same system as my high school counselor. For years, I had been fighting a battle to prove to myself and everyone else that I was not just a girl. I now began to see that the battle should be fought against the system and not against myself.

A month after the debacle at the *Free Press,* I had almost slid all the *33* way back into my former state of innocent arrogance when the city editor of *The Washington Post* extended his hand after a fifteen-minute interview and said I was hired—for general assignment. *He* wasn't concerned about sending me out on assignment at night, and the *Post* was a much better paper than the *Free Press*. Perhaps the "woman problem" had reared its head for the last time.

On the way out of the building, I had to stop by the personnel de-   *34* partment to fill out forms and take routine tests required of every new employee. Part of the test was a five-hundred-word essay. The personnel director assigned me the topic: "How I Plan to Combine Being a Career Woman and a Wife."

So the problem wasn't going to go away. But at least it was no longer   *35* a Problem That Had No Name.

Study Questions

1. Susan Jacoby opens "The Education of a Feminist: Part One" with a quotation from Betty Friedan's *The Feminine Mystique*. What, in particular, makes this passage appropriate as an opening for Jacoby's essay? What vocabulary in the quotation serves to establish the context for the rest of the essay?
2. Early in the essay, Jacoby discusses the word *intellectual*. How is that discussion relevant to the topic? What methods of organization does she use to connect this discussion to the surrounding paragraphs?
3. What dominant organizational method does Jacoby use for the body of the essay? Why is this method particularly appropriate for the topic of the essay as signalled by its title? Underline some of the major words and phrases that characterize this organization.
4. How does Jacoby's ending meet the requirement that a conclusion should leave the reader with a sense of the significance of the message? What does the incident at *The Washington Post* highlight?

Suggestion for Drafting

In "The Education of a Feminist: Part One," Susan Jacoby uses temporal organization to tie together the many stages she went through as she learned what it was like to be "a woman in a man's world." This method of organization becomes a convenient frame within which she can make specific comments as she presents each incident. In this way, she periodically interrupts her chronological account to give her opinion of what an incident now means to her.

Choose an incident in your own life that has had an important effect on you. Describe it to an audience that does not know you, and explain how it has changed you. Your goal in this exercise is to describe only enough of the incident to let the reader know what happened. Emphasize your opinion of the significance of the event in your own life.

On the Need for Oblivion

Samuel Johnson

A mong the innumerable mortifications that *1* way-lay human arrogance on every side may well be reckoned our ignorance of the most common objects and effects, a defect of which we become more sensible by every attempt to supply it. Vulgar and inactive minds confound familiarity with knowledge, and conceive themselves informed of the whole nature of things when they are shewn their form or told their use; but the Speculatist, who is not content with superficial views, harrasses himself with fruitless curiosity, and still as he enquires more perceives only that he knows less.

Sleep is a state in which a great part of every life is passed. No animal *2* has been yet discovered, whose existence is not varied with intervals of insensibility; and some late Philosophers have extended the empire of Sleep over the vegetable world.

Yet of this change so frequent, so great, so general, and so necessary, *3* no searcher has yet found either the efficient or final cause; or can tell by what power the mind and body are thus chained down in irresistible stupefaction; or what benefits the animal receives from this alternate suspension of its active powers.

Whatever may be the multiplicity or contrariety of opinions upon this *4* subject, Nature has taken sufficient care that Theory shall have little influence on Practice. The most diligent enquirer is not able long to keep his eyes open; the most eager disputant will begin about midnight to desert his argument; and once in four and twenty hours, the gay and the gloomy, the witty and the dull, the clamorous and the silent, the busy and the idle, are all overpowered by the gentle tyrant, and all lie down in the equality of Sleep.

Philosophy has often attempted to repress insolence, by asserting that *5* all conditions are levelled by Death; a position which, however it may deject the happy, will seldom afford much comfort to the wretched. It is far more pleasing to consider that Sleep is equally a leveller with Death; that the time is never at a great distance, when the balm of rest shall be effused alike upon every head, when the diversities of life shall stop their operation, and the high and the low shall lie down together.

It is somewhere recorded of *Alexander,* that in the pride of conquests, *6* and intoxication of flattery, he declared that he only perceived himself to be a man by the necessity of Sleep. Whether he considered Sleep as necessary to his mind or body, it was indeed a sufficient evidence of human infirmity; the body which required such frequency of renovation gave but faint promises of immortality; and the mind which, from time to time, sunk gladly into insensibility, had made no very near approaches to the felicity of the supreme and self-sufficient Nature.

I know not what can tend more to repress all the passions that disturb *7* the peace of the world, than the consideration that there is no height of happiness or honour, from which man does not eagerly descend to a state of unconscious repose; that the best condition of life is such, that we contentedly quit its good to be disentangled from its evils; that in a few hours splendor fades before the eye, and praise itself deadens in the ear; the senses withdraw from their objects, and reason favours the retreat.

What then are the hopes and prospects of covetousness, ambition, *8* and rapacity? Let him that desires most have all his desires gratified, he never shall attain a state, which he can, for a day and a night, contemplate with satisfaction, or from which, if he had the power of perpetual vigilance, he would not long for periodical separations.

All envy would be extinguished if it were universally known that there *9* are none to be envied, and surely none can be much envied who are not pleased with themselves. There is reason to suspect that the distinctions of mankind have more shew than value, when it is found that all agree to be weary alike of pleasures and of cares; that the powerful and the weak, the celebrated and obscure, join in one common wish, and implore from Nature's hand the nectar of oblivion.

Such is our desire of abstraction from ourselves, that very few are *10* satisfied with the quantity of stupefaction which the needs of the body force upon the mind. *Alexander* himself added intemperance to sleep, and solaced with the fumes of wine the sovereignty of the world; and almost every man has some art, by which he steals his thoughts away from his present state.

It is not much of life that is spent in close attention to any important *11* duty. Many hours of every day are suffered to fly away without any traces left upon the intellects. We suffer phantoms to rise up before us, and amuse ourselves with the dance of airy images, which after a time we dismiss for ever, and know not how we have been busied.

Many have no happier moments than those that they pass in solitude, *12* abandoned to their own imagination, which sometimes puts sceptres in their hands or mitres on their heads, shifts the scene of pleasure with endless variety, bids all the forms of beauty sparkle before them, and gluts them with every change of visionary luxury.

It is easy in these semi-slumbers to collect all the possibilities of *13* happiness, to alter the course of the Sun, to bring back the past, and anticipate the future, to unite all the beauties of all seasons, and all the blessings of all climates, to receive and bestow felicity, and forget that

misery is the lot of man. All this is a voluntary dream, a temporary
recession from the realities of life to airy fictions; and habitual subjection
of reason to fancy.

Others are afraid to be alone, and amuse themselves by a perpetual *14*
succession of companions: but the difference is not great; in solitude we
have our dreams to ourselves, and in company we agree to dream in
concert. The end sought in both is forgetfulness of ourselves.

Study Questions

1. Johnson begins "On the Need for Oblivion" with an extended discussion about sleep, but by the time he has concluded his essay, he has
   considerably expanded this original topic. What is Johnson's final
   message to his readers? What reasons might he have had for beginning
   with the narrower topic of sleep?
2. What kind of an educational background does Johnson assume his
   audience has? Point to specific passages that support your characterization. If he were writing today, would Johnson realistically be able
   to make the same assumptions? Why or why not?
3. The major form of organization that Johnson uses in the body of his
   essay is conceptual. He does not, however, use many of the words
   we normally expect to signal this method (e.g., *therefore, however,
   thus, nevertheless*). How, then, can we still identify this method
   in the organization? In an essay like "On the Need for Oblivion,"
   why may it be redundant to use "transition words" to signal the
   organization?
4. Look up the words *vulgar* and *Speculatist* in the *Oxford English
   Dictionary* to find the meanings that were current when Samuel Johnson was writing. How does knowing these definitions change your
   understanding of the first paragraph? What other words in the essay
   may have had different meanings from those they have now?

Suggestion for Drafting

Johnson ends "On the Need for Oblivion" with this observation: "In
solitude we have our dreams to ourselves, and in company we agree to
dream in concert. The end sought in both is forgetfulness of ourselves."
Do you agree that all people need time to forget themselves? Using a
conceptual organization, write a one- or two-paragraph response to this
question.

Resistance to Civil Government

Henry David Thoreau

I heartily accept the motto,—"That government *1* is best which governs least;" and I should like to see it acted up to more rapidly and systematically. Carried out, it finally amounts to this, which also I believe,— "That government is best which governs not at all;" and when men are prepared for it, that will be the kind of government which they will have. Government is at best but an expedient; but most governments are usually, and all governments are sometimes, inexpedient. The objections which have been brought against a standing army, and they are many and weighty, and descrve to prevail, may also at last be brought against a standing government. The standing army is only an arm of the standing government. The government itself, which is only the mode which the people have chosen to execute their will, is equally liable to be abused and perverted before the people can act through it. Witness the present Mexican war, the work of comparatively a few individuals using the standing government as their tool; for, in the outset, the people would not have consented to this measure.

This American government,—what is it but a tradition, though a recent *2* one, endeavoring to transmit itself unimpaired to posterity, but each instant losing some of its integrity? It has not the vitality and force of a single living man; for a single man can bend it to his will. It is a sort of wooden gun to the people themselves; and, if ever they should use it in earnest as a real one against each other, it will surely split. But it is not the less necessary for this; for the people must have some complicated machinery or other, and hear its din, to satisfy that idea of government which they have. Governments show thus how successfully men can be imposed on, even impose on themselves, for their own advantage. It is excellent, we must all allow; yet this government never of itself furthered any enterprise, but by the alacrity with which it got out of its way. *It* does not keep the country free. *It* does not settle the West. *It* does not educate. The character inherent in the American people has done all that has been accomplished; and it would have done somewhat more, if the government had not sometimes got in its way. For government is an expedient by which men would fain succeed in letting one another alone; and, as has been said, when it is most expedient, the governed are most let alone by it. Trade and commerce, if they were not made of India rubber, would never manage to bounce over the obstacles which legislators are continually putting in their way; and, if one were to judge these men wholly by the effects of their actions, and not partly by their intentions, they would deserve to be classed and punished with those mischievous persons who put obstructions on the railroads.

But, to speak practically and as a citizen, unlike those who call them- *3* selves no-government men, I ask for, not at once no government, but *at once* a better government. Let every man make known what kind of government would command his respect, and that will be one step toward obtaining it.

After all, the practical reason why, when the power is once in the *4* hands of the people, a majority are permitted, and for a long period continue, to rule, is not because they are most likely to be in the right, nor because this seems fairest to the minority, but because they are physically the strongest. But a government in which the majority rule in all cases cannot be based on justice, even as far as men understand it. Can there not be a government in which majorities do not virtually decide right and wrong, but conscience?—in which majorities decide only those questions to which the rule of expediency is applicable? Must the citizen ever for a moment, or in the least degree, resign his conscience to the legislator? Why has every man a conscience, then? I think that we should be men first, and subjects afterward. It is not desirable to cultivate a respect for the law, so much as for the right. The only obligation which I have a right to assume, is to do at any time what I think right. It is truly enough said, that a corporation has no conscience; but a corporation of conscientious men is a corporation *with* a conscience. Law never made men a whit more just; and, by means of their respect for it, even the well-disposed are daily made the agents of injustice. A common and natural result of an undue respect for law is, that you may see a file of soldiers, colonel, captain, corporal, privates, powder-monkeys and all, marching in admirable order over hill and dale to the wars, against their wills, aye, against their common sense and consciences, which makes it very steep marching indeed, and produces a palpitation of the heart. They have no doubt that it is a damnable business in which they are concerned; they are all peaceably inclined. Now, what are they? Men at all? or small moveable forts and magazines, at the service of some unscrupulous man in power? Visit the Navy Yard, and behold a marine, such a man as an American government can make, or such as it can make a man with its black arts, a mere shadow and reminiscence of humanity, a man laid out alive and standing, and already, as one may say, buried under arms with funeral accompaniments, though it may be

"Not a drum was heard, nor a funeral note,
    As his corse to the ramparts we hurried;
Not a soldier discharged his farewell shot
    O'er the grave where our hero we buried."*

* From Charles Wolfe's *Burial of Sir John Moore at Corunna* (1817), a song
  Thoreau liked to sing.

The mass of men serve the State thus, not as men mainly, but as 5 machines, with their bodies. They are the standing army, and the militia, jailers, constables, *posse comitatus,** &c. In most cases there is no free exercise whatever of the judgment or of the moral sense; but they put themselves on a level with wood and earth and stones; and wooden men can perhaps be manufactured that will serve the purpose as well. Such command no more respect than men of straw, or a lump of dirt. They have the same sort of worth only as horses and dogs. Yet such as these even are commonly esteemed good citizens. Others, as most legislators, politicians, lawyers, ministers, and office-holders, serve the State chiefly with their heads; and, as they rarely make any moral distinctions, they are as likely to serve the devil, without intending it, as God. A very few, as heroes, patriots, martyrs, reformers in the great sense, and *men,* serve the State with their consciences also, and so necessarily resist it for the most part; and they are commonly treated by it as enemies. A wise man will only be useful as a man, and will not submit to be "clay," and "stop a hole to keep the wind away,"† but leave that office to his dust at least:—

"I am too high-born to be propertied,
To be a secondary at control,
Or useful serving-man and instrument
To any sovereign state throughout the world."‡

He who gives himself entirely to his fellow-men appears to them 6 useless and selfish; but he who gives himself partially to them is pronounced a benefactor and philanthropist.

How does it become a man to behave toward this American govern- 7 ment to-day? I answer that he cannot without disgrace be associated with it. I cannot for an instant recognize that political organization as *my* government which is the *slave's* government also.

All men recognize the right of revolution; that is, the right to refuse 8 allegiance to and to resist the government, when its tyranny or its inefficiency are great and unendurable. But almost all say that such is not the case now. But such was the case, they think, in the Revolution of '75. If one were to tell me that this was a bad government because it taxed certain foreign commodities brought to its ports, it is most probable that I should not make an ado about it, for I can do without them: all machines have their friction; and possibly this does enough good to counterbalance the evil. At any rate, it is a great evil to make a stir about it. But when the friction comes to have its machine, and oppression and robbery are organized, I say, let us not have such a machine any longer. In other words, when a sixth of the population of a nation

* Sheriff's posse.
† Shakespeare's *Hamlet,* 5.1.236–37.
‡ Shakespeare's *King John,* 5.1.79–82.

which has undertaken to be the refuge of liberty are slaves, and a whole country is unjustly overrun and conquered by a foreign army, and subjected to military law, I think that it is not too soon for honest men to rebel and revolutionize. What makes this duty the more urgent is the fact, that the country so overrun is not our own, but ours is the invading army.

Paley, a common authority with many on moral questions, in his 9 chapter on the "Duty of Submission to Civil Government," resolves all civil obligation into expediency; and he proceeds to say, "that so long as the interest of the whole society requires it, that is, so long as the established government cannot be resisted or changed without public inconveniency, it is the will of God that the established government be obeyed, and no longer." —"This principle being admitted, the justice of every particular case of resistance is reduced to a computation of the quantity of the danger and grievance on the one side, and of the probability and expense of redressing it on the other." Of this, he says, every man shall judge for himself. But Paley appears never to have contemplated those cases to which the rule of expediency does not apply, in which a people, as well as an individual, must do justice, cost what it may. If I have unjustly wrested a plank from a drowning man, I must restore it to him though I drown myself. This, according to Paley, would be inconvenient. But he that would save his life, in such a case, shall lose it.* This people must cease to hold slaves, and to make war on Mexico, though it cost them their existence as a people.

In their practice, nations agree with Paley; but does any one think that 10 Massachusetts does exactly what is right at the present crisis?

"A drab of state, a cloth-o'-silver slut,
To have her train borne up, and her soul trail in the dirt."†

Practically speaking, the opponents to a reform in Massachusetts are not a hundred thousand politicians at the South, but a hundred thousand merchants and farmers here, who are more interested in commerce and agriculture than they are in humanity, and are not prepared to do justice to the slave and to Mexico, *cost what it may.* I quarrel not with far-off foes, but with those who, near at home, cooperate with, and do the bidding of those far away, and without whom the latter would be harmless. We are accustomed to say, that the mass of men are unprepared; but improvement is slow, because the few are not materially wiser or better than the many. It is not so important that many should be as good as you, as that there be some absolute goodness somewhere; for that will

* Matthew 10.39; Luke 9.24.
† Cyril Tourneur (1575?–1626), *The Revenger's Tragedy,* IV.iv.

leaven the whole lump.* There are thousands who are *in opinion* opposed to slavery and to the war, who yet in effect do nothing to put an end to them; who, esteeming themselves children of Washington and Franklin, sit down with their hands in their pockets, and say that they know not what to do, and do nothing; who even postpone the question of freedom to the question of free-trade, and quietly read the prices-current along with the latest advices from Mexico, after dinner, and, it may be, fall asleep over them both. What is the price-current of an honest man and patriot to-day? They hesitate, and they regret, and sometimes they petition; but they do nothing in earnest and with effect. They will wait, well disposed, for others to remedy the evil, that they may no longer have it to regret. At most, they give only a cheap vote, and a feeble countenance and God-speed, to the right, as it goes by them. There are nine hundred and ninety-nine patrons of virtue to one virtuous man; but it is easier to deal with the real possessor of a thing than with the temporary guardian of it.

All voting is a sort of gaming, like chequers or backgammon, with a *11* slight moral tinge to it, a playing with right and wrong, with moral questions; and betting naturally accompanies it. The character of the voters is not staked. I cast my vote, perchance, as I think right; but I am not vitally concerned that that right should prevail. I am willing to leave it to the majority. Its obligation, therefore, never exceeds that of expediency. Even voting *for the right* is *doing* nothing for it. It is only expressing to men feebly your desire that it should prevail. A wise man will not leave the right to the mercy of chance, nor wish it to prevail through the power of the majority. There is but little virtue in the action of masses of men. When the majority shall at length vote for the abolition of slavery, it will be because they are indifferent to slavery, or because there is but little slavery left to be abolished by their vote. *They* will then be the only slaves. Only *his* vote can hasten the abolition of slavery who asserts his own freedom by his vote.

I hear of a convention to be held at Baltimore, or elsewhere, for the *12* selection of a candidate for the Presidency, made up chiefly of editors, and men who are politicians by profession; but I think, what is it to any independent, intelligent, and respectable man what decision they may come to, shall we not have the advantage of his wisdom and honesty, nevertheless? Can we not count upon some independent votes? Are there not many individuals in the country who do not attend conventions? But no: I find that the respectable man, so called, has immediately drifted from his position, and despairs of his country, when his country has more reason to despair of him. He forthwith adopts one of the candidates thus selected as the only *available* one, thus proving that he is himself *available* for any purposes of the demagogue. His vote is of no more worth

* 1 Corinthians 5.6.

than that of any unprincipled foreigner or hireling native, who may have been bought. Oh for a man who is a *man,* and, as my neighbor says, has a bone in his back which you cannot pass your hand through! Our statistics are at fault: the population has been returned too large. How many *men* are there to a square thousand miles in this country? Hardly one. Does not America offer any inducement for men to settle here? The American had dwindled into an Odd Fellow,—one who may be known by the development of his organ of gregariousness, and a manifest lack of intellect and cheerful self-reliance, whose first and chief concern, on coming into the world, is to see that the alms-houses are in good repair; and, before yet he has lawfully donned the virile garb,* to collect a fund for the support of the widows and orphans that may be; who, in short, ventures to live only by the aid of the mutual insurance company, which has promised to bury him decently.

It is not a man's duty, as a matter of course, to devote himself to the   13
eradication of any, even the most enormous wrong; he may still properly have other concerns to engage him; but it is his duty, at least, to wash his hands of it, and, if he gives it no thought longer, not to give it practically his support. If I devote myself to other pursuits and contemplations, I must first see, at least, that I do not pursue them sitting upon another man's shoulders. I must get off him first, that he may pursue his contemplations too. See what gross inconsistency is tolerated. I have heard some of my townsmen say, "I should like to have them order me out to help put down an insurrection of the slaves, or to march to Mexico,—see if I would go;" and yet these very men have each, directly by their allegiance, and so indirectly, at least, by their money, furnished a substitute. The soldier is applauded who refuses to serve in an unjust war by those who do not refuse to sustain the unjust government which makes the war; is applauded by those whose own act and authority he disregards and sets at nought; as if the State were penitent to that degree that it hired one to scourge it while it sinned, but not to that degree that it left off sinning for a moment. Thus, under the name of order and civil government, we are all made at last to pay homage to and support our own meanness. After the first blush of sin, comes its indifference; and from immoral it becomes, as it were, *un*moral, and not quite unnecessary to that life which we have made.

The broadest and most prevalent error requires the most disinterested   14
virtue to sustain it. The slight reproach to which the virtue of patriotism is commonly liable, the noble are most likely to incur. Those who, while they disapprove of the character and measures of a government, yield to it their allegiance and support, are undoubtedly its most conscientious supporters, and so frequently the most serious obstacles to reform. Some are petitioning the State to dissolve the Union, to disregard the requisi-

---

* Adult garb allowed a Roman boy on reaching 14.

tions of the President. Why do they not dissolve it themselves,—the union between themselves and the State,—and refuse to pay their quota into its treasury? Do not they stand in the same relation to the State, that the State does to the Union? And have not the same reasons prevented the State from resisting the Union, which have prevented them from resisting the State?

How can a man be satisfied to entertain an opinion merely, and enjoy *15* *it?* Is there any enjoyment in it, if his opinion is that he is aggrieved? If you are cheated out of a single dollar by your neighbor, you do not rest satisfied with knowing that you are cheated, or with saying that you are cheated, or even with petitioning him to pay you your due; but you take effectual steps at once to obtain the full amount, and see that you are never cheated again. Action from principle,—the perception and the performance of right,—changes things and relations; it is essentially rev- olutionary, and does not consist wholly with any thing which was. It not only divides states and churches, it divides families; aye, it divides the *individual,* separating the diabolical in him from the divine.

Unjust laws exist: shall we be content to obey them, or shall we *16* endeavor to amend them, and obey them until we have succeeded, or shall we transgress them at once? Men generally, under such a govern- ment as this, think that they ought to wait until they have persuaded the majority to alter them. They think that, if they should resist, the remedy would be worse than the evil. But it is the fault of the government itself that the remedy *is* worse than the evil. *It* makes it worse. Why is it not more apt to anticipate and provide for reform? Why does it not cherish its wise minority? Why does it cry and resist before it is hurt? Why does it not encourage its citizens to be on the alert to point out its faults, and *do* better than it would have them? Why does it always crucify Christ, and excommunicate Copernicus and Luther, and pronounce Washington and Franklin rebels?

One would think that a deliberate and practical denial of its authority *17* was the only offence never contemplated by government; else, why has it not assigned its definite, its suitable and proportionate penalty? If a man who has no property refuses but once to earn nine shillings* for the State, he is put in prison for a period unlimited by any law that I know, and determined only by the discretion of those who placed him there; but if he should steal ninety times nine shillings from the State, he is soon permitted to go at large again.

If the injustice is part of the necessary friction of the machine of *18* government, let it go, let it go: perchance it will wear smooth,—certainly the machine will wear out. If the injustice has a spring, or a pulley, or a rope, or a crank, exclusively for itself, then perhaps you may consider whether the remedy will not be worse than the evil; but if it is of such a

---

* The amount of the poll tax Thoreau had refused to pay.

nature that it requires you to be the agent of injustice to another, then, I say, break the law. Let your life be a counter friction to stop the machine. What I have to do is to see, at any rate, that I do not lend myself to the wrong which I condemn.

As for adopting the ways which the State has provided for remedying 19 the evil, I know not of such ways. They take too much time, and a man's life will be gone. I have other affairs to attend to. I came into this world, not chiefly to make this a good place to live in, but to live in it, be it good or bad. A man has not every thing to do, but something; and because he cannot do *every thing,* it is not necessary that he should do *something* wrong. It is not my business to be petitioning the governor or the legislature any more than it is theirs to petition me; and, if they should not hear my petition, what should I do then? But in this case the State has provided no way: its very Constitution is the evil. This may seem to be harsh and stubborn and unconciliatory; but it is to treat with the utmost kindness and consideration the only spirit that can appreciate or deserves it. So is all change for the better, like birth and death which convulse the body.

I do not hesitate to say, that those who call themselves abolitionists 20 should at once effectually withdraw their support, both in person and property, from the government of Massachusetts, and not wait till they constitute a majority of one, before they suffer the right to prevail through them. I think that it is enough if they have God on their side, without waiting for that other one. Moreover, any man more right than his neighbors, constitutes a majority of one already.*

I meet this American government, or its representative the State gov- 21 ernment, directly, and face to face, once a year, no more, in the person of its tax-gatherer; this is the only mode in which a man situated as I am necessarily meets it; and it then says distinctly, Recognize me; and the simplest, the most effectual, and, in the present posture of affairs, the indispensablest mode of treating with it on this head, of expressing your little satisfaction with and love for it, is to deny it then. My civil neighbor, the tax-gatherer,† is the very man I have to deal with,—for it is, after all, with men and not with parchment that I quarrel,—and he has voluntarily chosen to be an agent of the government. How shall he ever know well what he is and does as an officer of the government, or as a man, until he is obliged to consider whether he shall treat me, his neighbor, for whom he has respect, as a neighbor and well-disposed man, or as a maniac and disturber of the peace, and see if he can get over this obstruction to his neighborliness without a ruder and more impetuous thought or speech corresponding with his action? I know this well, that

* John Knox (1505?–72), the Scottish religious reformer who said that "a man with God is always in the majority."
† Sam Staples, who sometimes assisted Thoreau in his surveying.

if one thousand, if one hundred, if ten men whom I could name,—if ten *honest* men only,—aye, if *one* HONEST man, in this State of Massachusetts, *ceasing to hold slaves,* were actually to withdraw from this copartnership, and be locked up in the county jail therefor, it would be the abolition of slavery in America. For it matters not how small the beginning may seem to be: what is once well done is done for ever. But we love better to talk about it: that we say is our mission. Reform keeps many scores of newspapers in its service, but not one man. If my esteemed neighbor, the State's ambassador,* who will devote his days to the settlement of the question of human rights in the Council Chamber, instead of being threatened with the prisons of Carolina, were to sit down the prisoner of Massachusetts, that State which is so anxious to foist the sin of slavery upon her sister,—though at present she can discover only an act of inhospitality to be the ground of a quarrel with her,—the Legislature would not wholly waive the subject the following winter.

Under a government which imprisons any unjustly, the true place for a just man is also a prison. The proper place to-day, the only place which Massachusetts has provided for her freer and less desponding spirits, is in her prisons, to be put out and locked out of the State by her own act, as they have already put themselves out by their principles. It is there that the fugitive slave, and the Mexican prisoner on parole, and the Indian come to plead the wrongs of his race, should find them; on that separate, but more free and honorable ground, where the State places those who are not *with* her but *against* her,—the only house in a slave-state in which a free man can abide with honor. If any think that their influence would be lost there, and their voices no longer afflict the ear of the State, that they would not be as an enemy within its walls, they do not know by how much truth is stronger than error, nor how much more eloquently and effectively he can combat injustice who has experienced a little in his own person. Cast your whole vote, not a strip of paper merely, but your whole influence. A minority is powerless while it conforms to the majority; it is not even a minority then; but it is irresistible when it clogs by its whole weight. If the alternative is to keep all just men in prison, or give up war and slavery, the State will not hesitate which to choose. If a thousand men were not to pay their tax-bills this year, that would not be a violent and bloody measure, as it would be to pay them, and enable the State to commit violence and shed innocent blood. This is, in fact, the definition of a peaceable revolution, if any such is possible. If the tax-gatherer, or any other public officer, asks me, as one has done, "But what shall I do?" my answer is, "If you

22

* Samuel Hoar (1778–1856), local political figure who as agent of the state of Massachusetts had been expelled from Charleston, South Carolina, in 1844 while interceding on behalf of imprisoned Negro seamen from Massachusetts. The South Carolina legislature had voted to ask the Governor to expel Hoar.

really wish to do any thing, resign your office." When the subject has refused allegiance, and the officer has resigned his office, then the revolution is accomplished. But even suppose blood should flow. Is there not a sort of blood shed when the conscience is wounded? Through this wound a man's real manhood and immortality flow out, and he bleeds to an everlasting death. I see this blood flowing now.

I have contemplated the imprisonment of the offender, rather than the   23 seizure of his goods,—though both will serve the same purpose,—because they who assert the purest right, and consequently are most dangerous to a corrupt State, commonly have not spent much time in accumulating property. To such the State renders comparatively small service, and a slight tax is wont to appear exorbitant, particularly if they are obliged to earn it by special labor with their hands. If there were one who lived wholly without the use of money, the State itself would hesitate to demand it of him. But the rich man—not to make any invidious comparison—is always sold to the institution which makes him rich. Absolutely speaking, the more money, the less virtue; for money comes between a man and his objects, and obtains them for him; and it was certainly no great virtue to obtain it. It puts to rest many questions which he would otherwise be taxed to answer; while the only new question which it puts is the hard but superfluous one, how to spend it. Thus his moral ground is taken from under his feet. The opportunities of living are diminished in proportion as what are called the "means" are increased. The best thing a man can do for his culture when he is rich is to endeavour to carry out those schemes which he entertained when he was poor. Christ answered the Herodians according to their condition. "Show me the tribute-money," said he;—and one took a penny out of his pocket;—If you use money which has the image of Cæsar on it, and which he has made current and valuable, that is, *if you are men of the State,* and gladly enjoy the advantages of Cæsar's government, then pay him back some of his own when he demands it: "Render therefore to Cæsar that which is Cæsar's, and to God those things which are God's,"*—leaving them no wiser than before as to which was which; for they did not wish to know.

When I converse with the freest of my neighbors, I perceive that,   24 whatever they may say about the magnitude and seriousness of the question, and their regard for the public tranquillity, the long and the short of the matter is, that they cannot spare the protection of the existing government, and they dread the consequences of disobedience to it to their property and families. For my own part, I should not like to think that I ever rely on the protection of the State. But, if I deny the authority of the State when it presents its tax-bill, it will soon take and waste all my property, and so harass me and my children without end. This is

---

* Matthew 22.16–21.

hard. This makes it impossible for a man to live honestly and at the same time comfortably in outward respects. It will not be worth the while to accumulate property; that would be sure to go again. You must hire or squat somewhere, and raise but a small crop, and eat that soon. You must live within yourself, and depend upon yourself, always tucked up and ready for a start, and not have many affairs. A man may grow rich in Turkey even, if he will be in all respects a good subject of the Turkish government. Confucious said,—"If a State is governed by the principles of reason, poverty and misery are subjects of shame; if a State is not governed by the principles of reason, riches and honors are the subjects of shame."* No: until I want the protection of Massachusetts to be extended to me in some distant southern port, where my liberty is endangered, or until I am bent solely on building up an estate at home by peaceful enterprise, I can afford to refuse allegiance to Massachusetts, and her right to my property and life. It costs me less in every sense to incur the penalty of disobedience to the State, than it would to obey. I should feel as if I were worth less in that case.

Some years ago, the State met me in behalf of the church, and com- 25 manded me to pay a certain sum toward the support of a clergyman whose preaching my father attended, but never I myself. "Pay it," it said, "or be locked up in the jail." I declined to pay. But, unfortunately, another man saw fit to pay it. I did not see why the schoolmaster should be taxed to support the priest, and not the priest the schoolmaster; for I was not the State's schoolmaster, but I supported myself by voluntary subscription. I did not see why the lyceum should not present its tax-bill, and have the State to back its demand, as well as the church. However, at the request of the selectmen, I condescended to make some such statement as this in writing:—"Know all men by these presents, that I, Henry Thoreau, do not wish to be regarded as a member of any incorporated society which I have not joined." This I gave to the town-clerk; and he has it. The State, having thus learned that I did not wish to be regarded as a member of that church, has never made a like demand on me since; though it said that it must adhere to its original presumption that time. If I had known how to name them, I should then have signed off in detail from all the societies which I never signed on to; but I did not know where to find a complete list.

I have paid no poll-tax for six years. I was put into a jail once on this 26 account, for one night; and, as I stood considering the walls of solid stone, two or three feet thick, the door of wood and iron, a foot thick, and the iron grating which strained the light, I could not help being struck with the foolishness of that institution which treated me as if I were mere flesh and blood and bones, to be locked up. I wondered that it should have concluded at length that this was the best use it could put me to,

* *Analects,* VIII.13.

and had never thought to avail itself of my services in some way. I saw that, if there was a wall of stone between me and my townsmen, there was a still more difficult one to climb or break through, before they could get to be as free as I was. I did not for a moment feel confined, and the walls seemed a great waste of stone and mortar. I felt as if I alone of all my townsmen had paid my tax. They plainly did not know how to treat me, but behaved like persons who are underbred. In every threat and in every compliment there was a blunder; for they thought that my chief desire was to stand the other side of that stone wall. I could not but smile to see how industriously they locked the door on my meditations, which followed them out again without let or hinderance, and *they* were really all that was dangerous. As they could not reach me, they had resolved to punish my body; just as boys, if they cannot come at some person against whom they have a spite, will abuse his dog. I saw that the State was half-witted, that it was timid as a lone woman with her silver spoons, and that it did not know its friends from its foes, and I lost all my remaining respect for it, and pitied it.

Thus the State never intentionally confronts a man's sense, intellectual   27 or moral, but only his body, his senses. It is not armed with superior wit or honesty, but with superior physical strength. I was not born to be forced. I will breathe after my own fashion. Let us see who is the strongest. What force has a multitude? They only can force me who obey a higher law than I. They force me to become like themselves. I do not hear of *men* being *forced* to live this way or that by masses of men. What sort of life were that to live? When I meet a government which says to me, "Your money or your life," why should I be in haste to give it my money? It may be in a great strait, and not know what to do: I cannot help that. It must help itself; do as I do. It is not worth the while to snivel about it. I am not responsible for the successful working of the machinery of society. I am not the son of the engineer. I perceive that, when an acorn and a chestnut fall side by side, the one does not remain inert to make way for the other, but both obey their own laws, and spring and grow and flourish as best they can, till one, perchance, overshadows and destroys the other. If a plant cannot live according to its nature, it dies; and so a man.

The night in prison was novel and interesting enough. The prisoners   28 in their shirt-sleeves were enjoying a chat and the evening air in the doorway, when I entered. But the jailer said, "Come, boys, it is time to lock up;" and so they dispersed, and I heard the sound of their steps returning into the hollow apartments. My room-mate was introduced to me by the jailer, as "a first-rate fellow and a clever man." When the door was locked, he showed me where to hang my hat, and how he managed matters there. The rooms were whitewashed once a month; and this one, at least, was the whitest, most simply furnished, and probably the neatest apartment in the town. He naturally wanted to know where I came from, and what brought me there; and, when I had told him, I asked him in my turn how he came there, presuming him to be an honest man, of course; and, as the world goes, I believe he was. "Why," said he, "they accuse me of burning a barn; but I never did it." As near as I could discover, he had probably gone to bed in a barn when drunk, and smoked his pipe there; and so a barn was burnt. He had the reputation of being a clever man, had been there some three months waiting for his trial to come on, and would have to wait as much longer; but he was quite domesticated and contented, since he got his board for nothing, and thought that he was well treated.

He occupied one window, and I the other; and I saw, that, if one 29 stayed there long, his principal business would be to look out the window. I had soon read all the tracts that were left there, and examined where former prisoners had broken out, and where a grate had been sawed off, and heard the history of the various occupants of that room; for I found that even here there was a history and a gossip which never circulated beyond the walls of the jail. Probably this is the only house in the town where verses are composed, which are afterward printed in a circular form, but not published. I was shown quite a long list of verses which were composed by some young men who had been detected in an attempt to escape, who avenged themselves by singing them.

I pumped my fellow-prisoner as dry as I could, for fear I should never 30 see him again; but at length he showed me which was my bed, and left me to blow out the lamp.

It was like travelling into a far country, such as I had never expected 31 to behold, to lie there for one night. It seemed to me that I never had heard the town-clock strike before, nor the evening sounds of the village; for we slept with the windows open, which were inside the grating. It was to see my native village in the light of the middle ages, and our Concord was turned into a Rhine stream, and visions of knights and castles passed before me. They were the voices of old burghers that I heard in the streets. I was an involuntary spectator and auditor of whatever was done and said in the kitchen of the adjacent village-inn,— a wholly new and rare experience to me. It was a closer view of my native town. I was fairly inside of it. I never had seen its institutions before. This is one of its peculiar institutions; for it is a shire town. I began to comprehend what its inhabitants were about.

In the morning, our breakfasts were put through the hole in the door, 32 in small oblong-square tin pans, made to fit, and holding a pint of chocolate, with brown bread, and an iron spoon. When they called for the vessels again, I was green enough to return what bread I had left; but my comrade seized it, and said that I should lay that up for lunch or dinner. Soon after, he was let out to work at haying in a neighboring field, whither he went every day, and would not be back till noon; so he bade me good-day, saying that he doubted if he should see me again.

When I came out of prison,—for some one interfered, and paid the *33* tax,—I did not perceive that great changes had taken place on the common, such as he observed who went in a youth, and emerged a tottering and gray-headed man; and yet a change had to my eyes come over the scene,—the town, and State, and country,—greater than any that mere time could effect. I saw yet more distinctly the State in which I lived. I saw to what extent the people among whom I lived could be trusted as good neighbors and friends; that their friendship was for summer weather only; that they did not greatly purpose to do right; that they were a distinct race from me by their prejudices and superstitions, as the Chinamen and Malays are; that, in their sacrifices to humanity, they ran no risks, not even to their property; that, after all, they were not so noble but they treated the thief as he had treated them, and hoped, by a certain outward observance and a few prayers, and by walking in a particular straight though useless path from time to time, to save their souls. This may be to judge my neighbors harshly; for I believe that most of them are not aware that they have such an institution as the jail in their village.

It was formerly the custom in our village, when a poor debtor came *34* out of jail, for his acquaintances to salute him, looking through their fingers, which were crossed to represent the grating of a jail window, "How do ye do?" My neighbors did not thus salute me, but first looked at me, and then at one another, as if I had returned from a long journey. I was put into jail as I was going to the shoemaker's to get a shoe which was mended. When I was let out the next morning, I proceeded to finish my errand, and, having put on my mended shoe, joined a huckleberry party, who were impatient to put themselves under my conduct; and in half an hour,—for the horse was soon tackled,—was in the midst of a huckleberry field, on one of our highest hills, two miles off; and then the State was nowhere to be seen.

This is the whole history of "My Prisons." *35*

I have never declined paying the highway tax, because I am as desirous *36* of being a good neighbor as I am of being a bad subject; and, as for supporting schools, I am doing my part to educate my fellow-countrymen now. It is for no particular item in the tax-bill that I refuse to pay it. I simply wish to refuse allegiance to the State, to withdraw and stand aloof from it effectually. I do not care to trace the course of my dollar, if I could, till it buys a man, or a musket to shoot one with,—the dollar is innocent,—but I am concerned to trace the effects of my allegiance. In fact, I quietly declare war with the State, after my fashion, though I will still make what use and get what advantage of her I can, as is usual in such cases.

If others pay the tax which is demanded of me, from a sympathy with *37* the State, they do but what they have already done in their own case, or rather they abet injustice to a greater extent than the State requires. If they pay the tax from a mistaken interest in the individual taxed, to save his property or prevent his going to jail, it is because they have not considered wisely how far they let their private feelings interfere with the public good.

This, then, is my position at present. But one cannot be too much on *38* his guard in such a case, lest his action be biassed by obstinacy, or an undue regard for the opinions of men. Let him see that he does only what belongs to himself and to the hour.

I think sometimes, Why, this people mean well; they are only ignorant; *39* they would do better if they knew how: why give your neighbors this pain to treat you as they are not inclined to? But I think, again, this is no reason why I should do as they do, or permit others to suffer much greater pain of a different kind. Again, I sometimes say to myself, When many millions of men, without heat, without ill-will, without personal feeling of any kind, demand of you a few shillings only, without the possibility, such is their constitution, of retracting or altering their present demand, and without the possibility, on your side, of appeal to any other millions, why expose yourself to this overwhelming brute force? You do not resist cold and hunger, the winds and the waves, thus obstinately; you quietly submit to a thousand similar necessities. You do not put your head into the fire. But just in proportion as I regard this as not wholly a brute force, but partly a human force, and consider that I have relations to those millions as to so many millions of men, and not of mere brute or inanimate things, I see that appeal is possible, first and instantaneously, from them to the Maker of them, and secondly, from them to themselves. But, if I put my head deliberately into the fire, there is no appeal to fire or to the Maker of fire, and I have only myself to blame. If I could convince myself that I have any right to be satisfied with men as they are, and to treat them accordingly, and not according, in some respects, to my requisitions and expectations of what they and I ought to be, then, like a good Mussulman and fatalist, I should endeavor to be satisfied with things as they are, and say it is the will of God. And, above all, there is this difference between resisting this and a purely brute or natural force, that I can resist this with some effect; but I cannot expect, like Orpheus, to change the nature of the rocks and trees and beasts.

I do not wish to quarrel with any man or nation. I do not wish to *40* split hairs, to make fine distinctions, or set myself up as better than my neighbors. I seek rather, I may say, even an excuse for conforming to the laws of the land. I am but too ready to conform to them. Indeed I have reason to suspect myself on this head; and each year, as the tax-gatherer comes round, I find myself disposed to review the acts and position of the general and state governments, and the spirit of the people, to discover a pretext for conformity. I believe that the State will soon be able to take all my work of this sort out of my hands, and then I shall be no better a patriot than my fellow-countrymen. Seen from a lower point of view, the Constitution, with all its faults, is very good; the law and the courts are very respectable; even this State and this American government are, in many respects, very admirable and rare things, to be thankful for, such as a great many have described them; but seen from a point of view a little higher, they are what I have described them; seen from a higher still, and the highest, who shall say what they are, or that they are worth looking at or thinking of at all?

However, the government does not concern me much, and I shall *41* bestow the fewest possible thoughts on it. It is not many moments that I live under a government, even in this world. If a man is thought-free, fancy-free, imagination-free, that which *is not* never for a long time appearing *to be* to him, unwise rulers or reformers cannot fatally interrupt him.

I know that most men think differently from myself; but those whose *42* lives are by profession devoted to the study of these or kindred subjects, content me as little as any. Statesmen and legislators, standing so completely within the institution, never distinctly and nakedly behold it. They speak of moving society, but have no resting-place without it. They may be men of a certain experience and discrimination, and have no doubt invented ingenious and even useful systems, for which we sincerely thank them; but all their wit and usefulness lie within certain not very wide limits. They are wont to forget that the world is not governed by policy and expediency. Webster* never goes behind government, and so cannot speak with authority about it. His words are wisdom to those legislators who contemplate no essential reform in the existing government; but for thinkers, and those who legislate for all time, he never once glances at the subject. I know of those whose serene and wise speculations on this theme would soon reveal the limits of his mind's range and hospitality. Yet, compared with the cheap professions of most reformers, and the still cheaper wisdom and eloquence of politicians in general, his are almost the only sensible and valuable words, and we thank Heaven for him. Comparatively, he is always strong, original, and, above all, practical. Still his quality is not wisdom, but prudence. The lawyer's truth is not Truth, but consistency, or a consistent expediency. Truth is always in harmony with herself, and is not concerned chiefly to reveal the justice that may consist with wrong-doing. He well deserves to be called, as he has been called, the Defender of the Constitution.

* Daniel Webster (1782–1852), prominent Whig politician of the second quarter of the 19th century.

There are really no blows to be given by him but defensive ones. He is not a leader, but a follower. His leaders are the men of '87.* "I have never made an effort," he says, "and never propose to make an effort; I have never countenanced an effort, and never mean to countenance an effort, to disturb the arrangement as originally made, by which the various States came into the Union."† Still thinking of the sanction which the Constitution gives to slavery, he says, "Because it was a part of the original compact,—let it stand." Notwithstanding his special acuteness and ability, he is unable to take a fact out of its merely political relations, and behold it as it lies absolutely to be disposed of by the intellect,— what, for instance, it behoves a man to do here in America to-day with regard to slavery, but ventures, or is driven, to make some such desperate answer as the following, while professing to speak absolutely, and as a private man,—from which what new and singular code of social duties might be inferred?—"The manner," says he, "in which the government of those States where slavery exists are to regulate it, is for their own consideration, under their responsibility to their constituents, to the general laws of propriety, humanity, and justice, and to God. Associations formed elsewhere, springing from a feeling of humanity, or any other cause, have nothing whatever to do with it. They have never received any encouragement from me, and they never will."

They who know of no purer sources of truth, who have traced up its 43 stream no higher, stand, and wisely stand, by the Bible and the Constitution, and drink at it there with reverence and humility; but they who behold where it comes trickling into this lake or that pool, gird up their loins once more, and continue their pilgrimage toward its fountain-head.

No man with a genius for legislation has appeared in America. They 44 are rare in the history of the world. There are orators, politicians, and eloquent men, by the thousand; but the speaker has not yet opened his mouth to speak, who is capable of settling the much-vexed questions of the day. We love eloquence for its own sake, and not for any truth which it may utter, or any heroism it may inspire. Our legislators have not yet learned the comparative value of free-trade and of freedom, of union, and of rectitude, to a nation. They have no genius or talent for comparatively humble questions of taxation and finance, commerce and manufactures and agriculture. If we were left solely to the wordy wit of legislators in Congress for our guidance, uncorrected by the seasonable experience and the effectual complaints of the people, America would not long retain her rank among the nations. For eighteen hundred years, though perchance I have no right to say it, the New Testament has been written; yet where is the legislator who has wisdom and practical talent

* The writers of the Constitution, who convened at Philadelphia in 1787.
† From Webster's speech on *The Admission of Texas* (December 22, 1845).

enough to avail himself of the light which it sheds on the science of legislation?

The authority of government, even such as I am willing to submit 45 to,—for I will cheerfully obey those who know and can do better than I, and in many things even those who neither know nor can do so well,— is still an impure one: to be strictly just, it must have the sanction and consent of the governed. It can have no pure right over my person and property but what I concede to it. The progress from an absolute to a limited monarchy, from a limited monarchy to a democracy, is a progress toward a true respect for the individual. Is a democracy, such as we know it, the last improvement possible in government? Is it not possible to take a step further towards recognizing and organizing the rights of man? There will never be a really free and enlightened State, until the State comes to recognize the individual as a higher and independent power, from which all its own power and authority are derived, and treats him accordingly. I please myself with imagining a State at last which can afford to be just to all men, and to treat the individual with respect as a neighbor; which even would not think it inconsistent with its own repose, if a few were to live aloof from it, not meddling with it, nor embraced by it, who fulfilled all the duties of neighbors and fellow-men. A State which bore this kind of fruit, and suffered it to drop off as fast as it ripened, would prepare the way for a still more perfect and glorious State, which also I have imagined, but not yet anywhere seen.

Study Questions

1. In "Resistance to Civil Government," is Thoreau's purpose to explain his behavior, to convince others to act as he has, or to do both? What words or phrases help you to identify that purpose?
2. Thoreau opens his essay by directly stating his opinion concerning the best kind of government. What effect does this statement have on you? What effects might it have on other readers? Based on your reading of the entire essay, what reasons do you think Thoreau may have had for such an opening?
3. In paragraphs 26–35, Thoreau tells the story of "My Prisons." What purpose does this passage serve? Identify the chief words and phrases that signal the method of organization used in these paragraphs.
4. Thoreau's statements on government are often radical, not only for his time but for ours as well. How does he try to show his readers that his ideas are not unreasonable? How does he express his concern that his audience might refuse to read his essay all the way through?

Suggestion for Drafting

In paragraph 5 Thoreau uses classification to list the various categories of citizens that a state might contain and discusses their characteristics. Obviously he favors those citizens who "serve the State with their conscience also." Draft a paragraph in which you use definition to discuss this kind of citizen.

Corn-Pone Opinions

Mark Twain

Fifty years ago, when I was a boy of fifteen and 1
helping to inhabit a Missourian village on the
banks of the Mississippi, I had a friend whose
society was very dear to me because I was forbidden by my mother to
partake of it. He was a gay and impudent and satirical and delightful
young black man—a slave—who daily preached sermons from the top of
his master's woodpile, with me for sole audience. He imitated the pulpit
style of the several clergymen of the village, and did it well, and with
fine passion and energy. To me he was a wonder. I believed he was the
greatest orator in the United States and would some day be heard from.
But it did not happen; in the distribution of rewards he was overlooked.
It is the way, in this world.

He interrupted his preaching, now and then, to saw a stick of wood; 2
but the sawing was a pretense—he did it with his mouth; exactly imitating
the sound the bucksaw makes in shrieking its way through the wood.
But it served its purpose; it kept his master from coming out to see how
the work was getting along. I listened to the sermons from the open
window of a lumber room at the back of the house. One of his texts was
this:

"You tell me whar a man gits his corn pone, en I'll tell you what his 3
'pinions is."

I can never forget it. It was deeply impressed upon me. By my 4
mother. Not upon my memory, but elsewhere. She had slipped in upon
me while I was absorbed and not watching. The black philosopher's
idea was that a man is not independent, and cannot afford views which
might interfere with his bread and butter. If he would prosper, he must
train with the majority; in matters of large moment, like politics and
religion, he must think and feel with the bulk of his neighbors, or suffer
damage in his social standing and in his business prosperities. He must
restrict himself to corn-pone opinions—at least on the surface. He must
get his opinions from other people; he must reason out none for himself;
he must have no first-hand views.

I think Jerry was right, in the main, but I think he did not go far 5
enough.

1. It was his idea that a man conforms to the majority view of his locality 6
   by calculation and intention.
   This happens, but I think it is not the rule.   7

2. It was his idea that there is such a thing as a first-hand opinion; an *8*
original opinion; an opinion which is coldly reasoned out in a man's
head, by a searching analysis of the facts involved, with the heart
unconsulted, and the jury room closed against outside influences. It
may be that such an opinion has been born somewhere, at some time
or other, but I suppose it got away before they could catch it and stuff
is and put it in the museum.

I am persuaded that a coldly-thought-out and independent verdict upon *9*
a fashion in clothes, or manners, or literature, or politics, or religion, or
any other matter that is projected into the field of our notice and interest,
is a most rare thing—if it has indeed ever existed.

A new thing in costume appears—the flaring hoop skirt, for example— *10*
and the passers-by are shocked, and the irreverent laugh. Six months
later everybody is reconciled; the fashion has established itself; it is
admired, now, and no one laughs. Public opinion resented it before,
public opinion accepts it now, and is happy in it. Why? Was the resentment reasoned out? Was the acceptance reasoned out? No. The instinct
that moves to conformity did the work. It is our nature to conform; it
is a force which not many can successfully resist. What is its seat? The
inborn requirement of self-approval. We all have to bow to that; there
are no exceptions. Even the woman who refuses from first to last to
wear the hoop skirt comes under the law and is its slave; she could not
wear the skirt and have her own approval; and that she *must* have, she
cannot help herself. But as a rule our self-approval has its source in but
one place and not elsewhere—the approval of other people. A person
of vast consequences can introduce any kind of novelty in dress and the
general world will presently adopt it—moved to do it, in the first place,
by the natural instinct to passively yield to that vague something recognized as authority, and in the second place by the human instinct to train
with the multitude and have its approval. An empress introduced the
hoop skirt, and we know the result. A nobody introduced the bloomer,
and we know the result. If Eve should come again, in her ripe renown,
and reintroduce her quaint styles—well, we know what would happen.
And we should be cruelly embarrassed, along at first.

The hoop skirt runs its course and disappears. Nobody reasons about *11*
it. One woman abandons the fashion; her neighbor notices this and
follows her lead; this influences the next woman; and so on and so on,
and presently the skirt has vanished out of the world, no one knows how
nor why; or cares for that matter. It will come again, by and by, and in
due course will go again.

Twenty-five years ago, in England, six or eight wine glasses stood *12*
grouped by each person's plate at a dinner party, and they were used,
not left idle and empty; today there are but three or four in the group,
and the average guest sparingly uses about two of them. We have not

adopted this new fashion yet, but we shall do it presently. We shall not think it out; we shall merely conform, and let it go at that. We get our notions and habits and opinions from outside influences; we do not have to study them out.

Our table manners, and company manners, and street manners change   13 from time to time, but the changes are not reasoned out; we merely notice and conform. We are creatures of outside influences, as a rule we do not think, we only imitate. We can not invent standards that will stick; what we mistake for standards are only fashions, and perishable. We may continue to admire them, but we drop the use of them. We notice this in literature. Shakespeare is a standard, and fifty years ago we used to write tragedies which we couldn't tell from—from somebody else's; but we don't do it any more, now. Our prose standard, three-quarters of a century ago, was ornate and diffuse; some authority or other changed it in the direction of compactness and simplicity, and conformity followed, without argument. The historical novel starts up suddenly, and sweeps the land. Everybody writes one, and the nation is glad. We had historical novels before; but nobody read them, and the rest of us conformed—without reasoning it out. We are conforming in the other way, now, because it is another case of everybody.

The outside influences are always pouring in upon us, and we are   14 always obeying their orders and accepting their verdicts. The Smiths like the new play; the Joneses go to see it, and they copy the Smith verdict. Morals, religions, politics, get their following from surrounding influences and atmospheres, almost entirely; not from study, not from thinking. A man must and will have his own approval first of all, in each and every moment and circumstance of his life—even if he must repent of a self-approved act the moment after its commission, in order to get his self-approval *again*: but, speaking in general terms, a man's self-approval in the large concerns of life has its source in the approval of the peoples about him, and not in a searching personal examination of the matter. Mohammedans are Mohammedans because they are born and reared among that sect, not because they have thought it out and can furnish sound reasons for being Mohammedans; we know why Catholics are Catholics; why Presbyterians are Presbyterians; why Baptists are Baptists; why Mormons are Mormons; why thieves are thieves; why monarchists are monarchists; why Republicans are Republicans and Democrats, Democrats. We know it is a matter of association and sympathy, not reasoning and examination; that hardly a man in the world has an opinion upon morals, politics, or religion which he got otherwise than through his associations and sympathies. Broadly speaking, there are none but corn-pone opinions. And broadly speaking, corn-pone stands for self-approval. Self-approval is acquired mainly from the approval of other people. The result is conformity. Sometimes conformity has a sordid business interest—the bread-and-butter interest—but not in most cases, I think. I think that in the majority of cases it is unconscious and not calculated; that it is born of the human being's natural yearning to stand well with his fellows and have their inspiring approval and praise—a yearning which is commonly so strong and so insistent that it cannot be effectually resisted, and must have its way.

A political emergency brings out the corn-pone opinion in fine force *15* in its two chief varieties—the pocketbook variety, which has its origin in self-interest, and the bigger variety, the sentimental variety—the one which can't bear to be outside the pale; can't bear to be in disfavor; can't endure the averted face and the cold shoulder; wants to stand well with his friends, wants to be smiled upon, wants to be welcome, wants to hear the precious words, "*He's* on the right track!" Uttered, perhaps by an ass, but still an ass of high degree, an ass whose approval is gold and diamonds to a smaller ass, and confers glory and honor and happiness, and membership in the herd. For these gauds many a man will dump his life-long principles into the street, and his conscience along with them. We have seen it happen. In some millions of instances.

Men think they think upon great political questions, and they do; but *16* they think with their party, not independently; they read its literature, but not that of the other side; they arrive at convictions, but they are drawn from a partial view of the matter in hand and are of no particular value. They swarm with their party, they feel with their party, they are happy in their party's approval; and where the party leads they will follow, whether for right and honor, or through blood and dirt and a mush of mutilated morals.

In our late canvass half of the nation passionately believed that in *17* silver lay salvation, the other half as passionately believed that that way lay destruction. Do you believe that a tenth part of the people, on either side, had any rational excuse for having an opinion about the matter at all? I studied that mighty question to the bottom—came out empty. Half of our people passionately believe in high tariff, the other half believe otherwise. Does this mean study and examination, or only feeling? The latter, I think. I have deeply studied that question, too—and didn't arrive. We all do no end of feeling, and we mistake it for thinking. And out of it we get an aggregation which we consider a boon. Its name is public opinion. It is held in reverence. It settles everything. Some think it the voice of God.

Study Questions

1. Mark Twain is popularly known as a humorist. How humorous do you find "Corn-Pone Opinions"? Identify specific passages that illustrate his humor, or lack of it.
2. What is Twain's opinion of his fellow human beings? Would he consider that view a "corn-pone opinion"? Why?

3. In the first paragraph, Twain briefly sketches the character who coined the words of the title. Then Twain expresses his opinion of this man and his life. How does his opinion create a context for the rest of the essay?
4. List the kinds of examples of corn-pone opinions that Twain gives us in the order in which they appear. Is there any logic to that order? How does the order allow Twain to make stronger statements toward the end of the essay than he could have made at the beginning?
5. What would Twain say about the enormous use of opinion polls in politics today? Would he be surprised by their widespread use?

Suggestion for Drafting

The following "paragraph" is from "Corn-Pone Opinions," but we have jumbled the order of the sentences. Without referring to the original, reorder these sentences so that they follow a logical sequence:

(1) Even the woman who refuses from first to last to wear the hoop skirt comes under the law and is its slave; she could not wear the skirt and have her own approval; and that she *must* have, she cannot help herself. (2) A nobody introduced the bloomer, and we know the result. (3) If Eve should come again, in her ripe renown, and reintroduce her quaint styles—well, we know what would happen. (4) A new thing in costume appears—the flaring hoop skirt, for example—and the passers-by are shocked, and the irreverent laugh. (5) It is our nature to conform; it is a force which not many can successfully resist. (6) An empress introduced the hoop skirt, and we know the result. (7) Six months later everybody is reconciled; the fashion has established itself; it is admired, now, and no one laughs. (8) And we should be cruelly embarrassed, along at first. (9) Why? Was the resentment reasoned out? Was the acceptance reasoned out? (10) But as a rule our self-approval has its source in but one place and not elsewhere—the approval of other people. (11) What is its seat? The inborn requirement of self-approval. (12) We all have to bow to that; there are no exceptions. (13) A person of vast consequences can introduce any kind of novelty in dress and the general world will presently adopt it—moved to do it, in the first place, by the natural instinct to passively yield to that vague something recognized as authority, and in the second place by the human instinct to train with the multitude and have its approval. (14) Public opinion resented it before, public opinion accepts it now, and is happy in it. (15) No. The instinct that moves to conformity did the work.

After you have reordered these sentences, underline the words and phrases that signaled the organization to you, and discuss how they aided you in choosing the order you did.

The Lost Dimension in Religion

Paul Tillich

E very observer of our Western civilization is *1*
aware of the fact that something has happened
to religion. It especially strikes the observer
of the American scene. Everywhere he finds symptoms of what one has
called religious revival, or more modestly, the revival of interest in religion. He finds them in the churches with their rapidly increasing membership. He finds them in the mushroomlike growth of sects. He finds
them on college campuses and in the theological faculties of universities.
Most conspicuously, he finds them in the tremendous success of men
like Billy Graham and Norman Vincent Peale, who attract masses of
people Sunday after Sunday, meeting after meeting. The facts cannot be
denied, but how should they be interpreted? It is my intention to show
that these facts must be seen as expressions of the predicament of Western man in the second half of the twentieth century. But I would even
go a step further. I believe that the predicament of man in our period
gives us also an important insight into the predicament of man generally—
at all times and in all parts of the earth.

There are many analyses of man and society in our time. Most of *2*
them show important traits in the picture, but few of them succeed in
giving a general key to our present situation. Although it is not easy to
find such a key, I shall attempt it and, in so doing, will make an assertion
which may be somewhat mystifying at first hearing. The decisive element
in the predicament of Western man in our period is his loss of the
dimension of depth. Of course, "dimension of depth" is a metaphor. It
is taken from the spatial realm and applied to man's spiritual life. What
does it mean?

It means that man has lost an answer to the question: What is the *3*
meaning of life? Where do we come from, where do we go to? What
shall we do, what should we become in the short stretch between birth
and death? Such questions are not answered or even asked if the "dimension of depth" is lost. And this is precisely what has happened to
man in our period of history. He has lost the courage to ask such
questions with an infinite seriousness—as former generations did—and
he has lost the courage to receive answers to these questions, wherever
they may come from.

I suggest that we call the dimension of depth the religious dimension *4*
in man's nature. Being religious means asking passionately the question
of the meaning of our existence and being willing to receive answers,

even if the answers hurt. Such an idea of religion makes religion universally human, but it certainly differs from what is usually called religion. It does not describe religion as the belief in the existence of gods or one God, and as a set of activities and institutions for the sake of relating oneself to these beings in thought, devotion and obedience. No one can deny that the religions which have appeared in history are religions in this sense. Nevertheless, religion in its innermost nature is more than religion in this narrower sense. It is the state of being concerned about one's own being and being universally.

There are many people who are ultimately concerned in this way who 5 feel far removed, however, from religion in the narrower sense, and therefore from every historical religion. It often happens that such people take the question of the meaning of their life infinitely seriously and reject any historical religion just for this reason. They feel that the concrete religions fail to express their profound concern adequately. They are religious while rejecting the religions. It is this experience which forces us to distinguish the meaning of religion as living in the dimension of depth from particular expressions of one's ultimate concern in the symbols and institutions of a concrete religion. If we now turn to the concrete analysis of the religious situation of our time, it is obvious that our key must be the basic meaning of religion and not any particular religion, not even Christianity. What does this key disclose about the predicament of man in our period?

If we define religion as the state of being grasped by an infinite concern 6 we must say: Man in our time has lost such infinite concern. And the resurgence of religion is nothing but a desperate and mostly futile attempt to regain what has been lost.

How did the dimension of depth become lost? Like any important 7 event, it has many causes, but certainly not the one which one hears often mentioned from ministers' pulpits and evangelists' platforms, namely that a widespread impiety of modern man is responsible. Modern man is neither more pious nor more impious than man in any other period. The loss of the dimension of depth is caused by the relation of man to his world and to himself in our period, the period in which nature is being subjected scientifically and technically to the control of man. In this period, life in the dimension of depth is replaced by life in the horizontal dimension. The driving forces of the industrial society of which we are a part go ahead horizontally and not vertically. In popular terms this is expressed in phrases like "better and better," "bigger and bigger," "more and more." One should not disparage the feeling which lies behind such speech. Man is right in feeling that he is able to know and transform the world he encounters without a foreseeable limit. He can go ahead in all directions without a definite boundary.

A most expressive symbol of this attitude of going ahead in the hori- 8 zontal dimension is the breaking through of the space which is controlled by the gravitational power of the earth into the world-space. It is interesting that one calls this world-space simply "space" and speaks, for instance, of space travel, as if every trip were not travel into space. Perhaps one feels that the true nature of space has been discovered only through our entering into indefinite world-space. In any case, the predominance of the horizontal dimension over the dimension of depth has been immensely increased by the opening up of the space beyond the space of the earth.

If we now ask what does man do and seek if he goes ahead in the *9* horizontal dimension, the answer is difficult. Sometimes one is inclined to say that the mere movement ahead without an end, the intoxication with speeding forward without limits, is what satisfies him. But this answer is by no means sufficient. For on his way into space and time man changes the world he encounters. And the changes made by him change himself. He transforms everything he encounters into a tool; and in doing so he himself becomes a tool. But if he asks, a tool for what, there is no answer.

One does not need to look far beyond everyone's daily experience in *10* order to find examples to describe this predicament. Indeed our daily life in office and home, in cars and airplanes, at parties and conferences, while reading magazines and watching television, while looking at advertisements and hearing radio, are in themselves continuous examples of a life which has lost the dimension of depth. It runs ahead, every moment is filled with something which must be done or seen or said or planned. But no one can experience depth without stopping and becoming aware of himself. Only if he has moments in which he does not care about what comes next can he experience the meaning of this moment here and now and ask himself about the meaning of his life. As long as the preliminary, transitory concerns are not silenced, no matter how interesting and valuable and important they may be, the voice of the ultimate concern cannot be heard. This is the deepest root of the loss of the dimension of depth in our period—the loss of religion in its basic and universal meaning.

If the dimension of depth is lost, the symbols in which life in this *11* dimension has expressed itself must also disappear. I am speaking of the great symbols of the historical religions in our Western world, of Judaism and Christianity. The reason that the religious symbols became lost is not primarily scientific criticism, but it is a complete misunderstanding of their meaning; and only because of this misunderstanding was scientific critique able, and even justified, in attacking them. The first step toward the nonreligion of the Western world was made by religion itself. When it defended its great symbols, not as symbols, but as literal stories, it had already lost the battle. In doing so the theologians (and today many religious laymen) helped to transfer the powerful expressions of the dimension of depth into objects or happenings on the horizontal plane. There the symbols lose their power and meaning and become an easy prey to physical, biological and historical attack.

If the symbol of creation which points to the divine ground of every- *12* thing is transferred to the horizontal plane, it becomes a story of events in a removed past for which there is no evidence, but which contradicts every piece of scientific evidence. If the symbol of the Fall of Man, which points to the tragic estrangement of man and his world from their true being is transferred to the horizontal plane, it becomes a story of a human couple a few thousand years ago in what is now present-day Iraq. One of the most profound psychological descriptions of the general human predicament becomes an absurdity on the horizontal plane. If the symbols of the Saviour and the salvation through Him which point to the healing power in history and personal life are transferred to the horizontal plane, they become stories of a half-divine being coming from a heavenly place and returning to it. Obviously, in this form, they have no meaning whatsoever for people whose view of the universe is determined by scientific astronomy.

If the idea of God (and the symbols applied to Him) which expresses *13* man's ultimate concern is transferred to the horizontal plane, God becomes a being among others whose existence or nonexistence is a matter of inquiry. Nothing, perhaps, is more symptomatic of the loss of the dimension of depth than the permanent discussion about the existence or nonexistence of God—a discussion in which both sides are equally wrong, because the discussion itself is wrong and possible only after the loss of the dimension of depth.

When in this way man has deprived himself of the dimension of depth *14* and the symbols expressing it, he then becomes a part of the horizontal plane. He loses his self and becomes a thing among things. He becomes an element in the process of manipulated production and manipulated consumption. This is now a matter of public knowledge. We have become aware of the degree to which everyone in our social structure is managed, even if one knows it and even if one belongs himself to the managing group. The influence of the gang mentality on adolescents, of the corporation's demands on the executives, of the conditioning of everyone by public communication, by propaganda and advertising under the guidance of motivation research, et cetera, have all been described in many books and articles.

Under these pressures, man can hardly escape the fate of becoming *15* a thing among the things he produces, a bundle of conditioned reflexes without a free, deciding and responsible self. The immense mechanism, set up by man to produce objects for his use, transforms man himself into an object used by the same mechanism of production and consumption.

But man has not ceased to be man. He resists this fate anxiously, *16* desperately, courageously. He asks the question, for what? And he realizes that there is no answer. He becomes aware of the emptiness which is covered by the continuous movement ahead and the production of means for ends which become means again without an ultimate end. Without knowing what happened to him, he feels that he has lost the meaning of life, the dimension of depth.

Out of this awareness the religious question arises and religious an- *17* swers are received or rejected. Therefore, in order to describe the contemporary attitude toward religion, we must first point to the places where the awareness of the predicament of Western man in our period is most sharply expressed. These places are the great art, literature and, partly, at least, the philosophy of our time. It is both the subject matter and the style of these creations which show the passionate and often tragic struggle about the meaning of life in a period in which man has lost the dimension of depth. This art, literature, philosophy is not religious in the narrower sense of the word; but it asks the religious question more radically and more profoundly than most directly religious expressions of our time.

It is the religious question which is asked when the novelist describes *18* a man who tries in vain to reach the only place which could solve the problem of his life, or a man who disintegrates under the memory of a guilt which persecutes him, or a man who never had a real self and is pushed by his fate without resistance to death, or a man who experiences a profound disgust of everything he encounters.

It is the religious question which is asked when the poet opens up the *19* horror and the fascination of the demonic regions of his soul, or if he leads us into the deserts and empty places of our being, or if he shows the physical and moral mud under the surface of life, or if he sings the song of transitoriness, giving words to the ever-present anxiety of our hearts.

It is the religious question which is asked when the playwright shows *20* the illusion of a life in a ridiculous symbol, or if he lets the emptiness of a life's work end in self-destruction, or if he confronts us with the inescapable bondage to mutual hate and guilt, or if he leads us into the dark cellar of lost hopes and slow disintegration.

It is the religious question which is asked when the painter breaks the *21* visible surface into pieces, then reunites them into a great picture which has little similarity with the world at which we normally look, but which expresses our anxiety and our courage to face reality.

It is the religious question which is asked when the architect, *22* in creating office buildings or churches, removes the trimmings taken over from past styles because they cannot be considered an honest expression of our own period. He prefers the seeming poverty of a purpose-determined style to the deceptive richness of imitated styles of the past. He knows that he gives no final answer, but he does give an honest answer.

The philosophy of our time shows the same hiddenly religious traits. *23* It is divided into two main schools of thought, the analytic and the existentialist. The former tries to analyze logical and linguistic forms which are always used and which underlie all scientific research. One may compare them with the painters who dissolve the natural forms of bodies into cubes, planes and lines; or with those architects who want the structural "bones" of their buildings to be conspicuously visible and not hidden by covering features. This self-restriction produces the almost monastic poverty and seriousness of this philosophy. It is religious— without any contact with religion in its method—by exercising the humility of "learned ignorance."

In contrast to this school the existentialist philosophers have much to *24* say about the problems of human existence. They bring into rational concepts what the writers and poets, the painters and architects, are expressing in their particular material. What they express is the human predicament in time and space, in anxiety and guilt and the feeling of meaninglessness. From Pascal in the seventeenth century to Heidegger and Sartre in our time, philosophers have emphasized the contrast between human dignity and human misery. And by doing so, they have raised the religious question. Some have tried to answer the question they have asked. But if they did so, they turned back to past traditions and offered to our time that which does not fit our time. Is it possible for our time to receive answers which are born out of our time?

Answers given today are in danger of strengthening the present situa- *25* tion and with it the questions to which they are supposed to be the answers. This refers to some of the previously mentioned major representatives of the so-called resurgence of religion, as for instance the evangelist Billy Graham and the counseling and healing minister, Norman Vincent Peale. Against the validity of the answers given by the former, one must say that, in spite of his personal integrity, his propagandistic methods and his primitive theological fundamentalism fall short of what is needed to give an answer to the religious question of our period. In spite of all his seriousness, he does not take the radical questions of our period seriously.

The effect that Norman Peale has on large groups of people is rooted *26* in the fact that he confirms the situation which he is supposed to help overcome. He heals people with the purpose of making them fit again for the demands of the competitive and conformist society in which we are living. He helps them to become adapted to the situation which is characterized by the loss of the dimension of depth. Therefore, his advice is valid on this level; but it is the validity of this level that is the true religious question of our time. And this question he neither raises nor answers.

In many cases the increase of church membership and interest in *27* religious activities does not mean much more than the religious consecration of a state of things in which the religious dimension has been lost. It is the desire to participate in activities which are socially strongly approved and give internal and a certain amount of external security. This is not necessarily bad, but it certainly is not an answer to the religious question of our period.

Is there an answer? There is always an answer, but the answer may *28* not be available to us. We may be too deeply steeped in the predicament out of which the question arises to be able to answer it. To acknowledge this is certainly a better way toward a real answer than to bar the way to it by deceptive answers. And it may be that in this attitude the real answer (within available limits) is given. The real answer to the question of how to regain the dimension of depth is not given by increased church membership or church attendance, nor by conversion or healing experiences. But it is given by the awareness that we have lost the decisive dimension of life, the dimension of depth, and that there is no easy way of getting it back. Such awareness is in itself a state of being grasped by that which is symbolized in the term, dimension of depth. He who realizes that he is separated from the ultimate source of meaning shows by this realization that he is not only separated but also reunited. And this is just our situation. What we need above all—and partly have—is the radical realization of our predicament, without trying to cover it up by secular or religious ideologies. The revival of religious interest would be a creative power in our culture if it would develop into a movement of search for the lost dimension of depth.

This does not mean that the traditional religious symbols should be *29* dismissed. They certainly have lost their meaning in the literalistic form into which they have been distorted, thus producing the critical reaction against them. But they have not lost their genuine meaning, namely, of answering the question which is implied in man's very existence in powerful, revealing and saving symbols. If the resurgence of religion would produce a new understanding of the symbols of the past and their relevance for our situation, instead of premature and deceptive answers, it would become a creative factor in our culture and a saving factor for many who live in estrangement, anxiety and despair. The religious answer has always the character of "in spite of." In spite of the loss of dimension of depth, its power is present, and most present in those who are aware of the loss and are striving to regain it with ultimate seriousness.

Study Questions

1. In "The Lost Dimension in Religion," Paul Tillich deals with a topic that might alienate a large number of readers. Given the potential for angering his audience, how does he anticipate the problem and try to moderate readers' reactions? How does his opening question help in this moderation?
2. Tillich follows his opening paragraph with a discussion of the concept he calls *dimension of depth*. What does he mean by this term? What method of organization does he use to present the topic?
3. Starting with paragraph 18, Tillich introduces a set of parallel statements that begin with the words "It is the religious question . . ." How is his message strengthened by his use of this kind of structuring? What kind of organization does he employ here?
4. In paragraph 23 the author introduces a new topic and signals a new method of organization as well. What is that organization? How does the organization also show his feelings toward the new topic?

Suggestion for Drafting

In a rather interesting form of conceptual organization, Tillich first poses a problem and then tries to solve it. Each time he begins a new paragraph with *if* he signals that he is posing a new problem and that in the paragraphs to follow he will attempt to solve it. By breaking down his topic into a series of problems to pose and solve, he is able to cover the issue step by step in a highly controlled fashion.

In the suggestion for prewriting following Fromm's "The Nature of Symbolic Language," you were asked to practice clustering by making a diagram of your associations with a universal symbol, such as fire. Write the draft of the body of an essay in which you present these associations by first posing a question about each of the words or phrases directly connected with the symbol and then answering each question by explaining how these "meanings" came to you. For example, based on the clustering represented in fig. 2.1 (p. 98), one of the questions we might ask would be, "If fire is potentially so destructive, why do I think of it as comforting?" We could then go on to answer it by discussing our images of fireplaces, campfires, loving couples, and winter nights.

Information for Those Who Would Remove to America

Benjamin Franklin

M any Persons in Europe, having directly or by *1* Letters, express'd to the Writer of this, who is well acquainted with North America, their Desire of transporting and establishing themselves in that Country; but who appear to have formed, thro' Ignorance, mistaken Ideas and Expectations of what is to be obtained there; he thinks it may be useful, and prevent inconvenient, expensive, and fruitless Removals and Voyages of improper Persons, if he gives some clearer and truer Notions of that part of the World, than appear to have hitherto prevailed.

He finds it is imagined by Numbers, that the Inhabitants of North *2* America are rich, capable of rewarding, and dispos'd to reward, all sorts of Ingenuity; that they are at the same time ignorant of all the Sciences, and, consequently, that Strangers, possessing Talents in the Belles-Lettres, fine Arts, &c., must be highly esteemed, and so well paid, as to become easily rich themselves; that there are also abundance of profitable Offices to be disposed of, which the Natives are not qualified to fill; and that, having few Persons of Family among them, Strangers of Birth must be greatly respected, and of course easily obtain the best of those Offices, which will make all their Fortunes; that the Governments too, to encourage Emigrations from Europe, not only pay the Expence of personal Transportation, but give Lands gratis to Strangers, with Negroes to work for them, Utensils of Husbandry and Stocks of Cattle. These are all wild Imaginations; and those who go to America with Expectations founded upon them will surely find themselves disappointed.

The Truth is, that though there are in that Country few People so *3* miserable as the Poor of Europe, there are also very few that in Europe would be called rich; it is rather a general happy Mediocrity that prevails. There are few great Proprietors of the Soil, and few Tenants; most People cultivate their own Lands, or follow some Handicraft or Merchandise; very few rich enough to live idly upon their Rents or Incomes, or to pay the high Prices given in Europe for Paintings, Statues, Architecture, and the other Works of Art, that are more curious than useful. Hence the natural Geniuses, that have arisen in America with such Talents, have uniformly quitted that Country for Europe, where they can be more suitably rewarded. It is true, that Letters and Mathematical Knowledge are in Esteem there, but they are at the same time more common than is apprehended; there being already existing nine Colleges or Universities, viz. four in New England, and one in each of the Provinces of New York, New Jersey, Pensilvania, Maryland, and Virginia, all furnish'd with learned Professors; besides a number of smaller Academies; these educate many of their Youth in the Languages, and those Sciences that qualify men for the Professions of Divinity, Law, or Physick. Strangers indeed are by no means excluded from exercising those Professions; and the quick Increase of Inhabitants everywhere gives them a Chance of Employ, which they have in common with the Natives. Of civil Offices, or Employments, there are few; no superfluous Ones, as in Europe; and it is a Rule establish'd in some of the States, that no Office should be so profitable as to make it desirable. The 36th Article of the Constitution of Pennsilvania, runs expressly in these Words; "As every Freeman, to preserve his Independence, (if he has not a sufficient Estate) ought to have some Profession, Calling, Trade, or Farm, whereby he may honestly subsist, there can be no Necessity for, nor Use in, establishing Offices of Profit; the usual Effects of which are Dependance and Servility, unbecoming Freemen, in the Possessors and Expectants; Faction, Contention, Corruption, and Disorder among the People. Wherefore, whenever an Office, thro' Increase of Fees or otherwise, becomes so profitable, as to occasion many to apply for it, the Profits ought to be lessened by the Legislature."

These Ideas prevailing more or less in all the United States, it cannot 4 be worth any Man's while, who has a means of Living at home, to expatriate himself, in hopes of obtaining a profitable civil Office in America; and, as to military Offices, they are at an End with the War, the Armies being disbanded. Much less is it adviseable for a Person to go thither, who has no other Quality to recommend him but his Birth. In Europe it has indeed its Value; but it is a Commodity that cannot be carried to a worse Market than that of America, where people do not inquire concerning a Stranger, *What is he?* but, *What can he do?* If he has any useful Art, he is welcome; and if he exercises it, and behaves well, he will be respected by all that know him; but a mere Man of Quality, who, on that Account, wants to live upon the Public, by some Office or Salary, will be despis'd and disregarded. The Husbandman is in honor there, and even the Mechanic, because their Employments are useful. The People have a saying, that God Almighty is himself a Mechanic, the greatest in the Univers; and he is respected and admired more for the Variety, Ingenuity, and Utility of his Handyworks, than for the Antiquity of his Family. They are pleas'd with the Observation of a Negro, and frequently mention it, that *Boccarorra* (meaning the White men) *make de black man workee, make de Horse workee, make de Ox workee, make ebery ting workee; only de Hog. He, de hog, no workee; he eat, he drink, he walk about, he go to sleep when he please, he libb* *like a Gentleman.* According to these Opinions of the Americans, one of them would think himself more oblig'd to a Genealogist, who could prove for him that his Ancestors and Relations for ten Generations had been Ploughmen, Smiths, Carpenters, Turners, Weavers, Tanners, or even Shoemakers, and consequently that they were useful Members of Society; than if he could only prove that they were Gentlemen, doing nothing of Value, but living idly on the Labour of others, mere *fruges consumere nati,** and otherwise *good for nothing,* till by their Death their Estates, like the Carcass of the Negro's Gentleman-Hog, come to be *cut up.*

With regard to Encouragements for Strangers from Government, they 5 are really only what are derived from good Laws and Liberty. Strangers are welcome, because there is room enough for them all, and therefore the old Inhabitants are not jealous of them; the Laws protect them sufficiently, so that they have no need of the Patronage of Great Men; and every one will enjoy securely the Profits of his Industry. But, if he does not bring a Fortune with him, he must work and be industrious to live. One or two Years' residence gives him all the Rights of a Citizen; but the government does not at present, whatever it may have done in former times, hire People to become Settlers, by Paying their Passages, giving Land, Negroes, Utensils, Stock, or any other kind of Emolument whatsoever. In short, America is the Land of Labour, and by no means what the English call *Lubberland,* and the French *Pays de Cocagne,* where the streets are said to be pav'd with half-peck Loaves, the Houses til'd with Pancakes, and where the Fowls fly about ready roasted, crying, *Come eat me!*

Who then are the kind of Persons to whom an Emigration to America 6 may be advantageous? And what are the Advantages they may reasonably expect?

Land being cheap in that Country, from the vast Forests still void of 7 Inhabitants, and not likely to be occupied in an Age to come, insomuch that the Propriety of an hundred Acres of fertile Soil full of Wood may be obtained near the Frontiers, in many Places, for Eight or Ten Guineas, hearty young Labouring Men, who understand the Husbandry of Corn and Cattle, which is nearly the same in that Country as in Europe, may easily establish themselves there. A little Money sav'd of the good Wages they receive there, while they work for others, enables them to buy the Land and begin their Plantation, in which they are assisted by the Good-Will of their Neighbours, and some Credit. Multitudes of poor People from England, Ireland, Scotland, and Germany, have by this means in a few years become wealthy Farmers, who, in their own Countries, where all the Lands are fully occupied, and the Wages of Labour

---

* ". . . born merely to eat up the corn."—WATTS [*Franklin's note.*]

low, could never have emerged from the poor Condition wherein they were born.

From the salubrity of the Air, the healthiness of the Climate, the plenty 8 of good Provisions, and the Encouragement to early Marriages by the certainty of Subsistence in cultivating the Earth, the Increase of Inhabitants by natural Generation is very rapid in America, and becomes still more so by the Accession of Strangers; hence there is a continual Demand for more Artisans of all the necessary and useful kinds, to supply those Cultivators of the Earth with Houses, and with Furniture and Utensils of the grosser sorts, which cannot so well be brought from Europe. Tolerably good Workmen in any of those mechanic Arts are sure to find Employ, and to be well paid for their Work, there being no Restraints preventing Strangers from exercising any Art they understand, nor any Permission necessary. If they are poor, they begin first as Servants or Journeymen; and if they are sober, industrious, and frugal, they soon become Masters, establish themselves in Business, marry, raise Families, and become respectable Citizens.

Also, Persons of moderate Fortunes and Capitals, who, having a Num- 9 ber of Children to provide for, are desirous of bringing them up to Industry, and to secure Estates for their Posterity, have Opportunities of doing it in America, which Europe does not afford. There they may be taught and practise profitable mechanic Arts, without incurring Disgrace on that Account, but on the contrary acquiring Respect by such Abilities. There small Capitals laid out in Lands, which daily become more valuable by the Increase of People, afford a solid Prospect of ample Fortunes thereafter for those Children. The writer of this has known several Instances of large Tracts of Land, bought, on what was then the Frontier of Pensilvania, for Ten Pounds per hundred Acres, which after 20 years, when the Settlements had been extended far beyond them, sold readily, without any Improvement made upon them, for three Pounds per Acre. The Acre in America is the same with the English Acre, or the Acre of Normandy.

Those, who desire to understand the State of Government in America, 10 would do well to read the Constitutions of the several States, and the Articles of Confederation that bind the whole together for general Purposes, under the Direction of one Assembly, called the Congress. These Constitutions have been printed, by order of Congress, in America; two Editions of them have also been printed in London; and a good Translation of them into French has lately been published at Paris.

Several of the Princes of Europe having of late years, from an Opinion 11 of Advantage to arise by producing all Commodities and Manufactures within their own Dominions, so as to diminish or render useless their Importations, have endeavoured to entice Workmen from other Countries by high Salaries, Privileges, &c. Many Persons, pretending to be skilled in various great Manufactures, imagining that America must be in Want of them, and that the Congress would probably be dispos'd to imitate the Princes above mentioned, have proposed to go over, on Condition of having their Passages paid, Lands given, Salaries appointed, exclusive Privileges for Terms of years, &c. Such Persons, on reading the Articles of Confederation, will find, that the Congress have no Power committed to them, or Money put into their Hands, for such purposes; and that if any such Encouragement is given, it must be by the Government of some separate State. This, however, has rarely been done in America; and, when it has been done, it has rarely succeeded, so as to establish a Manufacture, which the Country was not yet so ripe for as to encourage private Persons to set it up; Labour being generally too dear there, and Hands difficult to be kept together, every one desiring to be a Master, and the Cheapness of Lands inclining many to leave Trades for Agriculture. Some indeed have met with Success, and are carried on to Advantage; but they are generally such as require only a few Hands, or wherein great Part of the Work is performed by Machines. Things that are bulky, and of so small Value as not well to bear the Expence of Freight, may often be made cheaper in the Country than they can be imported; and the Manufacture of such Things will be profitable wherever there is a sufficient Demand. The Farmers in America produce indeed a good deal of Wool and Flax; and none is exported, it is all work'd up; but it is in the Way of domestic Manufacture, for the Use of the Family. The buying up Quantities of Wool and Flax, with the Design to employ Spinners, Weavers, &c., and form great Establishments, producing Quantities of Linen and Woollen Goods for Sale, has been several times attempted in different Provinces; but those Projects have generally failed, goods of equal Value being imported cheaper. And when the Governments have been solicited to support such Schemes by Encouragements, in Money, or by imposing Duties on Importation of such Goods, it has been generally refused, on this Principle, that, if the Country is ripe for the Manufacture, it may be carried on by private Persons to Advantage; and if not, it is a Folly to think of forcing Nature. Great Establishments of Manufacture require great Numbers of Poor to do the Work for small Wages; these Poor are to be found in Europe, but will not be found in America, till the Lands are all taken up and cultivated, and the Excess of People, who cannot get Land, want Employment. The Manufacture of Silk, they say, is natural in France, as that of Cloth in England, because each Country produces in Plenty the first Material; but if England will have a Manufacture of Silk as well as that of Cloth, and France one of Cloth as well as that of Silk, these unnatural Operations must be supported by mutual Prohibitions, or high Duties on the Importation of each other's Goods; by which means the Workmen are enabled to tax the home Consumer by greater Prices, while the higher Wages they receive makes them neither happier nor richer, since they only drink more and work less. Therefore the Governments in America do nothing to encourage such Projects. The People, by this Means, are not impos'd on, either by the Merchant or Mechanic. If the Merchant demands too much Profit on imported Shoes, they buy of the Shoemaker; and if he asks too high a Price, they take them of the Merchant; thus the two Professions are checks on each other. The Shoemaker, however, has, on the whole, a considerable Profit upon his Labour in America, beyond what he had in Europe, as he can add to his Price a Sum nearly equal to all the Expenses of Freight and Commission, Risque or Insurance, &c., necessarily charged by the Merchant. And the Case is the same with the Workmen in every other Mechanic Art. Hence it is, that Artisans generally live better and more easily in America than in Europe; and such as are good Œconomists make a comfortable Provision for Age, and for their Children. Such may, therefore, remove with Advantage to America.

In the long-settled Countries of Europe, all Arts, Trades, Professions, *12* Farms, &c., are so full, that it is difficult for a poor Man, who has Children, to place them where they may gain, or learn to gain, a decent Livelihood. The Artisans, who fear creating future Rivals in Business, refuse to take Apprentices, but upon Conditions of Money, Maintenance, or the like, which the Parents are unable to comply with. Hence the Youth are dragg'd up in Ignorance of every gainful Art, and oblig'd to become Soldiers, or Servants, or Thieves, for a Subsistence. In America, the rapid Increase of Inhabitants takes away that Fear of Rivalship, and Artisans willingly receive Apprentices from the hope of Profit by their Labour, during the Remainder of the Time stipulated, after they shall be instructed. Hence it is easy for poor Families to get their Children instructed; for the Artisans are so desirous of Apprentices, that many of them will even give Money to the Parents, to have Boys from Ten to Fifteen Years of Age bound Apprentices to them till the Age of Twenty-one; and many poor Parents have, by that means, on their Arrival in the Country, raised Money enough to buy Land sufficient to establish themselves, and to subsist the rest of their Family by Agriculture. These Contracts for Apprentices are made before a Magistrate, who regulates the Agreement according to Reason and Justice, and. having in view the Formation of a future useful Citizen, obliges the Master to engage by a written Indenture, not only that, during the time of Service stipulated, the Apprentice shall be duly provided with Meat, Drink, Apparel, washing, and Lodging, and, at its Expiration, with a compleat new Suit of Cloaths, but also that he shall be taught to read, write, and cast Accompts; and that he shall be well instructed in the Art or Profession of his Master, or some other, by which he may afterwards gain a Livelihood, and be able in his turn to raise a Family. A Copy of this Indenture is given to the Apprentice or his Friends, and the Magistrate keeps a Record of it, to which recourse may be had, in case of Failure by the Master in any Point of Performance. This desire among the Masters, to have more Hands employ'd in working for them, induces them to pay the Passages of young persons, of both Sexes, who, on their Arrival, agree to serve them one, two, three, or four Years; those, who have already learnt a Trade, agreeing for a shorter Term, in proportion to their Skill, and the consequent immediate Value of their Service; and those, who have none, agreeing for a longer Term, in consideration of being taught an Art their Poverty would not permit them to acquire in their own Country.

The almost general Mediocrity of Fortune that prevails in America 13 obliging its People to follow some Business for subsistence, those Vices, that arise usually from Idleness, are in a great measure prevented. Industry and constant Employment are great preservatives of the Morals and Virtue of a Nation. Hence bad Examples to Youth are more rare in America, which must be a comfortable Consideration to Parents. To this may be truly added, that serious Religion, under its various Denominations, is not only tolerated, but respected and practised. Atheism is unknown there; Infidelity rare and secret; so that persons may live to a great Age in that Country, without having their Piety shocked by meeting with either an Atheist or an Infidel. And the Divine Being seems to have manifested his Approbation of the mutual Forbearance and Kindness with which the different Sects treat each other, by the remarkable Prosperity with which He has been pleased to favour the whole Country.

Study Questions

1. The stated audience for this essay is "those who would remove to America," but is it possible that Franklin had other audiences in mind as well? What points does Franklin make that might be addressed to these other audiences?
2. In his opening paragraph, Franklin states that he wishes to give people who are thinking of coming to America accurate information, but in his concluding paragraph, he seems to deliver quite another message. What is that message? Why did he not begin his essay with it?
3. Throughout his essay Franklin contrasts the conditions in America with those in Europe. Identify some of the major words and phrases he uses to signal this kind of organization. What makes this organization particularly appropriate for the message he states at the end?
4. Besides contrast, what other form of additive organization does Franklin use? Choose a passage in which he makes use of this form, and discuss how it orders his ideas.

Suggestion for Drafting

Benjamin Franklin made extensive use of contrast in "Information for Those Who Would Remove to America" in order to emphasize the opportunities the new country offered the right kind of person. Contrast is not the only method he could have used. For example, he could have told the story of a typical man who came to America and became successful.

Reread Franklin's essay, paying particular attention to the features that Franklin considered most desirable in an immigrant and to the opportunities in America that he most recommended. Then write a draft of a passage in which you tell how a man with these qualities finds America to be the land of opportunity.

The Pocket Hunter

Mary Austin

I remember very well when I first met him. *1* Walking in the evening glow to spy the marriages of the white gilias, I sniffed the unmistakable odor of burning sage. It is a smell that carries far and indicates usually the nearness of a campoodie, but on the level mesa nothing taller showed than Diana's sage. Over the tops of it, beginning to dusk under a young white moon, trailed a wavering ghost of smoke, and at the end of it I came upon the Pocket Hunter making a dry camp in the friendly scrub. He sat tailorwise in the sand, with his coffee-pot on the coals, his supper ready to hand in the frying-pan, and himself in a mood for talk. His pack burros in hobbles strayed off to hunt for a wetter mouthful than the sage afforded, and gave him no concern.

We came upon him often after that, threading the windy passes, or by *2* water-holes in the desert hills, and got to know much of his way of life. He was a small, bowed man, with a face and manner and speech of no character at all, as if he had that faculty of small hunted things of taking on the protective color of his surroundings. His clothes were of no fashion that I could remember, except that they bore liberal markings of pot black, and he had a curious fashion of going about with his mouth open, which gave him a vacant look until you came near enough to perceive him busy about an endless hummed, wordless tune. He traveled far and took a long time to it, but the simplicity of his kitchen arrangements was elemental. A pot for beans, a coffee-pot, a frying-pan, a tin to mix bread in—he fed the burros in this when there was need—with these he had been half round our western world and back. He explained to me very early in our acquaintance what was good to take to the hills for food: nothing sticky, for that "dirtied the pots;" nothing with "juice" to it, for that would not pack to advantage; and nothing likely to ferment. He used no gun, but he would set snares by the water-holes for quail and doves, and in the trout country he carried a line. Burros he kept, one or two according to his pack, for this chief excellence, that they would eat potato parings and firewood. He had owned a horse in the foothill country, but when he came to the desert with no forage but mesquite, he found himself under the necessity of picking the beans from the briers, a labor that drove him to the use of pack animals to whom thorns were a relish.

I suppose no man becomes a pocket hunter by first intention. He *3* must be born with the faculty, and along comes the occasion, like the tap on the test tube that induces crystallization. My friend had been several things of no moment until he struck a thousand-dollar pocket in the Lee District and came into his vocation. A pocket, you must know, is a small body of rich ore occurring by itself, or in a vein of poorer stuff. Nearly every mineral ledge contains such, if only one has the luck to hit upon them without too much labor. The sensible thing for a man to do who has found a good pocket is to buy himself into business and keep away from the hills. The logical thing is to set out looking for another one. My friend the Pocket Hunter had been looking twenty years. His working outfit was a shovel, a pick, a gold pan which he kept cleaner than his plate, and a pocket magnifier. When he came to a watercourse he would pan out the gravel of its bed for "colors," and under the glass determine if they had come from far or near, and so spying he would work up the stream until he found where the drift of the gold-bearing outcrop fanned out into the creek; then up the side of the cañon till he came to the proper vein. I think he said the best indication of small pockets was an iron stain, but I could never get the run of miner's talk enough to feel instructed for pocket hunting. He had another method in the waterless hills, where he would work in and out of blind gullies and all windings of the manifold strata that appeared not to have cooled since they had been heaved up. His itinerary began with the east slope of the Sierras of the Snows, where that range swings across to meet the coast hills, and all up that slope to the Truckee River country, where the long cold forbade his progress north. Then he worked back down one or another of the nearly parallel ranges that lie out desertward, and so down to the sink of the Mojave River, burrowing to oblivion in the sand,—a big mysterious land, a lonely, inhospitable land, beautiful, terrible. But he came to no harm in it; the land tolerated him as it might a gopher or a badger. Of all its inhabitants it has the least concern for man.

There are many strange sorts of humans bred in a mining country, *4* each sort despising the queernesses of the other, but of them all I found the Pocket Hunter most acceptable for his clean, companionable talk. There was more color to his reminiscences than the faded sandy old miners "kyoteing," that is, tunneling like a coyote (kyote in the vernacular) in the core of a lonesome hill. Such a one has found, perhaps, a body of tolerable ore in a poor lead,—remember that I can never be depended on to get the terms right,—and followed it into the heart of country rock to no profit, hoping, burrowing, and hoping. These men go harmlessly mad in time, believing themselves just behind the wall of fortune—most likable and simple men, for whom it is well to do any kindly thing that occurs to you except lend them money. I have known "grub stakers" too, those persuasive sinners to whom you make allowances of flour and pork and coffee in consideration of the ledges they are about to find; but none of these proved so much worth while as the Pocket Hunter. He wanted nothing of you and maintained a cheerful preference for his own way of life. It was an excellent way if you had the constitution for it. The Pocket Hunter had gotten to that point where he knew no bad weather, and all places were equally happy so long as they were out of doors. I do not know just how long it takes to become saturated with the elements so that one takes no account of them. Myself can never get past the glow and exhilaration of a storm, the wrestle of long dust-heavy winds, the play of live thunder on the rocks, nor past the keen fret of fatigue when the storm outlasts physical endurance. But prospectors and Indians get a kind of a weather shell that remains on the body until death.

The Pocket Hunter had seen destruction by the violence of nature and 5 the violence of men, and felt himself in the grip of an All-wisdom that killed men or spared them as seemed for their good; but of death by sickness he knew nothing except that he believed he should never suffer it. He had been in Grape-vine Cañon the year of storms that changed the whole front of the mountain. All day he had come down under the wing of the storm, hoping to win past it, but finding it traveling with him until night. It kept on after that, he supposed, a steady downpour, but could not with certainty say, being securely deep in sleep. But the weather instinct does not sleep. In the night the heavens behind the hill dissolved in rain, and the roar of the storm was borne in and mixed with his dreaming, so that it moved him, still asleep, to get up and out of the path of it. What finally woke him was the crash of pine logs as they went down before the unbridled flood, and the swirl of foam that lashed him where he clung in the tangle of scrub while the wall of water went by. It went on against the cabin of Bill Gerry and laid Bill stripped and broken on a sand bar at the mouth of the Grape-vine, seven miles away. There, when the sun was up and the wrath of the rain spent, the Pocket Hunter found and buried him; but he never laid his own escape at any door but the unintelligible favor of the Powers.

The journeyings of the Pocket Hunter led him often into that myste- 6 rious country beyond Hot Creek where a hidden force works mischief, mole-like, under the crust of the earth. Whatever agency is at work in that neighborhood, and it is popularly supposed to be the devil, it changes means and direction without time or season. It creeps up whole hillsides with insidious heat, unguessed until one notes the pine woods dying at the top, and having scorched out a good block of timber returns to steam and spout in caked, forgotten crevices of years before. It will break up sometimes blue-hot and bubbling, in the midst of a clear creek, or make a sucking, scalding quicksand at the ford. These outbreaks had the kind of morbid interest for the Pocket Hunter that a house of unsavory reputation has in a respectable neighborhood, but I always found the accounts he brought me more interesting than his explanations, which were compounded of fag ends of miner's talk and superstition. He was a perfect gossip of the woods, this Pocket Hunter, and when I could get him away from "leads" and "strikes" and "contacts," full of fascinating small talk about the ebb and flood of creeks, the piñon crop on Black Mountain, and the wolves of Mesquite Valley. I suppose he never knew how much he depended for the necessary sense of home and companionship on the beasts and trees, meeting and finding them in their wonted places,—the bear that used to come down Pine Creek in the spring, pawing out trout from the shelters of sod banks, the juniper at Lone Tree Spring, and the quail at Paddy Jack's.

There is a place on Waban, south of White Mountain, where flat, wind- 7 tilted cedars make low tents and coves of shade and shelter, where the wild sheep winter in the snow. Woodcutters and prospectors had brought me word of that, but the Pocket Hunter was accessory to the fact. About the opening of winter, when one looks for sudden big storms, he had attempted a crossing by the nearest path, beginning the ascent at noon. It grew cold, the snow came on thick and blinding, and wiped out the trail in a white smudge; the storm drift blew in and cut off landmarks, the early dark obscured the rising drifts. According to the Pocket Hunter's account, he knew where he was, but couldn't exactly say. Three days before he had been in the west arm of Death Valley on a short water allowance, ankle-deep in shifty sand; now he was on the rise of Waban, knee-deep in sodden snow, and in both cases he did the only allowable thing—he walked on. That is the only thing to do in a snowstorm in any case. It might have been the creature instinct, which in his way of life had room to grow, that led him to the cedar shelter; at any rate he found it about four hours after dark, and heard the heavy breathing of the flock. He said that if he thought at all at this juncture he must have thought that he had stumbled on a storm-belated shepherd with his silly sheep; but in fact he took no note of anything but the warmth of packed fleeces, and snuggled in between them dead with sleep. If the flock stirred in the night he stirred drowsily to keep close and let the storm go by. That was all until morning woke him shining on a white world. Then the very soul of him shook to see the wild sheep of God stand up about him, nodding their great horns beneath the cedar roof, looking out on the wonder of the snow. They had moved a little away from him with the coming of the light, but paid him no more heed. The light broadened and the white pavilions of the snow swam in the heavenly blueness of the sea from which they rose. The cloud drift scattered and broke billowing in the cañons. The leader stamped lightly on the litter to put the flock in motion, suddenly they took the drifts in those long light leaps that are nearest to flight, down and away on the slopes of Waban. Think of that to happen to a Pocket Hunter! But though he had fallen on many a wished-for hap, he was curiously inapt at getting the truth about beasts in general. He believed in the venom of toads, and charms for snake bites, and—for this I could never forgive him—had all the miner's prejudices against my friend the coyote. Thief, sneak, and son of a thief were the friendliest words he had for this little gray dog of the wilderness.

Of course with so much seeking he came occasionally upon pockets 8 of more or less value, otherwise he could not have kept up his way of life; but he had as much luck in missing great ledges as in finding small ones. He had been all over the Tonopah country, and brought away float without happening upon anything that gave promise of what that district was to become in a few years. He claimed to have chipped bits off the very outcrop of the California Rand, without finding it worth while to bring away, but none of these things put him out of countenance.

It was once in roving weather, when we found him shifting pack on a 9 steep trail, that I observed certain of his belongings done up in green canvas bags, the veritable "green bag" of English novels. It seemed so incongruous a reminder in this untenanted West that I dropped down beside the trail overlooking the vast dim valley, to hear about the green canvas. He had gotten it, he said, in London years before, and that was the first I had known of his having been abroad. It was after one of his "big strikes" that he had made the Grand Tour, and had brought nothing away from it but the green canvas bags, which he conceived would fit his needs, and an ambition. This last was nothing less than to strike it rich and set himself up among the eminently bourgeois of London. It seemed that the situation of the wealthy English middle class, with just enough gentility above to aspire to, and sufficient smaller fry to bully and patronize, appealed to his imagination, though of course he did not put it so crudely as that.

It was no news to me then, two or three years after, to learn that he 10 had taken ten thousand dollars from an abandoned claim, just the sort of luck to have pleased him, and gone to London to spend it. The land seemed not to miss him any more than it had minded him, but I missed him and could not forget the trick of expecting him in least likely situations. Therefore it was with a pricking sense of the familiar that I followed a twilight trail of smoke, a year or two later, to the swale of a dripping spring, and came upon a man by the fire with a coffee-pot and frying-pan. I was not surprised to find it was the Pocket Hunter. No man can be stronger than his destiny.

Study Questions

1. In "The Pocket Hunter," Mary Austin's first words are: "I remember very well when I first met him." She does not, however, identify *him*. In the same paragraph she uses the term *Pocket Hunter,* but does not define it until two paragraphs later. What does Austin accomplish by being so vague in her opening? Why might this accomplishment be worth the risk of confusing readers?

2. In what kind of magazine would "The Pocket Hunter" most likely be published? Explain your answer by illustrating how the language and topic would suit your choice.
3. In paragraph 4 Austin describes the "sandy old miners" and the "grub stakers" as well as the Pocket Hunter. How are all three connected with each other? How does the comparison and contrast between the Pocket Hunter and these other two types lead to Austin's message? What is that message?
4. What is Austin's major method of organizing the body of the essay? Since the body contains a series of episodes in the life of the Pocket Hunter, how does this organization serve to connect all the episodes?

Suggestion for Drafting

Austin gives us a concrete picture of the life of people like the Pocket Hunter by concentrating on one man and telling his story. This method gives us a highly personalizd view of such a life. Suppose, however, that you want to write a more "factual" type of essay by concentrating on the general characteristics the Pocket Hunter represents rather than on the man himself. What are those general characteristics? How would you reorganize the essay to present them? Choose a method or methods of organization and draft a beginning and ending for the essay.

The Strange Elizabethans

Virginia Woolf

T here are few greater delights than to go back 1
three or four hundred years and become in
fancy at least an Elizabethan. That such fan-
cies are only fancies, that this "becoming an Elizabethan," this reading
sixteenth-century writing as currently and certainly as we read our own
is an illusion, is no doubt true. Very likely the Elizabethans would find
our pronunciation of their language unintelligible; our fancy picture of
what it pleases us to call Elizabethan life would rouse their ribald mer-
riment. Still, the instinct that drives us to them is so strong and the
freshness and vigor that blow through their pages are so sweet that we
willingly run the risk of being laughed at, of being ridiculous.

And if we ask why we go further astray in this particular region of 2
English literature than in any other, the answer is no doubt that Elizabethan prose, for all its beauty and bounty, was a very imperfect medium.
It was almost incapable of fulfilling one of the offices of prose which is
to make people talk, simply and naturally, about ordinary things. In an
age of utilitarian prose like our own, we know exactly how people spend
the hours between breakfast and bed, how they behave when they are
neither one thing nor the other, neither angry nor loving, neither happy
nor miserable. Poetry ignores these slighter shades; the social student
can pick up hardly any facts about daily life from Shakespeare's plays;
and if prose refuses to enlighten us, then one avenue of approach to the
men and women of another age is blocked. Elizabethan prose, still
scarcely separated off from the body of its poetry, could speak magnifi-
cently, of course, about the great themes—how life is short, and death
certain; how spring is lovely, and winter horrid—perhaps, indeed, the
lavish and towering periods that it raises above these simple platitudes
are due to the fact that it has not cheapened itself upon trifles. But the
price it pays for this soaring splendor is to be found in its awkwardness
when it comes to earth—when Lady Sidney, for example, finding herself
cold at nights, has to solicit the Lord Chamberlain for a better bedroom
at Court. Then any housemaid of her own age could put her case more
simply and with greater force. Thus, if we go to the Elizabethan prose-
writers to solidify the splendid world of Elizabethan poetry as we should
go now to our biographers, novelists, and journalists to solidify the world
of Pope, of Tennyson, of Conrad, we are perpetually baffled and driven
from our quest. What, we ask, was the life of an ordinary man or woman
in the time of Shakespeare? Even the familiar letters of the time give us

little help. Sir Henry Wotton is pompous and ornate and keeps us stiffly at arm's length. Their histories resound with drums and trumpets. Their broadsheets reverberate with meditations upon death and reflections upon the immortality of the soul. Our best chance of finding them off their guard and so becoming at ease with them is to seek one of those unambitious men who haunt the outskirts of famous gatherings, listening, observing, sometimes taking a note in a book. But they are difficult to find. Gabriel Harvey perhaps, the friend of Spenser and of Sidney, might have fulfilled that function. Unfortunately the values of the time persuaded him that to write about rhetoric, to write about Thomas Smith, to write about Queen Elizabeth in Latin, was better worth doing than to record the table talk of Spenser and Sir Philip Sidney. But he possessed to some extent the modern instinct for preserving trifles, for keeping copies of letters, and for making notes of ideas that struck him in the margins of books. If we rummage among these fragments we shall, at any rate, leave the highroad and perhaps hear some roar of laughter from a tavern door, where poets are drinking; or meet humble people going about their milking and their love-making without a thought that this is the great Elizabethan age, or that Shakespeare is at this moment strolling down the Strand and might tell one, if one plucked him by the sleeve, to whom he wrote the sonnets, and what he meant by Hamlet.

The first person whom we meet is indeed a milkmaid—Gabriel Har- 3 vey's sister Mercy. In the winter of 1574 she was milking in the fields near Saffron Walden accompanied by an old woman, when a man approached her and offered her cakes and malmsey wine. When they had eaten and drunk in a wood and the old woman had wandered off to pick up sticks, the man proceeded to explain his business. He came from Lord Surrey, a youth of about Mercy's own age—seventeen or eighteen that is—and a married man. He had been bowling one day and had seen the milkmaid; her hat had blown off and "she had somewhat changed her color." In short, Lord Surrey had fallen passionately in love with her; and sent her by the same man gloves, a silk girdle, and an enamel posy ring which he had torn from his own hat though his Aunt, Lady W——, had given it him for a very different purpose. Mercy at first stood her ground. She was a poor milkmaid, and he was a noble gentleman. But at last she agreed to meet him at her house in the village. Thus, one very misty, foggy night just before Christmas, Lord Surrey and his servant came to Saffron Walden. They peered in at the malthouse, but saw only her mother and sisters; they peeped in at the parlor, but only her brothers were there. Mercy herself was not to be seen; and "well mired and wearied for their labor," there was nothing for it but to ride back home again. Finally, after further parleys, Mercy agreed to meet Lord Surrey in a neighbor's house alone at midnight. She found him in the little parlor "in his doublet and hose, his points untrust, and his shirt lying round about him." He tried to force her on to the bed; but she cried out, and the good wife, as had been agreed between them, rapped on the door and said she was sent for. Thwarted, enraged, Lord Surrey cursed and swore, "God confound me, God confound me," and by way of lure emptied his pockets of all the money in them—thirteen shillings in shillings and testers it came to—and made her finger it. Still, however, Mercy made off, untouched, on condition that she would come again on Christmas Eve. But when Christmas Eve dawned she was up betimes and had put seven miles between her and Saffron Walden by six in the morning, though it snowed and rained so that the floods were out, and P., the servant, coming later to the place of assignation, had to pick his way through the water in patterns. So Christmas passed. And a week later, in the very nick of time to save her honor, the whole story very strangely was discovered and brought to an end. On New Year's Eve her brother Gabriel, the young fellow of Pembroke Hall, was riding back to Cambridge when he came up with a simple countryman whom he had met at his father's house. They rode on together, and after some country gossip, the man said that he had a letter for Gabriel in his pocket. Indeed, it was addressed "To my loving brother Mr. G. H.," but when Gabriel opened it there on the road, he found that the address was a lie. It was not from his sister Mercy, but to his sister Mercy. "Mine Own Sweet Mercy," it began; and it was signed "Thine more than ever his own Phil." Gabriel could hardly control himself—"could scarcely dissemble my sudden fancies and comprimitt my inward passions"—as he read. For it was not merely a love letter; it was more; it talked about possessing Mercy according to promise. There was also a fair English noble wrapped up in the paper. So Gabriel, doing his best to control himself before the countryman, gave him back the letter and the coin and told him to deliver them both to his sister at Saffron Walden with this message: "To look ere she leap. She may pick out the English of it herself." He rode on to Cambridge; he wrote a long letter to the young lord, informing him with ambiguous courtesy that the game was up. The sister of Gabriel Harvey was not to be the mistress of a married nobleman. Rather she was to be a maid, "diligent, and trusty and tractable," in the house of Lady Smith at Audley End. Thus Mercy's romance breaks off; the clouds descend again; and we no longer see the milkmaid, the old woman, the treacherous serving man who came with malmsey and cakes and rings and ribbons to tempt a poor girl's honor while she milked her cows.

    This is probably no uncommon story; there must have been many [4] milkmaids whose hats blew off as they milked their cows, and many lords whose hearts leapt at the sight so that they plucked the jewels from their hats and sent their servants to make treaty for them. But it is rare for the girl's own letters to be preserved or to read her own account of the story as she was made to deliver it at her brother's inquisition. Yet when we try to use her words to light up the Elizabethan field, the Elizabethan house and living room, we are met by the usual perplexities.

It is easy enough, in spite of the rain and the fog and the floods, to make a fancy piece out of the milkmaid and the meadows and the old woman wandering off to pick up sticks. Elizabethan song writers have taught us too well the habit of that particular trick. But if we resist the impulse to make museum pieces out of our reading, Mercy herself gives us little help. She was a milkmaid, scribbling love letters by the light of a farthing dip in an attic. Nevertheless, the sway of the Elizabethan convention was so strong, the accent of their speech was so masterful, that she bears herself with a grace and expresses herself with a resonance that would have done credit to a woman of birth and literary training. When Lord Surrey pressed her to yield she replied:

The thing you wot of, Milord, were a great trespass towards God, a great offence to the world, a great grief to my friends, a great shame to myself, and, as I think, a great dishonour to your lordship. I have heard my father say, Virginity is ye fairest flower in a maid's garden, and chastity ye richest dowry a poor wench can have. . . . Chastity, they say, is like unto time, which, being once lost, can no more be recovered.

Words chime and ring in her ears, as if she positively enjoyed the act 5 of writing. When she wishes him to know that she is only a poor country girl and no fine lady like his wife, she exclaims, "Good Lord, that you should seek after so bare and country stuff abroad, that have so costly and courtly wares at home!" She even breaks into a jog-trot of jingling rhyme, far less sonorous than her prose, but proof that to write was an art, not merely a means of conveying facts. And if she wants to be direct and forcible, the proverbs she has heard in her father's house come to her pen, the Biblical imagery runs in her ears: "And then were I, poor wench, cast up for hawk's meat, to mine utter undoing, and my friends' exceeding grief." In short, Mercy the milkmaid writes a natural and noble style, which is incapable of vulgarity, and equally incapable of intimacy. Nothing, one feels, would have been easier for Mercy than to read her lover a fine discourse upon the vanity of grandeur, the loveliness of chastity, the vicissitudes of fortune. But of emotion as between one particular Mercy and one particular Phillip, there is no trace. And when it comes to dealing exactly in a few words with some mean object— when, for example, the wife of Sir Henry Sidney, the daughter of the Duke of Northumberland, has to state her claim to a better room to sleep in, she writes for all the world like an illiterate servant girl who can neither form her letters nor spell her words nor make one sentence follow smoothly after another. She haggles, she niggles, she wears our patience down with her repetitions and her prolixities. Hence it comes about that we know very little about Mercy Harvey, the milkmaid, who wrote so well, or Mary Sidney, daughter to the Duke of Northumberland, who wrote so badly. The background of Elizabethan life eludes us.

But let us follow Gabriel Harvey to Cambridge, in case we can there 6
pick up something humble and colloquial that will make these strange
Elizabethans more familiar to us. Gabriel, having discharged his duty as
a brother, seems to have given himself up to the life of an intellectual
young man with his way to make in the world. He worked so hard and
he played so little that he made himself unpopular with his fellows. For
it was obviously difficult to combine an intense interest in the future of
English poetry and the capacity of the English language with card-play-
ing, bear-baiting, and such diversions. Nor could he apparently accept
everything that Aristotle said as gospel truth. But with congenial spirits
he argued, it is clear, hour by hour, night after night, about poetry, and
meter, and the raising of the despised English speech and the meager
English literature to a station among the great tongues and literatures of
the world. We are sometimes made to think, as we listen, of such
arguments as might now be going forward in the new Universities of
America. The young English poets speak with a bold yet uneasy arrogance—"England, since it was England, never bred more honorable
minds, more adventurous hearts, more valorous hands, or more excellent
wits, than of late." Yet, to be English is accounted a kind of crime—
"nothing is reputed so contemptible and so basely and vilely accounted
of as whatsoever is taken for English." And if, in their hopes for the
future and their sensitiveness to the opinion of older civilizations, the
Elizabethans show much the same susceptibility that sometimes puzzles
us among the younger countries today, the sense that broods over them
of what is about to happen, of an undiscovered land on which they are
about to set foot, is much like the excitement that science stirs in the
minds of imaginative English writers of our own time. Yet however
stimulating it is to think that we hear the stir and strife of tongues in
Cambridge rooms about the year 1570, it has to be admitted that to read
Harvey's pages methodically is almost beyond the limits of human patience. The words seem to run redhot, molten, hither and thither, until
we cry out in anguish for the boon of some meaning to set its stamp on
them. He takes the same idea and repeats it over and over again:

In the sovereign workmanship of Nature herself, what garden of flowers without weeds? what orchard of trees without worms? what field of
corn without cockle? what pond of fishes without frogs? what sky of
light without darkness? what mirror of knowledge without ignorance?
what man of earth without frailty? what commodity of the world without
discommodity?

It is interminable. As we go round and round like a horse in a mill, 7
we perceive that we are thus clogged with sound because we are reading
what we should be hearing. The amplifications and the repetitions, the
emphasis like that of a fist pounding the edge of a pulpit, are for the

benefit of the slow and sensual ear which loves to dally over sense and luxuriate in sound—the ear which brings in, along with the spoken word, the look of the speaker and his gestures, which gives a dramatic value to what he says and adds to the crest of an extravagance some modulation which makes the word wing its way to the precise spot aimed at in the hearer's heart. Hence, when we lay Harvey's diatribes against Nash or his letters to Spenser upon poetry under the light of the eye alone, we can hardly make headway and lose our sense of any definite direction. We grasp any simple fact that floats to the surface as a drowning man grasps a plank—that the carrier was called Mrs. Kerke, that Perne kept a cub for his pleasure in his rooms at Peterhouse; that "Your last letter . . . was delivered me at mine hostesses by the fireside, being fast hedged in round about on every side with a company of honest, good fellows, and at that time reasonable, honest quaffers"; that Greene died begging Mistress Isam "for a penny pot of Malmsey," had borrowed her husband's shirt when his own was awashing, and was buried yesterday in the new churchyard near Bedlam at a cost of six shillings and fourpence. Light seems to dawn upon the darkness. But no; just as we think to lay hands on Shakespeare's coat-tails, to hear the very words rapped out as Spenser spoke them, up rise the fumes of Harvey's eloquence and we are floated off again into disputation and eloquence, windy, wordy, voluminous, and obsolete. How, we ask, as we slither over the pages, can we ever hope to come to grips with these Elizabethans? And then, turning, skipping and glancing, something fitfully and doubtfully emerges from the violent pages, the voluminous arguments—the figure of a man, the outlines of a face, somebody who is not "an Elizabethan" but an interesting, complex, and individual human being.

We know him, to begin with, from his dealings with his sister. We 8 see him riding to Cambridge, a fellow of his college, when she was milking with poor old women in the fields. We observe with amusement his sense of the conduct that befits the sister of Gabriel Harvey, the Cambridge scholar. Education had put a great gulf between him and his family. He rode to Cambridge from a house in a village street where his father made ropes and his mother worked in the malthouse. Yet though his lowly birth and the consciousness that he had his way to make in the world made him severe with his sister, fawning to the great, uneasy and self-centered and ostentatious, it never made him ashamed of his family. The father who could send three sons to Cambridge and was so little ashamed of his craft that he had himself carved making ropes at his work and the carving let in above his fireplace, was no ordinary man. The brothers who followed Gabriel to Cambridge and were his best allies there, were brothers to be proud of. He could be proud of Mercy even, whose beauty could make a great nobleman pluck the jewel from his hat. He was undoubtedly proud of himself. It was the pride of a self-made man who must read when other people are playing cards, who owns no undue allegiance to authority and will contradict Aristotle himself, that made him unpopular at Cambridge and almost cost him his degree. But it was an unfortunate chance that led him thus early in life to defend his rights and insist upon his merits. Moreover, since it was true—since he was abler, quicker, and more learned than other people, handsome in person too, as ever, his enemies could not deny ("a smudge piece of a handsome fellow it hath been in his days," Nash admitted) he had reason to think that he deserved success and was denied it only by the jealousies and conspiracies of his colleagues. For a time, by dint of much cabaling and much dwelling upon his own deserts, he triumphed over his enemies in the matter of the degree. He delivered lectures. He was asked to dispute before the Court when Queen Elizabeth came to Audley End. He even drew her favorable attention. "He lookt something like an Italian," she said when he was brought to her notice. But the seeds of his downfall were visible even in his moment of triumph. He had no self-respect, no self-control. He made himself ridiculous and his friends uneasy. When we read how he dressed himself up and "came ruffling it out huffty tuffty in his suit of velvet," how uneasy he was, at one moment cringing, at another "making no bones to take the wall of Sir Philip Sidney," now flirting with the ladies, now "putting bawdy riddles to them," how when the Queen praised him he was beside himself with joy and talked the English of Saffron Walden with an Italian accent, we can imagine how his enemies jeered and his friends blushed. And so, for all his merits, his decline began. He was not taken into Lord Leicester's service; he was not made Public Orator; he was not given the Mastership of Trinity Hall. But there was one society in which he succeeded. In the small, smoky rooms where Spenser and other young men discussed poetry and language and the future of English literature, Harvey was not laughed at. Harvey, on the contrary, was taken very seriously. To friends like these he seemed as capable of greatness as any of them. He too might be one of those destined to make English literature illustrious. His passion for poetry was disinterested. His learning was profound. When he held forth upon quantity and meter, upon what the Greeks had written and the Italians, and what the English might write, no doubt he created for Spenser that atmosphere of hope and ardent curiosity spiced with sound learning that serves to spur the imagination of a young writer and to make each fresh poem as it is written seem the common property of a little band of adventurers set upon the same quest. It was thus that Spenser saw him:

Harvey, the happy above happiest men,
I read: that, sitting like a looker-on
Of this world's stage, doest note, with critic pen,
The sharp dislikes of each condition.

Poets need such "lookers-on"; some one who discriminates from a watch tower above the battle; who warns; who foresees. It must have been pleasant for Spenser to listen as Harvey talked; and then to cease to listen, to let the vehement, truculent voice run on, while he slipped from theory to practice and made up a few lines of his own poetry in his head. But the looker-on may sit too long and hold forth too curiously and domineeringly for his own health. He may make his theories fit too tight to accommodate the formlessness of life. Thus when Harvey ceased to theorize and tried to practice there issued nothing but a thin dribble of arid and unappetizing verse or a copious flow of unctuous and servile eulogy. He failed to be a poet as he failed to be a statesman, as he failed to be a professor, as he failed to be a Master, as he failed, it might seem, in everything that he undertook, save that he had won the friendship of Spenser and Sir Philip Sidney.

But happily Harvey left behind him a commonplace book; he had the 9 habit of making notes in the margins of books as he read. Looking from one to the other, from his public self to his private, we see his face lit from both sides, and the expression changes as it changes so seldom upon the face of the Elizabethans. We detect another Harvey lurking behind the superficial Harvey, shading him with doubt and effort and despondency. For, luckily, the commonplace book was small; the margins even of an Elizabethan folio narrow; Harvey was forced to be brief, and because he wrote only for his own eye at the command of some sharp memory or experience he seems to write as if he were talking to himself. That is true, he seems to say; or that reminds me, or again: If only I had done this—We thus become aware of a conflict between the Harvey who blundered among men and the Harvey who sat wisely at home among his books. The one who acts and suffers brings his case to the one who reads and thinks for advice and consolation.

Indeed, he had need of both. From the first his life was full of conflict 10 and difficulty. Harvey the rope-maker's son might put a brave face on it, but still in the society of gentlemen the lowness of his birth galled him. Think, then, the sedentary Harvey counseled him, of all those unknown people who have nevertheless triumphed. Think of "Alexander, an Unexpert Youth"; think of David, "a forward stripling, but vanquished a huge Giant"; think of Judith and of Pope Joan and their exploits; think above all of that "gallant virago . . . Joan of Arc, a most worthy, valiant young wench . . . what may not an industrious and politic man do . . . when a lusty adventurous wench might thus prevail?" And then it seems as if the smart young men at Cambridge twitted the rope-maker's son for his lack of skill in the gentlemanly arts. "Leave writing," Gabriel counseled him, "which consumeth unreasonable much time. . . . You have already plagued yourself this way." Make yourself master of the arts of eloquence and persuasion. Go into the world. Learn swordsmanship, riding, and shooting. All three may be learnt in a week. And then the ambitious but uneasy youth began to find the other sex attractive and asked advice of his wise and sedentary brother in the conduct of his love affairs. Manners, the other Harvey was of opinion, are of the utmost importance in dealing with women; one must be discreet, self-controlled. A gentleman, this counselor continued, is known by his "Good entertainment of Ladies and gentlewomen. No salutation, without much respect and ceremony"—a reflection inspired no doubt by the memory of some snub received at Audley End. Health and the care of the body are of the utmost importance. "We scholars make an Ass of our body and wit." One must "leap out of bed lustily, every morning in ye whole year." One must be sparing in one's diet, and active, and take regular exercise, like brother H., "who never failed to breathe his hound once a day at least." There must be no "buzzing or musing." A learned man must also be a man of the world. Make it your "daily charge" "to exercise, to laugh; to proceed boldly." And if your tormentors brawl and rail and scoff and mock at you, the best answer is "a witty and pleasant Ironie." In any case, do not complain, "It is gross folly, and a vile Sign of a wayward and forward disposition, to be eftsoons complaining of this, or that, to small purpose." And if as time goes on without preferment, one cannot pay one's bills, one is thrust into prison, one has to bear the taunts and insults of landladies, still remember "Glad poverty is no poverty"; and if, as time passes and the struggle increases, it seems as if "Life is warfare," if sometimes the beaten man has to own, "But for hope ye Hart would burst," still his sage counselor in the study will not let him throw up the sponge. "He beareth his misery best, that hideth it most," he told himself.

So runs the dialogue that we invent between the two Harveys—Harvey the active and Harvey the passive, Harvey the foolish and Harvey the wise. And it seems on the surface that the two halves, for all their counseling together, made but a sorry business of the whole. For the young man who had ridden off to Cambridge full of conceit and hope and good advice to his sister returned empty-handed to his native village in the end. He dwindled out his last long years in complete obscurity at Saffron Walden. He occupied himself superficially by practicing his skill as a doctor among the poor of the neighborhood. He lived in the utmost poverty of buttered roots and sheep's trotters. But even so he had his consolations, he cherished his dreams. As he pottered about his garden in the old black velvet suit, purloined, Nash says, from a saddle for which he had not paid, his thoughts were all of power and glory; of Stukeley and Drake; of "the winners of gold and the wearers of gold." Memories he had in abundance—"The remembrance of best things will soon pass out of memory; if it be not often renewed and revived," he wrote. But there was some eager stir in him, some lust for action and glory and life and adventure that forbade him to dwell in the past. "The present tense only to be regarded" is one of his notes. Nor did he drug himself with the dust of scholarship. Books he loved as a true reader loves them, not as trophies to be hung up for display, but as living beings that "must be meditated, practiced and incorporated into my body and soul." A singularly humane view of learning survived in the breast of the old and disappointed scholar. "The only brave way to learn all things with no study and much pleasure," he remarked. Dreams of the winners of gold and the wearers of gold, dreams of action and power, fantastic though they were in an old beggar who could not pay his reckoning, who pressed simples and lived off buttered roots in a cottage, kept life in him when his flesh had withered and his skin was "riddled and crumpled like a piece of burnt parchment." He had his triumph in the end. He survived both his friends and his enemies—Spenser and Sidney, Nash and Perne. He lived to a very great age for an Elizabethan, to eighty-one or eighty-two; and when we say that Harvey lived we mean that he quarreled and was tiresome and ridiculous and struggled and failed and had a face like ours—a changing, a variable, a human face.

Study Questions

1. Why has Virginia Woolf called her essay "The Strange Elizabethans"? In what ways does Gabriel Harvey represent this "strangeness"?
2. Woolf seems to make her clearest statement of her message at the very end: "and when we say that Harvey lived we mean that he quarreled and was tiresome and ridiculous and struggled and failed and had a face like ours—a changing, a variable, a human face." Why do you think she waited so long to make this statement? Would readers have found the essay easier to understand if she had made such a statement earlier? Explain your answer.
3. In her description of the incident involving Mercy Harvey, the word *friend* is used several times. Check the *Oxford English Dictionary* for the most common meaning of *friend* in Elizabethan England. What other words in this essay should be checked for earlier definitions?
4. "The Strange Elizabethans" is difficult to read. The difficulty is in part caused by the kind of organization Woolf uses. What method of organization does Woolf use most often in this essay? How does it add to the readers' problems in understanding the writer's meaning?

Suggestion for Drafting

In "The Strange Elizabethans," Virginia Woolf uses her discussion of Gabriel Harvey to emphasize her point that all humans are too complex to be summed up in one or two quick phrases. As interesting as Harvey may be, Woolf's description of the man is secondary to this greater meaning. In this exercise, we want you to redraft part of the body of the essay so as to stress Harvey himself rather than Woolf's final message.

Suppose you were to write on how Harvey would appear to modern readers from his reaction to Lord Surrey's attempt to have an affair with Mercy Harvey. After rereading that section of the essay, draft a version in which you stress what can be learned of Gabriel Harvey by looking at how he handled the incident.

Of the Inconsistency of Our Actions

Michel de Montaigne

T hey who make a practice of comparing human *1* actions are never so perplexed as when they try to piece them together and place them in the same light, for they commonly contradict one another so strangely that it seems impossible they should have come out of the same shop. Marius the younger is now a son of Mars, now a son of Venus. Some one said that Pope Boniface the Eighth entered upon his charge like a fox, behaved therein like a lion, and died like a dog. And who could believe that it was Nero, the very image of cruelty, who, when the sentence of a condemned criminal was brought to him to be signed in the usual way, exclaimed, 'Would to God that I had never learned to write!' So grieved was he in his heart to doom a man to death!

The world is full of such examples, nay, any man may provide such *2* an abundance of them out of his own experience, that I sometimes wonder to see intelligent men at pains to sort the pieces, seeing that irresolution is, in my view, the most common and conspicuous defect of our nature: witness that famous line of Publilius the writer of low comedies,

Poor is the plan that never can be changed.   (Publilius Syrus.)*

It seems reasonable to judge a man by the most ordinary acts of his *3* life, but in view of the natural instability of our habits and opinions, I have often thought that even good authors are wrong in obstinately attributing to us a steadfast and consistent character. They hit upon a general feature in a man and arrange and interpret all his actions in accordance with this fanciful conception; and if they are unable to twist them sufficiently, set them down to dissimulation. Augustus has escaped them, for we see in this man, throughout the course of his life, so manifest, abrupt, and continual a variety of actions, that he has slipped through the fingers of even the most daring critics, and been left undecided. I find nothing more difficult to believe than man's consistency, and nothing more easy than his inconsistency. If we examine him in

* *Apothegms (Sententiae),* l. 362.

detail and judge of his actions separately, bit by bit, we shall most often find this true.

Throughout ancient history it would be difficult to choose a dozen *4* men who have steered their lives in one certain and constant course, which is the principal aim of wisdom. For, to comprise it all in one word, as an ancient writer* says, and to embrace all the rules of life in one, is 'to wish and not to wish always the same thing. I will not vouchsafe to add, he says, provided the wish be right; for if it be not right, it is impossible it should be always the same'. I once learned indeed that vice is no more than want of rule and moderation, and that it is consequently impossible to associate it with consistency. It is a saying attributed to Demosthenes, 'that the beginning of all virtue is consultation and deliberation; and the end and perfection, constancy'. If reason directed our course we should choose the fairest; but no one has thought of that:

He scorns that which he sought, seeks what he scorned of late;
He flows and ebbs, his whole life contradiction.   (Horace.)†

Our ordinary practice is to follow the inclinations of our appetite, to *5* right, to left, up hill, down dale, as we are borne along by the wind of opportunity. We do not consider what we wish except at the moment of wishing it, and we change like that animal which takes its colour from what it is laid upon. What we have but now determined we presently alter, and soon again we retrace our steps: it is nothing but wavering and uncertainty;

We are led as a puppet is moved by the strings.   (Horace.)‡

We do not go, we are carried along, like things floating, now smoothly, now perturbedly, according as the water is angry or calm;

   We see them, knowing not
What 'tis they want, and seeking ever and ever
A change of place, as if to drop the burden.
          (Lucretius.)§

Every day a new fancy; and our humours move with the changes of weather:

* Seneca, in *Epistles*, Epistle xx.
† *Epistles*, Book I, Epistle i, ll. 98 f.
‡ *Satires*, Book II, Satire vii, l. 82.
§ *On the Nature of Things*, Book III, ll. 1057 ff.

So change the minds of men, like days
That Father Jove sends down to earth,
To alternate 'twixt wet and fine.

(Homer.)*

We waver between different minds; we wish nothing freely, nothing 6
absolutely, nothing constantly. Should any man prescribe and establish
definite laws and a definite policy in his own head, he would present
throughout his life a shining example of even habits, an order and an
unfailing relation of one action to another.

(Empedocles remarked in the inhabitants of Agrigentum this discrep- 7
ancy, that they abandoned themselves to their pleasures as if they were
to die on the morrow, and that they built as if they were never to die.)†

The reason will be easily found, as we see in the case of the younger 8
Cato, he who touches one note of the keyboard touches all: there is a
harmony of sounds, all in perfect tune with each other, which is not to
be mistaken. With us, on the other hand, the rule is: so many actions,
so many particular judgements to be passed. The surest, in my opinion,
would be to refer them to the nearest circumstances, without seeking
any farther, and without drawing from them any other inferences.

It was told me, during the tumultuous times our poor State had to go 9
through, that a young woman who lived quite near to where I then was,
had thrown herself from a high window to avoid the forcible caresses of
a poor knave of a soldier who was quartered in her house; the fall did
not kill her, and, repeating the attempt on her life, she would have cut
her throat with a knife, but was prevented; not however without inflicting
a serious wound. She herself then confessed that the soldier had done
no more than importune her with gifts, entreaties, and solicitations, but
that she feared he would in the end proceed to violence. And all this,
her words, her mien, and the blood which testified to her virtue, in the
true manner of a second Lucretia!

Now I have heard, as a fact, that, both before and after, she was a 10
wench not very difficult to come by. As the tale has it, 'Be as handsome
and as fine a gentleman as you will, when you have failed in your pursuit,
do not immediately conclude an inviolable chastity in your mistress; it
does not follow that the muleteer will not find his opportunity.'

Antigonus, having taken a liking to one of his soldiers, on account of 11
his virtue and valour, ordered his physicians to attend him for a persistent
internal malady which had long tormented him, and perceiving that after
his cure he went much more coldly to work than before, asked him what
it was that had so altered and cowed him. 'You yourself, Sire, he replied,
by delivering me from the ill which made me indifferent to life.' A soldier

* *Odyssey,* Book XVIII, l. 135.
† from the life of the fifth-century Greek philosopher Empedocles, by Diogenes
Laertius.

of Lucullus, having been plundered by enemies, devised a bold stroke for his revenge; when he had retrieved his loss with interest, Lucullus, whose good opinion he had gained, tried to induce him, with the best persuasions he could think of, to undertake some risky business;

With words that might have stirred a coward's heart.

(Horace.)*

'Employ, he replied, some wretched soldier who has been plundered;'   *12*

Though but a rustic clown, he'll go
Who's lost his money-belt,' he said;   (Horace.)†

and resolutely refused to go.

When we read that Mahomet having furiously rated Chasan, chief of   *13* his Janissaries, for allowing his line of troops to be broken by the Hungarians, and bearing himself like a coward in the battle; and that Chasan made no reply but, alone and just as he was with his weapon in his hand, rushed furiously into the first body of enemies that he met with, and was immediately overwhelmed; it was not so much a justification of his conduct as a change of mood, not so much natural prowess as a new spite.

Do not think it strange that the man who was so venturesome yester-   *14* day should prove such a poltroon on the morrow; either anger, or necessity, or company, or wine, or the sound of the trumpet had put his heart into his belly; it was not a courage thus formed by reason, but a courage stiffened by those circumstances; it was no marvel if other contrary circumstances made a new man of him.

These so supple changes and contradictions which we manifest have   *15* made some to imagine that we have two souls, others, that we have two powers which, each in its own way, accompany and stir us, the one to good, the other to evil, since so abrupt a diversity is not to be reconciled with a single subject.

Not only does the wind of accidents stir me according to its blowing,   *16* but I am also stirred and troubled by the instability of my attitude; and he who examines himself closely will seldom find himself twice in the same state. I give to my soul now one face, now another, according to the side to which I turn it. If I speak differently of myself, it is because I regard myself differently. All the contradictions are to be found in me, according as the wind turns and changes. Bashful, insolent; chaste, lascivious; talkative, taciturn; clumsy, gentle; witty, dull; peevish, sweet-tempered; mendacious, truthful; knowing, ignorant; and liberal and avaricious and prodigal: all this I see in myself in some degree, according

* *Epistles,* Book II, Epistle ii, l. 36.
† *Epistles,* Book II, Epistle ii, ll. 39 f.

as I veer about; and whoever will study himself very attentively will find in himself, yea, in his judgement, this discordance and unsteadiness. I can say nothing of myself absolutely, simply, and steadily, without confusion and mixture, nor in one word. *Distinguo** is the most universal member of my logic.

Though I am ever inclined to speak well of what is good, and rather 17 to interpret favourably the things that are capable of such interpretation, yet such is the strangeness of our nature that we are often driven to do good, even by vice; if it were not that well-doing is judged by the intention alone.

Therefore a courageous deed ought not to imply a valiant man: the 18 man who is really brave will be always so, and on all occasions. If valour were a habit, and not a sudden eruption, it would make a man equally resolute for all emergencies, the same alone as in company, the same in single combat as in a battle; for let them say what they will, there is not one valour for the pavement and another for the field. As bravely would he bear sickness in his bed as a wound in camp, nor would he fear death in his own home any more than in an assault. We should not see the same man charge with brave assurance into the breach, and afterwards worrying like a woman, over the loss of a law-suit or a son. When, though afraid of infamy, he bears up against poverty; when, though wincing at a surgeon's lancet, he stiffly faces the enemy's sword, the action is praiseworthy, but not the man.

Many Greeks, says Cicero, cannot look upon an enemy, and are brave 19 in sickness. The Cimbrians and the Celtiberians, quite the contrary: *For nothing can be consistent that has not reason for its foundation* (Cicero).†

No valour could be more extreme in its kind than Alexander's; but it 20 is of one kind only, and is not complete enough, nor universal on all occasions. Incomparable though it be, it has its blemishes. So it is that we see him so desperately disturbed by the slightest suspicions that his subjects may be plotting against his life, and carried away in his investigations to such violent and indiscriminate acts of injustice, and haunted by a fear that upsets his natural good sense. The superstition too with which he was so strongly tainted bears some likeness to pusillanimity. And the excess of his penitence for the murder of Clytus is also evidence of uneven temper.

Our actions are but a patchwork (*they despise pleasure, but are cow-* 21 *ardly in pain; they are indifferent to fame, but infamy breaks their spirit‡*), and we try to gain honour by false pretences. Virtue will not be wooed but for her own sake, and if we sometimes borrow her mask for some other purpose, she will very soon snatch it from our face. When the soul

* I distinguish; I separate into its components.
† *Tusculan Disputations,* Book II, Chapter 27.
‡ Cicero, *Of Duties* (*De officiis*), Book I, Chapter 21.

is once steeped in it, the dye is strong and vivid, and will not go without taking the skin with it. Wherefore, to judge a man, we must long and carefully follow his traces. If constancy does not stand firm and wholly on its own foundation, *if the path of life has not been well considered and preconcerted* (Cicero);* if changing circumstances make him alter his pace (I should say his route, for the pace may be accelerated or retarded by them), let him go: that man will go *A vau le vent* (down the wind), as the motto of our Talebot has it.

It is no wonder, says an ancient writer,† that chance has so great a   22 hold over us, since we live by chance. Unless a man has directed his life as a whole to a certain fixed goal, he cannot possibly dispose his particular actions. Unless he have an image of the whole in his mind, he cannot possibly arrange the pieces. How can a painter lay in a stock of colours, if he knows not what he is going to paint? No man draws a definite outline of his life, and we only think it out in details. The archer must first know at what he is aiming, and then accommodate his hand, his bow, the string, the arrow, and his movements, accordingly. Our plans go wrong because they have neither aim nor direction. No wind serves the ship that has no port of destination.

I cannot agree with those judges who, on the strength of seeing one   23 of his tragedies, declared in favour of Sophocles, when accused by his son of being incapable of managing his domestic affairs. Nor do I hold with the conclusions arrived at by the Parians who were sent to reform the Milesians. Visiting the island, they remarked the best-cultivated lands and the best-kept country-houses, and made a note of their owners; and then, having called an assembly of the citizens in the town, they appointed these owners the new governors and magistrates, concluding that, being careful of their private affairs, they would be equally careful of those of the public.

We are all made up of bits, and so shapelessly and diversely put   24 together, that every piece, at every moment, plays its own game. And there is as much difference between us and ourselves, as between us and others. *Be sure that it is very difficult to be always the same man* (Seneca).‡ Since ambition can teach a man valour, temperance, and liberality, yea and justice too; since greed can implant in the heart of a shop-apprentice, bred up in obscurity and neglect, the confidence to entrust himself, so far from the domestic hearth, to the mercy of the waves and angry Neptune in a frail bark; since it teaches also discretion and prudence; and since Venus herself can put resolution and temerity into the boy who is still under the discipline of the rod, and embolden the heart of the tender virgin in her mother's arms,

* *Paradoxes (Paradoxa)*, Paradox v.
† Seneca, in *Epistles,* Epistle lxxi.
‡ *Epistles,* Epistle cxx.

> With Love for guide,
> Alone the maid steps o'er her prostrate guards,
> And steals by night into the young man's arms;   (Tibullus.)*

it is not enough for a sober understanding to judge us simply by our external actions: we must sound the innermost recesses, and observe the springs which give the swing. But since it is a high and hazardous undertaking, I would rather that fewer people meddled with it.

Study Questions

1. In "Of the Inconsistency of Our Actions," Montaigne deals with human inconsistency, a topic that most people take for granted. We have all heard one phrase or another to the effect that "it is human nature to be inconsistent." What is Montaigne's attitude toward this topic? How does he try to interest his readers in this attitude?
2. Where does Montaigne give his clearest statement of his feelings toward inconsistency? What effect do you think he was trying to achieve by placing his statement there?
3. Paragraphs 6–12 are connected by an additive organization. Identify the chief words and phrases that signal this method. In this case, the "list" contains a series of examples that illustrate his statement "We waver between different minds; we wish nothing freely, nothing absolutely, nothing constantly." How well do these examples illustrate this point?
4. Starting with paragraph 13, Montaigne shifts to a different method of organization. What change in his discussion of inconsistency leads to this shift? What is the new method of organization? How does it fit the new statement he wishes to make?

Suggestion for Drafting

A type of additive organization in which the writer uses examples or illustrations to make an essential point is known as *exemplification*. For the method to work, you must choose examples with an obvious relation to your point or those that are easily explained. Vague or overly elaborate examples will slow your discussion down and distract your readers from the statement you wish to illustrate.

Reread paragraph 21 as if it were part of a prewriting "list":

* *Elegies,* Book II, Elegy i, ll. 75 ff.

Our actions are but a patchwork (*they despise pleasure, but are cowardly in pain; they are indifferent to fame, but infamy breaks their spirit*), and we try to gain honour by false pretences. Virtue will not be wooed but for her own sake, and if we sometimes borrow her mask for some other purpose, she will very soon snatch it from our face. When the soul is once steeped in it, the dye is strong and vivid, and will not go without taking skin with it. Wherefore, to judge a man, we must long and carefully follow his traces. If constancy does not stand firm and wholly on its own foundation, *if this path of life has not been well considered and preconcerted* (Cicero), if changing circumstances make him alter his pace (I should say his route, for the pace may be accelerated or retarded by them), let him go: that man will go *A vau le vent* (down the wind), as the motto of our Talebot has it.

Write your own draft of an essay, in which you use two or more examples that exemplify the points made in this paragraph. Try to find examples from your own experience or that of people you know.

Man of the Future

Loren Eiseley

T here are days when I may find myself unduly *1* pessimistic about the future of man. Indeed, I will confess that there have been occasions when I swore I would never again make the study of time a profession. My walls are lined with books expounding its mysteries, my hands have been split and raw with grubbing into the quicklime of its waste bins and hidden crevices. I have stared so much at death that I can recognize the lingering personalities in the faces of skulls and feel accompanying affinities and repulsions.

One such skull lies in the lockers of a great metropolitan museum. It *2* is labeled simply: Strandlooper, South Africa. I have never looked longer into any human face than I have upon the features of that skull. I come there often, drawn in spite of myself. It is a face that would lend reality to the fantastic tales of our childhood. There is a hint of Wells's *Time Machine* folk in it—those pathetic, childlike people whom Wells pictures as haunting earth's autumnal cities in the far future of the dying planet.

Yet this skull has not been spirited back to us through future eras by *3* a time machine. It is a thing, instead, of the millennial past. It is a caricature of modern man, not by reason if its primitiveness but, startlingly, because of a modernity outreaching his own. It constitutes, in fact, a mysterious prophecy and warning. For at the very moment in which students of humanity have been sketching their concept of the man of the future, that being has already come, and lived, and passed away.

We men of today are insatiably curious about ourselves and desper- *4* ately in need of reassurance. Beneath our boisterous self-confidence is fear—a growing fear of the future we are in the process of creating. In such a mood we turn the pages of our favorite magazine and, like as not, come straight upon a description of the man of the future.

The descriptions are never pessimistic; they always, with sublime *5* confidence, involve just one variety of mankind—our own—and they are always subtly flattering. In fact, a distingushed colleague of mine who was adept at this kind of prophecy once allowed a somewhat etherealized version of his own lofty brow to be used as an illustration of what the man of the future was to look like. Even the bald spot didn't matter— all the men of the future were to be bald, anyway.

Occasionally I show this picture to students. They find it highly 6
comforting. Somebody with a lot of brains will save humanity at the
proper moment. "It's all right," they say, looking at my friend's picture
labeled "Man of the Future." "It's O.K. Somebody's keeping an eye on
things. Our heads are getting bigger and our teeth are getting smaller.
Look!"

Their voices ring with youthful confidence, the confidence engendered 7
by my persuasive colleagues and myself. At times I glow a little with
their reflected enthusiasm. I should like to regain that confidence, that
warmth. I should like to but . . .

There's just one thing we haven't quite dared to mention. It's this, 8
and you won't believe it. It's all happened already. Back there in the
past, ten thousand years ago. The man of the future, with the big brain,
the small teeth.

Where did it get him? Nowhere. *Maybe there isn't any future.* Or, 9
if there is, maybe it's only what you can find in a little heap of bones on
a certain South African beach.

Many of you who read this belong to the white race. We like to think 10
about this man of the future as being white. It flatters our ego. But the
man of the future in the past I'm talking about was not white. He lived
in Africa. His brain was bigger than your brain. His face was straight
and small, almost a child's face. He was the end evolutionary product
in a direction quite similar to the one anthropologists tell us is the road
down which we are traveling.

In the minds of many scholars, a process of "foetalization" is one of 11
the chief mechanisms by which man of today has sloughed off his ferocious appearance of a million years ago, prolonged his childhood, and
increased the size of his brain. "Foetalization" or "pedomorphism," as
it is termed, means simply the retention, into adult life, of bodily characters which at some earlier stage of evolutionary history were actually
only infantile. Such traits were rapidly lost as the animal attained
maturity.

If we examine the life history of one of the existing great apes and 12
compare its development with that of man, we observe that the infantile
stages of both man and ape are far more similar then the two will be in
maturity. At birth, as we have seen, the brain of the gorilla is close to
the size of that of the human infant. Both newborn gorilla and human
child are much more alike, facially, than they will ever be in adult life
because the gorilla infant will, in the course of time, develop an enor-
mously powerful and protrusive muzzle. The sutures of his skull will
close early; his brain will grow very little more.

By contrast, human brain growth will first spurt and then grow steadily 13
over an extended youth. Cranial sutures will remain open into adult life.
Teeth will be later in their eruption. Furthermore, the great armored

skull and the fighting characters of the anthropoid male will be held in abeyance.

Instead, the human child, through a more extended infancy, will ap-   *14*
proach a maturity marked by the retention of the smooth-browed skull of childhood. His jaws will be tucked inconspicuously under a forehead lacking the huge, muscle-bearing ridges of the ape. In some unknown manner, the ductless glands which stimulate or inhibit growth have, in the course of human evolution, stepped down the pace of development and increased the life span. Our helpless but well-cared-for childhood allows a longer time for brain growth and, as an indirect consequence, human development has slowly been steered away from the ape-like adulthood of our big-jawed forebears.

Modern man retains something of his youthful gaiety and nimble men-   *15*
tal habits far into adult life. The great male anthropoids, by contrast, lose the playful friendliness of youth. In the end the massive skull houses a small, savage, and often morose brain. It is doubtful whether our thick-skulled forerunners viewed life very pleasantly in their advancing years.

We of today, then, are pedomorphs—the childlike, yet mature products   *16*
of a simian line whose years have lengthened and whose adolescence has become long drawn out. We are, for our day and time, civilized. We eat soft food, and an Eskimo child can outbite us. We show signs, in our shortening jaws, of losing our wisdom teeth. Our brain has risen over our eyes and few, even of our professional fighters, show enough trace of a brow ridge to impress a half-grown gorilla. The signs point steadily onward toward a further lightening of the skull box and to additional compression of the jaws.

Imagine this trend continuing in modern man. Imagine our general   *17*
average cranial capacity rising by two hundred cubic centimeters while the face continued to reduce proportionately. Obviously we would possess a much higher ratio of brain size to face size than now exists. We would, paradoxically, resemble somewhat our children of today. Children acquire facial prominence late in growth under the endocrine stimulus of maturity. Until that stimulus occurs, their faces bear a smaller ratio to the size of the brain case. It was so with these early South Africans.

But no, you may object, this whole process is in some way dependent   *18*
upon civilization and grows out of it. Man's body and his culture mutually control each other. To that extent we are masters of our physical destiny. This mysterious change that is happening to our bodies is epitomized at just one point today, the point of the highest achieved civilization upon earth—our own.

I believed this statement once, believed it wholeheartedly. Sometimes   *19*
it is so very logical I believe it still as my colleague's ascetic, earnest, and ennobled face gazes out at me from the screen. It carries the lineaments of my own kind, the race to which I belong. But it is not, I

know now, the most foetalized race nor the largest brained. That game
had already been played out before written history began—played out in
an obscure backwater of the world where sails never came and where
the human horde chipped flint as our ancestors had chipped it northward
in Europe when the vast ice lay heavy on the land.

These people were not civilized; they were not white. But they meet 20
in every major aspect the physical description of the man of tomorrow.
They achieved that status on the raw and primitive diet of a savage.
Their delicate and gracefully reduced teeth and fragile jaws are striking
testimony to some strange inward hastening of change. Nothing about
their environment in the least explains them. They were tomorrow's
children surely, born by error into a lion country of spears and sand.

Africa is not a black man's continent in the way we are inclined to 21
think. Like other great land areas it has its uneasy amalgams, its genetically strange variants, its racial deviants whose blood stream is no longer
traceable. We know only that the first true men who disturbed the
screaming sea birds over Table Bay were a folk that humanity has never
looked upon again save as their type has wavered into brief emergence
in an occasional mixed descendant. They are related in some dim manner
to the modern Kalahari Bushman, but he is dwarfed in brain and body
and hastening fast toward eventual extinction. The Bushman's forerunners, by contrast, might have stepped with Weena out of the future eras
of the Time Machine.

Widespread along the South African coast, in the lowest strata of 22
ancient cliff shelters, as well as inland in Ice Age gravel and other
primeval deposits, lie the bones of these unique people. So remote are
they from us in time that the first archaeologists who probed their caves
and seashore middens had expected to reveal some distant and primitive
human forerunner such as Neanderthal man. Instead their spades uncovered an unknown branch of humanity which, in the words of Sir
Arthur Keith, the great English anatomist, "outrivals in brain volume
any people of Europe, ancient or modern . . ."

But that is not all. Dr. Drennan of the University of Capetown com- 23
ments upon one such specimen in anatomical wonder: "It appears ultramodern in many of its features, surpassing the European in almost every
direction. That is to say, it is less simian than any modern skull." This
ultramodernity Dr. Drennan attributes to the curious foetalization of
which I have spoken.

More fascinating than big brain capacity in itself, however, is the 24
relation of the cranium to the base of the skull and to the face. The skull
base, that is, the part from the root of the nose to the spinal opening, is
buckled and shortened in a way characteristic of the child's skull before
the base expands to aid in the creation of the adult face. Thus, on this
permanently shortened cranial base, the great brain expands, bulging the
forehead heavily above the eyes and leaving the face neatly retracted

beneath the brow. There is nothing in this face to suggest the protrusive facial angle of the true Negro. It is, as Dr. Drennan says, "ultramodern," even by Caucasian standards. The bottom of the skull grew, apparently, at a slow and childlike tempo while the pace-setting brain lengthened and broadened to a huge maturity.

When the skull is studied in projection and ratios computed, we find   25 that these fossil South African folk, generally called "Boskop" or "Boskopoids" after the site of first discovery, have the amazing cranium-to-face ratio of almost five to one. In Europeans it is about three to one. This figure is a marked indication of the degree to which face size had been "modernized" and subordinated to brain growth. It is true that Dr. Ronald Singer has recently contended that the "Boskop" people cannot be successfully differentiated from the Bushman because Boskopoid features can be observed in this latter group, but even he would not deny the appearance of the peculiarly pedomorphic and ultrahuman features we have been discussing. At best, he would contend, in contrast to Keith and Drennan, that these characters have emerged in a sporadic fashion throughout the racial history of South Africa. By contrast, the facial structure of existing Causasians, advanced though we imagine it, has only a mediocre rating.

The teeth vary a little from the usual idea about man of the future,   26 yet they, too, are modern. Our prophecies generally include the speculation that we will, in time, lose our third molar teeth. This seems likely indeed, for the tooth often fails to erupt, crowds, and causes trouble. The Boskop folk had no such difficulty. Their teeth are small, neatly reduced in proportion to their delicate jaws, and free from any sign of the dental ills that trouble us. Here, in a hunter's world that would seem to have demanded at least the stout modern dentition of the Congo Negro, nature had decreed otherwise. These teeth could have nibbled sedately at the Waldorf, nor would the customers have been alarmed.

With the face, however, it would have been otherwise. In its anatom-   27 ical structure we observe characters which relate these people both with the dwarf modern Bushman and to some ancient Negroid strain distinct from the West Coast blacks. We believe that they had the tightly-kinked "pepper-corn" hair of the Bushman as well as his yellow-brown skin. A branch of the Negro race has thus produced what is actually, so far as we can judge from the anatomical standpoint, one of the most ultrahuman types that ever lived! Had these characters appeared among whites, they would undoubtedly have been used in invidious comparisons with other "lesser" races.

We can, of course, repeat the final, unanswerable question: What did   28 this tremendous brain mean to the Boskop people? We can marvel over their curious and exotic anatomy. We can wonder at the mysterious powers hidden in the human body, so potent that once unleashed they brought this more than modern being into existence on the very threshold of the Ice Age.

We can debate for days whether that magnificent cranial endowment *29* actually represented a superior brain. We can smile pityingly at his miserable shell heaps, point to the mute stones that were his only tools. We can do this, but in doing it we are mocking our own rude forefathers of a similar day and time. We are forgetting the high artistic sensitivity which flowered in the closing Ice Age of Europe and which, oddly, blossomed here as well, lingering on even among the dwarfed Bushmen of the Kalahari. No, we cannot dismiss the Boskop people on such grounds, for even remarkable potential endowment cannot create high civilization overnight.

What we *can* say is that perhaps the unloosed mechanism ran too fast, *30* that these people may have been ill-equipped physically to compete against the onrush of more ferocious and less foetalized folk. In a certain sense the biological clock had speeded them out of their time and place— a time which ten thousand years later has still not arrived. We may speculate that even mentally they may have lacked something of the elemental savagery of their competitors.

Their evolutionary gallop has led precisely nowhere save to a dwarfed *31* and dying folk—if, with some authorities, we accept the later Bushmen as their descendants. This, then, was the logical end of complete foetalization: a desperate struggle to survive among a welter of more prolific and aggressive stocks. The answer to the one great question is still nowhere, still nothing. But there in the darkened laboratory, after the students have gone, I look once more at the exalted photograph of my friend upon the screen, noting character by character the foetalized refinement by which the artist has attempted to indicate the projected trend of future development—the expanded brain, the delicate face.

I look, and I know I have seen it all before, reading, as I have long *32* grown used to doing, the bones through the living flesh. I have seen this face in another racial guise in another and forgotten day. And once again I grow aware of that eternal flickering of forms which we are now too worldly wise to label progress, and whose meaning forever escapes us.

The man of the future came, and looked out among us once with *33* wistful, if unsophisticated eyes. He left his bones in the rubble of an alien land. If we read evolution aright, he may come again in another million years. Are the evolutionary forces searching for the right moment of his appearance? Or is his appearance itself destined always, even in the moment of emergence, to mark the end of the drama and foretell the extinction of a race?

Perhaps the strange interior clockwork that is here revealed as so *34* indifferent to environmental surroundings has set, after all, a limit to the human time it keeps. That is the real question propounded by my friend's fine face. That is the question that I sometimes think the Boskop folk have answered. I wish I could be sure. I wish I knew.

Whatever else these skulls or those of occasional variant moderns may   *35* tell us, one thing they clearly reveal: Those who contend that because of present human cranial size, and the limitations of the human pelvis, man's brain is no longer capable of further expansion, are mistaken. Cranial capacities of almost a third more than the modern average have been occasionally attained among the Boskop people and even in rare individuals among other, less foetalized races. The secret does not lie in the size of the brain before birth; rather, as we have seen, it is contained in that strange spurt which in the first year of life carries man upward and outward into a social world from which his fellow beings are excluded. Whether that postnatal expansion is destined to be further enhanced in the long eras to come there is no telling, nor, perhaps, does it matter greatly. For in the creation of the social brain, nature, through man, has eluded the trap which has engulfed in one way or another every other form of life on the planet. Within the reasonable limits of the brain that now exists, she has placed the long continuity of civilized memory as it lies packed in the world's great libraries. The need is not really for more brains, the need is now for a gentler, a more tolerant people than those who won for us against the ice, the tiger, and the bear. The hand that hefted the ax, out of some old blind allegiance to the past fondles the machine gun as lovingly. It is a habit man will have to break to survive, but the roots go very deep.

I once sat, a prisoner, long ago, and watched a peasant soldier just   *36* recently equipped with a submachine gun swing the gun slowly into line with my body. It was a beautiful weapon and his finger toyed hesitantly with the trigger. Suddenly to possess all that power and then to be forbidden to use it must have been almost too much for the man to contain. I remember, also, a protesting female voice nearby—the eternal civilizing voice of women who know that men are fools and children, and irresponsible. Sheepishly the peon slowly dropped the gun muzzle away from my chest. The black eyes over the barrel looked out at me a little wicked, a little desirous of better understanding.

"Thompson, Tome'-son'," he repeated proudly, slapping the barrel.   *37* "Tome'-son'." I nodded a little weakly, relaxing with a sigh. After all, we were men together and understood this great subject of destruction. And was I not a citizen of the country that had produced this wonderful mechanism? So I nodded again and said carefully after him. "Thompson, Tome-son'. *Bueno, si, muy bueno.*" We looked at each other then, smiling a male smile that ran all the way back to the Ice Age. In academic halls since, considering the future of humanity, I have never been quite free of the memory of that soldier's smile. I weigh it mentally against the future whenever one of those delicate forgotten skulls is placed upon my desk.

Study Questions

1. Loren Eiseley uses a comparatively long beginning section, paragraphs 1–18, as the introduction to "Man of the Future." What points does he establish in that opening that require such length? Why is it important that these points be established before he begins the body of the essay?
2. Is Eiseley's goal to explain to his readers why he finds himself "unduly pessimistic about the future of man" or is it to convince his readers that they should be pessimistic as well? Discuss how the way he has ordered his discussion supports your answer.
3. Eiseley frequently stops to define technical terms that he does not expect his readers to know. Why would he want to use these terms if he needs to define them? How does he define the terms without disrupting his discussion?
4. After discussing the similarities between the Boskop skulls and the Caucasian skulls that are predicted after future evolution, Eiseley ends his essay with a narrative that illustrates his fear for humanity's future: "The need is not really for more brains, the need is now for a gentler, a more tolerant people than those who won for us against the ice, the tiger, and the bear." Why has he waited so long to voice this message? What connection does this message have with the Boskop skulls? How reasonable do you think it is for Eiseley to expect his readers to make this connection?

Suggestion for Drafting

As we suggested in question 4, Eiseley has left his readers to make the connection between Boskop man and future man. Most readers will eventually be able to make that connection, but there is a danger that some will not. In order to practice conceptual organization, suppose that you were redrafting this section of "Man of the Future." Write a passage in which you explain how the similarities between the Boskop skulls and the skulls foreseen for future man lead to the conclusion that brains are not enough.

Come Eat

Patricia Hampl

F ood was the potent center of my grandmoth- *1*
er's life. Maybe the immense amount of time
it took to prepare meals during most of her
life accounted for her passion. Or it may have been her years of work
in various kitchens on the hill and later, in the house of Justice Butler:
after all, she was a professional. Much later, when she was dead and I
went to Prague, I came to feel the motto I knew her by best—*Come
eat*—was not, after all, a personal statement, but a racial one, the *cri de
coeur* of Middle Europe.

Often, on Sundays, the entire family gathered for dinner at her house. *2*
Dinner was at 1 P.M. My grandmother would have preferred the meal
to be at the old time of noon, but her children had moved their own
Sunday dinner hour to the more fashionable (it was felt) 4 o'clock, so
she compromised. Sunday breakfast was something my mother liked to
do in a big way, so we arrived at my grandmother's hardly out of the
reverie of waffles and orange rolls, before we were propped like rag dolls
in front of a pork roast and sauerkraut, dumplings, hot buttered carrots,
rye bread and rollikey, pickles and olives, apple pie and ice cream. And
coffee.

Coffee was a food in that house, not a drink. I always begged for *3*
some because the magical man on the Hills Brothers can with his turban
and long robe scattered with stars and his gold slippers with pointed toes,
looked deeply happy as he drank from his bowl. The bowl itself reminded
me of soup, Campbell's chicken noodle soup, my favorite food. The
distinct adultness of coffee and the robed man with his deep-drinking
pleasure made it clear why the grownups lingered so long at the table.
The uncles smoked cigars then, and the aunts said, "Oh, those cigars."

My grandmother, when she served dinner, was a virtuoso hanging on *4*
the edge of her own ecstatic performance. She seemed dissatisfied,
almost querulous until she had corralled everybody into their chairs
around the table, which she tried to do the minute they got into the
house. No cocktails, no hors d'oeuvres (pronounced, by some of the
family, "horse's ovaries"), just business. She was a little power crazed:
she had us and, by God, we were going to eat. She went about it like a
goose breeder forcing pellets down the gullets of those dumb birds.

She flew between her chair and the kitchen, always finding more this, *5*
extra that. She'd given you the *wrong* chicken breast the first time

around; now she'd found the *right* one: eat it too, eat it fast, because after the chicken comes the rhubarb pie. Rhubarb pie with a thick slice of cheddar cheese that it was imperative every single person eat.

We had to eat fast because something was always out there in the 6 kitchen panting and charging the gate, champing at the bit, some mound of rice or a Jell-O fruit salad or vegetable casserole or pie was out there, waiting to be let loose into the dining room.

She had the usual trite routines: the wheedlings, the silent pout 7 ("What! You don't like my brussels sprouts? I thought you liked *my* brussels sprouts," versus your wife's/sister's/mother's. "I made that pie just for you," etc., etc.) But it was the way she tossed around the old cliches and the overused routines, mixing them up and dealing them out shamelessly, without irony, that made her a pro. She tended to peck at her own dinner. Her plate, piled with food, was a kind of stage prop, a mere bending to convention. She liked to eat, she was even a greedy little stuffer, but not on these occasions. She was a woman possessed by an idea, given over wholly to some phantasmagoria of food, a mirage of stuffing, a world where the endless chicken and the infinite lemon pie were united at last at the shore of the oceanic soup plate that her children and her children's children alone could drain . . . if only they would try.

She was there to bolster morale, to lead the troops, to give the sharp 8 command should we falter on the way. The futility of saying no was supreme, and no one ever tried it. How could a son-in-law, already weakened near the point of imbecility by the once, twice, thrice charge to the barricades of pork and mashed potato, be expected to gather his feeble wit long enough to ignore the final call of his old commander when she sounded the alarm: "Pie, Fred?"

Just when it seemed as if the food-crazed world she had created was 9 going to burst, that she had whipped and frothed us like a sack of boiled potatoes under her masher, just then she pulled it all together in one easeful stroke like the pro she was.

She stood in the kitchen doorway, her little round Napoleonic self 10 sheathed in a cotton flowered pinafore apron, the table draped in its white lace cloth but spotted now with gravy and beet juice, the troops mumbling indistinctly as they waited at their posts for they knew not what. We looked up at her stupidly, weakly. She said nonchalantly, "Anyone want another piece of pie?" No, no more pie, somebody said. The rest of the rabble grunted along with him. She stood there with the coffeepot and laughed and said, "Good! Because there *isn't* any more pie."

No more pie. We'd eaten it all, we'd put away everything in that 11 kitchen. We were exhausted and she, gambler hostess that she was (but it was her house she was playing), knew she could offer what didn't exist, knew us, knew what she'd wrought. There was a sense of her having won, won something. There were no divisions among us now, no adults, no children. Power left the second and third generations and returned to the source, the grandmother who reduced us to mutters by her art.

That wasn't the end of it. At 5 P.M. there was "lunch"—sandwiches *12* and beer; the sandwiches were made from the leftovers (mysteriously renewable resources, those roasts). And at about 8 P.M. we were at the table again for coffee cake and coffee, the little man in his turban and his coffee ecstasy and his pointed shoes set on the kitchen table as my grandmother scooped out the coffee and dumped it into a big enamel pot with a crushed eggshell. By then everyone was alive and laughing again, the torpor gone. My grandfather had been inviting the men, one by one, into the kitchen during the afternoon where he silently (the austere version of memory—but he must have talked, must have said *something*) handed them jiggers of whiskey, and watched them put the shot down in one swallow. Then he handed them a beer, which they took out in the living room. I gathered that the *little* drink in the tiny glass shaped like a beer mug was some sort of antidote for the *big* drink of beer. He sat on the chair in the kitchen with a bottle of beer on the floor next to him and played his concertina, allowing society to form itself around him— while he lived he was the center—but not seeking it, not going into the living room. And not talking. He held to his music and the kindly, medicinal administration of whiskey.

By evening, it seemed we could eat endlessly, as if we'd had some *13* successful inoculation at dinner and could handle anything. I stayed in the kitchen after they all reformed in the dining room at the table for coffee cake. I could hear them, but the little man in his starry yellow robe was on the table in the kitchen and I put my head down on the oil cloth very near the curled and delighted tips of his pointed shoes, and I slept. Whatever laughter there was, there was. But something sweet and starry was in the kitchen and I lay down beside it, my stomach full, warm, so safe I'll live the rest of my life off the fat of that vast family security.

Study Questions

1. The first paragraph of Patricia Hampl's essay begins: "Food was the potent center of my grandmother's life." What words in the description of Sunday dinners contained in paragraphs 4–11 develop the connotation suggested by the opening sentence?
2. If "Come Eat" had ended with paragraph 11, what attitude toward her grandmother would Hampl have expressed? How is that attitude changed by the last paragraph?

3. Hampl describes her grandfather in paragraph 12. How does his behavior contrast with her grandmother's? How do these contrasts help readers understand the grandmother?

4. In paragraphs 3, 11, and 12, Hampl refers to "the magical man on the Hills Brothers can." What does this image represent? How is it related to her memories of her grandparents?

Suggestion for Drafting

Patricia Hampl tells the story of Sunday dinners at her grandmother's house from her own point of view. That is, she tells us what she thinks about the dinners. She could have chosen to use another point of view; for example, she could have tried to describe the dinners through the eyes of her grandfather. What did he feel during this time? What thoughts did he have? As an excrcise in revising, reformulate paragraphs 4–6 so that they describe the grandfather's reaction to the dinners. Start by changing "My grandfather" to "My wife" and then rewrite the words and sentences so that they portray a loving husband describing his wife.

The Artificial Universe

Vine Deloria, Jr.

T he justification for taking lands from Indian *1*
people has always been that the needs and
requirements of civilized people had to come
first. Settlers arriving on these shores saw a virtual paradise untouched
by the works of man. They drooled at the prospect of developing the
land according to their own dictates. Thus a policy of genocide was
advocated that would clear the land of the original inhabitants to make
way for towns, cities, farms, factories, and highways. This was progress.

Even today Indian people hold their land at the sufferance of the non- *2*
Indian. The typical white attitude is that Indians can have land as long
as whites have no use for it. When it becomes useful, then it naturally
follows that the land must be taken by whites to put to a better use. I
have often heard the remark "what happens to the Indian land base if
we decide we need more land?" The fact that Indian rights to land are
guaranteed by the Constitution of the United States, over four hundred
treaties, and some six thousand statutes seems irrelevant to a people
hungry for land and dedicated to law and order.

The major reason why whites have seen fit to steal Indian lands is that *3*
they feel that their method of using land is so much better than that of
the Indian. It follows that God would want them to develop the land.
During the Seneca fight against Kinzua Dam, sympathetic whites would
raise the question of Indian legal rights and they would be shouted down
by people who said that the Indians had had the land for two hundred
years and did *nothing* with it. It would be far better, they argued, to let
whites take the land and develop something on it.

From the days of the earliest treaties, Indians were shocked at the *4*
white man's attitude toward land. The tribal elders laughed contemptuously at the idea that a man could sell land. "Why not sell the air we
breathe, the water we drink, the animals we hunt?" some replied. It was
ludicrous to Indians that people would consider land as commodity that
could be owned by one man. The land, they would answer, supports all
life. It is given to all people. No one has a superior claim to exclusive
use of land, much less does anyone have the right to fence off a portion
and deny others its use.

In the closing decades of the last century, Indian tribes fought fiercely *5*
for their lands. Reservations were agreed upon and tribes held a fragment
of the once expansive hunting grounds they had roamed. But no sooner
had Indians settled on the reservations, than the government, ably led

by the churches, decided that the reservation areas should be divided into tiny plots of land for farming purposes. In many reservation areas it was virtually impossible to farm such lands. The situation in California was so desperate that a report was issued denouncing the government land policy for Indians. The report contained such detrimental material exposing the vast land swindles that it was pigeonholed in the Senate files and *has never been released and cannot be obtained today, nearly a century later!!!*

Tribe after tribe succumbed to the allotment process. After the little 6 plots of land were passed out to individual Indians, the remainder, which should have been held in tribal hands, was declared surplus and opened to settlement. Millions of "excess" acres of lands were thus casually transferred to federal title and given to non-Indian settlers. Churches rushed in and grabbed the choice allotments for their chapels and cemeteries, and in some cases simply for income-producing purposes. They had been the chief advocates of allotment—on the basis that creating greed and selfishness among the Indians was the first step in civilizing them and making them Christians.

For years the development of the land did make it seem as if the whites 7 had been correct in their theory of land use. Cities were built, productive farms were created, the wilderness was made safe, and superhighways were built linking one portion of the nation with the others. In some areas the very landscape was changed as massive earth-moving machines relocated mountains and streams, filled valleys, and created lakes out of wandering streams.

Where Indian people had had a reverence for the productiveness of 8 the land, whites wanted to make the land support their way of life whether it was suited to do so or not. Much of San Francisco Bay was filled in and whole areas of the city were built upon the new land. Swamps were drained in the Chicago area and large portions of the city were built on them. A great portion of Ohio had been swamp and grassland and this was drained and farmed. Land was the great capital asset for speculation. People purchased apparently worthless desert land in Arizona, only to have the cities grow outward to their doorstep, raising land prices hundreds of percents. Land worth pennies an acre in the 1930s became worth thousands of dollars a front foot in the 1960s.

The rapid increase of population, technology, and capital has produced 9 the present situation where the struggle for land will surpass anything that can be conceived. We are now on the verge of incredible development of certain areas into strip cities that will extend hundreds of miles along the coasts, major rivers, and mountain ranges. At the same time, many areas of the country are steadily losing population. Advanced farming techniques allow one man to do the work that several others formerly did, so that the total population needed in agricultural states continues to decline without a corresponding decline in productivity.

The result of rapid industrialization has been the creation of innumer- *10* able problems. Farm surpluses have lowered prices on agricultural prod- ucts so that the federal government has had to enter the marketplace and support prices to ensure an adequate income for farmers. Farm subsidies are no longer a small business. In nine wheat and feed grain-producing counties in eastern Colorado in 1968, $31.4 million was given in farm subsidies. In all of Colorado, $62.8 million was given in 1968 to support farmers. This was a state with a declining farm population. Under the Agricultural Stabilization Conservation Service, some $3.5 billion was paid out in 1968, $675 million paid to 33,395 individual farmers as farm "income maintenance," some receiving amounts in excess of $100,000.

For much of the rural farm areas the economy, the society, and the *11* very structure of life is completely artificial. It depends wholly upon government welfare payments to landowners, a thinly disguised guaran- teed annual income for the rich. If the payments were suddenly cut off, millions of acres would become idle because it would not pay to farm them and there would be no way to live on them without income. Our concern for the family farm and the rural areas is thus a desperate effort to maintain the facade of a happy, peace-loving nation of farmers, tillers of the soil who stand as the bastion of rugged individualism.

If rural areas have an artificial economy, the urban areas surpass them *12* in everything. Wilderness transformed into city streets, subways, giant buildings, and factories resulted in the complete substitution of the real world for the artificial world of the urban man. Instead of woods, large buildings rose. Instead of paths, avenues were built. Instead of lakes and streams, sewers and fountains were created. In short, urban man lives in a world of his own making and not in the world that his ancestors first encountered.

Surrounded by an artificial universe where the warning signals are not *13* the shape of the sky, the cry of the animals, the changing of seasons, but simply the flashing of the traffic light and the wail of the ambulance and police car, urban people have no idea what the natural universe is like. They are devoured by the goddess of progress, and progress is defined solely in terms of convenience within the artificial technological universe with which they are familiar. Technological progress totally defines the outlook of most of America, so that as long as newer buildings and fancier roads can be built, additional lighting and electric appliances can be sold, and conveniences for modern living can be created there is not the slightest indication that urban man realizes that his artificial universe is dependent on the real world.

Milk comes in cartons, and cows are so strange an animal that hunters *14* from large cities kill a substantial number of cattle every year on their annual hunting orgies. This despite the fact that in many areas farmers paint the word COW on the side of their animals to identify them. Food comes in plastic containers highly tinged with artificial sweeteners, col- ors, and preservatives. The very conception of plants, growing seasons, rainfall, and drought is foreign to city people. Artificial criteria of comfort define everything that urban areas need and therefore dominate the producing rural areas as to commercial products.

The total result of this strange social order is that there has been total *15* disregard for the natural world. The earth is considered simply another commodity used to support additional suburbs and superhighways. Plant and animal life are subject to destruction at the whim of industrial development. Rivers are no more than wasted space separating areas of the large cities. In many areas they are open sewers carrying off the millions of tons of refuse discarded by the urban consumer.

The Indian lived with his land. He feared to destroy it by changing *16* its natural shape because he realized that it was more than a useful tool for exploitation. It sustained all life, and without other forms of life, man himself could not survive. People used to laugh at the Indian respect for smaller animals. Indians called them little brother. The Plains Indians appeased the buffalo after they had slain them for food. They well understood that without all life respecting itself and each other no society could indefinitely maintain itself. All of this understanding was ruthlessly wiped out to make room for the white man so that civilization could progress according to God's divine plan.

In recent years we have come to understand what progress is. It is *17* the total replacement of nature by an artificial technology. Progress is the absolute destruction of the real world in favor of a technology that creates a comfortable way of life for a few fortunately situated people. Within our lifetime the difference between the Indian use of land and the white use of land will become crystal clear. The Indian lived with his land. *The white destroyed his land. He destroyed the planet earth.*

Non-Indians have recently come to realize that the natural world *18* supports the artificial world of which they are so fond. Destruction of nature will result in total extinction of the human race. There is a limit beyond which man cannot go in reorganizing the land to suit his own needs. Barry Commoner, Director of the Center for the Biology of Natural Systems at Washington University in St. Louis, has been adamant about the destruction of nature. He told a Senate Subcommittee on Intergovernmental Affairs that the present system of technology would destroy the natural capital, the land, air, water, and other resources within the next fifty years. He further pointed out that the massive use of inorganic fertilizers may increase crop yields for a time but inevitably changes the physical character of the soil and destroys the self-purifying capability of the rivers. Thus the rivers in Illinois have been almost totally destroyed, while the nitrate level of rivers in the Midwest and California has risen above the safe level for use as drinking water.

A conference on pollution in Brussels outlined the same problem and *19* had a much earlier deadline in mind. Scientists there predicted the end of life on the planet within a minimum of thirty-five years. Elimination of the oxygen in the atmosphere was credited to jet engines, destruction

of oxygen-producing forests, and fertilizers and pesticides such as DDT
that destroy oxygen-producing microorganisms. Combining all of the
factors that are eliminating the atmosphere, the scientists could not see
any future for mankind. Realization of the situation is devastating.

Even where forest and plant life exist, the situation is critical. In *20*
southern California millions of trees are dying from polluted air. A recent
aerial survey by the Forest Service in November, 1969, showed 161,000
acres of conifers already dead or dying in southern California. The
situation has been critical since 1955, when residents of the area discovered trees turning yellow, but no one even bothered to inquire until 1962.
In the San Bernardino forest 46,000 acres of pine are already dead and
close to 120,000 acres more are nearly dead.

With strip cities being developed that will belch billions of tons of *21*
pollutants skyward every day the pace will rapidly increase so that optimistic projections of fifty to a hundred years more of life must be
telescoped to account for the very rapid disappearance of plant life by
geometrically increasing pollution. The struggle for use of land has polarized between conservationists, who understand that mankind will
shortly become extinct, and developers, who continue to press for immediate short-term financial gains by land exploitation.

The Bureau of Land Management, alleged guardian of public lands, *22*
has recently been involved in several controversial incidents with regard
to its policies. In one case Bureau officials reversed themselves and
acceded to Governor Jack Williams' request to transfer 40,000 acres of
federal range to the state "so the land could be leased to ranchers."
Stewart Udall, the great conservationist, upheld the original decision of
the Bureau of Land Management because he thought that federal lands
closer to cities could be obtained for development purposes. The overall
effect of government policies on land is to silently give the best lands to
state or private development without regard for the conservation issue
or the public welfare.

We can be relatively certain that the federal and state governments *23*
will not take an objective view of land use. Agencies established to
protect the public interest are subject to heavy political pressure to allow
land to slip away from their trusteeship for short-sighted gains by interest
groups. This much is certain: at the moment there is not the slightest
chance that mankind will survive the next half century. The American
public is totally unconcerned about the destruction of the land base. It
still believes in the infallibility of its science, technology, and government.
Sporadic and symbolic efforts will receive great publicity as the future
administrations carefully avoid the issue of land destruction. Indian
people will find their lands under continual attack and will probably lose
most of them because of the strongly held belief that progress is inevitable
and good.

With the justification of progress supporting the destruction of Indian *24*
tribes and lands, the question of results becomes important. Four
hundred years of lies, cheating, and genocide were necessary in order

for American society to destroy the whole planet. The United States government is thus left without even the flimsiest excuse for what has happened to Indian people, since the net result of its machinations is to destroy the atmosphere, thus suffocating mankind.

There is a grim humor in the situation. People used to make fun of 25 Indians because of their reverence for the different forms of life. In our lifetime we may very well revert to panicked superstition and piously worship the plankton of the sea, begging it to produce oxygen so that we can breathe. We may well initiate blood sacrifices to trees, searching for a way to make them productive again. In our lifetime, society as a whole will probably curse the day that white men landed on this continent, because it will all ultimately end in nothingness.

Meanwhile, American society could save itself by listening to tribal 26 people. While this would take a radical reorientation of concepts and values, it would be well worth the effort. The land-use philosophy of Indians is so utterly simple that it seems stupid to repeat it: man must live with other forms of life on the land and not destroy it. The implications of this philosophy are very far-reaching for the contemporary political and economic system. Reorientation would mean that public interest, indeed the interest in the survival of humanity as a species, must take precedence over special economic interests. In some areas the present policies would have to be completely overturned, causing great political dislocations in the power structure.

In addition to cleaning up streams and rivers and cutting down on air 27 pollution, a total change in land use should be instituted. Increase in oxygen-producing plants and organisms should be made first priority. In order to do this, vast land areas should be reforested and bays should be returned to their natural state. At present, millions of acres of land lie idle every year under the various farm programs. A great many more acres produce marginal farming communities. Erosion and destruction of topsoil by wind reduces effectiveness of conservation efforts. All of this must change drastically so that the life cycle will be restored.

Because this is a total social problem and the current solutions such 28 as sporadic national and state parks and soil banks are inadequate answers, a land-use plan for the entire nation should be instituted. The government should repurchase all marginal farmlands and a substantial number of farms in remote areas. This land should be planted with its original growth, whether forest or grassland sod. The entire upper midwest plains area of the Dakotas and Montana and upper Wyoming should become open-plains range with title in public hands. Deer, buffalo, and antelope should gradually replace cattle as herd animals. Outside of the larger established towns, smaller towns should be merely residences for people employed to redevelop the area as a wilderness.

Creeks and streams should be cleared of mining wastes and their banks 29 replanted with bushes and trees. The Missouri should be returned to its primitive condition, except where massive dams have already been built.

These should remain primarily as power-generating sites without the corresponding increase in industry surrounding them. Mining and tourism should be cut to a minimum and eventually prohibited. The present population could well be employed in a total conservation effort to produce an immense grasslands filled with wildlife.

The concept is not impossible. Already a rancher in Colorado has *30* tried the idea of grazing wild animals and beef cattle on his range with excellent results. Tom Lasater has a 26,000-acre ranch east of Colorado Springs, Colorado. He has pursued a no-shooting, no-poisoning, no-killing program for his land. There has already been a substantial increase in game animals, primarily mule deer and antelope, without any disturbance to his beef animals. Lasater first decided to allow wild animals to remain on his land when his foreman remarked, after the prairie dogs had been exterminated, that the grass always grew better when the prairie dogs had been allowed to live on the land.

The result of Lasater's allowing the land to return to its primitive state *31* has been the notable decrease of weeds. Lasater feels that the smaller animals, such as gophers, ground squirrels, badgers, and prairie dogs, that dig holes all provided a better means of aerating the ground and introducing more oxygen into it than modern farming methods of periodically turning the sod by plowing. All of the wildlife use on the land produced better grazing land and reduced the danger of overgrazing in a remarkable way. The fantastic thing about Lasater's ranch is that it returns almost double the income from beef cattle, because of the improved conditions of the soil and the better grasses, than would the average ranch of comparable acreage using the so-called modern techniques of ranching.

The genius of returning the land to its original animals is that the whole *32* program cuts down on labor costs, maintains fertility far better than modern techniques, increases environmental stability, and protects the soil from water and wind erosion. The net result is that the land supports much more life, wild and domestic, and is in better shape to continue to support life once the program is underway. Returning the major portion of the Great Plains to this type of program would be the first step in creating a livable continental environment. But introduction of this kind of program would mean dropping the political platitudes of the rancher and farmer as America's last rugged individualists, admitting that they are drinking high on the public trough through subsidies, and instituting a new kind of land use for the areas involved.

In the East and Far West, all land that is not immediately productive *33* of agricultural products for the urban areas should be returned to forest. This would mean purchasing substantial acreage in Wisconsin, Ohio, Michigan, New York, New Jersey, and Pennsylvania and planting new forests. With the exception of settled urban areas, the remainder of those states would probably become vast woods as they were originally. Wildlife would be brought in to live on the land since it is an irreplaceable part of the forest ecology. With the exception of highspeed lanes for transportation facilities, the major land areas of the East Coast would become forest and woodlands. The presence of great areas of vegetation would give carbon-dioxide-consuming plants a chance to contribute to the elimination of smog and air pollution.

The social structure of the East would have to change considerably. *34* In New York City the number of taxicabs is limited because unimpeded registration of cabs would produce a city so snarled with traffic that there would be no transportation. In the same manner anyone owning a farm of substantial acreage would have to be licensed by the state. The rest of the land would become wilderness with a wildlife cycle supporting the artificial universe of the cities by producing relatively clean air and water. The countless millions now on welfare in the eastern cities could be resettled outside the cities with conservation jobs and in retirement towns to ensure that the green belt of oxygen-producing plants would be stabilized.

In the coal mining states strip mining would be banned and a substan- *35* tial number of people could be employed in work to return the land to its natural state. Additional people could harvest the game animals and the food supply would partially depend upon meat from wild animals instead of DDT-bearing beef animals. Mines would be filled in and vegetation planted where only ugly gashes in the earth now exist. People disenchanted with urban society would be allowed to live in the forests with a minimum of interference. Any who might want to live in small communities and exist on hunting and fishing economies would be permitted to do so.

On the seacoasts, pollution should be cut to a minimum. Where there *36* are now gigantic ports for world shipping, these would be limited to a select few large enough to handle the trade. Others would have to become simply ports for pleasure boats and recreation. Some of the large commercial centers on both coasts would have to change their economy to take into account the absence of world trade and shipping. Beaches would have to be cleaned and set aside as wilderness areas or used by carefully selected people as living areas. Lobster beds, oyster beds, and areas that used to produce edible seafood would have to be returned to their original condition.

The pollution crisis presents the ultimate question on tribalism. If *37* mankind is to survive until the end of the century, a substantial portion of America's land area must be returned to its original state of forest and grasslands. This is fundamentally because these plants produce oxygen and support the life cycle at the top of which is man. Without air to breathe it is ridiculous to speak of progress, culture, civilization, or technology. Machines may be able to live in the present environment, but it is becoming certain that people cannot.

By returning the land to its original state, society will have to acknowl- *38* edge that it can no longer support two hundred million people at an artificial level of existence in an artificial universe of flashing lights and instantaneous communications. To survive, white society must return the land to the Indians in the sense that it restores the land to the condition it was in before the white man came. And then to support the population we now have on the land that will be available, a great number of people will have to return to the life of the hunter, living in the forests and hunting animals for food.

Whenever I broach this subject to whites, they cringe in horror at the   *39* mere prospect of such a development. They always seem to ask how anyone could consider returning to such a *savage and unhappy state,* as the government reports always describe Indian life. Yet there is a real question as to which kind of life is really more savage. Does the fact that one lives in a small community hunting and fishing for food really indicate that one has no sensitive feelings for humanity? Exactly how is this kind of life primitive when affluent white hunters pay thousands of dollars every fall merely for the chance to roam the wilderness shooting at one another in the hopes of also bringing down a deer?

In 1967 I served on the Board of Inquiry for Hunger and Malnutrition   *40* in the United States. We discovered that a substantial number of Americans of all colors and backgrounds went to bed hungry every night. Many were living on less than starvation diets and were so weakened that the slightest sickness would carry them off. The black children in the Mississippi delta lands were eating red clay every other day to fill their stomachs to prevent hunger pains. Yet the Agricultural Department had millions of tons of food in giant storehouses that went undistributed every year. Is this type of society more savage than living simply as hunters and fishermen? Is it worth being civilized to have millions of people languishing every year for lack of food while the warehouses are filled with food that cannot be distributed?

Last Christmas in California a federal judge, disgusted at the snarls of   *41* red tape that prevented distribution of food to hungry people, ordered a warehouse opened and the food distributed in spite of the pleas of bureaucrats that it was against regulations. In the field of hunger alone the government had better act before hungry people take the law into their own hands.

For years Indian people have sat and listened to speeches by non-   *42* Indians that gave glowing accounts of how good the country is now that it is developed. We have listened to people piously tell us that we must drop everything Indian as it is impossible for Indians to maintain their life style in a modern civilized world. We have watched as land was stolen so that giant dams and factories could be built. Every time we have objected to the use of land as a commodity, we have been told that progress is necessary to the American way of life.

Now the laugh is ours. After four centuries of gleeful rape, the white   *43* man stands a mere generation away from extinguishing life on this planet. Granted that Indians will also be destroyed—it is not because we did not realize what was happening. It is not because we did not fight back. And it is not because we refused to speak. We have carried our responsibilities well. If people do not choose to listen and instead overwhelm us, then they must bear the ultimate responsibility.

What is the ultimate irony is that the white man must drop his dollar- 44 chasing civilization and return to a simple, tribal, game-hunting, berry-picking life if he is to survive. He must quickly adopt not just the contemporary Indian world view but the ancient Indian world view to survive. He must give up the concept of the earth as a divisible land area that he can market. The lands of the United States must be returned to public ownership and turned into wilderness if man is to live. It will soon be apparent that one man cannot fence off certain areas and do with the land what he will. Such activity will be considered too dangerous to society. Small animals and plants will soon have an equal and perhaps a greater value for human life than humans themselves.

Such a program is, of course, impossible under the American economic 45 and political system at the present time. It would interfere with vested economic interests whose motto has always been "the public be damned." Government policy will continue to advocate cultural oppression against Indian tribes, thinking that the white way of life is best. This past year, five powerful government agencies fought the tiny Lummi tribe of western Washington to prevent it from developing a bay that the tribe owned as a sealife sanctuary. The agenices wanted to build massive projects for commercial use on the bay, the Indians wanted it developed as a conservation area restoring its original food-producing species such as fish, clams, and oysters. Fortunately, the tribe won the fight, much to the chagrin of the Army Corps of Engineers, which makes a specialty of destroying Indian lands.

The white man's conception of nature can be characterized as obscene, 46 but that does not even begin to describe it. It is totally artificial and the very existence of the Astrodome with its artificial grass symbolizes better than words the world visualized by the non-Indian. In any world there is an aspect of violence that cannot be avoided; Nature is arbitrary and men must adjust to her whims. The white man has tried to make Nature adjust to his whims by creating the artificial world of the city. But even here he has failed. Politicians now speak reverently of corridors of safety in the urban areas. They are main lines of transportation where your chances of being robbed or mugged are greatly reduced. Everywhere else there is indiscriminate violence. Urban man has produced even an artificial jungle, where only the fittest or luckiest survive.

With the rising crime rate, even these corridors of safety will disap- 47 pear. People will only be able to go about in the urban areas in gangs, tribes if you will. Yet the whole situation will be artificial from start to finish. The ultimate conclusion of American society will be that even with respect to personal safety it was much safer and more humane when

Indians controlled the whole continent. The only answer will be to adopt Indian ways to survive. For the white man even to exist, he must adopt a total Indian way of life. That is really what he had to do when he came to this land. It is what he will have to do before he leaves it once again.

Study Questions

1. What context does Vine Deloria, Jr., create for "The Artificial Universe" in the opening paragraph? What response would readers have to this context? Why would Deloria wish for such a response?
2. In paragraphs 3–9, Deloria uses a temporal organization to structure his discussion of what has happened to Indian lands. Underline the words and phrases that signal this method. Why would he choose a temporal organization for this presentation?
3. Scattered throughout the essay are phrases that begin "the result of," "because this is," and "such a program is, of course." Such phrases signal conceptual organization. Identify a few of these paragraphs. Why are they placed where they are? What do they contribute to the readers' understanding of Deloria's meaning?
4. In paragraphs 24–28, Deloria uses an additive organization as he describes a series of incidents and reports on what has happened to the land as a result of industrialization. Why is this method appropriate for the point he wishes to make here?
5. Identify the paragraph in which Deloria begins his conclusion. What point does he emphasize? How does that emphasis explain the occasional use of conceptual organization in the body of the essay?

Suggestion for Drafting

In paragraph 17, Deloria writes: "In recent years we have come to understand what progress is. It is the total replacement of nature with artificial technology." In paragraphs 20–25, he presents a series of incidents that are meant to confirm his claim. Study these paragraphs, and imagine that the list of incidents is a prewriting list. Consider the methods of organization you might use to develop the list into a draft of the body of an essay in which you either agree or disagree with Deloria's statement. Write a first draft of that body.

Primitive Blues and Primitive Jazz

Imamu Amiri Baraka (LeRoi Jones)

A slave cannot be a man. A man does not, or *1* is not supposed to, work all of his life without recourse to the other areas of human existence. The emotional limitations that slavery must enforce are monstrous: the weight of his bondage makes impossible for the slave a great many alternatives into which the shabbiest of free men can project himself. There is not even a separate identity the ego can claim. "What are you going to be when you grow up?" "A slave."

The work song is a limited social possibility. The shouts and hollers *2* were strident laments, more than anything. They were also chronicles, but of such a mean kind of existence that they could not assume the universality any lasting musical form must have. The work songs and later blues forms differ very profoundly not only in their form but in their lyrics and *intent*.

Oh, Lawd, I'm tired, uuh
Oh, Lawd, I'm tired, uuh
Oh, Lawd, I'm tired, uuh
Oh, Lawd, I'm tired, a dis mess.

(*repeated*)

Primitive blues-singing actually came into being because of the Civil *3* War, in one sense. The emancipation of the slaves proposed for them a normal human existence, a humanity impossible under slavery. Of course, even after slavery the average Negro's life in America was, using the more ebullient standards of the average American white man, a shabby, barren existence: But still this was the black man's first experience of time when he could be alone. The leisure that could be extracted from even the most desolate sharecropper's shack in Mississippi was a novelty, and it served as an important catalyst for the next form blues took.

Many Negroes who were sharecroppers, or who managed to purchase *4* one of the tiny farms that dotted the less fertile lands of the South, worked in their fields alone or with their families. The old shouts and hollers were still their accompaniment for the arduous work of clearing land, planting, or harvesting crops. But there was a solitude to this work that had never been present in the old slave times. The huge plantation fields had many slaves, and they sang together. On the smaller farms with fewer slaves where the older African forms died out quicker, the eight- and sixteen-bar "ballits," imitations of the songs of the white masters, were heard along with the shouts. Of course, there must have been lyrics to some of the songs that the slave could not wisely sing in front of his master. But the small farms and sharecroppers' plots produced not only what I think must have been a less self-conscious work song but a form of song or shout that did not necessarily have to be concerned with, or inspired by, *labor*. Each man had his own voice and his own way of shouting—his own life to sing about. The tenders of those thousands of small farms became almost identified by their individual shouts. "That's George Jones, down in Hartsville, shoutin' like that."

Along with this leisure there was also that personal freedom to conduct 5 or ruin one's life as one saw fit. In the 1870's there were thousands of black migrant workers moving all through the South. There were also men who just moved around from place to place, not really migratory laborers, just footloose wanderers. There could come now to these ex-slaves a much fuller idea of what exactly America was. A slave on a Georgia plantation, unless he was sold or escaped, usually was born, grew to manhood, and died right in Georgia. To him, the whole of America would be Georgia, and it would have to conform strictly to what he had experienced. St. Louis, Houston, Shreveport, New Orleans, simply did not exist (and certainly not New York). But now for many Negroes there was a life of movement from farm to farm, or town to town. The limited social and emotional alternatives of the work song could no longer contain the growing experience of this country that Negroes began to respond to. Also, the entrance of Negroes into the more complicated social situation of self-reliance proposed multitudes of social and cultural problems that they never had to deal with as slaves. The music of the Negro began to reflect these social and cultural complexities and change.

Very early blues did not have the "classic" twelve-bar, three-line, AAB 6 structure. For a while, as I mentioned before, blues-type songs utilized the structure of the early English ballad, and sometimes these songs were eight, ten, or sixteen bars. The shout as much as the African call-and-response singing dictated the form blues took. Blues issued directly out of the shout and, of course, the spiritual. The three-line structure of blues was a feature of the shout. The first two lines of the song were repeated, it would seem, while the singer was waiting for the next line to come. Or, as was characteristic of the hollers and shouts, the single line could be repeated again and again, either because the singer especially liked it, or because he could not think of another line. The repeated phrase also carries into instrumental jazz as the *riff*.

Another reason for the changes in musical form was the change of 7
speech patterns among a great many Negroes. By now the language of
America was mastered for casual use by most Negroes. While the work
song or shout had only a few English words, or was composed of Afri-
canized English words or some patois-like language that seemed more a
separate language than an attempt at mastering English, early blues had
already moved toward pure American lyrics (with the intent that the song
be understood by other Americans). The endlessly repeated line of the
shout or holler might also have been due to the relative paucity of
American words the average field Negro possessed, the rhyme line being
much more difficult to supply because of the actual limitation singing in
American imposed. The lines came more easily as the language was
mastered more completely. Blues was a kind of singing that utilized a
language that was almost strictly American. It was not until the ex-
slaves had mastered this language in whatever appropriation of it they
made that blues began to be more evident than shouts and hollers.

The end of the almost exclusive hold of the Christian Church on the 8
black man's leisure also resulted in a great many changes of emphasis in
his music. The blues is formed out of the same social and musical fabric
that the spiritual issued from, but with blues the social emphasis becomes
more personal, the "Jordan" of the song much more intensely a *human*
accomplishment. The end of slavery could be regarded as a Jordan, and
not a metaphysical one either, although the analogy of the deliverance of
the Jews and the Emancipation must have been much too cogent a point
for proselytizing to be lost on the local black minister. There was a
definite change of *direction* in the primitive blues. The metaphysical
Jordan of life after death was beginning to be replaced by the more
pragmatic Jordan of the American master: the Jordan of what the ex-
slave could see vaguely as self-determination. Not that that idea or
emotion hadn't been with the very first Africans who had been brought
here; the difference was that the American Negro wanted some degree
of self-determination where he was living. The desperation to return to
Africa had begun to be replaced by another even more hopeless one.
The Negro began to feel a desire to be more in this country, America,
than chattel. "The sun's gonna shine in my back door someday!"

The leisure and movement allowed to Negroes after the Civil War 9
helped to standardize the new blues form as well as spread the best
verses that were made up. Although there were regional differences in
the way blues began to be sung, there were also certain recurring, soon
"classical," blues verses and techniques that turned up in a great many
places simply because a man had been there from Georgia or Louisiana
or South Carolina and shown the locals what his town or region produced.

But the thousands of black blues shouters and ballit singers who 10
wandered throughout the South around the turn of the century moved
from place to place not only because Negroes were allowed to travel

after the Civil War, but because for a great many Negroes, emancipation meant a constant desperate search for employment (although there must also have been those people who, having been released from their bondage, set out at once to see what this country was really about). Not only the migratory workers who followed the crop harvests but the young men who wanted any kind of work had to tramp all over the South in search of it. It is also a strange note that once the Negroes were free, it was always the men who had the harder time finding work. Women could always find work as domestics wherever they were. But the black man who had done agricultural labor, as most Negroes had, found it difficult to find work because the impoverished whites of the South suddenly had to pay wages to their workers. The Negro had to have wages to live: for the first time he needed money and had to enter into the fierce struggle for economic security like any other poor man in this country. Again, even the economic status of the Negro after his freedom proposed new changes for his music. "I never had to have no money befo'/And now they want it everywhere I go." The content of blues verse had become much changed from the strictly extemporized lyrics of the shouts and hollers.

It seems possible to me that some kind of graph could be set up using *11* samplings of Negro music proper to whatever moment of the Negro's social history was selected, and that in each grouping of songs a certain frequency of reference could pretty well determine his social, economic, and psychological states at that particular period. From the neo-African slave chants through the primitive and classical blues to the scat-singing of the beboppers: all would show definite insistences of reference that would isolate each group from the others as a social entity. No slave song need speak about the slave's lack of money; no early Afro-American slave song would make reference to the Christian Church; almost no classical blues song would, or could, make direct or *positive* mention of Africa. Each phase of the Negro's music issued directly from the dictates of his social and psychological environment. Hence the black man who began after slavery to eliminate as much of the Negro culture from his life as possible became by this very act a certain kind of *Negro*. And if this certain kind of Negro still endeavored to make music, albeit with the strict provision that this music not be a Negro music, he could still not escape the final "insult" of this music being evaluated socially, psychologically, and musically as a kind of *Negro* music. The movement of the Negro into a position where he would be able to escape even this separation from the white mainstream of America is a central theme of this book.

Even with the relative formalization of secular Negro music, blues *12* was still an extremely personal music. There were the songs extolling the merits and adventures of heroes or heroic archetypes, John Henry, Stagger Lee, Dupree, etc., but even as the blues began to expand its references it still remained a kind of singing that told about the exploits of the singer. Heroic archetypes or cowardly archetypes were used to point up some part of the singer's life.

In come a nigger named Billy Go-helf
Coon was so mean was skeered of hisself;
Loaded wid razors an' guns, so they say,
Cause he killed a coon most every day.

And this intensely personal nature of blues-singing is also the result of what can be called the Negro's "American experience." African songs dealt, as did the songs of a great many of the preliterate or classical civilizations, with the exploits of the social unit, usually the tribe. There were songs about the gods, their works and lives, about nature and the elements, about the nature of a man's life on the earth and what he could expect after he died, but the insistence of blues verse on the life of the individual and his individual trials and successes on the earth is a manifestation of the whole Western concept of man's life, and it is a development that could only be found in an American black man's music. From the American black leader's acceptance of Adam Smith "laissez faire" social inferences to some less fortunate black man's relegation to a lonely patch of useless earth in South Carolina, the weight of Western tradition, or to make it more specific and local, the weight of just what social circumstance and accident came together to produce the America that the Negro was part of, had to make itself part of his life as well. The whole concept of the *solo,* of a man singing or playing by himself, was relatively unknown in West African music.

But if the blues was a music that developed because of the Negro's *13* adaptation to, and adoption of, America, it was also a music that developed because of the Negro's peculiar position in this country. Early blues, as it came to differ from the shout and the Afro-Christian religious music, was also perhaps the most impressive expression of the Negro's individuality within the superstructure of American society. Even though its birth and growth seems connected finally to the general movement of the mass of black Americans into the central culture of the country, blues still went back for its impetus and emotional meaning to the individual, to his completely personal life and death. Because of this, blues could remain for a long time a very fresh and singular form of expression. Though certain techniques and verses came to be standardized among blues singers, the singing itself remained as arbitrary and personal as the shout. Each man sang a different blues: the Peatie Wheatstraw blues, the Blind Lemon blues, the Blind Willie Johnson blues, etc. The music remained that personal because it began with the performers themselves, and not with formalized notions of how it was to be performed. Early blues developed as a music to be sung for *pleasure,* a casual music, and that was its strength and its weakness.

I don't want you to be no slave,
I don't want you to work all day,
I don't want you to be true,
I just want to make love to you.

Since most Negroes before and after slavery were agricultural labor-   *14* ers, the corn songs and arwhoolies, the shouts and hollers, issued from one kind of work. Some of the work songs, for instance, use as their measure the grunt of a man pushing a heavy weight or the blow of a hammer against a stone to provide the metrical precision and rhythmical impetus behind the singer. ("Take this hammer, uh,/Take it to the captain, uh,/Take it to the captain, uh,/Tell him I'm gone.") Contemporary work songs, for example, songs recorded by Negro convicts working in the South—laying railroad ties, felling trees, breaking rocks, take their impetus from the work being done, and the form of the singing itself is dictated by the work. These workers for the most part do not sing blues. The labor is central to the song: not only is the recurring grunt or moan of these work songs some kind of metrical and rhythmical insistence, it is the very catalyst for the song. On one recent record, the Louisiana Folklore Society's, *Prison Worksongs* recorded in Angola, Louisiana, at the Louisiana State Penitentiary there, one song listed as *Take This Hammer* begins as that song, but lasts as that for only about three "bars" (three strokes of the hammer) and then wanders irresolutely into *Alberta, Berta,* several blues verses, and a few lines from a spiritual. The point is that the primitive blues was at once a more formal music since the three-line, twelve-bar song became rapidly standardized, and was also a more liberated music since there was literally *more* to sing about. In one's leisure one can begin to formalize a method of singing as well as find new things to sing about. (It is an interesting thought that perhaps all the music that Negroes in America have made might have been quite different if the work that they were brought here to do had been different. Suppose Negroes had been brought to this country to make vases or play basketball. How might the blues have developed then from the impetus of work songs geared to those occupations?)

Work songs and shouts were, of course, almost always *a capella*. It   *15* would have been extremely difficult for a man to pick cotton or shuck corn and play an instrument at the same time. For this reason pre-blues secular singing did not have the discipline or strict formality that a kind of singing employing instruments must have. But it is obvious from the very earliest form of the blues that instrumental accompaniment was beginning to be taken into consideration. The twelve-bar blues—the more or less final form of blues—is constructed so that each verse is of three lines, each line about four bars long. The words of the song usually occupy about one-half of each line, leaving a space of two bars for either a sung answer or an instrumental response.

It may seem strange that the formal blues should evolve *after* slavery, 16 after so many years of bondage and exposure by the slaves to the larger Western cultural unit, into a form that is patently non-Western; the three-line verse form of the blues springs from no readily apparent Western source. But the use of instruments on a large scale was also something that happened after the Emancipation; the very possession of instruments, except those few made from African models, was rare in the early days of slavery. The stereotyped pictures that many of the apologists for the Southern way of life used as flyleaves for their numerous novels after the Civil War, depicting a happy-go-lucky black existentialist strumming merrily on his banjo while sitting on a bale of cotton, were, I'm sure, more romantic fiction than fact. The slave would hardly have had the time to sit on his master's bale of cotton during the work day, and the only instruments that were in common usage among the slaves were drums, rattles, tambourines, scrapers (the jawbone of a horse over which a piece of wood was scraped), and the like; even such an African instrument as the banjo was very scarce. The guitar was not commonly played by Negroes until much after the Civil War. An instrument like the harmonica grew in popularity among a great many Negroes simply because it took up almost no space and was so easy to carry around. But even the harmonica did not come into common use until after slavery, and certainly the possession and mastery of European instruments did not occur until much later.

When primitive or country blues did begin to be influenced by instru- 17 ments, it was the guitar that had the most effect on the singers. And when the great masses of Negroes were just beginning to learn the instrument, the relatively simple chords of the country blues were probably what they learned. Conceivably, this also brought about another change: blues, a vocal music, was made to conform to an instrument's range. But, of course, the blues widened the range of the instrument, too. Blues guitar was not the same as classical or "legitimate" guitar: the strings had to make vocal sounds, to imitate the human voice and its eerie cacophonies. Perhaps the reason why the guitar was at once so popular was not only because it was much like the African instrument, the banjo (or *banjor*), but because it was an instrument that still permitted the performer to *sing*.

When the Negro finally did take up the brass instruments for strictly 18 instrumental blues or jazz, the players still persisted in singing in the "breaks." This could be done easily in the blues tradition with the call-and-response form of blues. Even much later in the jazz tradition, not only were instruments made to sound like the human voice but a great many of the predominantly instrumental songs were still partially sung. The first great soloist of jazz, Louis Armstrong, was a formidable blues singer, as was the great jazz pianist Jelly Roll Morton. Both men sang blues almost as beautifully as they played their instruments.

The primitive blues was still very much a vocal music; the singers *19* relied on the unpredictability and mobility of the human voice for their imaginative catalysts. But the growing use of European instruments such as brass and reeds almost precluded song, except as accompaniment or as an interlude. When Negroes began to master more and more "European" instruments and began to think musically in terms of their timbres, as opposed to, or in conjunction with, the voice, blues began to change, and the era of jazz was at hand.

"Jazz began in New Orleans and worked its way up the river to *20* Chicago," is the announcement most investigators of mainstream popular culture are apt to make when dealing with the vague subject of jazz and its origins. And while that is certainly a rational explanation, charmingly simple, etc., it is more than likely untrue. Jazz, or purely instrumental blues, could no more have begun in one area of the country than could blues. The mass migrations of Negroes throughout the South and the general liberating effect of the Emancipation make it extremely difficult to say just exactly where and when jazz, or purely instrumental blues (with European instruments), originated. It *is* easy to point out that jazz is a music that could not have existed without blues and its various antecedents. However, jazz should not be thought of as a *successor* to blues, but as a very original music that developed out of, and was concomitant with, blues and moved off into its own path of development. One interesting point is that although jazz developed out of a kind of blues, blues in its later popular connotation came to mean *a way of playing jazz,* and by the swing era the widespread popularity of the blues singer had already been replaced by the jazz player's. By then, blues was for a great many people no longer a separate music.

Even though New Orleans cannot be thought of with any historical *21* veracity as "the birthplace of jazz," there has been so much investigation of the jazz and earlier music characteristic there in the first part of the twentieth century, that from New Orleans conclusions may be drawn concerning the social and cultural phenomena that led to the creation of jazz. Also, the various effects of the development of this music upon Negroes in the area can be considered and certain essential analogies made.

I have mentioned Congo Square in New Orleans as a place where *22* African Negroes in the earlier years of slavery met to play what was certainly an African music. Marshall Stearns quotes an architect, Benjamin Latrobe, who visited Congo Square in 1819:

"The music consisted of two drums and a stringed instrument. An *23*
old man sat astride of a cylindrical drum about a foot in diameter, and
beat it with incredible quickness with the edge of his hand and fingers.
The other drum was an open staved thing held between the knees and
beaten in the same manner. . . . The most curious instrument, however,
was a stringed instrument which no doubt was imported from Africa.
On the top of the finger board was the rude figure of a man in a sitting
posture, and two pegs behind him to which the strings were fastened.
The body was a calabash . . . One, which from the color of the wood
seemed new, consisted of a block cut into something of the form of a
cricket bat with a long and deep mortice down the center . . . being
beaten lustily on the side by a short stick. In the same orchestra was a
square drum, looking like a stool . . . also a calabash with a round hole
in it, the hole studded with brass nails, which was beaten by a woman
with two short sticks."*

This kind of gathering in Congo Square was usually the only chance *24*
Negroes had to sing and play at length. And, of course, even this was
supervised by the local authorities: the slaves were brought to the square
and brought back by their masters. Still, the Congo Square sessions
were said to have included many African songs that were supposedly
banned by the whites for being part of the vodun or voodoo rites. The
slaves also danced French quadrilles and sang patois ditties in addition
to the more African chants that they shouted above the "great drums."

Nowhere else in the United States is the French influence so apparent *25*
as in New Orleans; it was this predominantly French culture that set the
tone for the Europeanization of African slaves in the area. The mulat-
toes, or light-skinned Negroes, in New Orleans, who were the result
usually of some less than legal union between the French masters and
black slave women, even adopted the name *Creole* to distinguish themselves from the other Negroes, although this term originally meant any
white settler of French or Spanish blood. The Creoles, in much the same
manner as the house Negroes on plantations in other areas, adopted as
much of the French culture as they could and turned their backs on the
"darker" culture of their half-brothers. It is safe to assume, for instance,
that there were no black Creoles dancing in Congo Square.

The black man must have been impressed not only by the words and *26*
dances of the quadrilles and minuets he learned from the French settlers
of New Orleans, but by the instruments the white Creoles employed to
play them. So New Orleans Negroes became interested in the tubas,
clarinets, trombones, and trumpets of the white marching bands, which
were also popular in New Orleans as well as in many other Southern
cities. (In the time of Napoleon, the popularity of the military band soon
spread from France to all the settlements in the New World influenced

* *The Story of Jazz* (New York, Oxford University Press, 1956), p. 43.

by French culture.) The "exotic" rhythms of the quadrilles (2/4 and 6/8) and the military marching bands (4/4) also made a great impression on the slaves, and they tried to incorporate these meters into their own music. The black Creoles, however, tried to adopt these elements of French culture completely, learning the quadrilles by rote. Still slavery and the circumstance of the Negroes' bondage played a big role in this kind of assimilation as well. Many of the Creoles were freedmen by virtue of the accident of their birth, or at least were house servants long before the Emancipation. They had direct access to European music and instruments long before the rest of the Negroes in the area.

The marching bands that were started by Negroes in imitation of the Napoleonic military marching bands of the white Creoles also fell into two distinct categories. There were the comparatively finely trained bands of the Creoles and the untutored, raw bands of the Uptown, darker New Orleans Negroes (which did not begin until well after slavery was abolished). These bands were used for all kinds of affairs; in addition to the famous funeral processions, they played for picnics, dances, boating trips, and the like. One reason for the formation of these bands was the organization of a great number of clubs and secret societies and fraternities in the Negro communities (white and black) after the Emancipation. These societies and fraternities were an important part of the Negro's life, and drained a lot of the black community away from the Christian Church, which had been the sole place the slaves could spend their leisure time. But it was not unusual for a Negro to belong to the Christian Church (in New Orleans, after the Black Codes of 1724, Negroes were only allowed to become Catholics) and to also belong to a number of secret societies. These societies still thrive today all over the country in most Negro communities, though for the most part their actual "secrecy" is the secrecy of any fraternal organization. The Masons and the Elks have claimed most urban and Northern Negroes, and the old vodun-tinged secret orders, sometimes banned by whites, have for the most part (except in the rural areas) disappeared completely.

One example of the way Negroes used European rhythms in conjunction with their own West African rhythms was the funeral processions. The march to the cemetery was played in slow, dirgelike 4/4 cadence. It was usually a spiritual that was played, but made into a kind of raw and bluesy Napoleonic military march. The band was followed by the mourners—relatives, members of the deceased's fraternal order or secret society, and well-wishers. (All night before the burial, or on as many nights as there were that intervened between the death and the burial, the mourners came into the house of the deceased to weep and wail and kiss the body. But these "wakes" or "mourning times" usually turned into house parties.) After the burial, the band, once removed some good distance from the cemetery, usually broke into the uptempo part of the march at some approximation of the 2/4 quadrille time. *Didn't He Ram-*

ble and *When the Saints Go Marchin' In* were two of the most frequently played tunes—both transmuted religious songs. Even in this kind of march music the influence of the blues was very heavy, at least for the Uptown or "darker" brass bands—the Downtown Creole bands would have nothing to do with the "raw and raucous playing of those dark folks." The form of the Creole funerals must have differed also if the Downtown mourners were emulating their white Creole models. Certainly a great many self-respecting Creoles must have frowned on the antics the darker Negroes performed when burying a member of their community. The long period of jovial mourning, complete with banquets and dancing, was certainly outside the pale of either Catholic or Protestant religious practice. Herskovits cites these burial customs as originating in West Africa, especially among the large Dahomey tribes. (An interesting note about the New Orleans funeral is that recently, in 1955, *Ebony,* the vehicle of American middle-class Negro aspirations, announced that when PaPa Celestin, the great New Orleans trumpet player, died, no jazz was played—"out of respect for PaPa.")

By the time the marching and brass bands were in vogue in New *29* Orleans and some other parts of the South, Negroes had already begun to master a great many other European instruments besides the guitar and the harmonica. The trumpets, trombones, and tubas of the brass bands were played with a varying amount of skill, though when a man has learned enough about an instrument to play the music he wants to play, "skill" becomes an arbitrary consideration. The black brass bands of New Orleans around the turn of the century had certainly mastered the European brass instruments as well as the Downtown Creole bands, but by now they were simply "doing it the way they felt it." By the time the first non-marching, instrumental, blues-oriented groups started to appear in numbers, *i.e.,* the "jass" or "dirty" bands, the instrumentation was a pastiche of the brass bands and the lighter quadrille groups. In 1897, Buddy Bolden's group consisted of cornet, trombone, clarinet (the first reed instrument Negroes began to play with any frequency), violin, guitar, string bass (already an innovation over the tuba, the first "time-keeping" instrument in these bands), and drums.

The repressive "white supremacy" measures that were put into effect *30* after the Civil War had a great deal of effect on the music of New Orleans. By 1894, there was a legislative act enforcing segregation which hit the black Creoles hardest. It also, in the long run, helped redirect their social and musical energies. Up until the time of the infamous discriminative codes, the Creoles enjoyed an autonomy of social and economic status; to a certain extent they had the same economic and social advantages as the whites. Many of them had been educated in France and also sent their children to France to be educated, where many remained. Quite a few Creole families were among the richest families in New Orleans, and still others were well-known artisans and craftsmen. In a great many cases Creoles worked side by side with whites. They also enjoyed the cultural side of eighteenth- and nineteenth-century New Orleans life: Creoles had their own boxes at the opera, and they participated in all the Downtown or white parades with their own highly trained military-style marching bands. But with the segregation acts of the late nineteenth century, Creoles began to lose the jobs where they had been working with whites, and they were no longer permitted to play Downtown, neither in the homes of the rich whites nor in the military parades.

It was about this time that the darker, blues-oriented musicians from *31* Uptown New Orleans were beginning to play their "dirty" instrumental music in saloons and dance halls, at parties, picnics, and some of the places where the older brass marching bands used to hold forth. It was still a "marchy" kind of music, but the strict 4/4 march tempo had given way to the ragged 2/4 tempo, and the timbres and tones that people like Bolden began to use were radically removed from the pure sonorities of European-style marching bands. Theirs was a much more vocal kind of playing compared to the way brass horns had been used before. Again, this seems part of a definable cycle in the response of the Negro to the cultural and social stimuli of this country. The blues moved through much the same cycle, developing out of what seemed like imitations of European music into a form (and content) that was relatively autonomous. Primitive blues is much more a Negro music than a great deal of the music it grew out of.

Miss Kemble in her diary reports hearing Negroes singing a song *32* "while they labored" on river boats that was very much like *Coming Through the Rye*. It is quite probable that it was *Coming Through the Rye*. Most slaves in the early part of the nineteenth century could not have sung the words to the song, but could change them into: "Jenny shake her toe at me,/Jenny gone away;/Jenny shake her toe at me,/Jenny gone away./Hurrah! Miss Susy, oh!/Jenny gone away;/Hurrah! Miss Susy, oh!/Jenny gone away." Also relevant are the best of Miss Kemble's observations about Negro music—presumably their work songs, since she would hardly have observed them at any other time:

"Except the extemporaneous chants in our honor . . . I have never *33* heard the Negroes . . . sing any words that could be said to have any sense. To one, an extremely pretty, plaintive, and original air, there was but one line, which was repeated with a sort of wailing chorus—

Oh! my massa told me, there's no grass in Georgia.

Upon inquiring the meaning of which, I was told it was supposed to be the lamentation of a slave from one of the more northerly states, Virginia or Carolina, where the labor of hoeing the weeds, or grass as they call it, is not nearly so severe as here, in the rice and cotton lands of Georgia.

Another very pretty and pathetic tune began with words that seemed to promise something sentimental—

Fare you well, and good-by, oh, oh!
I'm goin' away to leave you, oh! oh!

but immediately went off into nonsense verses about gentlemen in the parlor drinking wine and cordial, and ladies in the drawing room drinking tea and coffee, etc. I have heard that many of the masters and overseers on these plantations prohibit melancholy tunes or words, and encourage nothing but cheerful music and senseless words, deprecating the effect of sadder strains upon the slaves, whose peculiar musical sensibility might be expected to make them especially excitable by any songs of a plaintive character, and having any reference to their peculiar hardships."*

And so we have perhaps another reason why the Negro's secular 34 music matured only after the end of slavery. The blues, as it came into its own strict form, was the most plaintive and melancholy music imaginable. And the content, the meaning, Miss Kemble searched for in vain in the work songs, was certainly quite evident in the later music.

Although the instrumental music moved toward an autonomous form 35 only after the Emancipation, in only a few years after the beginning of the twentieth century, there was such a thing as a jazz band. And in a few more years this kind of band was throwing off most of its musical ties with the brass marching bands or the string groups of the white Creoles.

When the Creoles "of color" began to lose their Downtown jobs or 36 found that they were no longer permitted to play for white affairs, some of them began to make the trip Uptown to sit in with their darker half-brothers. By this time, near the turn of the century, there was a marked difference in the playing and music of the Uptown and Downtown Negroes. The Creoles had received formal musical training, sometimes under the aegis of white French teachers. They had mastered the European instrumental techniques, and the music they played was European. The Uptown Negroes, who had usually learned their instruments by ear and never received formal and technical training, developed an instrumental technique and music of their own, a music that relied heavily on the non-European vocal tradition of blues. Many Creoles who had turned their backs on this "darker" tradition now began to try to learn it again.

An important idea to consider here is that jazz as it developed was 37 predominantly a blues-based music. The blues timbre and spirit had come to jazz virtually unchanged, even though the early Negro musicians using European instruments had to learn to play them with the strict

* *Op. cit.,* pp. 163–64.

European march music as a model. The "classical" timbre of the trumpet, the timbre that Creoles imitated, was not the timbre that came into
jazz. The purity of tone that the European trumpet player desired was
put aside by the Negro trumpeter for the more humanly expressive sound
of the voice. The brass sound came to the blues, but it was a brass
sound hardly related to its European models. The rough, raw sound the
black man forced out of these European instruments was a sound he had
cultivated in this country for two hundred years. It was an American
sound, something indigenous to a certain kind of cultural existence in
this country.

Creoles like violinist Paul Domingues, when he said, "See, us Down- *38*
town people, we didn't think so much of this rough Uptown jazz until
we couldn't make a living otherwise. . . . I don't know how they do it.
But goddam, they'll do it. Can't tell you what's there on the paper, but
just play the hell out of it,"* were expressing perhaps the basic conflict
to arise regarding the way the ex-slave was to make his way in America.
Adaptation or assimilation? It was not much of a problem for most
Negroes in the nineteenth century, although, to be sure, there must have
been quite a few who had already disappeared (culturally) into the white
world. The Creoles, for instance, had already made that move, but New
Orleans was a special situation. Adaptation was the Negro's way earlier;
he had little choice. He had not sufficient knowledge of, or experience
in, the dominant culture to become completely assimilated within it. He
went along the path of least resistance, which was to fashion something
out of that culture for himself, girded by the strength of the still evident
African culture. The Uptown musicians made jazz in this manner. The
Creoles resisted "Negro" music because they thought they had found a
place within white society which would preclude their being Negroes.
But they were unsuccessful in their attempt to "disappear" because the
whites themselves reminded them that they were still, for all their assimilation, "coons." And this seems to me an extremely important idea
since it is just this bitter insistence that has kept what can be called
Negro culture a brilliant amalgam of diverse influences.

There was always a border beyond which the Negro could not go, *39*
whether musically or socially. There was always a possible limitation to
any dilution or excession of cultural or spiritual references. The Negro
could not ever become white and that was his strength; at some point,
always, he could not participate in the dominant tenor of the white man's
culture. It was at this juncture that he had to make use of other resources, whether African, subcultural, or hermetic. And it was this
boundary, this no man's land, that provided the logic and beauty of his
music.

* Alan Lomax, *Mr. Jelly Roll* (New York, Duell, Sloan & Pearce, 1950), pp.
  15–16.

Study Questions

1. Imamu Amiri Baraka opens "Primitive Blues and Primitive Jazz" with a description of the inhuman conditions of slavery. What context does this create for his discussion of blues and jazz? What information does this opening give the readers about Baraka's topic?
2. In paragraph 6, Baraka uses the form of conceptual organization called *explanation*. He gives reasons for the way blues developed after the Civil War. Underline the words and phrases that signal that explanations are being given. Why must Baraka include passages like this one throughout his essay?
3. One of the most noticeable forms of additive organization used by Baraka is comparison. Choose a passage in which Baraka uses comparison and identify his signals. Why does Baraka use comparison in the passage you have chosen? How does comparison help him make his point?
4. In the second half of his essay, Baraka describes a special situation for blacks in New Orleans. How does he organize this lengthy section? How is it connected with the other sections?

Suggestion for Drafting

In "Primitive Blues and Primitive Jazz," Baraka uses a description of the development of blues and jazz to discuss the life of black Americans in the nineteenth and early twentieth centuries. Although he is certainly interested in the music, Baraka focuses on the ways in which this music and its development symbolize the history of blacks in the United States. Thus, as Roger Angell used the description of a baseball as the occasion to discuss the sport itself, Baraka uses the history of blues and jazz as the occasion to discuss black history and culture.

In the suggestion for prewriting (p. 61) following Angell's "On the Ball," we asked you to do some prewriting for an essay describing a "perfect" piece of sporting equipment. We now want you to take that exercise a step further. Review your prewriting, and then consider how that piece of equipment and the sport it is used in remind you of the people who regularly play the game. For example, if you chose a tennis racquet, how would the racquet and the game of tennis seem to characterize the people who play tennis? Write a first draft of the body of an essay in which you present your ideas to readers who are familiar with the sport you have chosen.

Singapore's Patrimony
(and Matrimony)

Stephen Jay Gould

S ome historical arguments are so intrinsically *1* illogical or implausible that, following their fall from grace, we do not anticipate any subsequent resurrection in later times and contexts. The disappearance of some ideas should be as irrevocable as the extinction of species.

Of all invalid notions in the long history of eugenics—the attempt to *2* "improve" human qualities by selective breeding—no argument strikes me as more silly or self-serving than the attempt to infer people's intrinsic, genetically based "intelligence" from the number of years they attended school. Dumb folks, or so the argument went, just can't hack it in the classroom; they abandon formal education as soon as they can. The fallacy, of course, lies in a mix-up, indeed a reversal, of cause and effect. We do not deny that adults who strike us as intelligent usually (but by no means always) spent many years in school. But common sense dictates that their achievements are largely a result of the teaching and of the learning itself (and of the favorable economic and intellectual environments that permit the luxury of advanced education), not of a genetic patrimony that kept them on school benches. Unless education is a monumental waste of time, teachers must be transmitting, and students receiving, something of value.

This reversed explanation makes such evident sense that even the *3* staunchest of eugenicists abandoned the original genetic version long ago. The genetic argument was quite popular from the origin of IQ testing early in our century until the mid-1920s, but I can find scarcely any reference to it thereafter—although Cyril Burt, that grand old faker and discredited doyen of hereditarians, did write in 1947:

It is impossible for a pint jug to hold more than a pint of milk; and it is equally impossible for a child's educational attainments to rise higher than his educable capacity permits.

In my favorite example of the original, genetic version, Harvard psy- *4* chologist R. M. Yerkes tested nearly two million recruits to this man's army during World War I and calculated a correlation coefficient of 0.75 between measured intelligence and years of schooling. He concluded:

The theory that native intelligence is one of the most important conditioning factors in continuance in school is certainly borne out by this
accumulation of data.

Yerkes then noted a further correlation between low scores of blacks   5
on his tests and limited or absent schooling. He seemed on the verge of
a significant social observation when he wrote:

Negro recruits though brought up in this country where elementary education is supposedly not only free but compulsory on all, report no
schooling in astonishingly large proportion.

But he gave the data his customary genetic twist by arguing that a   6
disinclination to attend school can only reflect low innate intelligence.
Not a word did he say about the poor quality (and budgets) of segregated
schools or the need for early and gainful employment among the impoverished. (Ashley Montagu reexamined Yerkes's voluminous data twenty
years later and, in a famous paper, showed that blacks in several northern
states with generous school budgets and strong commitments to education tested better than whites in southern states with the same years of
schooling. I could almost hear the old-line eugenicists sputtering from
their graves, "Yes, but, but only the most intelligent blacks were smart
enough to move north.")
  I did not, in any case, ever expect to see Yerkes's argument revived   7
as a hereditarian weapon in the ongoing debate about human intelligence.
I was wrong. The reincarnation is particularly intriguing because it
comes from a place and culture so distant from the original context of
IQ testing in Western Europe and America. It should teach us—and this
is the main point I hope to convey in this column—that debates among
academics are not always the impotent displays of arcane mental gym-
nastics so often portrayed in our satires and stereotypes, but that ideas
can have important social consequences with impacts upon the lives of
millions. Old notions may emerge later, often in curiously altered contexts, but their source can still be recognized and traced to claims made
in the name of science yet never really supported by more than the social
prejudices (often unrecognized) of their proposers. Ideas matter in tangible ways.
  Natural History really gets around. I received last month from some   8
regular readers in Singapore, who knew of my interest in the IQ controversy from previous columns, a thick package of Xeroxed reports from
the English-language press of their nation. These pages covered a debate
that has raged in their country since August 1983, when in his annual
National Day Rally speech (an equivalent to our "state of the union"
message, I gather), Prime Minister Lee Kwan Yew abandoned his customary account of economic prospects and progress and, instead, de-

voted his remarks to what he regards as a great danger threatening his nation. The headline of the *Straits Times* for August 15 read (Singapore was once the primary city of a British colony named Straits Settlement): "Get Hitched . . . and don't stop at one. PM sees depletion of talent pool in 25 years unless better educated wed and have more children."

Prime Minister Lee had studied the 1980 census figures and found a   9 troubling relationship between the years that women spend in school and the number of children subsequently born. Specifically, Mr. Lee noted that women with no education have, on average, 3.5 children; with primary education, 2.7; with secondary schooling, 2.0; and with university degrees, only 1.65. He stated:

The better educated the people are, the less children they have. They can see the advantages of a small family. They know the burden of bringing up a large family. . . . The better educated the woman is, the less children she has.

So far, of course, Prime Minister Lee had merely noted for his nation   10 a demographic pattern common to nearly every modern technological society. Women with advanced degrees and interesting careers do not wish to spend their lives at home, bearing and raising large families. Mr. Lee acknowledged:

It is too late for us to reverse our policies and have our women go back to their primary role as mothers. . . . Our women will not stand for it. And anyway, they have already become too important a factor in the economy.

But why is this pattern troubling? It has existed for generations in   11 many nations, our own for example, with no apparent detriment to our mental or moral stock. The correlation of education with fewer children becomes a dilemma only when you add to it Yerkes's old and discredited argument that people with fewer years of schooling are irrevocably and biologically less intelligent, and that their stupidity will be inherited by their offspring. Mr. Lee made just this argument, thus setting off what Singapore's press then dubbed "the great marriage debate."

The prime minister is not, of course, unaware that years in school can   12 reflect economic advantages and family traditions with little bearing on inherited smarts. But he made a specific argument that deemphasized to insignificance the potential contribution of these environmental factors to years of schooling. Singapore has made great and recent advances in education: universal schooling was introduced during the 1960s and university places were opened to all qualified candidates. Before these reforms, Lee argued, many genetically bright children grew up in poor homes and never received an adequate education. But, he contends, this single generation of universal opportunity resolved all previous genetic inequities in one swoop. Able children of poor parents were discovered and educated to their level of competence. Society has sorted itself out along lines of genetic capacity—and level of education is now a sure guide to inherited ability.

We gave universal education to the first generation in the early 1960s. In the 1960s and '70s, we reaped a big crop of able boys and girls. They came from bright parents, many of whom were never educated. In their parents' generation, the able and not-so-able both had large families. This is a once-ever bumper crop which is not likely to be repeated. For once this generation of children from uneducated parents have received their education in the late 1960s and '70s, and the bright ones make it to the top, to tertiary [that is, university] levels, they will have less than two children per ever-married woman. They will not have large families like their parents.

Lee then sketched a dire picture of gradual genetic deterioration:

If we continue to reproduce ourselves in this lopsided way, we will be unable to maintain our present standards. Levels of competence will decline. Our economy will falter, the administration will suffer, and the society will decline. For how can we avoid lowering performance, when for every two graduates (with some exaggeration to make the point), in 25 years' time there will be one graduate, and for every two uneducated workers, there will be three?

So far, I have not proved my case—that the worst arguments raised *13* by hereditarians in the great nature-nurture wars of Western intellectuals can resurface with great social impact in later and quite different contexts. Mr. Lee's arguments certainly sound like a replay of the immigration debate in America during the early 1920s or of the long controversy in Britain over establishing separate, state-supported schools (it was done for many years) for bright and benighted children. But the arguments are evident, however flawed. Perhaps the prime minister of Singapore merely thought them up anew, with no input from older, Western incarnations.

But another key passage in Lee's speech—the one that set off waves *14* of recognition and inspired me to write this column—locates the source of his claims in old fallacies of the Western literature. I have left one crucial part of the argument out—the "positive" justification for a predominance of heredity in intellectual achievement (versus the merely negative claim that universal education should have smoothed out any environmental component). Lee stated, in a passage that sent a frisson of *déjà-vu* up my spine:

A person's performance depends on nature and nurture. There is increasing evidence that nature, or what is inherited, is the greater determinant of a person's performance than nurture (or education and environment). . . . The conclusion the researchers draw is that 80 percent is nature, or inherited, and 20 percent the differences from different environment and upbringing.

The giveaway phrase is "80 percent" (supplemented by Lee's specific   15
references to studies of identical twins reared apart). All cognoscenti of the Western debate will immediately recognize the source of this claim in the "standard figure" so often cited by hereditarians (especially by Arthur Jensen in his notorious 1969 article entitled "How Much Can We Boost IQ and Scholastic Achievement") that IQ has a measured heritability of 80 percent.

The fallacies of this 80 percent formula, both of fact and interpretation,   16
have also been thoroughly aired back home, but that part of the debate has, alas, apparently not penetrated to Singapore.

When Jensen advocated an 80 percent heritability, his primary support   17
came from Cyril Burt's study of identical twins separated early in life and raised apart. Burt, the grand old man of hereditarianism, wrote his first paper in 1909 (just four years after Binet published his initial IQ test) and continued, with steadfast consistency, to advance the same arguments until his death in 1971. His study of separated twins won special fame because he had amassed so large a sample for this rarest of all animals—more than fifty cases, where no previous researcher had managed to find even half that number. We now know that Burt's "study" was perhaps the most spectacular case of outright scientific fraud in our century—no problem locating fifty pairs of separated twins when they exist only in your own head.

Burt's hereditarian supporters first reacted to this charge of fraud by   18
attributing it to left-wing environmentalist ideologues out to destroy a man by innuendo when they couldn't overwhelm him by logic or evidence. Now that Burt's fraud has been established beyond any possible doubt (see L. S. Hearnshaw's biography, *Cyril Burt, Psychologist*), his erstwhile supporters advance another argument—the 80 percent figure is so well established from other studies that Burt's "corroboration" was irrelevant in any case.

In my reading, the literature on estimates of heritability for IQ is a   19
confusing mess—with values from 80 percent, still cited by Jensen and others, all the way down to Leon Kamin's contention (*The Science and Politics of IQ*) that existing information is not incompatible with a true heritability of flat zero. In any case, it hardly matters, for the real fallacy

of Lee's argument lies not in an inaccurate claim for heritability but in a false interpretation of what heritability means.

The problem lies in a common and incorrect equation of heritable with 20 "fixed and inevitable." Most people, when they hear that IQ is 80 percent heritable, conclude that four-fifths of its value is irrevocably set in our genes and only one-fifth is subject to improvement by good education and environment. Prime Minister Lee fell right into this old trap of false reason when he concluded that 80 percent heritability established the predominance of nature over nurture.

Heritability, as a technical term, is a measure of how much variation 21 in the appearance of a trait within a population (height, eye color, or IQ, for example) can be accounted for by genetic differences among individuals. It is simply not a measure of flexibility or inflexibility in the potential expression of a trait. A type of visual impairment, for example, might be 100 percent heritable but still easily corrected to normal vision by a pair of eyeglasses. Even if IQ were 80 percent heritable, it might still be subject to major improvement by proper education. (I do not claim that all heritable traits are easily altered; some inherited visual handicaps cannot be overcome by any available technology. I merely point out that heritability is not a measure of intrinsic and unchangeable biology.) Thus, I confess I have never been much interested in the debate over IQ's heritability—for even a very large value (which is far from established) would not speak to the main issue, so accurately characterized by Jensen in his title—how much can we boost IQ and scholastic achievement? And I haven't even mentioned (and won't discuss, lest this column become interminable) the deeper fallacy of this whole debate—the assumption that so wonderfully multifarious a notion as intelligence can be meaningfully measured by a single number, with people ranked thereby along a unilinear scale of mental worth. IQ may have a high heritability, but if this venerable measure of intelligence is (as I suspect) a meaningless abstraction, then who cares? The first joint of my right ring finger probably has a higher heritability than IQ, but no one bothers to measure it because the trait has neither independent reality nor importance.

In arguing that Prime Minister Lee has based his fears for Singapore's 22 intellectual deterioration upon a false reading of some dubious Western data, I emphatically disclaim any right to pontificate about Singapore's problems or their potential solutions. I am qualified to comment on Mr. Lee's nation only by the first criterion of the old joke that experts on other countries are those who have lived there for either less than a week or more than thirty years. Nonetheless, buttinsky that I am, I cannot resist two small intrusions. I question, first, whether a nation with such diverse cultural traditions among its Chinese, Malay, and Indian sectors can really expect to even out all environmental influences in just one generation of educational opportunity. Second, I wonder whether the world's most densely populated nation (excluding such tiny city-states as Monaco) should really be encouraging a higher reproductive rate in any segment of its population. Despite my allegiance to cultural relativism, I still maintain a right for comment when other traditions directly borrow my own culture's illogic.

The greatest barrier to understanding the real issue in this historical *23* debate may lie in the blinders erected by that euphonious contrast of supposed opposites—*nature* and *nurture*. (How I wish that English did not contain such an irresistible pair—for language channels thought, often in unfortunate directions. In previous centuries, the felicity of phrase underscoring a comparison between God's *words* and his *works* encouraged a misreading of nature as a mirror of biblical truth. In our times, an imagined antithesis of nature and nurture provokes a compartmentalization quite foreign to our world of interactions.) All complex human traits are built by an inextricable mixture of varied environments working upon the unfolding of a program bound in inherited DNA. Interaction begins at the moment of fertilization and continues to the instant of death; we cannot neatly divide any human behavior into a part rigidly determined by biology and a portion subject to change by external influence.

The real issue, as I have emphasized in several previous columns, is *24* *biological* potentiality versus *biological* determinism. We are all interactionists; we all acknowledge the powerful influence of biology upon human behavior. But determinists, like Arthur Jensen and Prime Minister Lee (at least in his August speech), use biology to construct a *theory of limits*. In Mr. Lee's version, lack of schooling implies ineradicable want of intelligence since the fault (or at least four-fifths of it) does indeed lie not in our stars but in ourselves if we are underlings. Potentialists acknowledge the importance of biology but stress that complexities of interaction, and the resultant flexibility of behavior, preclude rigid genetic programming as the basis of human achievement.

Biological determinism has a longstanding (and continuing) political *25* use as a tool for justifying the inequities of a status quo by blaming the victim—as John Conyers, Jr., one of our few black congressmen, states in a powerful Op-Ed piece in the *New York Times* on December 28, 1983. Conyers begins:

In the 1950s, much of the sociological literature on poverty attributed the economic plight of blacks and other minorities to what it said was inherent laziness and intellectual inferiority. This deflected attention from the virtually insurmountable walls of segregation that blocked social and economic mobility.

Conyers then analyzes a growing literature that seeks genetic causes *26* for high mortality rates among blacks, particularly for various forms of cancer. "In the workplace," Conyers writes, blacks have a 37 percent higher risk of occupationally induced disease and a 20 percent higher death rate from occupationally related diseases.

Now susceptibility to disease may be influenced by genetic constitu- 27
tion, and racial groups may vary in their average propensities. But if we focus on unsupported speculations about inheritance, we neglect the immediate root in racism and economic disadvantage—for these are surely major causes of the discrepancy, which could then be eradicated by social reform. (As an obvious political comment, location of the cause in intractable biology decreases pressure for the same reforms.) Conyers continues:

Just as in the 1950s, blacks are being told that their problems are largely self-inflicted, that their poor health is a manifestation of immoderate personal habits. Such blame-the-victim strategies . . . serve to divert attention from the fact that blacks are the targets of a disproportionate threat from toxins both in the workplace, where they are assigned the dirtiest and most hazardous jobs, and in their homes, which tend to be situated in the most polluted communities.

As an example, Conyers notes that black steelworkers in coke plants 28
display twice the cancer death rate of white workers, with eight times the white rate for lung cancer, in particular. "This disparity," Conyers argues,

is explainable by job patterns: 89 percent of black workers labor at coke ovens—the most dangerous part of the industry; only 32 percent of their white co-workers do.

Shall we strive directly to improve working conditions or speculate 29
about inherent racial differences? Even if we prefer genetic hypotheses, we could only test them by equalizing (and improving) our workplaces, and then assessing the impact upon mortality. Similarly, should we proclaim that women with little schooling must be intractably stupid or should we remove social and economic obstacles, push universal education a little bit harder, and see how well these women do? In the midst of Singapore's great marriage debate, the *Jakarta Post* peeked in on its neighbor's brouhaha and commented: "It would be more sensible and less controversial to build more schools."

Study Questions

1. In "Singapore's Patrimony (and Matrimony)," Stephen Jay Gould has an identifiable attitude toward his topic, eugenics, which colors every

part of his discussion. Find the opening and closing of the essay; show how in these sections Gould clearly communicates his attitude to his readers.

2. Gould begins the body of his essay with an example, the case of Prime Minister Lee Kwan Yew's flirtation with eugenics. Given Gould's attitude toward the topic, why is this an effective section? How does his description of the incident help to organize the rest of the essay?

3. Starting with paragraph 14, Gould switches from a basically additive organization to a conceptual one. What subject does Gould deal with in the earlier section that is best served by his using additive organization? In what ways does his emphasis change in the later section so that he must change structures? Why is conceptual organization more suitable for this new emphasis?

4. In "The Artificial Universe," Vine Deloria, Jr., also switches from an additive to a conceptual organization. What do the two essays have in common that would lead to similar organizations? What differences do you see in the ways each writer has used that organization? What differences in their messages might account for their different applications of the organization?

Suggestion for Drafting

Stephen Jay Gould in his essay tackles one of the more misunderstood concepts in our country: IQ. While the debate rages around us about exactly what IQ represents, IQ is measured, recorded, and used to predict how successful a student will be in school.

Using the information you have gathered from "Singapore's Patrimony (and Matrimony)," suppose that you are working on your own essay about the problems of using IQ measurements. Write a draft of your opening and closing sections.

Viking on the Plain of Gold

Arthur C. Clarke

I t is pure coincidence that the *Viking 1* Lander *1* made its historic touchdown in a region that astronomers had given the fanciful name *Planitia Chryse*—the plain of gold. No one expected to find gold in Chryse; Viking was looking for something much more valuable than that overrated metal—knowledge.

Yet it is very difficult for the layman, unaware of the way in which *2* the most esoteric scientific discoveries can save millions of lives and create whole new industries, to appreciate the importance of such a project. He is apt to take the short-term view and ask, very reasonably, why the billion dollars spent on Viking could not have been used instead on houses, schools, hospitals, roads, etc.?

It should be admitted at once that all the answers to this question *3* won't be in for a couple of centuries. But it is an act of faith among scientists, based on all past history, that every breakthrough into a new realm of knowledge invariably adds to the total potential—and hence, wealth and happiness—of mankind.

Sometimes the payoff is immediate: from Faraday's first experiments *4* with magnets, to telegraphs and electric motors, was only a few years. Sometimes it takes a little longer; the voyage of Columbus changed the destiny of the human race, but it was several lifetimes before this became apparent.

One can divide the motives behind any voyage of exploration— *5* manned or unmanned—into three main categories: scientific, practical (or commercial), and spiritual (or philosophical-religious). Sometimes it is not easy to separate them, and indeed they are seldom found in isolation, for in the past there have been missionary-scientists and tradesmen-naturalists.

Science first. All men, if their souls are not utterly destroyed by *6* poverty or bad education, have a natural curiosity about the world around them—not only this planet, but any others that may exist. In its purest form, science is simply an expression of this curiosity; any man who is even half-alive must have some interest in conditions on other worlds, even if the knowledge is of no conceivable practical importance.

For over a hundred years, since the development of modern tele- *7* scopes, Mars has been the center of such interest—though partly for reasons which we now know to be quite erroneous. The reported discovery in 1877 of a network of "canals" inspired millions of words of speculation about Martian civilizations—not to mention countless science fiction stories and movies, of which H. G. Wells' *The War of the Worlds* is the most famous (or most notorious, after it provoked the 1938 radio panic in the United States!).

The canals have turned out to be an illusion, but there was no way of proving this while we were confined to observations from Earth. Viking's precursors, particularly the orbiting *Mariner 9,* which produced the first complete photographic survey of the planet, swept into limbo all the fabled Martian cities and princesses. Instead, they revealed a world almost as fascinating as the fiction—a place of rolling multicolored deserts, of canyons that could swallow those of Arizona and Colorado without trace, and of volcanoes three times as high as Everest. *8*

But even the closest observations from space could not prove or disprove the existence of life on Mars, although they could eliminate many possibilities. Thus there were certainly no extensive areas of vegetation necessary to support animal life as we know it. Such life was in any case ruled out by the almost complete absence of oxygen in the extremely thin Martian atmosphere. Yet for all that *Mariner 9* could tell, there might still be living creatures on the planet, of any size from microbes to elephants, and the only way to settle the matter was by a landing on the surface. Hence Viking, with its pair of electronic cameras and its automated biology lab—an incredible tour de force of technology, containing forty thousand components in the volume of a biscuit tin. *9*

This marvelously compact and versatile type of instrumentation usually, within a very few years, has its impact upon a whole range of down-to-earth applications in medicine, science and industry. Unfortunately, by the time some space-inspired device gets to the general public, its origins are usually forgotten. The shopkeeper or accountant (or for that matter schoolboy or housewife) operating one of the miraculous little electronic calculators that have removed all the drudgery from arithmetic, seldom stops to ask how such a gadget came about. But without the stringent demands of space navigation, these tiny pocket brains would never have been developed. Soon we will find it impossible to imagine how we ever ran our lives without them—and their even more intelligent successors, already on the drawing board. *10*

Perhaps only 10 percent of the world's population can afford pocket calculators, or would know how to use them. But 100 percent of the world requires food, water and the basic necessities of life—and the type of survey equipment carried on space probes has already started to revolutionize the search for these things on Earth. After all, looking for life on Mars, and looking for its prerequisites on our own planet, involves much the same problems. *11*

Quite early in the Space Age, it was discovered that orbiting cameras and other instruments (very similar to those which gave us our first *12*

Martian's-eye view from *Viking 1)* could reveal astonishingly detailed information about crops, water supplies, snow cover, ocean fertility, mineral deposits. The list is enormous, and is still growing. As a result, the National Aeronautics and Space Administration has launched two "earth resources satellites," now rechristened Landsats—though Earthsats would have been a better name, because they are doing equally important work on land and sea. Between them, *Landsats 1* and *2* have produced millions of beautiful—and economically priceless—photographs, giving information about our planet that could have been obtained in no other way. This information is available cheaply to any country in the world, and has already enabled some developing nations to produce maps at a fraction of the cost of conventional aerial surveying.

In a very important and fundamental way, when we study Mars we 13 are also studying our own world . . . and what it may teach us about our planet may one day be a matter of life and death. This may seem surprising, but consider these facts:

For some years it has been known that the Martian atmosphere (mostly 14 carbon dioxide) is so thin that its pressure is about one hundredth of the Earth's. This means that even if it was warm enough (which it seldom is, except near noon on the equator) water cannot exist in the liquid form. There are clouds and snowfields on Mars, but no rivers or lakes, still less oceans. Yet to the astonishment of the scientists, the first good photos of Mars showed vast dried-up riverbeds and huge canyons that seemed to have been cut by torrential rains—on a planet now more desert than the Sahara.

What has happened to the lost lakes—and perhaps oceans—of Mars? 15 Is the same process occurring on Earth? There has been tragic evidence, in the past few years, that profound changes are taking place in the weather patterns of our planet. Mars may tell us what is happening here— and perhaps what to do about it. Few discoveries would be more important than unraveling the forces which control climate, and while we have only a single planet for study, our chance of understanding this process is small. We urgently need the tools of space to save our own world, midway, it would seem, in the evolutionary sequence between cold, low-pressure Mars and red-hot, high-pressure Venus.

During the last decade, we have learned more about our cosmic neigh- 16 bors than in the whole of previous history. We now have robot scouts reporting steadily from the Moon and Mars, and have obtained close-ups of Mercury and Jupiter. We have even received a couple of hours of observation from the surface of Venus, before the hellish conditions there destroyed the instruments. For the first time, therefore, we are beginning to develop a real science of the planets.

Why is that important? Because when we understand how our own 17 Earth works, we will know where to look for its mineral deposits, how to anticipate earthquakes and major changes in climate—and, perhaps, how to prevent them. Such knowledge may one day save millions of lives and create billions of dollars of wealth.

The engineer-visionary Buckminster Fuller once remarked that the 18 most important thing about Spaceship Earth is that it comes without an operating manual; hence many of our present troubles. Today's space explorers are helping us to write that manual.

Even if Mars had been known to be as lifeless as the Moon, most of 19 Viking's instruments and objectives would have been unchanged. But understandably, public interest has focused on the life-detecting experiment. And rightly so, because the discovery of even simple microbes on Mars would have the most profound implications not only to science, but to philosophy and even to religion.

After centuries of fruitless speculation, Viking gave us the first op- 20 portunity of settling that ancient question: "Is there life beyond the Earth?" True, it represented a gamble against very long odds, and many scientists considered that the biology experiments were a waste of money. They argued that conditions on Mars were so severe that life was impossible—or that if it did exist, we wouldn't know it when we saw it. But one has to start looking somewhere, and Viking's designers assumed that any life forms must eat and excrete certain basic chemicals, so that even if they were invisibly small, their presence could still be detected. The cameras, of course, would quickly spot anything comparable to plants or trees, though probably not animals, unless they were very slow-moving. For technical reasons, Viking takes many minutes to scan the whole Martian panorama; thus even a tortoise would only appear as a streak on its pictures.

The first question which we would want to ask of anything that crawls, 21 hops, burrows or walks within range of Viking is rather surprising and may even appear simple-minded. Whether it has three heads or four eyes or six tentacles, we would still want to know of any passing Martian: "Are you identical with us?"

One of the most profound discoveries of the past generation is that, 22 despite all appearances, there is in a sense only a single life form on the planet Earth. "We men, we microbes, we cabbages, we sharks . . ." to paraphrase Dr. Carl Sagan. The infinite diversity of the living world is an illusion. Deep down, we are all variations of the same very few biochemical themes. It is as if every creature on Earth was built from one huge organic Meccano set, with only a few basic components. It would be impossible to tell, purely from the disassembled fragments, what any original model was like. This fact, incidentally, is a far more conclusive proof of life's evolution from a single origin than the relatively superficial resemblances between men and apes which helped to launch Darwin's theory.

The great unanswered question which Viking may settle is this: Must 23
all life, everywhere, depend on the same handful of reactions as it does
on Earth? If we find that Martian life forms have just the same chemical
themes as we men, we microbes, etc., that will suggest that no other
arrangement is possible.

If, on the other hand, it turns out that Martian life has a fundamentally 24
different chemistry—or, to continue our analogy, that the Mars Meccano
set has quite different components—that would open up whole new vistas
in biology and, ultimately, medicine. Remember how many of the drugs
in the doctors' armory were discovered by travelers to strange places on
this planet. On a much more sophisticated level, this situation may be
repeated in space.

And beyond the sheer excitement and practical importance of finding 25
life elsewhere, there are philosophical implications which may change
the patterns of human thinking until the end of time. A single Martian
microbe would prove that life will arise on any world where it has the
slightest chance of survival. We will look up to the stars with new
emotions, in the virtual certainty that we are not alone, and that scattered
across the Milky Way galaxy of more than a hundred thousand million
suns there must be civilizations which could make us look like savages.
Perhaps that knowledge may be just what we need—to stop us from
behaving like savages.

And even if there is no life on Mars today—sometime in the next 26
century, there will be. Next to the Moon, Mars is the new frontier for
manned exploration—and, one day, settlement—using the tools of future
science to tame a world whose opportunities and challenges are as yet
almost wholly unknown.

Study Questions

1. Arthur C. Clarke opens his essay with the image of the *Viking 1*
   Lander on the *Planitia Chryse*—the Plain of Gold. In what ways is
   this an effective image for creating a context for Clarke's meaning?
   What associations can we expect readers to have with such words as
   Vikings, gold, and *voyages of expedition?*
2. What is the dominant method of organization in the body of the essay?
   Where does Clarke directly announce the scheme to his readers? What
   does he gain by so clearly signaling his method?
3. What function does the discussion of Mars in paragraphs 7–9 serve in
   developing Clarke's meaning? How does Clarke connect these paragraphs with those that precede and follow?
4. Clarke points to calculators and orbiting cameras as two benefits
   derived from the space program. What reasons might he have for

mentioning calculators first? What would these reasons suggest about Clarke's view of his potential audience? Who does he think might read his essay?
5. What is the importance of paragraph 19 in the organization of the essay? How does it complete the organizational scheme Clarke announced earlier?

Suggestion for Drafting

Arthur C. Clarke uses three types of argument in favor of "voyages of exploration": scientific, practical, and spiritual. Could Clarke have conveyed his message if he had used only one type?

Redraft the body of this essay so that only the practical advantages of space exploration are discussed. In doing so, consider these two questions before you begin: (1) What additional details will you need before you can devote your entire discussion to this one point? (2) What changes will you need to make in Clarke's organization?

Little Things That Tick Off Baboons

Glenn Hausfater and Reed Sutherland

O n the plains north of Mount Kilimanjaro, old *1* female Scar walked over and sat next to her daughter Cete in the shade of an acacia tree. After a few seconds, Scar turned her shoulder prominently toward Cete, who immediately responded by picking through her mother's fur. Cete shortly pulled from Scar's shoulder a large, black tick emblazoned with an *art nouveau* design. Both mother and daughter smacked their lips exaggeratedly at this sight. Cete placed the delicacy in her mouth and, while still chewing, resumed grooming her mother's coat.

Scar and Cete are two of the approximately 200 yellow baboons for *2* which the Amboseli National Park of Kenya serves as home. Similarly, this particular tick species, *Rhipicephalus pulchellus,* is one of many different kinds of parasites for which Amboseli baboons themselves provide a home, although in the parlance of parasitology they are more properly called hosts.

Since 1971, Amboseli baboons have been the focus of ecological and *3* behavioral studies by a team of scientists under the direction of Stuart and Jeanne Altmann of the University of Chicago and Glenn Hausfater of the University of Missouri. The Amboseli studies, like many that have been done of primates in their natural environment, have had a strong emphasis on what baboons eat (foraging ecology) and conversely, on what eats baboons (predator–prey relations). Only recently have researchers begun to explore the complex host–parasite dynamics involving Amboseli baboons and to understand how parasites both affect and are affected by the behavior and ecology of baboons. We would hardly be so brash as to claim that a *Rhipicephalus* tick scrambling through the grass toward a resting baboon is as spectacular a sight as the bounding charge of a snarling leopard. But the Amboseli studies suggest that these almost imperceptible creatures may be just as important as the large cats in influencing the ranging, feeding, and social behavior of baboons and several other primate species.

A parasite is a plant or animal that lives in prolonged, intimate contact *4* with another organism and can grow and reproduce only by feeding on that organism's tissues and resources. The parasites of wild mammals are generally divided into those that live inside the host's body (endoparasites) and those that live attached to the host's skin or fur (ectoparasites). In baboons and other nonhuman primates, common endoparasites include roundworms (or nematodes), tapeworms, and flukes, all three of which are referred to collectively as helminths. Various pathogenic species of protozoans and bacteria found in baboons are also generally considered intestinal parasites, even though other species of these same microorganisms in primate digestive systems are beneficial symbionts. Common ectoparasites of Amboseli baboons and other primates include fleas, ticks, lice, and mites, although a few of the latter (called lung mites) have actually managed to colonize the respiratory pathway and are thus technically endoparasites. Contrary to popular opinion, many endoparasites and ectoparasites cause little pain or damage to their host. This is particularly true of the more highly coevolved and evolutionarily older host–parasite relationships.

The Amboseli project has maintained a strict policy of noninterference with the subject animals, meaning that the baboons are not fed, trapped, or otherwise manipulated. Nevertheless, this did not prevent team members from collecting a small sample of feces from individual baboons shortly after they had defecated and gone on their way. Then, just as a veterinarian might look for parasites in a fecal smear from one's pet, B. Jean Meade and D. F. Watson of Virginia Polytechnic Institute similarly examined samples from each Amboseli study animal. Using other techniques, they were able to extract and identify intestinal parasite ova from small samples of preserved feces and thereby monitor changes over time in ova emissions by individual baboons. This information was then used to determine if the age, reproductive condition, or social status of a baboon influences the number and kinds of parasites that it harbors. 5

Since Amboseli baboons showed few clinical signs of parasite infection, research team members were surprised to discover that nearly all individuals, including young infants, have a large complement of intestinal helminths. In fact, the average adult animal harbors four to five species of helminths, as well as several species of protozoan parasites; a single fecal sample might contain as many as 100 nematode ova per gram. Several previous laboratory and field studies have shown that a well-fed host can often support large numbers of parasites without showing any external signs of blood loss, tissue damage, or inflammation. However, if a drought reduces the availability of food or an injury prevents the host from feeding, clinical symptoms appear rapidly and may kill the animal. More frequently, the weakened and malnourished host falls victim to one of its predators or to disease. 6

Far and away the most common intestinal parasites recovered from Amboseli baboons are helminths of the genera *Trichuris,* *Trichostrongylus,* and *Abbreviata.* The first two have very similar life cycles. Baboons become infected with *Trichuris* and *Trichostrongylus* by swallowing their eggs or larvae, which are found as contaminants in the soil adhering to the baboons' food plants. The larvae mature in the gut of the host baboon, then mate and produce eggs, which are dispersed via 7

the host's feces. The third common helminth, *Abbreviata,* undergoes
the first part of its development in an insect such as a grasshopper or
dung beetle. Baboons get infected with this parasite when they eat the
insect intermediate host, and the worm then spends the rest of its life in
the baboon's intestinal tract. Other helminths found in Amboseli baboons infect their host by penetrating the skin, the way hookworms do,
rather than by an oral route.

Clearly, baboons get infected with all these intestinal nematodes by   8
direct contact with larvae or ova. Thus, a major research effort has
focused on trying to determine the most likely site of this contact. Since
parasite ova and larvae are dispersed in the baboons' feces, members of
the research team faced the very nasty job of finding out where and how
frequently baboons defecate and if the choice of defecation site influenced
parasite transmission. Sparing the reader details of methodology, we will
say merely that fresh feces desiccate rapidly on the open savanna and
that this is generally lethal to parasite ova and larvae. In contrast, both
ova and larvae remain viable and infective for a substantially longer time
directly beneath the trees where baboons sleep.

Although baboons spend most of their waking hours feeding on the   9
open savanna, their day always begins and ends at one of several groves
of acacia trees within their home range. Baboons sleep in the trees at
night as a refuge from large cats, and in just a few nights they deposit a
considerable amount of fecal matter on the ground below.

Early in the morning, baboons spend some time resting, feeding,   10
grooming, and sunning themselves beneath their trees. During this period, which may last a few minutes or a few hours, they are exposed to
infective ova and larvae in their own feces. Multiple soil samples obtained beneath baboon sleeping trees averaged more than 100 adult and
larval nematodes per ounce. The yield from these samples was propor-
tional to the soil's distance from the center of the grove. Samples obtained just outside the shadow of the grove or in the open savanna
contained virtually no larvae at all. These data point to the obvious
conclusion that the baboons' own sleeping sites were the primary source
of contact with their intestinal parasites.

Even in the relatively moist soil beneath the baboons' sleeping trees,   11
parasite ova and larvae cannot live forever. The eggs are rapidly attacked
by soil fungi, and both eggs and larvae may be eaten by the myriad dung
beetles active in Amboseli. Hausfater and Meade wondered if baboons
might outsmart their parasites by avoiding a grove with a high density of
infective parasites until the natural causes of egg and larval mortality had
reduced parasite numbers to a minimum.

Through a series of controlled experiments, these researchers were   12
able to determine that the ova and larvae in baboon feces have a fairly
regular hatching and mortality schedule, based partly on environmental
conditions and partly on their species-specific life cycles. Larval hatching hits a peak two to four days after fecal deposition, and the larvae

become infective shortly thereafter. However, four to five days later, larvae will have died off to nearly the same level as when baboons first used the grove. Thus, approximately nine days from the first time baboons use a grove, it becomes "safe" for reuse.

Each of the two main study groups of Amboseli baboons—Alto's group 13 and Hook's group—uses about fifteen to twenty different acacia groves for sleeping. Often these groves are just a few hundred yards apart, although both groups use sites widely scattered throughout the thirty-square-mile study area. Amboseli baboons are not territorial, but each group has almost exclusive access to a number of groves. Thus, if a group returns to an acacia grove after foraging and sleeping on the other side of its range, the baboons can safely assume that another group has not used the trees in their absence.

Hausfater and Meade analyzed grove use by Amboseli baboons and 14 found that groups typically stayed at any given grove for only two nights and then moved on to another sleeping site. When they analyzed the patterns more closely, they found that the study animals not only avoided groves during times of peak larval hatching but also waited an average of nine days before using a grove again. In other words, grove-use patterns by the baboons seem to minimize the animals' exposure to infective ova and larvae.

The Amboseli team has uncovered no compelling evidence to sug- 15 gest that baboons actually perceive microscopic ova and larvae in the soil beneath their groves. More likely, the odor from the feces accumulated beneath their sleeping sites is their cue to change groves again. Ernest Hemingway seems to have noted this same phenomenon in his novel *The Green Hills of Africa:*

Instead of the cool early morning smell of the forest there was a nasty stink like the mess cats make.
"What makes the stink?" I whispered to Pop.
"Baboons," he said.
A whole tribe of them had gone on just ahead of us and their droppings were everywhere.

Although Amboseli researchers hypothesize that baboons leave groves 16 because of the buildup of feces and parasite larvae beneath their trees, there may be other reasons. For example, if the animals are attacked by a leopard or lions during the night, they may abandon their current grove immediately and stay away for a long time. Thus, one alternative hypothesis about sleeping site changes is that the moves help baboons and other primates avoid predators.

Another hypothesis about grove use evolves from the baboons' for- 17 aging behavior: when baboons wander on their home range during the day, they don't stray too far from their nightly rest sites. Some researchers think the baboons might switch groves as a way of getting at new feeding grounds.

Neither of these hypotheses seems very likely, however. When ba- 18 boons move to a new sleeping grove, it is frequently only a few hundred yards away, hardly far enough to give them access to entirely different foraging areas or to fool a leopard.

Thus, the grove-change pattern by Amboseli baboons may well be the 19 result of "fecal buildup" since that is the hypothesis that best accounts for the frequent, short-distance relocations of Amboseli baboons and of primates at other study sites.

In addition to their intestinal parasites, Amboseli baboons are also 20 host to a wide range of arthropod ectoparasites. Ticks, fleas, and similar small creatures give irritating bites and are vectors for a variety of diseases transmissible to animals and humans. Ticks are known to carry several forms of typhus, including an attenuated variety, appropriately called tick fever, that has laid low more than a few Amboseli researchers. One indication of the seriousness of ectoparasite-borne diseases is that baboons and other primates have a ritualized behavior for removal of ectoparasites—grooming.

Scar, Cete, and other female baboons spend more time grooming each 21 other than in any social activity except infant care. About 7 percent of their day is given over to grooming. Since baboon groups are basically made up of a series of matriarchies, females direct much of their grooming attention toward their offspring and siblings. This tendency is so strong that if an adult female and young female frequently groom each other, they are almost certainly a mother–daughter pair. Grooming is also one of the most important ways that baboons from different families build social bonds with each other, and the various matriarchs in a group often groom each other.

Adult males, by contrast, hardly spend any time at all grooming each 22 other. Unlike females, males generally leave their parental group and thus have few relatives available as grooming partners. However, males do spend an extraordinary amount of time grooming the rump fur of estrous females.

A grooming sequence generally begins when one baboon approaches 23 another and inclines its chest, neck, or cheek toward the prospective groomer. The "groomee" simultaneously assumes the characteristic stiff-legged solicitation posture, while cocking its head to the side and assiduously avoiding direct eye contact with the groomer. Avoiding eye contact is exceedingly important if the groomee ranks higher in dominance status than the groomer, for even a glance from the higher-ranking baboon may be perceived as a threat and the prospective groomer would then probably break off the interaction and move away.

According to the etiquette of grooming, the groomer and groomee 24 must exchange roles every few minutes. Baboons that fail to reciprocate in this manner or that consistently do a lackluster job of grooming have great difficulty finding partners.

Once a grooming bout begins in earnest, the groomer combs through 25 the groomee's fur with great concentration, using specific finger and hand movements to capture and remove ectoparasites. A groomer will often use his or her fingertips and nails to rake the groomee's skin in short strokes—movements called comb and scrape by Amboseli researchers— thereby loosening ectoparasites and other debris. Another pair of movements—termed lift and bite—are used to remove the loosened ectoparasite from the groomee's fur or skin and then transport it to the groomer's mouth, where it is eaten. Carol D. Saunders, who recently completed a study of the grooming behavior of Amboseli baboons and the ecology of their ectoparasites, has thus far identified more than a dozen such motor patterns.

The most common ectoparasites that Amboseli baboons remove from 26 each other during grooming are hard ticks of the family *Ixodidae*. Hard ticks generally have four life stages, of which three are spent on a succession of vertebrate hosts. Mating takes place while the adult ticks are riding about on a baboon or some other mammal. About a week later the gravid female drops to the ground and deposits thousands of eggs on the soil. The eggs hatch into tiny six-legged larvae, called pepper ticks in East Africa, and the larvae in turn climb to the top of grass plants and wait for any appropriate vertebrate host to walk by. The larvae feed on their hosts for about a week and then drop off prior to molting into larger eight-legged nymphs. The nymphs feed for about a week on yet another vertebrate host before they drop off one last time and undergo their final molt to adulthood.

As adults, these ticks are quite mobile. They are attracted to carbon 27 dioxide because it may be a cue to the presence of a living, breathing mammal in their vicinity. Saunders was able to capitalize on this attraction by slowly releasing CO_2 from metal cylinders and luring ticks from vegetation. Similarly she found that "questing" ticks, those perched high atop grass stems, would readily jump onto a sheet of wool flannel dragged through the grass. Both of these methods of collecting ticks were used to estimate seasonal changes in tick density in Amboseli and to determine where the greatest number of ticks lived.

Saunders found that tick densities in Amboseli have two major peaks. 28 The first is in January-February, following a rainy period late in the preceding year, and the second occurs between April and June, following a second rainy period that begins between March and May. As with helminth larvae, the baboons' own sleeping groves proved to be the major reservoir of ixodid ticks. Another important concentration of ticks was found directly beneath "umbrella" trees, the squat, flat-topped acacias scattered about the African savanna and under which baboons take their midday siestas.

The aim of obtaining such detailed information on the distribution of *29* ticks in the study area is to determine how tick densities in the baboons' home range influence their movements and grooming patterns. Although formal analyses are still in progress, casual examination of the data suggests that baboons often go into a "burst" of grooming after moving through a habitat infested with ticks. But at this point we cannot draw any conclusions beyond the obvious one: ticks seem to play an extremely important role in the social life and ecology of Amboseli baboons.

Analyses like the one described so far only tell one side of the host– *30* parasite coevolution story. Although none of the Amboseli researchers likes parasites very much, a spirit of fairness requires us to admit that parasites are entitled to make a living as much as baboons. From the parasites' point of view, the evolution by baboons of behavior to avoid them is unfortunate. On the other hand, parasites might have evolved a few tricks of their own. For example, parasites might time their reproduction and dispersion to maximize their chances of landing a baboon host, especially a relatively parasite-free infant.

One of the features of baboons that makes them convenient to study *31* is a flashy, hot-pink swelling, called the sexual skin, on the backsides of females. This peculiar anatomical structure (restricted to baboons and certain other Old World monkeys and apes) is an area of perineal skin that cyclically swells, deflates, and changes color in relation to female hormonal changes. By keeping daily records of the size, shape, and color of each female's sexual skin, one can obtain a fairly good idea of her hormonal and reproductive conditions on any given day.

When data on parasite ova emissions were compared with records on *32* sexual skin swelling, Amboseli researchers discovered that reproduction by the intestinal helminths of the study females was strongly influenced by the females' reproductive cycles. In particular, just after female baboons gave birth there was a very sharp rise in egg production by their intestinal helminths, apparently tied to a series of rapid changes in the female's progesterone level.

Such reproduction clearly facilitates an early assault on newborn in- *33* fants, but some baboons may develop parasites before they are even born. Amboseli researchers believe that one endoparasite species, *Strongyloides fulleborni,* is acquired by infants while still in the womb or possibly very shortly after birth, through the colostrum. This form of mother–infant parasite transmission has previously been recorded in domestic animals, but never in a wild primate.

One other aspect of our work at Amboseli has been to examine *34* whether baboons might be infecting other primate species with their parasites. Although most of the intestinal parasites of Amboseli baboons can infect many other host species, only half of the helminths found in the baboons are also found in the two other primates with which they share their home range—vervet monkeys (*Cercopithecus aethiops*) and the indigenous Masai pastoral people. The similarities and differences in the parasites of these three sympatric hosts can probably be accounted for by similarities and differences in diet.

For example, the Masai harbor tapeworms that they probably pick up *35* from eating meat. Baboons and vervet monkeys eat very little meat and thus rarely have tapeworms. On the other hand, baboons and vervets eat grasshoppers, an item not usually found on the Masai menu.

Such cross-species comparisons of parasites is a controversial subject, *36* for medical researchers in some tropical countries argue that wild non-human primates pose a serious health risk to humans who have traditional life styles. Some experts even go so far as to say that nonhuman primates such as baboons or vervets should be controlled, that is, trapped or shot, to reduce the frequency of parasite transmission to humans.

However, nearly the only finding of human health concern from Am- *37* boseli was that a few baboons carry the protozoan parasites *Balantidum coli* and *Entamoeba histolytica,* species that can cause dysentery in humans but that have little effect on baboons. Humans and baboons could potentially pass these dangerous protozoans to each other through their communal use of certain water holes. However, since Amboseli baboons fastidiously avoid defecating around their water holes, these protozoan parasites are probably transmitted only in one direction—from humans to monkeys. In sum, there seems to be little evidence that controlling wild primates in Amboseli would improve the health of the Masai people or other local inhabitants.

Much to their chagrin, several Amboseli researchers have begun to *38* find the parasites of baboons nearly as interesting as the baboons themselves. Although they cannot be sure where this strange fascination will lead, the goal of their ongoing work is to learn more about the behavioral and ecological factors responsible for the transmission of parasites and disease to primates in their natural environment. Of course, for Scar, Cete, and the other Amboseli baboons, the goal of their efforts is much more basic: to avoid both predators and parasites and thereby live a long and healthy life.

Study Questions

1. Glenn Hausfater and Reed Sutherland begin "Little Things That Tick Off Baboons" with an anecdote. What particular actions described in this anecdote are important for creating a context for their meaning? How does the story shape the readers' attitude toward the topic?
2. After introducing the various kinds of parasites that can infect the Amboseli baboons, the writers spend the first part of the body of the essay discussing the relationship of certain types of intestinal parasites

to the living habits of the baboons. What two types of organization are used to structure this discussion? How can you tell where the authors use each of them?

3. Paragraph 29 signals a shift in topics within the body of the essay. How do Hausfater and Sutherland prepare the readers for this shift? What part of this paragraph acts as a kind of "mini opening" to introduce the new topic? Why is such an introduction needed?

4. What technique do Hausfater and Sutherland use to end their essay? Given the variety of points they make in their discussion, is this an effective technique? Does it seem to round off the discussion and give a perspective to their meaning?

Suggestion for Drafting

Paragraph 4 of "Little Things That Tick Off Baboons" is organized by classification, an additive method. The writers use this form in order to present a large amount of information in a clear and efficient manner.

The following "paragraph" contains a series of basic sentences that describe a number of different kinds of essays. Combine these sentences to create a more "mature" passage and, when possible, add words and phrases that signal a classification organization. Feel free to rearrange statements within the paragraph, but maintain the original vocabulary. You may want to reread paragraph 4 before attempting this exercise.

Writers create essays. Some essays are personal. Some essays are descriptive. Some essays are expository. Personal essays are about the writer. Personal essays demand organization. Personal essays use transitions. The organization is usually chronological. The transitions are usually based on time. Descriptive essays are not about the writer. Descriptive essays are about subjects. The subjects are various. The subjects are specifically identified in the essays. Descriptive essays demand organization. Descriptive essays use transitions. The organization depends upon the subject. The transitions depend upon the organization. Expository essays are not about the writer. Expository essays are supposed to inform the readers. Expository essays explain topics. The topics are various. Expository essays demand organization. The organization must be obvious. The organization must be highly controlled. The writer makes the organization obvious. The writer controls the organization. The writer chooses the transitions. The transitions signal the organization. The transitions help the readers understand the explanation.

After you have rewritten this paragraph, underline the words and phrases in your version that show you are using classification.

Women Fight Back

Susan Brownmiller

O n the fourteenth of November, 1642, *a young* 1
Virgine, daughter to Mr. Adam Fisher, was
hurrying along a country road in Devonshire
so darke that she could scarce discerne her hand when the figure of a
Gentleman, Mr. Ralph Ashley, a debased Cavalier, approached on horseback. Inspired by the *Devill* himself, this gentleman told the trusting
maiden that he knew her father well and would be pleased to escort her
home in safety, for there were lustful soldiers in those parts.

And then, Dear Reader, as if you didn't know what next, he galloped 2
her off to a deserted spot and *went about to ravish her* while she fervently
prayed, *Help, Lord, or I perish.*

Just then *a fearefull Comet burst out in the ayre* and *strucke* the 3
rapacious Cavalier with *a streame of fire* so that *he fell downe staggering.*

According to some shepherds folding their flock who had witnessed 4
the *Blazing Starre* from a distance, Mr. Ashley expired within the night,
ranting and raving in terrible blasphemy about *that Roundheaded whore.*
Adam Fisher's daughter, aroused from a graceful faint, found her Virginity intact and thanked her lucky starres and God Almighty.

The original text of this Puritan fable, a seventeenth-century propa- 5
ganda pamphlet aimed at "those Cavaliers which esteem murder and
rapine the chiefe Principalls of their religion," is housed today in the
British Museum.

Three eventful centuries have passed since that fateful autumn night 6
when Mr. Ralph Ashley attempted to ravish Mr. Adam Fisher's nameless
daughter and was struck in his tracks by a bolt from the sky. Fewer of
us these days, we would all agree, are young Virgines. The automobile
has replaced the horse and blazing comets have proved fairly unpredictable after all. But the problem of rape, and how to deal with it, remains.

To a woman the definition of rape is fairly simple. A sexual invasion 7
of the body by force, an incursion into the private, personal inner space
without consent—in short, an internal assault from one of several avenues
and by one of several methods—constitutes a deliberate violation of
emotional, physical and rational integrity and is a hostile, degrading act
of violence that deserves the name of rape.

Yet by tracing man's concept of rape as he defined it in his earliest 8
laws, we now know with certainty that the criminal act he viewed with
horror, and the deadly punishments he saw fit to apply, had little to do
with an actual act of sexual violence that a woman's body might sustain.
True, the law has come some distance since its beginnings when rape

meant simply and conclusively the theft of a father's daughter's virginity, a specialized crime that damaged valuable goods before they could reach the matrimonial market, but modern legal perceptions of rape are rooted still in ancient male concepts of property.

From the earliest times, when men of one tribe freely raped women *9* of another tribe to secure new wives, the laws of marriage and the laws of rape have been philosophically entwined, and even today it is largely impossible to separate them out. Man's historic desire to maintain sole, total and complete access to woman's vagina, as codified by his earliest laws of marriage, sprang from his need to be the sole physical instrument governing impregnation, progeny and inheritance rights. As man understood his male reality, it was perfectly lawful to capture and rape some other tribe's women, for what better way for his own tribe to increase? But it was unlawful, he felt, for the insult to be returned. The criminal act he viewed with horror and punished as rape was not sexual assault *per se,* but an act of unlawful possession, a trespass against his tribal right to control vaginal access to all women who belonged to him and his kin.

Since marriage, by law, was consummated in one manner only, by *10* defloration of virginity with attendant ceremonial tokens, the act man came to construe as criminal rape was the illegal destruction of virginity outside a marriage contract of his making. Later, when he came to see his own definition as too narrow for the times, he broadened his criminal concept to cover the ruination of his wife's chastity as well, thus extending the law's concern to nonvirgins too. Although these legal origins have been buried in the morass of forgotten history, as the laws of rape continued to evolve they never shook free of their initial concept—that the violation was first and foremost a violation of *male* rights of possession, based on *male* requirements of virginity, chastity and consent to private access as the female bargain in the marriage contract (the underpinnings, as he enforced them, of man's economic estate).

To our modern way of thinking, these theoretical origins are peculiar *11* and difficult to fully grasp. A huge disparity in thought—male logic versus female logic—affects perception of rape to this very day, confounding the analytic processes of some of the best legal minds. Today's young rapist has no thought of capturing a wife or securing an inheritance or estate. His is an act of impermanent conquest, not a practical approach to ownership and control. The economic advantage of rape is a forgotten concept. What remains is the basic male-female struggle, a hit-and-run attack, a brief expression of physical power, a conscious process of intimidation, a blunt, ugly sexual invasion with possible lasting psychological effects on all women.

When rape is placed where it truly belongs, within the context of *12* modern criminal violence and not within the purview of ancient masculine codes, the crime retains its unique dimensions, falling midway between robbery and assault. It is, in one act, both a blow to the body and a blow to the mind, and a "taking" of sex through the use or threat of force. Yet the differences between rape and an assault or a robbery are as distinctive as the obvious similarities. In a prosecutable case of assault, bodily damage to the victim is clearly evident. In a case of rape, the threat of force does not secure a tangible commodity as we understand the term, although sex traditionally has been viewed by men as "the female treasure"; more precisely, in rape the threat of force obtains a highly valued sexual service through temporary access to the victim's intimate parts, and the intent is not merely to "take," but to humiliate and degrade.

This, then, is the modern reality of rape as it is defined by twentieth-   13
century practice. It is not, however, the reality of rape as it is defined by twentieth-century law.

In order for a sexual assault to qualify as felonious rape in an American   14
courtroom, there must be "forcible penetration of the vagina by the penis, however slight." In other words, rape is defined by law as a heterosexual offense that is characterized by genital copulation. It is with this hallowed, restrictive definition, the *sine qua non* of rape prosecutions, that our argument begins.

That forcible genital copulation is the "worst possible" sex assault a   15
person can sustain, that it deserves by far the severest punishment, equated in some states with the penalties for murder, while all other manner of sexual assaults are lumped together under the label of sodomy and draw lesser penalties by law, can only be seen as an outdated masculine concept that no longer applies to modern crime.

Sexual assault in our day and age is hardly restricted to forced genital   16
copulation, nor is it exclusively a male-on-female offense. Tradition and biologic opportunity have rendered vaginal rape a particular political crime with a particular political history, but the invasion may occur through the mouth or the rectum as well. And while the penis may remain the rapist's favorite weapon, his prime instrument of vengeance, his triumphant display of power, it is not in fact his only tool. Sticks, bottles and even fingers are often substituted for the "natural" thing. And as men may invade women through other orifices, so, too, do they invade other men. Who is to say that the sexual humiliation suffered through forced oral or rectal penetration is a lesser violation of the personal, private inner space, a lesser injury to mind, spirit and sense of self?

All acts of sex forced on unwilling victims deserve to be treated in   17
concept as equally grave offenses in the eyes of the law, for the avenue of penetration is less significant than the intent to degrade. Similarly, the gravity of the offense ought not be bound by the victim's gender. That the law must move in this direction seems clear.

A gender-free, non-activity-specific law governing all manner of sexual   18
assaults would be but the first step toward legal reform. The law must rid itself of other, outdated masculine concepts as well.

Since man first equated rape with the ruination of his wholly owned 19
property, the theft of his private treasure, he reflected his concern most
thunderously in the punishments that his law could impose. Today in
many states of the Union, a conviction for first-degree felonious rape
still draws a life sentence, and before the 1972 Supreme Court ruling that
abolished capital punishment, a number of Southern states set the penalty
at death. A modern perception of sexual assault that views the crime
strictly as an injury to the victim's bodily integrity, and not as an injury
to the purity or chastity of man's estate, must normalize the penalties
for such an offense and bring them in line more realistically with the
penalties for aggravated assault, the crime to which a sexual assault is
most closely related.

Here the law must move from its view that "carnal knowledge" is the 20
crux of the crime to an appreciation that the severity of the offense, and
the corresponding severity of the penalty that may be imposed, might
better be gauged by the severity of the objective physical injury sustained
by the victim during the course of the attack. Another criterion that the
law can reflect beyond objective physical injury in the imposition of
penalties is the manner in which the assault was accomplished. As the
current law distinguishes between the severity of an armed robbery versus an unarmed robbery, so must the law distinguish between the commission of a sexual assault with a deadly weapon—in which the threat
against the victim's life is manifest and self-evident—and a sexual assault
committed without a weapon. The participation of two or more offenders
is another useful indicator of the severity of a sexual assault, since a
number of assailants by their overwhelming presence constitutes a realistic threat of bodily harm.

Parenthetically I want to note at this point that I am one of those 21
people who view a prison sentence as a just and lawful societal solution
to the problem of criminal activity, the best solution we have at this time,
as civilized retribution and as a deterrent against the commission of future
crimes. Whether or not a term in jail is truly "rehabilitative" matters
less, I think, than whether or not a guilty offender is given the penalty
his crime deserves. It is important to be concerned with the treatment
offenders receive in prison, but a greater priority, it would seem, is to
ensure that offenders actually go to prison.*

Current feminist thinking on sexual assault legislation favors a system 22
of sentencing that ranges from six months to twenty years, depending on

* Since "Castrate Rapists" has become a slogan in certain circles, I guess I
  should say on the record that I am not "for" castration any more than I am
  "for" cutting off the ear of an informer or cutting off the hand of a thief. As
  for retaliatory killing, of which there have been a few recent cases, I would
  go along with the law and say that the concept of justifiable homicide in self-
  defense is sound, but premeditated murder some time after the act can never
  be condoned.

the severity of the crime. This approach strikes me as sound, even generous, for with good behavior, a prisoner may be paroled after one-third of his sentence is served. (As it stands now, a convicted rapist who goes to jail serves an average of forty-four months; the problem, however, is that few rapists actually reach jail.) A sexual assault case in which the victim has suffered permanent physical damage or disfigurement, or lasting psychological damage, should subject the offender to additional charges and penalties for aggravated assault as well.

Rape, as the current law defines it, is the forcible perpetration of an 23 act of sexual intercourse on the body of a woman *not one's wife.* The exemption from rape prosecutions granted to husbands who force their wives into acts of sexual union by physical means is as ancient as the original definition of criminal rape, which was synonymous with that quaint phrase of Biblical origin, "unlawful carnal knowledge." To our Biblical forefathers, any carnal knowledge outside the marriage contract was "unlawful." And any carnal knowledge within the marriage contract was, by definition, "lawful." Thus, as the law evolved, the idea that a husband could be prosecuted for raping his wife was unthinkable, for the law was conceived to protect *his* interests, not those of his wife. Sir Matthew Hale explained to his peers in the seventeenth century, "A husband cannot be guilty of rape upon his wife for by their mutual matrimonial consent and contract the wife hath given up herself in this kind to her husband, which she cannot retract." In other words, marriage implies consent to sexual intercourse at all times, and a husband has a lawful right to copulate with his wife against her will and by force according to the terms of their contract.

The most famous marital rape in literature, occurring onstage in the 24 popular television serial but offstage in the novel, is that of Irene by Soames in *The Forsyte Saga.* As Galsworthy presents the Soamesian logic, the logic of Everyhusband, although perhaps not of Galsworthy himself, the denied husband has "at last asserted his rights and acted like a man." In his morning-after solitude while he hears Irene still crying in the bedroom, Soames muses, "The incident was really of no great moment; women made a fuss about it in books; but in the cool judgment of right-thinking men, of men of the world, such as he recollected often received praise in the Divorce Court, he had but done his best to sustain the sanctity of marriage, to prevent her from abandoning her duty. . . . No, he did not regret it."

In the cool judgment of right-thinking women, compulsory sexual 25 intercourse is not a husband's right in marriage, for such a "right" gives the lie to any concept of equality and human dignity. Consent is better arrived at by husband and wife afresh each time, for if women are to be what we believe we are—equal partners—then intercourse must be construed as an act of mutual desire and not as a wifely "duty," enforced by the permissible threat of bodily harm or of economic sanctions.

In cases of rape within a marriage, the law must take a philosophic 26 leap of the greatest magnitude, for while the ancient concept of conjugal rights (female rights as well as male) might continue to have some validity in annulments and contested divorces—civil procedures conducted in courts of law—it must not be used as a shield to cover acts of force perpetrated by husbands on the bodies of their wives. There are those who believe that the current laws governing assault and battery are sufficient to deal with the cases of forcible rape in marriage, and those who take the more liberal stand that a sexual assault law might be applicable only to those men legally separated from their wives who return to "claim" their marital "right," but either of these solutions fails to come to grips with the basic violation.

Since the beginning of written history, criminal rape has been bound 27 up with the common law of consent in marriage, and it is time, once and for all, to make a clean break. A sexual assault is an invasion of bodily integrity and a violation of freedom and self-determination wherever it happens to take place, in or out of the marriage bed. I recognize that it is easier to write these words than to draw up a workable legal provision, and I recognize the difficulties that juries will have in their deliberations when faced with a wife who accuses her husband of forcing her into copulation against her will, but the principle of bodily self-determination must be established without qualification, I think, if it is to become an inviolable principle on any level. And revolutionary as this principle may appear to the traditions of Anglo-American jurisprudence, it is accepted as a matter of course and human dignity in the criminal codes of Sweden and Denmark and in the codes of the U.S.S.R. and other countries in the Communist bloc as well, although how it works out in practice I cannot say. (Certain of these European countries, including Switzerland and Yugoslavia, also equate economic threats, such as the threatened loss of a job, with threats of physical force in cases of rape.)

The concept of consent rears its formidable head in the much debated 28 laws of statutory rape, but here consent is construed in the opposite sense—not as something that cannot be retracted, as in marriage, but as something that cannot be given. Since the thirteenth-century Statutes of Westminster, the law has sought to fix an arbitrary age below which an act of sexual intercourse with a female, with or without the use of force, is deemed a criminal offense that deserves severe punishment because the female is too young to know her own mind. Coexistent with these statutory rape laws, and somewhat contradictory to them, have been the laws governing criminal incest, sexual victimization of a child by a blood relation, where the imposition of legal penalties has been charitably lenient, to say the least—yet another indication of the theoretical concept that the child "belongs" to the father's estate. Under current legislation, which is by no means uniform, a conviction for statutory rape may draw a life sentence in many jurisdictions, yet a conviction for incest rarely carries more than a ten-year sentence, approximately the same maximum penalty that is fixed by law for sodomy offenses.

If protection of the bodily integrity of all children is to be genuinely *29* reflected in the law, and not simply the protection of patriarchal interests, then the current division of offenses (statutory rape for outsiders; incest for members of the victim's family) must be erased. Retaining a fixed age of consent seems a necessary and humane measure for the protection of young girls and young boys alike, although it must be understood that any arbitrary age limit is at best a judicious compromise since sexual maturity and wisdom are not automatically conferred with the passage of time. Feminists who have applied themselves to this difficult question are in agreement that all children below the age of twelve deserve unqualified protection by a statutory age provision in sexual assault legislation, since that age is reasonably linked with the onset of puberty and awareness of sex, its biologic functions and repercussions. In line with the tradition of current statutory rape legislation, offenses committed against children below the age of twelve should carry the maximum penalty, normalized to twenty years. Recognizing that young persons above twelve and below sixteen remain particularly vulnerable to sexual coercion by adults who use a position of authority, rather than physical force, to achieve their aim (within the household or within an institution or a medical facility, to give three all-too-common examples), the law ought to be flexible enough to allow prosecutorial discretion in the handling of these cases under a more limited concept of "statutory sexual assault," with corresponding lesser penalties as the outer age limits are reached.

"Consent" has yet another role to play in a case of sexual assault. In *30* reviewing the act, in seeking to determine whether or not a crime was committed, the concept of consent that is debated in court hinges on whether or not the victim offered sufficient resistance to the attack, whether or not her will was truly overcome by the use of force or the threat of bodily harm. The peculiar nature of sexual crimes of violence, as much as man's peculiar historic perception of their meaning, has always clouded the law's perception of consent.

It is accepted without question that robbery victims need not prove *31* they resisted the robber, and it is never inferred that by handing over their money, they "consented" to the act and therefore the act was no crime. Indeed, police usually advise law-abiding citizens not to resist a robbery, but rather to wait it out patiently, report the offense to the proper authorities, and put the entire matter in the hands of the law. As a matter of fact, successful resistance to a robbery these days is considered heroic.

In certain middle-class neighborhoods in New York City, people who *32* must be out on the streets late at night, coming home from work, taking a trip to the deli, or walking the dog, have taken to carrying a ten-dollar bill as "mugger money" to satisfy the aims and rage of any robber who might accost them. Clearly, the feeling seems to be that the loss of a few bucks is a better bargain than the risk of physical violence. Handing over money at knife point, or dipping into one's wallet to assuage a weaponless but menacing figure on a dark, deserted street, may be financially painful or emotionally distressing, but it hardly compares to the massive insult to one's self-determination that is sustained during a sexual assault.

In a sexual assault physical harm is much more than a threat; it is a *33* reality because violence is an integral part of the act. Body contact and physical intrusion are the purpose of the crime, not appropriation of a physically detached and removable item like money. Yet the nature of the crime as it is practiced does bear robbery a close resemblance, because the sexual goal for the rapist resembles the monetary goal of the robber (often both goals are accomplished during the course of one confrontation if the victim is a woman), and so, in a sex crime, a bargain between offender and victim may also be struck. In this respect, a sexual assault is closer in victim response to a robbery than it is to a simple case of assault, for an assaultive event may not have a specific goal beyond the physical contest, and furthermore, people who find themselves in an assaultive situation usually defend themselves by fighting back.

Under the rules of law, victims of robbery and assault are not required *34* to prove they resisted, or that they didn't consent, or that the act was accomplished with sufficient force, or sufficient threat of force, to overcome their will, because the law presumes it highly unlikely that a person willingly gives away money, except to a charity or to a favorite cause, and the law presumes that no person willingly submits to a brutal beating and the infliction of bodily harm and permanent damage. But victims of rape and other forms of sexual assault do need to prove these evidentiary requirements—that they resisted, that they didn't consent, that their will was overcome by overwhelming force and fear—because the law has never been able to satisfactorily distinguish an act of mutually desired sexual union from an act of forced, criminal sexual aggression.

Admittedly, part of the law's confusion springs from the normal, bio- *35* logic, male procedural activity in an act of *unforced* copulation, but insertion of the penis (a descriptive phrase less semantically loaded than penetration, I think) is not in itself, despite what many men think, an act of male dominance. The real reason for the law's everlasting confusion as to what constitutes an act of rape and what constitutes an act of mutual intercourse is the underlying cultural assumption that it is the natural masculine role to proceed aggressively toward the stated goal, while the natural feminine role is to "resist" or "submit." And so to protect male interests, the law seeks to gauge the victim's behavior during the offending act in the belief that force or the threat of force is not conclusive *in and of itself.*

According to Menachem Amir's study, the assailant actually displays *36* a dangerous weapon in no more than one-fifth of all police-founded cases of rape. Clearly, these are the cases a jury would most likely believe. But most rapes are not accomplished by means of a knife, a gun, a lead pipe or whatever. The force that is employed more often consists of an initial stranglehold, manhandling, beating, shoving, tearing at clothes, a verbal threat of death or disfigurement, the sheer physical presence of two, three, four, five assailants, etc. Without doubt, any of these circumstances can and does produce immobilizing terror in a victim, terror sufficient to render her incapable of resistance or to make her believe that resistance would be futile.

Currently employed standards of resistance or consent *vis-à-vis* force *37* or the threat of force have never been able to accurately gauge a victim's terror, since terror is a psychological reaction and not an objective standard that can be read on a behavior meter six months later in court, as jury acquittal rates plainly show. For this reason, feminists have argued that the special burden of proof that devolves on a rape victim, that she resisted "within reason," that her eventual compliance was no indication of tacit "consent," is patently unfair, since such standards are not applied in court to the behavior of victims in other kinds of violent crime. A jury should be permitted to weigh the word of a victimized complainant at face value, that is what it boils down to—no more or less a right than is granted to other victims under the law.

Not only is the victim's response during the act measured and weighed, *38* her past sexual history is scrutinized under the theory that it relates to her "tendency to consent," or that it reflects on her credibility, her veracity, her predisposition to tell the truth or to lie. Or so the law says. As it works out in practice, juries presented with evidence concerning a woman's past sexual history make use of such information to form a moral judgment on her character, and here all the old myths of rape are brought into play, for the feeling persists that a virtuous woman either cannot get raped or does not get into situations that leave her open to assault. Thus the questions in the jury room become "Was she or wasn't she asking for it?"; "If she had been a decent woman, wouldn't she have fought to the death to defend her 'treasure'?"; and "Is this bimbo worth the ruination of a man's career and reputation?"

The crime of rape must be totally separated from all traditional con- *39* cepts of chastity, for the very meaning of chastity presupposes that it is a woman's duty (but not a man's) to refrain from sex outside the matrimonial union. That sexual activity renders a woman "unchaste" is a totally male view of the female as *his* pure vessel. The phrase "prior chastity" as well as the concept must be stricken from the legal lexicon, along with "prosecutrix," as inflammatory and prejudicial to a complainant's case.

A history of sexual activity with many partners may be indicative of 40 a female's healthy interest in sex, or it may be indicative of a chronic history of victimization and exploitation in which she could not assert her own inclinations; it may be indicative of a spirit of adventure, a spirit of rebellion, a spirit of curiosity, a spirit of joy or a spirit of defeat. Whatever the reasons, and there are many, prior consensual intercourse between a rape complainant and other partners of her choosing should not be scrutinized as an indicator of purity or impurity of mind or body, not in this day and age at any rate, and it has no place in jury room deliberation as to whether or not, in the specific instance in question, an act of forcible sex took place. Prior consensual intercourse between the complainant and *the defendant* does have some relevance, and such information probably should not be barred.

An overhaul of present laws and a fresh approach to sexual assault 41 legislation must go hand in hand with a fresh approach to enforcing the law. The question of who interprets and who enforces the statutes is as important as the contents of the law itself. At present, female victims of sexual crimes of violence who seek legal justice must rely on a series of male authority figures whose masculine orientation, values and fears place them securely in the offender's camp.

The most bitter irony of rape, I think, has been the historic masculine 42 fear of false accusation, a fear that has found expression in male folklore since the Biblical days of Joseph the Israelite and Potiphar's wife, that was given new life and meaning in the psychoanalytic doctrines of Sigmund Freud and his followers, and that has formed the crux of the legal defense against a rape charge, aided and abetted by that special set of evidentiary standards (consent, resistance, chastity, corroboration) designed with one collective purpose in mind: to protect the male against a scheming, lying, vindictive woman.

Fear of false accusation is not entirely without merit in any criminal 43 case, as is the problem of misidentification, an honest mistake, but the irony, of course, is that while men successfully convinced each other and us that women cry rape with ease and glee, the reality of rape is that victimized women have always been reluctant to report the crime and seek legal justice—because of the shame of public exposure, because of that complex double standard that makes a female feel culpable, even responsible, for any act of sexual aggression committed against her, because of possible retribution from the assailant (once a woman has been raped, the threat of a return engagement understandably looms large), and because women have been presented with sufficient evidence to come to the realistic conclusion that their accounts are received with a harsh cynicism that forms the first line of male defense.

A decade ago the FBI's *Uniform Crime Reports* noted that 20 percent   *44*
of all rapes reported to the police "were determined by investigation to
be unfounded." By 1973 the figure had dropped to 15 percent, while rape
remained, in the FBI's words, "the most under-reported crime." A 15
percent figure for false accusations is undeniably high, yet when New
York City instituted a special sex crimes analysis squad and put police-
women (instead of men) in charge of interviewing complainants, the
number of false charges in New York dropped dramatically to 2 percent,
a figure that corresponded exactly to the rate of false reports for other
violent crimes. The lesson in the mystery of the vanishing statistic is
obvious. Women believe the word of other women. Men do not.

That women have been excluded by tradition and design from all   *45*
significant areas of law enforcement, from the police precinct, from the
prosecutor's office, from the jury box and from the judge's bench, up to
and including the appellate and supreme court jurisdictions, has created
a double handicap for rape victims seeking justice under the laws of
man's devise. And so it is not enough that the face of the law be changed
to reflect the reality; the faces of those charged with the awesome responsibility of enforcing the law and securing justice must change as well.

I am convinced that the battle to achieve parity with men in the critical   *46*
area of law enforcement will be the ultimate testing ground on which full
equality for women will be won or lost. Law enforcement means quite
literally the use of force when necessary, to maintain the social order,
and force since the days of the rudimentary *lex talionis* has been a male
prerogative because of size, weight, strength, biologic construction and
deliberate training, training from which women have been barred by
custom as stern as the law itself.

If in the past women had no choice but to let men be our lawful   *47*
protectors, leaving to them not only the law but its enforcement, it would
now seem to be an urgent priority to correct the imbalance. For things
have come full circle. The biologic possibility that allows the threat and
use of rape still exists, but our social contract has reached a point of
sophistication whereby brute force matters less to the maintenance of
law and order, or so I believe. I am not unaware that members of the
police force in various cities have shown considerable reluctance to admit
that size and strength may not be the prime factor in the making of an
effective police officer, and they may be temporarily pardoned for sticking
to outdated male values. New studies show quite conclusively that
women police officers are as effective as men in calming a disturbance
and in making an arrest, and they accomplish their work in potentially
violent situations without resorting to the unnecessary force that deserves
its label, "police brutality."

I am not one to throw the word "revolutionary" around lightly, but   *48*
full integration of our cities' police departments, and by full I mean fifty-
fifty, no less, is a revolutionary goal of the utmost importance to women's

rights. And if we are to continue to have armies, as I suspect we will for some time to come, then they, too, must be fully integrated, as well as our national guard, our state troopers, our local sheriffs' offices, our district attorneys' offices, our state prosecuting attorneys' offices—in short, the nation's entire lawful *power* structure (and I mean power in the physical sense) must be stripped of male dominance and control—if women are to cease being a colonized protectorate of men.

A system of criminal justice and forceful authority that genuinely 49 works for the protection of women's rights, and most specifically the right not to be sexually assaulted by men, can become an efficient mechanism in the control of rape insofar as it brings offenders speedily to trial, presents the case for the complainant in the best possible light, and applies just penalties upon conviction. While I would not underestimate the beneficial effects of workable sex assault laws to "hold the line" and provide a positive deterrent, what feminists (and all right-thinking people) must look toward is the total eradication of rape, and not just an effective policy of containment.

A new approach to the law and to law enforcement can take us only 50 part of the way. Turning over to women 50 percent of the power to enforce the law and maintain the order will be a major step toward eliminating *machismo*. However, the ideology of rape is aided by more than a system of lenient laws that serve to protect offenders and is abetted by more than the fiat of total male control over the lawful use of power. The ideology of rape is fueled by cultural values that are perpetuated at every level of our society, and nothing less than a frontal attack is needed to repel this cultural assault.

The theory of aggressive male domination over women as a natural 51 right is so deeply embedded in our cultural value system that all recent attempts to expose it—in movies, television commercials or even in children's textbooks—have barely managed to scratch the surface. As I see it, the problem is not that polarized role playing (man as doer; woman as bystander) and exaggerated portrayals of the female body as passive sex object are simply "demeaning" to women's dignity and self-conception, or that such portrayals fail to provide positive role models for young girls, but that cultural sexism is a conscious form of female degradation designed to boost the male ego by offering "proof" of his native superiority (and of female inferiority) everywhere he looks.

Critics of the women's movement, when they are not faulting us for 52 being slovenly, straggly-haired, construction-booted, whiny sore losers who refuse to accept our female responsibilities, often profess to see a certain inexplicable Victorian primness and antisexual prudery in our attitudes and responses. "Come on, gals," they say in essence, "don't you know that your battle for female liberation is part of our larger battle for sexual liberation? Free yourselves from all your old hang-ups! Stop pretending that you are actually offended by those four-letter words and animal noises we grunt in your direction on the street in appreciation of your womanly charms. When we plaster your faceless naked body on the cover of our slick magazines, which sell millions of copies, we do it in sensual obeisance to your timeless beauty—which, by our estimation, ceases to be timeless at age twenty or thereabouts. If we feel the need for a little fun and go out and rent the body of a prostitute for a half hour or so, we are merely engaging in a mutual act between two consenting adults, and what's it got to do with you? When we turn our movie theaters into showcases for pornographic films and convert our book-stores to outlets for mass-produced obscene smut, not only should you marvel at the wonders of our free-enterprise system, but you should applaud us for pushing back the barriers of repressive middle-class mo-rality, and for our strenuous defense of all the civil liberties you hold so dear, because we have made obscenity the new frontier in defense of freedom of speech, that noble liberal tradition. And surely you're not against civil liberties and freedom of speech, now, are you?"

The case against pornography and the case against toleration of pros- 53 titution are central to the fight against rape, and if it angers a large part of the liberal population to be so informed, then I would question in turn the political understanding of such liberals and their true concern for the rights of women. Or to put it more gently, a feminist analysis approaches all prior assumptions, including those of the great, unquestioned liberal tradition, with a certain open-minded suspicion, for all prior traditions have worked against the cause of women and no set of values, including that of tolerant liberals, is above review or challenge. After all, the liberal *politik* has had less input from the feminist perspective than from any other modern source; it does not by its own considerable virtue embody a perfection of ideals, it has no special claim on goodness, rather, it is most receptive to those values to which it has been made sensitive by others.

The defense lawyer mentality had such a hold over the liberal tradition 54 that when we in the women's movement first began to politicize rape back in 1971, and found ourselves on the side of the prosecutor's office in demanding that New York State's rape laws be changed to eliminate the requirement of corroborative proof, the liberal establishment as rep-resented by the American Civil Liberties Union was up in arms. Two years later the ACLU had become sensitized to the plight of rape victims under the rules of law, thanks to the lobbying efforts of feminist lawyers, and once this new concern for rape victims was balanced against the ACLU's longstanding and just concern for the rights of all defendants, the civil-liberties organization withdrew its opposition to corroboration repeal. This, I believe, was a philosophic change of significant propor-tions, and perhaps it heralds major changes to come. In any event, those of us who know our history recall that when the women's liberation movement was birthed by the radical left, the first serious struggle we faced was to free ourselves from the structures, thought processes and priorities of what we came to call the *male* left—and so if we now find ourselves in philosophic disagreement with the thought processes and priorities of what has been no less a male liberal tradition, we should not find it surprising.

Once we accept as basic truth that rape is not a crime of irrational, 55 impulsive, uncontrollable lust, but is a deliberate, hostile, violent act of degradation and possession on the part of a would-be conqueror, designed to intimidate and inspire fear, we must look toward those elements in our culture that promote and propagandize these attitudes, which offer men, and in particular, impressionable, adolescent males, who form the potential raping population, the ideology and psychologic encouragement to commit their acts of aggression *without awareness, for the most part, that they have committed a punishable crime,* let alone a moral wrong. The myth of the heroic rapist that permeates false notions of masculinity, from the successful seducer to the man who "takes what he wants when he wants it," is inculcated in young boys from the time they first become aware that being a male means access to certain mysterious rites and privileges, including the right to buy a woman's body. When young men learn that females may be bought for a price, and that acts of sex command set prices, then how should they not also conclude that that which may be bought may also be taken without the civility of a monetary exchange?

That there *might* be a connection between prostitution and rape is 56 certainly not a new idea. Operating from the old (and discredited) lust, drive and relief theory, men have occasionally put forward the notion that the way to control criminal rape is to ensure the ready accessibility of female bodies at a reasonable price through the legalization of prostitution, so that the male impulse might be satisfied with ease, efficiency and a minimum of bother. Alas for these androcentric pragmatists, even Dr. Kinsey could unearth "no adequate data to prove the truth or falsity" of such a connection. Twenty years after Kinsey others of a similar mind were still trying, although the evidence still suggested that men who make frequent use of brothels are several years older than men who are usually charged with criminal rape. To my mind the experience of the American military in Vietnam, where brothels for GI's were officially sanctioned, even incorporated into the base-camp recreation areas, should prove conclusively that the availability of sex for a small price is no deterrent to the decision to rape, any more than the availability of a base-camp shooting range is a deterrent to the killing of unarmed civilians and children.

But my horror at the idea of legalized prostitution is not that it doesn't 57 work as a rape deterrent, but that it institutionalizes the concept that it is man's monetary right, if not his divine right, to gain access to the female body, and that sex is a female service that should not be denied the civilized male. Perpetuation of the concept that the "powerful male impulse" must be satisfied with immediacy by a cooperative class of women, set aside and expressly licensed for this purpose, is part and parcel of the mass psychology of rape. Indeed, until the day is reached when prostitution is totally eliminated (a millennium that will not arrive until men, who create the demand, and not women who supply it, are fully prosecuted under the law), the false perception of sexual access as an adjunct of male power and privilege will continue to fuel the rapist mentality.

Pornography has been so thickly glossed over with the patina of chic *58* these days in the name of verbal freedom and sophistication that important distinctions between freedom of political expression (a democratic necessity), honest sex education for children (a societal good) and ugly smut (the deliberate devaluation of the role of women through obscene, distorted depictions) have been hopelessly confused. Part of the problem is that those who traditionally have been the most vigorous opponents of porn are often those same people who shudder at the explicit mention of any sexual subject. Under their watchful, vigilante eyes, frank and free dissemination of educational materials relating to abortion, contraception, the act of birth, and female biology in general is also dangerous, subversive and dirty. (I am not unmindful that a frank and free discussion of rape, "the unspeakable crime," might well give these righteous vigilantes further cause to shudder.) Because the battle lines were falsely drawn a long time ago, before there was a vocal women's movement, the anti-pornography forces appear to be, for the most part, religious, Southern, conservative and right-wing, while the pro-porn forces are identified as Eastern, atheistic and liberal.

But a woman's perspective demands a totally new alignment, or at *59* least a fresh appraisal. The majority report of the President's Commission on Obscenity and Pornography (1970), a report that argued strongly for the removal of all legal restrictions on pornography, soft and hard, made plain that 90 percent of all pornographic material is geared to the male heterosexual market (the other 10 percent is geared to the male homosexual taste), that buyers of porn are "predominantly white, middle-class, middle-aged married males" and that the graphic depictions, the meat and potatoes of porn, are of the naked female body and of the multiplicity of acts done to that body.

Discussing the content of stag films, "a familiar and firmly established *60* part of the American scene," the commission report dutifully, if foggily, explained, "Because pornography historically has been thought to be primarily a masculine interest, the emphasis in stag films seems to represent the preferences of the middle-class American male. Thus male homosexuality and bestiality are relatively rare, while lesbianism is rather common."

The commissioners in this instance had merely verified what purveyors 61
of porn have always known: hard-core pornography is not a celebration
of sexual freedom; it is a cynical exploitation of female sexual activity
through the device of making all such activity, and consequently all
females, "dirty." Heterosexual male consumers of pornography are
frankly turned on by watching lesbians in action (although never in the
final scenes, but always as a curtain raiser); they are turned off with the
sudden swiftness of a water faucet by watching naked men act upon each
other. One study quoted in the commission report came to the unas-
tounding conclusion that "seeing a stag film in the presence of male peers
bolsters masculine esteem." Indeed. The men in groups who watch the
films, it is important to note, are *not* naked.

When male response to pornography is compared to female response, 62
a pronounced difference in attitude emerges. According to the commission, "Males report being more highly aroused by depictions of nude
females, and show more interest in depiction of nude females than [do]
females." Quoting the figures of Alfred Kinsey, the commission noted
that a majority of males (77 percent) were "aroused" by visual depictions
of explicit sex while a majority of females (68 percent) were not aroused.
Further, "females more often than males reported 'disgust' and 'offense.'"

From whence comes this female disgust and offense? Are females 63
sexually backward or more conservative by nature? The gut distaste
that a majority of women feel when we look at pornography, a distaste
that, incredibly, it is no longer fashionable to admit, comes, I think, from
the gut knowledge that we and our bodies are being stripped, exposed
and contorted for the purpose of ridicule to bolster that "masculine
esteem" which gets its kick and sense of power from viewing females as
anonymous, panting playthings, adult toys, dehumanized objects to be
used, abused, broken and discarded.

This, of course, is also the philosophy of rape. It is no accident (for 64
what else could be its purpose?) that females in the pornographic genre
are depicted in two cleanly delineated roles: as virgins who are caught
and "banged" or as nymphomaniacs who are never sated. The most
popular and prevalent pornographic fantasy combines the two: an innocent, untutored female is raped and "subjected to unnatural practices"
that turn her into a raving, slobbering nymphomaniac, a dependent sexual
slave who can never get enough of the big, male cock.

There can be no "equality" in porn, no female equivalent, no turning 65
of the tables in the name of bawdy fun. Pornography, like rape, is a
male invention, designed to dehumanize women, to reduce the female to
an object of sexual access, not to free sensuality from moralistic or
parental inhibition. The staple of porn will always be the naked female
body, breasts and genitals exposed, because as man devised it, her naked

body is the female's "shame," her private parts the private property of man, while his are the ancient, holy, universal, patriarchal instrument of his power, his rule by force over *her*.

Pornography is the undiluted essence of anti-female propaganda. Yet *66* the very same liberals who were so quick to understand the method and purpose behind the mighty propaganda machine of Hitler's Third Reich, the consciously spewed-out anti-Semitic caricatures and obscenities that gave an ideological base to the Holocaust and the Final Solution, the very same liberals who, enlightened by blacks, searched their own conscience and came to understand that their tolerance of "nigger" jokes and portrayals of shuffling, rolling-eyed servants in movies perpetuated the degrading myths of black inferiority and gave an ideological base to the continuation of black oppression—these very same liberals now fervidly maintain that the hatred and contempt for women that find expression in four-letter words used as expletives and in what are quaintly called "adult" or "erotic" books and movies are a valid extension of freedom of speech that must be preserved as a Constitutional right.

To defend the right of a lone, crazed American Nazi to grind out *67* propaganda calling for the extermination of all Jews, as the ACLU has done in the name of free speech, is, after all, a self-righteous and not particularly courageous stand, for American Jewry is not currently threatened by storm troopers, concentration camps and imminent extermination, but I wonder if the ACLU's position might change if, come tomorrow morning, the bookstores and movie theaters lining Forty-second Street in New York City were devoted not to the humiliation of women by rape and torture, as they currently are, but to a systematized, commercially successful propaganda machine depicting the sadistic pleasures of gassing Jews or lynching blacks?

Is this analogy extreme? Not if you are a woman who is conscious *68* of the ever-present threat of rape and the proliferation of a cultural ideology that makes it sound like "liberated" fun. The majority report of the President's Commission on Obscenity and Pornography tried to pooh-pooh the opinion of law enforcement agencies around the country that claimed their own concrete experience with offenders who were caught with the stuff led them to conclude that pornographic material is a causative factor in crimes of sexual violence. The commission maintained that it was not possible at this time to scientifically prove or disprove such a connection.

But does one need scientific methodology in order to conclude that *69* the anti-female propaganda that permeates our nation's cultural output promotes a climate in which acts of sexual hostility directed against women are not only tolerated but ideologically encouraged? A similar debate has raged for many years over whether or not the extensive glorification of violence (the gangster as hero; the loving treatment accorded bloody shoot-'em-ups in movies, books and on TV) has a causal effect, a direct relationship to the rising rate of crime, particularly among youth. Interestingly enough, in this area—nonsexual and not specifically related to abuses against women—public opinion seems to be swinging to the position that explicit violence in the entertainment media does have a deleterious effect; it makes violence commonplace, numbingly routine and no longer morally shocking.

More to the point, those who call for a curtailment of scenes of   *70* violence in movies and on television in the name of sensitivity, good taste and what's best for our children are not accused of being pro-censorship or against freedom of speech. Similarly, minority group organizations, black, Hispanic, Japanese, Italian, Jewish, or American Indian, that campaign against ethnic slurs and demeaning portrayals in movies, on television shows and in commercials are perceived as waging a just political fight, for if a minority group claims to be offended by a specific portrayal, be it Little Black Sambo or the Frito Bandito, and relates it to a history of ridicule and oppression, few liberals would dare to trot out a Constitutional argument in theoretical opposition, not if they wish to maintain their liberal credentials. Yet when it comes to the treatment of women, the liberal consciousness remains fiercely obdurate, refusing to be budged, for the sin of appearing square or prissy in the age of the so-called sexual revolution has become the worst offense of all.

A law that reflects the female reality and a social system that no longer   *71* shuts women out of its enforcement and does not promote a masculine ideology of rape will go a long way toward the elimination of crimes of sexual violence, but the last line of defense shall always be our female bodies and our female minds. In making rape a *speakable* crime, not a matter of shame, the women's movement has already fired the first retaliatory shots in a war as ancient as civilization. When, just a few years ago, we began to hold our speak-outs on rape, our conferences, borrowing a church meeting hall for an afternoon, renting a high-school auditorium and some classrooms for a weekend of workshops and discussion, the world out there, the world outside of radical feminism, thought it was all very funny.

"You're talking about *rape*? Incredible! A *political* crime against   *72* women? How is a sex crime political? You're actually having women give testimony about their own rapes and what happened to them afterwards, the police, the hospitals, the courts? Far out!" And then the nervous giggles that betray confusion, fear and shame disappeared and in their place was the dim recognition that in daring to speak the unspoken, women had uncovered yet another part of our oppression, perhaps the central key: historic physical repression, a conscious process of intimidation, guilt and fear.

Within two years the world out there had stopped laughing, and the   *73* movement had progressed beyond the organizational forms of speak-outs

and conferences, our internal consciousness-raising, to community out-
reach programs that were imaginative, original and unprecedented: rape
crisis centers with a telephone hot line staffed twenty-four hours a day
to provide counseling, procedural information and sisterly solidarity to
recent rape victims and even to those whose assault had taken place
years ago but who never had the chance to talk it out with other women
and release their suppressed rage; rape legislation study groups to work
up model codes based on a fresh approach to the law and to work with
legislators to get new laws adopted; anti-rape projects in conjunction with
the emergency ward of a city hospital, in close association with police-
women staffing newly formed sex crime analysis squads and investigative
units. With pamphlets, newsletters, bumper stickers, "Wanted" posters,
combative   slogans—"STOP   RAPE";   "WAR—WOMEN   AGAINST
RAPE"; "SMASH SEXISM, DISARM RAPISTS!"—and with classes in
self-defense, women turned around and seized the offensive.

   The wonder of all this female activity, decentralized grassroots organ- 74
izations and programs that sprung up independently in places like Seattle,
Indianapolis, Ann Arbor, Toronto, and Boulder, Colorado, is that none
of it had been predicted, encouraged, or faintly suggested by men anywhere in their stern rules of caution, their friendly advice, their fatherly
solicitude in more than five thousand years of written history. That
women should *organize* to combat rape was a women's movement invention.

   Men are not unmindful of the rape problem. To the contrary, their 75
paternalistic codes reserved the harshest penalties for a violation of their
property. But given an approach to rape that saw the crime as an illegal
encroachment by an unlicensed intruder, a stranger come into their midst,
the advice they gave (and still try to give) was all of one piece: a set of
rules and regulations designed to keep their property penned in, much
as a sheepherder might try to keep his flock protected from an outlaw
rustler by taking precautions against their straying too far from the fold.
By seeing the rapist always as a stranger, never as one of their own, and
by viewing the female as a careless, dumb creature with an unfortunate
tendency to stray, they exhorted, admonished and warned the female to
hide herself from male eyes as much as possible. In short, they told her
not to claim the privileges they reserved for themselves. Such advice—
well intentioned, solicitous and genuinely concerned—succeeded only in
further aggravating the problem, for the message they gave was to live a
life of fear, and to it they appended the dire warning that the woman who
did not follow the rules must be held responsible for her own violation.

   Clinton Duffy, the famous warden of San Quentin, couldn't understand 76
why women didn't imprison themselves under maximum security conditions for their own protection. He wrote, "Many break the most elementary rules of caution every day. The particularly flagrant violators,

those who go to barrooms alone, or accept pickups from strangers, or wear unusually tight sweaters and skirts, or make a habit of teasing, become rape bait by their actions alone. When it happens they have nobody to blame but themselves."

Duffy heaped scorn on women who "regularly break commonsense 77 rules of caution" by neglecting to draw the shades or put out the light while undressing, by forgetting to lock all doors and windows, by failing "to report telephone callers who hang up when they answer, or suspicious-looking loiterers," by letting a lone male stranger into the house, by walking home alone late at night. "If it's impossible for a woman to keep off lonely streets at night," he instructed, "she should walk near the curb with her head up and her eyes straight forward, move rapidly and keep going. . . . Women in these situations should carry a police whistle in the palm of their hand until they are out of the danger area. Ridiculous as it may sound," he concluded, "women should be careful to hang underwear out to dry in the least conspicuous places on the line. If a woman lives alone she shouldn't hang it outside at all."

A fairly decent article on rape in the March, 1974, issue of *The Read-* 78 *er's Digest* was written by two men who felt obliged to warn,

Don't broadcast the fact that you live alone or with another woman. List only your last name and initial on the mailbox and in the phone book. Before entering your car, check to see if anyone is hiding on the rear seat or on the rear floor. If you're alone in a car, keep the doors locked and the windows rolled up. If you think someone is following you . . . do not go directly home if there is no adult male there. Possible weapons are a hatpin, corkscrew, pen, keys, umbrella. If no weapons are available, fight back physically *only* if you feel you can do so with telling effect.

What immediately pops into mind after reading the advice of Warden 79 Duffy and *The Reader's Digest* is the old-time stand-up comedian's favorite figure of ridicule, the hysterical old maid armed with hatpin and umbrella who looks under the bed each night before retiring. Long a laughable stereotype of sexual repression, it now appears that the crazy old lady was a pioneer of sound mind after all.

But the negative value of this sort of advice, I'm afraid, far outweighs 80 the positive. What it tells us, implicitly and explicitly, is:

1. A woman alone probably won't be able to defend herself. Another 81 woman who might possibly come to her aid will be of no use whatsoever.

2. Despite the fact that it is men who are the rapists, a woman's 82 ultimate security lies in being accompanied by men at all times.

3. A woman who claims to value her sexual integrity cannot expect 83 the same amount of freedom and independence that men routinely enjoy.

Even a small pleasure like taking a spin in an automobile with the windows open is dangerous, reckless behavior.

4. In the exercise of rational caution, a woman should engage in an 84 amazing amount of pretense. She should pretend she has a male protector even if she hasn't. She should deny or obscure her personal identity, life-style and independence, and function on a sustained level of suspicion that approaches a clinical definition of paranoia.

Of course I think all people, female and male, child and adult, must 85 be alert and on guard against the warning signs of criminal violence and should take care in potentially hazardous situations, such as a dark, unfamiliar street at night, or an unexpected knock on the door, but to impose a special burden of caution on women is no solution at all. There can be no private solutions to the problem of rape. A woman who follows this sort of special cautionary advice to the letter and thinks she is acting in society's interest—or even in her own personal interest—is deluding herself rather sadly. While the risk to one potential victim might be slightly diminished (and I even doubt this, since I have known of nuns who were raped within walled convents), not only does the number of potential rapists on the loose remain constant, but the ultimate effect of rape upon the woman's mental and emotional health has been accomplished *even without the act.* For to accept a special burden of self-protection is to reinforce the concept that women must live and move about in fear and can never expect to achieve the personal freedom, independence and self-assurance of men.

That's what rape is all about, isn't it? And a possible deep-down 86 reason why even the best of our concerned, well-meaning men run to stereotypic warnings when they seek to grapple with the problem of rape deterrence is that they *prefer* to see rape as a woman's problem, rather than as a societal problem resulting from a distorted masculine philosophy of aggression. For when men raise the spectre of the unknown rapist, they refuse to take psychologic responsibility for the nature of his act.

We know, or at least the statistics tell us, that no more than half of all 87 reported rapes are the work of strangers, and in the hidden statistics, those four out of five rapes that go unreported, the percent committed by total strangers is probably lower. The man who jumps out of the alley or crawls through the window is the man who, if caught, will be called "the rapist" by his fellow men. But the known man who presses his advantage, who uses his position of authority, who forces his attentions (fine Victorian phrase), who will not take "No" for an answer, who assumes that sexual access is his right-of-way and physical aggression his right-on expression of masculinity, conquest and power is no less of a rapist—yet the chance that this man will be brought to justice, even under the best of circumstances, is comparatively small.

I am of the opinion that the most perfect rape laws in the land, strictly *88* enforced by the best concerned citizens, will not be enough to stop rape. Obvious offenders will be punished, and that in itself will be a significant change, but the huge gray area of sexual exploitation, of women who are psychologically coerced into acts of intercourse they do not desire because they do not have the wherewithal to physically, or even psychologically, resist, will remain a problem beyond any possible solution of criminal justice. It would be deceitful to claim that the murky gray area of male sexual aggression and female passivity and submission can ever be made amenable to legal divination—nor should it be, in the final analysis. Nor should a feminist advocate to her sisters that the best option in a threatening, unpleasant situation is to endure the insult and later take her case to the courts.

Unfortunately for strict constructionists and those with neat, orderly *89* minds, the male-female sexual dynamic at this stage in our human development lends itself poorly to objective arbitration. A case of rape and a case of unpleasant but not quite criminal sexual extortion in which a passive, egoless woman succumbs because it never occurred to her that she might, with effort, repel the advance (and afterward quite justifiably feels "had") flow from the same oppressive male ideology, and the demarcation line between the two is far from clear. But these latter cases, of which there are many, reflect not only the male ideology of rape but a female paralysis of will, the result of a deliberate, powerful and destructive "feminine" conditioning.

The psychologic edge men hold in a situation characterized by sexual *90* aggression is far more critical to the final outcome than their larger size and heavier weight. They *know* they know how to fight, for they have been trained and encouraged to use their bodies aggressively and competitively since early childhood. Young girls, on the other hand, are taught to disdain physical combat, healthy sports competition, and winning, because such activities dangerously threaten the conventional societal view of what is appropriate, ladylike, feminine behavior. The case for a strong mind in a strong body as a necessary step in the battle for equality (which Susan B. Anthony argued for vehemently in the earliest issues of her feminist newspaper, *The Revolution*) is being dramatically and effectively argued each day by our professional female athletes— who at long last are becoming female stars—and by recent struggles to integrate the Little League and to equalize expenditures for female sports programs in grade schools, high schools and colleges.

This sudden upsurge of interest in female athletics is more than a *91* matter of giving girls who like sports a chance to fully explore their potential. It is based on a new female recognition (something men have always known) that there are important lessons to be learned from sports competition, among them that winning is the result of hard, sustained and serious training, cool, clever strategy that includes the use of tricks and bluffs, and a positive mind-set that puts all reflex systems on "go." This knowledge, and the chance to put it in practice, is precisely what women have been conditioned to abjure.

It is no wonder, then, that most women confronted by physical aggres-   92 sion fall apart at the seams and suffer a paralysis of will. We have been trained to cry, to wheedle, to plead, to look for a male protector, but we have never been trained to fight and win.

Prohibitions against a fighting female go back to the Bible. In one of   93 the more curious passages in Deuteronomy it is instructed that when two men are fighting and the wife of one seeks to come to his aid and "drag her husband clear of his opponent, if she puts out her hand and catches hold of the man's genitals, you shall cut off her hand and show her no mercy." When the patriarchs wrote the law, it would seem, they were painfully cognizant of woman's one natural advantage in combat and were determined to erase it from her memory.

Man's written law evolved from a rudimentary system of retaliatory   94 force, a system to which women were not particularly well adapted to begin with, and from which women were deliberately excluded, osten- sibly for our own protection, as time went by. Combat has been such a traditional, exclusionary province of man that the very idea of a fighting woman often brings laughter, distaste or disbelief and the opinion that it must be "unnatural." In a confusion partially of their own making, local police precincts put out contradictory messages: they "unfound" a rape case because, by the rule of their own male logic, the woman did not show normal resitance; they report on an especially brutal rape case and announce to the press that the multiple stab wounds were the work of an assailant who was enraged because the woman resisted.

Unthinkingly cruel, because it is deceptive, is the confidential advice   95 given from men to women (it appears in *The Reader's Digest* article), or even from women to women in some feminist literature, that a sharp kick to the groin or a thumb in the eye will work miracles. Such advice is often accompanied by a diagram in which the vulnerable points of the human anatomy are clearly marked—as if the mere knowledge of these pressure spots can translate itself into devastating action. It is true that this knowledge has been deliberately obscured or withheld from us in the past, but mere knowledge is not enough. What women need is systematic training in self-defense that begins in childhood, so that the inhibition resulting from the prohibition may be overcome.

It would be decidedly less than honest if at this juncture I did not   96 admit that my researches for this book included a three-month training program in jujitsu and karate, three nights a week, two and a half hours a night, that ended summarily one evening when I crashed to the mat and broke my collarbone. I lost one month of writing and the perfect symmetry of my clavicular structure, but I gained a new identification with the New York Mets' injury list, a recognition that age thirty-eight is not the most propitious time in life *to begin* to learn how to kick and hit and break a stranglehold, and a new and totally surprising awareness of my body's potential to inflict real damage. I learned I had natural weapons that I didn't know I possessed, like elbows and knees. I learned how to kick backward as well as forward. I learned how to fight dirty, and I learned that I loved it.

Most surprising to me, I think, was the recognition that these basic aggressive movements, the sudden twists, jabs and punches that were so foreign to my experience and ladylike existence, were the stuff that all little boys grow up learning, that boy kids are applauded for mastering while girl kids are put in fresh white pinafores and patent-leather Mary Janes and told not to muss them up. And did that early difference in rearing ever raise its draconic head! At the start of our lessons our Japanese instructor freely invited all the women in the class, one by one, to punch him in the chest. It was not a foolhardy invitation, for we discovered that the inhibition against hitting was so strong in each of us that on the first try none of us could make physical contact. Indeed, the inhibition against striking out proved to be a greater hindrance to our becoming fighting women than our pathetic underdeveloped muscles. (Improvement in both departments was amazingly swift.) 97

Not surprisingly, the men in our class did not share our inhibitions in the slightest. Aggressive physical grappling was part of their heritage, not ours. And yet, and yet . . . we women discovered in wonderment that as we learned to place our kicks and jabs with precision we were actually able to inspire fear in the men. We *could* hurt them, we learned to our astonishment, and hurt them hard at the core of their sexual being—if we broke that Biblical injunction. 98

Is it possible that there is some sort of metaphysical justice in the anatomical fact that the male sex organ, which has been misused from time immemorial as a weapon of terror against women, should have at its root an awkward place of painful vulnerability? Acutely conscious of their susceptibility to damage, men have protected their testicles throughout history with armor, supports and forbidding codes of "clean," above-the-belt fighting. A gentleman's aggreement is understandable—among gentlemen. When women are threatened, as I learned in my self-defense class, "Kick him in the balls, it's your best maneuver." How strange it was to hear for the first time in my life that women could fight back, *should* fight back and make full use of a natural advantage; that it is *in our interest* to know how to do it. How strange it was to understand with the full force of unexpected revelation that male allusions to psychological defeat, particularly at the hands of a woman, were couched in phrases like emasculation, castration and ball-breaking because of that very special physical vulnerability. 99

Fighting back. On a multiplicity of levels, that is the activity we must *100*
engage in, together, if we—women—are to redress the imbalance and rid
ourselves and men of the ideology of rape.

Rape can be eradicated, not merely controlled or avoided on an indi- *101*
vidual basis, but the approach must be long-range and cooperative, and
must have the understanding and good will of many men as well as
women.

My purpose has been to give rape its history. Now we must deny it *102*
a future.

Study Questions

1. Susan Brownmiller begins her essay "Women Fight Back" with a
   narrative written in the seventeenth century. What does she gain by
   using an "historical" narrative instead of reporting on a recent attempted rape? How does the language of the narrative support this
   result?
2. Brownmiller's language suggests that she is writing specifically for
   women. Identify several passages that seem to illustrate this restriction to a female audience. For what reasons might she have limited
   her audience in such a way? What effect will this restriction have on
   men who do read the essay?
3. The definition of rape is central to Brownmiller's essay. Identify
   several passages that deal with definition and find the words or phrases
   that signal this form of additive organization. For each passage you
   identify, note the paragraph that follows it. What method of organization does Brownmiller use to relate the material in these paragraphs
   to her definitions? What does your answer show about how she uses
   definition in her essay?
4. At paragraph 41, Brownmiller shifts from a discussion of rape to a
   discussion of legislation and penalties having to do with sexual assault.
   Organization based on definition is, therefore, no longer useful. What
   form of organization does she shift to? Identify passages that are
   clear examples of this kind of organization.
5. The concluding section of "Women Fight Back" deals with self-defense and the "natural advantage" that women have over men in a
   fight. Why is this an appropriate topic for the end of the essay? How
   does Brownmiller use this topic to stress the significant points in her
   essay? (See in particular the final three paragraphs.)

Suggestion for Drafting

Susan Brownmiller's "Women Fight Back" pushes the upper limits of
length for an essay. Brownmiller deals with a multitude of factors as-

sociated with rape, yet manages to do so in an organized and coherent way. The relationship of each detail to her thesis is always clear. Given the number of details presented and the complexity of their relationships to one another and to the thesis, the extreme length of the essay is not surprising.

What would happen if you were to redraft the essay to discuss only the more narrow topic of how pornography contributes to rape? What changes would you need to make in the opening and closing sections? How would you reorganize the section dealing with pornography so that it could stand on its own?

Essay Assignments

1. In this section, we have dicussed how drafting can be used to help you discover further things to say about your topic and to develop an organization for your essay. In this assignment we would like you to review our suggestions by writing a short essay (400–500 words) in which you describe the purpose of drafting to someone who has not read our remarks. You should focus on what you believe drafting can do for the writer rather than on any specific techniques of drafting. Answering the following questions should help you to get started: What does drafting add to prewriting? Why should various methods of organization rather than only one or two be tried? Why shouldn't the final draft be considered the finished essay?

2. Many of us associate particular pleasures or fears with everyday objects. For example, a person who as a child once got sick after eating too much ice cream may not be able to look at ice cream without getting sick again. A person who was once awakened by a telephone call to hear terrible news may fear the ringing of a telephone from then on. Choose something that evokes a special reaction in you; write a short essay (400–500 words) describing that reaction and how it originated.

3. In "Dick Cook", John McPhee writes of the many people who "come into the country" each year (p. 122):

   In they come—young people in ones and twos—from all over the Lower Forty-eight. With general trapping catalogues under their arms, they walk around wondering what to do next. The climate and the raw Alaska wild will quickly sort them out. Some will flinch. Others will go back.

   Write a six- to eight-hundred-word essay in which you describe a friend by discussing whether he or she would "flinch" after coming into the country. Base your discussion on what you have learned in "Dick Cook" and what you know about your friend. When possible, illustrate your statements with accounts of specific incidents that exemplify your friend's character.

4. In "Information for Those Who Would Remove to America," Benjamin Franklin presents an America that is rich in opportunity for the hard-working, honest person who is willing to take a chance. We have decided to create an anthology of essays entitled *Removing to America: Two Hundred Years Later* to explore how accurate this picture of America is today. The anthology will begin with Franklin's essay and contain a series of original essays that give personal reactions to it.

Write an eight-hundred- to one-thousand-word essay for our anthology, describing your own idea of the opportunities now available
for young people in the United States. Do you share Franklin's
optimism? Have things changed so much since 1782 that his view is
no longer valid? Assume that your audience has already read "Information for Those Who Would Remove to America," and concentrate
on presenting your own view.

5. In "Viking on the Plain of Gold," Arthur C. Clarke defends our space
program, in part, because it gives our lives a spirit of adventure that
he feels is sorely missing in most of the things that occupy our attention. Like many other writers, Clarke feels that the human race must
face great challenges in order to grow, and he believes that space
offers humanity its greatest challenge.

Other writers, however, believe that there are still enough challenges left on our own planet to ensure the growth of our race. They
point to poverty, racism, the threat of nuclear war, and environmental
problems as deserving of the energy, imagination, and money now
being put into the space program. They argue that these problems
need quick solutions or there will be no human race to go into space.

Write an essay in which you present your own view of the importance of the space program. You need not take sides in this debate
and argue that one view is right and the other wrong. As with most
debates, there is much to be said for each side. Try, instead, to
discuss the space program in terms of how it should fit in with all the
other challenges now facing us. What do you find exciting about it?
How might it help us to face the other challenges? What do you find
wasteful in it? How might it be used as an excuse to ignore our
immediate problems?

6. There is trouble in Bay City. This resort town on the Atlantic coast
is faced with a crisis that could very well destroy it. Bay City, New
Jersey, is a small town with about ten thousand year-round residents.
During the summer, however, almost forty thousand tourists come
there to enjoy its beautiful beaches and fill its hotels, restaurants, and
shops. This flood of people may soon end, however, because of the
recent discovery by Dr. William Jackson that the waters off the
beaches are being polluted by raw sewage leaking from the town's
ancient treatment plant.

Dr. Jackson claims that the pollution is as serious as any ecological
problem in the United States and that it threatens the health of everyone in the area. He has recommended that the town council either
close the beaches immediately or build a new treatment plant. His
estimate of the cost of a new plant is millions of dollars more than the
town can afford, however, and a number of people have come forward
to dispute Jackson's claims.

Mr. Peter Shaw, president of the local chamber of commerce, states
that people should not panic at the words of only one man who is,

after all, simply a general practitioner with no experience in the environmental sciences. He points out that few of the small businesses could survive the loss of a tourist season nor could they alone afford the cost of immediately building a new treatment plant. Shaw recommends that the town continue with its plans for the coming tourist season and that next winter it conduct the necessary tests to find out how serious the problem actually is.

Professor George Hill of the Department of Biological Sciences at Bay City College denies that a serious problem exists. Hired by the local hotel owners to test the ocean waters, he has concluded that minor leakage is occurring but in insignificant amounts. The ocean waters soon dilute the sewage and take it far off the coast. Therefore, Hill claims, the town council does not need to take any action at all.

Finally, Mr. Andrew Jones, a Bay City real estate agent, speculates that Dr. Jackson has a personal reason for spreading a rumor about the quality of the waters. He has stated that Jackson is looking for a new house with beach-front property. If people believe that the waters are polluted, the doctor will be able to buy the property for far less than its true value.

Unfortunately, some decision must be reached soon. The tourist season is only a month away. The local environmentalists are picketing the beach, and the *New York Times* is sending down a team of reporters and photographers to cover the story.

You are to write for a weekly news magazine an eight-hundred- to one-thousand-word essay in which you discuss Bay City's troubles. You will not, however, simply describe what has happened; the reporters will take care of that. You will deal with the larger issue of what factors Bay City needs to consider before reaching a decision. You will discuss what you believe to be the most important questions in this case. For example, you might deal with one or more of the following questions:

Does Bay City have enough information to act on?

What guidelines should the town council use in reaching a decision?

Is the mere suggestion of a threat to human health a sufficient reason to take drastic action?

How important should the economic considerations be in reaching a decision?

What responsibility does Bay City have for the environment?

Or you may have questions of your own that can be answered in your essay. However you narrow your topic, keep in mind that instead of simply retelling the story, you should focus on the difficulties facing the people of Bay City as they try to decide what to do.

SECTION
FOUR

Style

umpty Dumpty took the book and looked at it carefully. "That seems to be done right—" he began.

"You're holding it upside down!" Alice interrupted.

"To be sure I was!" Humpty Dumpty said gaily as she turned it round for him. "I thought it looked a little queer. As I was saying, that *seems* to be done right—though I haven't time to look it over thoroughly just now—and that shows that there are three hundred and sixty-four days when you get unbirthday presents—"

"Certainly," said Alice.

"And only *one* for birthday presents, you know. There's glory for you!"

"I don't know what you mean by 'glory,'" Alice said.

Humpty Dumpty smiled contemptuously. "Of course you don't—till I tell you. I meant 'there's a nice knock-down argument for you!'"

"But 'glory' doesn't mean 'a nice knock-down argument,'" Alice objected.

"When *I* use a word," Humpty Dumpty said, in a rather scornful tone, "it means just what I choose it to mean—neither more nor less."

Lewis Carroll, *Through the Looking Glass*

H ow much easier writing would be if we were able to make words mean just what we choose them to mean. But this is not possible for either Humpty Dumpty or us, no matter how much we may wish it so. We must be concerned with how clear our meanings are to our readers.

The audience, as we pointed out in Section 3, is a key consideration in drafting. When you organize your material, you begin the process of sharing your thoughts with an audience. Concern for the audience is even more important in the final stage of the writing process, when you must imagine yourself in the place of the readers and decide how well you conveyed your meaning. Here, we will emphasize methods of judging a final draft and the language used in it.

The essays at the end of this section illustrate a variety of styles. As you read them, consider how the appropriate use of language helps the reader to understand the message. The following questions should help you to focus on each essay's style:

What are the key words in this essay?

What adjectives and adverbs are used to add further meaning to the key words?

Does the writer use some words in unusual ways?

Does the essay contain words for which you need definitions?

What personality does the writer project? Is it friendly, cheerful, distant, or something else?

Is this personality appropriate for the meaning of the essay?

How does the vocabulary fit the personality?

Does the sentence structure make the essay easier or harder to read?

How may the meaning of the essay have affected the writer's choice of sentence structure?

Is there a progression of ideas or are the same points merely repeated?

These questions can be applied to almost every phase of writing. The words you choose, the sentences you use, and the organizations you create all tell the reader something about your topic. When words, sentences, and organizations seem to work well together, you have a successful style. A good style does not necessarily mean that your essay is easy to read. Sometimes your style must be rather complicated in order for you to communicate your meaning appropriately. But a good style will not needlessly complicate your presentation. It will suit the topic and the message you wish to communicate. It will also give your readers a sense of your *personality*—who you are and what you feel toward the topic.

Revision

Revision requires you to consider the style of your final draft and explore methods of improving it. Since you must deal with so many different elements, it is best to divide your work into two steps: reformulation and editing. Reformulation has to do with word choice, sentence structure, and organization; editing, with the more technical matters of punctuation, spelling, and grammar. By dividing the process of revision in this way, you will have a better chance of identifying the changes you need to make, but this division is not absolute. You will frequently find misspellings and incorrect punctuations as you work on reformulation, and you will often change both words and sentences as you edit.

Reformulation

Word Choice

Anything in your essay that distracts your readers will diminish their chances of understanding your meaning. If your audience finds particular words annoying or repetitious, chances are the concepts these words were meant to express will not be communicated. Thus, the words you used in your final draft must now be examined for their effectiveness. Do they clearly express your meaning? Do they express your meaning without being needlessly long-winded or repetitious? Do they express your meaning in an interesting way? While you are drafting, you will often become so preoccupied with trying to get your thoughts down that you will be happy with any word that comes close to what you want. In reformulation you need to do more than simply settle for "close" meanings. You need to find words that will accurately convey your meaning to your readers.

As an example let us return to the final draft of "There Is Nothing like a Good Zoo" and examine the word choice in one of its paragraphs. While there is no passage in our draft that does not need some rewording, paragraph 3 needs considerable attention:

~~Zoos do have many diversions for people who wish to escape. I know~~
~~that as~~ soon as I enter the main gate of a zoo I feel I have left the ~~city~~ [*As*] [*and see the children holding their red and yellow balloons,*]
~~behind.~~ ~~The crowds gathered~~ around the gate and the souvenir ~~shops~~ [*drab city*] [*Anticipating adventure, crowds cheerfully wander*] [*stands.*]
~~seem somehow to be different to me than similar crowds on the city streets.~~
The ~~concrete~~ walks and the asphalt roads ~~of a zoo seem more wonderous~~ [*tree-lined*] [*they travel on beckon to exotic*]
~~than the walks and roads of a city.~~ The people ~~on them~~ are not the same [*places and colorful sights.*] [*These*]
~~threatening crowds blocking my way.~~ In the zoo ~~these people~~ become ~~to~~ [*dull masses I meet on city streets.*] [*they*]
~~me~~ families, loving couples, happy children, and ~~tired loners~~ who are all [*warm*] [*friendly individuals*]
caught up in the same excitement. ~~I like these people more~~ in the zoo than [*They seem brighter and happier*]
~~I do~~ in the city. [*anyone I meet,*]

This paragraph was meant to show the readers something of the excitement we feel at a zoo, but does it? In many ways the original wording shares the same problems as our very first draft of the essay. We spend too much time telling the readers that there is excitement without showing it. They are likely to remain unconvinced unless we find some words that will convey excitement.

A word usually has two kinds of meanings. The first, its *denotation*, is its dictionary meaning. The denotation of *diversion*, for example, is "something that distracts the mind and relaxes or entertains." Its denotation, therefore, does fit the meaning we wish to convey. However, its second kind of meaning, its *connotation*, does not. *Connotations* are meanings that we associate with words; they suggest or imply attitudes that are not part of a word's primary meaning. The connotations of *diversion* cause two problems. First, the word suggests a formality that contrasts awkwardly with the scene at the main gate. "Diversions" seem out of place in the spontaneous setting of a zoo. Second, the word often conveys the sense that the diversion has been planned. People consciously create diversions to distract themselves or others. In this case, however, it is the zoo that is doing the distracting, and its distractions depend more on individual reactions to the exhibits than on the builders' conscious planning.

In the same way, *shops* needs to be changed in line 3. Although the dictionary will define *shop* as "small retail store," we associate shops with buildings. Most souvenirs sold in zoos, however, are not sold in buildings. They are usually found in stalls or carts. The image of a row of shops selling souvenirs, therefore, diminishes the effect of the sentence. It suggests rows of stores that can be found on any city street rather than the more exotic displays of the zoos.

Faulty connotations are not the only way that words can go wrong in your writing. Frequently, it is not the connotation that is the problem but the fact that there is too little connotation. For example, we claim in the original paragraph that right inside the main gate we immediately sense the excitement of the zoo, yet we have little going on to show that excitement, and our adjectives and adverbs do little to describe it. In fact, some of the words we use seem to contradict that sense of excitement. Our crowds are simply "gathered," and we see "tired strangers." And when we try to describe the atmosphere of the zoo, we only write that it "seems somehow to be different." Such words and phrases were useful when we were trying to set down our thoughts during drafting, but now we need to refine them so that our readers will be interested in what we have to say. If we describe something that we think is extraordinary in very ordinary terms, will our readers believe us? We need to change some of the nouns and verbs in this passage and add some adjectives and adverbs. In effect we need to project a personality that matches the meaning we wish to convey.

Finally, during reformulation you need to check how frequently you use key words. Needless repetition of a word will distract your readers. They will start noticing how much you use it and ignore what you are trying to say. You should not, of course, change a word simply for the sake of changing it. Repetition can serve the important function of emphasizing a point you are trying to make. But this technique should be used sparingly. Too much repetition can suggest to your readers that you have become bored with your own topic, that you no longer have the energy to express your ideas carefully and interestingly. If you are tired of discussing your topic, why should the readers be any less tired of reading about it? Notice in the first version of our paragraph the frequent use of *I*, *my*, and *me*. Since a personal point of view has already been established in the first sentence, many of these words can be omitted with no loss of meaning. The repetition here gives the passage the appearance of a draft rather than a finished essay. The words seem to suggest we are still thinking things over to ourselves rather than presenting coherent thoughts to an audience. Attention to such details adds a polish to the final draft that readers appreciate. It shows them that the essay was written with their interests in mind.

Sentence Structure

The reformulation of paragraph 3 by refining its vocabulary illustrates how changes of one kind often lead to others. Because of the changes we made in word choice, we now need to rewrite some of the sentences. For example, in paragraphs 7 and 8 of our final draft, we need to eliminate unnecessary repetition and rewrite entire sentences.

> Lowland gorillas come in two types, ~~western and eastern.~~ The ~~western lowland~~ gorilla ~~aver-~~ most common people
> see in zoos is the western lowland gorilla. ~~ages about a hundred pounds less than mountain gorillas. This type~~
>
> ~~ranges in color from black to grayish brown and has very short hair. They~~
> With ~~are far more abundant, relatively speaking, than mountain gorillas with~~
> they are far more abundant than other
> about 35,000 now living in the wild, ~~Western lowland gorillas are the most~~
> gorillas. They are also the smallest, weighing about 400 pounds. Their very ~~common gorillas people see in the zoo.~~ short hair ranges in color from
> black to grayish brown. ¶
> Eastern lowland gorillas ~~have characteristics that place them somewhere~~
> are the other two types in weight, color, and hair length.
> between ~~western lowland gorillas and mountain gorillas. They weigh more~~
> ~~than the western but less than the mountain gorillas. It is darker than the~~
> ~~western but not as black as the mountain and the hair length is also in~~
> There are about living ~~between that of the other two types.~~ About 5,000 eastern gorillas now ~~live~~
> the San Diego Zoo has one of the few living in captivity.
> in the wild, and ~~very few zoos have them.~~

These two paragraphs illustrate many of the problems found in final drafts. Not only is there frequent repetition of key words, but there are many awkward sentences. The style of these paragraphs reflects the difficulty we had in organizing the material. As we wrote, we also had to think out the distinctive features of each species of gorilla and compare and contrast them in paragraph 8. The language we used shows that we were still concentrating on getting the information right as we drafted the section. Choice of words and sentence structure did not receive as much attention as getting the facts down.

In the original draft, the most obvious result of our lack of attention to language is a feeling of standing still. We seem to be using a lot of words to say very little. Now we must move to a revision in which we concentrate as much on presenting the information effectively to the readers as we do on accuracy. We can accomplish this by reworking the original sentences to eliminate repetition and combining the results into a single paragraph. This reformulation presents the facts in language that reflects careful thought.

Avoiding repetition is not the only reason for restructuring sentences. One or more sentences may need to be changed because something in them may seem wrong to you. If you are not satisfied with a passage, your readers probably will not be satisfied either. The following sentences from paragraph 6 are grammatically correct but sound awkward:

It is always fun to watch the animals. ~~For example the San Diego Zoo has an elaborate gorilla exhibit that tries to reproduce the right habitat for the animals. While it is fun to spend the time simply watching the gorillas,~~ But this fun can be considerably increased ~~by~~ for me when I read the signs. ^ For example, I learned from a sign at the San ~~reading the large sign in front of the exhibit that explains to the viewers that~~ Diego Zoo that, two major (there are ~~actually three~~ kinds of gorillas, mountain and lowland.

The original sentences are awkward because they are unnecessarily long and complex. We have failed to match our language and meaning. All that we are trying to say here is that the information we read on the sign adds significantly to our enjoyment in watching the gorillas. Yet our expression of this relatively simple point is overblown and wordy. We need to reformulate these two sentences so that they directly state our meaning without the distraction of awkward sentences. In this case we need to simplify them.

Long sentences that use unnecessary words and phrases are distracting to the reader. In the drafting process, these words and phrases are part of our thinking out loud. We write them down in much the same way that we say "ah" or "you know" when we speak. They fill the space as we think of the next thing to say. Such "thinking noises," however, need to be removed before we finish the essay; their presence signals to the audience that we have not yet completed thinking through the topic.

At the same time, you should not go to the opposite extreme and assume that every complicated sentence needs to be simplified. Simple sentences can be just as awkward as complex ones. A large part of the awkwardness of paragraph 7 comes from the basic simplicity of each of the sentences. These follow a set formula of subject-verb-complement. Such a style is caused once again by the drafting process. We are listing here the particular traits that distinguish the western lowland gorilla from the others, but essays are not lists. We need to create a paragraph from this list, and paragraphs usually require more complex structures than a string of similar sounding sentences.

Reformulating sentences, like prewriting and drafting, is exploration. Finding the right structures for your meaning does not always come quickly, and it frequently forces you to reconsider what you thought you meant by a sentence or even a paragraph. Thus, you will occasionally find that in rewriting sentences you also omit some ideas that were in your draft and add others that were not.

Voice

The connotations of the words you choose help to determine the personality of your essay. Formal words distinguished by Latin or Greek roots will create a wholly different impression than casual words with native English roots. For example, we would be using a formal word if we called the crowd in paragraph 3 *amicable* and a more casual word if we used *friendly*. The level of formality that you choose should be consistent. Jumping from formal to casual words will be as much a distraction to your readers as awkward sentence structure or needless repetition.

Establishing a consistent level of formality (or informality) aids in giving your essay a personality, but your *voice,* or attitude you express toward the topic, is even more important. You have many voices to choose from: you can appear serious, flippant, or even neutral. When Aristotle pointed out that how a speaker sounds often determines whether an audience will believe his message, he was stating a truth not just for orators but for writers as well. You reveal something of yourself each time you write, and what you reveal will affect the readers' response to your meaning.

Deciding whether or not you want to appear objective or subjective is the first step in determining what voice to use. Do you wish to suggest that the points you make are true for all or most people? Do you wish to emphasize your attitudes and opinions? The more you want to focus on the topic, particularly a complicated one, the more you need a formal, objective style. Such a style is usually achieved by avoiding the use of personal pronouns such as *I* and by never directly addressing your readers. However, the more you want to focus on your own thoughts and express a personal opinion, the more you need a conversational style in which you use personal pronouns and directly address your audience.

No formula exists to tell you which of these voices or their many variations to use. Currently, the personal voice is preferred, but no voice should be considered better than any other. You need to decide by choosing the one that seems to best suit your purposes and the attitude you want to convey to your readers. Then, you must be sure that you use consistently the voice you have chosen.

During drafting it is almost impossible to write in a consistent voice. Thus, when you come to reformulation you will have a number of styles to select from. Paragraph 9 of our draft is much more formal than paragraph 3 or even paragraph 10, where we return to using personal pronouns. We must, therefore, choose between these voices and make the necessary changes:

Armed

~~Equipped~~ with this new information, ~~the visitor can now turn~~ to the game

I now look over the gorillas carefully and play,

of "Which is Which?". ~~Looking over the gorillas carefully, the game begins.~~

Which are the darker ones? Which have the longer hair? Is the one resting on that branch heavier than the ones at the base of this tree? Are all three gorillas feeding in that corner western lowland gorillas? Or is the middle one actually an eastern one? How black does a gorilla have to be before it qualifies as an eastern one? ~~People can quickly get caught up~~ [I become absorbed] in this [sort of] game as ~~they~~ [I] seek out that rare eastern lowland gorilla, and for that time [I] forget the city outside the zoo. Identifying a particular kind of gorilla will not pay ~~the~~ [my] bills, but it is a nice thing to do anyhow.

   The word *I* never appears in the original version of this paragraph, and instead of talking directly to the readers, we use such impersonal constructions as "the visitor can now turn." Clearly this voice does not fit with those of the earlier and later passages. Moreover, this formal voice is not even consistent with other parts of the same paragraph. Words and phrases like "will not pay the bills" and "it is nice to do anyhow" are too informal to fit with the earlier, impersonal phrases. Since most of the paragraphs in our final draft do stress a personal reaction, we have revised the paragraph to make it consistent with the others. Keep in mind, however, that voice, too, needs experimenting with. The voice you use in the majority of your draft may not always turn out to be the best.

Organization

Finally, during reformulation you should take another look at the order in which you present your ideas. Does that order help your readers? Is there another order you might use that would make your meaning clearer? In our final draft, for example, we need to reconsider where we have placed paragraph 10. This paragraph, in which we clearly state our own opinion of the importance of zoos, comes after our discussion of the rain forest and the gorillas. Its position in the essay may seem logical because it discusses material introduced in the paragraphs immediately preceding it. However, paragraph 10 can also be seen as an answer to the questions raised in paragraph 1 and an argument against the attitude expressed in paragraph 2 ("people are trying to escape the real world by visiting the zoos and acting like children for a while").
   We might move paragraph 10 forward to follow paragraph 2. We will then be able to show our serious intent immediately so that as we describe the rain forests and the gorillas, the readers will understand that we see them as more than excuses for reliving our childhoods. Since we can anticipate that many of our readers will believe that "zoos are for chil-

dren" and not expect any serious statement, it may be best to show them our intentions early.

Timing is the issue here. Making a point at just the right moment will support your style. The better the timing, the more likely your audience is to believe that you are in complete control of what you have written. Considering alternative orders for your paragraphs should become a regular part of your revision strategies.

Editing

Of all the parts of the revision stage, editing needs the least introduction. For many people, in fact, revising has become identical with editing. Most of us have learned that it is important to reread a paper for spelling, punctuation, and grammar errors. Most of us have also learned that these errors are often hard to catch. Our eyes and our minds are now so used to what we have written that we often no longer see what we have actually produced. We find it difficult or even impossible to concentrate on each word, each phrase, each punctuation mark, and each blank space. We are also in a hurry to be finally done.

Unhappily, editing does take time and concentration, and no one can afford to rush through it. Reading an essay filled with errors that editing should have corrected demands too much from the audience. Why should readers have to finish the writing process for the author? As tiresome as it may be, careful editing shows your concern for your essay and your readers. Editing is the last step before making your private message a public statement.

Writers have various methods of slowing down their reading as they search for errors. Some tap each word with a pencil so that the eye will focus on each word in the essay. Others read their essays aloud, again focusing on individual words. Some even go so far as to read their drafts backward, so that there will be no danger of the eye rushing ahead of the mind. Whatever the method, the intention is the same. You must find a way of slowing your attention so that you can see exactly what you have written.

As with any skill, you can learn to improve your editing from past mistakes. If you keep track of where your most common weaknesses lie, you can concentrate on them in future editing. As you concentrate on these problems, you may find that they recur less often.

To improve, however, you will need a good dictionary and a handbook that covers punctuation and grammar. And you must be willing to use them, even when after looking up a spelling or a punctuation rule you find that you were right in the first place. When in doubt, consult the dictionary or handbook.

Keep a record of the corrections you make in your writing. This record will show you where your most common problems lie and provide a convenient reference for corrections. As you increase the number of items with each editing, you will find that you will be checking the dictionary and handbook less and your own notes more.

Recording Spelling Errors

Fig. 4.1 illustrates one way of listing the words you misspell. It has been designed to help you do more than simply list correct spellings for incorrect ones. In the final column you must diagnose your misspellings so that you can anticipate what you need to be especially concerned with in later papers. If your chart reveals frequent problems with one or two types of spelling errors, you will know that you have a blind spot and

Word	Misspelling	Error	Type
pleasant	plesant	ea/e	1. wrong letters for the vowel
equipped	equiped	pp/p	2. failed to double a consonant
occasionally	occassionally	s/ss	2. incorrect doubling
length	lengh	gth/gh	2. left out part of a cluster
there	their	ere/eir	3. confused homonyms
something	somthing	met/mt	4. left out a letter
especially	especlly	=cially/ =clly	4. left out a syllable
though	through	ou/rou	5. confused two similar words
my	by	m/b	5. confused two similar words
receiving	recieving	ei/ie	6. reversed the order
bottle	bottel	le/el	6. reversed the order
wondrous	wonderous	dr/der	added a letter
rain forest	rainforest	n f/nf	ran two words together

Fig. 4.1: Chart of misspellings

that you must search for words in your draft that are susceptible to these mistakes.

The chart shows six basic reasons for spelling errors.

1. *Vowels:* The letters chosen to represent the vowel sound are incorrect.
2. *Double consonants or consonant clusters:* A consonant is not doubled when it should be or is doubled when it should not be. Use this category also for words in which you either add or omit a consonant in a consonant cluster.
3. *Homonyms:* A word with a similar pronunciation but a different spelling is used for the intended word.
4. *Missing letters or syllables:* A single letter or group of letters is missing.
5. *Word confusion:* A word that looks similar is used for the intended word.
6. *Letter reversal:* One or more letters are transposed; that is, they do not appear in their proper order.

You should not consider these categories exhaustive. As you chart your misspellings, you may want to add other groups that describe your own misspellings more accurately.

Recording Punctuation and Grammar Errors

Fig. 4.2 illustrates a way of recording your problems with punctuation and grammar. As in the case of misspelling, making a chart will help you to diagnose your most common weaknesses. Since it is not always easy to find the page or paragraph in your handbook with the advice you need for correcting your errors, the chart can become a convenient place to check first as you edit later essays.

Unlike spelling mistakes, punctuation and grammar errors do not usually fall into neat general categories. The conventions of written language are so diverse that no single set of labels and definitions would be sufficient. Moreover, different handbooks may treat the same point differently, especially punctuation marks like the comma and grammatical refinements like agreement between mass nouns and simple verbs. You need to use a respected handbook, and you need to use it consistently. When various handbooks disagree, find the alternative that you like best and then use that convention throughout your essay. Jumping from one convention of using commas to another, for example, will distract your readers.

The Finished Essay

We end this discussion of revision with our final version of "There Is No Place like a Good Zoo." We have also added questions and exercises

Sentence	Original	Rule
Not too long ago, a group of seven and eight year olds were on a tour of Woodland Park Zoo in Seattle.	Not too long ago a group of seven and eight year olds were on a tour of Woodland Park Zoo in Seattle.	Use a comma to set off an adverbial clause or phrase preceding the main clause.
There are only a few animals there, and they are too far back in their enclosures to see.	There are only a few animals there and they are too far back in their enclosures to see.	Use a comma to separate two main clauses joined by a coordinating conjunction.
In my own house I would find this climate uncomfortable; here it feels natural and I actually like it.	In my own house I would find this climate uncomfortable, here it feels natural and I actually like it.	Use a semicolon to separate closely related independent clauses not connected by a conjunction.
Zoos give me a place to go when I am tired of dealing with this overcomplicated world, a place that cannot be found anywhere else.	Zoos give me a place to go when I am tired of dealing with this overcomplicated world. A place that cannot be found anywhere else.	Avoid separating a subordinate clause or phrase from its main clause by a period.
Worrying about the bills, the next exam, how the boss feels, the repairs the car needs, the danger of walking the streets, or the quality of the air we breathe gives us all a warped view of our lives and the world we live in.	Worrying about the bills, the next exam, how the boss feels, the repairs the car needs, the danger of walking the streets, or the quality of the air we breathe give us all a warped view of our lives and the world we live in.	A singular subject followed by one or more prepositional phrases containing one or more plural nouns requires a singular verb.

Fig. 4.2: Chart of errors in grammar and punctuation

that will help you review the entire writing process and understand the role revision plays within it.

THE RESTING PLACE

It is December, and I am about to do something that you may consider irrational. At the same time I write out my checks for the utilities, credit card bills, and other monthly expenses, I will also use one of my credit cards to increase my debt. I am not going to use it for gifts, although December is the season of gift giving. I am going to use it to renew my membership in the New York Zoological Society. Why, you may ask, would I want to give money to a zoo, especially in December? What can I possibly see in a zoo that would encourage me to spend money I don't have at the very time when there are so many demands on what little I do have?

Some people might tell you that I am going through a second childhood. Zoos, they might say, are for children, and I am trying to escape the real world by acting like a child again. These "realists" might even point out that responsible adults would not act the way I am acting.

But they are wrong. I am, in fact, being very rational. Zoos are essential to my mental and physical health. Living each day forces all of us to deal with problems that can seriously depress us. Worrying about money, the next exam, what the boss is thinking, the repairs the car needs, the crime rate, and the quality of the air we breathe can give any of us a warped sense of the world we live in. I know that there are times when I become so preoccupied with my worries that I begin to think they are the only things in my life. I start to withdraw from the people around me, and, soon, nothing seems worthwhile. It is time to go to the zoo.

As soon as I enter the main gate and see the children holding their red and yellow balloons, I know I have left the drab city behind. Crowds cheerfully wander around the gate and the souvenir stands, eagerly anticipating adventure. The tree-lined walks and the dirt roads beckon to exotic places and colorful sights. The people are not the dull masses of city streets. In the zoo they become warm families, loving couples, and friendly individuals who are all sharing the same sense of excitement. They appear happier and brighter in the zoo than anyone I meet in the city.

The first exhibit I head for is the rain forest. Almost every zoo has one. No dictionary definition will ever be able to explain why rain forests have become so popular. The *American Heritage Dictionary*, for example, defines *rain forest* as "a dense evergreen forest occupying a tropical region with an annual rainfall of at least 100 inches." Such a description is only good for people who are stuck on "reality." The tropical rain forest of the Topeka zoo is certainly modelled on such a definition, although the rain comes from sprinklers and the Kansas climate can hardly be called tropical. Yet once inside, I know that moisture and temperature are not enough to describe a rain forest.

It is a world that is so far removed from where and how most of us live that it might as well be called a Venusian forest. I easily lose myself in a riot of greens, browns, yellows, and reds. Colorful flying birds fill the air, crawling reptiles inhabit the ground, and brilliantly patterned snakes hang from the branches. Everywhere there is something extraordinary to see, to hear, or to smell. If you look carefully, you will even see red flying foxes hanging from the roof supports. What is a rain forest? It is a place to go to forget problems for a time and enjoy the unique sights.

However, zoos have a lot more to offer me than exotic sights. It is always fun to watch the animals, but my pleasure is considerably increased when I read the signs. I learned from a sign at the San Diego Zoo, for example, that there are two major kinds of gorillas, mountain and lowland.

Mountain gorillas are the larger, often weighing more than five hundred pounds. They are black and have very long hair. As their name implies, they live in the mountains. Their black coloring and long hair keep them warm. According to the sign, there are only about five hundred of these gorillas now living in the wild, and no zoo has one.

Lowland gorillas are divided into two subtypes, western and eastern. The gorillas most commonly seen in zoos are western lowland gorillas. With about thirty-five thousand now living in the wild, they are far more abundant than the other type. They are also smaller, weighing about four hundred pounds. Their very short hair ranges in color from light black to grayish brown. Eastern lowland gorillas lie between mountain gorillas and western lowland gorillas in such characteristics as weight, color, and hair length. Only about five thousand eastern gorillas now live in the wild, and the San Diego Zoo has one of the few living in captivity.

Armed with this new information, I can now look over the gorillas carefully and play "which is which?". Which are the darker ones? Which have the longer hair? Is the one resting on that branch heavier than the ones at the base of this tree? Are all three gorillas feeding in that corner western lowland gorillas? Or is the middle one an eastern one? How black does a gorilla have to be before it qualifies as an eastern one? I become absorbed in the game of seeking out that rare eastern lowland gorilla, and for that time I forget the city outside the zoo. Identifying a particular kind of gorilla will not pay my bills, but it is a nice thing to do anyhow.

Rain forests and gorillas are for adults as well as for children. They give us a chance to wonder about our world, to go far beyond the limits of homes and jobs. In a sense, they do not so much give us an escape as they remind us that there is much more to life than the streets we live on and the headlines we read. Viewing a rain forest gives us the chance to be amazed; trying to identify the different kinds of gorillas provides us with the opportunity to learn for the pleasure of learning. Neither will give us any practical benefit, but we should be allowed to enjoy some things for their own sakes and to notice details simply because they are there.

Several years ago, the newspapers were filled with stories about a University of Michigan freshman who had suddenly dropped out of sight. He was a remarkably intelligent young man who had entered the university at the age of fifteen. The newspapers throughout the Midwest carried the story and his picture, but for three days there had been no new information.

Finally, a friend came forward and told one of the strangest stories imaginable. The missing student was a fanatic player of Dungeons and Dragons. He had decided to invent the ultimate playing field for this game and had entered the maze of heating tunnels that crisscrossed the campus. People immediately took up the search. The found him a day later happily wandering through the tunnels completely involved in his private game.

Wasn't this freshman doing what many of us do when we seek out new sights and experiences in order to escape from the pressures of our lives? Perhaps we all need to recognize the necessity for a rest before things become too much and our minds snap. Perhaps an occasional visit to the zoo would have helped the student. Perhaps he should have joined a zoological society.

Study Questions

1. In our final version, we have changed our working title, "There Is Nothing like a Good Zoo," to "The Resting Place." What does the new title suggest to the readers that the working title did not? What may the working title have suggested that the new title does not?
2. What changes have been made in the first two paragraphs between the final draft and the finished essay? How do these changes fit with our discussion of voice when we reformulated paragraph 9 of the final draft? What is gained by switching to this more conversational voice?
3. Compare the final draft with the finished version. What paragraphs have been greatly reduced in the final version? What reasons could there have been for such reductions?
4. What knowledge of zoos do we assume that our readers have? Point to specific passages that illustrate your answer. In particular, reread the paragraphs in which the various kinds of gorillas are described. Do you think these paragraphs could have been shortened? Do they contain too much information for the point we are trying to make?

The essays that follow have been selected for their notable use of style, the ways in whch the language projects both meaning and personality. These readings and the questions based on them will illustrate the rich variety of ways in which you can use words, sentences, and voice to make your meaning more interesting and understandable.

As demanding as the writing process may be, there is one reward we hope that you will enjoy as you gaze at the finished pages of your essay. Throughout the process you have been discovering a great deal about yourself, your opinions, and your topic. You should savor these discoveries. Like Alice at the end of her adventures in wonderland, you may even find that the difficulties you have had to overcome were really not so bad after all.

A Modest Proposal

for Preventing the Children of Poor People in Ireland from Being a Burden on Their Parents or Country, and for Making Them Beneficial to the Public

Jonathan Swift

I t is a melancholy object to those who walk *1* through this great town, or travel in the country, when they see the streets, the roads and cabin-doors crowded with beggars of the female sex, followed by three, four, or six children, all in rags, and importuning every passenger for an alms. These mothers, instead of being able to work for their honest livelihood, are forced to employ all their time in strolling, to beg sustenance for their helpless infants, who, as they grow up, either turn thieves for want of work, or leave their dear native country to fight for the Pretender in Spain, or sell themselves to the Barbadoes.

I think it is agreed by all parties that this prodigious number of chil- *2* dren, in the arms, or on the backs, or at the heels of their mothers, and frequently of their fathers, is in the present deplorable state of the kingdom a very great additional grievance; and therefore whoever could find out a fair, cheap, and easy method of making these children sound and useful members of the commonwealth would deserve so well of the public as to have his statue set up for a preserver of the nation.

But my intention is very far from being confined to provide only for *3* the children of professed beggars; it is of a much greater extent, and shall take in the whole number of infants at a certain age who are born of parents in effect as little able to support them as those who demand our charity in the streets.

As to my own part, having turned my thoughts for many years upon *4* this important subject, and maturely weighed the several schemes of other projectors, I have always found them grossly mistaken in their computation. It is true a child just dropped from its dam may be supported by her milk for a solar year with little other nourishment, at most not above the value of two shillings, which the mother may certainly get, or the value in scraps, by her lawful occupation of begging, and it is exactly at one year old that I propose to provide for them, in such a manner as, instead of being a charge upon their parents, or the parish, or wanting food and raiment for the rest of their lives, they shall, on the contrary, contribute to the feeding and partly to the clothing of many thousands.

There is likewise another great advantage in my scheme, that it will 5 prevent those voluntary abortions, and that horrid practice of women murdering their bastard children, alas, too frequent among us, sacrificing the poor innocent babes, I doubt, more to avoid the expense than the shame, which would move tears and pity in the most savage and inhuman breast.

The number of souls in Ireland being usually reckoned one million and 6 a half, of these I calculate there may be about two hundred thousand couples whose wives are breeders, from which number I subtract thirty thousand couples who are able to maintain their own children, although I apprehend there cannot be so many under the present distresses of the kingdom, but this being granted, there will remain an hundred and seventy thousand breeders. I again subtract fifty thousand for those women who miscarry, or whose children die by accident or disease within the year. There only remain an hundred and twenty thousand children of poor parents annually born: the question therefore is, how this number shall be reared, and provided for, which, as I have already said, under the present situation of affairs is utterly impossible by all the methods hitherto proposed, for we can neither employ them in handicraft or agriculture; we neither build houses (I mean in the country), nor cultivate land: they can very seldom pick up a livelihood by stealing until they arrive at six years old, except where they are of towardly parts, although I confess they learn the rudiments much earlier, during which time they can however be properly looked upon only as probationers, as I have been informed by a principal gentleman in the County of Cavan, who protested to me that he never knew above one or two instances under the age of six, even in a part of the kingdom so renowned for the quickest proficiency in that art.

I am assured by our merchants that a boy or a girl before twelve years 7 old, is no saleable commodity, and even when they come to this age, they will not yield above three pounds, or three pounds and half-a-crown at most on the Exchange, which cannot turn to account either to the parents or the kingdom, the charge of nutriment and rags having been at least four times that value.

I shall now therefore humbly propose my own thoughts, which I hope 8 will not be liable to the least objection.

I have been assured by a very knowing American of my acquaintance 9 in London, that a young healthy child well nursed is at a year old a most delicious, nourishing and wholesome food, whether stewed, roasted, baked, or boiled, and I make no doubt that it will equally serve in a fricassee, or a ragout.

I do therefore humbly offer it to public consideration, that of the 10
hundred and twenty thousand children already computed, twenty thousand may be reserved for breed, whereof only one fourth part to be
males, which is more than we allow to sheep, black-cattle, or swine, and
my reason is that these children are seldom the fruits of marriage, a
circumstance not much regarded by our savages, therefore one male will
be sufficient to serve four females. That the remaining hundred thousand
may at a year old be offered in sale to the persons of quality, and fortune,
through the kingdom, always advising the mother to let them suck plen-
tifully in the last month, so as to render them plump, and fat for a good
table. A child will make two dishes at an entertainment for friends, and
when the family dines alone, the fore or hind quarter will make a reasonable dish, and seasoned with a little pepper or salt will be very good
boiled on the fourth day, especially in winter.

I have reckoned upon a medium, that a child just born will weigh 11
twelve pounds, and in a solar year if tolerably nursed increaseth to
twenty-eight pounds.

I grant this food will be somewhat dear, and therefore very proper for 12
landlords, who, as they have already devoured most of the parents, seem
to have the best title to the children.

Infant's flesh will be in season throughout the year, but more plentiful 13
in March, and a little before and after, for we are told by a grave* author,
an eminent French physician, that fish being a prolific diet, there are
more children born in Roman Catholic countries about nine months after
Lent than at any other season; therefore reckoning a year after Lent, the
markets will be more glutted than usual, because the number of Popish
infants is at least three to one in this kingdom, and therefore it will have
one other collateral advantage by lessening the number of Papists among
us.

I have already computed the charge of nursing a beggar's child (in 14
which list I reckon all cottagers, labourers, and four-fifths of the farmers)
to be about two shillings *per annum,* rags included, and I believe no
gentleman would repine to give ten shillings for the carcass of a good fat
child, which, as I have said, will make four dishes of excellent nutritive
meat, when he hath only some particular friend or his own family to dine
with him. Thus the Squire will learn to be a good landlord and grow
popular among his tenants, the mother will have eight shillings net profit,
and be fit for work until she produces another child.

Those who are more thrifty (as I must confess the times require) may 15
flay the carcass; the skin of which artificially dressed, will make admirable
gloves for ladies, and summer boots for fine gentlemen.

As to our city of Dublin, shambles may be appointed for this purpose, 16
in the most convenient parts of it, and butchers we may be assured will

* Rabelais

not be wanting, although I rather recommend buying the children alive, and dressing them hot from the knife, as we do roasting pigs.

A very worthy person, a true lover of his country, and whose virtues *17* I highly esteem, was lately pleased, in discoursing on this matter to offer a refinement upon my scheme. He said that many gentlemen of this kingdom, having of late destroyed their deer, he conceived that the want of venison might be well supplied by the bodies of young lads and maidens, not exceeding fourteen years of age, nor under twelve, so great a number of both sexes in every county being now ready to starve, for want of work and service: and these to be disposed of by their parents if alive, or otherwise by their nearest relations. But with due deference to so excellent a friend, and so deserving a patriot, I cannot be altogether in his sentiments. For as to the males, my American acquaintance assured me from frequent experience that their flesh was generally tough and lean, like that of our schoolboys, by continual exercise, and their taste disagreeable, and to fatten them would not answer the charge. Then as to the females, it would, I think with humble submission, be a loss to the public, because they soon would become breeders themselves: and besides, it is not improbable that some scrupulous people might be apt to censure such a practice (although indeed very unjustly) as a little bordering upon cruelty, which I confess, hath always been with me the strongest objection against any project, howsoever well intended.

But in order to justify my friend, he confessed that this expedient was *18* put into his head by the famous Psalmanazar, a native of the island Formosa, who came from thence to London, above twenty years ago, and in conversation told my friend that in his country when any young person happened to be put to death, the executioner sold the carcass to persons of quality, as a prime dainty, and that, in his time, the body of a plump girl of fifteen, who was crucified for an attempt to poison the emperor, was sold to his Imperial Majesty's Prime Minister of State, and other great Mandarins of the Court, in joints from the gibbet, at four hundred crowns. Neither indeed can I deny that if the same use were made of several plump young girls in this town who, without one single groat to their fortunes, cannot stir abroad without a chair, and appear at the playhouse and assemblies in foreign fineries, which they never will pay for, the kingdom would not be the worse.

Some persons of a desponding spirit are in great concern about that *19* vast number of poor people, who are aged, diseased, or maimed, and I have been desired to employ my thoughts what course may be taken to ease the nation of so grievous an encumbrance. But I am not in the least pain upon that matter, because it is very well known that they are every day dying, and rotting, by cold, and famine, and filth, and vermin, as fast as can be reasonably expected. And as to the younger labourers they are now in almost as hopeful a condition. They cannot get work, and consequently pine away from want of nourishment, to a degree that if at any time they are accidentally hired to common labour, they have not strength to perform it; and thus the country and themselves are in a fair way of being soon delivered from the evils to come.

I have too long digressed, and therefore shall return to my subject. I *20* think the advantages by the proposal which I have made are obvious and many, as well as of the highest importance.

For first, as I have already observed, it would greatly lessen the *21* number of Papists, with whom we are yearly over-run, being the principal breeders of the nation, as well as our most dangerous enemies, and who stay at home on purpose with a design to deliver the kingdom to the Pretender, hoping to take their advantage by the absence of so many good Protestants, who have chosen rather to leave their country than stay at home and pay tithes against their conscience to an idolatrous Episcopal curate.

Secondly, the poorer tenants will have something valuable of their *22* own, which by law may be made liable to distress, and help to pay their landlord's rent, their corn and cattle being already seized, and money a thing unknown.

Thirdly, whereas the maintenance of an hundred thousand children, *23* from two years old, and upwards, cannot be computed at less than ten shillings a piece *per annum,* the nation's stock will be thereby increased fifty thousand pounds *per annum,* besides the profit of a new dish, introduced to the tables of all gentlemen of fortune in the kingdom, who have any refinement in taste, and the money will circulate among ourselves, the goods being entirely of our own growth and manufacture.

Fourthly, the constant breeders, besides the gain of eight shillings *24* sterling *per annum,* by the sale of their children, will be rid of the charge of maintaining them after the first year.

Fifthly, this food would likewise bring great custom to taverns, where *25* the vintners will certainly be so prudent as to procure the best receipts for dressing it to perfection, and consequently have their houses frequented by all the fine gentlemen, who justly value themselves upon their knowledge in good eating; and a skilful cook, who understands how to oblige his guests, will contrive to make it as expensive as they please.

Sixthly, this would be a great inducement to marriage, which all wise *26* nations have either encouraged by rewards, or enforced by laws and penalties. It would increase the care and tenderness of mothers towards their children, when they were sure of a settlement for life, to the poor babes, provided in some sort by the public to their annual profit instead of expense. We should soon see an honest emulation among the married women, which of them could bring the fattest child to the market. Men would become as fond of their wives, during the time of their pregnancy, as they are now of their mares in foal, their cows in calf, or sows when they are ready to farrow, nor offer to beat or kick them (as it is too frequent a practice) for fear of a miscarriage.

Many other advantages might be enumerated. For instance, the ad- 27
dition of some thousand carcasses in our exportation of barrelled beef;
the propagation of swine's flesh, and improvement in the art of making
good bacon, so much wanted among us by the great destruction of pigs,
too frequent at our tables, are no way comparable in taste or magnificence
to a well-grown, fat yearling child, which roasted whole will make a
considerable figure at a Lord Mayor's feast, or any other public entertainment. But this and many others I omit, being studious of brevity.

Supposing that one thousand families in this city would be constant 28
customers for infants flesh, besides others who might have it at merry
meetings, particularly weddings and christenings; I compute that Dublin
would take off annually about twenty thousand carcasses, and the rest
of the kingdom (where probably they will be sold somewhat cheaper) the
remaining eighty thousand.

I can think of no one objection that will possibly be raised against this 29
proposal, unless it should be urged that the number of people will be
thereby much lessened in the kingdom. This I freely own, and it was
indeed one principal design in offering it to the world. I desire the reader
will observe, that I calculate my remedy *for this one individual Kingdom
of* Ireland, *and for no other that ever was, is, or, I think, ever can be
upon earth.* Therefore let no man talk to me of other expedients: *Of
taxing our absentees at five shillings a pound: Of using neither clothes,
nor household furniture, except what is of our own growth and manufacture: Of utterly rejecting the materials and instruments that promote
foreign luxury: Of curing the expensiveness of pride, vanity, idleness,
and gaming in our women: Of introducing a vein of parsimony, prudence,
and temperance: Of learning to love our country, wherein we differ even
from* Laplanders, *and the inhabitants of* Topinamboo: *Of quitting our
animosities and factions, nor act any longer like the* Jews, *who were
murdering one another at the very moment their city was taken: Of being
a little cautious not to sell our country and consciences for nothing: Of
teaching landlords to have at least one degree of mercy towards their
tenants.* Lastly, *of putting a spirit of honesty, industry, and skill into
our shopkeepers, who, if a resolution could now be taken to buy only
our native goods, would immediately unite to cheat and exact upon us
in the price, the measure and the goodness, nor could ever yet be brought
to make one fair proposal of just dealing, though often and earnestly
invited to it.*

Therefore I repeat, let no man talk to me of these and the like expe- 30
dients, till he hath at least a glimpse of hope that there will ever be some
hearty and sincere attempt to put them in practice.

But as to myself, having been wearied out for many years with offering 31
vain, idle, visionary thoughts, and at length utterly despairing of success,
I fortunately fell upon this proposal, which as it is wholly new, so it hath
something solid and real, of no expense and little trouble, full in our own

power, and whereby we can incur no danger in disobliging England. For this kind of commodity will not bear exportation, the flesh being of too tender a consistence to admit a long continuance in salt, *although perhaps I could name a country which would be glad to eat up our whole nation without it.*

After all I am not so violently bent upon my own opinion as to reject 32 any offer, proposed by wise men, which shall be found equally innocent, cheap, easy and effectual. But before some thing of that kind shall be advanced in contradiction to my scheme, and offering a better, I desire the author, or authors, will be pleased maturely to consider two points. First, as things now stand, how they will be able to find food and raiment for a hundred thousand useless mouths and backs? And secondly, there being a round million of creatures in human figure, throughout this kingdom, whose whole subsistence put into a common stock would leave them in debt two millions of pounds sterling; adding those who are beggars by profession, to the bulk of farmers, cottagers, and labourers with their wives and children, who are beggars in effect; I desire those politicians who dislike my overture, and may perhaps be so bold to attempt an answer, that they will first ask the parents of these mortals whether they would not at this day think it a great happiness to have been sold for food at a year old, in the manner I prescribe, and thereby have avoided such a perpetual scene of misfortunes as they have since gone through, by the oppression of landlords, the impossibility of paying rent without money or trade, the want of common sustenance, with neither house nor clothes to cover them from the inclemencies of weather, and the most inevitable prospect of entailing the like, or greater miseries upon their breed for ever.

I profess in the sincerity of my heart that I have not the least personal 33 interest in endeavouring to promote this necessary work, having no other motive than the *public good of my country, by advancing our trade, providing for infants, relieving the poor, and giving some pleasure to the rich.* I have no children by which I can propose to get a single penny; the youngest being nine years old, and my wife past child-bearing.

Study Questions

1. In "A Modest Proposal," Jonathan Swift presents his message in an ironic manner. While seeming to propose seriously that one-year-old children be sold as meat animals, he argues that no one seems to care about the plight of the Irish poor. Where does he state that point most clearly? Why did he put his statement there?
2. Ironic or not, Swift's proposal has offended many readers. Do you think Swift was worried about being too offensive? Explain your answer by referring to the vocabulary he uses in specific passages.

3. What kind of person does Swift want his readers to think the writer of "A Modest Proposal" is? Do you think that Swift is actually like that person? Why or why not?
4. What is the major method of organization used in the essay? In what ways is it appropriate for the personality of the essay? How do Swift's vocabulary and sentence structure further fit both the organization and the "personality"?

Suggestion for Revising

In paragraph 29 Swift lists a large number of solutions to the problems of poverty in Ireland. Most of these solutions had, in fact, been suggested by him in other works. As a revising exercise, consider the list in paragraph 29 to be the result of previous prewriting and drafting you have done for an essay on the lives of the poor today. As part of that essay, plan to discuss possible solutions to their problems. Reformulate paragraphs 29–31 so that your attitude will be clear to your audience.

Heaven and Earth in Jest

Annie Dillard

I used to have a cat, an old fighting tom, who *1* would jump through the open window by my bed in the middle of the night and land on my chest. I'd half-awaken. He'd stick his skull under my nose and purr, stinking of urine and blood. Some nights he kneaded my bare chest with his front paws, powerfully, arching his back, as if sharpening his claws, or pummeling a mother for milk. And some mornings I'd wake in daylight to find my body covered with paw prints in blood; I looked as though I'd been painted with roses.

It was hot, so hot the mirror felt warm. I washed before the mirror *2* in a daze, my twisted summer sleep still hung about me like sea kelp. What blood was this, and what roses? It could have been the rose of union, the blood of murder, or the rose of beauty bare and the blood of some unspeakable sacrifice or birth. The sign on my body could have been an emblem or a stain, the keys to the kingdom or the mark of Cain. I never knew. I never knew as I washed, and the blood streaked, faded, and finally disappeared, whether I'd purified myself or ruined the blood sign of the passover. We wake, if we ever wake at all, to mystery, rumors of death, beauty, violence. . . . "Seem like we're just set down here," a woman said to me recently, "and don't nobody know why."

These are morning matters, pictures you dream as the final wave *3* heaves you up on the sand to the bright light and drying air. You remember pressure, and a curved sleep you rested against, soft, like a scallop in its shell. But the air hardens your skin; you stand; you leave the lighted shore to explore some dim headland, and soon you're lost in the leafy interior, intent, remembering nothing.

I still think of that old tomcat, mornings, when I wake. Things are *4* tamer now; I sleep with the window shut. The cat and our rites are gone and my life is changed, but the memory remains of something powerful playing over me. I wake expectant, hoping to see a new thing. If I'm lucky I might be jogged awake by a strange birdcall. I dress in a hurry, imagining the yard flapping with auks, or flamingos. This morning it was a wood duck, down at the creek. It flew away.

I live by a creek, Tinker Creek, in a valley in Virginia's Blue Ridge. *5* An anchorite's hermitage is called an anchor-hold; some anchor-holds were simple sheds clamped to the side of a church like a barnacle to a rock. I think of this house clamped to the side of Tinker Creek as an anchor-hold. It holds me at anchor to the rock bottom of the creek itself and it keeps me steadied in the current, as a sea anchor does, facing the stream of light pouring down. It's a good place to live; there's a lot to think about. The creeks—Tinker and Carvin's—are an active mystery, fresh every minute. Theirs is the mystery of the continuous creation and all that providence implies: the uncertainty of vision, the horror of the fixed, the dissolution of the present, the intricacy of beauty, the pressure of fecundity, the elusiveness of the free, and the flawed nature of perfection. The mountains—Tinker and Brushy, McAfee's Knob and Dead Man—are a passive mystery, the oldest of all. Theirs is the one simple mystery of creation from nothing, of matter itself, anything at all, the given. Mountains are giant, restful, absorbent. You can heave your spirit into a mountain and the mountain will keep it, folded, and not throw it back as some creeks will. The creeks are the world with all its stimulus and beauty; I live there. But the mountains are home.

The wood duck flew away. I caught only a glimpse of something like 6 a bright torpedo that blasted the leaves where it flew. Back at the house I ate a bowl of oatmeal; much later in the day came the long slant of light that means good walking.

If the day is fine, any walk will do; it all looks good. Water in particular 7 looks its best, reflecting blue sky in the flat, and chopping it into graveled shallows and white chute and foam in the riffles. On a dark day, or a hazy one, everything's washed-out and lack-luster but the water. It carries its own lights. I set out for the railroad tracks, for the hill the flocks fly over, for the woods where the white mare lives. But I go to the water.

Today is one of those excellent January partly cloudies in which light 8 chooses an unexpected part of the landscape to trick out in gilt, and then shadow sweeps it away. You know you're alive. You take huge steps, trying to feel the planet's roundness arc between your feet. Kazantzakis says that when he was young he had a canary and a globe. When he freed the canary, it would perch on the globe and sing. All his life, wandering the earth, he felt as though he had a canary on top of his mind, singing.

West of the house, Tinker Creek makes a sharp loop, so that the creek 9 is both in back of the house, south of me, and also on the other side of the road, north of me. I like to go north. There the afternoon sun hits the creek just right, deepening the reflected blue and lighting the sides of trees on the banks. Steers from the pasture across the creek come down to drink; I always flush a rabbit or two there; I sit on a fallen trunk in the shade and watch the squirrels in the sun. There are two separated wooden fences suspended from cables that cross the creek just upstream from my tree-trunk bench. They keep the steers from escaping up or down the creek when they come to drink. Squirrels, the neighborhood children, and I use the downstream fence as a swaying bridge across the creek. But the steers are there today.

I sit on the downed tree and watch the black steers slip on the creek 10 bottom. They are all bred beef: beef heart, beef hide, beef hocks. They're a human product like rayon. They're like a field of shoes. They have cast-iron shanks and tongues like foam insoles. You can't see through to their brains as you can with other animals; they have beef fat behind their eyes, beef stew.

I cross the fence six feet above the water, walking my hands down 11 the rusty cable and tightroping my feet along the narrow edge of the planks. When I hit the other bank and terra firma, some steers are bunched in a knot between me and the barbed-wire fence I want to cross. So I suddenly rush at them in an enthusiastic sprint, flailing my arms and hollering, "Lightning! Copperhead! Swedish meatballs!" They flee, still in a knot, stumbling across the flat pasture. I stand with the wind on my face.

When I slide under a barbed-wire fence, cross a field, and run over a 12 sycamore trunk felled across the water, I'm on a little island shaped like a tear in the middle of Tinker Creek. On one side of the creek is a steep forested bank; the water is swift and deep on that side of the island. On the other side is the level field I walked through next to the steers' pasture; the water between the field and the island is shallow and sluggish. In summer's low water, flags and bulrushes grow along a series of shallow pools cooled by the lazy current. Water striders patrol the surface film, crayfish hump along the silt bottom eating filth, frogs shout and glare, and shiners and small bream hide among roots from the sulky green heron's eye. I come to this island every month of the year. I walk around it, stopping and staring, or I straddle the sycamore log over the creek, curling my legs out of the water in winter, trying to read. Today I sit on dry grass at the end of the island by the slower side of the creek. I'm drawn to this spot. I come to it as to an oracle; I return to it as a man years later will seek out the battlefield where he lost a leg or an arm.

A couple of summers ago I was walking along the edge of the island 13 to see what I could see in the water, and mainly to scare frogs. Frogs have an inelegant way of taking off from invisible positions on the bank just ahead of your feet, in dire panic, emitting a froggy "Yike!" and splashing into the water. Incredibly, this amused me, and, incredibly, it amuses me still. As I walked along the grassy edge of the island, I got better and better at seeing frogs both in and out of the water. I learned to recognize, slowing down, the difference in texture of the light reflected from mudbank, water, grass, or frog. Frogs were flying all around me.

At the end of the island I noticed a small green frog. He was exactly half in and half out of the water, looking like a schematic diagram of an amphibian, and he didn't jump.

He didn't jump; I crept closer. At last I knelt on the island's winter- *14* killed grass, lost, dumbstruck, staring at the frog in the creek just four feet away. He was a very small frog with wide, dull eyes. And just as I looked at him, he slowly crumpled and began to sag. The spirit vanished from his eyes as if snuffed. His skin emptied and drooped; his very skull seemed to collapse and settle like a kicked tent. He was shrinking before my eyes like a deflating football. I watched the taut, glistening skin on his shoulders ruck, and rumple, and fall. Soon, part of his skin, formless as a pricked balloon, lay in floating folds like bright scum on top of the water: it was a monstrous and terrifying thing. I gaped bewildered, appalled. An oval shadow hung in the water behind the drained frog; then the shadow glided away. The frog skin bag started to sink.

I had read about the giant water bug, but never seen one. "Giant *15* water bug" is really the name of the creature, which is an enormous, heavy-bodied brown beetle. It eats insects, tadpoles, fish, and frogs. Its grasping forelegs are mighty and hooked inward. It seizes a victim with these legs, hugs it tight, and paralyzes it with enzymes injected during a vicious bite. That one bite is the only bite it ever takes. Through the puncture shoot the poisons that dissolve the victim's muscles and bones and organs—all but the skin—and through it the giant water bug sucks out the victim's body, reduced to a juice. This event is quite common in warm fresh water. The frog I saw was being sucked by a giant water bug. I had been kneeling on the island grass; when the unrecognizable flap of frog skin settled on the creek bottom, swaying, I stood up and brushed the knees of my pants. I couldn't catch my breath.

Of course, many carnivorous animals devour their prey alive. The *16* usual method seems to be to subdue the victim by downing or grasping it so it can't flee, then eating it whole or in a series of bloody bites. Frogs eat everything whole, stuffing prey into their mouths with their thumbs. People have seen frogs with their wide jaws so full of live dragonflies they couldn't close them. Ants don't even have to catch their prey: in the spring they swarm over newly hatched, featherless birds in the nest and eat them tiny bite by bite.

That it's rough out there and chancy is no surprise. Every live thing *17* is a survivor on a kind of extended emergency bivouac. But at the same time we are also created. In the Koran, Allah asks, "The heaven and the earth and all in between, thinkest thou I made them *in jest?*" It's a good question. What do we think of the created universe, spanning an unthinkable void with an unthinkable profusion of forms? Or what do we think of nothingness, those sickening reaches of time in either direction? If the giant water bug was not made in jest, was it then made in earnest? Pascal uses a nice term to describe the notion of the creator's, once having called forth the universe, turning his back to it: *Deus Absconditus*. Is this what we think happened? Was the sense of it there, and God absconded with it, ate it, like a wolf who disappears round the edge of the house with the Thanksgiving turkey? "God is subtle," Einstein said, "but not malicious." Again, Einstein said that "nature conceals her mystery by means of her essential grandeur, not by her cunning." It could be that God has not absconded but spread, as our vision and understanding of the universe have spread, to a fabric of spirit and sense so grand and subtle, so powerful in a new way, that we can only feel blindly of its hem. In making the thick darkness a swaddling band for the sea, God "set bars and doors" and said, "Hitherto shalt thou come, but no further." But have we come even that far? Have we rowed out to the thick darkness, or are we all playing pinochle in the bottom of the boat?

Cruelty is a mystery, and the waste of pain. But if we describe a *18* world to compass these things, a world that is a long, brute game, then we bump against another mystery: the inrush of power and light, the canary that sings on the skull. Unless all ages and races of men have been deluded by the same mass hypnotist (who?), there seems to be such a thing as beauty, a grace wholly gratuitous. About five years ago I saw a mockingbird make a straight vertical descent from the roof gutter of a four-story building. It was an act as careless and spontaneous as the curl of a stem or the kindling of a star.

The mockingbird took a single step into the air and dropped. His *19* wings were still folded against his sides as though he were singing from a limb and not falling, accelerating thirty-two feet per second per second, through empty air. Just a breath before he would have been dashed to the ground, he unfurled his wings with exact, deliberate care, revealing the broad bars of white, spread his elegant, white-banded tail, and so floated onto the grass. I had just rounded a corner when his insouciant step caught my eye; there was no one else in sight. The fact of his free fall was like the old philosophical conundrum about the tree that falls in the forest. The answer must be, I think, that beauty and grace are performed whether or not we will or sense them. The least we can do is try to be there.

Another time I saw another wonder: sharks off the Atlantic coast of *20* Florida. There is a way a wave rises above the ocean horizon, a triangular wedge against the sky. If you stand where the ocean breaks on a shallow beach, you see the raised water in a wave is translucent, shot with lights. One late afternoon at low tide a hundred big sharks passed the beach near the mouth of a tidal river in a feeding frenzy. As each green wave rose from the churning water, it illuminated within itself the six- or eight-foot-long bodies of twisting sharks. The sharks disappeared as each wave rolled toward me; then a new wave would swell above the horizon, containing in it, like scorpions in amber, sharks that roiled and heaved. The sight held awesome wonders: power and beauty, grace tangled in a rapture with violence.

We don't know what's going on here. If these tremendous events are 21 random combinations of matter run amok, the yield of millions of monkeys at millions of typewriters, then what is it in us, hammered out of those same typewriters, that they ignite? We don't know. Our life is a faint tracing on the surface of mystery, like the idle, curved tunnels of leaf miners on the face of a leaf. We must somehow take a wider view, look at the whole landscape, really see it, and describe what's going on here. Then we can at least wail the right question into the swaddling band of darkness, or, if it comes to that, choir the proper praise.

At the time of Lewis and Clark, setting the prairies on fire was a well- 22 known signal that meant, "Come down to the water." It was an extravagant gesture, but we can't do less. If the landscape reveals one certainty, it is that the extravagant gesture is the very stuff of creation. After the one extravagant gesture of creation in the first place, the universe has continued to deal exclusively in extravagances, flinging intricacies and colossi down aeons of emptiness, heaping profusions on profligacies with ever-fresh vigor. The whole show has been on fire from the word go. I come down to the water to cool my eyes. But everywhere I look I see fire; that which isn't flint is tinder, and the whole world sparks and flames.

I have come to the grassy island late in the day. The creek is up; icy 23 water sweeps under the sycamore log bridge. The frog skin, of course, is utterly gone. I have stared at that one spot on the creek bottom for so long, focusing past the rush of water, that when I stand, the opposite bank seems to stretch before my eyes and flow grassily upstream. When the bank settles down I cross the sycamore log and enter again the big plowed field next to the steers' pasture.

The wind is terrific out of the west; the sun comes and goes. I can 24 see the shadow on the field before me deepen uniformly and spread like a plague. Everything seems so dull I am amazed I can even distinguish objects. And suddenly the light runs across the land like a comber, and up the trees, and goes again in a wink: I think I've gone blind or died. When it comes again, the light, you hold your breath, and if it stays you forget about it until it goes again.

It's the most beautiful day of the year. At four o'clock the eastern 25 sky is a dead stratus black flecked with low white clouds. The sun in the west illuminates the ground, the mountains, and especially the bare branches of trees, so that everywhere silver trees cut into the black sky like a photographer's negative of a landscape. The air and the ground are dry; the mountains are going on and off like neon signs. Clouds slide east as if pulled from the horizon, like a tablecloth whipped off a table. The hemlocks by the barbed-wire fence are flinging themselves east as though their backs would break. Purple shadows are racing east; the wind makes me face east, and again I feel the dizzying, drawn sensation I felt when the creek bank reeled.

At four-thirty the sky in the east is clear; how could that big blackness 26 be blown? Fifteen minutes later another darkness is coming overhead from the northwest; and it's here. Everything is drained of its light as if sucked. Only at the horizon do inky black mountains give way to distant, lighted mountains—lighted not by direct illumination but rather paled by glowing sheets of mist hung before them. Now the blackness is in the east; everything is half in shadow, half in sun, every clod, tree, mountain, and hedge. I can't see Tinker Mountain through the line of hemlock, till it comes on like a streetlight, ping, *ex nihilo*. Its sandstone cliffs pink and swell. Suddenly the light goes; the cliffs recede as if pushed. The sun hits a clump of sycamores between me and the mountains; the sycamore arms light up, and *I can't see the cliffs*. They're gone. The pale network of sycamore arms, which a second ago was transparent as a screen, is suddenly opaque, glowing with light. Now the sycamore arms snuff out, the mountains come on, and there are the cliffs again.

I walk home. By five-thirty the show has pulled out. Nothing is left 27 but an unreal blue and a few banked clouds low in the north. Some sort of carnival magician has been here, some fast-talking worker of wonders who has the act backwards. "Something in this hand," he says, "something in this hand, something up my sleeve, something behind my back . . ." and abracadabra, he snaps his fingers, and it's all gone. Only the bland, blank-faced magician remains, in his unruffled coat, barehanded, acknowledging a smattering of baffled applause. When you look again the whole show has pulled up stakes and moved on down the road. It never stops. New shows roll in from over the mountains and the magician reappears unannounced from a fold in the curtain you never dreamed was an opening. Scarves of clouds, rabbits in plain view, disappear into the black hat forever. Presto chango. The audience, if there is an audience at all, is dizzy from head-turning, dazed.

Like the bear who went over the mountain, I went out to see what I 28 could see. And, I might as well warn you, like the bear, all that I could see was the other side of the mountain: more of same. On a good day I might catch a glimpse of another wooded ridge rolling under the sun like water, another bivouac. I propose to keep here what Thoreau called "a meteorological journal of the mind," telling some tales and describing some of the sights of this rather tamed valley, and exploring, in fear and trembling, some of the unmapped dim reaches and unholy fastnesses to which those tales and sights so dizzyingly lead.

I am no scientist. I explore the neighborhood. An infant who has *29*
just learned to hold his head up has a frank and forthright way of gazing
about him in bewilderment. He hasn't the faintest clue where he is, and
he aims to learn. In a couple of years, what he will have learned instead
is how to fake it: he'll have the cocksure air of a squatter who has come
to feel he owns the place. Some unwonted, taught pride diverts us from
our original intent, which is to explore the neighborhood, view the landscape, to discover at least *where* it is that we have been so startlingly
set down, if we can't learn why.

So I think about the valley. It is my leisure as well as my work, a *30*
game. It is a fierce game I have joined because it is being played anyway,
a game of both skill and chance, played against an unseen adversary—
the conditions of time—in which the payoffs, which may suddenly arrive
in a blast of light at any moment, might as well come to me as anyone
else. I stake the time I'm grateful to have, the energies I'm glad to direct.
I risk getting stuck on the board, so to speak, unable to move in any
direction, which happens enough, God knows; and I risk the searing,
exhausting nightmares that plunder rest and force me face down all night
long in some muddy ditch seething with hatching insects and crustaceans.

But if I can bear the nights, the days are a pleasure. I walk out; I see *31*
something, some event that would otherwise have been utterly missed
and lost; or something sees me, some enormous power brushes me with
its clean wing, and I resound like a beaten bell.

I am an explorer, then, and I am also a stalker, or the instrument of *32*
the hunt itself. Certain Indians used to carve long grooves along the
wooden shafts of their arrows. They called the grooves "lightning
marks," because they resembled the curved fissure lightning slices down
the trunks of trees. The function of lightning marks is this: if the arrow
fails to kill the game, blood from a deep wound will channel along the
lightning mark, streak down the arrow shaft, and spatter to the ground,
laying a trail dripped on broadleaves, on stones, that the barefoot and
trembling archer can follow into whatever deep or rare wilderness it
leads. I am the arrow shaft, carved along my length by unexpected lights
and gashes from the very sky, and this book is the straying trail of blood.

Something pummels us, something barely sheathed. Power broods *33*
and lights. We're played on like a pipe; our breath is not our own.
James Houston describes two young Eskimo girls sitting cross-legged on
the ground, mouth on mouth, blowing by turns each other's throat cords,
making a low, unearthly music. When I cross again the bridge that is
really the steers' fence, the wind has thinned to the delicate air of twilight;
it crumples the water's skin. I watch the running sheets of light raised
on the creek's surface. The sight has the appeal of the purely passive,
like the racing of light under clouds on a field, the beautiful dream at the
moment of being dreamed. The breeze is the merest puff, but you
yourself sail headlong and breathless under the gale force of the spirit.

Study Questions

1. Annie Dillard begins "Heaven and Earth in Jest" with a description of her occasionally awaking in the morning to find on her body the bloody paw prints of her cat. What is her reaction to those mornings? How do you react to them? How does she use this disturbing picture to introduce her topic?
2. In paragraphs 13–17, Dillard tells of how she once looked on as a giant water bug consumed a frog by dissolving everything inside the frog's skin and sucking it dry. What vocabulary does she use to describe this incident? What emotions do these words suggest Dillard felt on seeing it?
3. In paragraphs 18–22, Dillard describes things of grace and beauty. Compare the words she uses in these paragraphs with those she used in the story of the frog and the water bug. What differences do you see in the connotations? What similarities do you see? In what ways should these similarities and differences remind you of the bloody paw prints of the opening paragraphs?
4. In the last sentence of paragraph 2, Dillard quotes a popular view of life: "Seem like we're just set down here, and don't nobody know why." After reading the entire essay, what opinion do you think Dillard has of this view?
5. Dillard has filled her paragraphs with similes, figures of speech comparing two essentially unlike things, usually introduced by *like* or *as*. Keeping in mind the image of the bloody paw prints and Dillard's reaction to them, identify several of these similes and discuss how they help the readers understand Dillard's theme.

Suggestion for Revising

In paragraph 20, Dillard describes the "wonder" of seeing a group of sharks during a feeding frenzy. Reformulate this paragraph so that your words describe a "horror" rather than a "wonder." Notice that Dillard describes the sharks from a distance at which the specific details of what they do can be overlooked. In your reformulation, go in for a closer view (in order to describe the feeding in greater detail).

September 28

Peter Matthiessen

A t sunrise the small expedition meets beneath 1 a giant fig beyond Pokhara—two white sahibs, four sherpas, fourteen porters. The sherpas are of the famous mountain tribe of northeast Nepal, near Namche Bazaar, whose men accompany the ascents of the great peaks; they are Buddhist herders who have come down in recent centuries out of eastern Tibet—*sherpa* is a Tibetan word for "easterner"—and their language, culture, and appearance all reflect Tibetan origin. One of the porters is also a Sherpa, and two are refugee Tibetans; the rest are of mixed Aryan and Mongol stock. Mostly barefoot, in ragged shorts or the big-seated, jodhpur-legged pants of India, wearing all manner of old vests and shawls and headgear, the porters pick over the tall wicker baskets. In addition to their own food and blankets, they must carry a load of up to eighty pounds that is braced on their bent backs by a tump line around the forehead, and there is much hefting and denunciation of the loads, together with shrill bargaining, before any journey in these mountains can begin. Porters are mostly local men of uncertain occupation and unsteadfast habit, notorious for giving trouble. But it is also true that their toil is hard and wretchedly rewarded—about one dollar a day. As a rule, they accompany an expedition for no more than a week away from home, after which they are replaced by others, and the hefting and denunciation start anew. Today nearly two hours pass, and clouds have gathered, before all fourteen are mollified, and the tattered line sets off toward the west.

We are glad to go. These edges of Pokhara might be tropical outskirts 2 anywhere—vacant children, listless adults, bent dogs and thin chickens in a litter of sagging shacks and rubble, mud, weeds, stagnant ditches, bad sweet smells, vivid bright broken plastic bits, and dirty fruit peelings awaiting the carrion pig; for want of better fare, both pigs and dogs consume the human excrement that lies everywhere along the paths. In fair weather, all this flux is tolerable, but now at the dreg end of the rainy season, the mire of life seems leached into the sallow skins of these thin beings, who squat and soap themselves and wring their clothes each morning in the rain puddles.

Brown eyes observe us as we pass. Confronted with the pain of Asia, 3 one cannot look and cannot turn away. In India, human misery seems so pervasive that one takes in only stray details; a warped leg or a dead eye, a sick pariah dog eating withered grass, an ancient woman lifting her sari to move her shrunken bowels by the road. Yet in Varanasi there is hope of life that has been abandoned in such cities as Calcutta, which seems resigned to the dead and dying in its gutters. Shiva dances in the spicy foods, in the exhilarated bells of the swarming bicycles, the angry bus horns, the chatter of the temple monkeys, the vermilion tikka dot on the women's foreheads, even in the scent of charred human flesh that pervades the ghats. The people smile—that is the greatest miracle of all. In the heat and stench and shriek of Varanasi, where in fiery sunrise swallows fly like departing spirits over the vast silent river, one delights in the smile of a blind girl being led, of a Hindu gentleman in white turban gazing benignly at the bus driver who reviles him, of a flute-playing beggar boy, of a slow old woman pouring holy water from Ganga, the River, onto a stone elephant daubed red.

Near the burning ghats, and the industry of death, a river palace has *4* been painted with huge candy-striped tigers.

No doubt Varanasi is the destination of this ancient Hindu at the *5* outskirts of Pokhara, propped up on a basket borne on poles across the shoulders of four servants—off, it appears, on his last pilgrimage to the Mother Ganges, to the dark temples that surround the ghats, to those hostels where the pilgrim waits his turn to join the company of white-shrouded cadavers by the river edge, waits again to be laid upon the stacks of fired wood: the attendants will push this yellow foot, that shriveled elbow, back into the fire, and rake his remains off the burning platform into the swift river. And still enough scraps will remain to sustain life in the long-headed cadaverous dogs that haunt the ashes, while sacred kine—hugh white silent things—devour the straw thongs that had bound this worn-out body to its stretcher.

The old man has been ravened from within. That blind and greedy *6* stare of his, that caved-in look, and the mouth working, reveal who now inhabits him, who now stares out.

I nod to Death in passing, aware of the sound of my own feet upon *7* my path. The ancient is lost in a shadow world, and gives no sign.

Gray river road, gray sky. From rock to torrent rock flits a pied *8* wagtail.

Wayfarers: a delicate woman bears a hamper of small silver fishes, *9* and another bends low beneath a basket of rocks that puts my own light pack to shame; her rocks will be hammered to gravel by other women of Pokhara, in the labor of the myriad brown hands that will surface a new road south to India.

Through a shaft of sun moves a band of Magar women, scarlet- *10* shawled; they wear heavy brass ornaments in the left nostril. In the new sun, a red-combed rooster clambers quickly to the roof matting of a roadside hut, and fitfully a little girl starts singing. The light irradiates white peaks of Annapurna marching down the sky, in the great rampart

that spreads east and west for eighteen hundred miles, the Himalaya—
the *alaya* (abode, or home) of *hima* (snow).

Hibiscus, frangipani, bougainvillea: seen under snow peaks, these *11*
tropical blossoms become the flowers of heroic landscapes. Macaques
scamper in green meadow, and a turquoise roller spins in a golden light.
Drongos, rollers, barbets, and the white Egyptian vulture are the common
birds, and all have close relatives in East Africa, where GS* and I first
met; he wonders how this vulture would react if confronted with the egg
of an ostrich, which was also a common Asian bird during the Pleistocene. In Africa, the Egyptian vulture is recognized as a tool-using species, due to its knack of cracking the huge ostrich eggs by slinging rocks
at them with its beak.

Until quite recently, these Nepal lowlands were broadleaf evergreen *12*
sal forest (*Shorea robusta*), the haunt of elephant and tiger and the great
Indian rhinoceros. Forest-cutting and poaching cleared them out; except
in last retreats such as the Rapti Valley, to the southeast, the saintly
tread of elephants is gone. The last wild Indian cheetah was sighted in
central India in 1952, the Asian lion is reduced to a single small population
in the Gir Forest, northwest of Bombay, and the tiger becomes legendary
almost everywhere. Especially in India and Pakistan, the hoofed animals
are rapidly disapppearing, due to destruction of habitat by subsistence
agriculture, overcutting of the forests, overgrazing by the scraggy hordes
of domestic animals, erosion, flood—the whole dismal cycle of events
that acccompanies overcrowding by human beings. In Asia more than
all places on earth, it is crucial to establish wildlife sanctuaries at once,
before the last animals are overwhelmed. As GS has written, "Man is
modifying the world so fast and so drastically that most animals cannot
adapt to the new conditions. In the Himalaya as elsewhere there is a
great dying, one infinitely sadder than the Pleistocene extinctions, for
man now has the knowledge and the need to save these remnants of his
past."

The track along the Yamdi River is a main trading route, passing *13*
through rice paddies and villages on its way west to the Kali Gandaki
River, where it turns north to Mustang and Tibet. Green village com-
pounds, set about with giant banyans and old stone pools and walls, are
cropped to lawn by water buffalo and cattle; the fresh water and soft
shade give them the harmony of parks. These village folk own even less
than those of Pokhara, yet they are spared by their old economies from
modern poverty: one understands why "village life" has been celebrated
as the natural, happy domain of man by many thinkers, from Lao-tzu to
Gandhi. In a warm sun children play, and women roll clothes on rocks
at the village fountain and pound grain in stone mortars, and from all

* George Schaller: naturalist, scholar, and author of *Year of the Gorilla*.

sides come reassuring dung smells and chicken clatter and wafts of fire smoke from the low hearths. In tidy yards, behind strong stiles and walls, the clay huts are of warm earthen red, with thatched roofs, hand-carved sills and shutters, and yellow-flowered pumpkin vines. Maize is stacked in narrow cribs, and rice is spread to dry on broad straw mats, and between the banana and papaya trees big calm spiders hang against the sky.

A canal bridged here and there by ten-foot granite slabs runs through *14* a hamlet, pouring slowly over shining pebbles. It is midday, the sun melts the air, and we sit on a stone wall in the cool shade. By the canal is the village tea house, a simple open-fronted hut with makeshift benches and a clay oven in the form of a rounded mound on the clay floor. The mound has a side opening for inserting twigs and two holes on the top for boiling water, which is poured through a strainer of cheap tea dust into a glass containing coarse sugar and buffalo milk. With this *chiya* we take plain bread and a fresh cucumber, while children playing on the shining stones pretend to splash us, and a collared dove sways on a tall stalk of bamboo.

One by one the porters come, turning around to lower their loads onto *15* the wall. A porter of shy face and childlike smile, who looks too slight for his load, is playing comb music on a fig leaf. "Too many hot," says another, smiling. This is the Sherpa porter, Tukten, a wiry small man with Mongol eyes and outsized ears and a disconcerting smile—I wonder why this Tukten is a porter.

I set off ahead, walking alone in the cool breeze of the valley. In the *16* bright September light and mountain shadow—steep foothills are closing in as the valley narrows, and the snow peaks to the north are no longer seen—the path follows a dike between the reedy canal and the green terraces of rice that descend in steps to the margins of the river. Across the canal, more terraces ascend to the crests of the high hills, and a blue sky.

At a rest wall, two figs of different species were planted long ago; one *17* is a banyan, or nigrodha (*Ficus indica*), the other a pipal (*F. religiosa*), sacred to both the Hindus and the Buddhists. Wild flowers and painted stones are set among the buttressed roots, to bring the traveler good fortune, and stone terraces are built up around the trunks in such a way that the shade-seeking traveler may back up and set down his load while standing almost straight. These resting places are everywhere along the trading routes, some of them so ancient that the great trees have long since died, leaving two round holes in a stonework oval platform. Like the tea houses and the broad steppingstones that are built into the hills, the rest walls impart a blessedness to this landscape, as if we had wandered into a lost country of the golden age.

Awaiting the line of porters that winds through the paddies, I sit on *18* the top level of the wall, my feet on the step on which the loads are set and my back against a tree. In dry sunshine and the limpid breeze down from the mountains, two black cows are threshing rice, flanks gleaming in the light of afternoon. First the paddy is drained and the rice sickled, then the yoked animals, tied by a long line to a stake in the middle of the rice, are driven round and round in a slowly decreasing circle while children fling the stalks beneath their hooves. Then the stalks are tossed into the air, and the grains beneath swept into baskets to be taken home and winnowed. The fire-colored dragonflies in the early autumn air, the bent backs in bright reds and yellows, the gleam on the black cattle and wheat stubble, the fresh green of the paddies and the sparkling river— over everything lies an immortal light, like transparent silver.

In the clean air and absence of all sound, of even the simplest ma- *19* chinery—for the track is often tortuous and steep, and fords too many streams, to permit bicyles—in the warmth and harmony and seeming plenty, come whispers of a paradisal age. Apparently the grove of *sal* trees called Lumbini, only thirty miles south of this same tree, in fertile lands north of the Rapti River, has changed little since the sixth century B.C., when Siddhartha Gautama was born there to a rich clan of the Sakya tribe in a kingdom of elephants and tigers. Gautama forsook a life of ease to become a holy mendicant, or "wanderer"—a common practice in northern India even today. Later he was known as Sakyamuni (Sage of the Sakyas), and afterward, the Buddha—the Awakened One. Fig trees and the smoke of peasant fires, the greensward and gaunt cattle, white egrets and jungle crows are still seen on the Ganges Plain where Sakyamuni passed his life, from Lumbini south and east to Varanasi (an ancient city even when Gautama came there) and Rajgir and Gaya. Tradition says that he traveled as far north as Kathmandu (even then a prosperous city of the Newars) and preached on the hill of Swayam-bhunath, among the monkeys and the pines.

In Sakyamuni's time, the disciplines called yogas were already well *20* evolved. Perhaps a thousand years before, the dark-skinned Dravidians of lowland India had been overcome by nomad Aryans from the Asian steppes who were bearing their creed of sky gods, wind, and light across Eurasia. Aryan concepts were contained in their Sanskrit Vedas, or knowledge—ancient texts of unknown origin which include the Rig Veda and the Upanishads and were to become the base of the Hindu religion. To the wandering ascetic named Sakyamuni, such epic preachments on the nature of the Universe and Man were useless as a cure for human suffering. In what became known as the Four Noble Truths, Sakyamuni perceived that man's existence is inseparable from sorrow; that the cause of suffering is craving; that peace is attained by extinguishing craving; that this liberation may be brought about by following the Eight-fold Path: right attention to one's understanding, intentions, speech, and ac-tions; right livelihood, effort, mindfulness; right concentration, by which is meant the unification of the self through sitting yoga.

The Vedas already included the idea that mortal desire—since it im- *21*
plies lack—had no place in the highest state of being; that what was
needed was that death-in-life and spiritual rebirth sought by all teachers,
from the early shamans to the existentialists. Sakyamuni's creed was
less a rejection of Vedic philosophy than an effort to apply it, and his
intense practice of meditation does not content itself with the serenity of
yoga states (which in his view falls short of ultimate truth) but goes
beyond, until the transparent radiance of stilled mind opens out in *prajna,*
or transcendent *knowing,* that higher consciousness or "Mind" which is
inherent in all sentient beings, and which depends on the unsentimental
embrace of all existence. A true experience of *prajna* correponds to
"enlightenment" or liberation—not change, but transformation—a profound vision of his identity with universal life, past, present, and future,
that keeps man from doing harm to others and sets him free from fear of
birth-and-death.

In the fifth century B.C., near the town of Gaya, south and east of *22*
Varanasi, Sakyamuni attained enlightenment in the deep experience that
his own "true nature," his Buddha-nature, was no different from the
nature of the universe. For half a century thereafter, at such places as
the Deer Park in Sarnath, and Nalanda, and the Vulture's Peak near
present-day Rajgir, he taught a doctrine based upon the impermanence
of individual existence, the eternal continuity of becoming, as in the
morning river that appears the same as the river of the night before, now
passed away. (Though he preached to women and weakened the caste
system by admitting low-born brethren to his order, Sakyamuni never
involved himself in social justice, far less government; his way holds that
self-realization is the greatest contribution one can make to one's fellow
man.) At the age of eighty, he ended his days at Kusinagara (the modern
Kusinara), forty miles east of Gorakhpur and just west of the Kali Gandaki River.

This much is true; all else is part of the great Buddha legend, which *23*
is truth of a different order. In regard to his enlightenment, it is related
that this wanderer was in his thirties when he gave up the rigors of the
yogi and embraced the "Middle Path" between sensuality and mortifica-
tion, accepting food in a golden bowl from the daughter of the village
headman. Thereupon, he was renounced by his disciples. At dusk he
sat himself beneath a pipal tree with his face toward the East, vowing
that though his skin and nerves and bones should waste away and his
life-blood dry, he would not leave this seat until he had attained Supreme
Enlightenment. All that night, beset by demons, Sakyamuni sat in meditation. And in that golden daybreak, it is told, the Self-Awakened One
truly perceived the Morning Star, as if seeing it for the first time in his
life.

In what is now known as Bodh Gaya—still a pastoral land of cattle *24*
savanna, shimmering water, rice paddies, palms, and red-clay hamlets

without paved roads or wires—a Buddhist temple stands beside an ancient pipal, descended from that *bodhi* tree, or "Enlightenment Tree," beneath which this man sat. Here in a warm dawn, ten days ago, with three Tibetan monks in maroon robes, I watched the rising of the Morning Star and came away no wiser than before. But later I wondered if the Tibetans were aware that the *bodhi* tree was murmuring with gusts of birds, while another large pipal, so close by that it touched the holy tree with many branches, was without life. I make no claim for this event: I simply declare what I saw there at Bodh Gaya.

Already the Yamdi Khola narrows; soon it will vanish among moun- 25 tains. In a village on the northern slope, the huts are round or oval rather than rectangular, and Jang-bu, the head sherpa, says that this is a village of the Gurung, a people who came down long ago out of Tibet. In this region of southern Nepal live various hill peoples of Mongol and Aryan mix, most of them Paharis, or hill Hindus. For centuries, the Hindus have come up along the river valleys from the great plain of the Ganges, while Tibetans crossed the mountain passes from the north: the Tibetan-speaking Buddhist tribes, which include the Sherpas, are called Bhotes, or southern Tibetans. (Bhot or B'od is Tibet; Bhutan, which lies at the southern edge of Tibet, means "End of Bhot.") Of the tribes represented by the porters, the Gurungs and Tamangs tend toward Buddhism, while the Chetris and Magars are Hindus. Whether Hindu or Buddhist, most of these tribes—and the Gurung especially—pay respect to the animist deities of the old religions that persist in remote corners of the Asian mountains.

Some long-haired Tibetans, buttery flat faces red with ocher sheen, 26 descend the river barefoot on the silver stones. (Ocher is a traditional protection against cold and insects, and before the civilizing influence of Buddhism, Tibet was known as the Land of the Red-faced Devils.) These people are bound for Pokhara from Dhorpatan, a week away. When crops are harvested, the Tibetans, Mustang Bhotes, and other hill peoples follow the ridges and valleys south and east to Pokhara and Kathmandu, trading wool and salt for grain and paper, knives, tobacco, rice, and tea. One Tibetan boy has caught a rockfish in the shallows; he runs to show me, almond eyes agleam. The children all along the way are friendly and playful, even gay; though they beg a little, they are not serious about it, as are the grim Hindu children of the towns. More likely they will take your hand and walk along a little, or do a somersault, or tag and run away.

Where the valley narrows to a canyon, there is a tea house and some 27 huts, and here a pack train of shaggy Mongol ponies descends from the mountain in a melody of bells and splashes across the swift green water at the ford. From the tea house, a trail climbs steeply toward the southwest sky. In this land, the subsistence economies have always depended upon travel, and in its decades—centuries, perhaps—as a trade route for the hill peoples, broad steps have been worn into the mountain path. Wild chestnut trees overhang the trail; we pull down branches to pick the spiny nuts.

At sunset, the trail arrives at the hill village called Naudanda. Here I try out my new home, a one-man mountain tent, in poor condition. Phu-Tsering, our merry cook, in bright red cap, brings supper of lentils and rice, and afterward I sit outside on a wicker stool acquired at the tea house at the ford, and listen to cicadas and a jackal. This east-west ridge falls steeply on both sides to the Yamdi Valley in the north, the Marsa in the south; from Naudanda, the Yamdi Khola is no more than a white ribbon rushing down between dark walls of conifers into its gorge. Far away eastward, far below, the Marsa River opens out into Lake Phewa, near Pokhara, which glints in the sunset of the foothills. There are no roads west of Pokhara, which is the last outpost of the modern world; in one day's walk we are a century away.

28

Study Questions

1. "September 28" is an entry in the journal by Peter Matthiessen published as *The Snow Leopard*. On September 28, Matthiessen experienced a special moment of insight, which he tries to share with his readers. What has Matthiessen learned? How does he organize his entry around it? How does this organization resemble that of an essay?
2. The very last sentence of "September 28" suggests that some sort of contrast is implied: "There are no roads west of Pokhara, which is the last outpost of the modern world; in one day's walk we are a century away." What are the things being contrasted here? How is this contrast part of the insight Matthiessen has had this day?
3. Do you notice any differences among the adjectives Matthiessen uses to describe each area he travels through as he goes from Pokhara to Naundanda? Find a passage from the opening and one from the ending in which Matthiessen describes a scene that impresses him. What differences are there in the connotations of the words he uses in each? How might these differences be related to what he has learned during the day?
4. Matthiessen does occasionally use the pronouns *we* and *I* in this entry, but for the most part his voice seems to be impersonal. Point to specific passages that illustrate the characteristics of this voice. Why would Matthiessen choose such a style to present an account of his own journey?

Suggestion for Revising

In the suggestion for drafting following "Little Things That Tick Off Baboons" (p. 313), we asked you to rework a series of short sentences into a paragraph in which you describe three kinds of essays. If you followed the usual methods, your redraft of the opening sentence probably ended up something like this: "Writers create three kinds of essays: personal, descriptive, and expository." Such a sentence certainly fulfills the assignment, but it does not present the topic in an interesting manner. In this exercise, we will ask you to return to your draft and reformulate it so that it will convey an opinion or attitude that will interest your readers. For example, the sentence just quoted might be reformulated to read like this: "Boring writers produce three kinds of deadly essays: the egotistically personal, the endlessly descriptive, and the pointlessly expository." As you rework the original, don't be afraid to add new meanings. Writers frequently make such additions during reformulation as they try to emphasize an opinion or attitude.

People of the Ruined Hills

Skip Rozin

T he word is terracide. As in homicide, or gen- *1*
ocide. Except it's terra. Land.
It is not committed with guns and knives, but *2*
with great, relentless bulldozers and thundering dump trucks, with giant
shovels like mythological creatures, their girdered necks lifting massive
steel mouths high above the tallest trees. And with dynamite. They cut
and blast and rip apart mountains to reach the minerals inside, and when
they have finished there is nothing left but naked hills, ugly monuments
to waste, stripped of everything that once held them in place, cut off
from the top and sides and dug out from the inside and then left, restless,
to slide down on houses and wash off into rivers and streams, rendering
the land unlivable and the water for miles downstream undrinkable.

Terracide. Or, if you prefer, strip mining. *3*

It has become more and more common in the last fifteen years, in the *4*
South and the Southwest and the Far West, in Pennsylvania and Ohio
and Texas. But the worst is in Appalachia. In West Virginia, and
especially in Kentucky, Eastern Kentucky, in the mountains.

There is where the people live right on the steep, proud mountains, *5*
on the mountains and all through them, and in the hills and along streams
that form hollows and tiny valleys. They have lived there for five and
six and seven and eight generations. The same homes in the same
mountains.

To the mining companies the mountains are large, green coal mines, *6*
just as they were timber forests to the men who first bought the rights a
hundred years ago in questionable dealings for forty or fifty cents an
acre, then sold those rights when they were through.

The deeds are the same, infamous broad-form deeds that bought the *7*
rights to everything above and below the soil. Still being sold from
company to company, and still held legal. The prize is different. Now
it is coal, and the cost to the hills is greater than when they were cutting
timber. But the attitudes of the companies are the same—they take and
leave.

And the people, they are much the same. *8*

Mountain people tend to be slow to change. Not that they are against *9*
progress. They are not. They have cars, or trucks, and television sets,

some color. Few are paid for, of course, but that is not the point. They
accept the decorations of the 1970s.

But inside, deep inside where people decide who they are, they change *10*
very little. Men whose fathers and grandfathers were coal miners are
coal miners, as are their sons. A man born and reared on Turkey Creek
may have moved to Camp Branch or as far as Dry Fork, but the odds of
his having left Letcher County by the time he dies are slim.

Some do. Especially now, the younger ones are sifting away to the *11*
cities in greater and greater numbers, for school and work and for no
reason other than that they now know another world exists out there.

But their parents and their grandparents remain, in the same counties *12*
and the same hollows, and even in the same houses. It's the mountains,
they say—they hold a man. And of those who leave for a year or so, to
go to Cincinnati to work in the soap factory or to Detroit to the car
plants, most return to the mountains.

Bert Caudill spent two years in Detroit back in the fifties, and Bessie *13*
Smith twice went north with her husband and children, but they came
back. And Joe Begley worked for a while in Connecticut, but he came
back. Most of them come back, back to the mountains.

"I believe in this place," Joe Begley told me on the front porch of his *14*
general store in Blackey. It was after lunch one day early in the summer.
He likes to close for an hour or so just past noon, to work at his desk or
just sit on the squeaking front swing and look across highway seven, past
the creek and up into the hills.

"I believe in the mountains and the streams. I think they're Jesus *15*
Christ, or God maybe."

Those are not casual words; Joe Begley is not a casual man. He *16*
comes by his feelings honestly. His grandmother was a Cherokee Indian,
and though his father wanted to raise him as a white man, the old woman
taught her grandson to love the trees and the water and the hills as living
deities.

The lesson stuck, and has made the destruction he has witnessed in *17*
his fifty-three years in eastern Kentucky a repulsive sight, and it has
helped him choose a path.

He is a strange man, tall and lean and dark, with the dark eyes and *18*
black straight hair of an Indian. In his little office off the store are books
on trees and animals and the land, titles like *Nature and Wildlife, Environment and Cultural Behavior,* and *Yesterday's People,* and a dozen
more stacked up on the desk and on the floor and against the door, along
with copies of *The New Yorker* and *Audubon.*

His formal education has been sparse, and he dresses in blue jeans, *19*
but he is defending his land against the army of machines with the tools
of men whose walls are lined with degrees and who wear imported
neckties and double knits, fighting with lawsuits and courts.

From his store he has helped organize the people of the area, of 20
Blackey and Elk Creek and Jeremiah and Caudill's Branch, trying to
help those who live in the hollows and the mountains fight the broad-
form deeds, trying to make those who would sign new agreements aware
that ten cents a ton is not worth what will follow, trying to keep the
strippers off.

"This strip coal is cheap, dirty coal," he told me on the hard, metal 21
porch swing, "and 70 percent of it's bought by the TVA. The government. The government's scalping our land."

And looking out across the two-lane road, up into hills: "The game's 22
all gone, the streams is gone, the mountains is gone, all destroyed for
just a little bit of money by greedy people."

He says he isn't asking much, only that the people not sell away the 23
rights to their coal. But that is an odd request in these mountains, a
foreign idea. If ever there were a one-industry area, that area is eastern
Kentucky, and the industry is coal. That is the way it has been since
the end of the nineteenth century and the coming of the railroad.

Coal is everywhere. It is everybody's business.   24

In addition to the deep mines and the strip mines there are thousands 25
of truck mines, little mines by the side of the road and in people's
backyards. Coal lies in chunks by the side of every dirt road and highway, having fallen from or bounced out of the trucks that haul it. It lies
by the endless miles of railroad track, and dots the streets of downtown
Whitesburg and Hazard and Paintsville and a hundred other towns.

It is coal country, plain and simple. Even the little children play with 26
model dump trucks and bulldozers, making believe they are digging for
coal in the yard, strip mining under the front porch.

In such an environment it is difficult to convince people that digging 27
for coal is anything but the most natural of processes. Coal is a friend.
It always has been and always will be. That is the reality in these
mountains. No one entertains the notion that coal is an exhaustible
resource, that mining—deep or strip—can only continue for so long, and
that if the area is going to survive, alternate industries will have to be
developed.

That's not smart talk in country where King Coal is everybody's big 28
brother.

Whatever problems might result from an area being stripped, they are 29
viewed as isolated phenomena, totally unrelated to any other area being
stripped and certainly unconnected to the coal found deep in the ground
and reached through conventional means.

Bert Caudill certainly has nothing against coal. He has been a miner 30
all his adult life, as was his father and are his sons. It is what he does—
all he does.

He spent two years working in a Detroit assembly plant and earned *31* more money than in any other two years in his life, but he came back to the mines, back to the mines that took his father's life and his brother-in-law's life, the mines that have given him black lung disease and are slowly taking his life.

"That's the mines," says Caudill. "Some gets killed in airplanes and *32* some in cars."

But there was no philosophy in his voice when, after he sold the rights *33* to his land for stripping, the side of the mountain came sliding down one night in a rainstorm, tore away his barn and fence and covered his spring. That was two years ago, and still the mountain shifts, sending rocks and boulders dangerously close to the house he bought from his two years' work in Detroit, the first house he has ever owned.

"Everytime after it rains I climb up to the top of the mountain," said *34* Ruby, Caudill's wife, "just to see what's slid down and what's gonna be comin' next."

Bert and Ruby Caudill are not the only two to sell the rights to their *35* land, then regret it. Hundreds have done the same thing, even recently. Some only after being shown an old deed "Xed" by a long-dead relative and told the mining would go on regardless, that they might as well sign and get paid. Some without such pressure. But all thinking of bringing in a little extra money to pay the bills.

Columbus Sexton didn't think it was a bad idea to let them strip the *36* coal above his house, and Bill Bates figured his property on Elk Creek might bring in something extra. Now Columbus Sexton has had to abandon his house and build a new one, and Bill Bates swears they'll never get another inch of his land.

Both are intelligent, well-informed men holding responsible business *37* positions, and both had seen what the strippers had done to other men's land throughout the state. But, somehow, until it happened to them it meant nothing.

"You want to know who's to blame," Joe Begley said from his porch *38* swing. "It ain't the government or the strippers. They're crooked and you can't expect no better of them. I blame the people, the good people around here that lets 'em come and take their land."

In his way, Joe Begley has been fighting strip mining for a long time. *39* Like Tom Gish, editor of the Whitesburg *Mountain Eagle,* and Harry Caudill, lawyer and writer, he has been trying to stop the desecration of the mountains. It has been difficult, and every once in a while he gets impatient with those not so fervently committed as he, those who years ago did not hear the word.

But Joe Begley would be the first to tell you that the mountains are a *40* special place of special people. Things are not the same there as in the cities or even the plains. Thinking is different.

Ever since the days when the Cumberland Plateau was part of Amer-   *41*
ica's early frontier, its people have been staunchly independent, exercising a degree of privacy approaching isolation. Today, with pockets of
civilization still formed only around select streams and creeks, much of
that early attitude has remained.

It is not that mountain people are unfriendly toward their neighbors.   *42*
Mostly, in any particular hollow, everyone is related through one or a
number of genetic channels. There are half a dozen Nieces on Camp
Branch, twice that many Days on Cowan Creek, even more Sextons on
Sandlick Road, and Caudills in groups and bunches all over.

They exchange pleasantries on the road and will always offer a helping   *43*
hand. But there is also a great deal of letting alone. Breathing room,
some call it. The tendency is for a man to see to his own needs and
problems without bothering to step back for a long look at what repercussions might result.

For generations and generations, without interference from the out-   *44*
side, it was a good way. Strip mining has made it a dangerous luxury.
What is happening on Kingdom Come Creek tells it best.

Kingdom Come is a truly beautiful little hollow that runs for ten or   *45*
twelve miles along the creek from the point where it leaves Route 588,
crosses under the red metal bridge, and climbs to the headwaters deep
in the mountains. It is green and lush and thick, very cool and very
quiet, the only regular sounds the gurgling of the creek and the chirping
of birds, the only dissonant sight the old scavenged car bodies so common
to Appalachia that line the creek bed and peek out from deep in the
brush.

This is the place where, at the turn of the century, John Fox Jr. came   *46*
to write his novel about a young mountain man in the Civil War, *The
Little Shepherd of Kingdom Come*. Aside from the changing models of
abandoned cars, it is hard to believe that the hollow is very different
from what Fox saw as he traveled the dirt road that parallels and crosses
and occasionally becomes the creek.

Thirty-eight families live in the hollow, a large percentage of them   *47*
Isons or related to Isons. And for years coal companies have been trying
to buy the rights to the mountains at the head of the creek, the rights to
strip them for coal, but no one would sell. Not until last year, when a
family that once lived near the head but had moved sold the rights. Then
a second family, also moved, sold.

Still no stripping began, because the company needed more land.   *48*
Then, after several months of trying, the company convinced Sally Ison
to sell her rights to the coal. A large section of one mountain was left
to Sally by her father, who had inherited the same section of mountain
from his father.

She became the first person actually living on the creek to sell.   *49*

"They were after me for a long time to sell," Sally told me from her *50* wheelchair. A woman in her sixties, she is crippled with arthritis, so severely crippled that she requires the assistance of a wheelchair or walker to get around. "I kept telling 'em no, but last October they said the rest of it was theirs so I let 'em go ahead."

She used her arms to shift position in the chair. Then, again settled, *51* she looked from me to the bare, wooden floor where her five children, all grown now and gone from the hollow, once played.

"I didn't see how it would affect us," she said. "We weren't using *52* the mountain."

Sally Ison is as far from being a villain as one could imagine. A sweet, *53* lovable woman who wheels herself around the house, cleaning and cooking for her husband and two grandchildren spending the summer, she did what seemed logical with land she could see serving no immediate use, land for which no children or grandchildren were waiting.

Then it began. "They said they had to build a dam on the bottomland," *54* she said. "They hadn't said anything about that bottomland, not till after I signed."

She tried to stop them, but apparently they had a legal right. The *55* bottomland, considered to be among the best for planting in the hollow, immediately became useless. They also changed the course of the creek, and when they began moving in big machinery and blasting the following month, the once clear water of Kingdom Come Creek was ruined.

And all because a mining firm from California convinced Sally she *56* deserved some income from her land.

"I tried to stop her from selling, but it's her land," Sally's husband, *57* Marion, told me as we drove to the head of the creek in his old pickup, bouncing along the creek bed. He and Sally had known each other all their lives, both having grown up in the hollow.

"They put up a pitiful tale about getting that coal," he said, holding *58* tight to the jerking steering wheel. "Just kept on and kept on, telling her what it'd look like after it was over and what she'd get out of it. Said she'd rather have it that way than before. Said they'd fix it back up, sow grass and put in trees."

He spit out the open window, as if to comment on their promises. *59* "Even if they did fix what's ours, the rest of the hollow'll never be the same."

We went as far as we could by truck, then pulled up on a level piece *60* of land and walked up to the head of the creek. We climbed to a wide canyon, recently dug out of the hillside, flat on the bottom and lying at the base of high, straight walls. It was the bottomland, he said, where they were going to make their dam to catch the silt from mining.

"They cut it out and everything," he said, pointing to the scooped-out *61* walls nearly sixty feet high on each side, "then they run into clay and had to tear up some other land above." On three sides the mountains loomed around us, the mountains that had just begun to be strip mined. Slides had already scarred the face of one, ripping off trees and bushes as they came.

"I told her I didn't figure it would bother me and her," Marion Ison 62 said as he stood where his freshly cultivated field once stood. "We ain't got many more years, but later on, well . . ."

On the way back down toward the red metal bridge I stopped to talk 63 with Dewey Ison, cousin of Sally and Marion. A former miner nearly seventy, he had lived all his life on Kingdom Come Creek, as had his father and father's father, on back for five generations. He told me about the blasting, every evening about five o'clock, that shakes the windows and knocks jars off the shelf, and about the crystal-clear water that just isn't any more. But when I asked him about Sally selling the rights to the land he stopped, thought a minute, and pushed the hat back on his head.

"Her land," he said, "but I wished she hadn't done it." 64

And thinking another minute: "Not her fault. They didn't read her 65 the fine print. And they didn't say nothing about that bottomland. Best bottomland round here."

He pulled his hat back down over his eyes, told me again how it wasn't 66 Sally's fault, but that he doubted the hollow would ever be the same.

Every hollow in Eastern Kentucky is not Kingdom Come Creek. Men 67 like Tom Gish and Joe Begley have alerted enough people to the horrors of strip mining so that many have resisted.

When they came onto John Caudill's land he met them with his .38 68 and escorted them off, and the exploits of Dan Gibson holding forty strippers at gunpoint on Hardburly Ridge in Knott County are legend.

And in this year's Kentucky primary, Bessie Smith, a poorly educated 69 mother of nine, challenged incumbent U.S. Representative Carl Perkins to his seat on the issue of strip mining. Mrs. Smith, a fiery welfare recipient who last January led twenty-one women onto a strip-mining site and closed it down for fifteen hours, collected nearly three thousand votes, votes she feels will give her some leverage when the November election comes.

"Welfare and food stamps keeps the people quiet while the strippers 70 take their land," the chunky blond told me in a makeshift office in Hazard. And straightening up in her chair: "I have been asked for my support in the fall campaign, but before I give it I must hear the word on banning strip mining."

There are others who have tried to stop the devastation, both in the 71 courts and at their own property lines, but not enough, not nearly enough. Mostly, like Sally Ison, they give up.

Each story is more depressing than the last, with neighbor selling 72
mining rights for a couple of hundred dollars, only to ruin an entire
community. It happened in Johnnie Collins Hollow, where half a dozen
families besides Bert and Ruby Caudill were affected. And over on Elk
Creek, Bill Bates sold the rights to his land at the head of the creek, land
behind the house he had been renting to Tiny Walters and her seven
children for sixteen years.

"They started working up there in April," said Tiny, a large, blond 73
woman who says she has no idea how she got her name. "I'd already
had my garden cleaned up, and I wasn't about to leave." But then they
started to blast, and the first boulder came crashing through Tiny's garden, and she packed up her kids and left.

"I never thought Bill'd do me like he did," she said, "but you never 74
really know people till you comes down to a point."

Everybody loves Sally Ison, and except for Tiny Walters and maybe 75
three or four of her kids, nobody really hates Bill Bates. But both sold
the rights to their land, and the damage can never be repaired.

Both are sorry now, but it's late for that. The crime has been com- 76
mitted. In California and Texas and Florida, where it's flatter land that
is being stripped, reclamation at least is possible. In these mountains it
is not; they are simply too steep.

They could be helped, certainly. New topsoil brought in, permitted 77
to settle, the entire area seeded, and new trees planted. It would not
undo the damage, but it would help. It would also be a monumentally
expensive operation, requiring more time and money than any mining
company now in Appalachia has suggested spending.

What is left now when the strippers move on? Not much. Vast tracts 78
of land, restless land. Sliding, always sliding. Great mountains stripped
of everything living, left barren and naked, once as permanent as time
itself, now less steady than a child's sandpile.

And what of the water? Clear, pure wells and streams are now con- 79
taminated with mud and minerals, enough sulfur to alter the taste and
cause rashes and infections in the people who drink it and chase away
the wildlife that used to.

Not just at the source, not just where they are mining, but for miles 80
and miles downstream, far from Letcher and Perry and Knott counties,
down the Kentucky River, down Russell Fork and Poor Fork, down into
the Ohio and beyond.

And for how long? No one can tell that. 81

But there is no need to wait to see the effects of a land destroyed. 82
Not here, not in the Cumberlands. The mountains and the people are
too closely allied. Already in a severely depressed area, with massive
welfare rolls and one of the highest unemployment rates in the nation,
the people of eastern Kentucky are in growing trouble.

Walking down the streets of Whitesburg, seat of Letcher County, I *83*
was struck by the absence of vital life signs. A dearth of children playing
on the sidewalks, of the sound of young voices. And no music.

Old men stand on the street corner near the post office and in front of *84*
the New Daniel Boone Motel, congregate in the coffee shop and on the
steps of the courthouse. After dark there is nothing. No cars on the
main street, no lights in the shops. No restaurant is open past nine any
night, and none past midafternoon on Sunday.

No amusements are planned for the young, no place for roller skating *85*
or dancing. Of the town's two theaters, one is now a laundry and the
other, only recently re-opened, does not seem confident enough to advertise its programs on its own marquee.

It is an area that is losing its youth to the cities. And in those who *86*
remain there is an immense lethargy and lack of enthusiasm. Nothing
much is happening, and nobody seems to care.

"A lot of us are just wore out," Joe Begley told me. "Wore out *87*
worrying about the government and lawsuits, wore out worrying about
if the mountain's gonna sweep away our house."

And the stripping goes on. At the current pace over 60,000 acres of *88*
Letcher County alone will be "disturbed" by strip mining by 1990, leaving
less than 700 acres of farmland.

Eighteen years from now, in 1990. *89*

But this is the Cumberland Plateau—Daniel Boone country. *90*

These are mountain people, and the mountains hold a man in place. *91*
They always have. But what happens when the mountains are gone?

The word is genocide. As in terracide. *92*

Study Questions

1. Reread the first and last paragraphs of "People of the Ruined Hills."
   Skip Rozin obviously believes that strip mining is a form of murder
   both of the land and of the people who live on it. Why doesn't Rozin
   simply write that strip mining is killing the mountains and the residents? What do words like *terracide, homocide,* and *genocide* suggest
   that *murder* and *killing* do not?
2. Paragraphs 6–9 contain short, simple sentences or compound sentences in which *and* is used as the conjunction. What voice is created
   by the constant use of these sentence types? How does that voice
   emphasize Rozin's feelings about strip mining?
3. As his example of how strip mining is destroying the land and the
   people of eastern Kentucky, Rozin uses the story of Sally Ison, whose
   sale of her land to a company allowed strip mining to start on Kingdom
   Come Creek. After the destruction of the area through strip mining,
   one of the inhabitants says of Sally Ison, "Not her fault." How does

the language Rozin uses in this section show his agreement or disagreement with that speaker? Point to the words or phrases suggesting
that Sally Ison is guilty or innocent.
4. Paragraph 78 contains a series of sentence fragments. Why would
   Rozin want to use incomplete sentences here? What effect do they
   have upon the reader? How is his use of sentence fragments consistent with his use of short paragraphs?

Suggestion for Revising

In question 3 we asked you to consider how Rozin's choice of words
expressed his attitude toward Sally Ison and her sale of the land at
Kingdom Come Creek. Rewrite that passage of the essay, choosing
words and phrases that describe the same actions but that connote an
opinion opposite to Rozin's. You will find that it will not be sufficient
to simply substitute one word or phrase for another. Be prepared to
rewrite whole sentences and paragraphs.

How It Feels to Be Colored Me

Zora Neale Hurston

I am colored but I offer nothing in the way of *1* extenuating circumstances except the fact that I am the only Negro in the United States whose grandfather on the mother's side was *not* an Indian chief.

I remember the very day that I became colored. Up to my thirteenth *2* year I lived in the little Negro town of Eatonville, Florida. It is exclusively a colored town. The only white people I knew passed through the town going to or coming from Orlando. The native whites rode dusty horses, the Northern tourists chugged down the sandy village road in automobiles. The town knew the Southerners and never stopped cane chewing when they passed. But the Northerners were something else again. They were peered at cautiously from behind curtains by the timid. The more venturesome would come out on the porch to watch them go past and got just as much pleasure out of the tourists as the tourists got out of the village.

The front porch might seem a daring place for the rest of the town, *3* but it was a gallery seat for me. My favorite place was atop the gatepost. Proscenium box for a born first-nighter. Not only did I enjoy the show, but I didn't mind the actors knowing that I liked it. I usually spoke to them in passing. I'd wave at them and when they returned my salute, I would say something like this: "Howdy-do-well-I-thank-you-where-you-goin?" Usually automobile or the horse paused at this, and after a queer exchange of compliments, I would probably "go a piece of the way" with them, as we say in farthest Florida. If one of my family happened to come to the front in time to see me, of course negotiations would be rudely broken off. But even so, it is clear that I was the first "welcome-to-our-state" Floridian, and I hope the Miami Chamber of Commerce will please take notice.

During this period, white people differed from colored to me only in *4* that they rode through town and never lived there. They liked to hear me "speak pieces" and sing and wanted to see me dance the parse-me-la, and gave me generously of their small silver for doing these things, which seemed strange to me for I wanted to do them so much that I needed bribing to stop. Only they didn't know it. The colored people gave no dimes. They deplored any joyful tendencies in me, but I was their Zora nevertheless. I belonged to them, to the nearby hotels, to the county—everybody's Zora.

But changes came in the family when I was thirteen, and I was sent 5 to school in Jacksonville. I left Eatonville, the town of the oleanders, as Zora. When I disembarked from the river-boat at Jacksonville, she was no more. It seemed that I had suffered a sea change. I was not Zora of Orange County any more, I was now a little colored girl. I found it out in certain ways. In my heart as well as in the mirror, I became a fast brown—warranted not to rub nor run.

But I am not tragically colored. There is no great sorrow dammed up 6 in my soul, nor lurking behind my eyes. I do not mind at all. I do not belong to the sobbing school of Negrohood who hold that nature some-how has given them a lowdown dirty deal and whose feelings are all hurt about it. Even in the helter-skelter skirmish that is my life, I have seen that the world is to the strong regardless of a little pigmentation more or less. No, I do not weep at the world—I am too busy sharpening my oyster knife.

Someone is always at my elbow reminding me that I am the grand- 7 daughter of slaves. It fails to register depression with me. Slavery is sixty years in the past. The operation was successful and the patient is doing well, thank you. The terrible struggle that made me an American out of a potential slave said "On the line!" The Reconstruction said "Get set!"; and the generation before said "Go!" I am off to a flying start and I must not halt in the stretch to look behind and weep. Slavery is the price I paid for civilization, and the choice was not with me. It is a bully adventure and worth all that I have paid through my ancestors for it. No one on earth ever had a greater chance for glory. The world to be won and nothing to be lost. It is thrilling to think—to know that for any act of mine, I shall get twice as much praise or twice as much blame. It is quite exciting to hold the center of the national stage, with the spec-tators not knowing whether to laugh or to weep.

The position of my white neighbor is much more difficult. No brown 8 specter pulls up a chair beside me when I sit down to eat. No dark ghost thrusts its leg against mine in bed. The game of keeping what one has is never so exciting as the game of getting.

I do not always feel colored. Even now I often achieve the uncon- 9 scious Zora of Eatonville before the Hegira. I feel most colored when I am thrown against a sharp white background.

For instance at Barnard. "Beside the waters of the Hudson" I feel 10 my race. Among the thousand white persons, I am a dark rock surged upon, and overswept, but through it all, I remain myself. When covered by the waters, I am; and the ebb but reveals me again.

Sometimes it is the other way around. A white person is set down in   *11*
our midst, but the contrast is just as sharp for me. For instance, when
I sit in the drafty basement that is The New World Cabaret with a white
person, my color comes. We enter chatting about any little nothing that
we have in common and are seated by the jazz waiters. In the abrupt
way that jazz orchestras have, this one plunges into a number. It loses
no time in circumlocutions, but gets right down to business. It constricts
the thorax and splits the heart with its tempo and narcotic harmonies.
This orchestra grows rambunctious, rears on its hind legs and attacks
the tonal veil with primitive fury, rending it, clawing it until it breaks
through to the jungle beyond. I follow those heathen—follow them ex-
ultingly. I dance wildly inside myself; I yell within, I whoop; I shake
my assegai* above my head, I hurl it true to the mark yeeeeooww! I am
in the jungle and living in the jungle way. My face is painted red and
yellow and my body is painted blue. My pulse is throbbing like a war
drum. I want to slaughter something—give pain, give death to what, I
do not know. But the piece ends. The men of the orchestra wipe their
lips and rest their fingers. I creep back slowly to the veneer we call
civilization with the last tone and find the white friend sitting motionless
in his seat, smoking calmly.

"Good music they have here," he remarks, drumming the table with   *12*
his fingertips.

Music. The great blobs of purple and red emotion have not touched   *13*
him. He has only heard what I felt. He is far away and I see him but
dimly across the ocean and the continent that have fallen between us.
He is so pale with his whiteness then and I am *so* colored.

At certain times I have no race, I am *me*. When I set my hat at a   *14*
certain angle and saunter down Seventh Avenue, Harlem City, feeling as
snooty as the lions in front of the Forty-Second Street Library, for
instance. So far as my feelings are concerned, Peggy Hopkins Joyce on
the Boule Mich with her gorgeous raiment, stately carriage, knees knock-
ing together in a most aristocratic manner, has nothing on me. The
cosmic Zora emerges. I belong to no race nor time. I am the eternal
feminine with its string of beads.

I have no separate feeling about being an American citizen and col-   *15*
ored. I am merely a fragment of the Great Soul that surges within the
boundaries. My country, right or wrong.

Sometimes, I feel discriminated against, but it does not make me angry.   *16*
It merely astonishes me. How *can* any deny themselves the pleasure of
my company? It's beyond me.

* A light spear used by tribesmen in southern Africa.

But in the main, I feel like a brown bag of miscellany propped against 17
a wall. Against a wall in company with other bags, white, red and yellow.
Pour out the contents, and there is discovered a jumble of small things
priceless and worthless. A first-water diamond, an empty spool, bits of
broken glass, lengths of string, a key to a door long since crumbled away,
a rusty knife-blade, old shoes saved for a road that never was and never
will be, a nail bent under the weight of things too heavy for any nail, a
dried flower or two still a little fragrant. In your hand is the brown bag.
On the ground before you is the jumble it held—so much like the jumble
in the bags, could they be emptied, that all might be dumped in a single
heap and the bags refilled without altering the content of any greatly. A
bit of colored glass more or less would not matter. Perhaps that is how
the Great Stuffer of Bags filled them in the first place—who knows?

Study Questions

1. What tone does Zora Neale Hurston set in the opening sentence of
   "How It Feels to Be Colored Me"? What does this tone tell you about
   her attitude toward her topic?
2. What do you think Hurston means when she writes in paragraph 2,
   "I remember the very day that I became colored"? How does this
   statement fit the tone you identified in question 1? How does
   this statement fit in with what you believe is the message she wants
   to convey to her readers?
3. "How It Feels to Be Colored Me" was written in 1928. What words
   show that it could not have been written by a black writer of the
   1980s? How do you think white readers of today will react to these
   words? How will black readers react to them? How will the reactions
   of each group of readers affect the way they understand Hurston's
   essay?
4. In paragraph 6, Hurston writes, "I am not tragically colored." Do
   you think Hurston would be able to say the same thing about being
   black today? What changes have taken place since 1928 that might
   lead her to alter this statement? Given the attitude she expressed in
   the final paragraph, how, if at all, would Hurston alter her remark?

Suggestion for Revising

"How It Feels to Be Colored Me" was written by a strong woman with
a sure sense of her identity. She is able to look back at her childhood
with humor and pleasure. Paragraphs 2–5 show this ability particularly

well. Suppose, however, that disappointment and bitterness were mixed with Hurston's strength and certainty. For example, suppose she "became colored" through a series of personal experiences that instilled in her a great deal of resentment. What changes would have to be made in the wording of paragraphs 2–5 to reflect this new feeling? Reformulate this passage to reflect the bitterness, but make sure that your revision still describes the same incidents as the original.

The Hollow Miracle

George Steiner

A greed: post-war Germany is a miracle. But it *1* is a very queer miracle. There is a superb frenzy of life on the surface; but at the heart, there is a queer stillness. Go there: look away for a moment from the marvel of the production lines; close your ears momentarily to the rush of the motors.

The thing that has gone dead is the German language. Open the daily *2* papers, the magazines, the flood of popular and learned books pouring off the new printing presses; go to hear a new German play, listen to the language as it is spoken over the radio or in the Bundestag. It is no longer the language of Goethe, Heine, and Nietzsche. It is not even that of Thomas Mann. Something immensely destructive has happened to it. It makes noise. It even communicates, but it creates no sense of communion.

Languages are living organisms. Infinitely complex, but organisms *3* nevertheless. They have in them a certain life-force, and certain powers of absorption and growth. But they can decay and they can die.

A language shows that it has in it the germ of dissolution in several *4* ways. Actions of the mind that were once spontaneous become mechanical, frozen habits (dead metaphors, stock similes, slogans). Words grow longer and more ambiguous. Instead of style, there is rhetoric. Instead of precise common usage, there is jargon. Foreign roots and burrowings are no longer absorbed into the blood stream of the native tongue. They are merely swallowed and remain an alien intrusion. All these technical failures accumulate to the essential failure: the language no longer sharpens thought but blurs it. Instead of charging every expression with the greatest available energy and directness, it loosens and disperses the intensity of feeling. The language is no longer adventure (and a live language is the highest adventure of which the human brain is capable). In short, the language is no longer lived; it is merely spoken.

That condition can last for a very long time; observe how Latin re- *5* mained in use long after the springs of life in Roman civilization had run dry. But where it has happened, something essential in a civilization will not recover. And it has happened in Germany. That is why there is at the center of the miracle of Germany's material resurrection such a profound deadness of spirit, such an inescapable sense of triviality and dissimulation.

What brought death to the German language? That is a fascinating *6*
and complicated piece of history. It begins with the paradoxical fact that
German was most alive before there was a unified German state. The
poetic genius of Luther, Goethe, Schiller, Kleist, Heine, and in part that
of Nietzsche, predates the establishment of the German nation. The
masters of German prose and poetry were men not caught up in the
dynamism of Prussian-Germanic national consciousness as it developed
after the foundation of modern Germany in 1870. They were, like
Goethe, citizens of Europe, living in princely states too petty to solicit
the emotions of nationalism. Or, like Heine and Nietzsche, they wrote
from outside Germany. And this has remained true of the finest German
literature even in recent times. Kafka wrote in Prague, Rilke in Prague,
Paris, and Duino.

The official language and literature of Bismarck's Germany already *7*
had in them the elements of dissolution. It is the golden age of the
militant historians, of the philologists and the incomprehensible meta-
physicians. These mandarins of the new Prussian empire produced that
fearful composite of grammatical ingenuity and humorlessness which
made the word "Germanic" an equivalent for dead weight. Those who
escaped the Prussianizing of the language were the mutineers and the
exiles, like those Jews who founded a brilliant journalistic tradition, or
Nietzsche, who wrote from abroad.

For to the academicism and ponderousness of German as it was written *8*
by the pillars of learning and society between 1870 and the First World
War, the imperial regime added its own gifts of pomp and mystification.
The "Potsdam style" practiced in the chancelleries and bureaucracy of
the new empire was a mixture of grossness ("the honest speech of soldiers") and high flights of romantic grandeur (the Wagnerian note). Thus
university, officialdom, army, and court combined to drill into the German language habits no less dangerous than those they drilled into the
German people: a terrible weakness for slogans and pompous clichés
(*Lebensraum,* "the yellow peril," "the Nordic virtues"); an automatic
reverence before the long word or the loud voice; a fatal taste for saccharine pathos (*Gemütlichkeit*) beneath which to conceal any amount of
rawness or deception. In this drill, the justly renowned school of German
philology played a curious and complex role. Philology places words in
a context of older or related words, not in that of moral purpose and
conduct. It gives to language formality, not form. It cannot be a mere
accident that the essentially philological structure of German education
yielded such loyal servants to Prussia and the Nazi Reich. The finest
record of how the drill call of the classroom led to that of the barracks
is contained in the novels of Heinrich Mann, particularly in *Der Untertan*.

When the soldiers marched off to the 1914 war, so did the words. The *9*
surviving soldiers came back, four years later, harrowed and beaten. In
a real sense, the words did not. They remained at the front and built

between the German mind and the facts a wall of myth. They launched the first of those big lies on which so much of modern Germany has been nurtured: the lie of "the stab in the back." The heroic German armies had not been defeated; they had been stabbed in the back by "traitors, degenerates, and Bolsheviks." The Treaty of Versailles was not an awkward attempt by a ravaged Europe to pick up some of the pieces but a scheme of cruel vengeance imposed on Germany by its greedy foes. The responsibility for unleashing war lay with Russia or Austria or the colonial machinations of "perfidious England," not with Prussian Germany.

There were many Germans who knew that these were myths and who 10 knew something of the part that German militarism and race arrogance had played in bringing on the holocaust. They said so in the political cabarets of the 1920's, in the experimental theater of Brecht, in the writings of the Mann brothers, in the graphic art of Käthe Kollwitz and George Grosz. The German language leapt to life as it had not done since the Junkers and the philologists had taken command of it. It was a brilliant, mutinous period. Brecht gave back to German prose its Lutheran simplicity and Thomas Mann brought into his style the supple, luminous elegance of the classic and Mediterranean tradition. These years, 1920–1930, were the *anni mirabiles* of the modern German spirit. Rilke composed the *Duino Elegies* and the *Sonnets to Orpheus* in 1922, giving to German verse a wing-stroke and music it had not known since Hölderlin. *The Magic Mountain* appeared in 1924, Kafka's *Castle* in 1926. *The Three-Penny Opera* had its premiere in 1928, and in 1930 the German cinema produced *The Blue Angel*. The same year appeared the first volume of Robert Musil's strange and vast meditation on the decline of Western values, *The Man Without Qualities*. During this glorious decade, German literature and art shared in that great surge of the Western imagination which encompassed Faulkner, Hemingway, Joyce, Eliot, Proust, D. H. Lawrence, Picasso, Schoenberg, and Stravinsky.

But it was a brief noontime. The obscurantism and hatreds built into 11 the German temper since 1870 were too deep-rooted. In an uncannily prophetic "Letter from Germany," Lawrence noted how "the old, bristling, savage spirit has set in." He saw the country turning away "from contact with western Europe, ebbing to the deserts of the east." Brecht, Kafka, and Thomas Mann did not succeed in mastering their own culture, in imposing on it the humane sobriety of their talent. They found themselves first the eccentrics, then the hunted. New linguists were at hand to make of the German language a political weapon more total and effective than any history had known, and to degrade the dignity of human speech to the level of baying wolves.

For let us keep one fact clearly in mind: the German language was not 12 innocent of the horrors of Nazism. It is not merely that a Hitler, a Goebbels, and a Himmler happened to speak German. Nazism found in the language precisely what it needed to give voice to its savagery. Hitler heard inside his native tongue the latent hysteria, the confusion, the quality of hypnotic trance. He plunged unerringly into the undergrowth of language, into those zones of darkness and outcry which are the infancy of articulate speech, and which come before words have grown mellow and provisional to the touch of the mind. He sensed in German another music than that of Goethe, Heine, and Mann; a rasping cadence, half nebulous jargon, half obscenity. And instead of turning away in nauseated disbelief, the German people gave massive echo to the man's bellowing. It bellowed back out of a million throats and smashed-down boots. A Hitler would have found reservoirs of venom and moral illiteracy in any language. But by virtue of recent history, they were nowhere else so ready and so near the very surface of common speech. A language in which one can write a "Horst Wessel Lied" is ready to give hell a native tongue. (How should the word "*spritzen*" recover a sane meaning after having signified to millions the "spurting" of Jewish blood from knife points?)

And that is what happened under the Reich. Not silence or evasion, *13* but an immense outpouring of precise, serviceable words. It was one of the peculiar horrors of the Nazi era that all that happened was recorded, catalogued, chronicled, set down; that words were committed to saying things no human mouth should ever have said and no paper made by man should ever have been inscribed with. It is nauseating and nearly unbearable to recall what was done and spoken, but one must. In the Gestapo cellars, stenographers (usually women) took down carefully the noises of fear and agony wrenched, burned, or beaten out of the human voice. The tortures and experiments carried out on live beings at Belsen and Matthausen were exactly recorded. The regulations governing the number of blows to be meted out on the flogging blocks at Dachau were set down in writing. When Polish rabbis were compelled to shovel out open latrines with their hands and mouths, there were German officers there to record the fact, to photograph it, and to label the photographs. When the SS elite guards separated mothers from children at the entrance to the death camps, they did not proceed in silence. They proclaimed the imminent horrors in loud jeers: *"Heida, heida, juchheisassa, Scheissjuden in den Schornstein!"*

The unspeakable being said, over and over, for twelve years. The *14* unthinkable being written down, indexed, filed for reference. The men who poured quicklime down the openings of the sewers in Warsaw to kill the living and stifle the stink of the dead wrote home about it. They spoke of having to "liquidate vermin." In letters asking for family snapshots or sending season's greetings. Silent night, holy night, *Gemütlichkeit*. A language being used to run hell, getting the habits of hell into its syntax. Being used to destroy what there is in man of man and to restore to governance what there is of beast. Gradually, words lost their original meaning and acquired nightmarish definitions. *Jude, Pole, Russe* came to mean two-legged lice, putrid vermin which good Aryans must squash, as a party manual said, "like roaches on a dirty wall." "Final solution," *endgültige Lösung,* came to signify the death of six million human beings in gas ovens.

The language was infected not only with these great bestialities. It *15* was called upon to enforce innumerable falsehoods, to persuade the Germans that the war was just and everywhere victorious. As defeat began closing in on the thousand-year Reich, the lies thickened to a constant snowdrift. The language was turned upside down to say "light" where there was blackness and "victory" where there was disaster. Gottfried Benn, one of the few decent writers to stay inside Nazi Germany, noted some of the new definitions from the dictionary of Hitler German:

In December 1943, that is to say at a time when the Russians had driven us before them for 1,500 kilometers, and had pierced our front in a dozen places, a first lieutenant, small as a hummingbird and gentle as a puppy, remarked: "The main thing is that the swine are not breaking through." "Break through," "roll back," "clean up," "flexible, fluid lines of combat"—what positive and negative power such words have; they can bluff or they can conceal. Stalingrad—tragic accident. The defeat of the U-boats—a small, accidental technical discovery by the British. Montgomery chasing Rommel 4,000 kilometers from El Alamein to Naples—treason of the Badoglio clique.

And as the circle of vengeance closed in on Germany, this snowdrift *16* of lies thickened to a frantic blizzard. Over the radio, between the interruptions caused by air-raid warnings, Goebbels' voice assured the German people that "titanic secret weapons" were about to be launched. On one of the very last days of Götterdämmerung, Hitler came out of his bunker to inspect a row of ashen-faced fifteen-year-old boys recruited for a last-ditch defense of Berlin. The order of the day spoke of "volunteers" and elite units gathered invincibly around the Führer. The nightmare fizzled out on a shameless lie. The *Herrenvolk* was solemnly told that Hitler was in the front-line trenches, defending the heart of his capital against the Red beasts. Actually, the buffoon lay dead with his mistress, deep in the safety of his concrete lair.

Languages have great reserves of life. They can absorb masses of *17* hysteria, illiteracy, and cheapness (George Orwell showed how English is doing so today). But there comes a breaking point. Use a language to conceive, organize, and justify Belsen; use it to make out specifications for gas ovens; use it to dehumanize man during twelve years of calculated bestiality. Something will happen to it. Make of words what Hitler and Goebbels and the hundred thousand *Untersturmführer* made: conveyors of terror and falsehood. Something will happen to the words. Something of the lies and sadism will settle in the marrow of the language. Imperceptibly at first, like the poisons of radiation sifting silently into the bone. But the cancer will begin, and the deep-set destruction. The language will no longer grow and freshen. It will no longer perform, quite as well as it used to, its two principal functions: the conveyance of humane order which we call law, and the communication of the quick of the human spirit which we call grace. In an anguished note in his diary of 1940, Klaus Mann observed that he could no longer read new German books: "Can it be that Hitler has polluted the language of Nietzsche and Hölderlin?" It can.

But what happened to those who are the guardians of a language, the 18 keepers of its conscience? What happened to the German writers? A number were killed in the concentration camps; others, such as Walter Benjamin, killed themselves before the Gestapo could get at them to obliterate what little there is in a man of God's image. But the major writers went into exile. The best playwrights: Brecht and Zuckmayer. The most important novelists: Thomas Mann, Werfel, Feuchtwanger, Heinrich Mann, Stefan Zweig, Hermann Broch.

This exodus is of the first importance if we are to understand what 19 has happened to the German language and to the soul of which it is the voice. Some of these writers fled for their lives, being Jews or Marxists or otherwise "undesirable vermin." But many could have stayed as honored Aryan guests of the régime. The Nazis were only too anxious to secure the luster of Thomas Mann's presence and the prestige that mere presence would have given to the cultural life of the Reich. But Mann would not stay. And the reason was that he knew exactly what was being done to the German language and that he felt that only in exile might that language be kept from final ruin. When he emigrated, the sycophantic academics of the University of Bonn deprived him of his honorary doctorate. In his famous open letter to the dean, Mann explained how a man using German to communicate truth or humane values could not remain in Hitler's Reich:

The mystery of language is a great one; the responsibility for a language and for its purity is of a symbolic and spiritual kind; this responsibility does not have merely an aesthetic sense. The responsibility for language is, in essence, human responsibility. . . . Should a German writer, made responsible through his habitual use of language, remain silent, quite silent, in the face of all the irreparable evil which has been committed daily, and is being committed in my country, against body, soul and spirit, against justice and truth, against men and man?

Mann was right, of course. But the cost of such integrity is immense 20 for a writer.

The German writers suffered different degrees of deprivation and re- 21
acted in different ways. A very few were fortunate enough to find asylum
in Switzerland, where they could remain inside the living stream of their
own tongue. Others, like Werfel, Feuchtwanger, and Heinrich Mann,
settled near each other to form islands of native speech in their new
homeland. Stefan Zweig, safely arrived in Latin America, tried to resume
his craft. But despair overcame him. He was convinced that the Nazis
would turn German into inhuman gibberish. He saw no future for a man
dedicated to the integrity of German letters and killed himself. Others
stopped writing altogether. Only the very tough or most richly gifted
were able to transform their cruel condition into art.

Pursued by the Nazis from refuge to refuge, Brecht made of each of 22
his new plays a brilliant rear-guard action. *Mother Courage* was first
produced in Zurich in the dark spring of 1941. The further he was
hounded, the clearer and stronger became Brecht's German. The language seemed to be that of a primer spelling out the ABC of truth.
Doubtless, Brecht was helped by his politics. Being a Marxist, he felt
himself a citizen of a community larger than Germany and a participant
in the forward march of history. He was prepared to accept the desecration and ruin of the German heritage as a necessary tragic prelude to
the foundation of a new society. In his tract "Five Difficulties Encountered When Writing the Truth," Brecht envisioned a new German language, capable of matching the word to the fact and the fact to the dignity
of man.

Another writer who made of exile an enrichment was Hermann Broch. 23
The Death of Virgil is not only one of the most important novels European
literature has produced since Joyce and Proust; it is a specific treatment
of the tragic condition of a man of words in an age of brute power. The
novel turns on Virgil's decision, at the hour of his death, to destroy the
manuscript of the *Aeneid*. He now realizes that the beauty and truth of
language are inadequate to cope with human suffering and the advance
of barbarism. Man must find a poetry more immediate and helpful to
man than that of words: a poetry of action. Broch, moreover, carried
grammar and speech beyond their traditional confines, as if these had
become too small to contain the weight of grief and insight forced upon
a writer by the inhumanity of our times. Toward the close of his rather
solitary life (he died in New Haven, nearly unknown), he felt increasingly
that communication might lie in modes other than language, perhaps in
mathematics, that other face of silence.

Of all the exiles, Thomas Mann fared best. He had always been a 24
citizen of the world, receptive to the genius of other languages and
cultures. In the last part of the *Joseph* cycle, there seemed to enter into
Mann's style certain tonalities of English, the language in the midst of
which he was now living. The German remains that of the master, but
now and again an alien light shines through it. In *Doctor Faustus,* Mann

addressed himself directly to the ruin of the German spirit. The novel is shaped by the contrast between the language of the narrator and the events which he recounts. The language is that of a classical humanist, a touch laborious and old-fashioned, but always open to the voices of reason, skepticism, and tolerance. The story of Leverkühn's life, on the other hand, is a parable of unreason and disaster. Leverkühn's personal tragedy prefigures the greater madness of the German people. Even as the narrator sets down his pedantic but humane testimony to the wild destruction of a man of genius, the Reich is shown plunging to bloody chaos. In *Doctor Faustus* there is also a direct consideration of the roles of language and music in the German soul. Mann seems to be saying that the deepest energies of the German soul were always expressed in music rather than in words. And the history of Adrian Leverkühn suggests that this is a fact fraught with danger. For there are in music possibilities of complete irrationalism and hypnosis. Unaccustomed to finding in language any ultimate standard of meaning, the Germans were ready for the sub-human jargon of Nazism. And behind the jargon sounded the great dark chords of Wagnerian ecstasy. In *The Holy Sinner,* one of his last works, Mann returned to the problem of the German language by way of parody and pastiche. The tale is written in elaborate imitation of medieval German, as if to remove it as far as possible from the German of the present.

But for all their accomplishment, the German writers in exile could 25 not safeguard their heritage from self-destruction. By leaving Germany, they could protect their own integrity. They witnessed the beginnings of the catastrophe, not its full unfolding. As one who stayed behind wrote: "You did not pay with the price of your own dignity. How, then, can you communicate with those who did?" The books that Mann, Hesse, and Broch wrote in Switzerland or California or Princeton are read in Germany today, but mainly as valuable proof that a privileged world had lived on "somewhere else," outside Hitler's reach.

What, then, of those writers who did stay behind? Some became 26 lackeys in the official whorehouse of "Aryan culture," the *Reichsschrifttumskammer.* Others equivocated till they had lost the faculty of saying anything clear or meaningful even to themselves. Klaus Mann gives a brief sketch of how Gerhart Hauptmann, the old lion of realism, came to terms with the new realities:

"Hitler . . . after all, . . . My dear friends! . . . no hard feelings! . . . Let's try to be . . . No, if you please, allow me . . . objective . . . May I refill my glass? This champagne . . . very remarkable, indeed—the man Hitler, I mean . . . The champagne too, for that matter . . . Most extraordinary development . . . German youth . . . About seven million votes . . . As I often said to my Jewish friends . . . Those Germans . . . incalculable nation . . . very mysterious indeed . . . cosmic impulses . . .

Goethe . . . Nibelungen Saga . . . Hitler, in a sense, expresses . . . As I tried to explain to my Jewish friends . . . dynamic tendencies . . . elementary, irresistible. . . ."

Some, like Gottfried Benn and Ernst Jünger, took refuge in what Benn 27 called "the aristocratic form of emigration." They entered the German Army, thinking they might escape the tide of pollution and serve their country in the "old, honorable ways" of the officer corps. Jünger wrote an account of the victorious campaign in France. It is a lyric, elegant little book, entitled *Gärten und Strassen*. Not a rude note in it. An old-style officer taking fatherly care of his French prisoners and entertaining "correct" and even gracious relations with his new subjects. Behind his staff car come the trucks of the Gestapo and the elite guards fresh from Warsaw. Jünger does not mention any such unpleasantness. He writes of gardens.

Benn saw more clearly, and withdrew first into obscurity of style, then 28 into silence. But the sheer fact of his presence in Nazi Germany seemed to destroy his hold on reality. After the war, he set down some of his recollections of the time of night. Among them, we find an incredible sentence. Speaking of pressures put on him by the régime, Benn says: "I describe the foregoing not out of resentment against National Socialism. The latter is now overthrown, and I am not one to drag Hector's body in the dust." One's imagination dizzies at the amount of confusion it must have taken to make a decent writer write that. Using an old academic cliché, he makes Nazism the equivalent of the noblest of Homeric heroes. Being dead, the language turns to lies.

A handful of writers stayed in Germany to wage a covert resistance. 29 One of these very few was Ernst Wiechert. He spent some time in Buchenwald and remained in partial seclusion throughout the war. What he wrote he buried in his garden. He stayed on in constant peril, for he felt that Germany should not be allowed to perish in voiceless suffering. He remained so that an honest man should record for those who had fled and for those who might survive what it had been like. In *The Forest of the Dead* he gave a brief, tranquil account of what he saw in the concentration camp. Tranquil, because he wished the horror of the facts to cry out in the nakedness of truth. He saw Jews being tortured to death under vast loads of stone or wood (they were flogged each time they stopped to breathe until they fell dead). When Wiechert's arm developed running sores, he was given a bandage and survived. The camp medical officer would not touch Jews or Gypsies even with his glove "lest the odor of their flesh infect him." So they died, screaming with gangrene or hunted by the police dogs. Wiechert saw and remembered. At the end of the war he dug the manuscript out of his garden, and in 1948 published it. But it was already too late.

In the three years immediately following the end of the war, many   *30*
Germans tried to arrive at a realistic insight into the events of the Hitler
era. Under the shadow of the ruins and of economic misery, they considered the monstrous evil Nazism had loosed on them and on the world.
Long rows of men and women filed past the bone heaps in the death
camps. Returned soldiers admitted to something of what the occupation
of Norway or Poland or France or Yugoslavia had been like—the mass
shootings of hostages, the torture, the looting. The churches raised their
voice. It was a period of moral scrutiny and grief. Words were spoken
that had not been pronounced in twelve years. But the moment of truth
was rather short.

The turning point seems to have come in 1948. With the establishment   *31*
of the new Deutschmark, Germany began a miraculous ascent to renewed
economic power. The country literally drugged itself with hard work.
Those were the years in which men spent half the night in their rebuilt
factories because their homes were not yet viable. And with the upward
leap of material energy came a new myth. Millions of Germans began
saying to themselves and to any foreigner gullible enough to listen that
the past had somehow not happened, that the horrors had been grossly
exaggerated by Allied propaganda and sensation-mongering journalists.
Yes, there were some concentration camps, and *reportedly* a number of
Jews and other unfortunates were exterminated. "But not six million,
lieber Freund, nowhere near that many. That's just propaganda, you
know." Doubtless, there had been some regrettable brutalities carried
out on foreign territory by units of the S.S. and S.A. "But those fellows
were *Lumpenhunde,* lower-class ruffians. The regular army did nothing
of the kind. Not our honorable German Army. And, really, on the
Eastern Front our boys were not up against normal human beings. The
Russians are mad dogs, *lieber Freund,* mad dogs! And what of the
bombing of Dresden?" Wherever one traveled in Germany, one heard
such arguments. The Germans themselves began believing them with
fervor. But there was worse to come.

Germans in every walk of life began declaring that they had not known   *32*
about the atrocities of the Nazi régime. "We did not know what was
going on. No one told us about Dachau, Belsen, or Auschwitz. How
should we have found out? Don't blame us." It is obviously difficult to
disprove such a claim to ignorance. There *were* numerous Germans who
had only a dim notion of what might be happening outside their own
backyard. Rural districts and the smaller, more remote communities
were made aware of reality only in the last months of the war, when the
battle actually drew near them. But an immense number *did* know.
Wiechert describes his long journey to Buchenwald in the comparatively
idyllic days of 1938. He tells how crowds gathered at various stops to
jeer and spit at the Jews and political prisoners chained inside the Gestapo
van. When the death trains started rolling across Germany during the

war, the air grew thick with the sound and stench of agony. The trains waited on sidings at Munich before heading for Dachau, a short distance away. Inside the sealed cars, men, women, and children were going mad with fear and thirst. They screamed for air and water. They screamed all night. People in Munich heard them and told others. On the way to Belsen, a train was halted somewhere in southern Germany. The prisoners were made to run up and down the platform and a Gestapo man loosed his dog on them with the cry: "Man, get those dogs!" A crowd of Germans stood by watching the sport. Countless such cases are on record.

Most Germans probably did not know the actual details of liquidation. 33 They may not have known about the mechanics of the gas ovens (one official Nazi historian called them "the anus of the world"). But when the house next door was emptied overnight of its tenants, or when Jews, with their yellow star sewn on their coats, were barred from the air-raid shelters and made to cower in the open, burning streets, only a blind cretin could not have known.

Yet the myth did its work. True, German audiences were moved not 34 long ago by the dramatization of *The Diary of Anne Frank*. But even the terror of the *Diary* has been an exceptional reminder. And it does not show what happened to Anne *inside* the camp. There is little market for such things in Germany. Forget the past. Work. Get prosperous. The new Germany belongs to the future. When recently asked what the name Hitler meant to them, a large number of German schoolchildren replied that he was a man who had built the *Autobahnen* and had done away with unemployment. Had they heard that he was a bad man? Yes, but they did not really know why. Teachers who tried to tell them about the history of the Nazi period had been told from official quarters that such matters were not suitable for children. Some few who persisted had been removed or put under strong pressure by parents and colleagues. Why rake up the past?

Here and there, in fact, the old faces are back. On the court benches 35 sit some of the judges who meted out Hitler's blood laws. On many professorial chairs sit scholars who were first promoted when their Jewish or Socialist teachers had been done to death. In a number of German and Austrian universities, the bullies swagger again with their caps, ribbons, dueling scars, and "pure Germanic" ideals. "Let us forget" is the litany of the new German age. Even those who cannot, urge others to do so. One of the very few pieces of high literature to concern itself with the full horror of the past is Albrecht Goes's *The Burnt Offering*. Told by a Gestapo official that there will be no time to have her baby where *she* is going, a Jewish woman leaves her baby carriage to a decent Aryan shopkeeper's wife. The next day she is deported to the ovens. The empty carriage brings home to the narrator the full sum of what is being committed. She resolves to give up her own life as a burnt offering to God. It is a superb story. But at the outset, Goes hesitates whether it should be told: "One has forgotten. And there must be forgetting, for how could a man live who had not forgotten?" Better, perhaps.

Everything forgets. But not a language. When it has been injected *36* with falsehood, only the most drastic truth can cleanse it. Instead, the post-war history of the German language has been one of dissimulation and deliberate forgetting. The remembrance of horrors past has been largely uprooted. But at a high cost. And German literature is paying it right now. There are gifted younger writers and a number of minor poets of some distinction. But the major part of what is published as serious literature is flat and shoddy. It has in it no flame of life.* Compare the best of current journalism with an average number of the *Frankfurter Zeitung* of pre-Hitler days; it is at times difficult to believe that both are written in German.

This does not mean that the German genius is mute. There is a brilliant *37* musical life, and nowhere is modern experimental music assured of a fairer hearing. There is, once again, a surge of activity in mathematics and the natural sciences. But music and mathematics are "languages" other than language. Purer, perhaps; less sullied with past implications; abler, possibly, to deal with the new age of automation and electronic control. But not language. And so far, in history, it is language that has been the vessel of human grace and the prime carrier of civilization.

Study Questions

1. George Steiner chooses an impersonal voice for "The Hollow Miracle." Identify the characteristics of this style and illustrate them by referring to specific sentences and paragraphs. Why would Steiner want to use the impersonal voice in this essay?

2. According to Steiner (paragraph 12), the German language "was not innocent of the horrors of Nazism." He believes that Hitler saw within the language ways for him to obscure the truth and to confuse people while appearing to tell the truth. Reread paragraph 12 and discuss how Steiner uses language to do the opposite. What words and phrases does he use to clearly state what he believes the truth to be? How do the connotations of these words and phrases support that truth?

3. Compare the lengths of the paragraphs in "The Hollow Miracle" and Skip Rozin's "People of the Ruined Hills" (pp. 386–394). How can

---

* This statement was valid in 1959; not today. It is precisely by turning to face the past that German drama and fiction have resumed a violent, often journalistic, but undeniable force of life.

the difference in length be explained by the topics? How can the difference be explained by the voices?
4. What is the major form of organization used in "The Hollow Miracle"? How does this organization match the topic?

Suggestion for Revising

The way an essay "sounds" is frequently decided by the kinds of sentence structures you use to express your meaning. The sentence structures create a feeling of simplicity or complexity, which suggests to the readers your own view of the topic. Therefore, by changing the structure of a sentence, you will often change the view that sentence projects.

The following series of simple sentences is based on paragraph 12 of "The Hollow Miracle." Reformulate these sentences into a coherent paragraph. Do not refer to paragraph 12 as you rewrite these sentences. The object of this exercise is to create your own version, not Steiner's.

The soldiers marched off to war. The war was in 1914. The words marched off to war. The surviving soldiers came back. They came back four years later. They were harrowed. They were beaten. The words did not return in a real sense. The words remained at the front. The words built a wall of myth between the German mind and the facts. The words launched the first of the big lies. The big lies have nurtured much of modern Germany. The lie was the lie of "the stab in the back." The German armies were heroic. The German armies had not been defeated. "Traitors, degenerates, and Bolsheviks" had stabbed the German armies in the back. Ravaged Europe did not attempt in the Treaty of Versailles to pick up some of the pieces. It was not even an awkward attempt. The Treaty of Versailles was a cruel scheme of vengeance. Greedy foes imposed the scheme on Germany. Russia or Austria were responsible for unleashing the war. The colonial machinations of "perfidious England" were responsible. Prussian Germany was not responsible for unleashing the war.

Compare your reformulation with Steiner's original. What differences do you see in the two versions? How do these differences create a difference in the voices?

Marrakech

George Orwell

A s the corpse went past the flies left the restau- 1
rant table in a cloud and rushed after it, but
they came back a few minutes later.

The little crowd of mourners—all men and boys, no women—threaded 2
their way across the market-place between the piles of pomegranates and
the taxis and the camels, wailing a short chant over and over again.
What really appeals to the flies is that the corpses here are never put into
coffins, they are merely wrapped in a piece of rag and carried on a rough
wooden bier on the shoulders of four friends. When the friends get to
the burying-ground they hack an oblong hole a foot or two deep, dump
the body in it and fling over it a little of the dried-up, lumpy earth, which
is like broken brick. No gravestone, no name, no identifying mark of
any kind. The burying-ground is merely a huge waste of hummocky
earth, like a derelict building-lot. After a month or two no one can even
be certain where his own relatives are buried.

When you walk through a town like this—two hundred thousand in- 3
habitants, of whom at least twenty thousand own literally nothing except
the rags they stand up in—when you see how the people live, and still
more how easily they die, it is always difficult to believe that you are
walking among human beings. All colonial empires are in reality founded
upon that fact. The people have brown faces—besides, there are so
many of them! Are they really the same flesh as yourself? Do they
even have names? Or are they merely a kind of undifferentiated brown
stuff, about as individual as bees or coral insects? They rise out of the
earth, they sweat and starve for a few years, and then they sink back
into the nameless mounds of the graveyard and nobody notices that they
are gone. And even the graves themselves soon fade back into the soil.
Sometimes, out for a walk, as you break your way through the prickly
pear, you notice that it is rather bumpy underfoot, and only a certain
regularity in the bumps tells you that you are walking over skeletons.

I was feeding one of the gazelles in the public gardens. 4

Gazelles are almost the only animals that look good to eat when they 5
are still alive, in fact, one can hardly look at their hindquarters without
thinking of mint sauce. The gazelle I was feeding seemed to know that
this thought was in my mind, for though it took the piece of bread I was
holding out it obviously did not like me. It nibbled rapidly at the bread,
then lowered its head and tried to butt me, then took another nibble and

then butted again. Probably its idea was that if it could drive me away the bread would somehow remain hanging in mid-air.

An Arab navvy working on the path nearby lowered his heavy hoe   6
and sidled slowly towards us. He looked from the gazelle to the bread and from the bread to the gazelle, with a sort of quiet amazement, as though he had never seen anything quite like this before. Finally he said shyly in French:

"*I* could eat some of that bread."   7

I tore off a piece and he stowed it gratefully in some secret place   8
under his rags. This man is an employee of the Municipality.

When you go through the Jewish quarters you gather some idea of   9
what the medieval ghettoes were probably like. Under their Moorish rulers the Jews were only allowed to own land in certain restricted areas, and after centuries of this kind of treatment they have ceased to bother about overcrowding. Many of the streets are a good deal less than six feet wide, the houses are completely windowless, and sore-eyed children cluster everywhere in unbelievable numbers, like clouds of flies. Down the centre of the street there is generally running a little river of urine.

In the bazaar huge families of Jews, all dressed in the long black robe   10
and little black skull-cap, are working in dark fly-infested booths that look like caves. A carpenter sits crosslegged at a prehistoric lathe, turning chair-legs at lightning speed. He works the lathe with a bow in his right hand and guides the chisel with his left foot, and thanks to a lifetime of sitting in this position his left leg is warped out of shape. At his side his grandson, aged six, is already starting on the simpler parts of the job.

I was just passing the coppersmiths' booths when somebody noticed   11
that I was lighting a cigarette. Instantly, from the dark holes all round, there was a frenzied rush of Jews, many of them old grandfathers with flowing grey beards, all clamouring for a cigarette. Even a blind man somewhere at the back of one of the booths heard a rumour of cigarettes and came crawling out, groping in the air with his hand. In about a minute I had used up the whole packet. None of these people, I suppose, works less than twelve hours a day, and every one of them looks on a cigarette as a more or less impossible luxury.

As the Jews live in self-contained communities they follow the same   12
trades as the Arabs, except for agriculture. Fruit-sellers, potters, silver-smiths, blacksmiths, butchers, leatherworkers, tailors, water-carriers, beggars, porters—whichever way you look you see nothing but Jews. As a matter of fact there are thirteen thousand of them, all living in the space of a few acres. A good job Hitler wasn't here. Perhaps he was on his way, however. You hear the usual dark rumours about the Jews, not only from the Arabs but from the poorer Europeans.

"Yes, mon vieux, they took my job away from me and gave it to a   13
Jew. The Jews! They're the real rulers of this country, you know.

They've got all the money. They control the banks, finance—everything."

"But," I said, "isn't it a fact that the average Jew is a labourer working 14 for about a penny an hour?"

"Ah, that's only for show! They're all moneylenders really. They're 15 cunning, the Jews."

In just the same way, a couple of hundred years ago, poor old women 16 used to be burned for witchcraft when they could not even work enough magic to get themselves a square meal.

All people who work with their hands are partly invisible, and the 17 more important the work they do, the less visible they are. Still, a white skin is always fairly conspicuous. In northern Europe, when you see a labourer ploughing a field, you probably give him a second glance. In a hot country, anywhere south of Gibraltar or east of Suez, the chances are that you don't even see him. I have noticed this again and again. In a tropical landscape one's eye takes in everything except the human beings. It takes in the dried-up soil, the prickly pear, the palm tree and the distant mountain, but it always misses the peasant hoeing at his patch. He is the same colour as the earth, and a great deal less interesting to look at.

It is only because of this that the starved countries of Asia and Africa 18 are accepted as tourist resorts. No one would think of running cheap trips to the Distressed Areas. But where the human beings have brown skins their poverty is simply not noticed. What does Morocco mean to a Frenchman? An orange-grove or a job in Government service. Or to an Englishman? Camels, castles, palm trees, Foreign Legionnaires, brass trays, and bandits. One could probably live there for years without noticing that for nine-tenths of the people the reality of life is an endless, back-breaking struggle to wring a little food out of an eroded soil.

Most of Morocco is so desolate that no wild animal bigger than a hare 19 can live on it. Huge areas which were once covered with forest have turned into a treeless waste where the soil is exactly like broken-up brick. Nevertheless a good deal of it is cultivated, with frightful labour. Everything is done by hand. Long lines of women, bent double like inverted capital L's, work their way slowly across the fields, tearing up the prickly weeds with their hands, and the peasant gathering lucerne for fodder pulls it up stalk by stalk instead of reaping it, thus saving an inch or two on each stalk. The plough is a wretched wooden thing, so frail that one can easily carry it on one's shoulder, and fitted underneath with a rough iron spike which stirs the soil to a depth of about four inches. This is as much as the strength of the animals is equal to. It is usual to plough with a cow and a donkey yoked together. Two donkeys would not be quite strong enough, but on the other hand two cows would cost a little more to feed. The peasants possess no harrows, they merely plough the soil several times over in different directions, finally leaving it in rough furrows, after which the whole field has to be shaped with hoes into small oblong patches to conserve water. Except for a day or two after the rare rainstorms there is never enough water. Along the edges of the fields channels are hacked out to a depth of thirty or forty feet to get at the tiny trickles which run through the subsoil.

Every afternoon a file of very old women passes down the road outside　20 my house, each carrying a load of firewood. All of them are mummified with age and the sun, and all of them are tiny. It seems to be generally the case in primitive communities that the women, when they get beyond a certain age, shrink to the size of children. One day a poor old creature who could not have been more than four feet tall crept past me under a vast load of wood. I stopped her and put a five-sou piece (a little more than a farthing) into her hand. She answered with a shrill wail, almost a scream, which was partly gratitude but mainly surprise. I suppose that from her point of view, by taking any notice of her, I secmed almost to be violating a law of nature. She accepted her status as an old woman, that is to say as a beast of burden. When a family is travelling it is quite usual to see a father and a grown-up son riding ahead on donkeys, and an old woman following on foot, carrying the baggage.

But what is strange about these people is their invisibility. For several　21 weeks, always at about the same time of day, the file of old women had hobbled past the house with their firewood, and though they had registered themselves on my eyeballs I cannot truly say that I had seen them. Firewood was passing—that was how I saw it. It was only that one day I happened to be walking behind them, and the curious up-and-down motion of a load of wood drew my attention to the human being beneath it. Then for the first time I noticed the poor old earth-coloured bodies, bodies reduced to bones and leathery skin, bent double under the crushing weight. Yet I suppose I had not been five minutes on Moroccan soil before I noticed the overloading of the donkeys and was infuriated by it. There is no question that the donkeys are damnably treated. The Moroccan donkey is hardly bigger than a St. Bernard dog, it carries a load which in the British Army would be considered too much for a fifteen-hands mule, and very often its pack-saddle is not taken off its back for weeks together. But what is peculiarly pitiful is that it is the most willing creature on earth, it follows its master like a dog and does not need either bridle or halter. After a dozen years of devoted work it suddenly drops dead, whereupon its master tips it into the ditch and the village dogs have torn its guts out before it is cold.

This kind of thing makes one's blood boil, whereas—on the whole—　22 the plight of the human beings does not. I am not commenting, merely pointing to a fact. People with brown skins are next door to invisible.

Anyone can be sorry for the donkey with its galled back, but it is generally owing to some kind of accident if one even notices the old woman under her load of sticks.

As the storks flew northward the Negroes were marching southward— 23 a long, dusty column, infantry, screwgun batteries, and then more infantry, four or five thousand men in all, winding up the road with a clumping of boots and a clatter of iron wheels.

They were Senegalese, the blackest Negroes in Africa, so black that 24 sometimes it is difficult to see whereabouts on their necks the hair begins. Their splendid bodies were hidden in reach-me-down khaki uniforms, their feet squashed into boots that looked like blocks of wood, and every tin hat seemed to be a couple of sizes too small. It was very hot and the men had marched a long way. They slumped under the weight of their packs and the curiously sensitive black faces were glistening with sweat.

As they went past a tall, very young Negro turned and caught my eye. 25 But the look he gave me was not in the least the kind of look you might expect. Not hostile, not contemptuous, not sullen, not even inquisitive. It was the shy, wide-eyed Negro look, which actually is a look of profound respect. I saw how it was. This wretched boy, who is a French citizen and has therefore been dragged from the forest to scrub floors and catch syphilis in garrison towns, actually has feelings of reverence before a white skin. He has been taught that the white race are his masters, and he still believes it.

But there is one thought which every white man (and in this connection 26 it doesn't matter twopence if he calls himself a socialist) thinks when he sees a black army marching past. "How much longer can we go on kidding these people? How long before they turn their guns in the other direction?

It was curious, really. Every white man there had this thought stowed 27 somewhere or other in his mind. I had it, so had the other onlookers, so had the officers on their sweating chargers and the white N.C.O.'s marching in the ranks. It was a kind of secret which we all knew and were too clever to tell; only the Negroes didn't know it. And really it was like watching a flock of cattle to see the long column, a mile or two miles of armed men, flowing peacefully up the road, while the great white birds drifted over them in the opposite direction, glittering like scraps of paper.

Study Questions

1. Both in the introduction to "Marrakech" and in the section describing the Jewish ghetto, Orwell describes the flies that cluster around the people. What similarities in the description of flies are there in the

two sections? How do these similarities guide the readers to a recognition of the common point made in these sections?
2. George Orwell ends the essay by comparing the long column of black
soldiers to "a flock of cattle." What attitude toward the soldiers is
implied by this comparison? How is the attitude he projects pertinent
to the questions he asks in the next to the last paragraph?
3. In the same comparison, Orwell talks of "the great white birds" that
drift over the cattle, "glittering like scraps of paper." Who do these
birds represent? What might their connection be to the flies of the
first two sections?
4. In the final section of "Marrakech," Orwell expresses a common fear
of the Europeans living in Africa during the 1920s and 1930s: the fear
that the Africans would finally awake and "turn their guns in the other
direction." What is Orwell's attitude toward the natives of Marrakech? What words and phrases does he use in his descriptions of
them to express this attitude?

Suggestion for Revising

In "Marrakech," Orwell achieves most of his goals through description.
So carefully has he chosen his scenes and the words to describe them
that his meaning is usually clear without the need for a direct statement.
The comparison of the soldiers to cattle in the final paragraph is a fine
example of this technique.

What if Orwell had wished to reorganize his essay to make paragraphs
23–27 the introduction? Then his readers would have had the image of
the soldiers as cattle in mind as they read the rest. What would you
have to change in paragraphs 23–27 to make them suitable as an introduction? Revise these paragraphs so that they open rather than close
"Marrakech."

The Sound of Eating

Calvin Trillin

A t least I'll know what to say if a marriage 1 counselor ever asks whether we have one subject that seems to provoke tension in our marriage again and again. "New Orleans," I will say. "Eating in New Orleans, counselor."

"Do you mean that the Chez Helène Incident was not an isolated 2 incident?" the marriage counselor will say.

"Hardly," I will reply, as Alice sits without comment in the corner, 3 stuffing herself with Prestat truffles covered with Devonshire cream.

"Would you like to talk about it?"   4

"Nothing would give me more pleasure," I will say. "Except perhaps 5 eating in New Orleans, which nobody around here ever seems to let me do in peace." I will then present, in a calm and detached way, what the marriage counselor will come to know as the Jazz Festival Incident.

We had just decided to take in the New Orleans Jazz & Heritage 6 Festival one spring when Alice said, "It would be a great time to visit some of those lovely plantation houses along the river."

I have nothing against plantation houses. I have gone without com- 7 plaint once or twice to a plantation house outside New Orleans that has been made into a restaurant serving a passable copy of the baked oyster dish whose original inspired me to suggest that a statue be erected in Jackson Square of the inventor—Mrs. Lila Mosca, of Mosca's roadhouse, in Waggaman, Louisiana. (My proposal calls for the statue to be carved out of fresh garlic.) I had to face the possibility, though, that Alice might be talking about visiting plantation houses that served no food whatsoever. Part of marriage, after all, is trying to protect one's husband or wife from potential weaknesses or excesses, and it occurred to me that Alice was in danger of developing an unhealthy interest in exteriors.

"How can you decide to go to a jazz festival in New Orleans, the 8 birthplace of jazz, and then talk about spending any of your time staring at a bunch of façades?" I asked Alice.

"Are you claiming that you're going there to listen to jazz?" she asked. 9

"Well," I said, confidently. I didn't think I should go any further than 10 that. I do like jazz. I particularly like the sort of New Orleans street jazz heard at, say, a funeral held for a member of the Eagle Eye Benevolent Mutual Association or a Founder's Day Parade staged by the Jolly Bunch Social Aid & Pleasure Club—the sort of jazz nobody can hear without falling in behind the band and half-dancing down the street in a movement New Orleans people call "second-lining." I like the way jazz can be used in New Orleans to make what could be an ordinary event special. In fact, I once hired a jazz band to meet Alice as she arrived at the New Orleans airport from New York—a gesture, I might feel compelled to tell any marriage counselor, that was not made under the assumption that she would start talking about plantation houses or diet plans the moment she got off the plane. In fact, the jazz festival happened to be going on during the weekend I hired the band—although we were able to stop in only briefly, having a previously made engagement at the Crawfish Festival in Breaux Bridge. There was some difficulty finding a band that was free at the time Alice's airplane was scheduled to arrive, I remember, and an friend who was acting as what I suppose would be described as my band broker said, "How would you feel about having foreigners?"

"You mean from Houma or Morgan City or someplace like that?"   *11*

What my band broker meant, it turned out, was a band made up of *12* musicians from abroad who had come to New Orleans for the festival. There has always been a strong interest in New Orleans jazz in Europe and Japan; in the late fifties, when not many white people in New Orleans itself seemed very interested in New Orleans music, it used to be said that no jazz funeral was complete without a body, a band of music, and two Englishmen. The band that broke into "Hello Dolly" as Alice came down the ramp was led by a London antiques dealer who played trumpet as if he had grown up on Toulouse Street. I was not surprised. I have always believed that New Orleans jazz can be exported; it's the oyster loaves that won't travel.

Whatever my interest in jazz, though, it was true that my interest in *13* attending the New Orleans Jazz & Heritage Festival had been aroused when a New Orleans friend of ours named Allan Jaffe told me what was available at the festival food booths. According to Jaffe, the eating side of the festival had developed over the years in a way that might make it possible for a jazz fan to eat jambalaya from Gonzales just a few steps from the booth where he had eaten andouille gumbo from Laplace on the way to eat boiled crawfish from Breaux Bridge.

My conversation with Jaffe had taken place over some baked oysters, *14* cracked crab salad, barbecued shrimp, spaghetti Bordelaise, and chicken Grande at Mosca's—Jaffe and his wife, Sandy, having whisked me to that Louisiana Italian shrine from the airport one evening after I had figured out that a traveler who truly wanted to get stuck between planes in New Orleans on the way from Mobile to New York could arrange it. Jaffe is thought of by most people in New Orleans as the manager of Preservation Hall, a jazz hall that was an important element of the New Orleans jazz revival in the early sixties, but he thinks of himself as a tuba player. He certainly has the sort of appetite that might be associated with a tuba player. Before Buster Holmes retired, Alice felt pretty much the same way about my going to Buster's restaurant on Burgundy Street with Jaffe as she did about my going to Kansas City with Fats Goldberg—although, as far as I can remember, none of the meals I ate at Buster's with Jaffe lasted more than four or five hours. Jaffe, who was raised in Pennsylvania, is not shy about eating outside of Louisiana—when he is travelling with the Preservation Hall band, he is apparently quite gifted at devising reasons for detours that take the bus past Pat's, the cheese-steak emporium in South Philadephia, or past Arthur Bryant's Barbe-cue—but, given his appetite for New Orleans food, he has been struck on the road with cravings so desperate that Buster has to rush to his side by first available jet, laden with red beans and rice. "As much as I eat in New Orleans, though, I've only gained five pounds a year since I came here," Jaffe told me in the late sixties. "The only trouble is that I've been here nine years."

"Could it be that Allan Jaffe mentioned something about the food at *15* the jazz festival that night you stopped to eat at Mosca's on the way back from Mobile?" Alice asked.

That is what I mean by suspicious questions. I can't imagine what *16* led Alice to believe that Jaffe and I talked about the jazz festival at that dinner; as I remember, I reported to her at the time that our conversation had consisted mainly of speculation on whether or not Mrs. Mosca maintained her own garlic ranch hidden away somewhere in St. Bernard Parish. (Alice had raised the subject of garlic herself the morning after I arrived home from my Mosca's layover; she had not heard me when I crept quietly into the bedroom at two or three in the morning, she said, but while stirring in her sleep sometime before dawn, she had gathered from the presence of a strange odor that a wild beast had somehow found its way into the room.)

Confronted with the truth about my conversation with Jaffe, I told *17* Alice that eating all sorts of Louisiana specialties at the festival instead of having to drive all over the state to find them should appeal to any citizen eager to do his or her part in conserving our country's limited supply of fossil fuel.

"To you a jazz festival is just eating with background music," Alice *18* said.

"Jazz and *heritage* festival," I reminded her. "It's called the New *19* Orleans Jazz & Heritage Festival. And what do you think the heritage of New Orleans is—macramé? In New Orleans, heritage means eating."

"With so much going on at the Fairgrounds, one has to be fairly well *20* prepared ahead of time to catch as many good acts as possible on a given day," I read in *The Courier,* a New Orleans weekly, after we got into our hotel room. "This year there are five stages, three smaller gazebos (labeled A–C), a jazz tent, and a gospel tent." I could see the problem. In the eight years since we had stopped briefly at the jazz festival on our way to Breaux Bridge to eat crawfish (or, really, on our way to Opelousas to eat roast duck and dirty rice on our way to Breaux Bridge to eat crawfish), the festival had grown from a two-day event held at a local square to a huge undertaking that covered the Fairgrounds Race Track with people for two three-day weekends in a row. Since we had come for the second weekend, we had the opportunity to prepare ourselves by telephoning a New Orleans friend named Gail Lewis for whatever tips she could offer from having attended the first round. "The crawfish is expensive but good," Gail told me. "There's O.K. red beans and rice. Stay away from the oyster pie. Also skip the fettucine unless you're nostalgic for your mother's macaroni-and-cheese."

"Gail says the red beans and rice are O.K.," I told Alice. "She didn't 21 try the oyster loaves, so we might have to stop at the Acme to have two or three before we go out, just in case. The ladies from the Second Mount Triumph Missionary Baptist Church have a booth again selling the fried chicken that apparently caused Jaffe to seek salvation last year. I think everything's going to be all right."

Alice was on the other side of the room, looking at an old-fashioned 22 map that decorated the wall. I went over to read the map's inscription. It said, "Plantations on the Mississippi River from Natchez to New Orleans, 1858."

"Don't pay any attention to that map, Alice," I said. "It's nothing but 23 a reproduction."

During another planning session that evening—a planning session held 24 at Mosca's with fourteen of our closest advisers in attendance—I realized that the jazz festival had intensified a problem we always have in New Orleans: we never seem to have time for enough meals. There are simply too many restaurants in town that have been mentioned in sentences that begin, "We can't leave without going to . . ." The problem is serious under the best of circumstances—partly, of course, because of Alice's strange fixation on having only three meals a day—and the necessity of eating for a couple of hours each day at the jazz festival would make it even more acute.

"Anthropologists have found that in many societies four or five meals 25 a day are the norm," I told Alice, halfway through dinner, just after someone at the table had mentioned a smashing soul-food rival to Chez Helène that had been unearthed in Gretna since our previous visit.

"Don't feel you have to keep up with Jaffe tonight," Alice said, ig- 26 noring what I thought had been a rather interesting anthropological fact for a layman to have invented. "Remember, he's a tuba player."

The meal was magnificent. After we were through, Jaffe, who had 27 done the ordering, confided to me his suspicion that we had just ordered precisely the same meal for sixteen that we had ordered for three the night he and Sandy had rescued me from the airport.

"There must be some mistake," I said.   28
"Maybe," Jaffe said. "But tonight I'm not too full."   29

At some point in its development, the New Orleans Jazz & Heritage 30
Festival turned into the sort of pleasantly unstructured, laissez-faire celebration that Mardi Gras used to be before it absorbed successive body
blows from the youth cultures associated with Fort Lauderdale and
Woodstock. Some people stand in front of a stage all day, clapping to
bluegrass or amen-ing to gospel. Some people stake out a small section
of Fairgrounds grass and hold an eight- or nine-hour family picnic, probably listening to nothing much beyond the sound of their own chewing
unless one of the marching brass bands happens to wander within earshot.
Some people stroll from traditional jazz to Cajun to contemporary jazz,
stopping between tents and stages now and then to watch a brass band
or some of the brightly dressed high-steppers the jazz festival calls Scene-
boosters. Cajun happens to be a type of music I find particularly appealing—partly, I must admit, because for me it carries memories of
crawfish, the first good Cajun band I ever heard having been Celbert
Cormier and his Musical Kings at the Breaux Bridge Crawfish Festival.
    "It's hard to know where to begin," Alice said, when the music started. 31
    "I know what you mean," I said. "There are thirty-two different food 32
booths."
    By that time I had already paid my respects to the ladies of the Second 33
Mount Triumph Missionary Baptist Church, whose potato salad turned
out to be even better than their chicken, and, not wanting to provoke
any schisms among the Baptists, I had also sampled the barbecued
chicken being sold by the ladies of the Second True Love Baptist Church.
I also felt I should try both versions of jambalaya being offered, and both
versions of red beans and rice. Fair is fair.
    Three hours after we had arrived at the Fairgrounds I was settled 34
under a tree, almost too full to finish my second hot-sausage po' boy.
    "I think you've eaten just about everything that's for sale here," Alice 35
said.
    "Not quite," I said. "I refused to eat the avocado-cheese-and-sprout 36
sandwich as a matter of principle. If health food is part of the heritage
around here, so is the polka."
    "I'm beginning to think we're not going to make it out to the plantation 37
houses this trip," Alice said.
    "Probably not," I said. "That would mean we wouldn't have time to 38
go to the lakefront for boiled crabs. Of course, if we treated that lakefront
crab eating as a snack rather than as a meal, sort of like tea—"
    "I suppose we can at least take a drive to the Garden District," Alice 39
said, paying no attention to what I thought was an extremely sensible
solution to one of our scheduling problems.

"Good idea," I said. "There's a place in the Irish Channel whose po' *40*
boys I want to try—just a taste, not for dinner or anything—and we could
cut through the Garden District on the way."

"Do you want to hear some more music first?" Alice asked.   *41*

"Let's go to the gospel tent for a while," I said, rising with some *42*
difficulty. "I want to pray for a good harvest."

Study Questions

1. After reading "The Sound of Eating," what do you think makes Trillin's title particularly appropriate for the topics he covers? What does
"the sound of eating" signify in this essay? How is it connected with
the New Orleans Jazz & Heritage Festival?
2. What is Trillin's attitude toward food? Find a passage in which he
describes one of his meals, and examine the words and phrases he
uses. What connotations does he usually associate with food and
eating?
3. What is Trillin's attitude toward himself? How does he describe his
love affair with fine food? Is he aware of the lengths to which he
carries his love of food? What tone (serious, amused, distant, intimate) does he use when he describes himself as he eats and as he
talks about eating?
4. Personal obsessions often make interesting reading if the writer first
establishes his or her own character and then shows how the obsessions control that character. Choose several passages in which Trillin
describes how his love of food controls his life. How does this information increase your enjoyment of the essay?

Suggestion for Revising

Calvin Trillin and his wife, Alice, represent two different attitudes toward
eating. Each of these views is clearly stated in the essay, but Alice's
more "traditional" one is certainly less discussed. As an exercise in
reformulation, let us try to restore the balance. Choose one of the scenes
at the New Orleans Jazz & Heritage Festival, and describe what happens
from Alice's point of view instead of Trillin's. Be sure to use adjectives
and adverbs that would fit her attitude toward food and eating.

Stranger in the Village

James Baldwin

F rom all available evidence no black man had *1*
ever set foot in this tiny Swiss village before
I came. I was told before arriving that I would
probably be a "sight" for the village; I took this to mean that people of
my complexion were rarely seen in Switzerland, and also that city people
are always something of a "sight" outside of the city. It did not occur
to me—possibly because I am an American—that there could be people
anywhere who had never seen a Negro.

It is a fact that cannot be explained on the basis of the inaccessibility *2*
of the village. The village is very high, but it is only four hours from
Milan and three hours from Lausanne. It is true that it is virtually
unknown. Few people making plans for a holiday would elect to come
here. On the other hand, the villagers are able, presumably, to come
and go as they please—which they do: to another town at the foot of the
mountain, with a population of approximately five thousand, the nearest
place to see a movie or go to the bank. In the village there is no movie
house, no bank, no library, no theater; very few radios, one jeep, one
station wagon; and, at the moment, one typewriter, mine, an invention
which the woman next door to me here had never seen. There are about
six hundred people living here, all Catholic—I conclude this from the
fact that the Catholic church is open all year round, whereas the Protestant chapel, set off on a hill a little removed from the village, is open
only in the summertime when the tourists arrive. There are four or five
hotels, all closed now, and four or five *bistros,* of which, however, only
two do any business during the winter. These two do not do a great
deal, for life in the village seems to end around nine or ten o'clock.
There are a few stores, butcher, baker, *épicerie,** a hardware store, and
a moneychanger—who cannot change travelers' checks, but must send
them down to the bank, an operation which takes two or three days.
There is something called the *Ballet Haus,* closed in the winter and used
for God knows what, certainly not ballet, during the summer. There
seems to be only one schoolhouse in the village, and this for the quite
young children; I suppose this to mean that their older brothers and
sisters at some point descend from these mountains in order to complete
their education—possibly, again, to the town just below. The landscape
is absolutely forbidding, mountains towering on all four sides, ice and

---

* épicerie: (Fr.) grocery store

snow as far as the eye can reach. In this white wilderness, men and women and children move all day, carrying washing, wood, buckets of milk or water, sometimes skiing on Sunday afternoons. All week long boys and young men are to be seen shoveling snow off the rooftops, or dragging wood down from the forest in sleds.

The village's only real attraction, which explains the tourist season, *3* is the hot spring water. A disquietingly high proportion of these tourists are cripples, or semicripples, who come year after year—from other parts of Switzerland, usually—to take the waters. This lends the village, at the height of the season, a rather terrifying air of sanctity, as though it were a lesser Lourdes. There is often something beautiful, there is always something awful, in the spectacle of a person who has lost one of his faculties, a faculty he never questioned until it was gone, and who struggles to recover it. Yet people remain people, on crutches or indeed on deathbeds; and wherever I passed, the first summer I was here, among the native villagers or among the lame, a wind passed with me—of astonishment, curiosity, amusement, and outrage. That first summer I stayed two weeks and never intended to return. But I did return in the winter, to work; the village offers, obviously, no distractions whatever and has the further advantage of being extremely cheap. Now it is winter again, a year later, and I am here again. Everyone in the village knows my name, though they scarcely ever use it, knows that I come from America—though this, apparently, they will never really believe: black men come from Africa—and everyone knows that I am the friend of the son of a woman who was born here, and that I am staying in their chalet. But I remain as much a stranger today as I was the first day I arrived, and the children shout *Neger! Neger!* as I walk along the streets.

It must be admitted that in the beginning I was far too shocked to *4* have any real reaction. In so far as I reacted at all, I reacted by trying to be pleasant—it being a great part of the American Negro's education (long before he goes to school) that he must make people "like" him. This smile-and-the-world-smiles-with-you routine worked about as well in this situation as it had in the situation for which it was designed, which is to say that it did not work at all. No one, after all, can be liked whose human weight and complexity cannot be, or has not been, admitted. My smile was simply another unheard-of phenomenon which allowed them to see my teeth—they did not, really, see my smile and I began to think that, should I take to snarling, no one would notice any difference. All of the physical characteristics of the Negro which had caused me, in America, a very different and almost forgotten pain were nothing less than miraculous—or infernal—in the eyes of the village people. Some thought my hair was the color of tar, that it had the texture of wire, or the texture of cotton. It was jocularly suggested that I might let it all grow long and make myself a winter coat. If I sat in the sun for more than five minutes some daring creature was certain to come along and gingerly put his fingers on my hair, as though he were afraid of an electric shock, or put his hand on my hand, astonished that the color did not rub off. In all of this, in which it must be conceded there was the charm of genuine wonder and in which there was certainly no element of intentional unkindness, there was yet no suggestion that I was human: I was simply a living wonder.

I knew that they did not mean to be unkind, and I know it now; it is 5 necessary, nevertheless, for me to repeat this to myself each time that I walk out of the chalet. The children who shout *Neger!* have no way of knowing the echoes this sound raises in me. They are brimming with good humor and the more daring swell with pride when I stop to speak with them. Just the same, there are days when I cannot pause and smile, when I have no heart to play with them; when, indeed, I mutter sourly to myself, exactly as I muttered on the streets of a city these children have never seen, when I was no bigger than these children are now: *Your* mother *was a nigger.* Joyce is right about history being a nightmare— but it may be the nightmare from which no one *can* awaken. People are trapped in history and history is trapped in them.

There is a custom in the village—I am told it is repeated in many 6 villages—of "buying" African natives for the purpose of converting them to Christianity. There stands in the church all year round a small box with a slot for money, decorated with a black figurine, and into this box the villagers drop their francs. During the *carnaval* which precedes Lent, two village children have their faces blackened—out of which bloodless darkness their blue eyes shine like ice—and fantastic horsehair wigs are placed on their blond heads; thus disguised, they solicit among the villagers for money for the missionaries in Africa. Between the box in the church and the blackened children, the village "bought" last year six or eight African natives. This was reported to me with pride by the wife of one of the *bistro* owners and I was careful to express astonishment and pleasure at the solicitude shown by the village for the souls of black folk. The *bistro* owner's wife beamed with a pleasure far more genuine than my own and seemed to feel that I might now breathe more easily concerning the souls of at least six of my kinsmen.

I tried not to think of these so lately baptized kinsmen, of the price 7 paid for them, or the peculiar price they themselves would pay, and said nothing about my father, who having taken his own conversion too literally never, at bottom, forgave the white world (which he described as heathen) for having saddled him with a Christ in whom, to judge at least from their treatment of him, they themselves no longer believed. I thought of white men arriving for the first time in an African village, strangers there, as I am a stranger here, and tried to imagine the astounded populace touching their hair and marveling at the color of their skin. But there is a great difference between being the first white man to be seen by Africans and being the first black man to be seen by whites.

The white man takes the astonishment as tribute, for he arrives to conquer and to convert the natives, whose inferiority in relation to himself is not even to be questioned; whereas I, without a thought of conquest, find myself among a people whose culture controls me, has even in a sense, created me, people who have cost me more in anguish and rage than they will ever know, who yet do not even know of my existence. The astonishment with which I might have greeted them, should they have stumbled into my African village a few hundred years ago, might have rejoiced their hearts. But the astonishment with which they greet me today can only poison mine.

And this is so despite everything I may do to feel differently, despite 8 my friendly conversations with the *bistro* owner's wife, despite their three-year-old son who has at last become my friend, despite the *saluts* and *bonsoirs** which I exchange with people as I walk, despite the fact that I know that no individual can be taken to task for what history is doing, or has done. I say that the culture of these people controls me— but they can scarcely be held responsible for European culture. America comes out of Europe, but these people have never seen America, nor have most of them seen more of Europe than the hamlet at the foot of their mountain. Yet they move with an authority which I shall never have; and they regard me, quite rightly, not only as a stranger in their village but as a suspect latecomer, bearing no credentials, to everything they have—however unconsciously—inherited.

For this village, even were it incomparably more remote and incredibly 9 more primitive, is the West, the West onto which I have been so strangely grafted. These people cannot be, from the point of view of power, strangers anywhere in the world; they have made the modern world, in effect, even if they do not know it. The most illiterate among them is related, in a way that I am not, to Dante, Shakespeare, Michelangelo, Aeschylus, Da Vinci, Rembrandt, and Racine; the cathedral at Chartres says something to them which it cannot say to me, as indeed would New York's Empire State Building, should anyone here ever see it. Out of their hymns and dances come Beethoven and Bach. Go back a few centuries and they are in their full glory—but I am in Africa, watching the conquerors arrive.

The rage of the disesteemed is personally fruitless, but it is also 10 absolutely inevitable; this rage, so generally discounted, so little understood even among the people whose daily bread it is, is one of the things that makes history. Rage can only with difficulty, and never entirely, be brought under the domination of the intelligence and is therefore not susceptible to any arguments whatever. This is a fact which ordinary representatives of the *Herrenvolk*,† having never felt this rage and being

* saluts and bonsoirs: (Fr.) greetings and good evenings
† Herrenvolk: (Ger.) people of status

unable to imagine it, quite fail to understand. Also, rage cannot be hidden, it can only be dissembled. This dissembling deludes the thoughtless, and strengthens rage and adds, to rage, contempt. There are, no doubt, as many ways of coping with the resulting complex of tensions as there are black men in the world, but no black man can hope ever to be entirely liberated from this internal warfare—rage, dissembling, and contempt having inevitably accompanied his first realization of the power of white men. What is crucial here is that, since white men represent in the black man's world so heavy a weight, white men have for black men a reality which is far from being reciprocal; and hence all black men have toward all white men an attitude which is designed, really, either to rob the white man of the jewel of his naïveté, or else to make it cost him dear.

The black man insists, by whatever means he finds at his disposal, *11* that the white man cease to regard him as an exotic rarity and recognize him as a human being. This is a very charged and difficult moment, for there is a great deal of will power involved in the white man's naïveté. Most people are not naturally reflective any more than they are naturally malicious, and the white man prefers to keep the black man at a certain human remove because it is easier for him thus to preserve his simplicity and avoid being called to account for crimes committed by his forefathers, or his neighbors. He is inescapably aware, nevertheless, that he is in a better position in the world than black men are, nor can he quite put to death the suspicion that he is hated by black men therefore. He does not wish to be hated, neither does he wish to change places, and at this point in his uneasiness he can scarcely avoid having recourse to those legends which white men have created about black men, the most usual effect of which is that the white man finds himself enmeshed, so to speak, in his own language which describes hell, as well as the attributes which lead one to hell, as being as black as night.

Every legend, moreover, contains its residuum of truth, and the root *12* function of language is to control the universe by describing it. It is of quite considerable significance that black men remain, in the imagination, and in overwhelming numbers in fact, beyond the disciplines of salvation; and this despite the fact that the West has been "buying" African natives for centuries. There is, I should hazard, an instantaneous necessity to be divorced from this so visibly unsaved stranger, in whose heart, moreover, one cannot guess what dreams of vengeance are being nourished; and, at the same time, there are few things on earth more attractive than the idea of the unspeakable liberty which is allowed the unredeemed. When, beneath the black mask, a human being begins to make himself felt one cannot escape a certain awful wonder as to what kind of human being it is. What one's imagination makes of other people is dictated, of course, by the laws of one's own personality and it is one of the ironies of black-white relations that, by means of what the white man imagines the black man to be, the black man is enabled to know who the white man is.

I have said, for example, that I am as much a stranger in this village *13* today as I was the first summer I arrived, but this is not quite true. The villagers wonder less about the texture of my hair than they did then, and wonder rather more about me. And the fact that their wonder now exists on another level is reflected in their attitudes and in their eyes. There are the children who make those delightful, hilarious, sometimes astonishingly grave overtures of friendship in the unpredictable fashion of children; other children, having been taught that the devil is a black man, scream in genuine anguish as I approach. Some of the older women never pass without a friendly greeting, never pass, indeed, if it seems that they will be able to engage me in conversation; other women look down or look away or rather contemptuously smirk. Some of the men drink with me and suggest that I learn how to ski—partly, I gather, because they cannot imagine what I would look like on skis—and want to know if I am married, and ask questions about my *métier*.* But some of the men have accused *le sale nègre*†—behind my back—of stealing wood and there is already in the eyes of some of them that peculiar, intent, paranoiac malevolence which one sometimes surprises in the eyes of American white men when, out walking with their Sunday girl, they see a Negro male approach.

There is a dreadful abyss between the streets of this village and the *14* streets of the city in which I was born, between the children who shout *Neger!* today and those who shouted *Nigger!* yesterday—the abyss is experience, the American experience. The syllable hurled behind me today expresses, above all, wonder: I am a stranger here. But I am not a stranger in America and the same syllable riding on the American air expresses the war my presence has occasioned in the American soul.

For this village brings home to me this fact: that there was a day, and *15* not really a very distant day, when Americans were scarcely Americans at all but discontented Europeans, facing a great unconquered continent and strolling, say, into a marketplace and seeing black men for the first time. The shock this spectacle afforded is suggested, surely, by the promptness with which they decided that these black men were not really men but cattle. It is true that the necessity on the part of the settlers of the New World of reconciling their moral assumptions with the fact— and the necessity—of slavery enhanced immensely the charm of this idea, and it is also true that this idea expresses, with a truly American bluntness, the attitude which to varying extents all masters have had toward all slaves.

---

* métier: (Fr.) profession
† le sale nègre: (Fr.) the dirty Negro

But between all former slaves and slave-owners and the drama which 16
begins for Americans over three hundred years ago at Jamestown, there
are at least two differences to be observed. The American Negro slave
could not suppose, for one thing, as slaves in past epochs had supposed
and often done, that he would ever be able to wrest the power from his
master's hands. This was a supposition which the modern era, which
was to bring about such vast changes in the aims and dimensions of
power, put to death; it only begins, in unprecedented fashion, and with
dreadful implications, to be resurrected today. But even had this supposition persisted with undiminished force, the American Negro slave
could not have used it to lend his condition dignity, for the reason that
this supposition rests on another: that the slave in exile yet remains
related to his past, has some means—if only in memory—of revering and
sustaining the forms of his former life, is able, in short, to maintain his
identity.

This was not the case with the American Negro slave. He is unique 17
among the black men of the world in that his past was taken from him,
almost literally, at one blow. One wonders what on earth the first slave
found to say to the first dark child he bore. I am told that there are
Haitians able to trace their ancestry back to African kings, but any
American Negro wishing to go back so far will find his journey through
time abruptly arrested by the signature on the bill of sale which served
as the entrance paper for his ancestor. At the time—to say nothing of
the circumstances—of the enslavement of the captive black man who
was to become the American Negro, there was not the remotest possibility that he would ever take power from his master's hands. There
was no reason to suppose that his situation would ever change, nor was
there, shortly, anything to indicate that his situation had ever been different. It was his necessity, in the words of E. Franklin Frazier,* to find
a "motive for living under American culture or die." The identity of the
American Negro comes out of this extreme situation, and the evolution
of this identity was a source of the most intolerable anxiety in the minds
and the lives of his masters.

For the history of the American Negro is unique also in this: that the 18
question of his humanity, and of his rights therefore as a human being,
became a burning one for several generations of Americans, so burning
a question that it ultimately became one of those used to divide the
nation. It is out of this argument that the venom of the epithet *Nigger!*
is derived. It is an argument which Europe has never had, and hence
Europe quite sincerely fails to understand how or why the argument
arose in the first place, why its effects are so frequently disastrous and
always so unpredictable, why it refuses until today to be entirely settled.
Europe's black possessions remained—and do remain—in Europe's col-

* E. Franklin Frazier: (1894–1962) Howard University sociologist

onies, at which remove they represented no threat whatever to European identity. If they posed any problem at all for the European conscience, it was a problem which remained comfortingly abstract: in effect, the black man, *as a man,* did not exist for Europe. But in America, even as a slave, he was an inescapable part of the general social fabric and no American could escape having an attitude toward him. Americans attempt until today to make an abstraction of the Negro, but the very nature of these abstractions reveals the tremendous effects the presence of the Negro has had on the American character.

When one considers the history of the Negro in America it is of the *19* greatest importance to recognize that the moral beliefs of a person, or a people, are never really as tenuous as life—which is not moral—very often causes them to appear; these create for them a frame of reference and a necessary hope, the hope being that when life has done its worst they will be enabled to rise above themselves and to triumph over life. Life would scarcely be bearable if this hope did not exist. Again, even when the worst has been said, to betray a belief is not by any means to have put oneself beyond its power; the betrayal of a belief is not the same thing as ceasing to believe. If this were not so there would be no moral standards in the world at all. Yet one must also recognize that morality is based on ideas and that all ideas are dangerous—dangerous because ideas can only lead to action and where the action leads no man cay say. And dangerous in this respect: that confronted with the impossibility of remaining faithful to one's beliefs, and the equal impossibility of becoming free of them, one can be driven to the most inhuman excesses. The ideas on which American beliefs are based are not, though Americans often seem to think so, ideas which originated in America. They came out of Europe. And the establishment of democracy on the American continent was scarcely as radical a break with the past as was the necessity, which Americans faced, of broadening this concept to include black men.

This was, literally, a hard necessity. It was impossible, for one thing, *20* for Americans to abandon their beliefs, not only because these beliefs alone seemed able to justify the sacrifices they had endured and the blood that they had spilled, but also because these beliefs afforded them their only bulwark against a moral chaos as absolute as the physical chaos of the continent it was their destiny to conquer. But in the situation in which Americans found themselves, these beliefs threatened an idea which, whether or not one likes to think so, is the very warp and woof of the heritage of the West, the idea of white supremacy.

Americans have made themselves notorious by the shrillness and the *21* brutality with which they have insisted on this idea, but they did not invent it; and it has escaped the world's notice that those very excesses of which Americans have been guilty imply a certain, unprecedented uneasiness over the idea's life and power, if not, indeed, the idea's validity. The idea of white supremacy rests simply on the fact that white men are the creators of civilization (the present civilization, which is the only one that matters; all previous civilizations are simply "contributions" to our own) and are therefore civilization's guardians and defenders. Thus it was impossible for Americans to accept the black man as one of themselves, for to do so was to jeopardize their status as white men. But not so to accept him was to deny his human reality, his human weight and complexity, and the strain of denying the overwhelmingly undeniable forced Americans into rationalizations so fantastic that they approached the pathological.

At the root of the American Negro problem is the necessity of the 22 American white man to find a way of living with the Negro in order to be able to live with himself. And the history of this problem can be reduced to the means used by Americans—lynch law and law, segregation and legal acceptance, terrorization and concession—either to come to terms with this necessity, or to find a way around it, or (most usually) to find a way of doing both these things at once. The resulting spectacle, at once foolish and dreadful, led someone to make the quite accurate observation that "the Negro-in-America is a form of insanity which overtakes white men."

In this long battle, a battle by no means finished, the unforeseeable 23 effects of which will be felt by many future generations, the white man's motive was the protection of his identity; the black man was motivated by the need to establish an identity. And despite the terrorization which the Negro in America endured and endures sporadically until today, despite the cruel and totally inescapable ambivalence of his status in his country, the battle for his identity has long ago been won. He is not a visitor to the West, but a citizen there, an American; as American as the Americans who despise him, the Americans who fear him, the Americans who love him—the Americans who became less than themselves, or rose to be greater than themselves by virtue of the fact that the challenge he represented was inescapable. He is perhaps the only black man in the world whose relationship to white men is more terrible, more subtle, and more meaningful than the relationship of bitter possessed to uncertain possessor. His survival depended, and his development depends, on his ability to turn his peculiar status in the Western world to his own advantage and, it may be, to the very great advantage of that world. It remains for him to fashion out of his experience that which will give him sustenance, and a voice.

The cathedral at Chartres, I have said, says something to the people 24 of this village which it cannot say to me; but it is important to understand that this cathedral says something to me which it cannot say to them. Perhaps they are struck by the power of the spires, the glory of the windows; but they have known God, after all, longer than I have known him, and in a different way, and I am terrified by the slippery bottomless well to be found in the crypt, down which heretics were hurled to death, and by the obscene, inescapable gargoyles jutting out of the stone and seeming to say that God and the devil can never be divorced. I doubt that the villagers think of the devil when they face a cathedral because they have never been identified with the devil. But I must accept the status which myth, if nothing else, gives me in the West before I can hope to change the myth.

Yet, if the American Negro has arrived at his identity by virtue of the 25 absoluteness of his estrangement from his past, American white men still nourish the illusion that there is some means of recovering the European innocence, of returning to a state in which black men do not exist. This is one of the greatest errors Americans can make. The identity they fought so hard to protect has, by virtue of that battle, undergone a change: Americans are as unlike any other white people in the world as it is possible to be. I do not think, for example, that it is too much to suggest that the American vision of the world—which allows so little reality, generally speaking, for any of the darker forces in human life, which tends until today to paint moral issues in glaring black and white—owes a great deal to the battle waged by Americans to maintain between themselves and black men a human separation which could not be bridged. It is only now beginning to be borne in on us—very faintly, it must be admitted, very slowly, and very much against our will—that this vision of the world is dangerously inaccurate, and perfectly useless. For it protects our moral high-mindedness at the terrible expense of weakening our grasp of reality. People who shut their eyes to reality simply invite their own destruction, and anyone who insists on remaining in a state of innocence long after that innocence is dead turns himself into a monster.

The time has come to realize that the interracial drama acted out on 26 the American continent has not only created a new black man, it has created a new white man, too. No road whatever will lead Americans back to the simplicity of this European village where white men still have the luxury of looking on me as a stranger. I am not, really, a stranger any longer for any American alive. One of the things that distinguishes Americans from other people is that no other people has ever been so deeply involved in the lives of black men, and vice versa. This fact faced, with all its implications, it can be seen that the history of the American Negro problem is not merely shameful, it is also something of an achievement. For even when the worst has been said, it must also be added that the perpetual challenge posed by this problem was always, somehow, perpetually met. It is precisely this black-white experience which may prove of indispensable value to us in the world we face today. This world is white no longer, and it will never be white again.

Study Questions

1. In "Stranger in the Village," what tone does James Baldwin use as he describes the villagers' reactions to seeing him? Does he express anger, bitterness, surprise, sadness, or a combination of these emotions? Choose a passage that clearly illustrates the emotion you have identified and show how the vocabulary conveys that feeling.
2. Why does Baldwin begin his essay by describing the people of the Swiss village instead of discussing racism in the United States? What does his choice indicate about the kind of readers he has in mind?
3. In paragraphs 10–11, Baldwin associates the racism of whites with naïveté. What are the usual connotations of the word naïveté? Is Baldwin's use of this word a way of excusing or condemning racism? What new connotations has he given the word?
4. The landmark Supreme Court decision in Brown v. Topeka Board of Education was issued in 1954, one year after Baldwin wrote "Stranger in the Village." Suppose that Baldwin wanted to fully integrate this new material into his essay instead of simply tacking on a new paragraph. How would he change his treatment of the "American Negro problem" in paragraphs 19–24 to include a discussion of the decision and its consequences?

Suggestion for Revising

We have made the point that in revising a final draft you must play the roles of both writer and audience. In this final stage of the writing process, you must judge how effectively your words will convey your message to the readers you have in mind. James Baldwin seems to have written "Stranger in the Village" for white readers, whose "naïveté" is at the heart of "the American Negro problem." As a revising exercise, let us pretend that his essay was written for the villagers. Reformulate paragraphs 1–5 as if they were part of an essay that was going to be published in the local newspaper. Wherever possible, cover the same incidents mentioned in the original, but adjust the vocabulary and sentence structure to reflect the change in audience.

The Man Made of Words

N. Scott Momaday

I want to try to put several different ideas to- 1
gether this morning. I hope to indicate something about the nature of the relationship be-
tween language and experience. It seems to me that in a certain sense
we are all made of words; that our most essential being consists in
language. It is the element in which we think and dream and act, in
which we live our daily lives. There is no way in which we can exist
apart from the morality of a verbal dimension.

In one of the discussions yesterday the question "What is an American 2
Indian?" was raised.

The answer of course is that an Indian is an idea which a given man 3
has of himself. And it is a moral idea, for it accounts for the way in
which he reacts to other men and to the world in general. And that idea,
in order to be realized completely, has to be expressed.

I want to say some things then about this moral and verbal dimension 4
in which we live. I want to say something about such things as ecology
and storytelling and the imagination. Let me tell you a story:

One night a strange thing happened. I had written the greater part of 5
The Way to Rainy Mountain—all of it, in fact, except the epilogue. I
had set down the last of the old Kiowa tales, and I had composed both
the historical and the autobiographical commentaries for it. I had the
sense of being out of breath, of having said what it was in me to say on
that subject. The manuscript lay before me in the bright light. Small,
to be sure, but complete, or nearly so. I had written the second of the
two poems in which that book is framed. I had uttered the last word, as
it were. And yet a whole, penultimate piece was missing. I began once
again to write.

During the first hours after midnight on the morning of November 13, 6
1833, it seemed that the world was coming to an end. Suddenly the
stillness of the night was broken; there were brilliant flashes of light in
the sky, light of such intensity that people were awakened by it. With
the speed and density of a driving rain, stars were falling in the universe.
Some were brighter than Venus; one was said to be as large as the moon.
I went on to say that that event, the falling of the stars on North America,
that explosion of meteors which occurred 137 years ago, is among the
earliest entries in the Kiowa calendars. So deeply impressed upon the
imagination of the Kiowas is that old phenomenon that it is remembered
still; it has become a part of the racial memory.

"The living memory," I wrote, "and the verbal tradition which tran- *7* scends it, were brought together for me once and for all in the person of Ko-sahn." It seemed eminently right for me to deal, after all, with that old woman. Ko-sahn is among the most venerable people I have ever known. She spoke and sang to me one summer afternoon in Oklahoma. It was like a dream. When I was born she was already old; she was a grown woman when my grandparents came into the world. She sat perfectly still, folded over on herself. It did not seem possible that so many years—a century of years—could be so compacted and distilled. Her voice shuddered, but it did not fail. Her songs were sad. An old whimsy, a delight in language and in remembrance, shone in her one good eye. She conjured up the past, imagining perfectly the long continuity of her being. She imagined the Sun Dance:

There was an old, old woman. She had something on her back. The *8* boys went out to see. The old woman had a bag full of earth on her back. It was a certain kind of sandy earth. That is what they must have in the lodge. The dancers must dance upon the sandy earth. The old woman held a digging tool in her hand. She turned towards the south and pointed with her lips. It was like a kiss, and she began to sing:

We have brought the earth.
    Now it is time to play.

As old as I am, I still have the feeling of play. That was the beginning *9* of the Sun Dance.

By this time I was back into the book, caught up completely in the *10* act of writing. I had projected myself—imagined myself—out of the room and out of time. I was there with Ko-sahn in the Oklahoma July. We laughed easily together; I felt that I had known her all of my life—all of hers. I did not want to let her go. But I had come to the end. I set down, almost grudgingly, the last sentences:

It was—all of this and more—a quest, a going forth upon the way of *11* Rainy Mountain. Probably Ko-sahn too is dead now. At times, in the quiet of evening, I think she must have wondered, dreaming, who she was. Was she become in her sleep that old purveyor of the sacred earth, perhaps, that ancient one who, old as she was, still had the feeling of play? And in her mind, at times, did she see the falling stars?

For some time I sat looking down at these words on the page, trying *12* to deal with the emptiness that had come about inside of me. The words did not seem real. I could scarcely believe that they made sense, that they had anything whatsoever to do with meaning. In desperation almost, I went back over the final paragraphs, backwards and forwards, hurriedly. My eyes fell upon the name Ko-sahn. And all at once everything seemed suddenly to refer to that name. The name seemed to humanize the whole complexity of language. All at once, absolutely, I had the sense of the magic of words and of names. Ko-sahn, I said, and I said again KO-SAHN.

Then it was that that ancient, one-eyed woman Ko-sahn stepped out 13 of the language and stood before me on the page. I was amazed. Yet it seemed entirely appropriate that this should happen.

"I was just now writing about you," I replied, stammering. "I 14 thought—forgive me—I thought that perhaps you were . . . that you had . . ."

"No," she said. And she cackled, I thought. And she went on. "You 15 have imagined me well, and so I am. You have imagined that I dream, and so I do. I have seen the falling stars."

"But all of this, this imagining," I protested, "this has taken place—is 16 taking place in my mind. You are not actually here, not here in this room." It occurred to me that I was being extremely rude, but I could not help myself. She seemed to understand.

"Be careful of your pronouncements, grandson," she answered. "You 17 imagine that I am here in this room, do you not? That is worth something. You see, I have existence, whole being, in your imagination. It is but one kind of being, to be sure, but it is perhaps the best of all kinds. If I am not here in this room, grandson, then surely neither are you."

"I think I see what you mean," I said meekly. I felt justly rebuked. 18 "Tell me, grandmother, how old are you?"

"I do not know," she replied. "There are times when I think that I 19 am the oldest woman on earth. You know, the Kiowas came into the world through a hollow log. In my mind's eye I have seen them emerge, one by one, from the mouth of the log. I have seen them so clearly, how they were dressed, how delighted they were to see the world around them. I must have been there. And I must have taken part in that old migration of the Kiowas from the Yellowstone to the Southern Plains, near the Big Horn River, and I have seen the red cliffs of Palo Duro Canyon. I was with those who were camped in the Wichita Mountains when the stars fell."

"You are indeed very old," I said, "and you have seen many things." 20

"Yes, I imagine that I have," she replied. Then she turned slowly 21 around, nodding once, and receded into the language I had made. And then I imagined I was alone in the room.

Once in his life a man ought to concentrate his mind upon the remem- 22 bered earth, I believe. He ought to give himself up to a particular landscape in his experience, to look at it from as many angles as he can, to wonder about it, to dwell upon it. He ought to imagine that he touches it with his hands at every season and listens to the sounds that are made upon it. He ought to imagine the creatures that are there and all the faintest motions in the wind. He ought to recollect the glare of noon and all the colors of the dawn and dusk.

The Wichita Mountains rise out of the Southern Plains in a long 23 crooked line that runs from east to west. The mountains are made of

red earth, and of rock that is neither red nor blue but some very rare
admixture of the two like the feathers of certain birds. They are not so
high and mighty as the mountains of the Far West, and they bear a
different relationship to the land around them. One does not imagine
that they are distinctive in themselves, or indeed that they exist apart
from the plain in any sense. If you try to think of them in the abstract
they lose the look of mountains. They are preeminently in an expression
of the larger landscape, more perfectly organic than one can easily imagine. To behold these mountains from the plain is one thing; to see the
plain from the mountains is something else. I have stood on the top of
Mt. Scott and seen the earth below, bending out into the whole circle of
the sky. The wind runs always close upon the slopes, and there are
times when you can hear the rush of it like water in the ravines.

Here is the hub of an old commerce. A hundred years ago the Kiowas *24*
and Comanches journeyed outward from the Wichitas in every direction,
seeking after mischief and medicine, horses and hostages. Sometimes
they went away for years, but they always returned, for the land had got
hold of them. It is a consecrated place, and even now there is something
of the wilderness about it. There is a game preserve in the hills. Animals
graze away in the open meadows or, closer by, keep to the shadows of
the groves: antelope and deer, longhorn and buffalo. It was here, the
Kiowas say, that the first buffalo came into the world.

The yellow grassy knoll that is called Rainy Mountain lies a short *25*
distance to the north and west. There, on the west side, is the ruin of
an old school where my grandmother went as a wild young girl in blanket
and braids to learn of numbers and of names in English. And there she
is buried.

     Most is your name the name of
this dark stone.
     Deranged in death, the mind to
be inheres
     Forever in the nominal unknown,
     Who listens here and now to
hear your name.
     The early sun, red as a hunter's
moon,
     Runs in the plain. The mountain
burns and shines;
     And silence is the long approach
of noon
     Upon the shadow that your name
defines—
     And death this cold, black
density of stone.

I am interested in the way that a man looks at a given landscape and 26
takes possession of it in his blood and brain. For this happens, I am
certain, in the ordinary motion of life. None of us lives apart from the
land entirely; such an isolation is unimaginable. We have sooner or later
to come to terms with the world around us—and I mean especially the
physical world; not only as it is revealed to us immediately through our
senses, but also as it is perceived more truly in the long turn of seasons
and of years. And we must come to moral terms. There is no alternative,
I believe, if we are to realize and maintain our humanity; for our humanity
must consist in part in the ethical as well as the practical ideal of preservation. And particularly here and now is that true. We Americans need
now more than ever before—and indeed more than we know—to imagine
who and what we are with respect to the earth and sky. I am talking
about an act of the imagination essentially, and the concept of an American land ethic.

It is no doubt more difficult to imagine in 1970 the landscape of 27
America as it was in, say, 1900. Our whole experience as a nation in
this century has been a repudiation of the pastoral ideal which informs
so much of the art and literature of the nineteenth century. One effect
of the Technological Revolution has been to uproot us from the soil. We
have become disoriented, I believe; we have suffered a kind of psychic
dislocation of ourselves in time and space. We may be perfectly sure of
where we are in relation to the supermarket and the next coffee break,
but I doubt that any of us knows where he is in relation to the stars and
to the solstices. Our sense of the natural order has become dull and
unreliable. Like the wilderness itself, our sphere of instinct has diminished in proportion as we have failed to imagine truly what it is. And
yet I believe that it is possible to formulate an ethical idea of the land—
a notion of what it is and must be in our daily lives—and I believe
moreover that it is absolutely necessary to do so.

It would seem on the surface of things that a land ethic is something 28
that is alien to, or at least dormant in, most Americans. Most of us in
general have developed an attitude of indifference toward the land. In
terms of my own experience, it is difficult to see how such an attitude
could ever have come about.

Ko-sahn could remember where my grandmother was born. "It was 29
just there," she said, pointing to a tree, and the tree was like a hundred
others that grew up in the broad depression of the Washita River. I
could see nothing to indicate that anyone had ever been there, spoken
so much as a word, or touched the tips of his fingers to the tree. But in
her memory Ko-sahn could see the child. I think she must have remembered my grandmother's voice, for she seemed for a long moment to
listen and to hear. There was a still, heavy heat upon that place; I had
the sense that ghosts were gathering there.

And in the racial memory, Ko-sahn had seen the falling stars. For her *30*
there was no distinction between the individual and the racial experience,
even as there was none between the mythical and the historical. Both
were realized for her in the one memory, and that was of the land. This
landscape, in which she had lived for a hundred years, was the common
denominator of everything that she knew and would ever know—and her
knowledge was profound. Her roots ran deep into the earth, and from
those depths she drew strength enough to hold still against all the forces
of chance and disorder. And she drew strength enough to hold still
against all the forces of change and disorder. And she drew therefrom
the sustenance of meaning and of mystery as well. The falling stars were
not for Ko-sahn an isolated or accidental phenomenon. She had a great
personal investment in that awful commotion of light in the night sky.
For it remained to be imagined. She must at last deal with it in words;
she must appropriate it to her understanding of the whole universe. And,
again, when she spoke of the Sun Dance, it was an essential expression
of her relationship to the life of the earth and to the sun and moon.

In Ko-sahn and in her people we have always had the example of a *31*
deep, ethical regard for the land. We had better learn from it. Surely
that ethic is merely latent in ourselves. It must now be activated, I
believe. We Americans must come again to a moral comprehension of
the earth and air. We must live according to the principle of a land ethic.
The alternative is that we shall not live at all.

Ecology is perhaps the most important subject of our time. I can't *32*
think of an issue in which the Indian has more authority or a greater
stake. If there is one thing which truly distinguishes him, it is surely his
regard of and for the natural world.

But let me get back to the matter of storytelling.   *33*

I must have taken part in that old migration of the Kiowas from the *34*
Yellowstone to the Southern Plains, for I have seen antelope bounding
in the tall grass near the Big Horn River, and I have seen the ghost
forests in the Black Hills. Once I saw the red cliffs of Palo Duro Canyon.
I was with those who were camped in the Wichita Mountains when the
stars fell. "You are very old," I said, " and you have seen many things."
"Yes, I imagine that I have," she replied. Then she turned slowly around,
nodding once, and receded into the language I had made. And then I
imagined that I was alone in the room.

Who is the storyteller? Of whom is the story told? What is there in *35*
the darkness to imagine into being? What is there to dream and to relate?
What happens when I or anyone exerts the force of language upon the
unknown?

These are the questions which interest me most: *36*

If there is any absolute assumption in back of my thoughts tonight, it *37*
is this: We are what we imagine. Our very existence consists in our
imagination of ourselves. Our best destiny is to imagine, at least, com-

pletely, who and what, and *that* we are. The greatest tragedy that can befall us is to go unimagined.

Writing is recorded speech. In order to consider seriously the meaning 38 of language and of literature, we must consider first the meaning of the oral tradition.

By way of suggesting one or two definitions which may be useful to 39 us, let me pose a few basic questions and tentative answers:

(1) What is the oral tradition?   40

The oral tradition is that process by which the myths, legends, tales, 41 and lore of a people are formulated, communicated, and preserved in language by word of mouth, as opposed to writing. Or, it is a *collection* of such things.

(2) With reference to the matter of oral tradition, what is the relation- 42 ship between art and reality?

In the context of these remarks, the matter of oral tradition suggests 43 certain particularities of art and reality. Art, for example . . . involves an oral dimension which is based markedly upon such considerations as memorization, intonation, inflection, precision of statement, brevity, rhythm, pace, and dramatic effect. Moreover, myth, legend, and lore, according to our definitions of these terms, imply a separate and distinct order of reality. We are concerned here not so much with an accurate representation of actuality, but with the realization of the imaginative experience.

(3) How are we to conceive of language? What are words?   44

For our purposes, words are audible sounds, invented by man to 45 communicate his thoughts and feelings. Each word has a conceptual content, however slight; and each word communicates associations of feeling. Language is the means by which words proceed to the formulation of meaning and emotional effect.

(4) What is the nature of storytelling? What are the purposes and 46 possibilities of that act?

Storytelling is imaginative and creative in nature. It is an act by which 47 man strives to realize his capacity for wonder, meaning and delight. It is also a process in which man invests and preserves himself in the context of ideas. Man tells stories in order to understand his experience, whatever it may be. The possibilities of storytelling are precisely those of understanding the human experience.

(5) What is the relationship between what a man is and what he says— 48 or between what he is, and what he thinks he is?

This relationship is both tenuous and complicated. Generally speak- 49 ing, man has consummate being in language, and there only. The state of human *being* is an idea, an idea which man has of himself. Only when he is embodied in an idea, and the idea is realized in language, can man take possession of himself. In our particular frame of reference, this is to say that man achieves the fullest realization of his humanity in such an art and product of the imagination as literature—and here I use the term "literature" in its broadest sense. This is admittedly a moral view of the question, but literature is itself a moral view, and it is a view of morality.

Now let us return to the falling stars. And let me apply a new angle 50 of vision to that event—let me proceed this time from a slightly different point of view:

In this winter of 1833 the Kiowas were camped on Elm Fork, a branch 51 of the Red River west of the Wichita Mountains. In the preceding summer they had suffered a massacre at the hands of the Osages, and Tai-me, the sacred Sun Dance Doll and most powerful medicine of the tribe, had been stolen. At no time in the history of their migration from the north, and in the evolution of their plains culture, had the Kiowas been more vulnerable to despair. The loss of Tai-me was a deep psychological wound. In the early cold of November 13 there occurred over North America an explosion of meteors. The Kiowas were awakened by the sterile light of falling stars, and they ran out into the false day and were terrified.

The year the stars fell is, as I have said, among the earliest entries in 52 the Kiowa calendars, and it is permanent in the Kiowa mind. There was symbolic meaning in that November sky. With the coming of natural dawn there began a new and darker age for the Kiowa people; the last culture to evolve on this continent began to decline. Within four years of the falling stars the Kiowas signed their first treaty with the government; within twenty, four major epidemics of smallpox and Asiatic cholera destroyed more than half their number; and within scarcely more than a generation their horses were taken from them and the herds of buffalo were slaughtered and left to waste upon the plains.

Do you see what happens when the imagination is superimposed upon 53 the historical event? It becomes a story. The whole piece becomes more deeply invested with meaning. The terrified Kiowas, when they had regained possession of themselves, did indeed imagine that the falling stars were symbolic of their being and their destiny. They accounted for themselves with reference to that awful memory. They appropriated it, recreated it, fashioned it into an image of themselves—imagined it.

Only by means of that act could they bear what happened to them 54 thereafter. No defeat, no humiliation, no suffering was beyond their power to endure, for none of it was meaningless. They could say to themselves, "yes, it was all meant to be in its turn. The order of the world was broken, it was clear. Even the stars were shaken loose in the night sky." The imagination of meaning was not much, perhaps, but it was all they had, and it was enough to sustain them.

One of my very favorite writers, Isak Dinesen, said this: "All sorrows 55 can be borne if you put them into a story or tell a story about them."

Some three or four years ago, I became interested in the matter of 56 "oral tradition" as that term is used to designate a rich body of preliterate storytelling in and among the indigenous cultures of North America. Specifically, I began to wonder about the way in which myths, legends, and lore evolve into that mature condition of expression which we call "literature." For indeed literature is, I believe, the end-product of an evolutionary process, a stage that is indispensable and perhaps original as well.

I set out to find a traditional material that should be at once oral only, 57 unified and broadly representative of cultural values. And in this undertaking, I had a certain advantage, because I am myself an American Indian, and I have lived many years of my life on the Indian reservations of the southwest. From the time I was first able to comprehend and express myself in language, I heard the stories of the Kiowas, those "coming out" people of the Southern plains from whom I am descended.

Three hundred years ago the Kiowa lived in the mountains of what is 58 now western Montana, near the headwaters of the Yellowstone River. Near the end of the 17th century they began a long migration to the south and east. They passed along the present border between Montana and Wyoming to the Black Hills and proceeded southward along the eastern slopes of the Rockies to the Wichita Mountains in the Southern Plains (Southwestern Oklahoma).

I mention this old journey of the Kiowas because it is in a sense 59 definitive of the tribal mind; it is essential to the way in which the Kiowas think of themselves as a people. The migration was carried on over a course of many generations and many hundreds of miles. When it began, the Kiowas were a desperate and divided people, given up wholly to a day-by-day struggle for survival. When it ended, they were a race of centaurs, a lordly society of warriors and buffalo hunters. Along the way they had acquired horses, a knowledge and possession of the open land, and a sense of destiny. In alliance with the Comanches, they ruled the southern plains for a hundred years.

That migration—and the new golden age to which it led—is closely 60 reflected in Kiowa legend and lore. Several years ago I retraced the route of that migration, and when I came to the end, I interviewed a number of Kiowa elders and obtained from them a remarkable body of history and learning, fact and fiction—all of it in the oral tradition and all of it valuable in its own right and for its own sake.

I compiled a small number of translations from the Kiowa, arranged 61 insofar as it was possible to indicate the chronological and geographical progression of the migration itself. This collection (and it was nothing more than a collection at first) was published under the title *"The Journey of Tai-me"* in a fine edition limited to 100 hand printed copies.

This original collection has just been re-issued, together with illustra- 62 tions and a commentary, in a trade edition entitled *"The Way to Rainy Mountain."* The principle of narration which informs this latter work is in a sense elaborate and experimental, and I should like to say one or two things about it. Then, if I may, I should like to illustrate the way in which the principle works, by reading briefly from the text. And finally, I should like to comment in some detail upon one of the tales in particular.

There are three distinct narrative voices in *"The Way to Rainy Moun-* 63 *tain"*—the mythical, the historical, and the immediate. Each of the translations is followed by two kinds of commentary; the first is documentary and the second is privately reminiscent. Together, they serve, hopefully, to validate the oral tradition to an extent that might not otherwise be possible. The commentaries are meant to provide a context in which the elements of oral tradition might transcend the categorical limits of prehistory, anonymity, and archaeology in the narrow sense.

All of this is to say that I believe there is a way (first) in which the 64 elements of oral tradition can be shown, dramatically, to exist within the framework of a literary continuance, a deeper and more vital context of language and meaning than that which is generally taken into account; and (secondly) in which those elements can be located, with some precision on an evolutionary scale.

The device of the journey is peculiarly appropriate to such a principle 65 of narration as this. And *"The Way to Rainy Mountain"* is a whole journey, intricate with notion and meaning; and it is made with the whole memory, that experience of the mind which is legendary as well as historical, personal as well as cultural.

Without further qualification, let me turn to the text itself.   66

The Kiowa tales which are contained in *"The Way to Rainy Mountain"* 67 constitute a kind of literary chronicle. In a sense they are the milestones of that old migration in which the Kiowas journeyed from the Yellowstone to the Washita. They recorded a transformation of the tribal mind, as it encounters for the first time the landscape of the Great Plains; they evoke the sense of search and discovery. Many of the tales are very old, and they have not until now been set down in writing. Among them there is one that stands out in my mind. When I was a child, my father told me the story of the arrowmaker, and he told it to me many times, for I fell in love with it. I have no memory that is older than that of hearing it. This is the way it goes:

If an arrow is well made, it will have tooth marks upon it. That is 68 how you know. The Kiowas made fine arrows and straightened them in their teeth. Then they drew them to the bow to see that they were straight. Once there was a man and his wife. They were alone at night in their tipi. By the light of a fire the man was making arrows. After a while he caught sight of something. There was a small opening in the tipi where two hides had been sewn together. Someone was there on the outside, looking in. The man went on with his work, but he said to his wife, "Someone is standing outside. Do not be afraid. Let us talk easily, as of ordinary things." He took up an arrow and straightened it in his teeth; then, as it was right for him to do, he drew it to the bow and took aim, first in this direction and then in that. And all the while he was talking, as if to his wife. But this is how he spoke: "I know that you are there on the outside, for I can feel your eyes upon me. If you are a Kiowa, you will understand what I am saying, and you will speak your name." But there was no answer, and the man went on in the same way, pointing the arrow all around. At last his aim fell upon the place where his enemy stood, and he let go of the string. The arrow went straight to the enemy's heart.

Heretofore the story of the arrowmaker has been the private posses- 69 sion of a very few, a tenuous link in that most ancient chain of language which we call the oral tradition; tenuous because the tradition itself is so; for as many times as the story has been told, it was always but one generation removed from extinction. But it was held dear, too, on that same account. That is to say, it has been neither more nor less durable than the human voice, and neither more nor less concerned to express the meaning of the human condition. And this brings us to the heart of the matter at hand: The story of the arrowmaker is also a link between language and literature. It is a remarkable act of the mind, a realization of words and the world that is altogether simple and direct, yet nonetheless rare and profound, and it illustrates more clearly than anything else in my own experience, at least, something of the essential character of the imagination—and in particular of that personification which in this instance emerges from it: the man made of words.

It is a fine story, whole, intricately beautiful, precisely realized. It is 70 worth thinking about, for it yields something of value; indeed, it is full of provocation, rich with suggestion and consequent meaning. There is often an inherent danger that we might impose too much of ourselves upon it. It is informed by an integrity that bears examination easily and well, and in the process it seems to appropriate our own reality and experience.

It is significant that the story of the arrowmaker returns in a special 71 way upon itself. It is about language, after all, and it is therefore part and parcel of its own subject; virtually, there is no difference between the telling and that which is told. The point of the story lies, not so much in what the arrowmaker does, but in what he says—and indeed that he says it. The principal fact is that he speaks, and in so doing he places his very life in the balance. It is this aspect of the story which interests me most, for it is here that the language becomes most conscious of itself; we are close to the origin and object of literature, I believe; our sense of the verbal dimension is very keen, and we are aware of something in the nature of language that is at once perilous and compelling. "If you are a Kiowa, you will understand what I am saying, and you will speak your name." Everything is ventured in this simple declaration, which is also a question and a plea. The conditional element with which it begins is remarkably tentative and pathetic; precisely at this moment is the arrowmaker realized completely, and his reality consists in language, and it is poor and precarious. And all of this occurs to him as surely as it does to us. Implicit in that simple occurrence is all of his definition and his destiny, and all of ours. He ventures to speak because he must; language is the repository of his whole knowledge and experience, and it represents the only chance he has for survival. Instinctively, and with great care, he deals in the most honest and basic way with words. "Let us talk easily, as of ordinary things," he says. And of the ominous unknown he asks only the utterance of a name, only the most nominal sign that he is understood, that his words are returned to him on the sheer edge of meaning. But there is no answer, and the arrowmaker knows at once what he has not known before; that his enemy is, and that he has gained an advantage over him. This he knows certainly, and the certainty itself is his advantage, and it is crucial; he makes the most of it. The venture is complete and irrevocable, and it ends in success. The story is meaningful. It is so primarily because it is composed of language, and it is in the nature of language in turn that it proceeds to the formulation of meaning. Moreover, the story of the arrowmaker, as opposed to other stories in general, centers upon this procession of words toward meaning. It seems in fact to turn upon the very idea that language involves the elements of risk and responsibility; and in this it seeks to confirm itself. In a word, it seems to say, everything is a risk. That may be true, and it may also be that the whole of literature rests upon that truth.

The arrowmaker is preeminently the man made of words. He has *72* consummate being in language; it is the world of his origin and of his posterity, and there is no other. But it is a world of definite reality and of infinite possibility. I have come to believe that there is a sense in which the arrowmaker has more nearly perfect being than have other men, by and large, as he imagines himself, whole and vital, going on into the unknown darkness and beyond. And this last aspect of his being is primordial and profound.

And yet the story has it that he is cautious and alone, and we are *73* given to understand that his peril is great and immediate, and that he confronts it in the only way he can. I have no doubt that this is true, and I believe that there are implications which point directly to the determination of our literary experience and which must not be lost upon us. A final word, then, on an essential irony which marks this story and gives peculiar substance to the man made of words. The storyteller is nameless and unlettered. From one point of view we know very little about him, except that he is somehow translated for us in the person of an arrowmaker. But, from another, that is all we need to know. He tells us of his life in language, and of the awful risk involved. It must occur to us that he is one with the arrowmaker and that he has survived, by word of mouth, beyond other men. We said a moment ago that, for the arrowmaker, language represented the only chance of survival. It is worth considering that he survives in our own time, and that he has survived over a period of untold generations.

Study Questions

1. The wording in the first two paragraphs of "The Man Made of Words" indicates that N. Scott Momaday originally delivered his piece as a speech. What other passages show how he tried to involve his listeners in what he was saying? What information does Momaday and his audience share?
2. In Paragraph 49, Momaday states, "Generally speaking, man has consummate being in language, and there only. The state of human *being* is an idea, an idea which man has of himself." In paragraphs 7–21, Momaday describes his imagined encounter with Ko-sahn. What idea of man is presented here? How is this idea related to Momaday's interpretation of the story of the arrow maker?
3. Two other essays in this text, Vine Deloria's "The Artificial Universe" (pp. 264–274) and Skip Rozin's "People of the Ruined Hills" (pp. 386–394), deal with the relationship of people to the land. Which of these three works seems most "Indian"? To explain your choice, point to particular ways in which the writer uses language.
4. Compare "The Man Made of Words" with Arthur C. Clarke's "Viking on the Plain of Gold" (pp. 299–303). How is each writer's attitude toward modern technology reflected in the words and sentence structures he uses? Which of these two attitudes is more likely to be understood by the readers?

Suggestion for Revising

In his speech, Momaday returns frequently to the meteor shower that occurred on November 13, 1833, each time adding more information to explain its significance to himself and the Kiowa. Reread these passages; then try to reorganize them into a single passage that will tell the entire story. Where would you place your passage in "The Man Made of Words"? Compare what you have written with the original. What is gained by combining all the references to the meteor shower? What effect is lost? How important is that loss to the work?

Essay Assignments

1. A number of essayists in this section describe events in their lives to explain a personal belief or attitude. The events, usually presented as short anecdotes, give the reader a personal glimpse into how and why the writers came to hold those opinions. In a short essay (400–500 words), describe an incident in your own life that has influenced your attitudes toward a person or group. For example, a friend may have lied to you, or remained honest despite the cost; a parent may have disappointed you, or came through when you were most in need. Make sure that the words you choose to describe the incident convey your feelings about it. Did you feel anger, disappointment, frustration, joy, love, satisfaction? Instead of writing "that made me happy," choose nouns, verbs, adjectives, and adverbs that express the feeling.

2. More than forty essays are collected in this text, and by now you will have read quite a few of them. Choose one that you particularly liked or disliked, and discuss (in 400–500 words) your feelings toward it. Your essay should not be so much an analysis of the work as an explanation of your reaction. For example, you may have disliked one of the essays because you found its vocabulary and sentence structure too difficult to follow. Describe your confusion, and, giving specific examples, explain how the vocabulary and sentence structure contributed to your perplexity. You do not have to convince your readers to like or dislike the essay you have chosen. Your goal is to produce such a clear presentation of your attitude that even a person who disagrees with you will understand how you feel and why you feel that way.

3. In their descriptions of landscapes, Annie Dillard, Skip Rozin, and N. Scott Momaday try to communicate the emotions they feel when they look at the hills, streams, and trees. As a result, these descriptions are more than catalogs of the scenes. They are illustrations of the writers' feelings about nature.

   Choose a picture or photograph that evokes in you a strong emotion (e.g., love, hate, loyalty, pleasure, pain). In a six-hundred- to eight-hundred-word essay, describe the picture or photograph using terms that communicate that emotion to an audience. Include the picture or photograph with your finished essay so that your readers can have it in front of them as they read your description. Your goal is not to exhaustively describe the scene, but rather to concentrate on those features that make you feel a certain way.

4. No doubt you have heard people claim that there is a difference between going to college and living in the "real" world beyond the classroom. "Wait until you have to earn a living," they say, as if college life were somehow easier and more carefree than life on the

job. Yet these people seem to forget the hours spent listening to lectures, taking examinations, and following the same day-after-day routine.

Write an eight-hundred- to one-thousand-word essay in which you describe for these people what college life is like. Your goal is not to simply itemize the activities of a typical day, week, or year. Instead, select those features that best illustrate your feelings about attending a college or university so that your audience will better understand the demands and pressures you must endure.

5. Saint Matthew's church is an inner-city church that has long been recognized as an outstanding example of American Gothic architecture. Both in its overall design and its refined details, it is a tribute to American planners and craftsmen. Its stained-glass windows are considered to be the finest in the United States. Almost every textbook on the history of American art contains photographs of the church and its windows.

Saint Matthew's is not simply an architectural monument; it is an active church with progressive social programs. It runs a day-care center that is open to all the families in the neighborhood, no matter what their religious beliefs. It has a visiting nurses program as well as a program for serving meals to the poor and handicapped. Finally, Saint Matthew's has a family-counseling clinic that offers help to people with personal or interpersonal problems.

Saint Matthew's is now plagued by the problems that are typical for most inner-city churches. Younger people are leaving the community, and well over 70 percent of the dwindling congregation is fifty years old or older. The funds to run its various social programs are dangerously low, and the building is in need of extensive repair. There is some question of whether the church will be able to continue.

Across the street from Saint Matthew's is Darcy's Department Store. The store's management believes that it will be able to increase business if it is able to provide more convenient facilities. It has come up with a plan that it believes will solve its need for more parking space as well as Saint Matthew's need for more money. The management has offered an extremely generous sum to the church for its parking lot and some of the grounds surrounding it. On that land, the store plans to build a ten-story garage. The money Darcy's has offered the church would be sufficient to repair the building and to set up a trust fund that would ensure the continuation of the social programs.

There are, however, a few drawbacks to this offer. The day-care center is on the land Darcy's wants to buy. It would have to be torn down, and there would be neither space nor money for relocating it.

The ten-story garage would definitely clash with the architecture of the church, destroying its spiritual effect. Finally, the garage would be so high that it would completely block the sun from the stained-glass windows of the eastern wall.

Should Saint Matthew's accept the offer? Write an essay of eight hundred to one thousand words in which you defend your position. Assume that your audience is not aware of Saint Matthew's problems, and discuss what you believe to be the most important issues in the case and how the measures you recommend would affect them. There is probably no fully happy solution to Saint Matthew's problems; with or without the sale, some sacrifices will have to be made. Thus, before writing your essay, you must decide what you think is most important for Saint Matthew's to preserve.

Index

To the Student

We hope you will take a few minutes to fill out this questionnaire. Your responses will be helpful to us as we plan future editions of *The Essay*. Please tear out this sheet and mail it to: English Editor, College Division, Houghton Mifflin Company, One Beacon Street, Boston, MA 02108. Thank you.

Please rate the selections:	Excellent	Good	Fair	Poor	Didn't Read

Section One / Approaching Writing

	Excellent	Good	Fair	Poor	Didn't Read
Gold, *The Two Cultures and Dr. Franklin's Fly*	___	___	___	___	___
Walker, *The Unglamorous But Worthwhile Duties of the Black Revolutionary Artist*	___	___	___	___	___
Richards, *Centering as Dialogue*	___	___	___	___	___

Section Two / Meaning

	Excellent	Good	Fair	Poor	Didn't Read
Brandt, *The Gift of Gift-Giving*	___	___	___	___	
Angell, *On the Ball*	___	___	___	___	
Wilson, *The Old Stone House*	___	___	___	___	
Rich, *Teaching Language in Open Admissions*	___	___	___	___	
Fromm, *The Nature of Symbolic Language*	___	___	___	___	
Bacon, *Of Truth*	___	___	___	___	
Sontag, *The Image World*	___	___	___	___	
Ephron, *The Boston Photographs*	___	___	___	___	
Farb, *Man at the Mercy of His Language*	___	___	___	___	
McPhee, *Dick Cook*	___	___	___	___	
Ehrlich, *North America After the War*	___	___	___	___	___

Section Three / Structure

	Excellent	Good	Fair	Poor	Didn't Read
Royko, *Mary and Joe, Chicago-Style*	___	___	___	___	___
Stratton, *Days of Valor: Fighting the Wild*	___	___	___	___	___
Jacoby, *The Education of a Feminist: Part One*	___	___	___	___	___
Johnson, *On the Need for Oblivion*	___	___	___	___	___
Thoreau, *Resistance to Civil Government*	___	___	___	___	___
Twain, *Corn-Pone Opinions*	___	___	___	___	___

	Excellent	Good	Fair	Poor	Didn't Read
Tillich, *The Lost Dimension in Religion*	___	___	___	___	___
Franklin, *Information for Those Who Would Remove to America*	___	___	___	___	___
Austin, *The Pocket Hunter*	___	___	___	___	___
Woolf, *The Strange Elizabethans*	___	___	___	___	___
Montaigne, *Of the Inconsistency of Our Actions*	___	___	___	___	___
Eiseley, *Man of the Future*	___	___	___	___	___
Hampl, *Come Eat*	___	___	___	___	___
Deloria, *The Artifical Universe*	___	___	___	___	___
Baraka, *Primitive Blues and Primitive Jazz*	___	___	___	___	___
Gould, *Singapore's Patrimony (and Matrimony)*	___	___	___	___	___
Clarke, *Viking on the Plain of Gold*	___	___	___	___	___
Hausfater/Sutherland, *Little Things That Tick Off Baboons*	___	___	___	___	___
Brownmiller, *Women Fight Back*	___	___	___	___	___

Section Four / Style

	Excellent	Good	Fair	Poor	Didn't Read
Swift, *A Modest Proposal*	___	___	___	___	___
Dillard, *Heaven and Earth in Jest*	___	___	___	___	___
Matthiessen, *September 28*	___	___	___	___	___
Rozin, *People of the Ruined Hills*	___	___	___	___	___
Hurston, *How It Feels to Be Colored Me*	___	___	___	___	___
Steiner, *The Hollow Miracle*	___	___	___	___	___
Orwell, *Marrakech*	___	___	___	___	___
Trillin, *The Sound of Eating*	___	___	___	___	___
Baldwin, *Stranger in the Village*	___	___	___	___	___
Momaday, *The Man Made of Words*	___	___	___	___	___

Please add any additional comments or suggestions.

School _____

Course Title _____

Instructor's Name _____